THE RED BOOK

OF THE

PERSECUTED CHURCH

Published under the auspices of the Commission
for the Persecuted Church of the International
Catholic Organisations

THE RED BOOK

OF

THE PERSECUTED CHURCH

BY

ALBERT GALTER

This translation is published by arrangement with the proprietors
Editions Fleurus, Paris

SECOND EDITION

THE NEWMAN PRESS

WESTMINSTER, MD.

1957

M. H. GILL AND SON, LTD.,
ço UPPER O'CONNELL STREET, DUBLIN

AUSTRALIA AND NEW ZEALAND
E. J. DWYER, PTY., LTD.,
Cnr. Kippax and Waterloo Streets,
Surry Hills, Sydney, N.S.W.

U.S.A.
THE NEWMAN PRESS
Westminster, Md.

First Published June 1957.
Second Edition, October 1957.

Nihil Obstat :
             EDUARDUS GALLEN,
                  Censor Theol. Deput.

Imprimi Potest :
        ✠ IOANNES CAROLUS,
                  Archiep. Dublinen.,
                        Hiberniæ Primas.
DUBLINI, die 8a Septembris, anno 1957.

PRINTED IN THE REPUBLIC OF IRELAND BY M. H. GILL AND SON LTD., DUBLIN.

Contents

THE PERSECUTION OF THE CATHOLIC CHURCH

Preface

IN PRESENTING the *Red Book* to world public opinion the Commission for the Persecuted Church of the International Catholic Organisations fulfils the duty of offering objective information on the Communist persecution to those who are prepared to examine without prejudice documents and facts.

The truth is irresistible; but it must be known.

There is already an extensive literature on the Church of Silence: information which it has been possible to gather from behind the Iron and Bamboo Curtains; personal experiences of refugees; written accounts of certain events in particular countries; books on the religious situation in some nations. This material however has not hitherto been collected in a single volume. Sometimes too it was incomplete and was often based on the testimony of witnesses, trustworthy no doubt but isolated, so that they presented a view of the persecution which was too personal to allow the reader to draw conclusions of a general nature. In such conditions the difficulty or rather the impossibility of verifying the reported facts, the shameless ease with which Communism dares to deny even the most obvious truths and the tendency, conscious or unconscious, which is in each one of us to disregard whatever might disturb our agreeable aloofness can only too easily stand between us and our desire to act.

The *Red Book* is intended to fill this gap. It presents in a systematic manner a great many irrefutable facts, most carefully chosen and verified; it studies them and compares them one with the other wherever possible in the light of official documents which the persecutors themselves have drawn up. We believe that it is impossible to escape from the logic of the deductions drawn from the main outlines of the contemporary persecution.

Those who will study the revelations and proofs set out in the present work—which, while it is not official, has yet the character of a solemn warning—will very soon realise the true aim of the Marxist persecution.   If they are told that the struggle is not so fierce and that its purpose is not to combat religion, but only to strike at " outbreaks of fanaticism " or to repress " political resistance," it will be enough for them to recall the undeniable facts presented in the *Red Book*. The facts will speak for themselves to the unprejudiced inquirer.

Of the faithful who read this book, the Commission for the persecuted Church asks a prayer :* to unite themselves with the Commission in beseeching God to grant strength to the persecuted, grace to the persecutors, light and charity to a world so deeply divided, in order that at length it may find peace.

May those who do not share our Faith take with them from this book the conviction that the Catholic Church defends the most essential universal human rights, engraved on the conscience of every human being, respected by every power worthy of the name and consecrated by the most solemn declarations of the United Nations' Organisation.   Fighting in the forefront to safeguard the highest spiritual values of humanity the Catholic Church merits the sympathy, admiration, gratitude and active support of all.

JEAN BERNARD,

President of the Commission for the
Persecuted Church.

Luxembourg, Easter 1956.

---

* For prayer composed by His Holiness Pope Pius XII for " The Church of Silence " see page 467.

Foreword

THE AIM OF THIS BOOK is to give a summary but well-documented account of the persecution of the Catholic Church by the Communist governments of certain countries. In the following pages the reader is invited to consider the facts in themselves; commentary is dispensed with except in so far as it is judged necessary for a better understanding of how the persecution developed.

It is not asserted that the documentation here presented is complete, but it is nevertheless sufficient to give a clear idea of Communist aims as regards the Catholic Church. As is well known, information coming from countries behind the Iron Curtain is rather fragmentary. This being the case, we have drawn on Communist sources themselves to the degree that this was possible, completing the picture where necessary by the evidence of reliable eye-witnesses.

For the most part the chronological order of events is followed. The period reviewed begins with 1939 for the USSR and the territories occupied by the Soviets as a result of the Russo-German Pact of that year. For the other countries the period studied begins with the end of World War II. After an introduction dealing with the strategy and tactics of Communist persecution, each of the chapters that follow treats of a particular country and traces the sad story of its religious history until the death of Stalin in 1953—which, so to speak, marked the completion of a phase in the cycle of persecution. To the whole work is appended a bibliography for the benefit of those who wish to make further study of certain aspects of Marxist ideology and its anti-religious policy.

Conceived along these lines, the book is consciously restricted in its scope. It is important to realise that it does not claim to deal with the attitude adopted by Catholics in face of Communism in the " liberated " countries; nor is its object to remind

Catholics that the Church expects them to supplement their
persevering struggle against error by a positive effort to spread
the rich treasures of the Faith and to strive for a greater degree
of social justice; rather the mere fact of the persecution is
presented in its stark and irrefutable reality.

For this reason too there is no intention of analysing the
various causes and historical circumstances, though these could
shed greater light on the genesis, development and repercussions
of the persecution in each country. Such analyses, full of interest
and of undeniable value, have already been attempted for particular nations. The originality of the present volume and, we
hope, its usefulness, lie in the fact that it confronts the reader
with the evidence of a multiple and simultaneous persecution
of the Catholic Church in all the countries that have come under
Communist domination.

Viewed in this perspective it is seen that the following pages
do not purport to tell the story of the heroic resistance of the
Catholic Church in Communist-controlled countries. Neither
is it the purpose of the book to recount the genuine
cases of martyrdom which occurred in the ranks of both clergy
and laity. Wherever such happenings are reported, it is only
in passing and by indirect allusion. Furthermore, the book
makes no attempt to describe the Communist attitude to other
religions which though to a lesser degree than the Catholic
Church were the victims of persecution in some countries.

Least of all is there a desire to yield to a spirit of contention
or division. The Catholic Church as such rises above the world
of political vicissitudes. What she has condemned in the various
Communist régimes, and what she continues to condemn, is the
intrinsic error which vitiates Marxism-Leninism and the persecution which is the fruit of this error.

As it stands, the book purports to be:

   (1) a contribution towards the defence of those values
        which atheistic Communism rejects; and—for people
        who might be inclined to forget—a reminder of what
        Communism is doing to destroy those values;

(2) a description of the difficult situation—often a tangle
   of painful alternatives and soul-racking dilemmas—
   in which priests and faithful, but especially the bishops,
   have to live behind the Iron Curtain;

(3) an appeal addressed to all those who are interested in
   the cause of human liberty and the fundamental rights
   of man, to direct their attention anew to one of the
   most terrible tragedies of our time; an appeal not to
   ignore Communism or to minimise its dangers. Such
   ignoring or minimising (done sometimes even in
   highly-qualified international circles) is not only a
   mistake but also an act of ingratitude to those who
   suffer for their fidelity to God and for their defence
   of that Civilisation which takes its name from Christ.

ALBERT GALTER.

In this edition the story of Communist persecution is traced as far as July 1957.

Chapter 1

The Communist Persecution

" *Communism is intrinsically evil.*"
(Pope Pius XI, *AAS*, t. XIII, p. 96).
" *The philosophical basis of Marxism is
dialectical materialism . . . materialism
that is absolutely atheistic, and resolutely
opposed to all religion.*"
(Lenin, *Œuvres*, t. XV, p. 371).

B Y THE GREATER number of its opponents Communism is regarded as the mortal enemy of political and democratic liberty and is combatted on this account alone. Others, deeming themselves to have a deeper understanding of it, look on Communism as a social doctrine and a system of political economy divorced from all reference to spiritual realities but yet with a certain number of achievements to its credit.

Communism however as a philosophy denies the supernatural, putting in its place a pseudo-mystical cult of " progress " threatening the essential values of the Christian Revelation. Communism as a system rooted in Atheism is quite unknown to the majority despite the repeated pronouncements and warnings of the Church over many years.

Perhaps the apathy of so many Christians, in face of the Communist peril, is explained by the fact that they attach more importance to the social and political implications of Communism than to its spiritual significance. For them the Party is more important than the Party's ideology; the Party's programme, than the Party's principles. The end is forgotten in face of the tactics employed to achieve it.

This attitude explains perhaps the seductive influence which Communism continues to exercise over certain minds even after its reiterated condemnation by the Church. Communism in its spiritual and religious character is not well known.

The history of events since 1945 in those countries where the Communists succeeded in seizing power, shows plainly that religious persecution remains one of the fundamental and unchanging elements of Marxism. The classical Communist texts on the creation of a socialist society, beginning with the struggle against " all kinds of religious prejudice," have never been repudiated. The only change from the past has been in more methodical organisation, more strict application of the *Marxist dialectic*, and in more rigorous planning, all of which make a *truly scientific operation* of the persecution carried on in the " People's Democracies."

In their conquest of power and in their use of it the Communists—Slav, Latin, Balt, or Hungarian—have employed the same methods, methods inspired by dialectical Marxism, the doctrinal basis of Communism. In this there is obviously one " technique," the same for all Communist régimes. What can and does vary is the application of these methods, for it is an essential part of Marxist tactics to suit the use of them to the local historical circumstances, the mentality, institutions and traditions of each nation. But within the limits of this " tactical elasticity " the basic procedure remains essentially the same, for it is founded on that same Dialectical Materialism from which the Communists draw their practical norms of action with rigorous consistency.

The struggle against religion and the Church over the last ten years gives a further example of Communist methods. According to their principles Communists combat religion on three definite grounds. First, in the name of " science "; for religion is but a sham that turns man away from his true end, the realisation in himself of the evolution of matter. Secondly, in the name of " justice "; for religion is the ally of capitalist exploitation. Lastly, in the name of " social progress "; for religion is but the " opium of the people," and the promise it holds out of a world to come only helps to maintain the oppressed classes in their state of subjection. Without denying any of these principles, which directly inspire their system of procedure against the Church, and without losing sight of the ultimate purpose of the struggle—the simultaneous liquidation of religion and the capitalist society of which religion is an integral part—the Communists have always taken and continue to take strict account of the particular circumstances in each country.

It is for this reason that the history of the persecution since 1945 comprises on the one hand a series of identical measures against the Church in the different Communist-controlled countries, so that one is led to think of a single " plan of persecution," while on the other hand one may observe that within the framework of this common plan the Communists have in each case adapted their mode of action to the exigencies of varying concrete conditions. It is important to keep clearly in mind this twofold aspect of Communist persecution.

The following are the principal circumstances that may influence the mode of persecution in different countries:

(1) *The number of Catholics, their degree of organisation and the intensity of the Christian life of the country.*

These factors explain why the extreme severity of the persecution in China, Bulgaria and Romania has not been repeated to the same degree in Poland or in Yugoslavia. This fact has been seized upon by Communist propaganda and used *to impress world opinion* with the " exemplary religious liberty " which, they say, exists in Poland. These factors also explain why certain experiments, as for example the setting up of a Government Bureau for Ecclesiastical Affairs, were tried out in Czechoslovakia rather than in a country like Hungary.

If circumstances so suggest, the Communists are quite prepared to come forward as the protectors of religious liberty and of the Church. This has happened not infrequently before elections when the Marxist leaders realised that it would be to their advantage to assure the political neutrality of the Catholic population even if they could not hope to win its favour. In this connection it will be recalled that in Hungary the Communists at first acted as the staunch defenders of " freedom of education," and hence of the schools depending on ecclesiastical authority. They opposed on this point the left wing of the *Small-holders' Party* though it was the Communists themselves who had urged on the same left-wing members to demand nationalisation of the schools.

In almost every country, whenever it seemed expedient for the consolidation of their power, the Communists were quick to grant a temporary measure of religious freedom or to mitigate certain irksome laws, decrees or regulations.

(2) *The Rite professed by Catholics.*

In Romania for example Communist methods in dealing with Catholics of the Oriental Rite differed greatly from those employed against Catholics of the Latin Rite. Similarly in their struggle against the Uniate Church both in the Ukraine proper and in Subcarpathian Ukraine the Soviets used tactics quite different from those employed against the Latin Rite Catholics in the Baltic States and in the former Polish territories.

(3) *The existence of a more numerous and more stable denomination that might be used against the Church of the minority.*

Thus the Autonomous (Autocephalous) Russian and Romanian Orthodox [1] Churches were used in the struggle against the Catholic Church of the Oriental Rite in the Ukraine and Romania.

(4) *The strength of the Communist position within the country.*

It is a basic principle of Marxism that the liquidation of the Church should not be carried out if this would hinder in any way the "sovietisation" and economic development of the country. Consequently Communist tactics are always made subordinate to this principle.

Thus wherever the political and economic structure of Communism has been solidly established, as for example in the USSR, the régime proceeds in summary and radical fashion. But if, as in Hungary between 1953 and 1955, the country is faced with an economic crisis, anti-religious pressure is eased and the Government may even appeal to Catholics, pastors and

---

[1] In this book the term "orthodox" is taken in its usual historical acceptation, and not in its dogmatic sense.

faithful, to support the " National Popular Front " in the name of patriotism and for the welfare of the nation.

(5) *The possible impact abroad of the struggle against religion and the Church.*

In countries behind the Iron or the Bamboo Curtain, such as the USSR or China, where there was less fear of the bourgeois world, the campaign against religion was much more drastic than in countries like the " German Democratic Republic," which are in immediate contact with Western opinion, if only by reason of the continual exodus of refugees.

(6) *The psychological factor both within and without the country.*

Sometimes—as was often the case in Czechoslovakia—a Communist Government will deliberately arouse the indignation of the people by the extreme severity of the measures taken against the Church. The Government then gives way a little and the popular indignation abates. But in reality the Communists' purpose has been achieved. These tactics have been compared to those of a merchant who asks 6s. for an article which is worth only 4s. The customer finally agrees to buy for 5s. So at the end of the transaction both parties are satisfied; the merchant because he has got 5s. for an article worth only 4s., and the customer because he thinks he has saved 1s. Following this plan of action, Communists often adopt anti-Church measures which are much less severe than those called for by their propaganda.

On the international plane the Communists are careful not to alarm world opinion. For this reason they have perfected the " technique of the vice "—a tightening of the vice against the Church in one country, then a tightening in another, then a tightening in a third country followed by a tightening in the first country, and so on. In the meantime public opinion is conciliated by the granting of a concession in some other country.

Underlying this diversity of tactics there is always discernible a constant pattern of persecution, a kind of over-all planning, with but differences of degree in its practical application. There is reason to believe that the Communist Governments have at

their disposal a research organisation and psychological laboratories to aid them in their anti-religious or rather anti-Catholic
strategy.

* * *

What then are the great permanent features of every Communist persecution of the Catholic Church?

(1) First of all a propaganda campaign to discredit the Church
in the eyes of the people.

After World War II the Communists used for their anti-
Catholic propaganda the recent political history of the countries
" liberated " by the Red Army. In 1945 they accused the Church
in China of having helped *Chiang Kai-Chek* and the Japanese.
In Poland the Church was charged with having favoured the
Nazis. In Yugoslavia and Albania the Church had given protection
to the Fascists and Ustascia. In the Ukraine and Czechoslovakia
she had collaborated with the Nazis.

The propaganda machine spread gross accusations against
religion, the Church and the Pope. The Church was accused
of being the accomplice of Capitalism, the enemy of the workers
who are striving to break the chains that keep them slaves.
She was reproached with exacting payment even for the administration of the Sacraments. Scandals past and present were
served up to the people and a flood of coarse pamphlets distorted
the history of the Church.

The Pope was depicted as head of one of the world's greatest
financial powers; the Vatican, in the pay of the US, as the chief
instrument of " reactionary politics," and warmonger No. 1 in
the world.

The Slav peoples were reminded that the Holy See had always
been their enemy and that down through the centuries the Pope
had always sacrificed their interests to the interests of the
Germans. In Romania it was pointed out that the Vatican was
historically the chief obstacle to national unity, since it had protected the invaders of Transylvania. In China, Viet-Nam and
Korea the Holy See was charged with being the loyal ally of
colonialism.

Religious morality is for the Communists only a system of slavery and exploitation as is proved by the " reactionary activity of contemporary political Catholicism " and by its " co-operation with the dominant bourgeois class in the capitalist countries."

Once the Church has been discredited, Communist propaganda begins to prepare the minds of the people for active measures against Catholicism. All means are employed to justify these measures: the press, the radio, the cinema, mass-meetings, meetings of factory workers and of the workmen in particular urban areas, posters, cartoons, popular festivals, slogans, etc. In this campaign the worst sophisms and the most patent absurdities are quite in order. The persecutors do not mind. The deafening chorus of lying propaganda always produces results. A lie, through unending repetition, begins to look like the truth.[2] The man in the street begins to think that Communism is not against religion, but against the abuse of religion. In this way the Communist victims are cleverly led on to approve and defend decisions which in the end will spell their own destruction.

It is the Communist Party which inspires and directs the propaganda campaign the general themes of which are supplied by Marxist teaching. The Government's job is merely to set the propaganda machine in motion by all the means at its disposal.

(2) When public opinion has been sufficiently prepared, the first decrees against the Church make their appearance. Their purpose is twofold: firstly, to help to strengthen the Communist grip on power; and secondly, to " test " the resistance of the hierarchy and of the faithful.

In the People's Democracies from Poland to China, the first " legal " step is always the same: the Catholic press is suppressed, most frequently " because of paper shortage." This means the disappearance of one of the best means of offsetting the effects of Communist propaganda. Almost always and in the same order there follow:

(i) the dissolution of Catholic Associations. Frequently other political and cultural societies are suppressed at the same

---

[2] The following saying is almost an axiom with Communists: " A lie repeated twice is still a lie; repeated 100,000 times, it becomes for the greater number a truth."

time so as to take some of the sting out of the measures against
the Church;

(ii) the nationalisation of the free schools (which means in
reality of the Catholic schools). This process is presented as
a tribute to that free and gratuitous education which the State
alone can guarantee;

(iii) the nationalisation of Church property in the name of
greater " social justice." This is invariably pushed to the point
of depriving the Church of the indispensable means of subsistence;

(iv) the forbidding of the Church to engage in any kind of
social or charitable activity.

(3) A further stage in the persecution consists in obstructing
the relations of the hierarchy and the faithful with the centre
of Catholicism.

As a first step the " foreigner," who represents the Holy
See, is expelled. The decision is always justified by a preliminary propaganda campaign full of the noblest sentiments of
patriotic zeal. With the exception of North Viet-Nam no
Communist-dominated country to-day admits a representative
of the Holy See, whether he possesses diplomatic status or not.
The Apostolic Nuncio has been expelled from Hungary, Czechoslovakia, Yugoslavia and Romania. China lost no time in
getting rid of the Inter-nuncio. Bulgaria and Albania treated
the Apostolic Delegate in the same way. The Baltic States—
forcibly affiliated to the Union of Soviet Socialist Republics—
have followed the lead of the USSR in all that concerns relations
with the Holy See.

(4) The Church has been discredited, its social influence
undermined by severe restrictions and the relations between
the clergy and Rome rendered difficult, if not impossible.
The time has come for the Communists to compromise the
Church in the eyes of the people, and if possible in the eyes
of the world. It is the hour of the great court trials. Once
again the propaganda machine plays a dominant part in setting
the scene. An effort is made to strike at the Church through
her leaders whether it be a missionary subjected to a " People's

Judgment " in a Chinese village or the Cardinal Primate of Hungary whose very personality the Communists strove to undermine by a monstrous travesty of legality.

(5) These trials aim at destroying the prestige of bishops and priests and at weakening their influence among the people. But the Communists have also more direct and violent means of achieving the same ends, as for example the expulsion of missionaries from China, their extermination in Albania and Bulgaria; the concentration and forced labour camps of the USSR, and the prisons and " concentration monasteries " of Romania, Yugoslavia, Czechoslovakia and Poland.

(6) However the chief method used by Communism to undermine the influence and weaken the resistance of the clergy is to sow the seeds of division among them. Once they succeed in arousing in a certain number of priests a sympathetic attitude towards the régime, they immediately set up " Associations of Priests " under most harmless and often even pious titles. These are for the Communists a veritable " Fifth Column " in the Church and their mission is to bring about its dissolution from within through the play of " internal contrasts " (according to the Marxist terminology).

For this reason the following " Associations " have been set up: the *Union of National Priests* in Czechoslovakia; the *Union of Catholic Priests of Peace* in Hungary; the *Union of SS. Cyril and Methodius* in Croatia, with similar organisations in the other Federated Republics of Yugoslavia; the *Partisan Priests' Movement for Peace* in Romania; the *Association of Patriot Priests, supporters of the Triple Autonomy* in China, etc. The Communists are unreserved in their support of these associations—to the point even of seeming to deny their own principles. In Yugoslavia for example those priests who became members of the *Union of SS. Cyril and Methodius* were promised permission to teach religion in the schools.

Side by side with this system of dividing the clergy there is an attempt to gain control of the seminaries, and through them of the formation of future priests. In some countries the Communist Governments have even set up State seminaries of their own.

(7) Once the unity of the Church has been undermined, the hierarchy is faced with the dreadful alternative: complete paralysis of ecclesiastical life or the acceptance of the so-called Church " statutes."

By intimidation through the imprisonment of many priests and bishops, or *by promises* of personal freedom, free exercise of the sacred ministry, liberation of imprisoned religious, economic advantages, the Communists do all in their power to lead the bishops along the road of compromise, a road which they trust will finally end in schism in the true sense of the word.

The Communists do not openly ask the bishops to found a *National Independent Church*, and to renounce communion with the Holy See. That would most certainly meet with refusal. They merely ask the bishops to take into consideration the new democratic order in which the Church has to live. After all, the Church must adapt itself to the present-day political, social and economic situation. Hence it is only reasonable to sign an *accord* or *modus vivendi* with the State. In Communist terminology the Church, in this way, acquires official *statutes*. In reality however these statutes—for China, Albania, Bulgaria, Romania or any other Communist country—mean one thing only: a direct attack on the unity of the Church.

(8) Sometimes circumstances do not make this direct attack on the unity of the Church advisable. Still the Communists do not give up the idea of getting a grip on Church administration. The first step is an *accord* between the Episcopate and the State (the first such *accord* was that signed in Poland, 14 April 1950). This is followed by the establishment of a *Bureau for Ecclesiastical Affairs* (Poland, Hungary, Czechoslovakia, etc.). The function of the *Bureau* is to " regulate the relations between Church and State." In fact it quickly becomes a Communist instrument

(a) for reducing the Church, gradually to be sure, to the condition of a mere State department;

(b) for achieving the progressive elimination of those elements among the clergy who are considered " refractory." This is not difficult, since all nominations

to ecclesiastical offices are now under the authority
of the State;

(c) for making use of priests as political agents, after
having enslaved them economically;

(d) for giving the faithful the impression that the State is
carrying out the Church policy in the name of the
bishops.

The second of these four points needs further treatment.

One of the functions of the *Bureau for Ecclesiastical Affairs* is
to present to the bishops—or rather to impose on them—the
candidates for ecclesiastical offices. Thus " Vicars General "
and " Vicars Capitular " are nominated from the ranks of the
" patriot priests " subject to the control of State functionaries.
In these nominees the Communists are sure to possess docile
instruments, ready to co-operate with the Government. The
faithful priests are always set aside; there is never question of
nominating one of them. Thus too distrust and confusion are
begotten in the minds of the faithful.

By degrees the bishops find the direction of the dioceses
slipping from their control and being transferred to priests who
are known to be less intransigent than their bishops. Sometimes
of course the bishops are simply eliminated once and for all from
the government of the dioceses.

Another purpose of these appointments is to place bishops,
priests and faithful face to face with serious problems of conscience. If the bishops refuse to accept the Government
candidates, these in any case will be nominated without episcopal
consent, and the result will be confusion in the dioceses and
the obvious flouting of the bishops' authority. If however the
bishops accept such candidates, it is at once evident that they
are placing unworthy persons in positions of responsibility.
Dilemmas like this, and the systematic endeavours of the
Communists to disrupt the unity between the hierarchy and
Rome, between the members of the hierarchy themselves,
between priests and bishops, between clergy and faithful, are
all within the scope of Marxist dialectic Materialism. The
same dialectic—the *internal conflict*, in Marxist terminology—

explains also why Communist Governments protect the " lower " clergy against the " higher," the peace-loving priests against the " war-mongers," the secular against the regular clergy, those of the Oriental Rite against those of the Latin Rite, apostate priests against their ecclesiastical superiors. Just as social and economic structures are *destroyed and replaced from within*, so too the religious structure of the Church is subject to the same dialectical law. It is enough to sow the seed of disintegration and to cultivate it. This is the function of the *Bureau for Ecclesiastical Affairs*.

(9) The Church clamped as it were in this vice is practically eliminated from public life. This does not mean however that it is dispensed from *collaborating* in the " construction of the new social order." On the contrary this is a condition of its survival. For many reasons the Communists wish to have the collaboration of the Church once they have fashioned it to their will, for

(a) they need the influence of the clergy to aid their economic effort;

(b) such friendly co-operation proves to foreigners that the " People's Democracies " are not opposed to religion;

(c) they wish to divert the Church from its religious mission, or at least to impose limits on it. Thus the clergy must be engaged in secular occupations. By laicising the Church they make its final liquidation all the easier when the opportune time arrives.

The first act of collaboration is the " Oath of Fidelity " to the State demanded of bishops and priests. But they must also repeatedly declare their acceptance of Communist social principles, take part in " peace conferences," in re-education courses and in economic campaigns for the consolidation of the régime (encouragement of work-companies, praise of Stakhanovism, exhortations to the people not to evade the laws on " produce-collections," etc.). " Collaboration " means that the Church, like every other organisation, must be subject to the State, must adapt itself to the new Social Order and must co-operate positively with the régime. It is not enough for the priest to fulfil his civic duties faithfully; he must show that he accepts the régime. Here again the Marxist dialectic plays its part by creating a further dilemma for the conscience of the priest: either he refuses to co-operate and so deprives the faithful of his services, or he supports the régime and so gives bad example to the faithful.

Thus after imprisoning the Church within her sanctuaries, by suppressing all her external activities, the Communists force her to come out in the open again and engage in a type of activity planned according to the ideological and practical standards common to all Marxist régimes. In a word the Church is expected to forward the " Communist policy."

(10) Naturally there is " freedom of worship " under the *Bureau for Ecclesiastical Affairs*. But this freedom, sanctioned by all Marxist constitutions, and boasted about by Communists, can be exercised only within the walls of the churches, and even then it is fraught with risks and the ever present danger of denunciation for anyone wishing to avail himself of this freedom. Freedom of worship means for Communism only the temporary toleration of religion as a private affair; it can never be spread among the people, and it is necessarily accompanied by freedom of anti-religious propaganda. Communists see the strength of the Church in her *organisation*, and it is that organisation which must be destroyed. Worship may remain. When the right moment comes, Communist teaching will not fail to wean the faithful from it.

The Church as a hierarchically organised society, possessing recognised public rights, the Church as a socially active organisation, such a Church has no right to existence in a Communist country.

(11) When the Church has been separated from Rome and made the slave of the State, the rest can be left to time, for the passage of time is one of the recognised factors in the dialectical process. This passage of time will according to Communist principles lead gradually to the disintegration of both cult and clergy, and so in the end of the Church. In time the *homo religiosus* (" the superstitious man ") will evolve into the *homo economicus*. The Communist compulsory " re-education " scheme is especially important in this progressive transformation.

" Re-education " sows the seed of disintegration, for through it the Communist dialectic succeeds literally in emptying the minds, changing the wills and bringing about a complete overthrow of the accepted standards of its victims.

When Communists decide to " re-educate " a man, to convert him to the Communist *World-outlook*, they set about the task in radical fashion. The Chinese Communists call it " changing the brain," and the expression in the intellectual and moral senses is literally exact. It is in fact a man's whole mentality and activity that are to be changed. All the apparatus at the disposal of modern propaganda, all that comes under the title " socialist realism," is harnessed to the task of re-education: the press, the school, art, the theatre, the cinema . . . Life in all its aspects must be organised in harmony with the Communist ideology, for theory and practice must go hand in hand. In this work of transformation Communists, from China to Czechoslovakia, are unparalleled past-masters.

In so far as it comes within the scope of this book, this transformation consists in detaching Christians from their faith, and leading them to a sincere acceptance of Marxism. This is the final stage of the Communist persecution, very different from the well-known stereotyped pattern of persecution by condemnation to death, mass deportations and wholesale imprisonment.

Not being able to destroy the Church by direct attack, the Communists aim at transforming it gradually into an organisation whose Christian content will be replaced by Marxist ideology. This is the function of the re-education process; the Faith will die, and the new man, Communist man, will be born; the faithful one day and of their own accord will abandon the churches, and ecclesiastical organisation will disintegrate by a process of internal decomposition.

* * *

At the end of this analysis of constant factors common to all Communist persecution, one can see more clearly what distinguishes it from former persecutions; not only is there the astonishing synchronisation in countries so diverse in history and culture, but also and above all there are the methodical procedure (the logical application of Marxist theory), the desire to avoid making martyrs and the refusal to come to grips with Catholicism in the domain of faith.

It seems as though Communism has learned that physical force will never succeed in destroying religion, that faith in God cannot be suppressed by open persecution. Only the public and exterior manifestation of faith can be affected in this way.

Neither do Communists want to bring back the " Church of the Catacombs," for such a Church would escape the control of their Party organisations, and this they fear. They will tolerate a " Church of Silence," but their hopes go further—the emergence of a Church completely integrated into the Communist system.

The supreme tragedy of the contemporary persecution lies in this effort to enslave the Church to the godless ideology of Communism, to this theocracy without God, to this Marxist Josephism.

What are the results of ten years of Communist persecution? At first sight the results seem slight enough. According to information received, in all Communist countries there is a quite satisfactory attendance at those churches which are still open. This however proves merely that the Marxist re-education has not yet yielded all its fruit, and from the Communist viewpoint there is no need for excessive worry. The " time-factor " will eventually succeed in overcoming the resistance of the old bourgeois society. Under Communism even condemned institutions may carry on for a time, but their content and spirit will change gradually through a process the outcome of which is in Communist theory inevitable.

In fact there *has* been a real change in the life of the Church during the past ten years. People may still profess the faith to the extent of going to church. But the Christian community has no longer the right to live publicly according to its faith. Ecclesiastical organisation has been either undermined or abolished. The Church has been excluded from all activities which do not strictly pertain to worship. Indeed if the strength of the Church consisted solely in its external organisation, it would have to be admitted that the Communist régimes had got the upper hand. In no country behind the Iron Curtain does there exist a single independent ecclesiastical organisation. Everything is directed and controlled by the State.

Diocesan administration, as has been already pointed out, is often entrusted to Vicars General chosen directly or indirectly by the Government to replace the bishops who have been deprived of their authority or imprisoned. If it happens that a bishop is still theoretically at the head of his diocese, the *Bureau for Ecclesiastical Affairs* exercises a constant and strict control over his administration. It is the Bureau that *proposes* the transfer of parish priests and curates and even undertakes the publication of pastoral letters. The bishop at most is expected to give his consent so as to make valid the decisions taken by the State.

In addition, when a split has been caused among the clergy, the Government can maintain that the bishops and priests in prison are there for political reasons. After all, those who have shown themselves loyal members of the State enjoy perfect freedom.

Occasional changes in Communist religious policy may lead one to mistake the real intentions of the Communist régimes. There are periods of truce such as occurred everywhere after the death of Stalin when the new policy of " co-existence " came into being. Certain " gestures of relaxing pressure " may have given the impression that the Communists had decided not to push their anti-religious programme to its logical end, that they were satisfied with the results already obtained and so would not proceed to the total liquidation of the Church.

As examples of such " relaxing of pressure " may be mentioned the permission to consecrate two bishops in Lithuania, the liberation of Mgr. *Grösz* in Hungary, the conditional liberty granted to Cardinal *Mindszenty*, and to Cardinal *Stepinac* in Yugoslavia; the " act of clemency " towards Cardinal *Wyszynski* in Poland, the soft-pedalling of the *Triple Autonomy Movement* in China, the liberation of Bishop *Marton* and a certain easing of the pressure against the clergy in Romania, the gradual abolition of concentration camps for priests and religious in Czechoslovakia, the liberation of imprisoned priests in Viet-Nam after the signing of the Geneva Agreement (20 July 1954), etc.

Such gestures are not mere sporadic and isolated occurrences. They point to a single source of inspiration. Unfortunately there are good grounds for believing that there is no real change of heart, no true renunciation by the Communists of their " scientific " anti-religious principles. The interpretation is rather that to-day it is important to make the Catholic masses believe in the possibility of spiritual co-existence with Communism, so that the process of disintegration may meet with less opposition.

For the rest such " easing-off gestures " are—just gestures ! What could be done in Lithuania could not be done in Viet-Nam and Albania; the " clemency " shown to Cardinal *Wyszynski* in Poland was accompanied by the suppression of the faculties of Theology and Canon Law in the Catholic university of Lublin. And when bishops had been liberated " under conditions," the Communists did not revoke their unjust accusations against them; they have still to bear the burden of their unjust condemnation and are excluded from the exercise of their sacred ministry.

The plain truth forbids us to believe that the " Socialist States " or " People's Democracies " mean by this easing-off to give the Church juridical guarantees or a greater measure of independence. On the contrary it would seem nearer the truth to say that the new tactics mean for the Church a more disquieting process of slow attrition and enslavement. For while giving these signs, the Communist Governments favour in every way " progressivism " among the clergy, and give every assistance to the editors of the *Hungarian Catholic Bulletin*, *Dzis i Jutro* in Poland, the *Katolické Noviny* in Czechoslovakia, *Nova Pot* in Yugoslavia, etc. This is a new type of persecution carried on in the atmosphere of " co-existence " and " greater moderation."

The ten years' struggle which the Communist dictatorship has waged against the Catholic Church, and the heroic resistance of the latter, seem to indicate that the " limiting-point " foreseen by *Lenin* has been reached. *Lenin* affirmed that one day Communism and Christianity would have to stand alone face to face, as it were, in single combat.

In the West many Christians see no more in Communism than a threat to peaceful living and an attack on their political freedoms and economic security; others, with somewhat greater insight, think Communism can be fought on the merely social plane, but forget or do not see the magnitude of the religious drama that is going on before their eyes. The Communists however —and the persecution is proof positive of this—look on Christianity and fidelity to Christ's teaching as the greatest obstacle to the establishment and consolidation of their dictatorship and to the triumph of Materialism.

Communists see in Christianity their chief enemy much more clearly than Christians see their enemy in Communism.

To establish a Marxist régime systematic " re-education " of the masses is thought sufficient to overcome the psychological obstacles (" egoism " and the " bourgeois mentality "). Economic obstacles can be removed by transforming the economic structure of society, if necessary at the cost of bloodshed. " Purges," deportations, special courts, informers, strict police control, suppression of freedom of speech and of the press, and the " cordon sanitaire " along the frontiers of the corrupt bourgeois world—these are the means employed to rid the " new society " of the lukewarm at home and to silence adversaries abroad. But to overcome the resistance of a Christian, Communism must re-mould his soul, that unique reality which escapes the omnipresent control of the Totalitarian State, and whose faith is at the antipodes of the Communist world-outlook. The Christian as such cannot be fitted into the Communist scheme of the *homo economicus*. The history of Christianity cannot be explained by the theory of historical Materialism. The Sermon on the Mount and the work of Redemption wrought on Calvary are historical events that transcend the logic of dialectical Materialism.

But precisely because Christians, and above all Catholics, if they live up to their vocation, are the most refractory to Communism, they constitute for the Marxist leaders the main object of attack. When these latter succeed in " proving " to Catholics the " compatibility " which they allege exists between Christ and Marx—the classic case may be seen in the " re-education "

of Chinese Christians—they know that they have won over to
the Party precious elements, thanks to the " dogmatic and
disciplinary " formation received by Christians within the
Church.

" The Church of Silence " has sprung from the face-to-face
struggle between Christianity and Communism. The history of
that encounter shows that Communism is the greatest enemy
the Catholic Church has had to face in the 2,000 years of its
existence. At the present time the Church is enduring a
persecution aimed at her total destruction, and the scientific
and methodical planning of that persecution in no way cloaks
its brutality. This persecution rages over a large area of Christendom (nearly half of Europe) and over vast territories of Asia.
It exerts powerful ideological pressure in the economically
undeveloped regions, and is at the same time trying to stake
a claim in the West. Behind the persecution is a formidable
organisation such as was never in the hands of the persecutors
of the past.

It employs with exceptional—one might say with diabolical
—skill all the means offered by modern technology and all the
fruits of psychological research. The ranks of the persecutors
constitute a united militant force, knowing what its aims are,
merciless in the pursuit of its purpose, a force ready to sacrifice
all (family, fatherland, ambition, personal interests) for the
triumph of the Communist ideal and the establishment of the
Party in a position of power. Finally the persecution is backed
by one of the mightiest world powers which has succeeded
in linking its cause with the hopes of millions hungry for greater
social justice.

In the face of this persecution it is a prime duty to be aware
of the danger and to take steps to defend the Faith. What
spurious reasons of political, social or economic expediency
can cloak the primary importance of the religious and human
drama that is being enacted before our eyes? However powerful
may be the seductive appeal of Marxism for certain Christians,
must it not seem illusory in face of the manifest aim of the system,
an aim essential to atheistic Communism—the destruction of
the Church of Jesus Christ? Social action is indeed necessary.

But can one hope to be of service to mankind by siding with the self-confessed enemies of God and of the Church?

Let it be clearly understood however that what matters is the defence of the Faith. It would be a serious mistake to try to use the Church as an ally against Communism on the purely political plane. The Church condemned Nazism even though Nazism went to war with Communism, for Nazism was imbued with the same errors as Communism. The Apostolic Letter of 1952 to the peoples of Russia, *Sacro vergente anno*, recalled that the Church had refused to join the campaign against Russia in the last war, even though it was held up as a new " Crusade."

The Church combats error wherever it shows itself; she opposes injustice wherever it is perpetrated. Hers are weapons of peace. She denounces what is contrary to natural and divine law; she preaches the truth *opportune, importune*; she promotes justice with vigour and perseverance. The cause which the Church defends and for which 75 million persecuted Catholics are suffering in Communist-dominated countries is the cause of truth and of man's fundamental and entire freedom. It is the cause of God.

Chapter 2

Propaganda by Equivocation

THE " NEW ROAD " in Soviet international policy dates approximately from the " purges " which followed on Stalin's death. In dealing with this policy Communist propaganda has stressed in a marked manner the possibility of " co-existence " between the Communist régimes and religion. The different Communist-dominated countries have betrayed a great unanimity and an obstinacy not without significance in insisting in a very special way on the possibility of the existence—or rather of the co-existence—of Catholicism with Communism. If this co-existence has not so far become a reality, the blame is not to be laid at the door of the Democratic Progressive Governments; these have given ample and clear proof of their desire to put an " end to the state of tension."

The twentieth congress of the Soviet Communist Party, February 1956, supplied new material to this kind of propaganda with the declarations of *Nikita Kruschev* on " peaceful co-existence," with the " thaw " of Stalinist tyranny, with the introduction of " group direction " and the burial of the " cult of personality."

One result of this policy of the " new road " has been that the Western press has taken up the theme of " possible co-existence " and this has been echoed in public debates and controversies. There has been not a little talk about the possibility of " agreements," of " overtures," of " conversations " and " discussions," of the bringing about of " normal living relations " between Catholic communities and Communist régimes, and of the possibility of agreeing on a *modus vivendi*, if not of entering into Concordats at once. That Western public opinion has taken such an interest in this " leit-motiv " so dear to Communist propaganda for the past two years is surely a victory for the Communist propagandists.

The arguments which have served, and still serve, as the premises of Communist propaganda and which consciously or unconsciously are dutifully re-echoed by Western opinion, are of two orders: political and religious.

On the political plane Communist propaganda aims at establishing the belief that in the Marxist-ruled countries a change is taking place which makes peaceful international co-existence possible.

On the religious plane it is strongly insisted on that religious peace reigns in Communist-ruled countries; that there is full and absolute freedom for Christians and Catholics. Moreover it is pointed out that the frictions of the past, due not to religious but to political causes, can never be repeated, since " popular justice " has eliminated " the re-actionary, imperialist, war-mongering, traitorous " section of the clergy. If Catholics were only willing, so goes the propaganda, religious freedom could be exercised under Communism. The People's Governments have given ample proof of wanting a broad-minded policy. The premises then are there—and the facts show that they are there. Now it is up to the Catholics, and especially to the Vatican, to draw the conclusions and let the world see whether or not they are persons of " good-will." The people want to work in peace, and because they do, conclude the propagandists, each one must shoulder the consequences of his own attitude.

To demonstrate the Communists' will to " ease the strain " every little incident was good enough. The following are a few examples from among those which they have most often mentioned:

> the consecration of two bishops in Lithuania;
>
> the journey to the USSR in December 1955 of a priest from the faculty of Theology at Graz. He was received in Moscow by the Secretary for the Affairs of non-Orthodox communities and by *Mikoyan* himself;
>
> the " clemency " shown to some of the imprisoned prelates, especially to Cardinal *Mindszenty*, Primate of Hungary, and to the Archbishop of Kalocsa, Mgr. *Grösz*;

the statements of some of the bishops in countries behind the Iron Curtain particularly those of the Lithuanian prelate, Mgr. *Mazelis*, and of 87-year-old Mgr. *Picha*, Bishop of Hradec-Kralové in Czechoslovakia;

the journey to Vienna of two Polish emissaries to ask the ecclesiastical authorities to act as mediators with the Holy See;

the journey to Rome of two " progressive " Polish envoys (May 1956) in order " to establish contacts to bring about better conditions for the existence of the Catholic Church in the People's Republic ";

the meeting between the Apostolic Nuncio in Italy and the Soviet Chargé d'Affaires in August 1956 in order to hand over two Soviet diplomatic documents;

the favourable Soviet re-action towards the " convergence of view-points " on certain international problems between the teaching of *Pius XII* and the directives of Moscow, as for example, the Christmas radio broadcast in 1955.

In spite of the clear statements made from time to time by authorised sources on the true nature of the events which were supposed to point to the " easing of strained relations," [1]

---

[1] *L'Osservatore Romano* has not failed at each turn of Communist propaganda to put events in their true light. Thus with regard to the journey to the USSR of a professor of the faculty of Theology at Graz, it was pointed out that this was entirely on his own private and personal initiative. As for the acts of " clemency " it was remarked that these in no way made reparation for the acts of violence of the courts and of the police, which ended in the condemnation of cardinals, archbishops, bishops and priests, whose only crime was that they were faithful to their mission. The improvement in the lot of the few only threw into sadder relief the oppression which still weighs on thousands of others. Only two of the " liberated " bishops have been able to take possession of their sees again; for the others it is but a mockery of liberty, since they are either interned or placed in forced residence far from their dioceses, under the supervision of the police. With regard to the speculations attempted on the subject of the consecration of two Lithuanian bishops the Vatican paper recalled that, when Communism finds that it is not possible to destroy religion by a simple decree and that it can attain its end only by a process of attrition, it sometimes consents to allow the " surviving " Catholics to have their bishops. Concerning the " convergence " of the teaching of Pius XII and the international directives of the USSR, this is something lately discovered; the same teaching was scoffed at when the Sovereign Pontiff spoke of peace on occasions which were less equivocal.

The statements attributed to bishops in countries behind the Iron Curtain deserve

Communist propaganda did not fail to make profitable use of these both at home and abroad. They showed as proofs to foreign countries photographs of crowded churches, of public processions, and also of prelates side by side with leaders of the Communist Party and with Ministers of State.

From this can be judged the importance which Communist propaganda attached to this policy of " relaxation." Once the ecclesiastical organisation has been brought into complete subjection to the State, once Catholics themselves have been inoculated with the virus of discord and of real heresy, then the Church is destined according to Marxist theory to founder and to perish from " internal contrasts." Then there is no reason, while waiting for this slow disintegration, for not adopting a policy of " relaxation," or of " co-existence." In fact this will but make it easier for the atheistic State to get control over the few who still hold on to their " superstitions."

But what is not so easy to explain is the attitude of those non-Communists, and among them some Catholics, who hold that the " important " conciliatory advances of the Communists can no longer be ignored. According to them the policy of the past must be re-examined account being taken of the possibility of peaceful co-existence, above all in the present critical times in which, side by side with this new orientation of the policy of the USSR, an economic and social stabilisation in Eastern Europe is apparent.

To these Western partisans of a re-adjustment of the attitude of Catholics with regard to Communism are joined certain Catholic intellectuals who in countries under Marxist domination call themselves " progressives," and who are striving to spread the idea that the type of Communism being built up in their countries is fundamentally only a kind of practical Christianity

---

the same amount of credence as the self-accusations of the Communist leaders accused in the courts, and now re-habilitated. Finally the meeting between the Apostolic Nuncio in Italy was sought for by the Soviet Chargé d'Affaires and was confined to the handing over of documents already published in the press and given to the other members of the Diplomatic Corps. The Nuncio himself hastened to deny the unjustifiable conclusions that Communist propaganda tried to draw from this meeting. It must be remarked that it deliberately attempted to confuse the State of the Vatican City with the Holy See, since no one could say that the USSR had ever shown any consideration for the Catholic Church and its Head.

very close, if not to the letter, at least to the spirit of Christianity.

Other Catholics begin with " practical " considerations, that is to say, with the idea that Communism is a phenomenon in some way inevitable; the " fact that Communism exists " is undeniable; that must be taken into account and an understanding must be reached with it, if everything is not to be lost. Communism, they argue, to-day offers the possibility of saving whatever can still be saved. Advantage must be taken of this.

Other Catholics again, forgetting what is the very essence of Communism, live in the hope of a change of heart on the part of its adherents, merely because they know of one or other of these signs of " moderation " which have been mentioned.

And there are not wanting individuals who do not hesitate to accuse of " misplaced obstinacy " those who point out, with regard to co-existence, the irreconcilable opposition that exists between Marxism and Christianity. They have reproached Catholics and even the bishops of certain countries who had put the faithful on their guard against this Communist propaganda of deceptive soft-pedalling, for harbouring a fundamental and unjustifiable distrust of the possibility of the redemption of Communism.

To all those who live in the hope, if not of an ideological reconciliation between Marxist-Leninist Communism and Catholicism, at least of a practical *modus vivendi*, it is well to recall that, as long as the conditions of existence imposed on the Catholic Church in the People's Democracies remain unchanged, this *modus vivendi* can be nothing other than an unconditional surrender of the Church to the demands of Communism.

It would be well indeed to remember, in spite of the " easing of the strain," that

> Marxist-Leninist Communism, even under the new " group direction," is anchored firmly to its materialist principles and to its militant Atheism, according to which " co-existence " is granted on the basis of an unprecedented accomplished fact : the criminal physical and moral violence in the last ten years against the Catholic Church, which

has had no equal in extent and degree in twenty centuries of Christian history;

the Communist system and ideology give no guarantee of how long this change-over will last, which to-day it pleases these individuals to praise;

the Church continues to be oppressed, shut within its temples, cut off from the every-day life of men, while not one of its essential activities has yet been restored to it (religious apostolate, press, education of youth, social activities, works of charity . . .);

the Church can exercise its " acts of religious worship " only under severe control and within the limits of strict laws, which the Communist administration interprets as it wills; [2]

liberty of worship—sometimes only theoretical, for the reasons given already—continues to be synonymous with *religious liberty* in the eyes of the law and of Communist propaganda. Besides it is often granted only at the price of acceptance of the Communist political system;

the government of many dioceses is confided not to the lawful bishops but to priests, not very numerous indeed, whose collaboration the Communists have secured by a variety of methods;

even if all the bishops and all the priests in prison at the present moment were set free but still forbidden to exercise their ministry, the Communists would gain in two ways: they would show themselves generous, and at the same time would have taken care that the persecuted Church would not be able to take one step forward on the road to liberty.

---

[2] *L'Osservatore Romano* opportunely drew attention to the fact that these limitations of the liberty of the Church could be less severe in some countries than in others; but that did not depend on the will of the Communists, but on the strength of the Christian conscience of the faithful as a whole. When the moral resistance of millions of Catholics, continued the paper, shows itself stronger at least for the time being than the will of their oppressors, the Communists in their external propaganda claim merit for a leniency which is in reality a reverse for them.

It has been stated above that in practice Communism remains anchored to its atheistic and materialistic premises. On this point it is well to recall the " slant " given to anti-religious propaganda by the Central Committee of the Soviet Communist Party in the famous *Resolution* of November 1954, signed by the Secretary of the Party, *Kruschev*. This was the signal for " easing-off " and for tactical concessions. But the intrinsically atheistic sub-stratum of Communism was re-affirmed once again and with still more vigour than in the past.

The Resolution began by recognising that " serious errors " had been committed by the militants of the " Agit-Prop " and by certain over zealous members of the Party. The propagandists, so said the Resolution, had been badly chosen; many of them, according to *Kruschev*, were " persons barren of science and of atheistic propaganda " and their whole intellectual equipment consisted in " stupid stories and fables about the clergy."

The Resolution continued:

" Propaganda which is scientifically atheistic, used in a profound and patient manner and employed judiciously amongst the faithful, will eventually succeed in liberating them from their religious errors. On the other hand every administrative measure or illegal attack against the faithful and the clergy will turn only to our disadvantage and will definitely strengthen their religious prejudices . . . The Central Committee repeats that scientific atheistic propaganda ought to be based on the explanation of the most important phenomena of life, of nature and of society . . . and on the conquests of science which confirm the validity of the materialistic theses on the development of nature and of society." [3]

Therefore the struggle against religion should have developed from that point according to rigorously scientific principles and with flexible tactics.[4] This means that at the very beginning

---

[3] *Pravda*, 11 November 1954.

[4] The interpretation given by the Central Committee of the Soviet Communist Party was naturally the authority for the beginning of the " new " anti-religious propaganda in other countries. Everywhere " errors " of method were recognised and new directives given. Innumerable extracts from the Communist press in each country could be quoted:

of the easing-off of the religious situation there was deep down nothing but a refinement of the anti-religious struggle.

Kruschev was still more explicit when he declared on 22 September 1955:

> " Each citizen can do as he wishes with regard to religion ; profess whatever faith he likes; frequent his churches . . . But that does not at all mean that Communism has modified its fundamental attitude towards religion. We repeat as heretofore that religion is the " opium of the people " and that the greater the number of those who will be awakened from their pipe-dreams, the better it will be for progress. But we think that we should act by persuasion and by having recourse to reason." [5]

After the Resolution of November 1954 and the declarations of September 1955 the situation was stabilised in this manner and *Kruschev* made no mention of the anti-religious struggle in his full report to the twentieth congress of the Party. On the one hand the Soviet State repeats that it does not intend to interfere in the religious affairs (which are private matters) of the citizens and of the clergy, as long as these observe a loyal attitude towards the régime; on the other hand a more systematic and more rigorously scientific turn has been given to anti-religious propaganda. The Communist slogan, " The Party does not tolerate neutrality in religious matters," continues to be repeated incessantly.

Consequently the lines of action which have been strictly followed since then have been:

1. the struggle against religion is a difficult one; in order to be effective it must become more concrete, more systematic and less formal;

---

in Bulgaria (*Otecstven Front*); in Hungary (*Gyoer Sopronmegyei*); in the USSR (*Pravda*: the article entitled *The great strength of scientific Atheism as a world-outlook* in the issue of 30 June 1955, and *Kommunist*); in Germany (*Neues Deutschland*); in Yugoslavia (*Borba* and *Politika*); in Czechoslovakia (*Rudé Právo* and *Lidova demokracie*).

[5] *Russkie Novosti*, 30 September 1955.

2. this struggle must be undertaken by the whole Soviet intelligentsia (doctors, biologists, chemists, physicists, astronomers, philosophers, artists, ethnographers, etc.) and no longer solely by the " specialists in Atheism " and their papers and reviews.

To bring to a conclusion the discussion of the " co-existence " proposed to the Church and to Catholics, it must finally be noted that

1. With regard to religion " the true easing of the tension " does not depend on Catholicism and on the Church but solely on those who want the " tension."

2. The fact that Communism and Catholicism cannot be reconciled is not due to economic, social and political factors (in other words, to the fact that the Church is tied to an outdated view-point), but entirely to the fundamental antithesis formulated by the doctrinaires of Marxism and maintained with uncompromising inflexibility by those who act in the historical scene according to these " scientific " standards.[6] In other words authentic co-existence would be possible only if Communism renounced atheistic Materialism and the anti-religious engagements deriving therefrom. But in that case Communism would be no longer Communism in the Marxist-Leninist meaning of the word.[7]

3. The preliminary condition for a true " easing of the tension " must consist not in " gestures " but in freedom for the Church, recognition of those basic rights which are now denied her, abrogation of those laws which for years have paralysed every activity not strictly pertaining to worship, and the ending of the physical and moral violence constantly used against her ministers and against the faithful.

---

[6] *L'Osservatore Romano*, 14 December 1955.

[7] An article in the *Neues Deutschland*, 24 June 1956, stated on this point: " Peaceful co-existence does not at all mean that science will no longer oppose superstition, that Marxism-Leninism will no longer need to refute bourgeois economic theories, or that we must no longer defend the stand of our Party in the domain of cultural policy. What interests us is peaceful co-existence between the States, but to speak of co-existence between different ideologies does not make sense."

4. Unless Communism is on the point of revising, modifying or abandoning its own ideology, that is to say, unless it is definitely ready to give up being Marxist, one cannot but think that in promoting a policy of co-existence and of relaxation the true intention is to attempt to bring the Catholic masses, if not the Church itself, to accept an accomplished fact, a fact accomplished in the most brutal manner.

For the moment one can only observe with *Pius XII*:

" . . . The Catholic Church for decades and especially for the past ten years is undergoing one of the most serious, and taking everything into consideration, one of the most dangerous persecutions that she has ever known." [8]

---

[8] Message to the German Catholics on the occasion of the *Katholikentag* of September, 1956.

Chapter 3

THE PERSECUTION OF THE CATHOLIC CHURCH

IN

The Soviet Union

RUSSIA

THE SUCCESS OF the Bolshevik Revolution of 1917 marked the beginning of a new period not only in the history of Russia, but also in that of Christianity. The Communist leaders immediately adopted a clear-cut attitude towards religion and religious denominations, and to achieve their aims they made use of all the means provided by the absolute dictatorship they had established.

The anti-religious activity of the Soviet Union was destined to exercise a great influence on other countries, firstly through the directives issued by the Komintern to the Communist International, and then through the political prestige of the USSR after World War II. In its war on religion, particularly on the Christian faith, Bolshevik Communism varied its attack at different stages. As long as the revolutionary cause was threatened by Civil War (1917-1921), the measures adopted were sporadic and lacked co-ordination. Later the persecution was systematic, with periods of intense activity alternating with periods of relative calm. But at all times the Communists kept up an extremely active propaganda campaign.

According to Communist doctrine the factors which contribute to the survival of religion are the following: State protection; the influence of religion on the education of youth; its cherished place in family life and in the hearts of the masses among whom it acts as a spiritual " opium." Hence the Bolsheviks immediately directed their efforts to isolating the Churches from all aspects of public life.

By one of its first laws the Supreme Soviet declared the

separation of Church and State.[1] The Church was deprived of
all its estates and of all other sources of revenue and was thus
left at the mercy of the State. Religion was declared to be the
private affair of each citizen. Article 13 of the New Constitution
of July 1918 proclaimed: "Every citizen has the right to engage
in religious and anti-religious propaganda."

Other laws and decrees were aimed at weakening the bonds
of family life and undermining the authority of parents over their
children. Education was withdrawn from the authority of the
Church, and religious instruction was completely forbidden
during the entire period of youth formation. Until a child
reached his majority, Atheism was the keynote of his education.

It was in the treatment of adults however that the war on
religion reached its climax,[2] and the Bolshevik State threw all
its resources into the struggle. From the beginning conferences
were organised on the theme, "Religion and Communism," and
the best of these lectures were printed and widely distributed
among the people. Articles attacking religion appeared frequently
in the press. Anti-religious handbills were circulated. Even
poetry and music were pressed into service in the war against
God, and the cinema and theatre were used to popularise the
anti-religious campaign. The walls were plastered with posters
that caricatured religion.[3]

A seminary with a faculty of Atheism was established for the

---

[1] Decree of 23 January 1918. Cf. Boukharine-Preobrajensky, *ABC du Communisme*,
1920. Lenin in his so-called "testament" published in *The New York Times* of 8 October
1926 stated: "Bukharin is not only the greatest theoretician of the Party and the most
worthy of being listened to, but he can also be rightly considered the favourite of the
whole Party."

[2] Bukharin stated in 1919: "The separation of Church and State, and of school
and Church, has been relatively easy, almost an effortless task for the proletarian power.
But it is incomparably more difficult to fight against religious prejudices which have
already taken deep root in the conscience of the masses and which are extremely long-
lived ! The struggle will be long; patience must be accompanied by measures of extreme
firmness." Quoted from M. d'Herbigny, *L'âme religieuse des Russes*, in *Orientalia Christiana*,
III, 1 (1924), p. 8.

[3] Cf. Boukharine-Preobrajensky, *op. cit.* pp. 215-216 : "A war of maximum intensity
against religious prejudices must be waged at the present time when the Church,
revealing itself as a counter-revolutionary organisation is using all its religious influence
to launch the masses into a political struggle against the dictatorship of the proletariat.
The Orthodox Faith supported by the popes tends to ally itself with the monarchy.
Consequently the Soviet power should from the present moment engage in a most
intense campaign of anti-religious propaganda. This can be done by special conferences,
public discussions, publication of a whole new literature specially adapted for the purpose,

Communist Youth Party (*Komsomol*). From Christmas 1922, when the Bolsheviks were well established, the *Komsomol* took an active part in anti-religious processions and burlesque parades organised through the streets of Moscow, Leningrad and other large towns on the major Christian feast days. That same Christmas appeared the first edition of *Bezboznik* (" Godless "), an illustrated monthly containing blasphemous attacks on religion. The magazine was widely circulated and carried on its anti-God campaign under the banner of " science."

While Christianity was in process of liquidation, the Bolsheviks entrusted the Communist Party with the task of finding substitutes for religion. Party meetings were intended to act as substitutes for religious ceremonies, and were supposed to perform the same social function that religion had previously done in the collective life of the people. The theatre in particular underwent considerable development and became in some sort the temple of the new régime. Whereas in 1914 there were only 210 theatres in Russia, this number had reached 6,000 in 1920 and increased still more in the following years. It frequently happened that churches were transformed into theatres, where Russian ballet and other performances of less artistic value became vehicles of propaganda in favour of sensualism and of the new political order. Above all, the Soviet leaders took pains to establish the cult of Marx, Engels and Lenin among the masses, and even went so far as to organise " nocturnal adoration " at the tomb of Lenin.

The first target for Communist attack was the Russian Orthodox Church, considered as the ally *par excellence* of the Czarist régime. This phase however does not enter within the scope of this book and we shall confine ourselves to the persecution launched against the Catholic Church.

---

or by the widespread diffusion of scientific knowledge which will insensibly, gently, and inevitably, undermine the influence of religion. An excellent weapon in the struggle against the Church has been employed recently in many parts of the Republic, namely, the opening of " incorruptible " relics. This has revealed to huge throngs of fervent believers the gross charlatanism which is at the base of all religion and of Russian Orthodoxy in particular." Probably the reference is to some false reliquary of the Orthodox Church. The Communists would have been more than surprised had they tried the same experiment on the relics of St. Andrew Bobola. Cf. M. d'Herbigny, *op. cit.* p. 9.

The Famine

In the beginning of 1921 news reached Western Europe that a dreadful famine was raging in the South of Russia. The catastrophe was centred in the Volga basin, but it spread over almost the whole of Southern Russia, reaching as far as the gates of Moscow and Petrograd.

When the famished population could no longer find food in their villages they emigrated to the cities in their thousands, but were driven away again by detachments of police, lest overcrowding should lead to still greater disaster. Truly heart-rending was the spectacle of bands of children wandering through the country looking for bread. Deaths from starvation numbered hundreds of thousands.

Pope *Benedict XV* was profoundly moved by the news of such widespread suffering [4] and decided to share in the work of relief. In the summer of 1921 he sent a million lire to the *Œuvre de secours aux enfants* in Geneva and supported as well other charitable organisations in Europe which were engaged in sending relief to the people of Russia. [5] Not content with this, the Pope wished to send a Pontifical Relief Mission to Russia so that the beneficent activity of the Holy See might be more effectively administered. Over and beyond the sending of material aid, the concern of the Holy Father was primarily directed towards securing for the people of Russia a more humane system of government and better living conditions. The Pope negotiated for the admission of such a Pontifical Relief Mission into the USSR.

Pope *Pius XI* continued the work of his predecessor and in the summer of 1922 he addressed a memorandum to the States which had diplomatic representatives at the Vatican, asking them to work for the amelioration of conditions in Russia. He also

---

[4] On 5 August 1921 the Pope wrote to Cardinal Gasparri, Secretary of State: " We find ourselves in the presence of one of the most terrifying catastrophes known to history. An incalculable number of human beings, stricken with famine, exposed to typhus and cholera, are wandering in desperation across an arid country, hoping to find bread, and they are driven away by armed force. From the Volga basin thousands of human beings, doomed to a most cruel death, are calling upon humanity for aid." Cf. *AAS*, XIII, 1921, pp. 428-429.

[5] Cf. M. d'Herbigny, *L' aide pontificale aux enfants affamés de Russie*, in *Orientalia Christiana*. IV, 1 (1925), passim.

requested that, before they should admit the USSR into the circle of free peoples, they should ask the Soviet Government to guarantee " full and universal liberty of conscience," liberty for the public and private practice of religion and worship, and the right to private property which is entailed in liberty of religion.

In March 1922 the Communist Government permitted the sending of a Pontifical Mission, and on 14 July a group of twelve religious (9 priests and 3 lay-brothers) left Rome for the Crimea. The Soviets were anxious that the Mission be invested with a diplomatic character, hoping to use this as a lever to obtain world recognition for the revolutionary Government. But the Holy Father insisted that the Mission should remain a work of relief and nothing more. He undertook that it would not engage in works of the religious apostolate, but asked that it should enjoy the same privileges of inviolability as had been accorded the American Mission.

On 29 September 1922 the Pontifical Mission began its activity in the USSR with the distribution of food to the population and especially to the children. [6]

As has been said, the Soviet Government had forbidden the members of the Mission to engage in any religious or apostolic work during the accomplishment of their task. These conditions were respected and the priests in the group celebrated Mass behind closed doors. The Communist leaders however were not content with this and tried to impose further restrictions, hoping that in this way they would force the Holy See to grant the Mission full diplomatic status. The Soviet demand was impossible, and as a result of the restrictions imposed on the

---

[6] In the district of Eutropia (Crimea) 92 kitchens were installed in 92 villages in a single day. This was repeated in other regions of Southern Russia and the Pontifical Mission later spread its activity to Moscow and Petrograd. As supplies increased, it became possible to give a daily ration of food to 160,000 persons in over 400 localities. The members of the Mission were helped in their work by Russians, whose number rose at one time to 2,500. The distribution of relief was based on the needs of the people, and not on their political opinions or religious beliefs. This relief work reached its maximum development between March and September 1923.

In addition to the daily distribution of food, parcels of food each weighing 54.5 kilos were sent to needy families in various parts of Russia on the occasion of the great feasts (Christmas 1922, Easter 1923, etc.). The gift parcels also contained clothes and footwear. At its own expense the Mission opened clothing factories and bootmaking establishments,

Mission, some of its members had to leave the USSR in October 1923; the remainder left in September 1924. Thus without any fault on the part of the Holy See there came to an end an activity that had sprung from a desire to relieve the moral and physical sufferings of a great people.

Though it was impossible for the Holy See to aid the people of Russia during the famine of 1925, the Pope continued to take a paternal interest in their lot. Prevented from carrying on any relief work within the borders of Russia, the Holy See devoted its attention to aiding Russian emigrants who were no less the suffering members of the same great nation.[7]

The Catholic Church in Russia

The departure of the Pontifical Mission did not mean the disappearance of the Catholic Church within the territories of the Soviet Union. She continued to exist in the hearts of the faithful in spite of the bitter suffering which was their daily bread.

During the period preceding the Communist revolution, the Catholics had not enjoyed the same privileges as the Orthodox Church. They formed only 9% of the population dispersed through the country and they received but little legal protection. Under the influence of Liberalism there had been a slight improvement in the condition of the Catholic Church during the last period of the Czarist Empire, when the relations between the Church and State were regulated by the " Code for Ecclesiastical Affairs respecting Foreign Religions."[8]

According to article 66 of the Constitution, and article 1 of the Code, the Catholic Church, like the other religions, was guaranteed juridical liberty.

> " The principal and dominant religion in the Russian State is the Christian Catholic Oriental Orthodox Church. Nevertheless all subjects of the State and foreigners residing in the Russian State who do not belong to this Church, enjoy everywhere liberty of faith and of worship according to their own rite."

---

and was thus enabled to distribute tens of thousands of garments and boots. In all places where the Mission was operating, special care was taken to see that the sick got food and medicine. Monetary aid was allocated to several sanatoria for tubercular children and to hospitals and hospices.

[7] Cf. M. d'Herbigny, *op. cit.* pp. 25-73.

[8] Cf. *Svod Zakonov*, vol. XI, 1, and supplement up to 1916.

In spite of this solemn proclamation religious liberty was often restricted or suppressed by particular decrees so that the liberty was altogether relative.   Article 13 of the Code for Ecclesiastical Affairs reads:

" Within the general framework of State administration religious matters affecting Christians belonging to other rites, and those who profess other religions, are subject to the competence of the Ministry for the Interior."

The scope of this article was further defined in the Decree No. 1198 of 7 February 1912 which gave the Minister for the Interior " the right to be kept fully and everywhere informed about every manifestation of the religious life of heterodox religions."

In addition article 17 of the Code, dealing explicitly with the matter of correspondence between Catholics and the Holy See, placed serious limitations on their liberty:

" Christians of the Roman Catholic religion who are Russian subjects, be they ecclesiastics or lay persons, may not engage in correspondence with the Roman Curia about matters concerning their religion except through the Ministry for the Interior. No Bull, letter or instruction may be published in the Empire, or in the Grand Duchy of Finland, without permission from His Majesty the Emperor, and unless the Ministry for the Interior has been previously assured that these letters contain nothing contrary to the decisions, sacred rights and privileges of the supreme autocratic authority."

In spite of these restrictions the Catholic Church in Russia could still engage in some activity.   Catholic school children could receive religious instruction in the schools.   It was possible to open and maintain diocesan seminaries and there was an Ecclesiastical Academy at Petrograd.   There was even a certain amount of Catholic social activity.   Relief of the poor, the sick, the aged and orphans was carried on by confraternities, by St. Vincent de Paul conferences and by religious congregations. It was possible to establish new charitable associations, provided that the bishop got previous authorisation from the civil powers.

4

according to the terms of a circular issued by the Ministry for the Interior in 1910 (No. 1016). Likewise the Church might own property, but in this domain it was often harassed by the interference of the civil authorities. The Church was permitted to receive gifts and legacies and possess money; but on the other hand it was forbidden to send money out of the country without special authorisation. The administration of Church property was subjected to the control of lay boards and was not left to the diocesan councils.

From all this it can be seen that the juridical status of the Catholic Church in Czarist Russia was equivocal; one could not say that the State was openly hostile, but at the same time the position of the Church was not at all in conformity with her inalienable rights.

* * *

After the fall of the Empire there was a radical change in the religious situation. During the period of the Provisional Government (February—October 1917) the Catholic Church, as well as the Russian Orthodox Church, entertained great hopes. The Catholic hierarchy hoped for an improvement in the juridical status of the Church, and in 1917 they drew up a *pro memoria* in which were enumerated certain injustices that called for redress, such as the prohibition of both bishops and faithful from corresponding directly with the Holy See and vice versa; the censorship of the *Acta Apostolicae Sedis* by the Ministry for the Interior; and various difficulties that impeded the formation of the clergy, the existence of religious orders, the development of Catholic associations, religious instruction outside church and school, the erection of churches and chapels, etc.

These hopes gave way immediately to bitter disillusionment. As soon as the Bolshevik faction seized power as a result of the October Revolution (7 November 1917 according to the Gregorian Calendar) the Church was straightway " separated " from the State. The decree of 23 January 1918 was aimed in the first place against the Church of the majority, but the

Catholic Church and the other religions were no less affected. By virtue of this decree the Catholic Church was placed in the category of a mere religious " association " and no longer possessed even the same rights as professional and cultural organisations. By the same decree she was robbed of her material possessions and deprived of the right to possess anything in future; the churches became part of the " national patrimony." The " community of the faithful " could still make an agreement with the civil authority, and thereby be authorised to make use of the church building, on condition that they paid a public tax for its use and provided for its repair. The taxes imposed were so deliberately oppressive that most often the offerings of the faithful—the sole authorised source of church income—did not suffice. As an inevitable result their church was closed. Besides religion was banished from the schools. Anti-religious propaganda was spread abroad in every possible way, while the Church had no longer the means of counteracting it: press, films, libraries . . .

After these initial measures which did the Church consider-able damage, the Communists spared the Catholics somewhat, while they concentrated on the persecution of the Orthodox Church. Owing to their relatively small numbers the Catholics did not constitute a serious " counter-revolutionary " threat to the establishment of the new régime. Their numbers were further reduced when Russia ceded territories in the west by which Poland and the Baltic countries regained their independ-ence. In 1917-1918 while the western frontier was not yet defined and the Poles were still streaming eastwards, there were about 6,000,000 Catholics in Russia; after the Treaty of Riga, 18 March 1921, which defined the frontier between the USSR and Poland, there were no more than 1,600,000 left in Soviet territory.

There was a further reason for exercising a measure of diplomacy in handling the Catholic population. They constituted heterogeneous groups of different nationalities and it was im-portant to take account of the bonds of religion and nationality that linked them with the Catholics of Western Europe. Immediately after the war it was thought that Germany might incline towards the establishment of a Communist régime; rude treatment of German Catholic nationals in Russia would spoil this hope. Further, in an endeavour to maintain peace in the interior of Russia the Soviets had promised Poland, on the occasion of the Treaty of Riga, that they would improve the position of the Catholic Church in the USSR. For these reasons it was judged more prudent to postpone further attacks on the Catholic Church. We shall see what was the true worth of these Communist guarantees.

To meet the menace of Atheism the Catholic Church strengthened her ecclesiastical organisation. In 1917 there were five Catholic bishoprics of the Latin Rite (Mohilev, Kamienec, Minsk, Zytomir and Tiraspol) [9] with 896 priests, 614 churches and 581 chapels; in 1923 there were the following nine ecclesiastical circumscriptions:

1. The Archdiocese of Mohilev with 74 priests, 115 churches and 250,000 faithful;
2. The Diocese of Kamienec with 48 priests, 100 churches and 300,000 faithful;
3. The Diocese of Minsk with 14 priests, 46 churches and 150,000 faithful;
4. The Diocese of Zytomir with 66 priests, 107 churches and 350,000 faithful;
5. The Diocese of Tiraspol with 100 priests, 90 churches and 300,000 faithful;
6. The Diocese of Vladivostok erected 2 February 1923 with 6 priests, 6 churches and 20,000 faithful;
7. The Vicariate Apostolic of the Caucasian Crimea with 30 priests, 30 churches and 70,000 faithful;
8. The Vicariate Apostolic of Siberia erected 1 December 1921 with 12 priests, 35 churches and 75,000 faithful;
9. The Apostolic Administration for the faithful of the Armenian Rite, with 47 priests, 45 churches, 15 chapels and 66,618 faithful.

---

[9] In the north and west of the Soviet Union, as well as in the principal cities, the Catholic colonies were made up of Poles, White Russians, Lithuanians, Letts and Germans. In the southern and central regions of European Russia the Catholic communities consisted of Germans (80%), Poles of the Latin Rite, Ukrainians of the Slav Rite and Georgians of the Byzantine-Georgian Rite. In Asiatic Russia Catholics of Polish, German and Lithuanian origin were found along the railwayroutes.

From 1921 on, some 10 Ukranian and Russian priests, under the jurisdiction of an Exarch, catered for the needs of the few thousand Catholics of the Byzantine-Slav Rite.

Commenting on the political situation in the West and on the work of Pope *Pius XI* for the re-union of the Christian Churches, *Bezboznik* stated in March 1923 that the re-unification of Christendom appeared imminent since the Pope was planning a confederacy of all the " Black Internationales," and added: " If the conversations at present taking place between Rome and the Americans, English, Greeks and Russians meet with success, the ' Red Internationale ' will be in great peril." [10]

The same paper asserted that *Mussolini* had risen to power through Vatican aid and he was thereby pledged to support Vatican policy. It also called upon the Soviet tribunals to punish all Catholic priests, even with the death penalty. This demand was justified by explaining at great length that the Catholic Faith was the principal enemy of atheistic Communism.

The purpose of these articles in *Bezboznik* was to prepare public opinion for the repressive measures that were about to be launched. Only seven days after the publication of the above-mentioned articles, three prelates were condemned to sentences of extreme severity. They were Mgr. *John Cieplak*, Archbishop of Mohilev, Mgr. *Léonidas Feodoroff*, Exarch of the Russian Catholics of the Byzantine Rite, and Mgr. *Constantine Butkiewicz*. Twelve priests and a layman were also sentenced.

All of the accused had been arrested on 5 December 1922 on the charge of resisting the orders of the Soviet Government. The Government in its " anxiety " to succour the victims of the famine had ordered the surrender of all Church valuables, including the sacred vessels used in divine worship (chalices, patens, ciboria, monstrances, reliquaries, etc.) all of which had already in 1918 been declared part of the " patrimony of the people." To avert the execution of this Government order, which would have further impoverished the suffering Catholic community and made divine worship quasi-impossible, the Holy See offered to pay an equivalent sum of money, even in favour

---

[10] Cf. *Bezboznik*, 18 March 1923.

of the Orthodox Church. The Vatican offer was turned down by the Soviet Government.[11]

The ecclesiastical authorities in Russia, both Catholic and Orthodox, declared themselves ready to surrender the sacred vessels on condition that the sum realised by their sale should be administered for famine relief through the direct agency of ecclesiastical organisations and not through Government officials. Moscow called this request an " act of resistance " and proceeded to arrest those responsible.[12]

The charge was that the accused " from the end of 1918 until December 1920 had set up a counter-revolutionary organisation in Petrograd, to oppose the laws and decrees of the Soviet Government with regard to the relations between Church and State, and more particularly in opposition to the decree of the National Assembly of Commissars of 23 January 1918 relating to the separation of Church and State. By their action they tried to shake the loyalty of the people by exciting them at Petrograd in 1922 to oppose unanimously the nationalisation of Church property, the closing of churches and the requisition of articles of value. They also gave evidence of being categorically opposed to the legitimate demands of the Government . . . This opposition comes under articles 63 and 119 of the Penal Code." [13]

---

[11] Cf. *L'Osservatore Romano*, 18 June 1922, which published the Note of Mgr. Pizzardo, Substitute for the Cardinal Secretary of State, to Cicerin, Commissar for Foreign Affairs, as well as the latter's reply. The *NCWC News Service*, 21 May 1923, published the letter which Cardinal Gasparri, Secretary of State, wrote 7 June 1922 asking President Lenin for a reply.

[12] This account is based on authentic testimony and on copies of original documents, and particularly on information collected by the correspondent of the *NCWC News Service* who was present at the trial. Cf. the Note of the *NCWC News Service* of 21 May 1923 and the article of 6 April 1923 by *The New York Herald* correspondent, who was also at the trial.

[13] The following are the two articles in question:

> ART. 63: " Whoever takes part in an organisation which for counter-revolutionary aims opposes the normal activity of Soviet institutions and Soviet schemes, or whoever makes use of an organisation for counter-revolutionary aims, is liable to the penalties attached to Article 58, par. 1 and 2."
>
> ART. 119: " Whoever takes advantage of the religious superstitions of the masses to attack the Workers' and Peasants' Government, or to arouse resistance to its laws and decrees, is liable to the penalties mentioned in Article 69 of the Penal Code." (This Article is part of Chapter III of the Code which deals with " transgressions of the regulations governing the separation of Church and State ").

" Furthermore," continued the act of prosecution, " special charges have been preferred against each one of the accused : [14]

(a) *Cieplak* is accused of having aided the above-mentioned organisation by a Pastoral Letter to his clergy, in which he protested against the requisition of precious articles of Catholic worship without the authorisation of the Church authorities. To the question put by the priest *Rutkowski* of Jeroslav concerning the inventory of Church possessions demanded by the local Commissar, the bishop sent a telegram on 12 March 1922 which read: ' Demand illegal. Do not furnish inventory.' For this reason the priest *Rutkowski* refused to give the inventory. This crime comes under the Penal Code, Section I, Article 77.

(b) *Hodniewicz* is accused of resisting the expropriation of the valuables of the Church of St. Catherine at Petrograd on 24 June. When the Commissars *Kolesnikov* and *Ivanov* wished to examine a small altar furnishing (the tabernacle) he declared that they would do it only over his dead body. Then he said to the faithful who were in the church: ' Let us pray and let us keep them from touching the tabernacle except over our dead bodies.' For this reason the tabernacle could not be examined. This crime is punishable according to Article 119 of the Penal Code.

(c) *Juniewicz* is accused of having on 25 June 1922 offered resistance in the Church of St. Stanislas in Petrograd when Commissars *Kolesnikov* and *Ivanov* were examining the church valuables, and of having shouted ' Get out ! ' This crime is punishable under Article 62 of the Penal Code.

(d) *Rutkowski* and *Pronskietis* are accused of resistance when the Church of the Assumption of the Blessed Virgin was closed by Government order on 5 December. In spite of the formal order given by citizen *Smirnoff*, head of the administrative division of Moscow-Narva, and by the police representative, requiring all the people present to leave the church, the two above-mentioned accused instead of complying with the order incited the crowd in the church to resist the Government and threw themselves on their knees in a theatrical

---

[14] Cf. the complete text of the accusation, detailed list of the accused and the different charges in *La Civiltà Cattolica*, 1923, III, pp. 153-159.

gesture of prayer and called upon the parishioners to join them. By thus exploiting the religious prejudices of the throng present in the church, they incited them to offer passive resistance to the legitimate action of the Government. Article 119 of the Penal Code provides for the punishment of such acts.

(e) *Ciarnas*. In the same place and in the same circumstances described above, being in the middle of the crowd when the police under the orders of *Smirnoff* began to expel the demonstrators, *Ciarnas* along with others who could not be identified, opposed the action of the Government and insulted its representatives. This comes under Article 77 of the Penal Code."

Similar charges were preferred against Mgr. *Feodoroff*.[15] At the end of the trial, which took place at Niosca from 21 to 25 March 1923, the sentences pronounced were of the utmost severity. Mgr. *Cieplak* and Mgr. *Butkiewicz* were condemned to death and to the confiscation of their personal property;[16] Mgr. *Feodoroff* and four priests to 10 years' imprisonment, confiscation of property and loss of civil rights; Mgr. *Malecki* and seven priests to 3 years' imprisonment and loss of their civil rights.

The sentences were not fully carried out. Mgr. *Butkiewicz* was shot on Good Friday, 30 March 1923, but the Archbishop of Mohliev, Mgr. *John Cieplak*, had his sentence mitigated to 10 years' imprisonment and was later expelled from Russia. This difference in treatment may be explained by the fact that by executing Mgr. *Butkiewicz* the régime had given proof within the country of its implacable determination to suppress every " counter-revolutionary " act, whereas by sending Mgr. *Cieplak* to Western Europe they wished to prove to the outside world

---

[15] Cf. *La Civiltà Cattolica*, 1923, III, pp. 152-163; MacCullagh, *The Bolshevik Persecution of Christianity*, London, 1924, pp. 329-339.

[16] " Above all, these accused members of the Catholic clergy have admitted that if the orders of the Pope were in direct conflict with Soviet decrees, they would consider themselves obliged to obey the Pope's commands, and this too not only in matters of faith and morals, but also in what concerns ecclesiastical property that has been confiscated or nationalised. These priests have likewise admitted that contrary to article 121 of the Criminal Code they had instructed children in the so-called *Law of God*, and that they had the intention of continuing this instruction without either recognising or observing the said article of the Criminal Code which forbids such instruction." The various charges are reported by d'Herbigny in *L'Aide Pontificale*, p. 57.

that in Russia justice was tempered with clemency, and that there was no such thing as religious persecution.

Throughout the period of this trial the Communist propaganda organs directed their attacks not only against the accused, but also against the person of the Holy Father,[17] who at that very time was doing his utmost to alleviate the sufferings of the Soviet population. Obviously the Communist intention was to sabotage the moral effect of the Pontifical Mission by using the famine motive as a weapon against the Catholics so as to accuse them of hypocrisy.[18] How could the Catholics be sincere in their relief work if they refused to give up their valuables for the good of the people?

Very soon all the bishops were affected by the measures directed against the Catholic hierarchy. The Bishop of Minsk, Mgr. *Zygmunt Lozinski*, was arrested in 1922 and then expelled. Mgr. *Ignatius Dubowski*, Bishop of Zytomir, was arrested in June 1923 and exiled in 1925. The Bishop of Kamienec, Mgr. *Peter Mankowski*, was exiled in 1923 after a period of imprisonment in Moscow. The Administrator of the diocese of Tiraspol, Mgr. *Adrian Smets*, likewise passed some time in prison before being set free in the West. Mgr. *Charles Sliwowski* who had been but recently elected to the See of Vladivostok in 1923, had to take refuge in Shanghai, while the Vicar Apostolic of Siberia had to flee to Harbin (Manchuria).

The normal pattern of Bolshevik tactics was to banish the heads of the ecclesiastical circumscriptions after a period of imprisonment of longer or shorter duration. However Mgr. *Leonidas Feodoroff*, Exarch of the Russian Catholics of the

---

[17] Several sections of the Third International demanded the death sentence on the Pope. *Pravda*, 31 March 1923, the day after the execution of Mgr. Butkiewicz asked: " Why not institute a process against the Pope of Rome? The trial of Cieplak has shown that the person mainly responsible for the resistance organised by the counter-revolutionary priests to oppose the confiscation of Church property is the Pope of Rome. He should be tried by the revolutionary tribunal. The recent trial and the sentence pronounced . . . have proved . . . that the Catholic clergy are the bitter enemy of the poor and of the Peasants' and Workers' Government." The paper went on to accuse the Catholics of refusing aid to the famine victims.

[18] In the Consistory held in May 1923 Pope Pius XI said: " Nothing that has happened will stop the work of merciful relief which we have undertaken and continued all these months in an attempt to alleviate such profound distress. We shall continue it as long as we see the necessity for it and as long as it remains possible, according to the advice of the Apostle: *Noli vinci a malo*, but rather *Vince in bono malum*." (*AAS*, XV, 1923, p. 252).

Byzantine Rite (died 1935) and some others were dragged from prison to prison until their death.

Change of Tactics

By the end of 1923 all the episcopaı sees were vacant. At this stage the Russian Communists adopted a new plan of campaign. From 1924 to 1928 there was a period of relative calm. There was no interruption in the struggle against religion, and particularly against the Catholic Church, but less violent methods were adopted. In the administration and in the labour organisations the new plan called for a measure of respect for the religious feelings of the faithful and of the workers. There must be no martyrs, no heroes, in this persecution. Nevertheless anti-religious propaganda received wholehearted official support and was aimed at undermining basic Christian practice and belief " imperceptibly, without violence, but none the less persuasively."

The result of this propaganda was a dropping off in the number of the faithful in the ranks of the Orthodox Church and, to a lesser extent, in the ranks of the Catholic Church. Those who resisted became more strongly attached to their faith. The practice of the Christian life had indeed been rendered difficult because of a general anti-religious atmosphere and also because substantial sums of money had to be found to meet the Government tax for the use of the confiscated churches and to support the clergy. In spite of these sacrifices the faithful continued to maintain their clergy, their churches and divine worship.

During the same period there was a considerable drop in the number of priests. Since religious instruction was forbidden, vocations became less numerous. Many priests who were in Russia at the beginning of the Revolution had emigrated to the West. About seventy-five were in prison or had been deported to Siberia. In spite of this, in the diocese of Tiraspol for example, there were still 71 churches open in 1928, and only 23 of these churches were without a priest. It need scarcely be mentioned that the OGPU kept a strict watch on those priests who were still free.

After the first blast of persecution had ravaged the Church in Russia, the Holy See attempted a reorganisation of ecclesiastical circumscriptions that would be better adapted to the needs of the time. The old division into dioceses was no longer suited to the situation that had arisen. Moreover a large part of the territory contained in the circumscriptions which existed in the Czarist Empire had passed into the dioceses of the new countries emerging at the end of the war. Hence in 1926 new Apostolic Administrations were established in the Soviet Union. The following appointments were made: Moscow, Mgr. *Pius Eugene Neveu*; Leningrad, Mgr. *Anthony Malecki*; Mohilev and Minsk, Mgr. *Boleslav Sloskans*; Odessa, Mgr. *Alexander Frizon*; Kharkov, Mgr. *Vincent Ilyin*; Kazan, Samara and Simbirsk, Mgr. *Michael Juodokas*; Mgr. *Augustin Baumtorg* for the Apostolic Administration of the Volga and Mgr. *John Roth* for that of the Caucasus. The list is completed with Mgr. *Carapet Dirlughian*, Apostolic Administrator for the Armenian Catholics in all Russia, and the Reverend *Stephen Demurof*, Vicar *ad interim* of the Apostolic Administration of Tiflis and Georgia.

The new organisation however was robbed of success. Three of the new Apostolic Administrators were soon arrested: Mgr. *Ilyin* in December 1926, and Mgr. *Sloskans* and Mgr. *Neveu* in September 1927.[19]

* * *

It was not long until the Catholic Church in the USSR had to face a new offensive which in certain respects reached its climax in the years between 1929 and 1932. During this period anti-religious propaganda was promoted on a scale that surpassed all its previous efforts.[20] The organisation of the new propaganda campaign was the work of the Association of Militant Atheists, which at that time counted in its ranks more members than ever

---

[19] Mgr. Sloskans was expelled from Russia in 1933, after passing through 17 prisons, from the Solovki Islands to Siberia. Cf. *Dzimtenes Balsas*, No. 5,1951: *Boleslav Sloskans, The Life of an Enforced Labourer in a Concentration Camp in Russia*. Cf. also *The Catholic Church of Latvia under the Bolshevik Torturers*, Stockholm, 1950.

[20] Cf. *Krasnoia Gazeta*, 20 November 1929; *Pravda*, 1 December 1929. Documents relating to the period will also be found in *La Civiltà Cattolica*, 1930, I, pp. 280-283.

before. Possessed of a veritable arsenal of propaganda weapons (press, radio, theatre, cinema, school and administrative channels) the Association co-ordinated its activities in an intense, almost hysterical campaign that stopped little short of actual violence.[21] Here was an ideological war against God and religion, carried out on " scientific " lines in the name of Dialectical Materialism. Faith in the supernatural was classed *a priori* in a category beneath that of " science."

According to the programme envisaged by the Militant Atheists there would not be a single church still open by the year 1937, and by that time too all the priests and ministers of religion would be liquidated, deported or expelled from the country.

This anti-God campaign got official support from the *Law of 8 April 1929*, dealing with religious associations.[22] The 68 articles of the Law laid down the conditions under which these associations might function in the future. Article 13 of the Constitution of 1918, which had become Article 4 in the 1924 Constitution, was now remodelled. Instead of speaking of liberty " *to engage in religious and anti-religious propaganda* " the 1929 Law stipulated that " *religious profession and anti-religious propaganda are permitted to every citizen.*" Henceforth religious propaganda and the propagation of the faith are forbidden. Religion is a matter of " sentiment," not an expression of truth and cannot be allowed any place in public life outside the narrow domain of worship. Until 1929 religious propaganda was theoretically possible, even though in practice it was almost wholly curtailed by various administrative measures. The intention behind the Law of 1929 was to deprive the Churches of their last possible means of defence—possessed, up to the present, at least in theory—against atheistic propaganda.

Changes in the economic and social policy of the Communists likewise entailed grave consequences for the Church. To replace the NEP (New Economic Policy) the Soviets introduced the

---

[21] Cf. collection of documents in *Le front antireligieux en Russie Soviétique*, and in *La guerre antireligieuse en Russie Soviétique*, Paris, 1930.

[22] In the laws we must understand by " religious associations " parishes and other religious organisations. The preliminary draft of the law was presented on 8 April 1929, and approved by the 14th Soviets' Congress on 18 May of the same year. The law was inserted into the official Code of Laws, in 1929, no. 35.

Kolkoz and *Sovkoz* collectivist systems. The universal application of the new system meant that many churches and parishes, especially in villages through the country, were finally deprived of all means of livelihood. Under threat of deportation to Siberia priests were coerced into joining the *Kolkoz*, where of course Church activity was completely excluded.

To keep the churches open the Government taxes had still to be paid. At first the levies imposed on churches and on ministers of religion varied from place to place, but in 1931 the People's Commissariat for Finance introduced a uniform system of church taxation for the whole of the USSR, raising the rate to such an exorbitant figure that it was only a matter of time until every church in the Soviet Union would have to close.

The whole machinery of Soviet administration was thrown into the struggle to stamp out religion. Taking its stand on the law separating Church and State, the Communist Government sought to achieve its ends without attracting undue publicity. For this reason the rulers preferred to carry on their campaign through the administrative channels of the Commissariat for the Interior and through direct police action rather than expose themselves to the publicity of court-room procedure. It was a time of sudden and arbitrary arrests, of secret trials and pre-arranged verdicts, of speedy deportations, of condemnations to forced labour.

During this period the remaining Apostolic Administrators were arrested. Mgr. *Frizon* was imprisoned in 1929 and 1930, then again in 1935 and 1936. Arrested once more in 1937, he was shot in prison. Mgr. *Juodokas* was arrested in April 1929; Mgr. *Baumtorg* and Mgr. *Roth* in August 1930; Mgr. *Malecki* in November 1930. The last mentioned was deported to Siberia until 1934; in that year he was banished. He died in Poland in 1935. Mgr. *James Bagaratian*, who succeeded Mgr. *Dirlughian* as Apostolic Administrator for the Armenians, suffered the same fate as his predecessor and was arrested in 1930. The fate of Mgr. *Demurof* remains unknown.

Finally there was the case of Mgr. *Theophilus Skalski* who in May 1926 succeeded the exiled Bishop *Dubowski* as Apostolic Administrator of Zytomir. He was arrested in June 1926 and

suffered 18 months' imprisonment before being brought to trial
on 27 January 1928 on a charge of supporting counter-revolutionary activity and of espionage.   At a secret trial he was
sentenced to 10 years' imprisonment and 5 years' deprivation of
civic rights.   Eventually he was exiled in September 1932.
Mgr. *Skalski's* sole " crime " had been that he was conspicuous
for his zeal and charity.[23]

The years 1929-1932 saw the total liquidation of the Catholic
hierarchy in the Soviet Union. Priests shared the fate of their
bishops. Of the 66 priests in the diocese of Zytomir in 1918
there remained but one invalid priest in 1931. The roll of clergy
imprisoned or deported during the period contains 114 names.
In the whole of the USSR there were hardly 50 priests still at
liberty.[24]

In spite of the precautions taken by the Soviet Government
to conceal its campaign of persecution, the facts finally became
known in Western Europe. On 2 February 1930 Pope *Pius XI*
invited the whole Catholic world to unite in a crusade of
expiation.[25] Communist persecution was also stigmatised by the
Anglican Church.

The Soviet Government hastened to reply, through interviews
given by the Orthodox Metropolitan *Sergius*, that " complete
liberty of conscience " exists in the Soviet Union. There is no
such thing as religious " persecution " and only those who were
found guilty of counter-revolutionary activity have been condemned. Religious activity as such has not been punished and
" religious convictions are not tampered with." Foreign reports
of religious persecution in Russia are " calumnious fabrications "
and there was no justification for " the intervention of Rome
or Canterbury." [26] Such was the " official " reply. But in a
confidential letter of 20 June 1930, sent to the Holy See by the
supreme Russian ecclesiastical authority, it was stated that these
interviews (given to the *Tass* agency) though authentic, had been

---

[23] Cf. *La Civiltà Cattolica*, 1928, I, p. 377.
[24] Cf. note on the USSR persecution in *L'Osservatore Romano*, 7 April 1929.
[25] Personal letter to Cardinal Pompilj (*AAS*, XXII, 1930, pp. 89 *et seq.*).
[26] Interviews with the *Tass* Agency on 15 February 1930, and with foreign journalists
in Moscow, 17 February 1930.

given under pressure from the Soviet authorities. Here then was further proof of the existence of religious persecution.[27]

* * *

The year 1933 brought another period of relative calm, but there was no diminution in the violence of anti-religious propaganda, which could now be considered as having reached its maximum intensity. With the prospect of a conflict threatening the USSR, the Soviet leaders had to face a fresh problem—that of patriotism. The international bias of the Communist ideology began to yield to a more nationalistic, a more Russian concept. It was necessary to create a spirit of unity within the USSR as soon as possible, and for this purpose it was advisable to avoid measures that would further antagonise the faithful whose lot did not seem to demand the continuance of violent measures. Already almost everywhere they had been deprived of their priests and the constant and methodical pressure of atheistic propaganda was deemed sufficient to effect the gradual and total neglect of religion.

The activities of the Militant Atheists received a new impetus from the legislation of 1936. By article 124 of the Stalin Constitution [28] of that year religious liberty was restricted within still narrower limits. The Law of 1929, as has been mentioned, had stated: "*Liberty of religious profession and of anti-religious propaganda is permitted to every citizen.*" In the 1936 Constitution there is no mention of "religious profession." The text of article 124 reads: "Liberty of *worship* and of anti-religious propaganda is recognised as the right of all citizens." Henceforth only the exercise of "religious worship" is permitted; the Church can no longer raise her voice *in public*.[29]

---

[27] Cf. *La Documentation Catholique*, 23, 1930, col. 845-872.

[28] Stalin's constitution was published for the first time in the newspaper *Izvestia* on 6 December 1936. Cf. Giuseppe Schweigl, *Il Cristianesimo nell' Unione Sovietica*, Roma, 1948, p. 64.

[29] Cf. G. M. Schweigl, *L'article 124 de la Constitution Soviétique sur la liberté du culte.* Recueil des Lois, Rome, 1948. Published by *La Civiltà Cattolica*.

The number of believers continued to diminish but failed to reach the point expected by the Communists.[30] The census of 1937 contained some surprises for the authorities by revealing that 30% of the urban population declared themselves believers, and in the country the proportion rose to 60%.

During the late thirties also the Communists tried to avoid making martyrs for the Faith. Nevertheless on 2 August 1937 Mgr. *Alexander Frizon*, Apostolic Administrator of Odessa, who had already suffered several periods of imprisonment, was shot at Simferopol after a trial that lasted nine days.

The Expansion of Soviet Power ; Persecution in Soviet Occupied Territories.

The secret agreement concluded between the Nazi and Soviet Governments in 1939 had divided central Europe into two zones of influence. The USSR wanted the Baltic countries, that part of Poland east of the Ribbentrop-Molotov line, and the two Romanian provinces of Bessarabia and Bucovina. Germany had already brought Czechoslovakia under her yoke and had designs on Western Poland which she proceeded to realise by declaring war in September 1939.

The USSR emerged from World War II not only endowed with enormous military prestige, but also enriched by vast territories in Europe and Asia, and with a zone of influence in the East (China), which may prove of historic importance for the destiny of mankind.

The consequences of Soviet domination in the countries annexed or occupied in Central Europe were not confined to the political and economic planes. The religious life of these countries also came under Soviet control,[31] and the persecutions

---

[30] Cf. article in *Pravda*, 20 August 1939, entitled: " Plea for systematic anti-religious propaganda "—a significant title for an article in *Pravda*.

[31] The Central Council of the League of Atheists issued a call to arms shortly after the outbreak of World War II: " The twelfth hour has struck in the fight against religion in south-eastern Europe. Our soldiers are going forward under the banner of Atheism. The war against (the Christian) faith is entering a decisive phase. Backed by the bayonets of the Red Army, Militant Atheism is about to achieve a great triumph in south-eastern Europe. There will be no stop to our march on the West, since the National-Socialist State can oppose only a feeble resistance to the atheistic movement." *La Civiltà Cattolica*, quoting the above statement (1949, IV, p. 373) comments as follows: " The war against religion serves the Soviets as a means of political penetration."

launched after the war are still going on. First to fall victim
to the anti-religious campaign, conducted according to methods
that had proved their worth in Russia, were the countries
annexed as a result of the 1939 Ribbentrop-Molotov pact.
After the war came the turn of the satellite countries.

The anti-Church measures adopted by the Communists in the
Soviet-occupied territories varied in severity and thoroughness
from place to place. Factors determining this accidental variation
were: the nature of the union existing between a particular
country and the USSR, the numerical importance of the Catholic
population, and the rite to which they belonged.

ESTONIA

Estonia is the most northerly and the smallest of the three
Baltic States (pop. 1,100,000). In 1938 the Catholics numbered
about 2,000 or 0.2% of the total population. Lutheranism
claimed 78% and 19% belonged to the independent (autocephalous) Orthodox Church.

From 1721 to 1918 Estonia had been a part of Czarist Russia
and the position of the Catholic Church was more or less the
same as in the rest of the Empire. After the proclamation of
Estonian independence in 1919, complete liberty of conscience
was declared. In 1924 the Holy See established an Apostolic
Administration which embraced the whole country, and in 1926
Mgr. *Edward Profittlich* of the Society of Jesus was appointed
Apostolic Administrator. The Catholic population was served
by six parishes erected in the principal centres, and in 1937
there were 11 priests, assisted by about 20 members of religious
orders of both men and women, all of whom were foreigners.

The Catholic Church in Estonia was only twenty years old
when the Soviets arrived in 1940, and it would not have been
difficult for the Communists to crush the young Church utterly
by applying their well-tried methods of liquidation. They
refrained from this step but they succeeded in doing the Church
irreparable harm. From the beginning the attitude of the new
rulers was one of frank hostility to every form of religion.[32]

---

[32] The Lutheran Church and the self-governing Orthodox Church likewise endured
great suffering under the Soviet occupation. If one is to believe the Soviet press in recent

As a result of the events of 1940 the Apostolic Nuncio for Latvia and Estonia, Mgr. *Antonino Arata*, was compelled to leave his post and return to Rome. Priests of German nationality were also obliged to leave the country and so the tiny Catholic community lost half of its clergy.

The Soviet Government declared all churches State property and defined by law that the dwelling of an ecclesiastic could not cover an area of more than 6 *square metres*. Within a short time Mgr. *Profittlich* and one of the five priests who remained were arrested and later deported. The four remaining priests suffered frequent periods of imprisonment and were subjected to interrogations, with the usual accompaniment of threats and actual physical torture. There were many arrests and deportations among the laity, but lack of reliable testimony prevents us from giving the exact number.

Within a few months, but not at a single stroke of the axe lest public opinion might react too violently, every branch of Christian life was successively lopped off. It was forbidden to give religious instruction to those under 18 years of age. Heavy taxes were imposed on the clergy and there was a levy on the performance of religious ceremonies.[33] Church property, including cemeteries, was nationalised. The State confiscated the funds and all the property of Catholic charitable relief organisations, including the Widows' Pension Fund. Bookshops and libraries were " purged " of all religious literature, which then found its way into the central-heating furnaces. At the very beginning of the persecution the two Catholic papers had been suppressed and the printing of the first Catholic edition of the New Testament in Estonian was stopped.

After the relative truce of the German occupation (from 1941 to 1944) the second Soviet occupation brought fresh sufferings. In all Estonia there remained at the end of 1944 only four Catholic priests, reduced in 1945 to two, after the deportation

---

years, the Communist régime has succeeded in breaking the resistance of the Lutheran and Orthodox Churches, the latter being brought under the Patriarch of Moscow in 1945. It seems that they have become almost completely enslaved to the political set-up. The heads of both Churches took part in the Moscow Peace Congress in 1950 and signed the famous Peace Appeal.

[33] An ecclesiastic had to pay twenty times more per square metre than a workman.

to the USSR of the Jesuit Father *Henry Werling* and after the death from privations of the Capuchin Father *Ruszala* in January 1945. There have been no tidings of Archbishop *Profittlich*, who almost certainly must have ended his days in Siberia.

LATVIA

On the eve of World War II the agreement between *Ribbentrop* and *Molotov* made in August 1939 obliged the Latvian Government to sign the so-called " Mutual Aid Pact," by which Soviet troops were authorised to enter the country and set up military bases.

Undoubtedly in signing the pact the Soviets had undertaken to respect the sovereignty of the Latvian Republic; but when the Red Army arrived, it was accompanied by 300 " specialists " whose task it was to prepare the way for a Communist seizure of power. Shortly after their arrival a series of strikes broke out and incidents occurred which enabled the Communist press to describe the Latvian Government as " reactionary." The Kremlin seized the occasion to address an ultimatum to the Riga Government on 16 June 1940, alleging security reasons for its intervention. On the following day the commissar *Wyzinskij* presented a new panel of Government ministers, on which Communist members figured beside men who were well known supporters of the national tradition. At the same time there began the arrest of Lettish patriots, who were branded as " anti-Soviet elements." A general election was held and, as the list of candidates contained only Communist names, the result of the ballot was a foregone conclusion, a complete triumph for the Communist Party. The new parliament (and some persons not belonging to it) met on 21 July 1940. By a truly " democratic " show of hands it decided (1) to reorganise the country on Soviet lines; (2) to petition Moscow for incorporation into the Soviet Union; and (3) to adopt the Stalin Constitution. These measures naturally provoked some outbursts of nationalist feelings, but the slightest shadow of resistance was punished by imprisonment, deportation, and not infrequently by death. So ended Latvia's eighteen-year period of independence.

The Catholic Church in Latvia

The declaration of independence in 1918 had given rise to great hopes of religious freedom and in this case the hopes were realised. The Latvian Republic was founded on a renaissance of national sentiment, strangled under the Czarist rule, and in the respect paid by the new State to the traditional ideals of the Lett people, culture and religion were not neglected.

The Catholics were in a minority, embracing only a quarter of the 2,000,000 inhabitants; the majority were Lutherans. Nevertheless the Catholic Church received special consideration from the national Government. Before 1918 there were only two dioceses of Mohilev and Kaunas, but after the establishment of Latvian independence the former diocese of Riga was reconstituted, and in 1920 a Lett bishop was consecrated to that see, which was subsequently raised to the dignity of an archdiocese (1923). In 1927 a new bishopric was erected at Liepaja (Lietan), and at the same time the Archbishop of Riga received the title of Metropolitan. In 1922 the Latvian State concluded a Concordat with the Holy See, one of the provisions of which was that on the occasion of the agrarian reform of that year, each parish should receive sufficient land to provide for the support of the clergy. In all, 3,000 hectares (about 7,500 acres) were thus allotted. In addition the State allocated a yearly sum for the upkeep of divine worship. The economic prosperity of the country and the general spirit of freedom were manifest also in the external flowering of the Christian life, and in the period between the two World Wars twenty new Catholic churches were built.

The religious orders, breathing again the air of freedom, set about founding new houses. The Marianists, Capuchins and Jesuits and the Sisters of the Infant Jesus, the Sisters of the Holy Cross and the Poor Servants of Our Lady were able to engage in an increasing measure of cultural and charitable activity.

New Catholic periodicals made their appearance: the *Latgolas Vords* (circ. 10,000), the *Katolu Dzeive* (circ. 12,000), the *Rigas Vestnesis* (circ. 4,000), the *Gaisma* (circ. 3,000), not to mention five or six other bulletins and magazines.

On Sundays Holy Mass was broadcast by the national radio station. Religious instruction was obligatory in the State schools and colleges, and in addition the Church had direct control of two high schools (one for boys and the other for girls), a senior seminary (erected at Aglona in 1920, transferred to Riga in 1924), and a junior seminary at Iluksta in the diocese of Liepaja. Finally a faculty of theology was founded in 1938 at the University of Riga. There were numerous Catholic lay associations, such as *The Youth Association*, with a section in each parish which organised reunions, cultural séances, musical festivals, pilgrimages, etc.; *Fraternitas Catholica* for boys and *Terra Mariana* for girls; *Saule*, the Catholic Union Cultural Society; *Catholic Workers' Groups*; *Congregation of the Virgin Mary*; *Eucharistic Crusade*; *Apostolate of Prayer*; *Catholic Women Teachers' Society*; *Catholic Farmers' Union*. The Catholics also ran their own libraries, reading-rooms and convalescent homes.

Persecution; The First Phase

The entry of Latvia within the Soviet political orbit in June 1940 brought with it a new outlook on the rôle of the State, the family, the school, culture and religion. In all these domains the Soviets immediately imposed radical changes which were in contradiction to traditional Lettish ideas.

Deprived of an independent government, the people of Latvia were no longer able to pursue their own national and foreign policy, and so they were obliged by the Soviets to break off diplomatic relations with the Holy See. The Apostolic Nuncio at Riga, Mgr. *Antonino Arata*, was expelled in August 1940 and the Latvian representative at the Vatican, Professor *Hermans Albats*, was deported to Siberia where he died in 1943.

By the Soviet reform of Lett legislation and by the adoption of the Stalin Constitution, *the Church was excluded from public life*. The law indeed recognised " liberty of religious worship," but this was negatived in great part by the terms of the decree of June 1940, and subsequently by the nationalisation of all private property.

The following measures were directed specifically against the Church:

(a) Church property is declared the patrimony of the State.

(b) Not only church buildings and church estates are to be considered as nationalised, but everything that belongs to the Church, including bells, crosses and crucifixes, books of the Holy Scriptures, sacred vessels and vestments.

(c) The use of the church is permitted in return for the payment of a rent, which shall be assessed according to the capacity of the building and according to the schedule of taxes imposed on luxury restaurants and night-clubs.

(d) Rent shall also be paid for the use of bells, sacred vessels and vestments, etc.

(e) A tax shall be levied on every religious ceremony.

(f) It is forbidden to celebrate religious ceremonies outside the church, and the law inflicts grave penalties for the celebration of ceremonies in the open, in cemeteries and in private houses.

The obvious intention behind these measures, which had already been applied in the USSR, was to restrict religious worship in the greatest degree possible. In the case of large churches it was difficult and at times impossible to pay the government tax, as the people had been financially ruined by the nationalisation of their property. In an attempt to meet the levy on religious worship an effort was made to unite two or three parishes in one, and to rely on the services of one priest only. But even this solution became a heavy financial burden with the progressive plundering and impoverishment of the people. Churches which could no longer be maintained by the faithful were given over to profane use. Thus the Catholic church of Ozolmuiza (in the deanery of Rezekne) was requisitioned for service as part of an aerodrome, and on 1 May 1941 became a dance-hall. The church of St. Mary Magdalen at Riga was used by a ballet company who entertained the Soviet troops. In the country several churches were used as depots for agricultural machinery, while others were profaned, looted and burned.

In public life atheistic Communism was the order of the day. Communist Party members, State functionaries and army officers were not supposed to profess any religion. The broadcast of Holy Mass was stopped, and all Catholic publications were suppressed. Religious books were withdrawn from bookshops and libraries. Funeral rites and commemorative ceremonies for the dead, which were a cherished element in Latvian piety, were forbidden. Since the recurrence of Christian feasts, such as Christmas and Easter, was calculated to stimulate the devotion of the people, the Communist authorities decreed that all Church holydays should be abolished, and sanctions were imposed on workers who failed to present themselves on those days. As a substitute for the suppressed feast-days, Communist Party rallies were organised. All these measures were accompanied by a violent anti-religious campaign in the Marxist press, and in the towns there were frequent anti-religious demonstrations.

The Communists devoted special attention to bringing the educational régime into line with the Marxist spirit. Religious instruction was immediately suppressed. As a result the Catholic high schools and the faculty of Theology at Riga closed down. The professors were obliged to follow Soviet indoctrination courses, and subsequently to work for the destruction of the " bourgeois capitalist mentality " and the dissemination of the new philosophy. As a bait to ensnare the young, freedom from moral restraint was encouraged. The " new trend " in education undermined religious practice in the schools. The Catholic student organisations were dissolved, and the young people were forced to enlist as " pioneers " in one or other of the Party organisations.

The Communist attack was directed not only against the cultural prestige of the Church, *but also against its inner organisation*. Every form of Catholic Action was suppressed. By the end of 1940 the religious orders and congregations had been expelled from their houses and their members were forced to re-enter civil life. Monasteries and convents were confiscated by the State. An exception was made for the Poor Servants of Our Lady, who did not wear any special religious habit, and who were allowed to remain in their convent a little longer. Bishops had to give up their residences as a result of the nationalisation of church property; priests suffered the same fate and were in many cases removed by force from their presbyteries.

These repressive methods were not judged sufficient to ensure the triumph of Communism, and further means were adopted. The more zealous members of the clergy were " eliminated," but to avoid rousing too much public indignation the Government in the beginning took pains to make these arrests as secretly as possible, or else the priests marked down for arrest were accused of scandalous or criminal conduct, as for example the parish priest of Elerna, Father *Antons Lapotenoks*, who was accused of " debauchery." Father *V. Litauniks*, parish priest of Indra, was accused by Russian agents of having set fire to his residence (which had been appropriated by the State), whereas the Communists themselves had caused the fire; the curate of Rezekne, Father *Adolf Tarbunas*, was arrested because he had taken payment for cemetery plots; the parish priest of Nagli, Father *Mendriks*, was charged with having cheated the people by celebrating a church marriage. To convince public opinion of the truth of the charges brought against the clergy the confession of the accused was necessary. The extraction of such " confessions " was left to the Chekists and their torture methods.

The outbreak of war between Germany and the USSR was the signal for a wave of massacres and deportations in Latvia. We shall confine ourselves to a few examples. The sufferings of Father *Vladislavs Litauniks* surpassed most others; he was arrested in February 1941, eventually signed his " confession " of guilt and died in prison on 21 June of the same year. When his body was found it bore the marks of the torture he had endured. Another priest, Father *Vitolds Paskevics*, was struck down and killed by Communists when he was returning from a sick-call. Father *Sigismunds Tabore* and his sacristan were attacked in church on 30 June 1941 and both died in prison as a result of their tortures. Between 21 June and 10 July 1941 the following priests were arrested: Fathers *Stanislavs Kapacs*, *Edvards Bekers*, *Kazimirs Strods*, *Peters Aspiniks*, *Jazeps Pudans* and *Janis Zuks*. It is not known whether they were shot or whether they died in a concentration camp. Father *Filips Turks*, a

Capuchin, was arrested on 23 June 1941 and subjected to torture, but he survived until 8 January 1942. Amongst the laity too there were many victims who were imprisoned, deported or executed. The arrest of Mgr. *Joseph Rancans*, Mgr. *E. Stukels* and Mgr. *V. Strelevics* was already planned by the police when the German advance forced the Red army to retreat, leaving the prelates still at liberty.

It is estimated that during the Soviet occupation of Latvia in 1940-1941 a total of 34,000 Catholics and Lutherans were liquidated, especially in the days immediately before the Red retreat. Of this number 6,000 belonged to the Catholic intellectual élite.[34]

During the German military occupation (July 1941 to October 1944), the decrees governing the confiscation and nationalisation of property remained in force. Processions outside the churches were still forbidden and the Catholic press was not allowed to re-appear " through lack of paper." In the churches however there was no restriction on the celebration of religious ceremonies and it was permitted to give religious instruction in the schools, though not on the same scale as before, and with the exclusion of the Old Testament from the religious programme.

The Return of the Soviet Army

The Red army streamed into the streets of Riga on 13 October 1944 and the second Soviet occupation of Latvia had begun. That occupation has now lasted 13 years. Partisan resistance, which continued until May 1945, impeded the full re-introduction of Marxism. But from the beginning a wave of persecution broke over the country with sudden arrests and numerous deportations.

Among the first to fall victim to the new persecution was the young bishop, Mgr. *Kazimiris Dulbinskis*, consecrated in 1947 as Auxiliary to the aged Archbishop of Riga, Mgr. *Anthony Springovics*. The latter had been the only bishop in Latvia when the three Lett bishops, Mgr. *Joseph Rancans*, Auxiliary Bishop of Riga, Mgr. *Anthony Urbs*, Bishop of Liepaja and Mgr. *Boleslas Sloskans*, then spiritual director of the seminary of Riga, had

---

[34] Cf. *These Names Accuse*, Stockholm, 1951.

been deported to Germany. Mgr. *Dulbinskis* was arrested and
deported to Siberia where he still was in the Spring of 1953.
Mgr. *Springovics* was during the same period expelled from
his residence and forced to take refuge in a monastery of
Aglona. At present he is devoting himself, as well as he can, to
his pastoral duties despite his infirmities and the annoyances
occasioned him by the Communists. Many Catholic priests
suffered the same treatment. According to trustworthy information about 50 priests whose names are known, fell victims
to the Communist reign of terror. Forty-three are living in exile.
Heavy indeed (almost 30%) has been the loss suffered by the
Catholic Church in Latvia which formerly counted 187 priests
in the ranks of the clergy.

Religious rites in the strict sense of the word, that is, acts
of religious worship in church, have not been proscribed even
under the present Soviet régime in Latvia. Officially Mass may
be celebrated if the community has paid the fixed rents and taxes,
and if the priest has paid the levy imposed for the performance
of religious ceremonies. But the clergy are forbidden to
preach, give a Gospel commentary, or perform any act of the
missionary apostolate. Agents of the GPU follow the priest
wherever he goes, spying on his every act, ready to interpret
his every word in an unfavourable sense.

Meanwhile anti-religious propaganda has been organised for
a still more vigorous offensive. Following the Russian prototype,
the legal and administrative machinery of the Lett Socialist Soviet
Republic is at the disposal of the agents of persecution to help
them to strike at the Church in the most effective way possible.
To meet the Communist attack the Church finds herself severely
handicapped, since nothing has been left undone to undermine
and disrupt her organisation. The Communists seize on any and
every political pretext to bring charges against the clergy or to
impede their ministry. For the rest they rely on the " time-
factor " to operate in favour of dialectical Materialism and
ultimately to eradicate the Catholic faith from the soul of the
rising generation.[35]

---

[35] The present state of religion and of the Church has been thus described by some
refugees worthy of trust: The situation is better in the towns than in the country,

LITHUANIA

Throughout the nineteenth century the people of Lithuania looked forward to the day when they would be able to re-assert their national sovereignty. This hope was founded on the memory of their past glory, for in the fifteenth century the Grand Duchy of Lithuania stretched from the Baltic Sea to the Black Sea. The combined power of Lithuania and Poland had been a restraining bulwark against the growing might of Muscovite power, until with the partition of Poland Lithuania too lost her independence, and was occupied by the Russians in 1795. With the overthrow of the Czarist régime towards the end of the First World War the Lithuanians proclaimed an independent Republic (16 February 1918), thus creating a new State, whose life and political aspirations were imbued with the best ideals of the national heritage.

The Catholic Church in Lithuania

The period that followed the restoration of independence was one of prosperity for the Catholic Church. Working in perfect harmony, Church and State combined their efforts to resolve the problems consequent on two centuries of foreign occupation and to achieve the common good of the whole nation.

---

because the faithful in the towns still succeed, although at the cost of heavy sacrifices, in paying very high taxes for the *use* of the churches and in supporting the priests, who (considered dangerous elements by the Government) are excluded from any employment or remunerative work. It is strictly forbidden to take up any collection for religious purposes. In the country extremely few are the churches regularly open for worship; the faithful after the forcible introduction of the " Kolkoz " do not in fact succeed in paying the heavy taxes levied on them. The priests in the towns succeed only at intervals in visiting the country parishes and in organising religious functions there. At these functions, under pretext of maintaining order, a certain number of police always assist and note who are present. Among those exiled to Siberia and otherwise persecuted, are to be found always in the first place those who attend Church functions. Hence except for great feasts such as Christmas and Easter the churches are frequented chiefly by women and old people, that is, by persons who have least to fear from reprisals, especially economic ones. The Communist Government, so as better to destroy Christian customs, revive pagan ones. Thus for the feast of New Year, designed to take the place of Christmas, the Government set up at its own expense gigantic trees, called " trees of light," in the public squares. The press and the propagandists of the Party take pains to explain, in the Communistic sense, the meaning of these symbols. Catechism is studied chiefly at home, in view of the fact that Soviet legislation, now introduced, severely forbids any religious instruction whatever to be given to minors under 18. The priests are few in numbers, and their external aspect indicates material and spiritual sufferings.

In a population of about three million inhabitants 80% were Catholics of the Latin rite, organised in two archdioceses and four dioceses. Religion flourished throughout the country. Figures for the year 1939-40 show that in the six ecclesiastical circumscriptions there were three archbishops and eight bishops, 900 churches and chapels, 800 of which were parochial churches, and more than 1,500 priests.[36] Many religious belonging to various orders of men and women were engaged in teaching or devoted themselves to the care of orphanages, hospitals and homes for the aged, etc. There were about 600 students and seminarians studying in the four seminaries or at the faculty of theology in the university of Kaunas. The relations between Church and State were governed by a Concordat signed in 1927.[37]

Religious instruction was obligatory in all primary and secondary schools. Canon Law was recognised by the State and with the exception of the former German district of Memel church marriages only were recognised as valid. The Catholic press expanded rapidly and the Catholic daily *XX Amzius* (The XXth Century) had the largest circulation in the country. From the different Catholic publishing houses came a constant stream of new books.

Proclamation of the Lithuanian Soviet Socialist Republic

After the establishment of national independence the politicians of the new Lithuania set themselves to follow a sane realistic policy in their relations with their former masters. A Peace Treaty between Lithuania and the USSR recognising the complete independence of the new State was signed in Moscow on 12 July 1920. This Treaty was integrated in the Pact of non-Aggression signed in 1928, on which occasion the Soviet Foreign Minister, *Litvinov*, publicly stressed the peaceful intentions of the Soviet Union.

The political horizon darkened with the approach of World War II. By the Ribbentrop-Molotov Pact of 23 August 1939, dividing Central Europe into two spheres of influence, Lithuania

---

[36] *Elenchus omnium ecclesiarum et universi cleri Prov. Eccl. Lithuanae*, 1940.
[37] Cf. Jean Mauclère, *La situation de l'Eglise catholique en Lithuanie*, Le Raincy, 1950, pp. 1 et seqq.

was to remain within the German orbit. This arrangement was altered just one month later when on 28 September 1939 the same two signatories, *Ribbentrop* and *Molotov*, agreed that " the territory of the Lithuanian State should pass within the zone of influence of the USSR." As a result Lithuania had to agree to a Mutual Aid Pact (signed 10 October 1939) by the terms of which the USSR received the right to garrison an army of 20,000 in the country. On paper this was to have been a strictly military measure, and the terms of the Pact had specifically stated: " The execution of this Pact shall not in any way prejudice the sovereignty of the contracting parties, in particular as regards their political way of life, economic and social organisation and national defence " (art. 5). In reality the entrance of the Red army was but the first step towards the definitive annexation of Lithuania by the Soviet Union. When people had begun to accept the presence of the Soviet troops, and when the Lithuanian Communists had reached the required pitch of organisation, the situation was ripe for the second stage. On 14 June 1940 the Soviet Union presented the Government of Kaunas with an ultimatum demanding " that a government be formed immediately which shall be capable of guaranteeing the proper execution of the Mutual Aid Pact between the Soviet Union and Lithuania . . . and that free entry into Lithuanian territory be immediately accorded Soviet army units, which shall be garrisoned in the more important centres . . . in sufficient numbers to secure the effective application of the Mutual Aid Pact between the Soviet Union and Lithuania." [38]

The following day (15 June 1940) hundreds of Soviet tanks began pouring into Lithuania, reinforcing the Red troops who were already garrisoned in the country. The Government was forced to resign, and was immediately replaced by a new Cabinet drafted by the Soviet Legation in Kaunas. It was obvious from the composition of the new Government (Communists and patriots) that its rôle was to be purely provisional.[39] A general

---

[38] Cf. H. de Chambon, *La Tragédie des Nations Baltiques*, Paris, 1946, p. 49.
[39] The new Lithuanian Foreign Minister, Krévé-Mickevicius, tried to forestall the trend of events by openly expressing to Molotov the apprehension felt by the people of Lithuania (30 June 1940). Molotov is reported as saying, " If the Russian Czars, beginning with Ivan the Terrible, reached out towards the Baltic, this was in no wise

election was fixed for 14-15 July 1940, and to stifle all opposition about 2,000 intellectuals who might influence the popular vote were arrested on the night of 11-12 July. There was only a single list of candidates, prepared by the Communist Party, whose legal existence in Lithuania dates only from the previous month (26 June 1940). Although before the advent of the Russians there were no more than 2,000 Communists in the country, most of them belonging to non-Lithuanian elements of the population, the Parliament elected in July 1940 was nearly 60% Communist and the others were fellow-travellers. At the first meeting, held in the National Theatre in Kaunas on 21 July 1940, the deputies voted to adopt the Stalin Constitution of 1936, and endorsed a motion asking for the admission of Lithuania into the Soviet Union. A special delegation went to Moscow with this resolution, *and thus Lithuania became the 14th Soviet Republic.*

* * *

The Lithuanian clergy, though recognising the gravity of the political situation, were disposed to face the future with a measure of calm, confident in the loyalty of the Lithuanian Catholics to their Church. They hoped too that the good-neighbourly relations which had existed between their country and Russia since 1920 would continue, and they found it hard to believe that the Soviet Union was synonymous with atheistic Communism as condemned by the Church. Indeed during the first few weeks the Communists aimed their attacks rather at the capitalists and the Nationalist Party which during its long years in power had made such a boast of delivering the country from oppression. It was not long however until the onslaught

---

to satisfy mere personal aspirations, but solely because it was necessitated by the development of the aims of the Russian nation and the Russian people. It would be unforgivable if the Soviet Government failed to advance in the same direction especially in the present circumstances which may never again occur. The Government of the Soviet Union has decided to incorporate the Baltic States within the family of the Soviet Republics." When the Lithuanian minister reminded him of the determination of his people to keep their independence, Molotov is alleged to have said, " We shall know how to convince the Lithuanian people. You yourself will see that within a few months the people of Lithuania will ask for the incorporation of Lithuania in the Soviet Union." Cf. H. de Chambon, *op. cit.* pp. 54-56.

on the Church began. Even before the election of the new Government the Provisional Government imposed by the Russian ultimatum had decreed a separation of Church and State (25 June 1940). Five days later (1 July) it renounced the Concordat and the Apostolic Nuncio, Mgr. *Louis Centoz*, was asked to leave the country within two months.

On 22 July 1940 the Lithuanian Parliament, following the procedure of Soviet Communism, voted the nationalisation of all land which thus became State property. Though the law permitted former owners to retain 30 hectares (about 75 acres) in usufruct (so that they could not dispose of it by sale, donation, or legacy), the Catholic parishes were limited to three hectares ($7\frac{1}{2}$ acres) on the same conditions.[40] The State subsidies paid to the Church in compensation for Church property which had been confiscated by the Russians in the 19th century and inherited by the Lithuanian State, were immediately withdrawn.

On 6 August 1940 the Government nationalised all industrial concerns and business houses employing more than twenty persons. This figure was very soon reduced to five persons. In this way they were able to confiscate all the printing houses and bookshops of the diocesan Curiæ, religious congregations and various Catholic societies. All books of a religious character found on the premises—bibles, catechisms, prayer-books, etc. —were seized and destroyed. Objects of piety wherever discovered were also destroyed.

A decree of 31 October 1940 effected the nationalisation of private dwellings with an area of over 220 square metres in towns or 170 square metres in the country. Many parochial houses were thus confiscated.[41] In cases where " ministers of religion " were not expelled, they automatically became tenants of the State and their rent was calculated according to the rate fixed for capitalists, three roubles per square metre, whereas the rent

---

[40] A total area of 17,614 hectares, belonging to 690 churches was thus nationalised; 28 religious houses were despoiled of a total of 1,510 hectares. Cf. *Lietuviu Archyvas*, I, p. 219.

[41] A number of ecclesiastical buildings was confiscated even before the nationalisation of property. When the Red army entered Lithuania, many religious houses, Catholic schools and seminaries were occupied by the troops. By the nationalisation law these buildings automatically became State property.

of the working class was only one rouble per square metre. Each person had a right to 9 square metres, and if this area was exceeded, the rate was doubled.

The object of such measures was to deprive the Church of all property and of every source of revenue necessary for her activity. The Church and her ministers had to depend solely on the voluntary contributions of the faithful, whose financial means had been considerably reduced, and who were further prevented from effectively supplying the needs of the Church by a law of 1 November 1940. On that date the Russian rouble was imposed as the Lithuanian currency, and the rate of exchange of the Lithuanian *litas* was fixed on a par with it, although in reality the *litas* was worth three or four times more. The whole country suffered as a result and the general impoverishment of the people was aggravated soon afterwards by the nationalisation of all shares and bonds and the confiscation of bank and savings deposits of more than 1,000 roubles.

Education received special attention from the Communists. As from 28 June 1940 religious instruction was banished from the schools on the grounds that it was incompatible with dialectical Materialism; not long afterwards the crucifixes were removed from the classrooms, and the recitation of prayers in school was forbidden.[42] The faculties of philosophy and theology

---

[42] The following is the circular prescribing these measures (Cf. *Lietuviu Archyvas*, III, pp. 136-137) :

PEOPLE'S COMMISSARIAT OF EDUCATION

31 *August* 1940.

To the directors of primary and secondary schools

Beginning with the present school-year, prayers before and after classes are suppressed in all schools. All emblems of religion and of the former régime must be removed from the schools, as well as pictures of persons whose ideology and activity are opposed to the creation of a socialist Lithuania . . . Finally the schools must be adorned with the coat of arms of the Republic and with portraits of the guides of the working class throughout the world, Lenin and Stalin . . . The singing of the Lithuanian national anthem is forbidden; the *International* is the anthem of the Lithuanian Soviet Republic.

All inspectors are to convey the preceding instructions to all school directors and teachers.

Signed: A. Venclova,

People's Commissar for Education.

in the university of Kaunas were closed down. On 1 August the nationalisation of all private schools was effected, and thus the Church was deprived of several schools run by religious congregations and of many other educational establishments. Finally by a law of 29 August the whole scholastic programme from primary school to university was re-organised in harmony with the spirit of the new régime; history, literature, philosophy, law, biology and economics were to be taught henceforth according to the materialist doctrines of Marx and Lenin. Further the history of the Communist Party and the study of the Stalin Constitution became an integral part of the educational programme.

The Communist Government did not overlook the seminaries; they were either requisitioned to house Red army units or were used for other purposes. A section of the inter-diocesan seminary of Kaunas was taken over by a school for railway workers, but in spite of great difficulties the seminary was able to continue functioning until 12 January, when professors and students were expelled from the remainder of the house and obliged to find refuge with friendly families and use churches, sacristies and private houses for their classes.

The Lithuanian bishops were seriously perturbed by the loss of the Catholic schools and by the exclusion of religious instruction from the schools. Finally it was decided to ignore the prohibition, and small classes were organised in churches and sacristies where religion was taught as well as the other subjects on the official curriculum. Such a breach of the anti-God law could not be tolerated, and in the spring of 1941 the clergy of certain districts received copies of an official declaration which they were required to sign. The text was as follows:

" I, the undersigned .... minister of religion, residing at .... in the commune of .... and district of .... certify that I have on the ...... day of April 1941 received notice of the formal prohibition against teaching religion to students and also to children of preschool age in schools, or in their homes, or in my own house, in a word, anywhere. I have at the same time been warned

that in case of any infringement of this order I shall be liable
to prosecution . . . "

This last measure did not yield the results intended, for the
outbreak of war between Germany and the USSR on 22 June 1941
prevented its effective application.

To extirpate religion from the souls of the young was not
enough; the Communists aimed at making the adult population
forget their faith, and strove to drive the Church out of every
phase of public life. Membership of the Party was considered
incompatible with the profession of Catholicism; military and
prison chaplains were dismissed by a decree of 2 July 1940;
State functionaries and members of the armed forces were not
permitted to go to church, and Communist agents were appointed
to spy on those who attended religious ceremonies.

As a part of this attack on " the superstition of the masses " a
vigorous campaign was launched against the cherished traditions
of the Lithuanian Catholics. The first step was to ban public
processions on Corpus Christi, the official reason being to
prevent incidents between the faithful and non-believers. All
Saints' Day was declared a working day and the traditional
procession to the cemetery was forbidden. During Lent and
Advent the Communists did all in their power to promote
dances and public amusements in contradiction to the religious
customs of the people.

Of all the Church feasts Christmas was singled out for special
attention, as can be seen from a circular of 12 December 1940,
sent by *Guzevicius*, People's Commissar for Internal Affairs
of the Lithuanian Soviet Socialist Republic, and addressed to the
Chief of the Lithuanian NKVD of Vilna, and to district and
section heads of the same NKVD :

Comrades,

On 25 and 26 December the Catholics celebrate a feast which
they call Christmas. During this feast (beginning the night of
of 24-25 December) there are masses and sermons in the churches
and these two days are regarded by the believers as great feasts,
i.e. days on which they abstain from work.

The nationalist counter-revolutionary elements of the population, and especially the clergy, will attempt to make use of the feast of Christmas for their anti-Soviet activity, more particularly in the following domains:

(a) Attempts to stop work in factories and schools;

(b) Propaganda to dissuade the people from participating in the elections, in pulpit sermons of an apparently religious nature, or by attacks on individuals, or by organising groups of the faithful in the churches, sacristies and parochial houses;

(c) Propaganda in favour of counter-revolutionary literature, religious or other;

(d) Attempts to rouse the people to public demonstrations or to engage in other kinds of agitation.

To prevent incidents of this nature you must:

(1) Order the network of Secret Agents to report on the anti-Soviet preparations being made by the clergy and by Catholics who form part of the clerical milieu; from 20 to 27 December arrange to meet your agents as often as possible;

(2) Take the necessary measures to ensure that work goes on as usual in factories and schools;

(3) Organise motorised patrols and station sentries in the towns for the nights of 23, 24, 25 and 26 December. For this purpose, and in collaboration with the District Secretary of the Party, employ active members of the Party and of Communist Youth Organisations, and give them the necessary directives;

(4) Draw up charges for all incidents of an anti-Soviet nature, and send me the details as soon as possible. [43]

Signed: GUZEVICIUS.

Similar measures were adopted on the occasion of other church feasts, and the Communists did their best to make Sunday a work day. Sometimes the reason given was the war waged by the capitalists, and the argument went something like this: " While others are working for our destruction, we should be working for the good of the people and not waste our time in

[43] Cf. Jean Mauclère, *op. cit.* pp. 11-12.

celebrating feasts." Or again, Sunday was declared a work day by way of "compensation" if it happened that a Communist festival had been celebrated during the previous week.[44]

During the same period the Lithuanian Catholics suffered from a decree which suppressed all associations that had been in existence before the arrival of the Soviets. Most severely affected were the Catholic societies. Their archives, libraries and banners were confiscated; their insignia and religious books were destroyed.

Side by side with these repressive measures, the Communists undertook a positive campaign of anti-religious indoctrination. Marxist doctrine was universally taught and even university professors were obliged to follow special courses in Marxism as part of their "re-education." Darwinism held a place of honour in the colleges and even in the primary schools. The works of Lenin and Stalin and other Marxist and atheistic classics were freely distributed, and in the public libraries these took the place of religious literature which had been removed and destroyed. The whole Lithuanian press became the organ of laicism and of atheistic propaganda, while on its side the Church could not publish a single sheet. Under the new régime it was not even permitted to print prayer-books, and the faithful had to be content with whatever they had saved from destruction. The spoken word was the sole remaining means of expounding revealed truth and defending it against attack, but even this was a precarious weapon since one never knew when to expect arrest.

In their struggle against the Catholic Church in Lithuania the Communists aimed the spearhead of their attack against the clergy. In the propaganda sheets destined for the masses Catholic priests were represented as the worst exploiters and greatest enemies of the people, and in Party meetings they were spoken of as the implacable foes of Communism who must at all costs be exterminated. Judging that the moment had not come for open persecution, the Government seized on the slightest pretext to arrest a priest. A single criticism of the régime was sufficient. The GPU kept the clergy under constant

---

[44] Cf. *idem.* p. 12.

supervision and the agents of the secret police had recourse even to Sacramental Confession, in the hope that in the confessional they might trap the priest into pronouncing a judgment on Communism.

As part of the same campaign they neglected nothing that could diminish and if possible destroy the prestige of the clergy. The bishops were driven from their residences which were then taken over by Red army officers. Mgr. *K. Paltarokas* alone was allowed to remain in his palace, but he suffered harsh treatment in other ways. The Soviets likewise confiscated the homes for sick and indigent priests as well as the Clergy Relief Fund. The Museum of Religious Art in Kaunas was closed and the exhibits were confiscated and destroyed; Church vestments were used as door-mats.[45] Religious houses were confiscated and put at the service of the Red army or used for other Government purposes. Most of the religious were dispersed, and it was only in extremely rare cases that they were allowed to retain a few rooms in their houses.

As proof of the extent of the spying done by the Communists on the relations between clergy and people, the following is a secret document, sent on 2 October 1940 by Comrade *Gladkov*, Vice-Commissar for Interior Affairs of the Lithuanian SSR to the district chiefs of the secret police:

Absolutely Secret. Extremely Urgent.
To Comrade *Palevicius*, Head of the District of Alytus and to all District Chiefs of the State Security Police.

It appears from notes that are in the possession of the NKVD that some Lithuanian priests, former directors of Catholic parties and organisations, and some of the more active members of these organisations, have engaged in secret activities that threaten the USSR. They operate in the following three ways:

(1) In their sermons, sometimes openly, sometimes in veiled terms, the priests propagate nationalist ideas and try to create an anti-Soviet mentality among the people.

---

[45] Cf. *Lietuviu Archyvas*, I, p. 63.

(2) They pursue the same purpose in their relations with students whether in the university or in secondary and primary schools. Information that has come into our hands reveals that in conformity with the directives of Bishop *Brizgys*, several parochial houses harbour priests who are especially charged with exercising illegal activity among the young, so as to educate them in the spirit of nationalism and to inspire them with a hatred of the Communist system. Priests are engaged in this activity in almost all parts of Lithuania, not only in church on Sundays by means of sermons directed to the young, but also in their own houses where they hold meetings of young people in groups of 10 or 12; or again, they influence the parents to instil Catholic principles into their children.

(3) They engage in intense anti-Communist activity at meetings of confraternities and authorised Catholic societies (Men's Apostolate, Apostleship of Prayer, etc.), which are really political weapons in the hands of the clergy.

So as to organise the struggle against this hostile activity of the clergy, I hereby order:

(1) That you extend your vigilance over all the priests in your districts according to the official directions on this matter.

(2) That you inform yourselves of the personnel of the committee of Catholic organisations and confraternities and that you keep these persons under observation.

(3) That you immediately get information through your agents on all the members of the deanery and episcopal curiae in your district.

(4) To enable you to get sound information about the activity of Catholic parties, groups and confraternities, you should immediately try to bribe some of the priests and Church employees (sacristans, organists) who have close associations with the heads of the said groups. It would be well also to enlist such persons as secret agents in the service of the Party and get them to work for the disintegration of Catholic organisations.

(5) That you make a list of priests and confraternity leaders in

your district who keep up contact with Germans who leave the country; determine the nature of these relations and keep an active watch on both parties.

(6) That in all districts where there are monasteries, you keep the monks and especially the superior under observation, and that you form a branch of secret agents among the monks.

(7) That you find out the places where the priests meet students to carry on their anti-Soviet activity. Enlist the services of the senior classes in the high schools to organise and carry on subversive activities.

(8) In view of the fact that priests and active confraternity members are at present engaged in collecting signatures amongst the people for a petition asking the Government to permit the teaching of religion in the schools, you should find out who are the organisers of this activity and keep them under careful observation.

(9) When attempting bribery avoid rash mistakes; consequently get information about the candidates and lead them on gradually. Always remember that many priests are badly off financially.

(10) Keep a careful register of every case you discover of anti-Soviet and counter-revolutionary demonstrations engineered by the clergy and send all the pertinent documentation to my Commissariat.

(11) Before 10 October give a detailed report on the active opposition of the clergy in your district.

(12) By 15 October forward to the Headquarters of the State Secret Police (Section II) the extracts of the files of agencies dealing with ecclesiastics, or else the agency dossiers. These should be accompanied by an indication of the documents compiled by persons charged with the enquiries, and should indicate the measures which you intend to adopt in this matter in future.

Signed: GLADKOV. [46]

As can be seen from the above document the Communists went so far as to exploit the weakness of certain priests in their efforts to get useful information. When a priest was arrested

[46] Cf. *Lietuviu Archyvas*, I, pp. 29-31.

on some pretext or other, the police offered him the possibility of " regaining " his " liberty " if he signed an undertaking to perform certain services for the secret police. By refusing he ran the risk of an indefinite period of imprisonment, which ultimately meant deportation to Siberia. Many were the priests whose constancy in refusing collaboration cost them their liberty.

Proof that the plan to exterminate the Lithuanian clergy was conceived and elaborated not in Lithuania itself but in the Soviet Union (which had got rid of its clergy many years before) is furnished by the following document sent by Comrade *Guzevicius*, Commissar for the Interior, to all district heads of the State security forces:

Absolutely Confidential

Ministry for the Interior

To Comrade *Palevicius*, District Superintendent of Alytus.

Section II of the Commissariat for the Interior of the USSR is at present engaged in working out a plan for agencies dealing with the clergy in the new Soviet Republics.

Wherefore, I issue the following instructions:

(1) Draw up a list of all organisations and societies, Catholic, Orthodox or belonging to any other religious denomination, which existed in your district, either legally or not, during the Smetone régime.

(2) State the influence which each of these organisations exercised on the masses and the social life of the community (approximate number of members, political and social importance in the district).

(3) Draw up a list of Catholic and Orthodox churches and other places of worship in your district.

(4) Draw up a list of Catholic and Orthodox priests and ministers of any other sects in your district, and indicate the influence of each clergyman among the masses and in the social and political life of the country.

(5) Point out internal dissension existing within the religious organisations or among the clergy, indicating in detail the

reasons for the dissension and giving the names of the priests between whom strained relations exist.

(6) Offer your suggestions as to the best way to make use of these dissensions, so as to enlist certain people as secret agents and thus undermine the Church organisations in your district.

(7) Send on precise information on the results already obtained by your agents in their activity against Catholic and Orthodox priests and against ministers of other sects, enclosing the official forms duly completed and specify the plans followed in the operation.

(8) Give all the information you have on the ecclesiastics you have already enlisted as secret agents.

(9) On 30 January send me a detailed account of all the matters enumerated above.

Collect the necessary information by means of your secret agents among the clergy.

Signed: GUZEVICIUS,

Commissar for the Interior. [47]

21 January 1941, No. 2191.

As regards the actual number of clergy who were subjected to violent persecution, it is fully established that 18 priests were thrown into prison and that they owed their liberty to the hasty departure of the Soviet army before the German advance, which prevented the Communists from arranging for the transfer of their prisoners to Russia. Nine other priests were arrested and deported to Siberia either in the beginning of the Soviet occupation or during the first days of the Russo-German war. At the outbreak of hostilities between Germany and the USSR 15 priests were massacred in Lithuania. [48]

In addition to the clergy thousands of the faithful suffered the same treatment, the first victims being the leaders of Catholic Action. [49]

---

[47] Cf. *Lietuviu Archyvas*, I, pp. 33-43.
[48] Cf. *Lietuviu Archyvas*, I, pp. 70-73.
[49] According to well-founded calculations, the first Soviet occupation must have cost Lithuania more than 40,000 victims, deported or massacred by the Communists. (Cf. H. de Chambon, *op. cit.* p. 69). Apart from the deportation of individuals, which

The Second Soviet Occupation

During the German military occupation, which lasted until 1944, the situation of the Catholic Church in Lithuania improved slightly. The return of the Soviets brought a renewal of religious persecution. By a rigorous plan of mass deportations the Communists got rid of all those who on account of their attachment to the Catholic Church or for cultural, social or political reasons were regarded as " dangerous " elements that could not be absorbed into the system.[50]

The struggle against the clergy was renewed with greater intensity than before. Soon after their return the Soviets tried every means, but without any success, to establish a *Lithuanian National Church*. According to a letter of 1947 from the Lithuanian Catholics, the Communists " by lies and intrigues and by strategic arrests tried to entice active young Catholics to join the ranks of this national church.[51] They attempted to create among the clergy groups of agitators to carry on propaganda against the hierarchy and to constitute the nucleus of the new Church. At the same time they intensified their campaign against the Pope, and the people were obliged to read and listen to their litanies of lies." In the propagandist effort

---

continued during the whole period of the first occupation, there were mass deportations of Lithuanians to the USSR between 14 and 22 June 1941. During these days about 30,000 people were taken from their homes and packed into 800 goods wagons in such dreadful conditions that some died on the journey even before they had crossed the Lithuanian border. These deportations which took place just before the (Russo-German) war formed part of a vast Soviet plan to deport sections of the Baltic population to Russia. According to instructions from Moscow, signed by Serov, the Commissar of the NKVD which dealt with the deportation of anti-Soviet elements from Lithuania, Latvia and Estonia, Lithuania alone was to furnish a contingent of 700,000 persons, who were to include almost all the priests and the heads of Catholic associations. The war prevented the complete realisation of this plan.

[50] According to information recently received, the total number of persons deported, interned in concentration camps or condemned to forced labour was more than 500,000 in Lithuania alone.

[51] The letter is addressed to His Holiness, Pope Pius XII, and it denounces the chief crimes of the Soviet occupation, and of the anti-Catholic persecution. At the beginning the Communists appointed new " independent " priests, in place of the priests who had been deported, but the faithful immediately realised that it was a question of disguised agents of the NKVD. After the *Peace Conference of all Churches and Religions* which took place in the monastery of Zagorsk in the neighbourhood of Moscow in 1952, steps for the foundation of a National Church were speeded up. The Secretary of the Lithuanian Communist Party, A. Snieckus, convoked the ecclesiastical authorities several times more. He, as well as the Russian Smirnov, head of the MGB-OSZ. (formerly

directed at detaching the faithful from the unity of the Faith the Communist Party has not shrunk from falsifying letters of priests and even documents of the bishops. Furthermore in all Lithuania so-called " political seminaries " have been established, attendance at which is obligatory for all young men, and in which the teaching is principally aimed against the Church and the Vatican.[52]

The Communists next endeavoured to compromise the bishops and the priests by using them as political instruments. In 1946 when the activities of the NKVD were checked by a series of difficulties occasioned by the partisan guerilla war, the Minister for the Interior asked the bishops to condemn the resistance movement and to exhort the people to put an end to the underground struggle. When the bishops refused, the NKVD first threatened them and then went into action.[53] The first victim was Mgr. *Vincent Borisevicius*, Bishop of Telsiai, who was arrested at the beginning of 1946 and was condemned to death on 3 January 1947 by a secret tribunal held in the Lukiskes prison in Vilna. However it is not known for certain if in fact he died in a Russian forced labour camp. His auxiliary, Mgr. *Francis Ramanauskas*, was condemned in autumn 1946 and deported to Siberia; in the spring of 1955 he was undergoing forced labour at Abyz inside the USSR after having spent a long time in the gaols of Vladimir (180 kilometres from Moscow). Shortly afterwards the Bishop of Kaisedoris, Mgr. *Theophylus Matulionis* was arrested. According to some reports he was still in confinement at the beginning of 1955 in a hospice for the aged near Potma in

---

NKVD) tried, by means of religious links with countries abroad and of officials of the Council for Worship, to force the parochial committees to undertake a general movement among the faithful to create a *Lithuanian National Catholic Church.*

[52] The following are some of the subjects treated in such courses: " The struggle of youth against superstition"; " The Church in Lithuania is a product of obscurantism"; " The letter of Pius XII, dated 10 August 1941, to Archbishop Skvireckas as a document proving the collaboration of the Vatican with the Nazis ": " What does Marxism-Leninism say about the fight against religion?"; " Reactionary Christian morality"; " The Pope, servant of American Imperialists, etc." Those who attend the courses are subjected to an examination every three months, and the best essays composed by them are awarded prizes and published under the responsibility of the Minister for Education. To that must be added the intensified publication of anti-religious literature, which in 1952 alone went beyond 200,000 copies. Very widely distributed was a pamphlet by a certain N. *Seimanas*, entitled: " The Vatican, Enemy of Peace and Democracy."

[53] See, for instance, attacks of *Tiesa* (the organ of the PLC) of 25 September 1947.

the Republic of Mordovia.   Mgr. *Miecislao Reinys*, Apostolic
Administrator of the Archdiocese of Vilna, was also arrested
and died in Vladimir prison on 8 November 1953.   The only
Catholic Ordinary left in the country was Mgr. *Casimir Paltarokas*,
Bishop of Panevezys, who was nearly eighty.

In depriving the Catholic Church in Lithuania of its bishops,
by imprisonment, exile [54] and execution, the Soviets were
striking a direct blow at Church administration.   To achieve
their object more effectively they did not spare the priests.
At the beginning of 1948 there were only 700 priests in the
whole country, or 50% of the 1940 total.   By 1954 according
to certain sources the number had fallen to 400, while others
think that this figure is too high.

The lot of the priests who are still in Lithuania is a bitter
one.   The Communist régime treats them as outcasts and
excludes them as much as possible from social life.   In a Marxist
state, where everything is nationalised, a priest cannot obtain
employment no matter how straitened his financial circumstances,
because a State employee is not permitted to profess any religion,
more especially Catholicism.   He cannot set foot in the schools
to exercise his sacred ministry, for education is the province
of the Communist Party who ensure that it is carried on " scientifically," in other words, atheistically.   Nor can a priest enter
hospitals to visit the sick, since those who feel the need of the
consolations of religion should go to the church.   He cannot
have dealings with anyone, for whoever ventures to speak to
him becomes a suspect in the eyes of the police.   In spite of
this state of " moral siege " the priest must still attend to the
payment of his Government taxes, which for a parish priest
amount to 100,000 roubles per annum (equivalent to the annual
salary of 10 functionaries), while a curate is taxed at 50,000
roubles.   In addition to this the priests, as well as the religious,
have to pay the taxes on bachelors.   To these were added taxes
on religious edifices amounting to 50,000 roubles. [55]   When the

---

[54] Three of the Lithuanian bishops are since 1944 unwilling exiles.   They are Mgr.
Joseph Skvireckas, Bishop of Kaunas, Mgr. Vincent Brizgys, his auxiliary ; Mgr. Vincent
Padolskis, auxiliary to the Bishop of Vilkaviskis.
[55] Heavy taxes are imposed on churches since they are put in the same category
as theatres.   The cathedral of Panavezys, for example, is taxed at 40,000 roubles per

voluntary contributions of the faithful are insufficient to meet the Government tax, a priest is often forced to sell his belongings or church equipment so as to avoid being condemned to forced labour or deportation.   When finally all these resources are exhausted nothing remains but to close the church and watch the confiscation of the church and the other parish buildings.[56] In this way the Lithuanian Communists hope to effect the gradual destruction of the Catholic Church.

In 1952 a travelling " Museum of the History of Religion " was started.   In it, under direction of the leaders and active members of the Communist Party, was collected all that concerned " the reactionary activities of the Catholic Church " and the relations of the bishops and clergy with the Holy See.   The whole exhibit was divided into three periods: from antiquity to 1939; from 1941 to 1944 (the period of Nazi occupation); and the present time (the Church's contacts with the Resistance Movement).

The situation of the Church in Lithuania at the present time is very grave, and unfortunately there are no immediate prospects of an improvement.   This is especially true as regards fostering vocations.   Of the four seminaries that re-opened during the German occupation (Kaunas, Vilna, Vikaviskis and Telsiai) only two were tolerated by the Soviets when they returned in 1944 (Telsiai and Kaunas).   In 1946 the seminary of Telsiai was closed, so that the sole remaining seminary of Kaunas had to accommodate the seminarians from all the dioceses in the country. In December of that year (1946) the professorial staff of Kaunas was expelled, and the maximum number of seminarians was

---

annum, and that of Kaunas at 46,000 roubles. We must add that all ceremonies carried out in the church are taxed with a duty on " non-essentials." Thus, for instance, while a civil wedding costs 6 roubles, for a religious one it is necessary to pay 60.

[56] Many churches have been closed also by virtue of a law which permits only one church within a radius of 7 kilometres. Even in the towns many churches have been closed or transformed into shops, or into amusement halls. For instance, in the old part of Kaunas three churches were converted into grain-stores, and the imposing church of the Resurrection into a timber-shed. In Vilna ten of the twenty-five churches, including the Cathedral, were closed. Of 1,202 Catholic churches in Lithuania it is calculated that only one third remain open for worship to-day. Many sacred buildings were closed on the pretext that the " partisans " had entered them to perform acts of devotion.

fixed arbitrarily at 150 for all Lithuania. Subsequently this figure
was reduced to 75.

Of the external life of the Catholic Church, so flourishing in
Lithuania before the persecution, there remains very little sign
to-day. Of her 11 bishops there remains only one, and his
powers have been severely curtailed.[57]   All Catholic schools
have been despoiled, and religious instruction is banished from
every kind of educational establishment. The Catholic press
no longer exists, and public opinion is constantly being turned
against the clergy. The Soviet Union, while proceeding by stages
and avoiding as far as possible all impression of conducting a
violent persecution, has succeeded to an alarming degree in
making religion a purely private affair and in reducing the Church
to an institution for the " exercise of worship " in such buildings
only as the State still allows for such a purpose.

THE UKRAINE

When the Ribbentrop-Molotov Pact of 1939 ceded the east
of Poland to the Soviet Union, the Russian army occupied
White Ruthenia and Galicia. After withdrawing in face of the
German advance, the Russians returned in 1944 and retained
possession of these regions when the Allies agreed to the Curzon
Line as the western frontier of the Soviet Union.

The occupation of Galicia and of Carpatho-Ukraine marked
the last stage in the Russian conquest of the Ukraine. Since
the beginning of the 18th century Russia under Peter the Great
had begun its drive in this direction. Later she shared in the
partition of Poland in 1772, 1793 and 1795, and thus by
successive conquests and dismemberment she had gained
possession of the Ukraine proper and of a large part of White
Ruthenia. In 1939 she was presented with the opportunity of
completing her conquests by occupying the territory which had
been part of Poland since 1920.

The Ukrainians of Galicia were Catholics of the Byzantine-Slav
Rite and since 1596 were in union with the Church of Rome.
This however did not prevent Czarist Russia from imposing

---

[57] Later it was possible to consecrate two bishops.

her rights on the region in the name of Russian Orthodoxy. Even in the 18th century when the partition of Poland gave Russia possession of territories inhabited by members of the Uniate Church (White Ruthenia, for example), she had obliged them to embrace the Orthodox religion. Again during the First World War a persecution of the Uniates was begun under the protection of the Russian troops who had invaded Galicia, and with the connivance of the Orthodox Church *Andrew Szeptyckyj* was deported to Siberia and returned only after the overthrow of the Czarist dynasty.

When Galicia was attached to Poland after the first World War, the Catholic Church which had already reached a flourishing state under the Austro-Hungarian Empire continued to develop. The Church in Galicia was organised as an ecclesiastical province under the authority of the Metropolitan of Halicz-Lvov and comprised three dioceses: Lvov, Stanislav and Przemysl, to which was added the Apostolic Administration of Sanok. Before the second World War the faithful numbered 3,576,237 and there were 2,275 priests. Each diocese had its own seminary and facilities for ecclesiastical learning were abundant. The most prominent theological school was the Ecclesiastical Academy of Lvov. In addition to the secular clergy there were several religious orders engaged in various works of the apostolate: Basilians—with more than 600 members, Eudists, Redemptorists (of the Oriental branch), and eight congregations of nuns. There were large numbers of active members in the Catholic Action associations which were directed from a central institute in Lvov. Religious instruction was obligatory in all schools. Numerous publications catered for the religious and cultural life of the people, and in all phases of Ukrainian life the Uniate Church occupied a place of eminence.

When the Soviets occupied Galicia in 1939 they did not copy the Czarist régime in trying to justify their action by religious motives, but declared that their intention was simply to " liberate the Ukrainian people " and re-unite them with the " fatherland." The real sense of those phrases was soon clear, for shortly after the arrival of the Russian troops the sovietisation of Galicia began. It was intended to achieve in two years what had taken

twenty in the USSR. Accordingly the Soviets successively
introduced the Stalin Constitution of 1936, nationalisation of
heavy industry, collective farming and the suppression of all
existing organisations and societies. Prominent personalities,
who might impede the new trend, were thrown into prison.

The Soviet occupation and the reforms introduced by them
entailed hardship for the Catholic Church, but not to the same
degree for the different rites. The Latin Archbishop of Lvov, a
Pole, was brutally expelled and the episcopal See of the little
Armenian community was destroyed, but the Ukrainian hierarchy, presided over by the venerable Metropolitan *Andrew
Szeptyckyj*, was not interfered with. In this the Soviets were not
showing any deference to religion as such, but were merely
respecting the sentiment of the majority of the population who
were of Ukrainian origin.

As a result of the nationalisation of industrial concerns the
Church was deprived of her printing works, typewriters,
polycopying machines, etc., in a word, of every means of
propaganda. This was but the strict application of the new
Constitution imported from Russia which permitted liberty of
worship but not liberty to engage in religious propaganda. To
keep up some degree of contact with their numerous parishes
(1,276 in the archdiocese of Lvov alone) the bishops had to
have recourse to handwritten circulars, and this too at the very
moment when the clergy felt the extreme importance of keeping
in close touch with the faithful.

In complete conformity with Soviet legislation, decrees were
issued suppressing all religious houses and institutes and confiscating Church property, with all the usual consequences.
The expulsion of the religious was a severe blow to the Church
and the Metropolitan *Szeptyckyj* made a strong protest on the
subject in the autumn of 1939.[58] Likewise he tried to preserve
the conventual chapels for public worship by declaring them
parochial churches.

Although at the time of the occupation of Galicia the Uniate
dioceses had a considerable number of priests, the newly intro-

---

[58] Cf. *Documents*, A. LII, p. 2, notes p. 3, No. 13; and *Primi incatenati* (White Paper
on the religious persecution in the Ukraine), Rome, 1953.

duced social " outlook " gave rise to a certain amount of concern for the future. Accordingly the Metropolitan distributed among the parishes both seminarians and religious who had been expelled from their houses, and foreseeing the possibility of a sudden reduction in the numbers of priests, he wrote to his clergy:

> " I charge each one with the mission of teaching religion. Every priest will teach some intelligent and devout persons how to administer Baptism, so that if it happens that the priest should be removed, these will know how to baptise their infants." [59]

Furthermore the Metropolitan foresaw from the outset that the Soviet régime would do everything in its power to shake the fidelity of the young to the Church, and for that purpose he addressed this paternal letter especially to them:

> " My dear children, please make a copy of this letter and remember it from time to time. Recall these truths to other children too. In this letter I am saying ' Good-bye ' to you, for I do not know if God will allow *me to continue working and praying for you* . . . Keep yourselves from *sin against our Holy Faith. Be loyal to Holy Church.* Just as to betray the fatherland is a sin, so too to betray our Holy Mother the Church, who guides us from infancy to the grave, offering us a helping hand in all our needs, this too is a detestable sin . . . I also earnestly recommend you to receive the Sacraments frequently. Since at school you will not be reminded of this, *you must remind yourselves.*" [60]

The Soviet system of education was in fact immediately introduced into Galicia. Religious instruction was forbidden, crucifixes were banished from the classrooms and the most unbridled atheistic propaganda was permitted. In December 1939 the Metropolitan addressed an open letter of protest to Comrade *Zarcenko*, Head of the Department for Public Instruction at Lvov:

> " The violation of the conscience of children by a fanatical atheistic propaganda gives me occasion and reason to make a strong protest

---

[59] Cf. *Documents*, A. LII (1939, Nos. 9 and 10, p. 1).
[60] Cf. *Documents*, LII (1939), Nos. 9 and 10, pp. 7-8.

7

to the Provincial Education Office. I do not intend to single
out those responsible . . . For me it is a matter of principle.
Article 123 of the Stalin Constitution . . . guarantees to parents
liberty to bring up their children in their own religion and the
right to demand that the school respect their wishes in what
concerns the education of their children. In other words, the
school should not interfere in religious matters nor oppose the
religion of the children and their parents." [61]

This protest had no more effect than a similar one made by
the Metropolitan against the measures which excluded religion
from the hospitals and forbade priests to bring the consolations
of religion to the sick. Since he received no reply to his protests,
the Metropolitan asked the priests to ignore the Government
ban in so far as this was possible. [62] This decision was made in
view of the good of souls and did not conflict with that loyalty
to the Government, of which the Metropolitan spoke in his
Pastoral Letter of December 1939, when he addressed his clergy
in the following terms:

" This then is to be our programme. We shall obey the Government
and observe its laws in so far as they are not contrary to the law
of God. We shall keep out of politics and purely secular activities,
but we shall not cease to work zealously for the cause of Christ
and of our people." [63]

The Soviet Government however, though it should not have
been displeased by such a declaration of loyalty, wanted peace
only on its own terms.

After their efforts to disorganise the Ukrainian Church the
Communists were not going to tolerate any activity whose aim
was to remedy the situation they had created. Accordingly
when the Metropolitan *Szeptyckyj* convoked a Synod for 2 May
1940 to regulate the activity of the clergy in view of the changed
conditions imposed by the Soviets, the Government did not show
open opposition, but on the closing day of the Synod the participants heard these grave words from the lips of the Metro-

---

[61] Cf. *Documents*, LIII (1940), No. 3 pp. 38-39.
[62] Cf. *Documents*, LIII (1940), No. 2, p. 15.
[63] Cf. *Documents*, LII (1939), Nos. 9-10, p. 1.

politan: " Of the principal members of the Synod two priests have been executed and fourteen others arrested, victims of the conditions under which we live at the moment." [64]

Undoubtedly the Metropolitan *Andrew Szeptyckyj* constituted the greatest obstacle to the Soviet Government in its persecution of the Catholic Church in the Ukraine. The venerable prelate, who had suffered so much during his deportation in the course of the first World War, enjoyed enormous prestige in the eyes of the whole population and was admired as a national hero. As long as he remained at the head of the Catholic Church in the Ukraine, the machinations of the Government would fail to achieve the desired result. It was necessary to make an attack on the authority of the Metropolitan See. As their instrument, the Communists chose the Reverend *Gabriel Kostelnyk* who had written books on spirituality and philosophy and who directed the clergy's periodical *Nyva*. He was a well-known figure and enjoyed the esteem of the Uniate clergy. The Communists fastened on the weak point of this priest, namely, his affection for his seventeen year old son, *Bohdan*.[65] In February 1941, when *Kostelnyk* had refused to accept their proposition that he assume the Metropolitan See and oust *Szeptyckyj*, the NKVD had the boy arrested. From this moment the unfortunate priest was subjected to continuous pressure of all kinds. He had to submit to interviews during which he was urged to accept the position of Metropolitan and among the battery of arguments aimed at breaking his resistance there was the continual harping on the fate of his son.[66] But *Kostelnyk* refused to accept, even though the NKVD agents kept up the pressure until the day when the Soviets had to abandon Galicia before the German advance.

In their persecution of this unfortunate priest the Communists were convinced that *Kostelnyk*, whose weak character was well known to the NKVD, would eventually give in and consent to

[64] Cf. J. Nahurskyj, *Metropolite Szeptyckyj, de 1939 à 1949*, in *Zyttia i Slovo*, 1948-1949, pp. 167-168; and *Documents*, LIII (1940), No. 3, pp. 29-33; LV (1942), No. 1, pp. 11-17.

[65] For the Ukrainian clergy, as is general throughout the Church of the Byzantine Rite, marriage contracted before the reception of major orders does not constitute an impediment to the priesthood.

[66] Kostelnyk was a widower, and according to Oriental Canon Law his marriage had ceased to be an impediment to the reception of the episcopacy.

further the plan prepared by the Soviets for the liquidation of
the Uniate Church. For the rest they counted on the fact
that the eighty-year old Metropolitan had not long to live, and
were satisfied that their conversations with *Kostelnyk* would
weaken the morale of the prelate by keeping him under the
threat of removal. Their plans were interrupted by the war with
Germany in 1941.[67]

The retreat of the Soviet troops in 1941 was accompanied by
mass deportations from the Ukraine.[68] Thousands were
massacred just before the retreat, and there were many priests
among those deported or murdered.[69]

* * *

When the war reached the territory of the USSR there was
a noticeable change in the attitude of the civil authorities
towards religion. For this was " total " war, requiring the
mobilisation of all possible forces, and the Communists encouraged the Orthodox Church to take an active part in the
resistance movement against the German invader. The hope of
a greater degree of religious liberty was held out as a bait.

When in 1943 Soviet troops were once again approaching
Galicia, Radio Moscow repeatedly called upon the people of
the Ukraine: " Resist ! We are coming to restore your fatherland
and the faith of your ancestors." This allowed a change of position
in regard to the Church to be foreseen. In every respect it

---

[67] Cf. M. Chomiak, *La Lutte de l'Eglise catholique d'Ukraine contre le communisme*, " Logos,"
1 (1950), No. 4, pp. 285-286.

[68] The exodus of the Ukrainians from Galicia, imposed by the Soviet authorities,
had already begun in 1940 when many were transported to the main centres in western
and southern USSR. The Metropolitan tried to send priests with the workers for the
parishes of Kiev, Odessa, Vynncia, Kharkov, Poltava, etc., in the hope that the sacrifice
entailed in their new ministry would help towards re-union with our separated brethren
and influence even the atheists, whether baptised or not. Cf. *Documents*, LIII (1940),
No. 2, p. 12.

[69] It seems that there was a political motive behind the massacres. But the Metropolitan
saw motives of another kind in the activity of the NKVD when he declared, after the
withdrawal of the Soviet forces: " Under their rule God granted to many of our faithful
the grace to make great sacrifices, even that of life itself—we may speak even of martyrdom. It seems incontestable in our eyes that *the principal motive behind the persecution
was hatred of Christ and of His Church*. Those who laid down their lives were convinced
that they were *suffering for the Christian and Catholic faith*."

presaged nothing good for the Eastern Catholics, since by " ancestral faith " was meant naturally the Orthodox creed. And in reality when Galicia once more came under the control of Soviet troops (1944), a slight improvement in the attitude of the Communists could be observed. They showed respect for the Church. Soldiers, and even officers, assisted at religious worship. Anti-religious propaganda was almost non-existent. Crucifixes, which had been put back in the schools and hospitals during the German occupation, were allowed to remain.

The Stalin Constitution however was still in force and religious propaganda was still forbidden; the publication of religious books and tracts was not allowed to continue, and diocesan printing works had to close down for a second time. But there was liberty of worship and the observance of feast days was permitted. Although religious instruction was still excluded from the schools—since they were supposed to observe a strict "neutrality" on the subject—there was permission to teach Christian doctrine in the churches. The seminaries, which had re-opened under the Germans, were not troubled. Priests and theological students were exempted from military service and from compulsory labour. The churches were still State property, but the taxes for their use were reduced. Religious houses, restored during the German occupation, were not re-confiscated. There was no opposition to the public celebration of Easter and there were even certain measures taken to facilitate the popular rejoicing at such feasts.[70] When the Metropolitan *Andrew Szeptyckyj* died on 2 November 1944 solemn obsequies were allowed.[71]

In brief there was a general impression that as a result of the relaxation granted in the USSR during the years 1941-1943 the Catholic Church of the Oriental Rite could hope to lead a normal existence. The Soviets demanded of course that the ecclesiastical authorities make public profession of respect for the State, and that public prayers be offered for the success of the Red army. Nevertheless it is undeniable that in an attempt

---

[70] Cf. G. de Vries, *Les Catholiques ruthènes*, in *La Civiltà Cattolica*, 1946, I, p. 395.
[71] The obsequies were attended even by Kruschev, then Secretary of the Communist Party in the Ukraine and later Secretary General of the Soviet Communist Party.

to win over the sympathy of the Ukrainian population, the
Bolsheviks at this period changed their policy as regards religion;
for example the enthronement of Mgr. *Joseph Slipyj* as Metropolitan of the Ruthenian Church took place without incident.

As a precaution for the future however many people thought
that a *modus vivendi* should be established between the Church
and the State which would guarantee the Church the possibility
of exercising her ministry without hindrance. The New Metropolitan received the suggestion favourably and as a first step in
that direction he made a gift of 100,000 roubles as a contribution
from the Church in the Ukraine for the relief of the USSR
war-wounded.[72] The money was taken to Moscow by a delegation composed of the well-known *Kostelnyk* and the priests
Szeptyckyj, *Bucynskyj* and *Kotiw*. Contrary to their expectations
they were not received by *Stalin* but by Government officials
who made it clear that the favour of the Government towards
the Uniate Church in the Ukraine depended on the latter's
co-operation in the bitter struggle then in progress against
the partisan movement. The new Metropolitan had indeed
insisted on the Fifth Commandment, " Thou shalt not kill," and
on the duty of Christian charity, but the Soviet authorities did
not consider this an adequate proof of collaboration. The
impression left by this visit to Moscow was that though the
Soviet Government was ready to show consideration for the
religious feelings of the Ukrainian people, it had little time for
a hierarchy that was in union with Rome.

The first signs of what the Soviet intentions really were
became evident in the course of the autumn and winter of 1944-
45 when the Communist authorities began to hold regional
conferences for the clergy. In these meetings Party orators
treated either theoretical problems or aspects of Church history,
from which they invariably went on to attack the record of the
Ukrainian Church, Poland, the Papacy and the Catholic Church.
The priests were obliged to assist at these conferences which
were intended by the Communists to serve as " re-education "
courses to prepare the clergy for the future.

---

[72] Patriarch Sergius of the Orthodox Church made a similar gesture, but for the
purchase of munitions.

At this juncture certain events occurred in the USSR which seemed to presage a change in Communist tactics. Since the death of the Patriarch *Tykhon*, there had been only a " substitute " at the head of the Russian Orthodox Church. In September 1943 a Synod was held in Moscow and the Muscovite Metropolitan *Sergius* was elected as Patriarch. This nomination of a new head of the Russian Orthodox Church had been desired by the Soviet Government which intended to use him in its domestic and foreign policy. Not only must the new Patriarch pray for the victory of the Red army but through his prestige he must strive to rally Russian emigrants, entertain good relations with the other autonomous Orthodox Churches and above all win over the Ukrainian Catholics to the Orthodox Church.[73] After the death of the Patriarch *Sergius* on 15 May 1944 the Metropolitan *Alexyj* was elected to the patriarchal dignity (January 1945). He hastened to issue a proclamation to Catholics of the Oriental Rite urging them to reject Rome and to join up with the Russian Church. This proclamation made use in particular of political motives in support of what it urged.

The offensive against the Uniate Church in Galicia began on 8 April 1945 with the publication of a violent article by *Volodymyr Rosovyc*, entitled " With the cross or with the knife," in which he attacked the memory of the Metropolitan *Andrew Szeptyckyj*.[74] There was a purpose in selecting the deceased prelate as the first

---

[73] The Russian Orthodox Church zealously set about carrying out these directives. The message issued by the Moscow Synod, after prayers for victory over the national-socialist enemy, criticised the Catholic Church and in particular attacked the Holy Father's 1944 Christmas Message twisting the meaning of the Pope's exhortation not to obey the dictates of hatred. The April 1945 number of the *Patriarchal Review* carried two articles attacking the Catholic Church: one by the Metropolitan Benjamin bore the title " The Roman Catholic Church," with the sub-heading " Take heed that no one seduce you," (Matt. 24, 4-5)—a very unfair article; the other, under the signature of Bishop Nicholas of Volhynia, called " Militant Catholicism " was an attack on the Primacy of the Pope and the Union of the Ukrainians with Rome at Brest-Litovsk in 1595-1596. It concluded with " Time has not cured the Vatican of its ambitions. But the Orthodox Church throughout the course of its history has torn away the mask and has lost nothing of its hatred of the Vatican." Cf. No. 4, April 1945, pp. 19-20, in B. Schultze, *L'Attitude de L'Eglise patriarchale de Moscou envers Rome*, published in *La Civiltà Cattolica*, 1946, IV, p. 82. The attacks in the *Patriarchal Review* against the Catholic Church and the Union of 1596 were continued in the following issues (cf. B. Schultze, *op. cit.* pp. 80-89) and formed part of the campaign to do away with the Ukrainian Uniate Church.

[74] *Wolna Ucraina* (Free Ukraine) 8 April 1945.

target, because in the eyes of the people the late Metropolitan enjoyed not only the respect due to a confessor of the faith but also the prestige of a national hero. The Communists wished to undermine that prestige and so create a sense of inferiority among the Uniate Catholics. The article by *Rosovyc*, first published in the *Wolna Ucraina* (Free Ukraine) in Lvov, was later disseminated among the people in pamphlet form.

This psychological preparation was immediately followed by an attack on the Uniate Hierarchy. On 11 April 1945 the authorities arrested the five Ukrainian bishops who were then on Soviet territory: Mgr. *J. Slipyj*, the Metropolitan, and his Auxiliary, Mgr. *Niceta Budka*; Mgr. *Gregory Chomysyn*, Bishop of Stanislav and his Auxiliary, Mgr. *John Latysevskyj*; and the Apostolic Visitator of Volyn, Mgr. *Nicholas Carneckyj*. The Bishop of Przemsyl, Mgr. *Josaphat G. Kocylovskyj*, who was on Polish soil, was the only bishop who escaped arrest. Not long afterwards the members of the chapters and diocesan curiæ and the seminary directors were imprisoned. The clerical students of the two seminaries that remained open (Lvov and Stanislav) were drafted into the Red army. A police search of the cathedral and episcopal palace in Lvov lasted ten days, during which all the archives and many religious objects were carried off. The same happened in the other dioceses.

The bishops who had been arrested were next brought for trial before a secret court at Kiev. The indictment, drawn up by the Public Prosecutor of the Ukraine SSR was published at the beginning of March 1946 and specified that the bishops had been arrested for " treason and collaboration with the German occupation forces." [75] On these unjust charges the Metropolitan *Slipyj* was sentenced to deportation and to 8 years of forced

---

[75] On the subject of this charge an editor of the Information Service of the Congregation for the Oriental Church has stated that in 1941 (the year in which the events are alleged to have taken place) only one of the accused bishops was at the head of a diocese, namely Mgr. Gregory Chomysyn, who was Bishop of Stanislav. Mgr. Latysevakyj was Auxiliary, and Vicar General to Mgr. Chomysyn; Mgr. J. Slipyj and Mgr. N. Budka depended on the late Metropolitan Szeptyckyj who died on 2 November 1944. As regards Mgr. Nicholas Carneckyj, Apostolic Visitator for the Ukrainian Catholics at Volyn, the Germans had forbidden him to live within the territory of his jurisdiction and he had gone to Lvov. On the other hand it is well known that the Metropolitan Szeptyckyj was far from showing favour to the Germans who several times ransacked the episcopal residence. Cf. *L'Osservatore Romano*, 14 and 15 October 1946.

labour, while the others were condemned to penalties ranging from 5 to 10 years of forced labour.

By such means the Soviet authorities were manifestly attempting to disorganise the Church in the Ukraine, before carrying their plans a step further. Before their arrest the canons of Lvov had tried to place a Vicar Capitular at the head of the diocese, but he was immediately arrested.

The Ukrainian priests, deprived of the guidance of their bishops and disorganised by police intervention, were the next target of the Soviet authorities. The latter issued an order whereby only those priests who were " registered " in the competent *State Office*, could exercise their ministry in church. Likewise a parochial " committee " of 20 persons was set up in each parish with authority to administer Church property, movable and immovable, and even to obtain for the parish a " minister of worship" chosen from among the " authorised " or " registered " priests. The Communists took care to have their own men on these committees, and in this way they succeeded in depriving the priests of the support of the faithful, just as they had already deprived them of the support of the bishops.

Some weeks after the arrest of the bishops there came into being at the instigation of the Communists the so-called *Pioneer Group for the re-union of the Greek Catholic Church with the Orthodox Church*; the Reverend *Kostelnyk* re-appears as head of the group, chosen, no doubt, so that his cultural prestige might lend weight to the cause of the " re-union." Since all three Uniate dioceses formed his sphere of action, *Kostelnyk* chose as assistants the Reverend *John Melnyk* for the diocese of Przemsyl and the Reverend *Anthony Pelveckyj* for that of Stanislav.

When the group was first formed three " pastoral letters " were published simultaneously to inform the Ukrainian clergy and people of their exact position in the Soviet world. The first of these, signed by *Alexyj* the new Patriarch of Moscow, was addressed to the Catholics of Galicia and invited them to acknowledge the Patriarch as their pastor. In the second letter the Orthodox Bishop of Lvov and Tarnopil, Mgr. *Macaryj*, maintained that since the Uniate bishops had been imprisoned, the government of the Ukrainian Uniate Catholics devolved on

him.   The third letter dated 28 May 1945 was from the hand
of the Rev. *Kostelnyk* and was addressed to the clergy of " western
Ukraine." [76]   In it *Kostelnyk* announced the formation of the
Pioneer Group and defined its aim as the re-union of the
Ukrainian Church with the pan-Russian Orthodox Church. He
invited ecclesiastics and Church personnel to become members
of the Group and informed the clergy that the Soviet Government
would not in future recognise any administrative authority in
the Catholic Church in the Ukraine except that of the Group.
This statement is in itself a proof of the close relations maintained
by *Kostelnyk* with the Soviet political leaders.

But the Group went further, and not content with mere tacit
approval, sought explicit Government approbation to enable
them to establish the movement among the clergy and the faithful.
Accordingly *Kostelnyk* applied to the Council of Commissars of
the Ukrainian SSR for definite approval of the Group, [77] and
on 18 June 1945 the Government recognised the Group as the
sole organ charged with the provisional government of the
Catholic Church in the Ukraine. [78]   The Group was likewise
authorised to resolve in future all juridical questions concerning
the administration of the Catholic parishes and their re-union
with the Orthodox Church through recourse to the Plenipotentiary of the Council of Commissars.   Finally the Group
had to submit to the Plenipotentiary for the affairs of the
Orthodox Church a list of all the deans, parish priests and
superiors of monasteries who refused to submit to the jurisdiction
of the Group.   *Although the Stalin Constitution decreed the separation
of Church and State, the Soviet régime by a return to the methods
of the Czars put the State machinery at the service of the movement
for " re-union " with the Russian Orthodox Church.*

Throughout Galicia the Group engaged in a feverish campaign,
holding meetings, publishing anti-Catholic pamphlets and
threatening priests who held out against them with the loss of
their parishes and deportation to Siberia.   On these propaganda
tours *Kostelnyk* and his collaborators were always accompanied
and supervised by police agents who compelled the deans to

---

[76] *Acts* of the bogus ' synod of Lvov,' published in Lvov in 1946, pp. 20-24.
[77] *Acts*, pp. 16-19.   [78] *Acts*, pp. 19-20.

bring the priests together to listen to the propagandists. The purpose of the meetings was nothing less than to persuade the clergy to join the Orthodox Church. When a priest refused, the NKVD invited him to a private meeting and presented him with two declarations to sign. By the first he declared his willingness to join the Pioneer Group and by the second he stated that he freely identified himself with the Group activity. A priest who refused to sign was allowed to leave the building unhindered, but he was then arrested on some pretext or other and once he was in prison an attempt was made to force his consent. It was by such methods that many priests eventually gave their signatures, believing that they would satisfy the NKVD by a merely fictitious adherence to the Group.

To escape such treatment some priests joined the Poles who were returning from the Ukraine to Poland as the result of an agreed transfer of population. Others took refuge in the forests and joined the partisans. A large number was eventually caught and imprisoned. According to news received in 1946 more than 500 Ukrainian Catholic priests belonging to the diocese of Lvov alone were in prison. Other sources would put the total number of priests arrested during the year at about 800. In these difficult times many acts of courageous resistance both by individuals and by groups of priests were recorded. On 1 July 1945 more than 300 priests sent a message of protest to the Soviet Foreign Minister, *M. Molotov*, in which they denounced the activity of the Pioneer Group as harmful not only to the Church, but also to the State.[79] Though the protest failed to cause any change in Government tactics, it remains a precious testimony of the courage and conviction of the Uniate priests.

After the arrest and deportation of the priests who refused to submit, their churches were closed by the Government. The Communists however did not dare approach the people directly to ask them to abandon the Uniate Church. In all their measures they tried to give the impression that they were concerned solely with the priests. If churches were closed, they

---

[79] Cf. *La défense du Catholicisme en Ukraine*, pp. VI-VIII.

were only those administered by priests who had not conformed
to the " desires " of the Government.   The faithful for their
part, although they had been taught to baptise their infants and
to pray in their own homes on Sundays, were not unaffected
by the violent measures taken against the clergy.   At first,
whenever it was possible, they went to the Polish churches of
the Latin Rite; but when the Polish population was repatriated,
these churches were soon taken over by the Government and
after that the faithful had access to the Orthodox churches only.

When the Pioneer Group had been operating for about a year,
the time seemed ripe for the definitive completion of the
schism.[80]   A synod to establish the " union " was convoked at
Lvov for the 8, 9 and 10 March 1946—just after the publication
of the charges against the Uniate bishops.   The participants
comprised 216 priests and 19 laymen; no Catholic prelate was
present.   The synod was presided over by the apostate priests
of the Pioneer Group and in his inaugural speech *Kostelnyk* stated
that the Union with Rome in 1596 had been concluded for
purely political motives and in particular as a mark of favour
to Poland.   Henceforth however the Ukrainians intended to
cut themselves off from their " step-mother " Rome, and to
unite themselves with their true " mother," the patriarchal
Church of Moscow.   Another speaker accused the Holy Father
of collaborating with Hitler with a view to subjecting Russia
to Western slavery.

On 9 March the new " bishops " of the Pioneer Group, *Melnyk*
and *Pelveckyj*, together with the Orthodox Bishops *Macaryj* of
Lvov and *Nestor* of Mukaciv, received the " abjuration of Latin
errors " of the priests present at the synod.   Telegrams conveying
the respects of the assembly were sent to the Patriarch *Alexij*
of Moscow and to the Orthodox Patriarch of Constantinople.[81]
A letter [82] was also sent to the faithful of western Ukraine
and an address of homage to Generalissimo *Stalin* and to the head

---

[80] Besides holding meetings and making personal contacts, Kostelnyk published at
this period a tract entitled *The Apostle Peter and the Roman Popes*, or *The dogmatic basis
of the Papacy*.   Borrowing the old arguments of the Protestant and Orthodox Churches
he attacked the Primacy of Peter and of the Bishop of Rome.   The tract was meant to
prepare the ground for the solemn act of " reunion " with the Orthodox Church.

[81] *Acts*, pp. 133-134.   [82] *Acts*, pp. 129-132.

of the Government of the Ukrainian SSR.[83] To celebrate the "union" a solemn ceremony was held in the ancient Uniate Cathedral of St. George in Lvov, at which the Orthodox Metropolitan of Kiev presided. The latter declared that the original union with Rome had been effected under pressure from the Polish nobility, but that now, thanks to the heroic exploits of the Red army, the Ukrainian people formed a united block. It would have been sheer folly, he said, to remain in union with the Vatican which had kept up relations with Fascism.[84]

It is interesting to note that, during the whole process of liquidating the Uniate Church, the union of 1596 was repeatedly denounced as a political manœuvre, and this too at the very moment when the "union" with Moscow was being realised with the aid of the "atheistic theocracy" and the persuasive force of Soviet prison camps.

After the synod, at the beginning of April 1946, a delegation headed by *Kostelnyk*, who was now "archpriest"[85] set out for Moscow. They were welcomed at the airport by a member of the Soviet for the Affairs of the Orthodox Church. On 8 April the delegation was received by the Patriarch of Moscow who two days later celebrated a solemn office in the Orthodox cathedral, assisted by the "Bishops" *Melnyk* and *Pelveckyj*. The delegates were fêted at a banquet which was also attended by *Karpov*, head of the Soviet for the Affairs of the Orthodox Church.

Although the mission of the delegation to the Patriarch of Moscow was intended to represent the entire Uniate Church in the Ukraine, a large section of the Ukrainian clergy and laity refused to side with the "synodal members." In the official bulletin of the diocese of Lvov the Orthodox Bishop *Macaryj* published statistics of the number of priests who joined the Orthodox Church, giving the total as 1,111 (532 from the diocese of Lvov, 302 from Przemysl, 277 from Stanislav).

---

[83] *Acts*, pp. 141-144.
[84] Cf. *Le Christianisme en Union Soviétique*, p. 289; *Acts*, pp. 47-50.
[85] Kostelnyk was killed on 21 September 1948 by a young man who took his own life so as to avoid falling into the hands of the police, and the crime was as usual laid at the door of the Vatican, although everyone knew the hatred of the nationalist partisans for the slain man.

Considering that before the war there were 2,300 priests in Galicia, and taking account of the fact that about 300 of them had escaped from the Communist persecution by fleeing abroad, if one accepts as accurate the figures furnished by the Orthodox Church, *there would still remain almost 900 priests faithful to the Roman Church*. Many of those who gave their signatures as supporters of the Pioneer Group did so through weakness rather than through conviction; without judging them for what they did, let us remember those others who preferred suffering to apostasy.

The following shows the fate of the Uniate hierarchy at the beginning of 1956: Mgr. *Josaphat J. Kocylovskyj*, Bishop of Przemysl, his Vicar-General, Mgr. *Gregory Lakota*, and Mgr. *Gregory Chomysyn*, Bishop of Stanislav, died in prison; the Metropolitan Archbishop of Lvov, Mgr. *Joseph Slipyj*, after several years of forced labour, is now confined in the inhospitable territory of Krasnojarsk; his Auxiliary, Mgr. *Niceta Budka*, is in prison, as is also Mgr. *Nicholas Carneckyj*, Apostolic Visitator; Mgr. *John Latyseckyj*, the Auxiliary Bishop of Stanislav, after serving a forced labour sentence, is not allowed to exercise his pastoral ministry.

Not a few priests have been murdered. The faithful have shared in no small measure the fate of the hierarchy and the clergy. Without bishops and without priests the Catholic Ukrainian people are also deprived of their churches, which are either closed or handed over to the Orthodox ministers. The liturgy is not celebrated except in secret. Every external trace of Catholic life (schools, press, works of charity, associations, etc.) has been blotted out.

CARPATHO-UKRAINE [86]

As a result of the several partitions of Poland, Galicia and Carpatho-Ukraine became part of the Austrian Empire, and later, in the Austro-Hungarian monarchy, formed a separate administrative district. By the peace treaties at the end of the First World War, while Galicia was integrated in the new Polish

---

[86] This region is also called Subcarpathia or Transcarpathia.

State, Carpatho-Ukraine was made one of the constituent territories of the new Czechoslovak Republic. During World War II Carpatho-Ukraine was restored to Hungary, and Galicia to the USSR; in 1944 both areas were re-united under Soviet domination.

The Catholic Church in Carpatho-Ukraine

It was in 1646, exactly fifty years after the Church in Galicia had done so, that the Church in Carpatho-Ukraine effected its union with the Church of Rome.

When the Soviets arrived Carpatho-Ukraine did not represent an ecclesiastical unit of the same importance as Galicia, either in the number of dioceses or in the number of faithful. It is true that the Ukrainian population south of the Carpathians was served by three dioceses;[87] but in 1944 the diocese of Presov remained in Czechoslovak territory and that of Hajdudorog (Hungarian-speaking) was attached to Hungary. Hence in the territory ceded to the USSR there was only one diocese, the ancient see of Mukachevo with the episcopal residence at Uzhgorod. Catholicism was strong in this diocese of 461,000 souls. There were 281 parishes and 459 churches and chapels [88] served by 354 priests, while in the seminary 85 students were preparing for the priesthood. In addition the diocese had 8 religious houses with a total of 85 religious of both sexes. The Church played a large part in the education of the young and had about 2,300 pupils in its 31 schools. Religious instruction was also given in the State schools.

On 31 May 1943 the zealous Bishop of Mukachevo, Mgr. Stojka, " disappeared." This marked for the Catholic Church in Carpatho-Ukraine the beginning of a crisis similar to that which was to come to Galicia a year later (after the death of the Metropolitan Szeptyckyj in November 1944). The Government of the diocese was temporarily entrusted to an Apostolic Adminis-

---

[87] In 1646, when the union was concluded, there existed only the ecclesiastical circumscription of Mukachevo.

[88] The total population was 851,889. Apart from the Catholics of the Oriental Rite there were 81,412 of the Latin Rite, 108,907 Orthodox, 77,833 Protestants, 112,653 Jews and 9,529 belonging to various sects.

trator, Mgr. *Nicholas Dudas*, who displayed great foresight and wisdom in meeting the ever-increasing difficulties occasioned by the war. On 24 September 1944 Mgr. *Theodore George Romza* was consecrated Bishop of Mukachevo, and from the beginning of his episcopacy he had to confront the military and political vicissitudes that attended the last phase of the war.

The Soviet Occupation

At the request of the new bishop the German troops had retired from Uzhgorod without putting up any resistance. Neither was there any hostility on the part of the inhabitants of Uzhgorod. The populace were grateful for the intervention of their bishop and the Russians were equally pleased at being spared the necessity of engaging in street fighting. So in the beginning the Soviet occupation did not give rise to serious cause for concern.

Since it was the first time that they had ever penetrated this region, the Soviets made a special effort to win the sympathies of the population whom the Kremlin had already marked out for annexation to the Soviet Union. They avoided any manifestation of hostility towards religion or the clergy. Although the Soviet commanders had transformed ecclesiastical institutes into military hospitals (with the exception of the orphanage in Chust), they refrained from attacks on the clergy and the Catholic Church. Further on 27 October 1944, just a few days after the entry of the Red troops, the Soviet Commander went to visit Mgr. *Romza* and assured him of the goodwill of the Red army towards the Catholic Church in the Ukraine.

This demonstration of goodwill and the initial period of calm were part of a well devised plan. The local Communist Party was too weak. There was then need of a short period of calm for growth in strength before Soviet plans could be effectively carried out. In addition the favour shown to the Ukrainian clergy and the bishop was a political move, as was seen on 6 November 1944 when Mgr. *Romza* was invited by the military commander to participate in the anniversary ceremonies for

31052

the October Revolution, and was even asked to make a speech on the occasion.[89]

It was in this very month (November 1944) that the Catholic Church in Carpatho-Ukraine experienced the first assaults of the new régime. The Red army itself did not take any direct action, but the People's Committees which had been recently formed, relying on the support of the army, began to arrest priests. Some of these were later freed as a result of an appeal to the competent military authorities. Acts of major violence were perpetrated and one of the arrested priests, Fr. *Peter Damianovic*, was shot. During this same month the members of the Orthodox Church, confident of Soviet support, began a campaign against the Roman Catholics, and in the villages where they were numerically strong they took over Catholic churches and expelled the priests.

Annexation of Carpatho-Ukraine by the Soviet Union

No time was lost in imposing a new political order on Carpatho-Ukraine. One month after the arrival of the Soviet troops in Uzhgorod the time was judged ripe to decide on the future destiny of the territory. On 26 November 1944 a general re-union of the delegates from the People's Committees was held at Mukachevo under the presidency of the occupation authorities, with a view to choosing a National Council which would temporarily assume the government of Carpatho-Ukraine. Composed completely of Communists, the National Council immediately proclaimed the independence of the country, and sent a telegram to *Stalin* asking him to grant Carpatho-Ukraine

---

[89] The Communists had succeeded in taking root in Carpatho-Ukraine and had built up their organisation. In the towns and villages People's Committees (composed mostly of Communists) were formed to collaborate with the Red army in the administration of the country. But the Communists met with less success in their attempts to drag the Catholic Church into the political arena. The speech made by Mgr. Romza in answer to the Communist invitation was very brief. He gave thanks to God that the war had passed them by without causing many victims or much destruction. He also exhorted the people to receive the new army in a peaceable way and asked them to pray for the speedy arrival of the peace they all desired. The text of the speech appeared later in the press, but it was so distorted that the bishop made a protest against the falsification of his words. The Soviet authorities replied that they had published what he ought to have said in accordance with the instructions he had received !

8

the honour of being received into the Soviet Union.[90]   Using
threats where necessary, the Council called upon the whole
population to sign a Manifesto requesting union with Russia.
The Manifesto was subsequently brought to Moscow by a delegation, but there was no immediate response from the Kremlin.
Not until 29 June 1945, at the end of the war, was Carpatho-
Ukraine formally received into the Soviet Union.   But since
November 1944 the Soviet Government in Carpatho-Ukraine
acted as if the country were already part of the USSR.

The Manifesto had been presented to Mgr. Romza for his
signature. He was also asked to declare that there was no religious
persecution in the Soviet Union, and to condemn the reign of
terror that existed during the German and Hungarian occupation.
The bishop replied that since he had never engaged in politics
he did not see why he should do so then. This provoked a storm
of indignation. The press called the bishop a Fascist and accused
him of being the enemy of the people, and a violent campaign
was started against the Uniate Church and against the Ukrainian
clergy. Mgr. Romza was summoned before General Petrov.
With Petrov was General Mechlis, the political representative of
the Soviets, who proceeded to attack the Church and the Catholic
clergy. He said that only one form of religion could be tolerated
in the State and hence it was better to break off relations with
Rome so as to be independent of the Vatican. He stated that the time
had come to omit the commemoration of the Pope of Rome
in liturgical ceremonies since the Pope had always supported
the Fascists and for that reason was an object of hatred to
everyone. The bishop decided on the only course possible, that
of fidelity to the Catholic Church.

The Persecution of the Greek-Catholic Church

From that time on the Soviets showed increasing favour
towards the Orthodox Church in Carpatho-Ukraine. Since the
bishop and the more zealous priests showed no inclination to
join the ranks of the Orthodox Church, the Communists thought

---

[90] Cf. G. de Vries, Suppression de l'Eglise grecque-catholique en Subcarpathie, in La
Civiltà Cattolica, 1950, II, p. 392

they might attain their ends by backing the Orthodox Christians who were the minority Church in Carpatho-Ukraine. Accordingly a delegation from the Carpatho-Ukrainian Orthodox Church was sent to Moscow (7-13 December 1944) to ask the Muscovite Patriarch to take their Church under his protection. In this way Carpatho-Ukraine was united to Russia by both political and religious affiliation. During this time the Government press in Carpatho-Ukraine intensified its campaign against the Uniate clergy, accusing them of having collaborated with the Germans. Meanwhile the Orthodox Church enjoyed the support of the Government administration.

In the beginning of 1945 a Department for Worship was established at Uzhgorod under the presidency of a Communist. Shortly afterwards came the promulgation of the famous law on the " liberty to change one's religion without any formality," followed by a law for the confiscation of the goods of Catholic parishes in cases where two-thirds of the parish population adhered to the Orthodox Church. But thanks to the support of local Communist groups, Catholic churches were seized even in villages with a small Orthodox population. During the first months of Soviet occupation the Catholics were thus deprived of 15 parish churches and chapels.

The agrarian reform introduced by the Soviets became an instrument in the persecution of the Catholic parishes. The various commissions charged with carrying out the reform acted as propagandists for the Orthodox Church, collecting signatures which could be used at a later date to remove the Catholic priests, on the pretext that the people had " voluntarily " gone over to the Orthodox Church.[91]

With intrepid courage Mgr. *Romza* protested to the military and civil authorities on the unjust spoliation of Catholic churches. On 11 January 1945 he went to the civil authorities to refute the accusations alleged against his priests and to try to reach some

---

[91] It is to be noted that while in Galicia the Soviets adopted special measures against the clergy and refrained from pressing the faithful to pass over to the Orthodox Church, they reversed the process in Carpatho-Ukraine. There they began by rousing popular feeling, closing churches, seizing ecclesiastical property and then expelling priests from their parishes; during this period the bishop was still left free to engage in a certain amount of pastoral activity.

measure of agreement. Whatever hope there was of coming to an understanding was quickly dispelled. The churches remained in the hands of the Orthodox sect and there was no change in the trend of events. The bishop therefore decided to defend every violated right, every confiscated church, every imprisoned priest.[92]

The Communists continued nonetheless to assail the Uniate Church with increasing violence. By adopting the Stalin Constitution they were enabled to confiscate all educational and charitable establishments. Religious instruction which had been tolerated during the scholastic year 1944-45 to the extent of an optional period of one hour per week was now suppressed, and it was forbidden to teach religious doctrine even in the churches. Sermons were always and everywhere subject to the control of the NKVD, who asked the priests why they preached that the Church of Christ would never be vanquished and why they were so fond of proposing the example of the martyrs. Secret agents demanded that the clergy speak from the pulpit about the happiness of life in the Soviet Union and on the duty of the young men to join the Red army. In the press, and especially on Sundays, there was always an article attacking the Faith or the Vatican and the Holy Father, or some Catholic priest. Alongside these attacks were published articles in praise of the Orthodox Church, depicting it as the victim of previous Governments and the model of loyalty to the new Government.[93]

In their haste to liquidate the Uniate Catholic Church in Carpatho-Ukraine the Communists thought that since the Pioneer Group led by the apostate *Kostelnyk* had yielded such results in Galicia, they might make quicker progress if they found a Catholic priest who would fall in line with their plans. The NKVD met with no success in their attempts to force Mgr. *Alexander Chira* and the Basilian Fathers of Mukachevo to collaborate with the régime. Accordingly they abandoned this

---

[92] To encourage both clergy and faithful, the bishop began in March 1945 to visit the parishes in turn, travelling in a horse-drawn coach which was his sole means of transport. This pastoral visitation lasted a month and everywhere it aroused demonstrations of loyalty to the Church and to the Holy Father.

[93] Many of the Orthodox had already joined the Communist Party.

plan of defeating the Greek-Catholic Church by a movement from within, and concentrated once more on the Orthodox Church. On 22 October 1945 the synod of the Patriarchal Orthodox Church of Moscow appointed Bishop *Nestor* as Bishop of Mukachevo-Presov to supplant the Catholic Ordinary. As his cathedral *Nestor* selected that of Mukachevo, the ancient episcopal residence of Carpatho-Ukraine, and there he set about organising a dissident Church. In this task he was helped by the régime. The local press published articles in his favour and there was even an official declaration to the effect that the jurisdiction of the Catholic bishop ended with the coming of the Orthodox bishop, whose administration extended over the whole diocese of Mukachevo including the Catholic cathedral in Uzhgorod. By creating opposition between the two bishops according to the Marxist theory of " internal contrasts," and by their systematic support of the Orthodox prelate, the Soviets felt sure of victory without having to arrest Mgr. *Romza* or make him a martyr in the eyes of the people.

The plan did not work out as the Soviets would have wished. *Nestor* was not well received even by the Orthodox faithful and this for two reasons: the heavy taxes which were imposed, and the ban on religious demonstrations.[94] His reception by the Catholics was much more reserved. The tracts of *Kostelnyk*, which had been imported from Galicia and distributed throughout Carpatho-Ukraine, had no effect. The threats and deportations of priests and faithful, instead of inducing them to go over to the Orthodox Church, had the effect of strengthening their resistance. The confiscation of Church property, even though it reduced the clergy to great financial straits, did not break down their opposition, and the priests were aided in part by the voluntary contributions of the faithful.

After the synod of Lvov, 8-10 March 1946, which declared the union of the Uniate Church in Galicia with the Orthodox Church of Moscow, the Communists intensified their efforts against the Greek-Catholic Church in Carpatho-Ukraine. The hour had struck to bring Mgr. *Romza* to order. He was several

---

[94] There was a rumour, even among the Orthodox, that the new bishop was an officer in the NKVD.

times brought before the NKVD and the subject of these " conversations " was certain " faults " of the Catholic Church, of the
papacy and of the hierarchy. The bishops were accused among
other things of collaborating with Fascism and of displaying
hostility towards Communism and the Soviet Union. All these
meetings ended with an invitation to join the Orthodox Church.
The reply of Mgr. *Romza* was always the same: " Better death
and every kind of suffering than to betray the Church."

Nor did the passage of time help to realise the Soviet intentions
among the mass of the people. In spite of Government backing
the Orthodox Church did not grow in prestige. On 22 March
1947 the local Communist Committee of Mukachevo thought
they could make a breach in the Catholic resistance by sum-
moning two superiors of the Basilian Fathers, Father *Anthony
Mondyk* (Provincial) and Father *John Satmari* (Superior of the
monastery of Mukachevo) and demanding that they sign their
acceptance of the Orthodox Church. Both priests refused and
two days later the NKVD transferred them to another monastery
where they were kept under supervision. Mgr. *Romza* protested
in vain to the Soviet Government. On Good Friday and Easter
Sunday (11 and 13 April 1947) the bishop preached two sermons
in the cathedral of Uzhgorod in which he denounced the anti-
Catholic intrigues of the Government. Then he recommended
the pastoral visitation of his diocese.

Meanwhile the " zeal " of the Orthodox Bishop *Nestor*, aided
by the Communist authorities, had produced some " results,"
and in July 1947 about two years after his nomination by
Moscow the Orthodox Church had already taken over 73
Catholic churches. In the process 15 Uniate priests were
deported, 3 condemned for " political reasons " and 36 had to
flee to avoid arrest.[95] The Soviets judged that it was now the
time to abandon more restrained methods and to organise a mass
manifestation and finish with the Greek-Catholic Church once
and for all.

It was decided to take advantage of the Feast of the Assumption
to accomplish the " re-union " of the Uniate Catholics with the

---

[95] Cf. G. de Vries, *op. cit.*, p. 394.

Orthodox Church.   On that day crowds of pilgrims usually thronged to the monastery of the Basilian Fathers in Mukachevo (Cerneca Hora).   Mgr. *Romza* was forbidden to go there under pain of arrest.   On the other hand the Orthodox Bishop *Nestor* invited the Orthodox Exarch of Kiev, who had himself represented by three mitred archpriests.   From Lvov came *Kostelnyk* and the Orthodox Bishop *Macaryj*; from Odessa, the Orthodox Bishop *Sergius*; from Volyn, Bishop *Varlaam*; from Stanislav, Bishop *Anthony*, as well as numerous delegates from various parts of the Ukraine.   This gathering of so many Orthodox prelates was to be an impressive spectacle, well calculated to appeal to a people who were fond of ritual splendour and solemn ceremony.   Such a manifestation of the " prestige " of the Orthodox Church would surely dissuade the people from showing respect and obedience to a young bishop like Mgr. *Romza*, who travelled about in a plain horse carriage and who had not even been able to make the journey to Mukachevo.   What would they think of their bishop who, on this solemn feast, had left the celebration of the ceremonies—in their own Byzantine Slav Rite—to so many bishops who lived in harmony with the Soviet authorities and were untroubled by persecution?

Nevertheless, the faithful had the courage to make the distinction for themselves.   On 15 August 1947, although 80,000 had come to Mukachevo for the feast, the entourage of the Orthodox bishops numbered only 3,000.   It was a public defeat for the Orthodox bishop in his own town.

Mgr. *Romza* was held responsible for the attitude of the faithful. It was now clear in the minds of the Communists that as long as he remained at liberty, they would never realise their plan, and the decision was taken to remove the Catholic bishop from the scene.[96]   To avoid creating the impression that he was a martyr for the Faith, he was removed by a " road accident." [97]

[96] Mgr. Romza loved to repeat, " Everywhere and always we are in the hands of God, and if we suffer for the Faith we ought to thank Him for the grace that is preparing us for martyrdom."

[97] "For the honour of our martyr," writes a person worthy of credence, "you must be informed of the exact circumstances of his death.   On 27 October 1947 he was returning in his carriage from Lavky where he had consecrated a church the previous day.   He was accompanied by two priests and two seminarians.   On the road between Cereivsti and Ivanovsti a bus crowded with soldiers and police crashed into the carriage

Now that Mgr. *Romza* was dead the Communists recommenced their attempts to win over the Uniate clergy and they used all the means at their disposal to find accomplices among the priests themselves. Finally they discovered a second *Kostelnyk* in the person of *Irenaeus Michael Kondratovich* who had been involved in some difficulty with the authorities. As a result of moral pressure and physical torture he apostatised and recognised the authority of the Orthodox Patriarch of Moscow. His efforts however met with little success, and in spite of the added pressure of the public authorities he could find only 35 priests to follow his example. They too had been imprisoned and set at liberty on condition that they recognised the Orthodox Patriarch.

Bishop *Nestor* was succeeded at Mukachevo in 1948 by Bishop *Macaryj*, transferred from Lvov where he had worked for the " union " with Moscow. On his arrival in Carpatho-Ukraine he found only one Uniate priest who had gone over to the Orthodox Church. The people were frankly hostile to *Macaryj* and commenting on this the Moscow *Patriarchal Review* said he ought to show " great understanding and great love for his sons who were sunk in error, so as to free them from Vatican slavery." [98]

The final assault on the Uniate Church in Carpatho-Ukraine came in February 1949. On the 22nd of that month the cathedral of Uzhgorod was confiscated and given over to the Orthodox Bishop *Macaryj* who had meanwhile been named Bishop of Uzhgorod by the Patriarch of Moscow. During the same month all Uniate churches were closed and the Uniate priests were forbidden to celebrate liturgical ceremonies, on the grounds that the Greek-Catholic Church, as it was generally called, was

---

with the obvious intention of overturning it and killing the bishop, so that it could be said that he had been the victim of an accident. But Providence thwarted their designs. The horses were killed instantly and the carriage wrecked, but the occupants emerged unhurt from the collision. The Communists in their rage did what the accident had failed to do; they beat the bishop about the head with iron bars. They then went away unconcerned. At the moment of the attack the bishop was saying his rosary. The victims were brought to the hospital in Munhacs where it was discovered that the bishop's jaw was fractured in two places, that he had lost all his teeth and bore multiple bruises all over his body. His injured companions recovered fairly soon, but there was no hope for the bishop. On 29 October a new nursing sister was appointed to the hospital and was detailed to attend the bishop; the nuns were sent away . . . the bishop died half an hour after midnight on 1 November."

[98] Cf. *Année 1949*, no. 10, p. 5.

not officially registered in accordance with the law. There followed a mass deportation of both faithful and clergy after the latter had been driven from their presbyteries by the police to make way for their Orthodox successors. Five Catholic priests were put into prison and one of them was condemned to 25 years' forced labour. Those who were interned in the hospital of Uzhgorod had to follow " re-education courses," while those who would not conform to the new directions were deported to Siberia.

The annexation of the Uniate Catholics by the Orthodox Church had been achieved by the persuasive force of genuine police methods. It was deemed necessary to invest the event with a solemn religious character, and the Feast of the Assumption 1949 was chosen for the purpose. There was little fear of a recurrence of the 1947 fiasco. Bishop *Macaryj* celebrated a solemn office in the monastery of Mukachevo, during which *Kondratovich* read a formal declaration of adherence to the Russian Orthodox Church. All ties with Rome were abjured. Then a telegram was read conveying the congratulations of the Patriarch *Alexij* of Moscow to the clergy and people. Commenting on the event, the Moscow *Patriarchal Review* [99] called it a triumph, but in an article published in the very same number of the review, Bishop *Macaryj* expressed himself in more modest terms.

According to news received from other sources the success obtained by the Orthodox Church, pressed into service as a Communist instrument, is really very slight, in spite of the use of force and of the illegality of its methods. Priests who did not conform, do what they can to assist the faithful in secret. They are forced to work in factories in order to earn a wretched pittance. The *suppression of the Greek-Catholic Church in Carpatho-Ukraine is no more than a legal formality imposed by the " atheistic theocracy " of the Soviets for purely political ends.*

---

[99] *Ibid.*

Chapter 4

THE PERSECUTION OF THE CATHOLIC CHURCH

UNDER

Communist Rule in Albania

THE DATE OF the definitive Communist accession to power in Albania can be fixed as November 1944, that is, just after the Germans had evacuated Tirana. However the election of deputies to the Constituent Assembly did not take place until 2 December of the same year. This election, carried out as a formality with only a single list of candidates prepared by the Communist Party, gave according to information coming from Government sources 95% of the votes to the *Democratic Front* (Communist).

As early as May 1944 there had been held at Parmeti a predominantly Communist Congress which had issued a decree investing a *National Anti-Fascist Committee of Liberation* with legislative and executive powers. After declaring defunct the Regency Council, set up after 8 September 1943, the Congress placed the Communist, *Enver Hoxa*, at the head of the Committee. On 22 October 1944 the committee met at Berat, and acting as Provisional Government, issued a proclamation that guaranteed respect for the basic rights of man, freedom of religion, of the press, of association, etc.[1] But the Committee had scarcely been installed at Tirana, November 1944, when it became quite clear that the Communists were ready to get rid of everything that might constitute an obstacle to their ultimate attainment to absolute power. On 11 January 1945 the Constituent Assembly proclaimed the *People's Republic of Albania*,[2] whose clearly

---

[1] The Congress of Parmeti had also guaranteed, over and above the other democratic liberties, " freedom of religion and of conscience, with equality of rights for all religions."

[2] *Bashkimi* (organ of the Albanian Democratic Front), extraordinary edition of 11 January 1945.

" democratico-progressive " Constitution also guaranteed liberty of speech, of the press, of assembly, of manifestation and profession of faith as well as inviolability of domicile. At the same time the Constitution decreed the separation of the Church from the State, the school and " politics."

The Catholic Church in Albania

Until the advent of the Communist administration the Catholic Church in Albania, despite its small numerical importance, was one of the active and constructive forces in the social and cultural life of the country.[3] In 1944 there were in Albania:

(a) 2 archdioceses: Durazzo and Scutari;

(b) 3 dioceses: Paluti, Sappa and Lissus;

(c) 1 abbacy *nullius*: St. Alexander of Oroshi;

(d) 1 apostolic administration: Southern Albania.

Out of a total population of about 1,100,000 (comprising 730,000 Mohammedans and 220,000 members of the Orthodox Church) there were 124,000 Catholics in 131 parishes, cared for by 93 secular priests and 94 members of religious orders.

The following figures give an idea of the position in Northern Albania as regards *religious institutions and houses* of both men and women:

(1) *Franciscans*, 52 in number, all Albanians. 27 resided at Scutari, while the rest were distributed, as the needs of the ministry demanded, among different parishes and religious houses in the north.

(2) *Jesuits*, numbering 25 priests of whom 9 were Albanians and 16 Italians.

(3) *Society of Don Orione*, 5 priests assisted by some Brothers.

(4) *Sisters of the Holy Stigmata*, with 48 nuns nearly all Albanians.

---

[3] On the subject of the great prestige which the Catholic Church had acquired in Albania, see *La Civiltà Cattolica*, 1947, II, pp. 409 *seqq.*

(5) *Servite Nuns*, numbering 27, nearly all Albanian.

(6) *Salesian Nuns*, numbering 10.

(7) *Sisters of Charity of Brescia*, 71 Italians and 5 Albanians.

These diverse institutes were dedicated either to the parochial ministry or to works of education and charity, such as schools, refuges, orphanages, hospitals, nursing homes, maternity clinics, diffusion of good literature, etc.

More recently in Southern Albania various institutions and works had been established for the care of the sick, education, pastoral ministry, etc. The whole vast area of Southern Albania constituted a single *apostolic administration* containing more than 4,000 Catholics with 6 secular priests (all Albanians) 7 Conventuals, 4 Basilians and 2 Lazarists, all of Italian nationality. Besides there were about 70 nuns, 20 of whom were Albanians, as well as 15 Basilian Sisters of the Oriental Rite, all of Italo-Albanian extraction.

All Catholic activities were under the direction of the Albanian hierarchy, composed exclusively of bishops of Albanian origin who ruled over the six dioceses of Northern Albania. Southern Albania, as has been stated, formed a single ecclesiastical circumscription under the Apostolic Delegate.

The Persecution of 1944-1945

In the form of a diary is given the sad chronicle of the war of extermination waged by the Albanian Communist Government against the Catholics, whose small numbers magnify the guilt of the oppressor who to-day boasts of the destruction he has accomplished.

The beginning; December 1944: The three Catholic printing works then existing in Albania were commandeered; that of the Jesuits, the oldest in Albania, founded secretly in 1870 when the Turks were in power, which had served the cause of culture, education and religion; that of the Franciscans, no less deserving though dating only from 1916; and finally the printing-house, " Scanderberg." Without any semblance of a decree, and solely in virtue of an arbitrary decision inspired by reasons of " public utility," the Catholic Church was suddenly deprived of its entire press. It was in fact forced to suspend the publication of the two Catholic cultural reviews *Hylli i Drites* and *Leka*, of the two popular monthly reviews *Zani* and *Majmtari i Zemres se Krishtit* (The Messenger of the Sacred Heart) and of the Catholic weekly *Kumbona e se dielles* (The Sunday Bell).

Shortly afterwards the right of association was dealt with in just as arbitrary and brutal a manner. Without the sanction of law, without even a police regulation, but solely on the accusation that they were " Fascist societies," the Catholic Action groups (flourishing under the direction of the Franciscans, the Jesuits and the cathedral clergy of Scutari) were subjected to a violent campaign of intimidation, threats and suspicion.[4] Communist violence was directed in a special manner against the Youth Organisations of *St. Anthony*, *St. John Bosco* and *St. Prosper*, several members of which were arrested, beaten or deported.

15 December 1944: Armed search of Catholic institutions, especially of the Pontifical seminary [5] and the Jesuit house at Scutari. In this town numerous Catholics were arrested, among them several secular priests and two Franciscans.

2 February 1945: Sixteenth search of the Jesuit Fathers' house. Hundreds of soldiers armed with machine-guns surrounded the residence where everything was ransacked for about six hours. While the religious and students were shut up in the refectory, ceilings and floors were staved in, the library and museum damaged, archæological specimens broken and the labels scattered; even the tombs of the church were violated. The searches continued at the Franciscan house, the Mantelate convent, the episcopal residence at Scutari and at the Apostolic Delegation.[6]

---

[4] Cf. *Rinia*, organ of *Brash* (Albanian Anti-Fascist Youth Front), 2 January 1946, and *Bashkimi*, 8 January 1947, article signed Tuk Jakova.

[5] The institution in which the future priests of the six Albanian dioceses received their formation.

[6] Before undertaking the elimination of the Catholic cultural centres at Scutari, the Communists inaugurated a spate of propaganda in the grand manner with its ridiculous arguments, illustrated with caricatures and faked photographs. This propaganda reached the whole of Albania. The aim was to prepare public opinion. These caricatures and

Mid-March 1945: There were already 1,000 people in the prisons of Scutari (population 30,000).

At the end of the month a People's Court began to pronounce the first death sentences and four priests were executed:

(1) Fr. *Lazarus Shantoja*, on 19 March 1945, accused of being Italophile. He was tortured and then hanged.

(2) Fr. *Andrew Zadeja*, on 25 March 1945, accused of having favoured the *Balli Kombetar*.[7] He was considered the greatest Albanian poet of recent times.

(3) Fr. *Anthony Harapj*, Franciscan, ex-member of the Regency, shot on 7 April 1945.

(4) Fr. *John Shallaku*, Franciscan, shot on 13 April 1945, charged with having worked for the formation of a party opposed to the Communist régime.

March 1945: A whole series of measures was inaugurated which ultimately caused the complete disappearance of Catholic social activities in Southern Albania.[8]

In the space of two months (March and April 1945) refuges, schools, hospitals, orphanages and missions vanished one after another, so that in Southern Albania no vestige of Catholic life remained.[9]

---

photographs purported to show religious hearing confessions in confessionals crammed with rifles and machine-guns, altars covered with arms and ammunition, religious armed to the teeth, statues of Saints filled with strategical plans and dangerous documents etc.

[7] The *Balli Kombetar* (National Front) was the party which, during the union of the Albanian and Italian Crowns and the German occupation, aimed at re-establishing Albanian freedom, and, once the war was at an end, the complete independence of the country.

[8] Cf. *Bashkimi*, 3 January 1946, article *Professors in the Dock*, and the article of 17 January 1946, signed Gjovalin Luka: *Fascist Models in Soutane*.

[9] Here are some facts :

At *Korcia* the Sisters of the Holy Stigmata, all Albanians (hence there was no question of nationality), were the first to be sent away from the orphanage ; they were then forced to close the kindergarten, and finally deprived of the house in which they lived.

At *Valona* and *Argirocastro* the eleven Sisters of Charity of Brescia were driven from the hospital where they worked, and forced to quit Albania because they were Italians.

At *Elbasan* the kindergarten was closed, and the Servite Sisters, all Albanians, had to leave the town.

At *Berat* the church was closed and the houses of the missionaries and of the nuns were taken over.

At *Lushnja* the nuns were at first prevented from carrying out their usual work, and finally repatriated.

The Apostolic Delegate, Mgr. *Leo Nigris*, did not hesitate to call the attention of the head of the Government, both by word and writing, to the existence of such abuses of power. Far from procuring the desired result his intervention only hastened his own departure from the country.

24 May 1945: The Apostolic Delegate, Mgr. *Nigris*, in Albania since 1938 as representative of the Holy See to the local episcopate,[10] was expelled as " undesirable " by order of the Albanian Communist Government.

May 1945: A Government decree ordered the closing of kindergartens conducted by nuns, the substitution of State teachers for teachers employed in private schools, and the introduction in the schools of materialist programmes.

June 1945: A law declares that elementary schools are exclusively a State concern.[11] The pupils of Catholic schools (the only private schools then in Albania) are thus forced to attend the State schools.

At *Fieri* the nuns' residence was occupied and the priest in charge of the mission arrested. After six months in prison without trial he was repatriated.

At *Dhrimades, Vuno* and *Pogradec* workshops and kindergartens were closed and the nuns were forbidden to proceed with their ordinary employments.

The six secular priests, all Albanians, who worked in Southern Albania, were sent away from these parts. The seven Conventuals, four were Basilians and two Lazarists, who were also in this area, were arrested, and a short time afterwards repatriated.

[10] On his departure for Rome at the end of March 1945 to ask help for the population whose plight had become miserable, Mgr. Nigris was assured by the General Secretary of the Ministry that there would be no difficulty about his return to Albania. Indeed the Albanian Government had asked the Apostolic Delegate to make known to the Holy See that it would like to have a representative of the Vatican to the Albanian Government. The Prime Minister, Enver Hoxa, desired his personal respects to be conveyed to the Holy Father, and that it be made known to him how much he admired his great philanthropic work. But scarcely had he left the plane at Tirana, on his return from Rome, than the Apostolic Delegate was put apart in a room at the airport. Seven hours later, without the sign of a farewell, he had to set out again for Italy. Cf. *La Civiltà Cattolica*, 1947, II, pp. 419-420.

[11] According to article 28 of the Constitution of 1945 the schools depend on the State which alone has the right to authorise the opening of private schools. The school is separated from the Church. The State guarantees to all social classes the right to frequent the schools and other cultural institutions.

On the spirit and work of the school, cf. Albanie—Ministère des Affaires étrangères —Section de Presse—*L'Instruction publique dans l'Albanie nouvelle*, Tirana, 1948—*Conseil génréal de la jeunesse populaire d'Albanie*, Tirana, 1947.

The law of 17 August 1946 laid the foundation of the " democratisation " of the new Albanian school. The programmes, manuals and methods of teaching were radically modified to bring them into line with the principles of Marxist-Leninist theory.

Cf. also: *Albánsky dvoulety hospodársky plán*, Prague, Orbis 1951.

Following on these enactments, Communist teachers began to teach in the Jesuit schools at Scutari. The religious of Don Orione were removed from the boys' orphanage, while in the girls' orphanage, conducted by the Sisters of Marie Auxiliatrice, the positions of director and sub-director were filled by two Communist girls aged 15 and 17 years respectively, both Mohammedans and both of notorious conduct.

Meanwhile in the Catholic colleges, which had so far escaped State control because of the shortage of lay professors, sections of the Brash organisation (Anti-Fascist Albanian Youth Front) were compulsorily introduced. With this went of necessity lectures of a political character given by special propagandists. At these lectures freedom to contradict was admitted; yet for having dared to criticise one of the propagandists in a public discussion the Jesuit Fathers *Gardin* and *Vata* (an Albanian) were arrested on 25 July and condemned by a People's Court, the former to six years', the latter to sixteen months' forced labour.

The Campaign against the Catholic Clergy

January-February 1946: The Jesuit Fathers, *Daniel Dajani* (an Albanian), rector of the Pontifical seminary of Scutari, and *John Fausti* (an Italian), vice-Provincial, were arrested [12] on a false charge of having spread leaflets and engaged in propaganda against the Government at the political elections of 1945.

The trial called *The Albanian Union Trial* lasted nearly a month. It ended on February 22 with the reading of the following sentences:

Condemned:

(1) *to death;* besides the two Jesuit priests, Father *Shallaku,* a Franciscan, and two seminarians;

(2) *to life imprisonment:* three seminarians;

(3) *to ten years' forced labour:* one other accused.

Those condemned to death were executed on 4 March and

---

[12] Cf. exhaustive article in *Bashkimi,* 4 January 1946: *For the Defence of Independence and Democracy:* "Fascist dogs must be eliminated; the arrest of Fathers Dajani and Fausti proves that some of them still exist." This is the gist of all current argument.

with them ten leading Catholics of Scutari and its neighbourhood. The bodies were left lying in the rain for a whole day in the Kiri torrent.

19 January 1946: All the religious of Italian nationality residing at Scutari got orders to go to police headquarters. There they were told that orders had been issued from Tirana that they were to leave Scutari within twenty four hours and get to Durazzo as best they could carrying with them only their personal effects. On the next day the refugees were led to Durazzo where they found the other Italian religious from all parts of Albania. After waiting for more than a month, during which they were subjected repeatedly to searches of their luggage and person, eighty Italian missionaries (nearly all the Italians present in Albania) [13] were put on a ship sailing for Italy. Only a few Sisters of Charity of Brescia remained in Albania. They were practically interned in the hospitals where they served until a Communist staff could be found to take their place. They were expelled in the spring of 1948.

March-December 1946: Once the Italians had been driven out, the Communists launched an attack on the Albanian clergy still at liberty, with the obvious intention of completely wiping out the Catholic Church in Albania.

At the end of 1946, the sad balance sheet of the struggle was as follows:

32 priests and religious imprisoned on the most varied and improbable charges; 15 priests and religious killed, these last being among the youngest of the clergy.[14]

---

[13] *Radio Belgrade,* 14 November 1945, citing the *Albanian Telegraphic Agency,* had spoken of the repatriation of priests and religious of Italian nationality who had come to Albania " during the occupation, to serve the Italian army and population sent for the purpose of colonisation." In reference to this statement it must be underlined that, with the exception of some of the missionary personnel of Southern Albania who had arrived after 1939 to undertake works of relief and charity in favour of the Albanian people, the Italian missionaries were in Albania quite a number of years before 1939. The Sisters of Charity of Brescia had served in the Albanian hospitals since 1924; the Salesian Sisters were in the country over 40 years; the Servite Sisters, more than 50 years; the Society of Don Orione, since 1928; the Jesuits, since 1848, and the Franciscans, for almost seven centuries.

[14] For list of victims and evidence of heroism see: *La Civiltà Cattolica,* 1947, III, pp. 138-141; and *Fides* 14 March 1953, p. 224.

9

April 1947: Sensational trial of some of the most outstanding of the clergy.[15] The trial ended on 18 April with the following sentences:

Fr. *Stephen Curti*, a secular priest, twenty years' imprisonment; Fr. *Meshkalla*, fifteen years; Mgr. *Bonati* and Fr. *Roch Oboti*, a secular priest, five years each. All were accused of having been " agents of the foreigner," of having worked " in the service of the Vatican " and of having taken part in " espionage and sabotage against the present Government's reconstruction scheme."

November 1947: Fr. *John Karma*, a secular priest, arrested and interned. After the expulsion of the Italian missionaries he had remained in Southern Albania with three other Albanian priests of whom there is no news.

February-March 1948: The elimination of the Catholic episcopate began. When the Archbishop of Scutari, Mgr. *Gaspard Thaci*, died in 1946, the Archbishop of Durazzo, Mgr. *Nicholas Vincent Prennhushi* had become head of the Catholic Church in Albania. At the beginning of January 1948 he was driven from his see and imprisoned. After torture by the police he was condemned to thirty years' forced labour and died in prison in August 1952.

Mgr. *George Volaj*, Bishop of Sappa, was arrested at the end of January 1948. Without any trial, without the least external semblance of justice the Communist Government had him horribly tortured and then shot on the morning of 3 February 1948.

The third victim among the Catholic hierarchy was Mgr. *Francis Gijni*, administrator of the Abbacy *nullius* of St. Alexander of Oroshi and of the diocese of Lissus, who had also directed the Apostolic Delegation after the expulsion of Mgr.

---

[15] The purpose of the trial was evidently to offer some justification in the eyes of the public both within and without the country for the wave of arrests and outrages against the Catholic Church. The account of the trial reached the public through the local Communist press and a special Sunday radio-transmission. It was the last official trial of Catholic clergy in Albania. Subsequently priests were " eliminated " without any pretence of a legal process, the general accusation of being "agents of the Vatican" sufficing to justify imprisonment, condemnation to a concentration camp or to forced labour.

Nigris. A year after his nomination as Regent of the Apostolic Delegation (towards the end of 1946), Mgr. *Gijni* was arrested and held in prison for about a year in a cell of little more than a square metre. Set free at the beginning of December 1947, he was arrested again after a short time and, together with 18 other persons, shot without trial on the morning of 11 March, 1948.

In March 1948 there remained only one member of the Catholic hierarchy, Mgr. *Bernardin Shallaku*, 80-year-old Bishop of Pulati. He was held prisoner in his own residence at Koder di Shën Gjergi in the mountains of the extreme north of Albania.

In the absence of the bishops the clergy elected Vicars Capitular to administer the dioceses: Mgr. *Thomas Laka* for the archdiocese of Scutari; Mgr. *Gaspard Gurakuqi* for the diocese of Sappa. No sooner were they elected than they were arrested and put in prison. The dioceses were once again without leadership. The Government may be considered to have reached its goal—the elimination of the Catholic hierarchy—by the end of 1948.

" The National Catholic Church of Albania "

June 1951: The Albanian Communist Government, following the example of the other Kominform countries, tried to establish a *National Catholic Church.*

In December 1949 the Government had promulgated a law on ecclesiastical communities.[16] According to the terms of this law any one of the three existing religions (Catholic, Orthodox and Mohammedan) which had not handed in the statutes of its organisation, management and administration within three months would be declared illegal.

The Orthodox Church and the Mohammedans presented these statutes within the prescribed time and were at once approved by the Government. After a period of nearly two years the statutes of the Catholics were still not forthcoming. Eventually after many threats and the detention of Mgr. *Shallaku* in police

---

[16] Cf. the Decree n. 743 in *Gazeta Zyrtare* (Official Journal), n. 90, 12 December 1949.

headquarters, where for three days he was humiliated and insulted, the Government succeeded in imposing statutes.

The clergy were in a dilemma: either they must accept the Government proposals or see the Catholic Church rendered completely inoperative even as regards the administration of the sacraments. The Government did not hesitate to arrest all those priests who, it was realised, would be absolutely opposed to accepting the statutes.[17]

After the necessary signatures were extorted, the statutes were presented to the Assembly of Deputies which on 3 August 1951 declared them approved and submitted them for the signature of the Præsidium of the Council of the People's Republic of Albania.

Thus was established the *National Catholic Church of Albania* in direct dependence on the Communist Government.

Here are the principal paragraphs of the document; their contents need no comment: [18]

1. The Catholic Church of Albania (C.C. of A.) is national in character, a juridical person, and comprises in its fold all Catholics in Albania. It is inspired by the religious principles of the Universal Catholic Church, instituted by Jesus Christ and having as its head the Pope, successor of the Apostle Peter.

   It has no dependence on the Pope in the domains of organisation, economics or politics.

2. The aim of the C.C. of A. is the external glory of God, the salvation of souls and the material prosperity of the people.

---

[17] According to the official radio report and *Zeri i Popullit* (Voice of the People) the statutes were supposed to have been signed by Mgr. Shallaku and 63 secular and regular priests. Of the latter, two certainly were dead in June 1951, while ten others were in prison. On the *Zeri i Popullit* list four Jesuit Fathers were given as secular priests. If there was any appearance of accepting the statutes, it had certainly been extorted by force and was of a purely external nature.

[18] The text of the statutes was published by *Zeri i Popullit*, 3 August 1951. There followed a violent comment on the Vatican " chief stronghold of world-reaction, grand agency of American espionage." The press represented the statutes as a " well-deserved reply " from the clergy and people to the Church of Rome and as " the concrete expression of the hate nurtured by the faithful and the Catholic priests of Albania against the Vatican which has given proof in the past of real enmity towards Albania."

3. As well as fostering their religious aspirations, the C.C. of A. shall promote among the faithful sentiments of loyalty towards the people's authority and the People's Republic of Albania (P.R. of A.), love of the fatherland, the cause of peace and of national prosperity.

4. The jurisdiction of the C.C. of A. extends to the whole territory of the P.R. of A. in which its members live. Its ministers and its personnel must be loyal subjects of the P.R. of A. and faithful to the people and the fatherland. It is their duty to exercise all their civic rights. The ecclesiastics constitute its directing body and the laymen are the faithful.

5. Albanian is the official language of the C.C. of A. It uses Latin however for worship according to the Latin Rite.

6. In the exercise of its ministry the C.C. of A. is bound to obey the laws of the P.R. of A. as well as the Divine Law. It obeys all the laws of the code of Canon Law of the Universal Catholic Church in so far as the enactments of said code do not contradict the laws of the P.R. of A. and are not contrary to established custom.

7. The C.C. of A., both from a religious and administrative point of view, is directed by the Albanian Catholic episcopate. The episcopate, composed of the ordinaries of the dioceses existing in the P.R. of A., is the directing organ of the C.C. of A. and its highest authority in all matters within its competency. At its head is the Ordinary of the metropolitan archdiocese of Scutari, who is its highest dignitary and resides at Scutari.

8. The rights and duties of the Catholic episcopate of Albania are as follows:

(a) to preserve inviolable the dogmatic unity and the canons of holy tradition of the C.C. of A.;

(b) to keep intact the unity of the C.C. of A. and preserve its national character;

(c) to direct and administer the dioceses of the C.C. of A.;

(d) to see to the provision of clergy through the medium of seminaries established and administered according to rules which must have the approval of the Council of Ministers of the P.R. of A.;

(e) to make provision for the setting up of a trust fund of the C.C. of A. and for the complete administration of its goods;

(f) the Government of the P.R. of A. subsidises the C.C. of A. taking into account the demands of the episcopate and the resources of the State;

(g) the episcopate shall see to the publication of pastoral letters, reviews, religious books for the formation of the Catholic clergy, in conformity with dogma and the holy canons as well as with the laws of the P.R. of A.;

(h) the episcopal body names the archbishops, bishops and other ministers of religion who, after being proposed, shall have their appointment confirmed by the Council of Ministers of the P.R. of A. The enthronement of new bishops or archbishops is the function of the bishop or archbishop authorised by the episcopate, in conformity with the dogmas of religion and with the approval of the Council of Ministers of the P.R. of A.;

9. The C.C. of A. comprises the following dioceses:

(a) the archdiocese of Scutari having as its head the Metropolitan Archbishop of Scutari;

(b) the archdiocese of Durazzo, having as its head an archbishop residing at Durazzo;

(c) the diocese of Lissus, with a suffragan bishop as its head, with the See provisionally at Kallmet;

(d) the diocese of Sappa, with a suffragan bishop of Scutari residing at Nenshat;

(e) the diocese of Pulati, with a suffragan bishop of Scutari residing at Koder di Shën Gjergi;

(f) the abbacy *nullius* of Mirdizia, having as head a bishop residing at Oroshi.
When these sees are vacant, vicars capitular will replace the archbishops and the bishops. The archdioceses and the dioceses are administered by their own ordinaries who have jurisdiction over all Catholic ecclesiastics exercising their ministry within the diocesan territory.

10. The ordinary of the metropolitan archdiocese, as head of the hierarchy of the C.C. of A. and leader of the episcopate, has authority to convoke at will the whole episcopal body and other ministers of religion as he deems necessary in

order to examine questions of the internal and external forum of the Church in general and of the dioceses in particular, keeping in mind Canon Law and the laws of the State then in force. He may take no important decision for the entire C.C. of A., nor inflict any disciplinary punishment on ecclesiastics not coming strictly within the limits of his episcopal jurisdiction. Important decisions for the whole C.C. of A. may be made only in complete agreement with the episcopal body. He represents the episcopate in all dealings with Government administration.

11. The metropolitan archbishop, and in his absence, the bishop chosen by the episcopal body, has power to keep in touch (in the name of the episcopate) with religious communities or official institutions situated outside the country.
These relations shall have no semblance of dependence or submission in the domains of organisation, economics or politics, but must exist solely for the purpose of *agreement on questions of religion* and must pass through the *official channels* of the P.R. of A. as required by section 25 of decree n. 743, dated 26-11-'49, relative to religious communities.

12. Residential bishops or in their absence the vicars capitular have the following rights and duties:

(a) to rule and administer their diocese;
(b) to ordain new priests according to the holy canons and the State laws in force;
(c) to convoke the diocesan synod to which are submitted special problems regarding the clergy and faithful of the diocese;
(d) to deal with all religious questions of their diocese;
(e) to name and change parish priests within the diocese after previous agreement with the diocesan consultors.

13. The bishops, and, in their absence, the vicars capitular, have at their disposal a diocesan Curia to help them in the management and administration of the diocese. The Curia is composed of the vicar general, the chancellor, the consultors, the secretary and other chancellery functionaries appointed by the bishop.

14. Each diocese is divided into parishes. In charge of each parish is a parish priest who depends on the ordinary of the place.

15. After taking canonical possession of his parish, the parish priest enjoys full rights, but at the same time *he is subject to all the duties* deriving from ecclesiastical tradition and the *laws* of the P.R. of A.

16. The parish priest has jurisdiction within the limits of his parish and over all his parishioners wherever they may be. Outside his parish he may exercise no jurisdiction except with the authorisation of the ordinary and, in certain cases, with the sole permission of the parish priest of the place. When a parish has more than one church, religious functions may be celebrated by a priest having the title of rector. If a parish is without a titular, a priest shall be appointed to celebrate Mass, preach the Gospel and perform all religious services in accordance with dogma, the holy canons and the Government laws then obtaining.

17. The ministers of religion, once chosen according to these statutes, are obliged to take the *Oath of Fidelity*. Celibacy is of obligation for all in Holy Orders.

18. Religious of both sexes form part of the C.C. of A., their aim being their own sanctification and the assistance of the clergy in religious offices. They live according to their Rule as approved by the ordinary and the Council of Ministers. Franciscans engaged in parochial ministry in various dioceses may be transferred according to the same rules as those in force for parish priests of the C.C. of A.

19. The patrimony of the dioceses and archdioceses constitutes the revenue of the ecclesiastics. Church property is divided into religious property and ordinary property. The former is made up of all goods destined for divine worship; the latter relates to all possessions needed for the upkeep of the Church and of persons in the service of the Church. Increase, conversion and administration of these goods, their control and supervision *are subject to the legislative provisions in force at the moment*, and in particular to the ruling on the administration of the goods of the C.C. of A. as approved by the Council of Ministers.

20. Expenses for divine worship and for religious functions are met by voluntary contributions of the faithful, by revenue from ecclesiastical property, and when forthcoming, by the State subsidy.

21. Within their dioceses the bishops may set up tribunals to examine dogmatic and canonical errors committed by priests and their helpers, and apply to them such disciplinary penalties as are of a religious character, *e.g.* warnings, suspension *a divinis*, degradation, according to Canon Law and § 14 of the decree on religious communities.

22, 23, 24 (om.).

25. These statutes, approved at the general meeting of the Albanian Catholic clergy, held on 26 June 1951 in the metropolitan archiepiscopal Curia of Scutari (elaborated according to the above mentioned principles and the general principles of Canon Law and in conformity with the existing rulings of the Council of the P.R. of A. and of the decrees on religious communities) for the purpose of establishing the procedure to be employed by the C.C. of A. in the regulation, management and administration of religious matters within its competency, come into force when they receive the approval of the Council of the P.R. of A.

Balance Sheet

After eight years of relentless persecution the position of the Catholic Church in Albania, compared with that of 1944, may be summarised as follows:

Secular Clergy:

(1) *Bishops:* 2 shot; 1 died in prison and 1 died a natural death; 1 old and in feeble health; the Apostolic Delegate expelled. In 1952 it was possible to consecrate two bishops, one of whom has since died.

(2) *Priests:* out of 94 priests 17 killed, 39 imprisoned, 3 forced to flee the country; 11 of the younger clergy called up for military service; 10 dead either from natural causes or ill-treatment; 14 still at liberty but under supervision.

(3) *Seminarians;* out of 60 in 1944 2 shot, 4 condemned to forced labour, 54 driven from the seminary and dispersed or drafted into the army.

Religious:

(1) *Jesuits:* 17 Fathers and 14 Brothers expelled; 3 Fathers shot; 3 Fathers and 5 Brothers in prison; 2 Fathers and 11 Brothers still at liberty but in hiding to avoid arrest.

(2) *Franciscans;* 13 priests killed; 27 imprisoned or condemned to forced labour; 6 dead from natural causes; the rest dispersed or in hiding.

(3) *Society of Don Orione:* being Italians all members were expelled.

(4) *Franciscan novices:* the whole 90 were dispersed.

There remains in Albania only a cruelly decimated clergy whose activity is restricted by the police and who are subjected to the worst elements of Communist propaganda.

Nuns: Of about 200 nuns engaged in 1944 in the different houses, schools and charitable institutions in Albania: 85 repatriated because they were non-Albanians; 43 interned or condemned to forced labour. The rest had to leave their houses and lay aside the religious habit.

Seminaries, Institutions and Religious Houses:

Closed or requisitioned: the seminary of Scutari, the Franciscan convent and novitiate of Scutari, the houses, printing-establishments and colleges of the Jesuits at Scutari and Tirana, the schools and kindergartens conducted by congregations of nuns, the orphanage managed by the Society of Don Orione at Scutari. Schools—all nationalised or closed.[19] Press—entirely suppressed. Charitable works—all destroyed.

In July 1955 the activity of the Church was still almost completely impeded by the " statutes of the Catholic Church in Albania " imposed by the Government in 1951. Since that date very little is known about the state of religion in the country. It is certain however that in spite of the havoc wrought by the Communist Government—whose brutality has not been equalled in any other country under Marxist rule [20]—considerable

---

[19] To understand in all its significance the suppression of the Catholic schools, the seizure of the buildings and the confiscation of their teaching and scientific equipment, it must be remembered that they, being by far the first of their kind, had remained in the forefront of all Albanian cultural activity. The two great institutes of the Jesuits and of the Franciscans at Scutari alone, had been able to publish about a thousand works (popular, scholastic, literary and scientific), the work almost entirely of their teaching staffs. A good half of the best writers of Albania were educated in these institutes, by which were also published two Catholic cultural reviews universally recognised in Albania as the best expression of the national culture.

[20] Concerning the methods used by the so-called " Sessions of Security " of the Albanian police, see the details given by *Tabor*, year VII, volume XIII, nos. 2-5, and the revelations made by an ex-member of the same police, Peter Kcira (who was afterwards executed), (*Ibidem*).

numbers frequented the churches that were still open. Three priests have died in prison and two others have been imprisoned. The two religious working in the parish of Tirana have been forced to abandon the religious habit and return to their families.

According to the latest reports (March 1957) Mgr. *Shallaku* died on 9 November 1956. At present there is in Albania only the Titular Bishop, Mgr. *Ernest Coba*, pro-Vicar Capitular of Scutari.

The losses of the Catholic Church in Albania have been great, but its prestige has not diminished in the eyes of the Albanian people (even Orthodox Christians and Moslems) who do not forget the heroic endurance of so many ecclesiastics and laymen.

Chapter 5

THE PERSECUTION OF THE CATHOLIC CHURCH

UNDER

Communist Rule in East Germany

AFTER THE UNCONDITIONAL surrender of the German armed forces in May 1945 the Allies placed the German territories " to the east of the Oder and Neisse " under Polish administration, and the Northern part of East Prussia under Soviet administration.[1] This was supposed to be an *ad interim* arrangement until definite frontiers would be established by the Peace Treaty.

Central Germany became the Soviet Zone of occupation, while the western part of the country was divided into American, French and British Zones. Berlin was broken up into four sectors, each controlled by one of the Allied Powers.

By the terms of the Potsdam Agreement the whole of Germany was to be under a uniform administration by the Four Powers

---

[1] The result of the advance of the Soviet troops, of the mutilation of German territory and of article 13 of the Potsdam Agreement, 2 August 1945, between the USA, Great Britain and the USSR—an agreement which provided for the transfer of the German population, or part of it, which lived in Poland, Czechoslovakia and Hungary—was the exodus, voluntary (autumn 1944—May 1945) or forced (from May 1945), of millions of Germans. This was one of the most serious and tragic transfers of population in history. For the Church it marked the beginning of very grave problems (from the points of view both of organisation and pastoral work) which are yet not fully solved. About 13 million Germans (7 million Protestants and 6 million Catholics) had to be divided up between the four occupation zones (10 million in the Western Zones and about 3 million in the Soviet Zone). This division, often carried out without any pre-established plan, led to the presence of Catholics in places which up to 1945 were almost exclusively Protestant and vice versa.

For example, of the total of " displaced persons " who found refuge in Bavaria (predominantly Catholic) 1,300,000 were Catholics and 500,000 Protestants. On the other hand, and especially in the Soviet Zone, hundreds of thousands of Catholics were settled in the midst of strongly Protestant communities. All this meant a new and extraordinary burden on the Church: need to provide spiritual assistance, to build churches, to see to religious instruction, etc.

based on democratic principles. But from the very beginning
the Soviets ignored this agreement and followed in their Zone
an occupation policy quite peculiar to themselves.

As a re-action to this Soviet policy in May 1949 the Western
Occupation Zones were united into the Federal Republic with
its capital at Bonn. The USSR replied to this manoeuvre by
favouring in its Zone the establishment of a German Democratic
Republic (Deutsche Demokratische Republik [DDR]) on the
lines of the eastern satellite " People's Democracies."

Twelve years after the end of the war Germany has not yet
succeeded in having a peace treaty signed. Although the
establishment of the Federal Republic gave it the standing of a
sovereign State, and allowed Germany once more to take its
place among the free peoples of Europe, the end of the partition
of its territory and of its people is not yet in sight. That
partition " has created in the heart of Europe a focus of disorder
and unrest." [2]

The Sovietisation of East Germany

Decree n. 1 of the Soviet Military Administration (SMA),
10 June 1945, was the beginning of a policy to create in the
Soviet Zone through *ukase* and the threat of arms a *de facto*
situation which later could be given the appearance of legality
" through the will of the people " expressed in actual fact through
the Communist organisations.

In 1946 the Military Administration authorised the formation
of the following four parties: the German Communist Party
(KPD), the German Social-Democrat Party (SPD), the Christian-
Democrat Party (CDU) and the Liberal-Democrat Party (LPD).
At the very first elections the Social-Democrat Party was
prevented from presenting its own list of candidates, because
it had been fused with the Communist Party under the name of
Unified Socialist Party (SED).

Besides the political parties the self-styled " Democratic

---

[2] Conrad Adenauer, Chancellor, so expresses himself in the preface to the book,
Germany To-day, Wiesbaden, 1955. He adds: " The re-unification of Germany can be
brought about solely by peaceful means; but without it the whole German people
can find neither peace nor economic vitality; *and that part of the population which is in
the Soviet Zone will find neither the dignity of human existence nor freedom of thought."*

Anti-Fascist Mass Organisations " were also authorised to have their own electoral lists. Such were: the Peasant Mutual Aid Union, the Free German Youth (FDJ), the German Federation of Free Unions (FDGB), the German Women's Democratic Union (DFD) and the Cultural Union for the Democratic Renewal of Germany. All these organisations were para-Communist. The Soviets aimed in this way at reaching their goal while keeping up a façade of normal parliamentary usage, tactics then common in other countries behind the Iron Curtain.

At the general elections in September 1946 the SED (Unified Socialist Party) polled only 52.4% of the votes, as against 39.9% for the other two parties. The " Mass Organisations " did not get even 1%.[3]

The Unified Socialist Party did not do any better in the elections to the local and regional Diets which followed.

After these last elections the Communists made up their minds that they could never get the parliamentary majority needed to enable them to follow out the Soviet policy in Germany. They then turned to extra-parliamentary methods. They prevented by force all legal political opposition and set up a " German People's Council " (Deutscher Volksrat) to which was given the task of drawing up a " pan-German " Constitution.[4]

The elections to the third congress of the German People's Council, carried out on even less democratic lines than the preceding elections, took place on 15 and 16 May 1949. They were decisive. The Unified Socialist Party got 90 seats, while the Christian-Democrat Party and the Liberal-Democrat Party got 45 each. Two new parties with Communist leanings got 15 seats each, and the " Mass Organisations " shared the remaining 120 between them. The strong minority (33.9%, that is, more

---

[3] This was the result in spite of the fact that the Unified Socialist Party's lists of candidates were presented in the 11,623 districts of the Soviet Zone, while the Christian-Democrat Party and the Liberal Party were allowed to present their lists only in 1,182 and 2,082 districts respectively. Besides, the Soviet Military Administration allotted some 886 tons of paper to the Unified Socialist Party, while the two other parties got only 9 tons. Cf. Wahlfälschungen, Wahlbehinderungen, Wahlbeeinflussungen, in der sowjetischen Besatzungszone, 1946-1950, Berlin 1950.

[4] This idea, considered at the time utopian, in fact formed the basis of the Constitution of the German Democratic Republic in 1949. Cf. Wegener, Die neuen deutschen Verfassungen, Essen 1947, pp. 301 seqq.

than one-third of the total poll) which was unwilling to accept the *system of one list of candidates*, was simply eliminated.

On 5 October 1949, on instructions from the Soviet Military Administration, the Deutscher Volksrat became the *People's Parliament* (Volkskammer); and proceeded at once to proclaim the German Democratic Republic (DDR). A provisional Government was set up with *Otto Grotewohl* (Unified Socialist Party) as President of the Council, and *Walter Ulbricht* (Secretary of the Unified Socialist Party) as Vice-President. *Wilhelm Pieck*, President of the Unified Socialist Party, was elected head of the State. The Soviet Military Administration " handed over " the legislative and administrative functions to the new State, now under Soviet domination.[5]

Finally in a message sent by *Stalin*, 13 October 1949,[6] the Kremlin gave its sanction to the Constitution of the German Democratic Republic, approved by the Volksrat on 30 May and like that of Bonn valid for the whole territory of the Reich.[7]

---

[5] The Soviet Military Administration (SMA) was replaced by a *Soviet Commission of Control* (SKK) with General Zhukov and political adviser Semionof at its head. Besides, Moscow sent to Berlin ambassador *Pusckin* as " Head of the Diplomatic Mission of the USSR."

[6] Cf. *L'Osservatore Romano*, 15 October 1949.

[7] Cf. *Die Verfassung der Deutschen Demokratischen Republik*, published by the Secretariate of the *Volksrat* with a Preface by Otto Grotewohl, Berlin 1949.

Although at first sight the Constitution seems innocent enough, in reality it is very dangerous. In it everything as in the Soviet dictatorship centres in a State system based essentially on the central power (Staatsgewalt). First place is not given to the State as a community and much less to the citizen and his inalienable natural rights, but to the State conceived on totalitarian principles. The following articles deal with the interests of the Church:

Arts. 8 and 9 guarantee the following basic rights: personal liberty, inviolability of domicile, secrecy of the post, freedom from censorship, free expression of thought, right of assembly.

There is however the limiting clause: " within the limits of the law in force for all." This same restriction applies also to the right to found associations and organisations.

Art. 16 lays down that Sundays and Feast Days are to be considered days of rest.

Art. 30 states that the family and marriage are the basis of the social community, and that they are under State protection. This of course is equivalent to laicisation of both institutions.

Art. 31 recognises the parents' right to choose the type of education the children are to receive. But in the remaining articles it is useless to look for the practical application of this right. The end assigned to education is to form youth in the democratic spirit (i.e. in accordance with the teachings of Marx, since *democracy* for the Communists means " progressive " democracy).

The new State, with *Pieck* and the Unified Socialist Party as its mouthpieces, hastened to state that the Oder-Neisse line constituted once and for all the peace frontier (Friedensgrenze) of Germany with the East.

On 27 March 1954 the USSR, obviously with a view to propaganda, stated that the German Democratic Republic was an independent State with sovereign rights. In fact it was abundantly clear that despite the formal recognition of its sovereign character the Government of the Soviet Zone, like that of all other satellites of the USSR, and maybe more so, was in every sphere wholly subject to the political and ideological directives of Moscow.

The sovietisation of East Germany continued in the following years, but was speeded up after the elections of 15 October 1950 which were a complete success for the Unified Socialist Party, 99.7% of the votes being in favour of the *single list*.[8] This spectacular success was repeated in the " People's " elections on

---

Art. 34, dealing with freedom of teaching, is a fine example of the way in which a right affirmed in a proposition is then emptied of content by the next phrase: " Teaching, art and science are free . . .; the State guarantees to safeguard them so that they may not be used for ends opposed to the spirit of the Constitution."

The provisions relating to religious instruction deserve special mention; the parents decide whether or not their children are to get such instruction (art. 44); but this instruction is not considered a school subject, and is the business of the Churches which choose the teachers. School buildings are only " put at their disposal " (arts. 40-44).

Art. 41 states:

(1) Every citizen has full freedom of religion and of conscience. The normal exercise of religion is guaranteed by the Republic.

(2) Religious institutions and organisations, religious activities and religious instruction may not be exploited for purposes opposed to the Constitution, or so as to profit political parties. There remains however the undisputed right of religious societies to take up their stand on fundamental problems in accordance with their own special ideologies.

This paragraph was introduced by the Communists with the clear intention— for those who know Communist methods—of provoking division among the clergy. The last phrase is especially significant.

Cf. Herderkorrespondenz, June 1951, pp. 408 seqq. on *Die rechtliche Lage der Kirche in der Ostzonen Republik*.

[8] The electors could not vote freely. There was only a single list of candidates, and the voting paper did not leave even the choice between " yes " and " no," for the result was in any case a foregone conclusion. The " free and democratic elections " became a non-secret vote. The ballot papers were without envelopes, openly placed in the polling stations reserved for the inhabitants of the same building, for all the workmen of the same company, for all the members of the same organisation, etc. . . . One need not vote at all, but abstention was looked on as an act hostile to the State and exposed the person responsible to serious retaliation.

17 October 1954 when the Unified Socialist Party polled 99.46% of the votes.

Soviet " progressive " efforts could in future be pursued in peace. The " building up of socialism " was pushed ahead, and brought with it the methodical and merciless change of East Germany into a " People's Democracy " with all its ensuing spiritual and religious consequences.

During the last six years more than one million East Germans have fled to the Federal Republic. There could hardly be a more eloquent proof of the efficiency of the New Gestapo, the *State-Security-Service* (SSD), (Staatssicherheitsdienst) of *East Germany*.

The Catholic Church in East Germany

At the end of the war the efficiency of the Catholic Church in Germany had been seriously affected by its twelve-year courageous fight under the Nazi Government, and by the loss of a great number of the clergy who had been mobilised during the war.

The results of the persecution which the Church had undergone in the Third Reich (a persecution vigorously denounced by the Encyclical " Mit Brennender Sorge," 1937) were strongly felt in the years that followed the downfall of National-Socialism. The Hitler régime tried in every way to paralyse Catholic associations. Many of them were dissolved or kept under strict watch; their directors were systematically accused of acting as enemies of the State.

The religious press too had suffered severely for its opposition to Nazi paganism. Denominational schools and Catholic social, cultural and charitable works were all seriously affected. The pressure brought to bear on Catholic priests took many forms: strict supervision of preachers, questionings and searches, warnings and reproofs, prohibition to teach, to give lectures, to organise religious ceremonies in public, arbitrary imprisonment in the notorious concentration camps, and even condemnation to death.[9]

---

[9] Cf. *Kreuz und Hakenkreuz*, Munich 1946, in which Neuhäusler has gathered together an extensive and exhaustive documentation on this matter.

In May 1945 the rebuilding of the *Civitas Christiana* (*Christian City*) had to be undertaken practically from the foundation, and that in a country devastated by frightful material and spiritual ruin and divided between four different occupying powers. It was generally said that Germany had become a " missionary country."

At the moment the following ecclesiastical circumscriptions of East Germany are under Polish administration: the dioceses of Ermland, the prelacy *nullius* of Schneidemühl, and the greater part of the archdiocese of Breslau. Juridically there has been no change in these circumscriptions; even though they are governed by apostolic administrators,[10] they continue to be dioceses. But besides having been deprived of their German ordinaries, they have suffered too by the expulsion of nearly all the German-speaking faithful.

From the point of view of ecclesiastical law the former administration has been maintained also in the Soviet Zone. The dioceses of Misnia and Berlin have continued to exist. Yet while the Bishop of Berlin lived in the Western sector, the greater part of his diocese was in the Soviet sector and the Soviet (Eastern) Zone. Small parts of the archdiocese of Breslau (Görlitz and Neuzelle), notable parts of the archdiocese of Paderborn and of the dioceses of Osnabrück, Fulda and Wurtzburg were also part of the Soviet Zone. It is of great importance for the ecclesiastical administration that the auxiliary bishops of Paderborn and Fulda have been able to keep their residences in the Soviet Zone, at Magdeburg and Erfurt.

A little reflection on the events that have marked the twelve years since the end of the war will show what trials the Church in the Soviet Zone has undergone under a régime as totalitarian as Nazism, and furthermore openly atheistic and materialist.

It must be noted however that, if on the international plane Communism looks on the Catholic Church as its first and most redoubtable enemy, in the Soviet Zone of East Germany the Communists see their main enemy in the Protestant (Evangelical)

---

[10] Although the Archbishop of Breslau, the Bishop of Ermland and the Prelate *nullius* of Schneidemühl have died since then, the Holy See has not appointed successors. These dioceses are now governed by administrators of Polish nationality.

Church. It is easy to see the reason for this. Catholics in the Soviet Zone number only 12.2% of the population while 81.6% are Protestants.

The aim of this book necessarily limits it to a consideration of the measures taken against religion in so far as they affect the Catholic Church.

The Struggle against the Catholic Church in the Soviet Zone

During a rather short period of " truce," due mainly to the need for economic and political re-organisation of the country, religion enjoyed a relative freedom in spite of serious difficulties.

The Soviet Military Administration, and then the Government of Pankow which replaced it, remained all the time faithful to the ideology of Marx and Lenin. Consequently it ordered a whole series of measures aimed at hindering an ordered development of religious activity.

The chief steps taken were:

1. Suppression of religious instruction in the schools by an order dated 31 May 1946. Such instruction had to be given outside of class hours. Care was taken at the same time to make the diffusion of religious knowledge more difficult for the Churches.

2. Compulsory teaching of atheistic Materialism in the State schools.

3. Regulations aimed at withdrawing the youth from family influences. The instrument used for this end was the official youth organisations: Free German Youth (Freie Deutsche Jugend: FDJ) and Pioneer Youth.

4. Efforts to wipe out the memory of Christian customs and traditions, especially on the occasions of great feasts.

5. Organisation of political meetings at the same hour as religious ceremonies.

6. Exclusion of the Church from all activity not of a strictly religious character.

7. Measures to make the economic situation of the clergy precarious.

8. Subjection of priests to severe political pressure (by threats, extortion, etc.), in order to force them to give their support to the Communist propaganda campaigns.

9. Obstacles of all kinds to the entry of priests from West Germany, even when they had been officially appointed by their bishops to the care of souls in the Eastern Zone.

The ecclesiastical authorities re-acted vigorously to these destructive measures. But the Communists only made this a pretext to accuse them of acting for political ends or out of hostility towards the people.

The Bishop of Berlin, Cardinal *Conrad von Preysing*, addressed to the Vice-President of the Council of Ministers, *Otto Nuschke*, a *Memorandum* entitled " Right to existence and possibility of life for the Catholic Church in the territory of the German Democratic Republic," dated 29 December 1949. In this *Memorandum* he deplored the fact that despite the Potsdam Agreements and the Constitution, liberty of religion and conscience did not exist in the German Democratic Republic, Atheism was the aim of official education, the Catholic press was not free, and the exercise of religion was in every way hindered. On 21 January 1950 the Cardinal received a reply in which it was stated that the *Memorandum* had raised serious problems and could not be studied until Parliament had been consulted. When at the end of four months no reply had been received and restrictions on freedom of religion had reached the point of making it almost impossible for Catholics to live according to their conscience, the Cardinal wrote directly to the President of the Council, *Grotewohl* (22 April 1950).

Here is the text of the document: [11]

" I wish to point out some facts and conditions that constitute a true oppression of the Christian conscience. At the same time I wish to make certain demands in connection with the situation and which should they not be taken into consideration would go to prove that one cannot speak of liberty of religion and of conscience in the Republic.

" (1) In the German Democratic Republic Materialism is in fact the exclusive world-outlook (Weltanschauung) professed by the State; it is the exclusive religion of the State, to which both

---

[11] When he got no direct answer to his letter the Bishop of Berlin brought the matter before the public in *Gibt es Glaubens-und Gewissensfreiheit in der Deutschen Demokratischen Republik? Eine kirchenamtliche Stellungnahme.* Berlin 1950 (Is there Freedom of Religion and Conscience in the German Democratic Republic?).

in theory and in practice all activities of the nation are subject. A clear tendency to look upon and judge life solely from the point of view of Materialism is manifest. In kindergartens, in schools and in universities, in obligatory professional formation, in the FDJ, and in the Association of Young Pioneers, in a word, everywhere only the materialist outlook on life and on the world is tolerated in the education of individuals.

" To withdraw Christians from this inadmissible state of affairs, I make the following demands:

(a) In the German Democratic Republic Materialism must cease to be considered the exclusive State world-outlook.

(b) Instruction given to pupils in the public schools, which they have to frequent, must no longer follow the principles of this anti-Christian outlook.

(c) All constraint, aimed at forcing children and adolescents to join the Organisations of Young Pioneers and of Free German Youth must cease.

" (2) Liberty of religion, in so far as it is allowed in the German Democratic Republic, is being limited to an ever greater degree according to a pre-established plan to the interior of the churches. Whenever religious life goes outside the framework of purely liturgical rites—a process natural to it—the Ordinance of 1 July 1949 on ' the obligation of announcing meetings beforehand,' allows the police to exercise control over these meetings.

" The restricting of religious activity solely to acts of worship, together with the development of the materialist spirit in public and private life, is part—this is admitted in materialist literature —of the processes that of their nature bring about the liquidation of religion.

" In the face of this situation I make the following demands:

(a) The attempts, undertaken with police help, to limit religion in the German Democratic Republic to acts of worship within the consecrated edifices, must cease.

(b) Christians should have the unrestricted right to pursue, even outside of religious functions, those aims which are according to their conscience. Among these latter we note especially the Apostolate of Youth in parishes, religious instruction and charitable works.

" (3) Materialist principles in their bearing on all human activity are being explained more and more to the public. To this end every means of propaganda is being employed.

" Adults too are being urged to take part in meetings or to become members of organisations whose spirit and methods are not reconcilable with the duties of the Christian conscience.

" Taking my stand on the Constitution of the German Democratic Republic, I present the following demands:

(a) The compulsion being used by means of official propaganda to make Christians join these organisations or take part in these meetings must cease.

(b) Neither the family life nor the social position of those who, for reasons which seem to them well founded, refuse to join such and such an organisation, ought to be endangered.

" (4) The monopoly which Materialism enjoys in the formation and direction of public opinion destroys in practice liberty of religion and of conscience. To give only a few examples, I point out the following: in the German Democratic Republic the Catholic Church has not a single periodical; the police have again intervened when there was question of circulating Catholic periodicals printed outside the Republic.

" Not infrequently the discourses and declarations of the ecclesiastical authorities have been for propaganda purposes grossly distorted by the authorised newspapers in the territory of the German Democratic Republic. In face of this situation Catholics have no opportunity of making public certain explanations which may be necessary.

" To safeguard liberty of religion and of conscience I am forced to present the following demands:

(a) The Catholic Church should be able to publish journals which would be at the service of its teaching and its world-outlook. These journals should enjoy liberty of the press, that is, in our case the materialist outlook should not be imposed on them in controverted questions. They should also have the right to defend the Church, its teaching and its hierarchy, at least to the same extent as the organs authorised by the German Democratic Republic claim the right to defame them.

(b) I demand further that Catholics be allowed to get periodicals
printed outside the Republic without the police or a
one-sided censorship intervening in a despotic manner.

" Finally I wish to point out that rape of Christian consciences
is becoming more and more frequent in the German Democratic
Republic.

" The discontent called forth by this *de facto* situation is growing.
The demands presented by me in this document are not privileges,
but are founded on the Potsdam Agreements and on the Constitution of the German Democratic Republic. Considering the
seriousness of the situation and the importance of my statement,
I dare to hope for a speedy and clear reply.

CONRAD CARDINAL VON PREYSING,
Bishop of Berlin."

The reply to this strong stand of the Bishop of Berlin was
given by the Politburo of the Unified Socialist Party in a resolution
passed at the Third Congress 14 May 1950:

" The Constitution of the German Democratic Republic guarantees
full liberty of religion. The greater part of the faithful is even
enrolled in the democratic organisations and parties within which
together with hundreds of priests they fight in the National Front
for the peace and unity of Germany. However the heads of the
Churches have paved the way for a re-actionary struggle against
the peace and the democratic order of the German Democratic
Republic by making use of *arguments not of a nature to serve the
interests of the Church*, but rather tending to upset the existing
political order. While claiming for themselves liberty of teaching
in the theological faculties, they want to forbid the same liberty
to Dialectical Materialism. They take disciplinary measures
against priests who join the National Front, but have no objections
if from the pulpit someone undertakes to utter re-actionary
propaganda. They protest because youth as a whole is turning
towards the National Front, and they would like to refuse it the
free exercise of its civic rights guaranteed by the Constitution.
This has happened because up to the present we have not paid
much attention to them, and have given only little encouragement
to the activity of progressive priests. Hundreds of priests have
taken sides with the people; we must help them."

The President of the State, *Wilhelm Pieck*, declared :

" Recently Church dignitaries have begun a struggle against progressive youth because of the materialist teaching given in the schools.   There is no doubt that they thus fight against the national interests of the people and push them in the direction of new wars." [12]

From the middle of 1952 [13] the position of the Church began to get worse.   Communist propaganda kept harping on the points that the religious denominations, and especially their heads, were subject to foreign influences, that they had secret ties with Western politics against which they never uttered a word, while they were ever ready to accept Western criticism of the German Democratic Republic and to use such criticism against the Government.[14]

Responsible Communist leaders stated that the Church would have to remain subject to " the special laws in force " and that she could not claim " special favourable treatment," as for example, international passports, facilities for communicating between Berlin and the Eastern Zone, dispensation from the

---

[12] Speech made at the inauguration of the "Republic of Young Pioneers." The President of the Council, Grotewohl, also made a threatening speech on the occasion of a press conference held after the Curia of Berlin had declared that the tension between the Church and State was not due to any restrictions on the liberty of the priests imposed by ecclesiastical authorities, but rather to the restrictions imposed by the State on the liberty of priests and faithful: " Ecclesiastics taking part in the struggle for peace and in the National Front fear the re-actions of the Church. Exercise of religion is guaranteed by the Constitution, as is also guaranteed the collaboration of the citizens (with the authorities). If an ecclesiastic happens to be hindered in the free exercise of his civic rights and duties, he will be protected by the Government." Cf. *Neues Deutschland* (official organ of the Unified Socialist Party), 17 June 1952.

Lehmann, member of the Secretariate of the Unified Socialist Party also stated at the Third Congress of this Party that it would occupy itself with the Churches and the " renegade priests," who were fighting against the National Front, and that a strong blow had been struck against these " renegades." Cf. *Der Kreuzberg*, 16 June 1950.

[13] In a speech on 9 July 1952 to a Congress of the Unified Socialist Party Walter Ulbricht stated: " The Church can no longer hide its true position under the mask of neutrality. The Church of the German Democratic Republic must resolutely and without distinction break with all the American and English agencies, even if their contact man is the Kaiser or Adenauer. The Christian teaching on human nature cannot be reconciled with the policy of enslavement of the Adenauer Government and with the yoke of the American, English and French occupation troops in Western Germany and West Berlin. It follows from this that the representatives of the Church in the DDR and in the democratic sector of Berlin can in no way take their instructions from those who act in the interests of the American occupation forces."

[14] Cf. *L'Osservatore Romano*, 3 September 1952.

obligation of forewarning the police of sacred functions and religious instruction (actually the police must be warned beforehand of every meeting that has been arranged) etc. . . . . Meanwhile in churches within the " protection zone " (a strip of land 500 metres deep along the frontier) no sacred function could be celebrated, and in the " forbidden zone " (a second strip 5 kilometres deep immediately behind the " protection zone ") the sacred ministry could be exercised only by special permission. It was made impossible for the Bishop of Berlin to visit the districts outside the city limits; three times the required permission was refused. In some other places the administration of Confirmation had to be put off at the last moment. Great difficulties also were put in the way of celebrating the *Katholikentag* which took place that year (1952) in Berlin.

In order to spread the Marxist-Leninist teaching among masters and teachers in East Germany some 80,000 teachers of the district schools received free copies of the October-November 1952 issue of the Bulletin of the German *Central Institute of Pedagogy*. This issue was consecrated entirely to a study of the theme: " Die sittliche Erziehung in der Deutschen Demokratischen Schule " (Moral Education in the German Democratic School), and was distributed on the initiative of the Institute itself.[15] Many teachers thus found themselves in a situation that was not only getting more difficult but was becoming incompatible with their duties as Christians. Towards the end of 1952 some 1,400 teachers had been " purged " by the Communist authorities. Nearly 2,000 had voluntarily resigned.[16]

At the same time the East Berlin authorities announced that as from 1 January 1953 the State would no longer undertake the collection of taxes for worship.[17] This meant that in future the Catholic and Evangelical Churches would themselves have to provide for all their needs.

Catholic priests and Protestant pastors were kept under

[15] The bulletin condemned the eternal moral laws, qualifying them as " false maxims," the fruit of bourgeois mentality, and proposed as a subject for discussion the following: " There is no eternal, definite, immutable moral law which is superior to the history of the people."

[16] Cf. *Informationsbüro West*, 4 December 1952.

[17] Cf. *Berliner Morgenpost*, 29 November 1952.

stricter watch both in the exercise of their ministry and in their personal conduct. This odious task was purposely entrusted to the members of the Christian-Democrat Party of the Eastern Zone.[18] In the meantime the Government was assiduous in calling priests to various congresses and meetings " for understanding and peace." [19]

In the first months of 1953 the religious position grew still worse. The following are a few of the measures taken against the Catholic Church at that time:

(1) Confiscation of Church property the proprietors of which lived in West Berlin or in the Federal Republic.[20] In the eastern sector of Berlin this meant for the Catholic Church alone confiscation of eleven buildings, three of which were important institutes, a hospital, an infant school and an orphanage.

(2) Occupation by Government authorities, under pretexts contrary to the law, of the House of Retreats at Berlin-Biesdorf.

(3) Taking over by the district authorities of Fürstenwalde of the " pedagogical and administrative management" of the kindergarten of Bad-Saarow, and the expulsion of the nuns.[21]

(4) Persecution, in order to force them to dissolve, of the Catholic Youth associations which were looked upon as the most dangerous adversaries of Communism. At first this persecution aimed only at the Protestant association, *Junge Gemeinde*, but later embraced also the Catholic Youth.[22] The first step was

---

[18] Cf. *Informationsbüro West*, 3 December 1952.

[19] Cf. *Märkische Union*, 3 December 1952.

[20] Cf. *Neues Deutschland*, 30 April 1953.

[21] The confiscation followed the usual course adopted by all Communist régimes. In the kindergarten, which was the property of *Caritas* of Berlin, there was a community of the Sisters of St. Hedwig, 130 children and the parish priest; the chapel of the Institute also served as the parish church. To take over the property the Communists first sent a control commission which went through every part of the premises, holding a veritable inquisition and questioning every one present; they then led a violent campaign of slander in the periodical *Junge Welt* (organ of the Free German Youth); they organised hostile manifestations; finally they ordered the nuns to leave the place within a few days.

Control commissions like that mentioned above went into action in every district examining the kindergartens in a rather objectionable manner and closing some of them. Their pretext was the education systems employed in them, the lack of food supplies and the manner in which the children were treated.

[22] Cf. concerning the propaganda campaign, the Communist papers of April-May 1953. Doctor Dibelius, Protestant Bishop of Berlin, protested against the *Junge Welt*, organ of the Free German Youth " for continual slandering of the *Junge Gemeinde*."

" ideological examinations " in the High Schools and student associations so as to get the youth to accept the Communist theses after they had been very cleverly explained. On the admission of the Communists themselves the High Schools should serve only one purpose, the formation of future State functionaries. Later the ideological examination was extended to all teaching establishments. The Free German Youth declared that it was ready to do everything in its power to free and to safeguard youth " from religious infection."

To sustain the young people during this campaign the Catholic ordinaries of the Soviet Zone addressed to them a particularly forceful Pastoral Letter.[23]

(5) Restrictions on the right of assembly. The police have to be informed beforehand of any assembly of more than five persons. Meetings of a specifically religious nature, held in buildings belonging to the Churches, were not bound by this formality. But a secret circular of the State Security Service restricted considerably under most varied pretexts religious ceremonies. In fact they were reduced to the performance of sacred rites alone.

(6) Restrictions on the press. The Catholic press, already notably reduced, was made the object of new restrictions. The *Tag des Herrn*, sole church periodical in the German Democratic Republic, found itself in a very difficult position because of the insufficiency of its allocation of paper. It had to reduce its circulation from 100,000 to 50,000 copies. The *Petrusblatt* (Berlin diocesan weekly) was forbidden in the East Berlin sector. The review *Christophorus* was also forbidden. Permission was sought on several occasions to publish an ecclesiastical periodical for East Berlin and Brandenburg, but was never granted.

(7) Restrictions on the activity of *Caritas*. Besides what has already been said about the buildings and institutes of *Caritas*, the distributing of assistance and the sending of parcels were being made constantly more difficult. Moreover in virtue of the

---

[23] Cf. *Bischoefliches Grusswort an die katholische Jugend*, published in the *Petrusblatt* under the title: " You have the right to be Christians ! " which was read in all the churches of the German Democratic Republic 3 May 1953. The letter bore the signatures of the following prelates: Mgr. William Weskamm, Bishop of Berlin, Mgr. Henry Wienken, Bishop of Misnia, Mgr. Ferdinand Piontek, Vicar Capitular of Görlitz, Mgr. Joseph Freusberg, Auxiliary Bishop of Erfurt, Mgr. Bernard Schräder, Episcopal Commissioner of Schwerin, and Mgr. Joseph Schönauer, Episcopal Commissioner of Meiningen. (Cf. *L'Osservatore Romano*, 31 May 1953).

Communist principle that children are the monopoly of the State, it was no longer allowed to organise holiday camps.

(8) Measures against ecclesiastics. Numerous priests were sentenced to several years' imprisonment. Reasons: " instigation to sabotage," " ill-treatment of children," " distribution of prayer-books coming from the West."

(9) Economic difficulties. State help for the Churches was reduced by about one-third. At the same time it was made more difficult to gather the Church taxes.

It became practically impossible to put up new buildings for ecclesiastical use, either owing to the slow economic strangling of the Church or because the Communist Government would not give the necessary authorisation.

The West German press denounced the persecution in the Eastern Zone.[24] *Grotewohl*, head of the Communist Government, in replying set himself out to prove the contrary. According to him everyone in East Germany enjoyed full liberty of thought and worship as guaranteed by the Constitution. Furthermore the Church profited by the protection and support of the State, since the Government gave 900,000 DM [25] each year as a contribution for the reconstruction of the churches.

Dr. *Dibelius*, Head of the German Evangelical Church, answered *Grotewohl* in an open letter in which he stated that " unfortunately the anti-religious struggle does exist; anyone with eyes can see it." [26]

Relations between Church and State were becoming worse than under the National-Socialist Government. The Communist Government, urged not by any consideration of principle but by the needs of the existing political situation (on 17 June 1953 the German workers rose against the rule of terror then prevailing

---

[24] Cf. the reports published by the KNA 13 April 1953 and by the *Informationsbüro West*, 10 April 1953.

[25] Cf. *Neue Zeit*, 24 April 1953. There was question of " East German " marks, that is to say something of little value compared with the 80 million marks that Catholics and Protestants had themselves collected for the repair of the sacred edifices. Moreover the Government contribution was ear-marked for those edifices classified as " historical monuments."

[26] Cf. among others, the newspaper *Weser-Kurier*, 29 April 1953.

in Berlin and in the Soviet Zone), asked that negotiations be begun with representatives of the two denominations.[27]

Thus was reached the " truce " of 10 July 1953 that led to the abolition of at least some of the restrictions in force, and which had as a direct result a certain easing of the situation.

But this did not hinder the Vice-President of the Council and Secretary of the Unified Socialist Party, *Ulbricht*, from stating a little later that youth must " be formed to a politico-scientific, fundamental, systematic outlook on culture, and more especially on the natural sciences, against the re-actionary influence of the Church and the clergy." [28]

The year 1954 went by without too serious trouble from the Communist Government. In 1955 however the news became very alarming, and it seemed as if the Government had deliberately violated the " truce " of the summer of 1953.

The Church was once again back in the position of two years before : [29]

(a) The State claimed once more, and now with greater insistence, an ideological monopoly in education which from the spiritual point of view meant great harm to both teachers and pupils.

(b) New difficulties were put in the way of building churches, collecting church taxes, changing priests (especially between West and East Germany).

(c) Efforts of all kinds (including threats and pressure on their families) were made to draw youth to atheistic Communism.

---

[27] The *Pro Memoria* addressed to the Government by the Catholics contained a list giving examples of the points which ought to be the subject of the discussions. It was demanded that on the terms of articles 9, 12, 41, 42 of the Constitution of the German Democratic Republic and of the Note of the USSR of 10 March 1952, the following should be granted:
  1. Liberty of action to the Church, particularly in what concerns religious instruction, the religious care of the sick in hospitals, prisoners, etc.
  2. Liberty in the formation and the appointment of priests according to the needs of diocesan organisation.
  3. Liberty in the collection and diffusion of information among the faithful by means of the press.
  4. Liberty concerning ecclesiastical property, with the possibility of meeting new needs by the construction of churches, chapels, etc.

[28] Cf. *Die Neue Zeitung*, 31 July 1953.

[29] Cf. the statements of the Bishop of Berlin, Mgr. Weskamm, to the representatives of the foreign press 31 December 1954 in *Neue Zürcher Zeitung*, 31 December 1954.

This was especially noticeable on the occasion of the
Jugendweihe.

(d) Pressure of various kinds was brought to bear on priests and
the Catholic press in order to get them to support the
Government policy of opposition to European unification.

(e) Catholics were threatened, for this purpose use being made
of the Christian-Democrat Party, to make them create an
ecclesiastical organisation independent of the Vatican should
the Paris Treaty be ratified.[30]   Attempts of the same kind
were repeated the following year.   Workmen and other
employees were sounded by propagandists, often under the
direction of the Ministry for the Interior, with a view to
provoking them to set up a " national Church " independent
of Rome.[31]

The Jugendweihe (Consecration of Youth)

The latest tension showed itself suddenly in its full force at
the beginning of 1955 as a result of the official Government
propaganda in favour of the *Jugendweihe.*   Starting in April this
Consecration was to take place for the third time, but with much
greater solemnity than before, in all the big towns of East
Germany.

On 13 November 1954 the press of the Soviet Zone published
an appeal from the " Central Committee for the Consecration
of the Youth (Jugendweihe) of the German Democratic
Republic."   The appeal insisted on " the radical difference
between this initiative and any other taken in the past or present."
It was furthermore claimed that this step was asked for " not
by this or that particular organisation or institution, but by the
whole people."

The first statement was near enough to the truth, for the
Communists had in mind by this step to use means much more
radical than those of Nazism " to sow the seed of their ideology "
in the soul of youth.   Take for example the programme of 20
lessons (Jugendstunden),[32] the study of which was to precede

---

[30] Cf. KNA, 28 December 1954.
[31] Cf. KNA, 9 March 1954—*Die Zeit*, 6 January 1955.
[32] Cf. *Themenplan der Jugendstunde* in *Deutsche Lehrerzeitung* (organ of the German
Democratic School) 9 January 1955.

the " rite " of the so-called Consecration: " cosmogony "
lessons on the " origin of life," on " human society and woman's
place in it," etc.[33] The importance of the appeal is also proved
by the names of the 22 signatories, all from among the best-
known upholders of atheistic Materialism in science (*Meusel*),
in literature and art (*Becher, Hermlin, Seghers*), and in education
(*Wandel, Laabs, Becher, Dorst*). There was even the name of a
secretary of the Central Committee of the Unified Socialist
Party side by side with that of an apostate priest.

The appeal defined the *Jugendweihe* as " a solemn ceremony
marking the passage of youths to adult life . . . far surpassing
any other rite of this kind, even the *Konfirmation*." [34] The
allusion to the Protestant ceremony with which, it was said,
the *Jugendweihe* was not meant to compete evidently aimed at
forestalling the opposition of the Churches. But the re-action
was quick and unmistakable from both Protestants and Catholics.
In a meeting of 9 and 10 December 1954 the Catholic episcopate
condemned the *Jugendweihe* as an " attempt to complete the
materialist education of the State schools with special courses
and solemnity." As a consequence of this condemnation the
hierarchy ordered that a special Pastoral Letter be read in the
whole territory of the German Democratic Republic.

This re-action of the episcopate, as much to the point as it
was timely, aroused the anger of the Unified Socialist Party
which in its organ, *Neues Deutschland*, accused the Church of
" terrorising the consciences of youth, of destroying the efforts
made to bring about peaceful co-existence of all citizens, and
of giving once more pretexts to the war-loving Western press
for its campaign against the German Democratic Republic." [35]

During February and March propaganda among youth became

---

[33] Cf. KNA, 27 December 1954.

[34] There is question here rather of the Protestant *Konfirmation*, a solemn engagement
of fidelity to the Christian faith. Besides the Appeal referred a second time to this religious
rite, observing that " all young people without distinction of *Weltanschauung* could
freely participate in this new rite, which has nothing to do with the Konfirmation."
The heads of the Protestant Church condemned at the beginning of December 1954
this pseudo-consecration: " Parents and young people ought to know," it was said in
this Protestant warning, " that the profession of evangelical faith cannot be reconciled
with participation in the *Jugendweihe*."

[35] Cf. the article " A clear word on the Jugendweihe " in *Neues Deutschland*, 8 January
1955.

very intense in an effort to recruit as many as possible for the
courses preparatory to the *Jugendweihe*. This " rite " was to take
place about two months before the end of the scholastic year
for boys aged 14 years who were to leave the elementary schools.

Once again the Catholic Church re-acted. A declaration of
the Bishop of Berlin was read in all the churches on 6 March.[36]
In his Letter the Bishop pointed out that he had protested against
all pressure to make young people take part in the *Jugendweihe*.[37]
For, wrote the Bishop, this ceremony is contrary to Christian
teaching and to participate in it is to deny the Faith. Absolution
could not be given to those taking part unless they signed a
solemn retractation.

The book, *Weltall Erde Mensch*, was given as " a bible " to all
youths preparing for the *Jugendweihe*. This book explained the
materialist view of the universe and of life.[38]

In spite of the fact that the whole State propaganda machine
was set in motion [39] and in spite of the efforts made in the
schools by the members of the " Young Pioneers," the *Jugendweihe*
in 1955 did not meet with much success among Catholic youth
and among a part of the Protestant youth.[40] Many youths of

---

[36] Cf. *Beilage zum Amtsblatt des Bischoefl. Ordinariates Berlin*, 1 February 1955.

[37] Knowing Communist methods parents feared above all lest, since the Jugendweihe
was to take place two months before the end of the school year, the Communist masters
would take into account in the examinations at the end of the year the absence of pupils
from this " consecration." On their part those masters who were not Communists feared
they would be dismissed, and parents feared the loss of their positions when these
depended on the State. Cf. on this subject KNA, 17 February 1955.

[38] Cf. *Weltall Erde Mensch*, Verlag Neues Leben, Berlin, 1954. This book had a preface
by the Secretary of the Unified Socialist Party, Walter Ulbricht, and an introduction by
Professor Havemanns. It gave a clear exposition of the necessity for training the young in
Atheism. Beginning by stating that certain theories had been given to the human race by
Marx and Engels, and that Lenin and Stalin had shown the practical application of these
theories, the book stated young people ought to be taught to discover that the future
of humanity lay in Communism. To sum up: historical and dialectical Materialism
should be made familiar to young people of 14 years by the aid of methods adapted to
their age and studies. They should be " formed " to see the salvation of the world only
in the Communist Party.

[39] The Communists exacted collaboration not only from the functionaries of the
Party but also from those of the State, particularly schoolmasters. These latter,
accompanied and supervised by a Party member, were obliged to go from house to house
to convince the parents and to strive in their propaganda work to keep the ideological
aspect intentionally in the shade while insisting on the economic and national side.

[40] Cf. KNA, numbers 31, 42, 43, 93, 98, February-April 1955.

between 14 and 15 preferred to leave the Soviet Zone so as to escape the Communist rite.[41]

The promoters of the *Jugendweihe* had only one way to re-act in the face of this failure of their " substitute " for religion. They began making the usual accusations against the Church: intransigence and moral pressure on the consciences of the young; they declared through their Central Committee: " We shall never rest until there is set up a lasting front of members of the *Jugendweihe*."

This explains why from the end of May 1955 the Unified Socialist Party set about making comprehensive plans for the *Jugendweihe* of the following year. Instead of being dissolved the local Committees previously established were multiplied. Besides it was decided to increase the number of " hours of preparation of youth," as they were called, and to make them more practical and attractive. The Central Committee also announced at the end of May 1955 that the next " hours of preparation " would begin in October (that is, at the beginning of the scholastic year, and not as heretofore, two months before the end), and that they would be held each week. It was agreed that in 1956 the Consecration would be of a yet more remarkable character and that it would be clearly distinct from all other religious or cultural demonstrations.

Position at the End of the First Quarter of 1956

The year 1956 opened with a comprehensive attack, carried on by the Central Committee of Communist Youth, against the observance of Sundays and religious Feast days. It was decided that all the leaders and militant members of the Association would be at its disposal at least two Sundays each month, and that the offices of the Communist Youth, Youth Circles, places reserved for youths in the factories and in the work-yards, and recreation centres, would be opened on Sundays but would remain closed on other days. This obviously aimed at keeping young people away from Mass and from evening devotions.[42]

---

[41] According to the reckoning of the chaplain of the refugee Camp at Marienfeld the numbers were, in April 1955, 4,665 boys and 1,973 girls. Cf. KNA 25 April 1955.
[42] Cf. KNA, 19 January 1956.

The Government of the German Democratic Republic is still creating obstacles to prevent bishops living in West Germany from entering the Soviet Zone.

Religious instruction may still be given outside of class periods for one hour each week to pupils in the elementary schools. But the position is very serious for students—and they are the greater number and the more intelligent—who enter the Professional State Institutes. The priest cannot enter these and in them atheistic and political propaganda is intense.

High School pupils most often have to go to State schools a long distance away, and so return home very late. It is extremely difficult to arrange for them to follow courses in religious instruction. And so the Communists reach the goal they have set themselves: to have in the future an educated class, Catholic in name, but in fact ignorant of religion.

The laws affecting the press,[43] works of charity [44] and Church property [45] are still in force. This State hostility obviously hits not only the Catholic Church but also all religious denominations.

What is the future of the Catholic Church after twelve years of conflict with the dialectic Materialism of a totalitarian Government?

Although the clergy have remained unbelievably steadfast in face of all the difficulties, nevertheless those twelve years of pressure, persecution and extortion have been a grave danger for the body of the faithful, even for those whose faith is strongest. And as is known, unfortunately the Communists put their trust in the *time factor* to reach their goal.

There are many Catholics (even among children and youths) who stand firm for the Church despite every effort and sacrifice that this may call for. But unfortunately this number grows ever less because many Catholic families emigrate to West Germany

---

[43] For example, in March 1956 the ecclesiastical bulletin of East Berlin *St. Hedwigsblatt* was seized because it published the collective Pastoral Letter for Lent of the German bishops against dialectical Materialism.

[44] For example, in the State institutions for old people and for children religious ceremonies continued to be forbidden.

[45] For example, in this way it has not been possible to make legal by the usual notary deeds the acquisition of property destined for ecclesiastical uses; the importation of material for necessary constructions has not been authorised.

and because State employees and those working in public administration or in industry dare not practise their religion if they want to hold their positions.

The Catholic Church looks with apprehension towards the future, for despite the " re-assuring " news spread from time to time by the Government press, the religious policy of the Communist authorities, far from having changed, forbodes no good for the time to come.

Chapter 6

THE PERSECUTION OF THE CATHOLIC CHURCH

UNDER

Communist Rule in Bulgaria

SOVIET TROOPS ENTERED Sofia on 9 September 1944 and hastened to set up a *predominantly Communist* Government in spite of its official label: " Patriotic Front."

After active hostilities between Bulgaria and the USSR had ceased (October 1944), but especially after the Republic was proclaimed (15 September 1945), the Communists began to eliminate their political opponents. At the same time they made sure of a strong majority in the elections to the Constituent Assembly (October 27 1946) by an electoral system which would guarantee their success.

In December 1948, a year after the " traitor " *Nicholas Petkov*, head of the Agrarian Opposition Party, was hanged (27 November 1947), Communism was in undisputed control in Bulgaria.

Then began the systematic struggle against whatever opposition still remained, chiefly against the different religious denominations.

The Constitution promulgated on 6 December 1947 pointed clearly to the intention of subordinating completely the religious rights of the people to the power of the State.

> ARTICLE 71 declared that privileges based on nationality, birth, religion and material status were no longer recognised. Racial discrimination and religious discrimination were punishable by law.

ARTICLE 76 recognised as valid only civil marriage.

ARTICLE 78 guaranteed " freedom of conscience and of religion " under the system of " separation of Church and State," and within the framework of a special law. It forbade " political organisations with a religious basis."

ARTICLE 79 gave sanction to the people's right to " lay education, democratic and progressive in spirit." The right to educate however belonged only to the State. Private schools could be authorised only by the laws of the State. Even in this case the schools must be under State control.

The elections of 18 December 1949 gave the Government after manipulation 97.76% of the votes. After this, Communist aims showed themselves in full conformity with the implacable exigencies of Marxist-Leninist ideology.

The Catholic Church in Bulgaria

At the advent of Communist rule in Bulgaria, out of a population of 6,078,000 the Catholic Church counted about 57,000 members in three ecclesiastical circumscriptions :

(a) the diocese of Nikopol,

(b) the vicariate of Sofia and Plovdiv,

(c) the exarchate apostolic for Bulgarians of the Byzantine Rite.

About 6,000 of the faithful belonged to the Byzantine-Slav Rite, the remainder to the Latin Rite.

Catholic religious houses and institutions numbered 18: 10 schools, 2 large hospitals, and 6 orphanages.

In 1944 there were 127 priests and 200 religious of both sexes.

Notwithstanding their small number the Catholics in Bulgaria were a very active body, not so much by reason of their efforts to bring new members into the Church, as by reason of the intensity of their Christian life which knitted them into a marvellous unity.

The Holy See was represented by an Apostolic Delegate. This representation was not of a diplomatic character.

First measures against the Catholic Church

During the years 1945-1948 the new *political* atmosphere created at the end of the war did not bring in its wake in Bulgaria a systematic persecution of the Church as it did in other countries under Marxist rule. Acts of violence although few in number and abuse of power against ecclesiastics and ecclesiastical institutions were not altogether wanting.

Priests were harassed in various ways: some were deprived of ration cards, others were imprisoned; a few disappeared mysteriously, efforts were made to lead others into traps by proposals incompatible with their religious mission; all were encircled by an ever-tightening network of espionage.

Two priests, *Kupen Michailoff* and *Gabriel Belovejdoff*, on returning to Bulgaria after eight years' study in Rome were arrested and after spending some time in gaol, were sent to a concentration camp.

During the years 1945-1948 attacks against the Church and the Pope were inaugurated so as to create a hostile atmosphere against the Catholic Church. At the same time *the expulsion of all foreign priests and nuns was begun*, so that none of them might witness the persecution which the Communists had decided to carry out according to a definite plan and which might be called a persecution in successive stages.

All persons who attended Catholic religious functions or who visited the residence of the Apostolic Delegation were, amongst other annoyances, watched and shadowed.

The Government authorities suggested to the editors of *Istina* (the only Catholic weekly in Bulgaria) that they insert in each number an article supplied by them. They arrested Dr. *Karagioff*, one of the paper's collaborators. In view of these facts the bishops decided to suspend the publication of *Istina* so that the Government would have no pretext for interference.

The Government however went on systematically with the

persecution of the Catholic Church. Here are the sad stages
of the process:

An intense press and propaganda campaign was set on foot.
It was meant to give credence to the idea that private schools
were henceforth intolerable in the new " progressivist " atmosphere.[1]   Then a decree of the Præsidium of the National
Assembly, dated 3 August 1948, ordered that from 1 November
1948 " *all foreign schools, religious and lay, be closed, whatever their
standard or cultural activity*." [2]

Consequently nine colleges conducted by religious had to
cease work: three at Sofia, two at Ruse, two at Plovdiv, one
at Varna and one at Burgas. These schools were attended by
more than 5,000 boys and girls. The buildings were taken over
by the Government and the Party. The foreign personnel was
expelled from the country and Bulgarian teachers were dismissed.
Later almost all the Bulgarian teaching staff was arrested.

In the meantime, *from 1948-1950*, the Communist Government
confiscated all ecclesiastical property, on the pretext that all
property was to be nationalised.[3]

In December 1948, taking advantage of the visit to Italy of
the Regent of the Apostolic Delegation, Mgr. *Francis Galloni*, the
Government *refused him a visa to return to Bulgaria* in spite of the
most formal guarantees to the contrary before his departure.[4] The

---

[1] Cf. *Novini* (News) 17 November 1947. The same paper had already published
(3 November) a resolution of the Higher Council of Public Education asking that a
law be passed obliging all pupils to attend the State schools. Only citizens of other
countries were to be allowed to frequent foreign schools. Cf. also the attacks on the
private schools in *Rabotnitchesko Delo*, official organ of the Bulgarian Communist Party,
7 and 10 December 1947; also *Novini*, 7 December 1947.

[2] Cf. *Otecstven Front* (National Front) 3 August 1948 for text of the Decree.

[3] At first, so as to force the ecclesiastical authorities to collectivise the Church's
landed estate, the administrators were obliged to pay into the people's reserve fund
a percentage of the produce far beyond what the land could produce even in the best
of circumstances. The administrators, finding it impossible to fulfil this absurd imposition,
had to collectivise the land to escape being accused of sabotage.

The Government had an easier task with the nationalisation of buildings. It simply
invoked public utility. Under this pretext, hospitals, schools, institutions and boarding
schools were confiscated. To complete the irony the former proprietors were left
the disposal of the cellars and attics.

[4] Only a few days after Mgr. Galloni's departure a Government-instigated campaign
began in the press and on the radio calling for the expulsion of the representative of
the Holy See. On 23 February 1949 the vice-president of the Council and Minister
for External Affairs, Vassil Kolarov declared in the National Assembly that the closing
of the Apostolic Delegation had put an end to " a humiliating episode for Bulgaria and
its people." Cf. *La Bulgarie nouvelle*, 25 February 1949.

Bulgarian Minister at Rome actually communicated to Mgr. *Galloni* that he had received instructions from his Government forbidding the prelate's return to the country, adding that orders of the same nature had been issued to the frontier authorities. The authorities would not consent to his return, even for a few hours, to collect his effects.

The Law on Worship

On 17 February 1949 the National Assembly approved a *Law on Religious Denominations*,[5] containing a whole series of enactments which would one day mark the end of Catholicism in Bulgaria.

The freedom of conscience and of worship ratified by the first article of this law was illusory. This freedom could never be in opposition to the Constitution, to " the laws, social order and ethical standards " of the Communist Government. Furthermore it was in practice suppressed by nearly every subsequent article, and especially by the following:

ARTICLE 2: Religious denominations, in as much as they are religious associations, are separated from the State.

ARTICLE 3: The Bulgarian Orthodox Church is the traditional denomination of the Bulgarian people and is linked with its history; as such, by its form, content and spirit, it may be considered as a people's democratic Church.

ARTICLE 9: Every denomination must have a directing body responsible to the State. Ministers of religion may remain in office, be dismissed or changed, only after receiving the *nihil obstat* of the Ministry for External Affairs. Ministers of a religion having foreign economic relations may be nominated only after being approved by the Ministry for External Affairs. On entering office they shall make a solemn promise of loyalty to the Government of the Republic.

ARTICLE 10: Only Bulgarian citizens may be ministers of religion or fill ecclesiastical offices. They must be men of good conduct, inspiring confidence and not deprived of those rights set out in Article 30 of the Penal Code.[6]

---

[5] The text appeared in *Otecstven Front* (official paper of the Party), 17 February 1949.
[6] This meant that all foreign priests were banished from Bulgaria.

ARTICLE 13: Ministers of religion and other ecclesiastical functionaries who violate the law, offend against public order or ethical standards or oppose the democratic institutions of the State, may be immediately suspended from the exercise of their office on the proposal of the Ministry for External Affairs. This measure must be applied by the directing body of the denomination in question immediately the Ministry for External Affairs gives intimation of its decisions. Should the religious authority fail in this matter, the minister of religion shall be suspended by an administrative measure.

ARTICLE 16: The directing bodies of the different denominations are bound to send in due time to the Ministry for External Affairs for its information, pastoral letters, encyclicals, circulars and other official publications. The Ministry can forbid the circulation of or the execution of the directives contained in these letters, circulars, documents or other official publications, should it deem them contrary to law, public order or recognised ethical standards.

ARTICLE 19: Because of the supreme authority of the State and of its official organisations the different religious associations may organise no ceremonies or solemnities which have not had the previous and express approval of the Ministry for External Affairs.

ARTICLE 21: The formation of religious associations, their organisation, and the printing of religious books, are subject to the general laws and to the particular ordinances of the administration. The education and organisation of children and youths are specially reserved to the State, and are in no way the concern of the denominations and their ministers.

ARTICLE 22: The denominations may not open hospitals, orphanages or other like institutions. Works of this kind in existence when the present law comes into force are to be taken over by the Ministries for Public Health, Labour and Social Welfare. Their property, movable and non-movable, shall become the property of the State. The Ministry for External Affairs will name a Commission to take the place of the present proprietors; this Commission will include a representative of the People's Council of the district in which the properties are situated.

ARTICLE 24: Religious denominations may have relations with

other denominations, institutions, organisations or persons situated outside the country, but only with the previous approval of the Ministry for External Affairs.[7]

ARTICLE 25: Denominations or their orders, congregations, missions, etc., having their administrative seat *outside* the country may not open houses in the People's Republic of Bulgaria. All those now in existence shall be closed within a month of the coming into force of this present law.

All the property of houses closed in accordance with the dispositions of the preceding paragraph, and all charitable or other works, will become the property of the State, as provided for by Article 22 of this law; compensation in the form of an equitable indemnity is guaranteed.

ARTICLE 30: Whoever organises political associations with a *religious basis*, or in any way whatsoever (by word or writing or action) uses the Church and religion to engage in propaganda against the authority of the State is liable to imprisonment and other severe penalties.

Finally article 32 imposes on the Church the obligation of drawing up its own " statutes " to be presented for the approval of the Ministry for External Affairs. The Minister is empowered to demand modification of any points he may deem contrary to " the laws, public order or recognised ethical standards."

The Catholic bishops hastened to point out to the President of the National Assembly that the law was a violation of the divine order on which the Church was founded.[8]

* * *

After a violent press campaign against the decree of the Holy Office condemning membership of the Marxist-Communist Party,[9] steps were taken to annihilate progressively the Catholic

---

[7] This article is specially directed against the Catholic Church, seeing that it aims at separating the Bulgarian Catholics from the living Body of the Church and above all from its head, the Roman Pontiff.

[8] Cf. *L'Osservatore Romano*, 26 March 1949, on the impossibility for the Catholic Church of accepting this law. Cavalli, *Persecuzione religiosa nella Repubblica Popolare Bulgara*, Roma 1953, pp. 11-13.

[9] Cf. *Izgreff*, 6 August 1949, article by G. Kulisceff: *A Medieval Procedure*; *ibidem* article by the Archimandrite Stefa; *Otecstven Front*, 4 August 1949, article by N. Ninoff: *Vatican Provocation*; *Rabotnitchesko Delo*, 4 August 1949, article by Boris Leontieff, taken from *Pravda*.

Church. Among these steps the following merit special mention:

Confiscation of the Catholic hospitals at Sofia and Plovdiv. From the latter 20 Sisters of Charity of Zagreb were expelled.

Expulsion of the Sisters of the Blessed Eucharist (a Bulgarian foundation) from the orphanage at Sofia and from their own novitiate. In the process they were subjected to all kinds of humiliations.

Closing of the Catholic seminary of Sofia directed by the Jesuit Fathers. The seminarians were received at Plovdiv, Stara-Zagora and Ruse. In 1952 the closing of these three junior seminaries was ordered.

Dispersal of the Congregation of the Annunciation.

Stifling of every form of apostolic work. Celebration of Mass was allowed, with a sermon which had to be reduced to the vaguest terms because of police supervision.

Multiplication of " agents provocateurs " to work on the clergy.

Radio Sofia did not fail to underline periodically the freedom of worship and the peaceful state of religion in Bulgaria.[10] *Kolarov* himself, Minister for External Affairs, in his discourse of 23 February 1949 pointed out with insistence that the People's Republic of Bulgaria " guaranteed full freedom of conscience and religion." [11]

The Trials

But the gravest steps against the Catholic Church were taken during 1952. The Bulgarian Government in that year staged three trials of Catholic clergy and laity:

First Trial: Father *Damian Ghiulov*, Superior of the Capuchins at Sofia, arrested 17 February 1950, was condemned to 12 years in prison on 14 January 1952.[12] Since then nothing more is known about him.

---

[10] For example, broadcast of 24 December 1951.
[11] Cf. *La Bulgarie nouvelle*, 25 February 1949.
[12] The twelve years were made up as follows: two years for defamation of the Bulgarian Government; one year for having disparaged the Soviet Government; two years for bad conduct in prison; the remainder for espionage in the interest of the Vatican and the Capitalist Powers.

Second Trial: Father *Robert Crustov* (Capuchin), arrested in May 1950,[13] was condemned to 20 years' imprisonment—the maximum penalty according to the Bulgarian Penal Code.

In August 1952 the Capuchin Father *Fortunatus Bakalscki* died in prison. The police reported that his death was due to double pneumonia. Father *Bakalscki* was aged 42 and up to the day of his arrest had been in excellent health.

Third Trial: 16 July 1952 the Passionist Mgr. *Eugene Bossilkov* was arrested at his episcopal residence at Nikopol.[14] Together with 26 priests, two nuns, and two Catholic laymen (former editors of *Istina*), he appeared for trial on 25 September 1952 in the Palace of Justice at Sofia. During the trial, staged in the grand style by the Communists, the charges ranged from espionage to illegal possession of arms and anti-Communist propaganda.[15]

On 3 October Mgr. *Bossilkov* was condemned to death. Three priests of the Society of the Assumption received a like sentence: Fathers *Kamen Vicev Ionkon*, *Pavel Gigiov* and *Josaphat Scisckov*. The other priests were condemned, two to twenty years in gaol; three to 15 years; two to 14 years; seven to 12 years; seven others to 10 years; one to 6 years and one to a year and a half. The two nuns were sentenced to 5 and 6 years respectively.

---

[13] This second trial was conducted right in the middle of the storm that had been unleashed against the Church. At Varna the church was closed, at Sofia the offices of the Catholic parish were searched, at Ruse the seminary was confiscated. Earlier the university hostel for girls had to close down. In the meantime, while Catholics were being forced to act as spies, especially against their own clergy, numbers of laymen and ecclesiastics were subjected to exhausting interrogations by the police. The arrests of priests, frequent since the beginning of the year, increased.

[14] See *Tabor*, Chapter I, pp. 142-143, for the facts about the heroic Mgr. Bossilkov, and about his attachment to the Holy See (which constituted for the Communists the " spying and plotting against the Bulgarian State " under pretext of which he was tried and condemned to death).

[15] Cf. *Rabotnitchesko Delo* 21 September 1952 for the Act of Accusation and Condemnation of the Catholic Spy and Terrorist Organisation in Bulgaria.

The press used this trial, following a predetermined plan, to discredit the little Catholic community, which it described as a nest of spies and traitors. See *Vecerni Novini* (Evening News) 20 September 1952, article by Hr. Totev; *Otecstven Front*, 24 September 1952, article signed Spas Ghergov: *The Obscurantists' Plot*. The principal accused at Sofia may be said to be Catholicism itself, so that the most tragic aspect of the trial was neither the complete disregard for the most elementary form of legal procedure and justice nor the cruelty of the sentences but the fact that it aimed at annihilating the Catholic Church in Bulgaria by reaching it through its bishops, priests and best laymen.

Cf. the Public Prosecutor's speech, delivered by Petriuski, in *Trud* (Work), organ of the Central Council of Professional Associations in Bulgaria, 4 October 1952.

Among the laymen the two editors of *Istina* were sentenced to 12 years each.[16]

During the trial the Public Prosecution demanded that Mgr. *John Romanov*, Vicar Apostolic of Sofia and Plovdiv, be brought to trial for having been in contact with Mgr. *Bossilkov*. Mgr. *Romanov* was arrested at once.

The Carmelite Sisters of Sofia, the only nuns not affected till then (because of their cloistered life), were arrested in October 1952. They occupied only a corner of the convent as the rest of the building had been requisitioned by the civil authorities. The sisters were all either condemned to prison, or in the case of foreigners deported.

Nothing had been heard for a long time about the third Catholic bishop in Bulgaria, Mgr. *Cyril Kurteff*, Exarch Apostolic for Bulgarians of the Eastern Rite. Then it was made known that he had been arrested again in December 1956, and was later released, but kept under police supervision.

Conclusion

Of the 127 secular priests in Bulgaria there can be scarcely more than a few dozen at liberty at the moment (March 1957). Some few of Bulgaria's regular priests and nuns are also free. We have already seen the position with regard to the three bishops. There remains only a scattered and terrified remnant of the one time 57,000 Catholics. The 18 religious houses, once the pride of Bulgarian Catholicism, are all gone. The destruction of the Catholic Church in Bulgaria could not have been more thorough or more cruel.

---

[16] Cf. sentence in *Rabotnitchesko Delo*, 4 October 1952. After the trial the just indignation of the Catholics of the world found a severe censor in the Bulgarian press. Cf. *La Bulgarie d'aujourd'hui*, November 1952.

According to news received at the end of 1955, Mgr. Bossilkov was in a prisoners' hospital; Mgr. Romanov was still in prison.

Chapter 7

THE PERSECUTION OF THE CATHOLIC CHURCH

UNDER

Communist Rule in China

THE IDEOLOGY OF Marx and Lenin was introduced into China towards 1920 by agents in Russian service. In thirty years it was imposed on a population of some 500,000,000, as a result of the clever way in which its prophets had insinuated themselves into the play of national events and had taken advantage of the international situation created in the Far East during and after World War II.

Founded in Shanghai in 1921, the Chinese Communist Party, aided by the mission of industrial and military experts sent by Russia in 1920, gave more and more precise expression to its revolutionary character.

When in 1927 *Chiang Kai-Chek* began the work of re-uniting the country by marching against the Nanking Government, the Communists, taking advantage of the Civil War, set up a Government at Hankow with *Mao Tse-Tung* at its head (1928).

Then followed the experiment of the sovietised State of Kiangsi (1928-1934); and after the Japanese invasion of Manchuria (1931) the Communists faced north to fight, as they put it, the common enemy. This operation was known as the " Long March " (1934-1935). Pursued by the Nationalists, their troops took their stand on the hills of Shensi, establishing there the independent State of Yenan (1936-1945). Using the propaganda slogan, " one Chinese cannot fight another when the Japanese are at the gates," the Communist leaders succeeded finally in having *Chiang Kai-Chek* arrested by his own generals on the charge of giving information to the enemy. Then as the price of his liberation, they got a free hand for their Party and a promise that *Chiang* would enter the war on their side at the first Japanese attack.

Thus in virtue of this agreement the Japanese attack in 1937 engaged the Nationalist Government in a long and bitter war for which China was not at all prepared and which exhausted considerably the material and moral resources of the country. On the other hand, through a plan of action against the enemy, cleverly reduced to sporadic guerilla engagements, the Communists were able during these years to consolidate their power in the North without any embarrassment to themselves. In this way they achieved a twofold purpose: they held in reserve for future use an ever greater number of fresh battle-trained troops, and they were able to sovietise slowly but relentlessly the territory they had occupied.

The end of hostilities in 1945 and the Russian occupation of Manchuria and Northern Korea put the Communist leaders in a position to further their revolutionary aims by turning Japanese arms and Soviet help to the advantage of their 2,000,000 well trained soldiers.

It was a new civil war. Mukden fell in 1948 after a two months' siege. By 1 October 1949 the Communists, now masters of a huge territory, could proclaim at Peking the *People's Republic of China.*

The Catholic Church in China

After World War II there were about four million Catholics in China out of a population of 463,500,000. In 1949 there were 20 archdioceses, 85 dioceses, and 39 prefectures apostolic, with 27 Chinese ordinaries. Foreign missionaries numbered 3,080, and native priests 2,557.

In 1926 the first Chinese bishops were consecrated at Rome, and in 1946 the ordinary hierarchy was established. In the same year the Archbishop of Peking was created China's first Cardinal. All efforts tended towards one day making the hierarchy completely Chinese.

The Catholic Church left nothing undone to honour and extol

the noblest cultural, artistic and moral traditions of this great people in the conviction that they would find new splendour in the light of Christian revelation. This task was confided particularly to the numerous schools of all kinds and degrees which flourished in China thanks to the missionaries and native clergy. But above all it was the task of the three universities of Shanghai, Peking and Tien-Tsin.

Since 1943 the Government had diplomatic relations with the Holy See.

* * *

Before 1945 the Communist attitude towards Christian missionaries was one of open though local and somewhat disorganised persecution in the territories under the Hankow Government (1929-1934). Churches were burned, schools and charitable institutions occupied. There were " proceedings " against missionaries, assassinations, demands of enormous ransoms for the liberation of hostages, etc. In the independent State of Yenan (1936-1945) missionaries were frequently molested and subjected to acts of violence. In fact the struggle properly so-called against the Catholic Church can be said to have begun at the end of the war with Japan and the beginning of the Civil War.[1]

For its plan, its methodical procedure, its refinement of technique, and the results obtained, the Chinese persecution may be cited as the prototype of persecutions in countries under Marxist rule.

Besides, the resurgence of national feeling offered to the Chinese Communists resources denied to the Communist persecutors of other countries.[2]

---

[1] The objectives remained all the time those fixed by Mao Tse-Tung in the *Report* which he presented on 22 January 1934 to the *Second National Congress of the Soviets of China*: " In the Chinese Soviet territories, Catholic priests and Protestant pastors have been expelled by the masses. Property held by the imperialist missionaries has been returned to the people. Missionary schools have been turned into Soviet schools. In short the Chinese Soviet districts are the only ones that have been liberated from the imperialist yoke."

[2] On this see the documented article in *L'Osservatore Romano*, 30 January 1955.

The Party chiefs in China were more anxious for action than for spectacular demonstrations. Methodically, almost silently, and with clear knowledge of what they wanted, they effected in the space of six years *an immense work of destruction*. They proved themselves past masters at minimising the bad impression which news of the persecution produced outside the country. They repeated, in all keys, that the Government considered it a duty to respect *Article 88 of the Constitution* [3] on the freedom of religion. They insisted that the steps they had taken had been forced on them by a " spontaneous " reaction of the Nation's conscience to an imperialism that was hiding under the cloak of religion.[4]

The Persecution from 1945—1950

In spite of many skilful changes of tactics necessitated from time to time by circumstances in the areas occupied by Communist troops, it was plain that Chinese Communist doctrine did not differ from that of international Marxism even if the Chinese Communists' tactics in its application did.

---

[3] Cf. *Agency Hsin Hwa* (New China), 5 October 1954. *Constitution of the Chinese People's Republic*, French edition, Peking, 1954.

[4] A thorough study of the method " adopted by the Chinese Communists " is to be found in a book by A. Bonnichon, S.J.: *La persecuzione in Cina et l'enciclica Ad Sinarum gentem*, Rome, 1955. Among other things the author says: " A man (in China) is not merely solicited and pursued by propaganda, as was the case in certain European totalitarian régimes. The study of Communism was imposed on all as a religious duty. Each section (bureau, office administration, village, school, university, shop, hospital, etc.) has its personnel divided into little groups of a dozen persons and each group is obliged to meet several times a week to ' learn.' And this is not limited to the beginning of the conquest, called ' liberation,' but continues all through life. It is not enough to learn the principles of Marxism, which could be done quickly; one must keep oneself in constant contact with Government views. Marxist doctrine may be badly known or not known at all, but every citizen at every moment must feel himself enlightened, guided and supported by living contact with Marxism. Indoctrinated permanently in this way, the faithful follower is strictly obliged to believe. To refuse to be convinced or to manifest slothfulness in this matter constitutes the crime of ' reaction ' or ' counter-revolution.' With this as a principle it is obvious that no Christian may seek what he is to think, or may take moral lessons and directives for his life from any authority but the Government. To act otherwise is not acceptable or rather it is unthinkable. Catholicism, the exponent of truth and of hierarchical society, is more than a rival to Communism; it is a usurper of the power of the State. And this is true not only of the Pope, who lives outside the country, but of the bishop, even if he be Chinese, and even of the parish priest. A form of worship, Buddhist or Catholic, can indeed be tolerated, and that is what is meant by ' freedom of religion ' but it is impossible to accept a *Church*."

The struggle against religion unfolded itself in a series of phases clearly determined beforehand and applied according to plan.

1. In the first phase religious freedom and tolerance (*hsing chiao-tse-yu*) were proclaimed. For this reason, in the months immediately following the entry of the Red army, it was still possible to keep churches open, to preach and to teach in the schools.

2. Then began the second phase, the war on " superstitions " (*fang pei mi hsing*). A violent campaign of speeches and writings was initiated. It was pointed out that religion was on the same footing as bourgeois society, and was therefore one of the worst evils of humanity.

By clever propaganda an attempt was made before all else to destroy the profound esteem in which Catholicism was held. Slogans were employed which were calculated to kill respect for religion and to stir up the masses against the missions. Three times a week young orators held meetings which all were obliged to attend. On Sundays these meetings were timed to coincide with Church functions. Exploiting old " topics," as e.g., greater freedom of conscience, each one's right to hold atheistic views, etc., the Communists created an atmosphere hostile to the Catholic religion. Catholicism was represented as an instrument of conquest in the hands of the Capitalist States and as a mass of superstitions invented by the priests and nuns so as to assure for themselves a good life at the expense of the poor. Allusions were made to the speculations of the clergy (masked under the name of charitable works, hospitals, schools, etc.), to the extent of the land taken from the people by the missionaries and exploited to their own advantage, to their hidden funds. And all this was neatly embellished by a series of calumnies on the celibacy of priests and nuns.

In support of this propaganda a number of journals, reviews, books and novels was spread among the people. These were written in an easy, attractive and popular style and contained fantastic descriptions of the prosperity that awaited the people after their complete liberation from the oppression of the Central

National Government and the yoke of absurd moral laws and religious superstitions.

The greatest effort of all was aimed at youth. In every village schools were opened in which tried Communist masters showed religion as a collection of absurdities, and as immoral. Morality, whether Christian or Confucian, was but an accumulation of ancient formulae opposed to individual liberty. The indissolubility of marriage was a Capitalist invention, while the absolute equality of the sexes was a conquest of " social progress."

3. The third phase was the *campaign for re-education*. This aimed at the progressive creation of the " new man." The press, lectures, State festivals, the radio, the cinema, daily mass meetings, extraordinary meetings for lower grade employees, study-weeks for directors of organisations, three-week sessions for functionaries and intellectuals, grand gatherings of several weeks or even months—everything was turned to this work of re-education. Periods of " education " are still obligatory whenever the Government launches a new plan or demands a new effort. The " educational sessions," often purposely held in churches or religious institutes, were repeated at intervals. These did not include the weekly meetings for the self-criticism and confession of Party members, nor those for the army and schools. In the universities Communist formation went on for years.

4. After a period of " re-education," carefully thought out, measures were put into force to paralyse completely the work of the missionaries. This was *the phase of active opposition (ta tao T'ien Chu Chiao).*

Under the cover of greater liberty in education the schools began to pass under the control of the Party which undertook to have them approved, to arrange their programmes from which religious instruction was excluded, and to choose their teaching personnel. So as not to co-operate in the spread of atheistic Materialism, the Catholic schools had to close down.

Next all land belonging to the missions was confiscated. Already this land was burdened with taxes far in excess of its actual value.

Then came an order requiring possession of a " pass " for travel between one town and another. As the " pass " was regularly refused, often with exquisite politeness, the missionaries were practically confined to their own residences. At the same time they had to give an account of their every act to the Communist authorities.

Frequent " questioning " of mission personnel, veiled and anonymous threats to the masters of Catholic schools, to catechists and their helpers, followed. Churches were put to all kinds of profane uses; they became lecture halls for the Party, dance halls, sometimes even sheds for animals. [5]

5. The organisation of " People's Courts " [6] put the finishing touches to all these measures.

In July 1946 the Communist headquarters, installed at Yenan, issued an " appeal " to all the inhabitants, inviting them to denounce in public the misdeeds of the foreigners. The " appeal " was enthusiastically welcomed by the Party sections which set about making the accomplishment of this duty as easy as possible for the people.

From the lowest quarters of the towns and villages, the most dissatisfied elements of the population were recruited to stage nightly demonstrations against the missions. Their purpose was to provoke the missionaries to lodge complaints with the local Party head.

At the very beginning the Communist leaders were quick to offer excuses for the population as " yet little educated " and to make protestations of their own personal esteem for the Church. They assured the missionaries of their support in calming the anger of the people, but suggested that " in their own interest " it would be better that the missionaries leave the district.

The demonstrations grew in frequency and violence. Naturally in the end the Party was forced " in the name of the people " to arrest the bishop, the missionaries, the nuns and the more prominent members of the faithful.

Some days later the *trial* took place before thousands of people.

---

[5] Cf. *China Missionary Bulletin*, November 1950, pp. 929-930.
[6] Cf. L. Legrand, *Le Communisme arrive au village chinois*, Peiping, 1947, pp. 12 *seqq.*

The organisation of the trial was entirely in the hands of the Party which had in the meantime appointed its most trusted members to the various rôles to be played. Some were to act the part of the " oppressed," others the part of " mob-agitators." After the " supervisor " had read a list of the many grave misdeeds of the missionaries, the " accusations " of the people were heard. These accusations, false for the most part, or trifling facts travestied and ridiculously exaggerated, came generally under the following heads:

Forced conversion of children to Catholicism.
Torture of the sick in hospitals.
Refusal of food to children in orphanages.
Removal of eyes for experimental purposes.
Murder of Chinese to eat their hearts.
Hiding of enormous quantities of gold in the churches.

To crown the process, the emissaries of the Party brought forward their own accusations: collaboration with the Japanese, spying for the Kuomintang and imperialist America, unspecified " offences against the people."

Although the right of defence was refused to the accused,[7] and these tragic farces were sometimes repeated two, three or four times, the hoped-for results were not always forthcoming. If the " culprit " did not repent of his errors, he was brought before the Communist chief who reminded him, often most paternally, of the " gravity of the accusations formulated against him by the people." It was pointed out *that according to the law* this should mean sentence of death. But the Party was merciful. The penalty would be reduced to a fine. This fine reached immense figures—sometimes half a million American dollars. As it could scarcely ever be paid, it was replaced by confiscation of all the goods of the accused, and restriction of his civil and religious liberties. This " lenient treatment " sometimes forced the bishop to go to the free zone to find the money in order not to have to abandon the faithful. The Party willingly granted the pass. It had attained its purpose. The missionary had been removed.

[7] Even when the accused is allowed to speak in his own defence (which is very exceptional), the result is the same, for no account is taken of anything he may have to say.

If the accused acknowledged his errors and repented he was allowed to remain at his post but his liberty and the exercise of his ministry were restricted in various ways. In general however Chinese priests were either sent to gaol or condemned to forced labour for a more or less prolonged period, while foreign missionaries were ordered to leave the country, or as sometimes happened, were liquidated by one or other of the well-known Chinese Communist methods.

These trials were often accompanied by acts of cruelty,[8] as for example, making the condemned person run through the streets while the mob insulted and beat him. Churches and mission residences were sacked—sometimes while the trial was still going on. Sacred vessels and images were sacrilegiously exposed to let the people see the "vulgar superstitions of the Catholics."

During 1946-1947 more than 100 priests [9] were put to death, often under the most inhuman conditions.[10]

Because of the pillage that followed the trials several dioceses were left without the bare essentials for carrying on their work. The missions of the North (Hopei, Shensi, Shantung and Ninghsia) were the first and generally the most severely hit. It is estimated that during 1946-1947 in these Provinces and in Mongolia (Inner) and Manchuria, 183 churches were turned into offices and 123 into theatres and cinemas, 166 were plundered, 25 destroyed, 101 closed, 12 burned, not to mention 549 mission houses which were occupied or destroyed.

With the ever increasing Communist occupation of new provinces the persecution through "People's Courts" increased

---

[8] Cf. *New Review*, Calcutta, November 1947, pp. 340-352.

[9] Cf. *China Missionary Bulletin*, I, 1948, which gives names and details.

[10] The "popular trial" of the Cistercian monks of Yangkiaping, near Peking, is notorious. This trial, to which were invited " ex officio " the inhabitants of some 30 neighbouring villages, ended on 17 August 1947 with the condemnation to death of a number of the monks. They were accused of conniving with the Japanese in the first instance, and then of collaborating with the Nationalist Government. The other monks were at first sentenced to prison. Tried again however on August 23 they were ordered to leave the monastery. They were forced to leave with their hands tied behind their backs. During a stop at Tang Kia-yao, after frightful torture 12 of them were buried alive. In all there were 26 victims (priests and brothers) from this monastery.

Chinese priests were treated with special cruelty after condemnation. When they were not tortured, the courses in Marxism, at which they had to assist regularly and which lasted six to eight hours a day, had in the end disastrous psychological effects on them.

in extent, and with it grew the number of victims and the extent of the destruction.[11]

The Persecution after 1950

Once political power had been seized, the Communists had proclamations of freedom posted almost everywhere, and there was a momentary slackening off in the open and bloody attack on religion.

Article 1 of the " Common Programme," approved by the *Political Consultative Congress* of 29 September 1949, guaranteed to all citizens " freedom of thought, speech, the press, meeting, association, correspondence, choice of domicile, travel, religious denomination, procession or other public demonstration (whether as organisers or participants.") [12]

Although this article was modelled on that of the Soviet Constitution and could be interpreted as freedom either to believe in religion or to oppose it, there were some signs of a certain " broad-mindedness " in the big towns. In the country districts however the old intolerance and repression were maintained.

But the *Law on counter-revolutionary activities*, published on 23 July 1950 [13] and coming into force in February 1951,[14] sought to put into the hands of the Government the " juridical " arms needed for a more intense attack on the Churches in general and on the Catholic Church in particular. Under cover of a " struggle " (*t'ou tcheng*) for the defence of Marxist principles and institutions, the clergy were kept isolated and under constant supervision. They were refused permission to travel. Thus priests and bishops had to ply most humble trades to procure the necessities of life. Missionaries were accused of anti-Government activity, of spreading superstition, of treason in favour of American imperialism. Here and there an attempt

---

[11] Cf. *China Missionary Bulletin*, February 1951.
[12] Cf. *Agency Hsin Hwa*, 1 October 1949. Also ch. III art. 87 and 88 of the *Constitution* approved by the *National Congress* at Peking, 20 September 1954.
[13] Cf. *Agency Hsin Hwa*, 23 July 1950—*Decree on the Repression of counter-revolutionary activity.*
[14] Cf. *Agency Hsin Hwa*, 21 February 1951—*Directions of the People's Republic of China on penalties for counter-revolutionaries.*

was made to prohibit religious ceremonies which were considered
" a waste of time and harmful to the national production."

By degrees the freedom sanctioned in the " Common Programme " was reduced to nothing. This was effected by a series
of restrictive measures, more or less severe as the temper of
international politics and the strength of the Communist
Government dictated.

Since 1950 25 charitable and relief institutions have been
suppressed on the ridiculous and calumnious accusation that
children had been put to death in them, or on other like
accusations.

The *65th Council of Political Affairs* ordered a census and the
registration of all social, cultural, religious and educational
works, subsidised from abroad. The evident purpose of this
step was to prepare the way for their confiscation and suppression
after careful inventory.[15]

The *Law on counter-revolutionary activity* also sounded the death
knell of all Catholic journals and reviews. *Vox Cleri* was the last
to disappear, following on a Government Order of 8 June 1951
dissolving the Catholic Central Bureau responsible for its
publication.

In July 1951 the *Legion of Mary* was outlawed as a secret and
anti-revolutionary organisation.

The State continued to take over the Catholic schools, over
which was placed a " Committee of professors, pupils and
superintendents," named by the Party and charged with the
administration of the schools.[16] The three Catholic universities
(*Aurora* of Shanghai, *Fugen* of Peking, and *Tsinku* of Tien-Tsin)
were confiscated, as was also the greater number of the 156
secondary and 1,546 primary schools. All of the 2,742 catechetical schools were closed.[17]

---

[15] The Council's decree obliged these organisations:
    (a) to have themselves registered with the competent Chinese authorities;
    (b) to give each week an exact account of their financial situation, of financial
       transactions carried out by them, of all other operations affecting their capital,
       and of all money, whatever the sum, received from abroad.
  Failure to comply with these regulations entailed suppression of the organisation.
[16] Cf. *China Missionary Bulletin*, November 1950 and December 1950.
[17] In spite of long and laborious efforts to save it, the Catholic university " Fugen "
at last came under the complete control of the Government (12 October 1950). It
was immediately made a seat of Marxism.

From the autumn of 1950, when Chinese Communism began to reveal its real intentions towards Catholicism,[18] the most shameful insults and unprecedented calumnies were directed against the Catholic Church.[19]

The Movement for Triple Autonomy

After a violent campaign of accusations against the Vatican,[20] charged with directing under cover of cultural activities a powerful anti-Government spy-network, the Government of Peking, wishing to support the ardent and " spontaneous " aspirations of Chinese Christianity, launched in January 1951 the Movement of " Triple Independence " or " Triple Autonomy."[21] This movement demanded for the Chinese Church:

   (a) Self-government (*Tze-Chih*)
   (b) Self-support (*Tze-Yang*)
   (c) Self-propagation (*Tze-ch'uan*).

For the Communists these " Autonomies," deliberately expressed in ambiguous terms, had an essentially political and insidious meaning, the purpose of which was to create a schism within the Catholic Church.

"Autonomy of Government " (self-government) meant for the Communists that the Church, governed by Chinese, was to recruit its own personnel in its own way without any control on the part of the Pope.[22]

---

[18] The official daily of the capital, *Jen Min Je Pao* (People's Daily), pointed the way with a series of articles discrediting the Catholic Church and showing it to the people as the " long arm " of foreign imperialism in the past, and of present American imperialism.

[19] Cf. Propaganda Bulletin, *People's China*, Peking, 16 April 1951, for the atrocities supposedly committed by nuns in the orphanages.
Cf. also: *New China*, 5 June 1951; the *Shanghai News*, 6 June 1951; *Ta Kung Pao* (Daily of Justice), 12 March 1951. During the *trial* of the Franciscan Missionaries of Mary of the Sacred Heart Orphanage at Nanking, some 100 little corpses buried near the orphanage were exhumed and exposed in public to show the people " the wickedness of the foreign religious."

[20] Cf. *Ta Kung Pao*, 6 January 1951, also *People's Daily*, reproduced in *China Missionary Bulletin*, 1951, pp. 148-149.

[21] On 7 January 1951 the Prime Minister, Chou En-Lai, invited some 40 Catholic leaders to a meeting in a Peking hotel " for an exchange of views on the movement for Catholic reform." Cf. *Agency Hsin Hwa*, 20 January 1951.

[22] Cf. *Agency Hsin Hwa*, 14 January 1951: " It is a question of freeing oneself from western traditions and of creating a new system, a new legialstion and a new liturgy."
Ta Kung Pao, 6 January 1951: " The Church of China will have to be self-governing, with no dependence on foreign bishops, and with still less on the Pope."

" Economic Autonomy " (self-support) signified that the Catholic Church in China was to receive no subsidy from outside (i.e. no imperialist money). The Communist Government undertook to provide for its needs.[23]

"Autonomy of Propagation " (self-propagation): the Chinese themselves were to spread their religion. There were to be no more foreign missionaries. The subject-matter of sermons was to be adapted to the Chinese mentality and to conditions in the " New China." A new theology, conformable to the ideology of the Communist Government, must be developed.[24]

During the whole of 1951 the Communists were busy setting up " Reform Committees " (diocesan and parochial) for the following purposes:

(a) to promote the establishment of a " truly Chinese Church ";

(b) to accuse the Catholic Church and its organisations of being instruments of imperialist penetration;

(c) to have arrested and sentenced bishops and priests " refusing to accept the reform ";

(d) to administer the " New Church ";

(e) to undertake and actively to pursue the " indoctrination " [25] of priests and faithful through the study of

---

[23] " The Church of China must be self-sufficient and must not beg money from abroad" —*Ta Kung Pao*, 6 January 1951.

[24] Cf. *Agency Hsin Hwa*, 14 January 1951: " Chinese Christians must discover for themselves and by themselves the treasures of the Gospel of Christ. They must get rid of Western theology and create a new theological system suitable to themselves. That is the only way of putting into practice in our " New China " the (revolutionary) spirit of the Gospel of Christ."

Jen Min ie Pao, 8 January 1951: " Our aim is to bring the Church of Christ back to its primitive state and, from a political point of view, to adapt it resolutely to the aspirations of the people."

Ta Kung Pao, 6 January 1951: " In future only Chinese may engage in religious propaganda among their fellow-citizens."

[25] The Communists pay special attention to Chinese priests. Father Gerbier, a French missionary, relates the words of a Communist official, an apostate Christian and former student of the university of Fugen: " We consider Chinese priests as a ' social value ' which, far from wanting to destroy, we wish on the contrary to retrieve. They represent a ' social value,' for in general they have received a good education and an excellent formation; besides they are accustomed to severe discipline, and to live according to well-determined principles. From the beginning they have instilled into them absolute devotion to an ideal, a devotion which means renunciation, unhesitating acceptance

Marxism, in order to sow the seeds of " self-destruction " within the Catholic Church.

In the beginning all these committees had not the same statutes. While all agreed in affirming the Three Autonomies, some were more radical, others, at least in words, more moderate. The statute of Tien-Tsin (8 March 1951), the first to be published, contains clearly schismatic statements. On the contrary the statute of Chungking (July 1951) was of a more moderate tone, but more coldly realistic. It seems to be the prototype of all the other statutes published about the same time.

" The purpose of the Committee," says article 1, " is to unite the clergy and faithful in the love of their country and their religion, to uphold the ' Common Programme ' (i.e. the Constitution), to act in accordance with Government policy, to sever radically every tie with imperialism, while keeping at the same time a purely religious link with the Vatican, to oppose all Vatican interference in internal Chinese politics so as to bring to full development the movement of reformation of the Chinese Catholic Church."

Article 3 states that " The Committees have power to found ' branches,' which means that the diocesan committees may found as many sub-committees as there are parishes."

Article 13 lays down as " obligations of members ":

(a) to study zealously; to raise their own political level; to know clearly the difference between the Church and imperialism; to take an active part in the opposition to America; to love the country and religion, because Chinese Catholicism has broken the link with imperialism, has freed itself from its influence, and has brought about the reform of the Three Autonomies;

---

of directives coming from a hierarchy, permanent orientation towards the common good of the organisation to which they belong. The Communist Party does not demand anything different from its adherents. But in China persons trained in this way are rather rare. That is why, once we have freed them from their foreign ' preceptors,' we hope to ' retrieve ' the priests easily and to use them with profit in the social field. We shall send them to re-education camps to change their ' brain ' . . . And when this is changed, those priests will become ardent promoters of the new order. Their first task will then be to change the mind of the faithful who like themselves have gone astray after Christ." (Quoted by *L'Osservatore Romano*, 30 January 1955).

(b) to take an active part in the work of building up the New Republic; to be dedicated to production; to become good citizens;

(c) always to observe Sundays and other Feasts; to go to confession and communion; to be good and pious Christians; to combat every activity that hides behind religion, sabotages the interests of the people, ruins public order . . . ”

It is to be noted also that articles 4 to 8 delegated to the diocesan committee, founded on democratic principles, the right to direct the activities of the faithful. The statutes make no mention of the bishop, and it is evident that they aim at *destroying the hierarchical principle* within the Church.[26]

In China the parochial and diocesan committees were called the “ renewed Church.” Every disciplinary link between the bishops and the clergy was destroyed, the parishes were subjected to the good pleasure of the local Communist authorities. Christians were called upon to “ renew ” their dogmatic and moral patrimony in accordance with the Third Autonomy. Already there are many martyrs from the ranks of those who refused to accept the “ Renewed Church.” [27]

* * *

From March 1951 [28] Mgr. *Anthony Riberi*, Internuncio in China, was the object of violent attacks in the Communist press. He had put the bishops on their guard against the schismatic

---

[26] Cf. *L'Osservatore Romano*, 30 January 1951.

[27] We recall here only the case of Father *Beda Chang*, S.J., who died of privations (11 November 1951) after spending three months in prison for refusing to retract the statement that the Church is “ one, holy, catholic and apostolic.” Many other names might be added: Fathers *Matthew Chen*; *Joseph Seng*, etc.

[28] As usual, the official organ, *Jen Min Je Pao*, 2 May 1951, showed the way. The following days in all the papers there were petitions to the Government demanding “ expulsion of the ‘ foreigner from Monaco ’ (Mgr. *Riberi* comes from the Principality of Monaco), of Riberi, the imperialist.”

Cf. also *Jen Min Je Pao*, 4 June 1951 ; *Chi Fang Pao* (The Liberator), Shanghai, 9 June 1951.

Signatures for the expulsion of the Internuncio were gathered during a campaign which accused the Vatican of imperialism, spying, Hitlerism, war-mongering, etc. Speeches, newspaper articles, caricatures, films and every other means of propaganda were used to “ smear ” the Papacy and the Sovereign Pontiff. Cf. *People's Daily*, 29 August 1951.

nature of the " reform " movement.[29] On 26 June he was put under house arrest. On 4 September the press announced that the Nanking *Military Committee of Control of the People's Army of Liberation* had finally ordered the expulsion from China of "*Anthony Riberi* from Monaco." On the following day the *New China News Agency* remarked that the order had been carried out at once.[30] All this was done without the slightest respect for common diplomatic usage.[31]

Situation of the Catholic Church at the end of 1955

At the end of 1955 practically all priests and bishops in China were forced to live in extreme poverty. The priest had become one of the many " democratic citizens " who kept his dispensary, cultivated a garden, worked as a bus-driver or, if Communist freedom allowed him, took up the job of itinerant hawker as the only way of bringing help to the scattered faithful and of administering the sacraments to them.

All Catholic works had been destroyed; hundreds of schools from primary to university status had been confiscated; " taken back " by the Government was the official formula. Only one seminary according to some, three according to others, had been able to carry on in some fashion.

All this was done *without the promulgation of a single legislative act*. Local administrative decisions carried out by the police have sufficed, for these are the reputed interpreters of the will of the people.[32]

The Government has not decreed the closing of the churches. At present the faithful may still assist at Mass in the large towns, but in the country districts the churches are being gradually and quietly closed.

---

[29] He was accused of " having urged the Catholics to oppose the People's Government." To this the following accusations were added: protecting agents and spies of foreign countries, engaging himself in spying, having organised " clandestine " counter-revolutionary associations, especially the *Legion of Mary*.

[30] Cf. *Agency Hsin Hwa*, 5 September 1951.

[31] Cf. *China Missionary News*, No. 34, 12 September 1951, for the infamous treatment reserved for diplomats of the Holy See.

[32] The Catholic press was completely suppressed. Before the Communist regime there were 3 dailies, 3 weeklies, 16 monthly and 3 two-monthly reviews. Besides the Communist Government confiscated 216 hospitals with 86,000 beds, 254 orphanages with 15,700 orphans, 781 dispensaries, all the kindergartens, nursing homes and other charitable institutions.

Nearly all foreign bishops and priests have been either imprisoned or expelled. *Of the 6,000 missionaries who ministered in China in 1943 only 35 remained on 5 October 1955 : 2 bishops, 18 priests and 15 sisters.*

More than 100 Chinese priests and bishops have died in prison. Greater numbers are still in prison, of whom many have completed their sentences of forced labour. Those still at liberty are continually spied upon and fear that they too may find themselves in gaol at any moment.

Despite threats, arrests, condemnations and expulsions the Catholic Church has firmly resisted the Peking Government from 1951 to the present time. Pope *Pius XII* has re-affirmed this resistance in his Encyclical, *Ad Sinarum gentem,* of 7 October 1954 :

> " Those who profess or teach truths other than those briefly outlined by us above, can neither be considered nor honoured as Catholics. This is the case for example of those who give their consent to the disastrous principles called the ' Three Autonomies ' or principles of the same kind." [33]

It need scarcely be remarked that the Communist authorities considered such resistance as " imperialist " and " counter-revolutionary." It afforded an excuse for renewing the persecution against Catholics in accordance with the second national campaign of " repression of counter-revolutionary elements " begun by the Government in April 1955.[34]

In August a communiqué announced the arrest at Paoting, Hopei, of the " counter-revolutionaries " of the *Association of Christian Youth.* They were accused of having insulted patriotic Christians favourable to the *Movement of Triple Autonomy* by treating them as " rebels." [35]   In the night of 8-9 September

---

[33] As in the case of the Apostolic Letter, *Cupimus imprimis,* 18 January 1952, the Communist Government did all in its power to prevent the Encyclical from reaching the clergy and faithful.

[34] Cf. *Agency Hsin Hwa,* 29 July 1955. Report of *Lo Jui-ching,* Minister for Public Security. As already stated, the first offensive was launched in July 1950.

[35] Cf. *Agency Hsin Hwa,* 28 August 1955.

the Bishop of Shanghai, Mgr. *Kung Pin-mei*, and 27 Chinese Catholic priests, with about 300 laymen, were arrested. There can be no doubt about the resistance of the Catholics of Shanghai to the *Movement of Triple Autonomy*. [36]

" *Kung Pin-mei's* counter-revolutionary clique has refused to obey the decree suppressing the *Legion of Mary* (promulgated on 8 October 1951 by the *Commission of Military Control* of Shanghai) and has prevented its members from resigning or registering themselves in Government offices. *Kung Pin-mei* and his clique have urged on the counter-revolutionaries to fight against patriotic Catholics." [37]

On 9 September 1955 *Chen I*, Mayor of Shanghai and President of the *Commission of Military Control* fixed 20 September 1955 as the last day for the " registration " (i.e. dissolution) of members of the *Legion of Mary*, which according to Peking is a " political, secret, international spy-organisation." Whoever does not obey this order for " the dissolution of this revolutionary organisation " will be " punished without pity." [38]

Following this decree there was a wave of arrests throughout China on the excuse of " counter-revolutionary activity consisting in opposition to the movement of Triple Autonomy, and in membership of the *Legion of Mary*." Mgr. *Hu Jo-san*, Chinese Catholic Bishop of Taichow (Tchekiang), and a number of priests and faithful [39] were arrested on 10 September. Arrests followed in the provinces of Anhwei, Fukien and Kiangsu, in

---

[36] " To eliminate counter-revolutionary elements hidden within the Catholic Church is a very difficult task. These counter-revolutionaries have acquired vast experience in the course of their long struggle and know perfectly every form of strategy and tactics. So we must take our enemy seriously and treat him accordingly." Editorial in *Sin Wen Je Pao* (Daily News), Shanghai, 9 September 1955.

[37] *Sin Wen Je Pao*, 9 September 1955. The paper added: " As regards religion the policy of the People's Government is clear and precise; as long as they act in accordance with the laws and the policy (!) of the Government, all Catholics and all the faithful of other religions may be protected in their religious beliefs and respected in their customs and traditions. This is known to all. But in the case of Kung Pin-mei, since his clique has engaged in counter-revolutionary activity, our duty is to suppress it with energy."

[38] Proclamation signed by Chen I and Shu Yu, President and vice-President respectively of the *Commission of Military Control* of Shanghai. Cf. *Sin Wen Je Pao*, 9 September 1955.

[39] Cf. *Sin Wen Je Pao*, 12 September 1955.

which the discovery was made of " a voluminous correspondence (carried on) with *Kung Pin-mei's* counter-revolutionary clique at Shanghai." [40] There were mass arrests at Shanghai.[41]

The tactics used five years previously were again employed: denunciations, mass-meetings, accusation-sessions and people's courts. Here is one report from Communist sources: "An accusation-session held in Shanghai on 12 September, attended by 1,900 Catholics, was quickly followed on 13, 14 and 15 September by other sessions in the 22 sub-districts, in which more than 30,000 Catholics took part. In the provinces of Anhwei, Tchekiang, Kiangsu and Fukien people of all social classes and Catholics themselves organised meetings to denounce and condemn the criminal activities of *Kung Pin-mei's* clique." [42]

The latest news from China (March 1957) indicated that the repression is still growing in extent. But it is very difficult to get exact figures. It would seem however that at least 70 priests and 3,000 Catholic laymen, all Chinese, have been arrested. There is no news as yet about the release of Mgr. *Ignatius Kung Pin-mei*.[43]

---

[40] Cf. *Anhwei Je Pao* (Anhwei Daily), 13 September 1955 (broadcast from Anhwei Radio). Cf. also *Fukien Je Pao*, 13 September 1955.

[41] Cf. broadcast from the People's Radio of Shanghai, 15 September 1955.

[42] *Sin Wen Je Pao*, Shanghai, 17 September 1955. The *Agency Fides* a little later reported some moving incidents, as when during a session of the public trial, Mgr. Kung Pin-mei shouted three times: " Long live Christ the King."

[43] An impressive testimony on the methods of Communist persecution in the very midst of the Catholic community of Shanghai is afforded by the book of Father J. Le Feuvre, S.J.: ' *Les Enfants de la Ville—Chronique de la vie Chrétienne à Shanghai 1949-1955.*' (' The Children of the City—Chronicle of Christian Life in Shanghai '). The ' Children of the City ' are the Christians of Shanghai and in particular the students of the Catholic university, Aurora. Fr. Le Feuvre, an eyewitness, relates how every Christian has to be on the alert and to have ready the light baggage which he will be permitted to bring with him when arrested. He describes the long questionings of young persons belonging to the *Legion of Mary* who were " invited˃ to present themselves as often as twelve or fifteen times before the police (p. 101); the cases of priests questioned for 40, 70, 92 hours (p. 337); the long detentions in prison (pp. 103-109).

In the diary written by Fr. Le Feuvre is to be found a description of many refined tortures, psychological and intellectual: the public interrogations directed at the prisoners in the dock, the slogans bellowed by loud-speakers and by the radio (pp. 100-112), the calumnies spread by the press (p. 189), Catholic students of Shanghai forced to attend ' re-education ' courses lasting for months (pp. 116, 118, 120). Nor are there lacking cases of moral pressure, from threats against the students' parents to refusal of diplomas to those who do not conform (pp. 305,343). All this alternates with the comedy of ' religious peace '—as for example, on the occasion of the Peking ' International Congress for Peace,' (pp. 157, 160)—or with treacherous offers of compromise. In an atmosphere of pressure, lies, spying, accusations, persecution

A Document

The following document, signed by many Catholic missionaries expelled from China and sent as a protest to the *Commission Internationale contre le Régime Concentrationaire* provides ample proof of the severity and extent of the ravages caused by the Communist persecution in China:[44]

" We, the undersigned, former Catholic missionaries in China, and victims of arbitrary arrest and imprisonment by the Government of the People's Republic of China, in our own name and in the name of our colleagues, both of China and of other nations, still held in prison at the present moment, address the following appeal to the *Commission Internationale contre le Régime Concentrationaire* (a non-governmental organisation with consultative voice accredited to the Economic and Social Council of the UNO):

" We were sent to China by our ecclesiastical authorities, that is to say, by our respective congregations, acting in dependence on the Central Congregations of the Holy See. We have never departed from the object of our mission, which is exclusively religious. In China we have never been the agents of any foreign power, either of our own country or of any other. When a new Government was established in China, we reminded the faithful of the teaching of the Church on obedience to established authority. Nevertheless we all suffered the same fate. One day, when we least expected, we were arrested and thrown into prison. We were accused of being ' counter-revolutionaries,' ' imperialists,' ' foreign agents ' and ' spies ' ! But we have never undertaken any political activity, and all our actions, well-known to a Government which nothing escaped, were confined to purely religious matters.

" The treatment to which we were subjected varied. Some of us were tortured. Others had their hands tied behind their backs day and night for months. Others were compelled to

---

and sometimes of defection, the Christian fortitude of the Catholic students of Shanghai is up to the present marvellous.

The Bishop of the city, when he was still in the midst of his people, had addressed this prayer to the Blessed Virgin: " We are not asking you for miracles; we are not asking you that this persecution may cease; we ask you only, O Holy Mother, to sustain our poor strength." (p. 224).

[44] CICRC, *Bulletin d'Information*, August-November 1955.

13

remain standing during interrogations, which in some cases went on continuously for five days and five nights. A great number had to remain crouched on the ground the whole day without speaking, without reading, without sleeping, occupied only with ' reflecting on their crimes.' Others had nothing more to complain about than the loss of their liberty, and had to sign each evening that ' they had not been ill-treated.'

" Many of us have known the common cells, where our companions, the Chinese prisoners, and ourselves were obliged to exhort each other mutually for several hours each day to ' reform our way of thinking,' that is to say, to make profession at least with our lips of Communist theories. We were told each day that the only way to get out of prison was to ' reform our way of thinking.' Every religious emblem and every prayer book were taken from us, and the usual gestures accompanying private prayer, even the simple sign of the Cross, were forbidden under threat of punishment.

" We remained like this for months, some even for years, without visits, without letters, without outside contacts, and with a few exceptions absolutely isolated, seeing only the faces of our fellow prisoners, among whom there were always one or more informers. In the cells there were no beds, no tables, no chairs. We slept on the bare wooden or cement floor.

" Denied all legal aid we appeared before the judges. Every question was asked with the sole intention of extracting from us lying confessions that we were imperialists, spies, enemies of the people. To make us lose control of ourselves we were subjected to the most impressive threats and cleverly designed pressure.

" Some of us were condemned to forced labour, labour which was generally hard, sometimes utterly nerve-racking, during which those condemned were themselves expected to increase ' spontaneously ' the rhythm of their output.

" We were set free by being expelled from Chinese territory, at a time when it seemed to the People's Government that our being set free would serve its policy better than our being kept in prison, no attention being paid as to whether our sentences were completed or not.

" Every principle of justice held by civilised peoples was violated in our regard; in nearly every case there were no definite

accusations, no proofs; in every case no defence or legal protection for the accused was permitted. In a word we were
delivered, bound hand and foot, to the absolutely arbitrary
decisions of the tribunal.

" Our sufferings are over. But the Government of the People's
Republic of China has still in its prisons several foreign missionaries,
our colleagues, whom we have known, with whom we have lived
and of whom we can state that they were no more guilty than
were we. Their American nationality alone merits for them a
harder fate than ours.

" Several hundreds of Chinese priests and thousands of Chinese
Christians are in prison at the present moment. Quite recently
(September 1955) the Chinese Bishop of Shanghai, 50 priests
and seminarians, some nuns and more than 1,400 lay people, all
Chinese, were arrested. For them as for us there is the same lack
of legal motives, the same procedure to get them to make lying
avowals, the same isolation; some of them have been deported
as convicts to the desert regions in the west. For them also
we can solemnly affirm that they are innocent of any crime,
either political or against common law. It is also in the name
of these, who have been reduced to silence, that we raise our
voices and make our protest.

" Our pity and our indignation as free men are not confined to
those of our own religion. We have lived in different prisons
or cells with dozens of Chinese companions of every social class
and of every religion. If some of them (which is possible) had
conspired against the Government, we are persuaded that the great
majority of them like ourselves are but victims of the arbitrary
use of power. All of them like us have been refused the most
elementary legal protection. It is also in the name of those
thousands, who to-day fill the prisons and who cannot make
themselves heard, in the name of their wives and children,
at the thought of whom we have often seen these men weep,
that we, who are now free to raise our voices, wish to protest
and to claim justice.

" This protest is completely independent of all political,
economic, social or religious theories. It is based on the plea
of simple humanity, whose every right has been systematically
violated. In order that this protest should not remain a merely

Platonic statement, we demand that the *Commission Internationale contre le Régime Concentrationaire* should hold an inquiry into the state of the prisons and labour camps in China, as well as into the methods of legal procedure in force there.

" We ask the *Commission* to exert its influence by representations to the Chinese Government and to international organisations and by appeals to public opinion throughout the world, that a remedy be found for such great sufferings to which we bear testimony." [45]

---

[45] Official Communist sources have given the following news on latest developments in the schism promoted in China by the Communist Government: a *Catholic National Conference* met at Peking in the middle of July 1957 and lasted for a fortnight. According to the same sources, the *Conference* is said to have been attended by " 241 delegates from some 100 dioceses: bishops, priests, nuns and laity." The *Conference* is alleged to have approved—among other items—" a protest against the decision of the Vatican not to recognise the new head of the Church in Shanghai, elected in March." (The reference is to the Communist-imposed " Vicar Capitular," Tsang). Furthermore, the report stated that the *Conference* concluded with the following decisions:

(a) the setting up of a "Patriotic Association" of Chinese Catholics, which undertook " to have with the Vatican only such relations as do not violate the interests and independence of China." Aim of the Association: " to take part in the building up of Socialism in China, and to work to safeguard peace ";

(b) the approval of a Resolution stating that Chinese Catholics " will obey the Vatican only in matters of dogma and morals," but will oppose " every plan devised by the Vatican in the guise of Religion which might interfere with the internal affairs of our country, violate its sovereignty or harm our patriotic movement against imperialism." Comment is scarcely necessary !

Chapter 8

THE PERSECUTION OF THE CATHOLIC CHURCH

UNDER

Communist Rule in Korea

SEVERAL FACTORS prepared the way for the establishment of a Communist régime in part of Korea:

The Cairo Conference (November 1943). The Four Powers (USA, Britain, USSR and China), regarding Korea as a friendly nation, undertook to restore the independence which she had lost when Japan annexed the country in 1910.

The Yalta Conference (January 1945). To facilitate its attack on Japan the USSR was authorised to move the Red army south into Korea as far as the 38th Parallel.

The USSR declaration of war on Japan (8 August 1945). The Soviet army occupied Manchuria and Korea. Even after the signing of the armistice between the Allies and Japan (15 August 1945) the Russians pressed south until they had reached the agreed limit, the 38th Parallel.

The Moscow Conference (27 December 1945). The Foreign Ministers of USSR, America and Britain envisaged the establishment of a Protectorate in Korea, but as a result of the opposition of the people of Korea they reached a compromise that would lead to the establishment of a provisional Government for the whole of Korea. This Government was to consist of democratically elected Koreans and the task of preparing the way for the elections was entrusted to an American and Russian " Joint Commission."

Between March 1946 and October 1947 the Joint Commission held only two meetings and achieved absolutely nothing.

The United Nations (14 November 1947) decided that a general election for the whole of Korea should be held under UN control as a first step towards the re-unification of the country.

On 10 May 1948 a general election was held in South Korea under the control of the *United Nations' Temporary Commission*. The USSR refused to allow the execution of the UN decision in the territory north of the 38th Parallel.

The representatives who were elected on 10 May met in the Constituent Assembly on 12 July 1948 to approve the Constitution of the Democratic Republic of Korea.   On 20th of the same month *Syngman Rhee* was elected President, and on 15 August a new Korean Government was officially inaugurated.

In North Korea too there had been elections.   Under Soviet pressure delegates had been elected in August to the People's Supreme Council and on 9 September 1948 they proclaimed the People's Democratic Republic of Korea.

On 8 December 1948 the General Assembly of the United Nations recognised the Seoul Government by 47 votes for, to 6 (the Soviet group) against, with one abstention (Sweden).

The USSR announced that she had effected the withdrawal of Soviet *troops* from North Korea (October 1948).

On 25 June 1950 the army of the People's Democratic Republic of Korea invaded South Korea.

The Catholic Church in Korea

In a population of 29,500,000 inhabitants Catholics numbered 182,000 at the end of World War II.   There were then 160 Korean and 39 foreign priests in the country.   Before war spread over the country there was a total of 615 missionaries (secular and religious clergy, lay brothers and nuns, both foreigners and Koreans) who were assisted by 1,400 catechists.[1]

---

[1] There were five missionary congregations working in Korea: L'Institut des Missions Etrangères de Paris, the German Benedictines of St. Ottilia, the American Maryknoll Fathers, the Irish Society of St. Columban, and the Canadian Franciscans.

Korea was divided into 8 ecclesiastical circumscriptions, comprising one abbacy *nullius*,[2] 4 vicariates apostolic and 4 prefectures apostolic, with 4 Korean ordinaries and 4 foreign prelates. There were two senior and two junior seminaries while Catholic schools and charitable institutions flourished.

On 7 April 1949 an Apostolic Delegation was erected in Seoul.

There were numerous Catholic papers and magazines. Dailies: the *Kyung-Hyang-Press* (70,000 copies, widely read throughout the country); the *Taegu-Mai-Il* (Daily of Taegu, 40,000). Weeklies: the *Kyung-Hyang* (The Country); the *Catholick-Shin-Bo* (Catholic News, 10,000). Among the monthly magazines there were the *Kyung-Hyang* (4,900) for the general public and the *Juvenis Catholicus*, a magazine that catered specially for students and a more educated circle of readers.

The slow progress made by Catholicism in Korea was due in part to the small number of missionaries (the percentage of missionaries in relation to the total population is one of the smallest in the world); but it was also due in part to the restrictions imposed on religious liberty,[3] which became more stringent when Japan entered the war.[4]

When hostilities ceased (15 August 1945) the Missionary Church in Korea had been greatly weakened. The American Maryknoll Fathers had been repatriated at the beginning of the war. The Irish priests of the Society of St. Columban and the Canadian Franciscans had been interned. All French priests were under constant police supervision. During the war 70% of the clergy had been mobilised in compulsory labour service, while 30 seminarians and 2 priests had been called to serve as privates in the army. By the end of the war many churches and church buildings had been transformed into barracks or other military establishments.

When Korea was divided into two zones there were two vicariates apostolic north of the 38th Parallel, that of *Wonsan*

---

[2] The abbacy *nullius* of Tok-Won. The Abbot, Mgr. Boniface Sauer, was also Vicar Apostolic of Wonsan.

[3] Cf. *L'Eglise catholique dans l'Empire Japonais*, Sapporo, 1935.

[4] Cf. *International Agency Fides*, 20 January 1940.

under German Benedictines and that of *Pyong-Yang* which was
confided to the native clergy.

The Persecution in North Korea

The Russian occupation authorities undertook the immediate
sovietisation of North Korea on the political and ideological
planes.[5] The first results were already seen on 3 November 1945
when the 41 members of the People's Provisional Government,
previously selected by the Russians, were elected with 92.2%
of the total votes, and the Communist, *Kim Il Sung*, became
President.

The real war on religion began when the Soviet occupation
troops withdrew in October 1948. The Soviets preferred to
leave this campaign in the hands of the North Koreans whom
they had already carefully indoctrinated; they had already taken
care that the Constitution of the People's Democratic Republic
proclaimed freedom of worship.[6] But even before the departure
of the Soviet troops there had been acts of hostility on the part
of the People's Provisional Government under *Kim Il Sung*.

First of all Catholic associations were dissolved and were
transformed into Communist organisations.[7] Catholics were
denied access to all public office and to teaching positions in
the schools. The study of Marxism was made compulsory in
all schools and particular care was taken to see that the seminarians also followed indoctrination courses.

Missionaries and nuns were deprived of their ration cards on
the grounds that their activity did not come under the heading
of work.[8]

---

[5] Cf. *Schicksal in Korea, Deutsche Missionaere Berichten* (no date). This is a collection of
memoirs by Benedictine priests and German nuns who were released from Red captivity
in January 1954. Published by the Abbey of St. Ottilia, this work is extremely interesting
as an account of the vicissitudes of the Catholic Church in North Korea. " This book,"
states the preface, " is neither an indictment nor a lament, but merely a factual account
of events in a country where, to quote the words of a Chinese Communist officer of the
Volunteer Legion in Korea, ' it is no longer permitted to believe in God.' "
    Cf. also *Trois ans de captivité d'une religieuse dans le Nord Coréen*, Annales des Soeurs
de Saint-Paul de Chartres, July 1953; *Gentes*, XXIII, n. 3, Rome, March 1949; *L'Osservatore Romano*, 5 June 1954.
[6] Cf. *Schicksal in Korea*, pp. 22-28.
[7] Cf. *Agency Fides*, 1947, p. 317.
[8] Cf. *Schicksal in Korea*, pp. 22-28.

It was forbidden to assemble in groups of more than three and every Sunday parish priests had to ask for permission to say Mass.

Immediately after the arrival of the Soviet troops the magnificent abbey and seminary at Tok-Won were seized and transformed into a Communist university. The seminarians had to transfer to Seoul to continue their studies. The house of the Maryknoll Sisters in Pyong-Yang was closed, as also that of the Benedictines in Wonsan. Korean nuns and lay brothers were compelled to lay aside the religious habit and return to their homes.

As soon as the Communist authorities took over the schools the new teachers obliged the pupils to come to school on Sundays, so that it would be impossible for them to assist at Mass.[9] At the same time all Catholic books were confiscated and Catholic periodicals were suppressed. The Benedictine library in Tok-Won which contained 50,000 volumes was likewise seized.

Christians were forced to join Communist associations and there were anti-religious film shows for the young in the halls of the seminary of Tok-Won.

A network of secret agents was organised to keep watch on the activity of the faithful and on all Catholic institutions in spite of the protests lodged by missionaries and Christians, including Protestants.[10]

It was not long until the persecution claimed its first victims. Father *Witmar Farenkopf*, a German Benedictine aged 39, was assassinated by Soviet troops during the occupation of North

---

[9] Cf. *Agency Fides*, 1947, p. 95.

[10] For examples of the kind of " liberty " restored by the Communists in North Korea, see *Schicksal in Korea* (pp. 22 *et seqq.*). " School teaching became grossly materialistic and religion was derided in the classroom. Every effort was made to alienate Catholic children from the Church. Christians working in offices and factories were under constant vigilance and were subjected to every kind of pressure which could make the profession of religion more difficult . . . One result of the intense anti-religious propaganda was that pagans began to show greater interest in religion . . . The situation became more critical as the days passed. We were aware that anti-Church measures were being prepared and that the Communists were only waiting for the opportune moment to strike the decisive blow . . . The Communist system followed a fixed and unalterable programme, of which agrarian reform was the first point and reform of religion the sixth. We realised that the time would come for the sixth point also. The only difference was that whereas the first five reforms had been introduced piecemeal from day to day,

Korea, while Father *Marc Baigner* died in his presbytery from a stroke during one of the many searches carried out by the Soviets.

All religious activity in the Vicariate Apostolic of Wonsan was terminated on 9 May 1949 by the mass arrest of 123 missionaries: the Vicar Apostolic, Mgr. *Boniface Sauer*; 18 German Benedictines; 17 Korean brothers; 27 German Benedictine lay-brothers; 5 Korean priests; 9 Korean novices and 46 German, French and Korean nuns.

When the Korean Bishop, Mgr. *Francis Hong*, Vicar Apostolic of Pyong-Yang, protested to the Ministry for the Interior about the arrests he was seized on the public road in the afternoon of 14 May 1949 when he was going to the convent of the Sisters of Se-Po to exercise his ministry.[11] Nothing certain is known of his fate but there is reason to believe that he was murdered by the Communists.[12]

There followed the arrest of the remaining 14 priests in the Vicariate Apostolic of Pyong-Yang. By the time the North

---

the war on religion developed slowly but methodically. Every citizen above the age of six had to declare his religion. This information was included on his identity card without which no one was allowed even to leave his home, and the question of religion was of special importance when a person was seeking employment. Observers took note of those who attended Church on Sundays and Feast days and passed on the information to the Communists. In public discussions about Marx and Hegel, whenever the descent of man or such subjects were in question, Catholics particularly were asked to express their views. When a person who was seeking employment appealed to the constitutional liberty of worship, he was told that such liberty did indeed exist, but that a person who had a divided mentality—a State and a Church outlook—could not hope to secure the same positions as a man who had the sole interests of the State at heart . . . The Communist net began to tighten and by the beginning of 1949 it was clear that we should not have long to wait for the inevitable. Meanwhile the domestic economy school opened in 1945 had been closed and without our being notified the building was used for the formation of young Communist executives. These future leaders got their first " practical training " by keeping a check on those who went in and out of the Church and the mission. Our elementary school was likewise seized without any notification and was transformed into a higher school of medicine. The kindergarten was equipped as a laboratory for chemical research. The hospice for the aged was taken over by the Party and a pretext was sought to close our pharmacy. During all this we lived surrounded by spies. By the end of March 1946 the agrarian law had reduced the lands of the abbey to 120 acres which were barely sufficient to support a normal peasant family, whereas the abbey had to support more than 100 persons. At the end of March 1949 the printing works in Tok-Won were closed."

[11] Cf. *Le Clocher de la Croix sur la terre rouge*, by Laurence Chang, Fusan, 1951, pp. 101-107, for a detailed account of the arrest of Mgr. Hong.

[12] According however to a report received in 1955 from a German prisoner who returned from Russia, Mgr. Hong was still alive in a USSR prison.

Koreans invaded the South, all priests north of the 38th Parallel had been either *killed or imprisoned*.[13]

The Communists in South Korea

The invasion of South Korea was the beginning of 15 months of war that utterly devastated the country. During those months the North Koreans overran part of the south, the zone of occupation shifting with the tide of battle. Wherever the Communist army penetrated it struck at the Catholic Church in her clergy, her institutions and her buildings.

No sooner had they entered Seoul than the Communists straightway took over all Catholic churches, schools, the seminary, and used the cathedral as a barracks.

The Apostolic Delegate, Mgr. *Patrick James Byrne*, of the Maryknoll Fathers, and his secretary, Father *Booth*, were interned on 30 June 1950 in the British Embassy. On 11 July they were arrested and when the Communists were forced to leave the capital they brought Mgr. *Byrne* with them as well as a number of foreign and native priests.[14] What is known as " the death march " began.

The French Sisters of St. Paul de Chartres were also arrested on 11 July.

At the beginning of the Korean war the Communists removed also from the scene Mgr. *Thomas Quinlan* (Irish), Prefect Apostolic of Chun-Chon, and Mgr. *Patrick Brennan* (American), Prefect Apostolic of Kwang-Ju.[15]

Although they foresaw that they would lack freedom for the exercise of their ministry, almost all the priests remained at their stations in the zones occupied by North Koreans. The Korean priests particularly had to endure great sufferings; many were shot, imprisoned or deported to unknown destinations.

---

[13] For an account of conditions in Communist captivity see the books already cited, as also the *NCWC News Service* of 25 January 1954, and the series of articles written by Father O'Connor for the NCWC in 1953, and which were published under the title *Faith behind Barbed Wires*.

[14] Cf. *Trois ans de captivité* which gives a good picture of the nobility and heroism of Mgr. Byrne. Cf. also Raymond A. Lane, *Ambassador in Chains*. The life of Bishop Patrick James Byrne, New York, 1955.

[15] Mgr. Quinlan was named Vicar Apostolic of Chun-Chon, on 20 September 1955; he is at present Regent of the Apostolic Delegation in Korea.

Balance Sheet

The release of a certain number of missionaries permits us to make a fairly exact reckoning of the losses sustained by the Church in Korea. (Information was received in January 1954 of the 42 survivors of the total of 67 German missionaries and nuns arrested on 9 May 1949).

The Abbacy *nullius* of Tok-Won, with episcopal seat in Wonsan, which was served by the German Benedictines of St. Ottilia, suffered the most grievous loss. Nineteen missionaries and nuns died in prison; of six others there is no news. Among those who died as a result of the maltreatment and privations endured in prison was the Lord Abbot, Mgr. *Sauer*.

Of the Korean clergy 43 priests were arrested; 7 of these were murdered and there is no news of what happened to the others. There is however grave reason to believe that they too were murdered. Of the 8 Korean nuns 3 were killed, 1 died in prison; the other 4 are unaccounted for. Two seminarians were put to death; two others have disappeared.

Of the 13 French priests of the Missions Etrangères de Paris who were arrested by the Communists, 2 died in prison, 2 were killed, 1 was released, and 8 are unaccounted for. Of the 8 French sisters who fell into the hands of the Communists 1 was murdered, 2 died in prison, 4 were released and there is no trace of another.

Of the 5 Irish missionaries 3 were killed, 1 died in prison and 1 was released.

Of the 4 American missionaries arrested by the Reds, Mgr. *Byrne* died in prison on 25 November 1950, 1 was murdered, 1 was released and there is no news of the fourth.

An Australian missionary has been released after suffering the rigours of Communist captivity.

* * *

Soeur *Eugénie du Sacre-Coeur*, one of the French nuns captured by the Communists, writes at the end of her *Journal de Captivité*:

" During our time in the prison camp the officers and guards often tried to indoctrinate us with Communist ideas, but always without success. I wonder had we any influence on them? God alone knows. It is certain that they watched us continually; our behaviour, our patience, our charity towards each other, the heroic deaths they witnessed, all this must have made a greater impression on them than their lectures and interrogations made on us. May all our sufferings, united to those of Christ Our Redeemer, one day obtain for them the grace of conversion." [16]

---

[16] Cf. *Trois ans de captivité*, p. 80.

Chapter 9

THE PERSECUTION OF THE CATHOLIC CHURCH

UNDER

Communist Rule in Hungary

IN 1944 HUNGARY became the theatre of Communist operations. Having occupied part of the country, the Russians set about establishing a Provisional Government which first met at Debrecen and was later transferred to Budapest. The Soviets insisted that in this Government the local "anti-Fascist" elements should be reinforced by a quota of members who had been specially trained in the USSR.

On 4 November 1945 Hungary went to the polls in the first post-war election in Central and Eastern Europe. The Small-holders' Party obtained an absolute majority in the new parliament with 57% of the votes; the Communists obtained only 17%.

In January 1946 the People's Republic of Hungary was proclaimed. The Constitution approved by the newly elected parliament guaranteed all democratic rights and liberties. In the coalition Government at this stage the Small-holders' Party had seven portfolios, the Communists three, the Social-Democrats three, and the Agrarian Party one. But the three leftist parties enjoyed the support of the High Command of the Soviet occupation forces with the result that the Small-holders' Party was unable to make normal use of its majority in the Government. Political life in Hungary became a tangle of crises which were manoeuvred so as to undermine the influence of the Small-holders. In this subversive campaign the Communists were particularly active and had an advantage in the fact that they had captured a key position in the Government, the Ministry for the Interior.

As a result of the crises which had developed a second general election was fixed for 31 August 1947. The purpose behind these elections was to ensure that before the cessation of Soviet military control the affairs of Hungary would be under the thumb of a cabinet and government which would be at the service of Soviet interests.[1]

Many citizens were deprived of the right to vote and various means were adopted to prevent others from the free exercise of the franchise.

According to published statistics the Government coalition gained 60% of the votes, while 40% went to the opposition. The Communists obtained 22%, but since this was the highest figure attained by a single party in the Government coalition, this low percentage was sufficient to let the Communists gain control.

A basically Communist Cabinet was formed, which thought itself strong enough to proceed immediately with the introduction of Marxist reforms without fear of too serious opposition from any of the other political parties.

The Peace Treaty of that same year (1947) was also a determining factor in the evolution of the political situation in Hungary. By the terms of the treaty the Soviet troops continued to occupy Hungary to enable them to maintain their link with occupied Austria. This enabled the Communists to proceed with the consolidation of their régime without taking too much account of either national opinion or western reactions.

From 31 August 1947 the history of Hungary is synonymous with the liquidation of all ideological and political opposition and the building up of a Communist society in strict accord with the theories of Marx and Lenin.

The position of the Catholic Church in Hungary in 1945

Since the time of King St. Stephen the Catholic Church occupied an eminent place in the religious, cultural and social life of the Hungarian nation. Even after the arrival of Protestant-

---

[1] Before these second elections the Communist Party changed its tactics. In 1945 the formation of a Catholic Party was forbidden. This resulted in the Small-holders' Party being greatly strengthened in the elections, for the non-Communist vote went to it. In 1947 however different opposition parties were authorised. This was done to split the anti-Communist front.

ism, Catholicism remained the religion of the majority of the people. In 1945, out of a population of 10,000,000, 7 millions were Catholics (68.1%). Protestants formed 26.8%, Jews 4.4% and the Orthodox Church, 0.6%. To speak of religion in Hungary was to speak in the first place of the Catholic Church.

The following are the details of Church organisation in Hungary in 1945:

3 archdioceses: Esztergom,[2] Kalocsa and Eger;

8 dioceses: Györ, Szombathely, Pécs, Veszprém, Székes-fehérvár, Vác, Csanád (with episcopal residence in Szeged) and Hajdudorog (Byzantine Rite);

2 apostolic administrations: Szatmar and Rozsnyo;

2 vicariates: Nagyvarad and Kassa (with their respective episcopal seats in Romania and Czechoslovakia);

1 abbacy *nullius* (Benedictine): Pannonhalma.

In these ecclesiastical circumscriptions there were 2,265 parishes and 4,012 priests.

The vast patrimony with which St. Stephen endowed the Church had been considerably reduced in the course of centuries,[3] but in 1945 the Church still possessed large estates which enabled her to engage in works of social and cultural importance to the whole nation.

In the sphere of education the Church was responsible for an imposing number of schools, colleges and other establishments. The following are some figures:

191 infant schools, 1,216 popular schools, 1,669 elementary schools, 86 training schools for girls, 3 kindergarten training schools, 32 training schools for men, 49 colleges, 27 professional

---

[2] The Archbishop of Esztergom is Primate of Hungary. In ancient times the Primate was the first dignitary in the kingdom. According to the Constitution no important decision could be taken without consulting the Primate. Even though this position ceased to exist *de jure* after World War I, the Primate was still looked upon as a prince, and in case of vacancy of the office of head of the State he was by right first member of the Regency Council.

[3] In 1919 for example during the second Republic the Church played its part in agrarian reform by contributing 71,000 hectares of land (177,500 acres).

schools, 22 schools of agriculture, industry, and commerce, 1 lyceum, 1 training school for nurses, 1 domestic economy training school, 1 girls' commercial high school, 3 industrial schools, 1 preparatory school attached to the commercial high school, 1 school of short-hand, 1 law academy, 4 training schools for secondary teachers, 22 senior seminaries, 8 junior seminaries, 20 popular high-schools, 167 colleges and boarding schools and 1 faculty of Theology. *Altogether the Catholic Church in Hungary had 3,344 schools of all kinds and at all educational levels.* Compared with the State schools, the Catholics had 75% of the kindergarten training schools, 55.2% of the teachers' training establishments and 28% of the colleges. Specialised schools being left out of account, it can be said that about 45% of Hungary's 8,150 schools depended on the Catholic Church. The cost of maintenance amounted to about 85.3 million florins (6 million dollars) each year.

The Catholic press in Hungary had developed to a truly remarkable extent. In 1945 there were 2 daily newspapers, 18 weeklies, 25 monthly magazines, 3 quarterlies, and about 20 other publications and topical journals. The total output came to 1,500,000 copies per month, not counting school texts and religious books.

In its vast religious, cultural and social activity the Catholic hierarchy counted on the invaluable support of the *religious orders and congregations*. In 1945 there were 18 orders and congregations of men with 187 religious houses and 2,459 members of whom 1,422 were priests. There were 39 religious orders and congregations of women in 456 houses with a total of 7,525 members. The contemplative life in these religious institutes was joined with the practice of various forms of the apostolate. They had 9 hospitals and 293 schools of their own and they also worked in another 100 Catholic schools, 90 hospitals, 120 orphanages, homes for the needy and other charitable institutions.

Catholic Action was flourishing and counted 5,000 groups which engaged in the apostolate along with other religious organisations, such as the various Marian societies (especially among the student population), the Company of the Rosary, the Guards of the Sacred Heart (organised in 800 parishes and numbering 170,000 members), the Blessed Sacrament Society, the Third Orders, etc. There were in addition certain organisations that engaged in more specialised forms of activity:

1. Catholic Social Circles.

2. Union of High School past students whose aim was to help young students through the universities;

3. Academy of St. Stephen and Society of St. Thomas Aquinas for Catholic scientists and writers;

4. KALOT and KALASZ: peasant youth movements comprising 700 groups with 100,000 members. On these depended 20 popular schools attended by 35,000 young country men.

5. Young Men's Catholic Association: an organisation for young people engaged in industry and commerce (Kolping) with 11,925 members, 32 houses and 6 other specialised institutes.

6. KIOE (National Association of Catholic Workers);

7. EMERICANA (University Youth Union) with 47 groups, 13 provincial sections and 10,000 members;

8. DL (Dolgozó Lanyok) for young Catholic working girls.

9. Friendly Protection Societies which cared for young girls coming to the cities from the villages;

10. The Association of St. Elizabeth for the care of the sick and the aged.

11. Catholic People's Associations: social benefit societies with 1,000 branches and about 300,000 members.

12. Social Missions and Society of Social Service Sisters. These prepared their members for various kinds of social activity, relief work, moral rehabilitation and various forms of econ- omic, political and cultural activity. When the members were trained they were put at the disposal of Catholic organisations, institutes, dioceses, etc.

This list is far from complete. One can say that there was no branch of social activity, no sphere of life but had its own association, making a definite contribution to the religious, moral and civic progress of the nation. Even this rapid sketch will enable the reader to understand the extent to which the Catholic Church inter-penetrated and leavened the life of the nation until 1945.

Communism undertook to destroy the whole fabric of the Church's religious and social organisation by means of progressive retrenchment of religious liberty and of the essential rights of the human person.

The pages that follow give, without any attempt at analytic commentary, a purely factual account of the sequence of events from the first threats to suppress the Catholic Associations (1945) to the effective denial of the rights and prerogatives of the Catholic Church in Hungary (1951).

The Years 1944 and 1945

The Government of Debrecen began by guaranteeing a large measure of civil liberty to the people of Hungary. Among other things it guaranteed complete respect for religion, the inviolability of private property and the restoration of provincial and municipal autonomies.

This Government propaganda was supported by the Soviet occupation authorities who were quite willing to show their respect for ecclesiastics. The Hungarian Communists on their side declared openly that there was nothing to prevent priests becoming members of the Party, and Communist leaders made a point of appearing in public in the company of the clergy. The official Government photographer was always on the spot to record the friendly relations that existed between Church and State, and such photographs were later used for propaganda purposes. It frequently happened that members of the local Party branch went to the parish priest and offered their services for the reconstruction of the church, school, or even the presbytery. They refused remuneration for their aid and were content with a written expression of thanks for their generosity. Whenever such a testimonial was received it inevitably appeared the following day in a prominent position in the newspapers.

Under the pretext of wishing to help in social welfare activities the Communists attempted to insinuate themselves into the Catholic organisations. Party members got orders even to infiltrate parochial life by getting themselves elected on parish councils.

At the same period there were many other examples of this manner of acting. Under the new agrarian reform—which did irreparable harm to the Church—needy parishes were endowed with allotments of land. Likewise an order of the Provisional Government restored bells that had been taken from some churches during the war. This display of interest by the Communist Party was a source of embarrassment to the hierarchy which would have been glad to escape from the apparent magnanimity of the régime.[4]

It was not long however before the favourable attitude of the Government and the occupation authorities was revealed in its true light as a mere façade thrown up to meet the actual circumstances. This conclusion is not based on the actions of some undisciplined occupation troops,[5] but on a whole series of legislative measures of the gravest import. Soon it was realised that the Communist display of respect for the Catholic Church was part and parcel of the scheme to subject the Church all the more thoroughly to the Communist ideology. It was all the result of deliberate planning and careful timing.[6]

One of the first anti-Christian measures was the expulsion of the Apostolic Nuncio. On 4 April 1945 two Russian officials presented Mgr. *Angelo Rotta*, the Papal representative, with an order to leave the country. The members of the diplomatic corps who had been accredited to the previous Hungarian Government were also ordered to leave. No consideration was shown for the special character of the Nunciature, nor

---

[4] Even in 1947 Mihály Farkas declared: " We, Hungarian Communists, have the greatest respect for the religious sentiments of our people," *Szabad Nép* (Free People), 12 August 1947. And Mátyás Rákosi, Secretary of the Party said, " We want everybody to know that we will continue in the future to be the defenders and supporters of liberty of conscience and of the true interests of the Church," *Szabad Nép*, 31 August 1947.

[5] It is enough to recall here the assassination of the Bishop of Györ, Mgr. Vilmos Apor, on Good Friday 1945, as he was going to the aid of some defenceless women. A Soviet soldier shot him down with a burst of machine-gun fire at the door of his residence. He died the following Easter Monday. The police forbade a solemn funeral as this in Government eyes would have the appearance of a protest against Soviet occupation.

[6] In a *Pastoral Letter* read in all the churches on 1 November 1945 Cardinal Mindszenty condemned in the name of the whole episcopate this bad faith of the adversaries of the Church. See the document in Péterffy, *Cardinal Mindszenty*, Rome, 1949, pp. 32-37.

was there any recognition of Mgr. *Rotta's* work for the Hungarian people. He had stayed on with them and shared their sufferings during the siege of Budapest and by his intervention had saved thousands of Hungarian Jews. One consideration alone swayed the Communists: the Catholic Church had to be cut off from the centre of Christendom, and for that purpose there was urgent need to get rid of the Nuncio.

The second step was to weaken the Church through the new agrarian reform measures.

The Hungarian Communists who were few in number before the arrival of the Russian army tried immediately to win the good graces of the people by various measures of economic and social reform. For this reason they inaugurated a redistribution of land [7] even while one third of Hungarian territory was still in German hands.

The Catholic Church was deprived of the greater part of its estates; the bishoprics were allowed to keep only about 143 acres. By this means the Church was suddenly impoverished with serious consequences for her religious, social and cultural activity. [8]

The third blow aimed at the Church consisted in the restrictions imposed on the press.

Until the arrival of the Soviets the Church, as has been seen, published about 1,500,000 copies per month between newspapers, magazines and periodicals. After the setting up of the Provisional Government a decree was issued (spring 1945) by which special authorisation and an official allocation of paper were necessary in order to continue publication. [9]

In April 1945 the inter-Allied Commission authorised the

---

[7] *Ministerial Decree* n. 600/1945, 15 March 1945.

[8] Agrarian reform was considered even before the arrival of the Soviets. Cardinal Serédi 12 December 1939 in the Upper Chamber declared in the name of the Church that he was in favour of the law then under discussion. The Catholic Church in Hungary gave proof in 1947 of the same spirit of conciliation although the Communist law was a serious blow to it. The Catholic paper, *Magyar Kurir* (Hungarian Courier), 13 February 1948 in a Note, inspired by Cardinal Mindszenty, indicated the position of the Church on the question of agrarian reform. This was in reply to the accusations of being " completely reactionary " contained in an interview given by Rákosi to the *Daily Worker*.

[9] It was at this period that the old Budapest Catholic newspaper, *Nemzeti Mjság*, was suppressed. The request for the publication of a new paper was rejected by the Communist Minister for the Interior.

publication of the weekly *A Sziv* (The Heart), which was a
purely religious paper; the following May they authorised
Uj Ember (New Man), a publication devoted to social and political
problems, which subsequently became the Catholic Action organ.
Finally in 1947 a third publication was permitted, *Vigilia*, a
literary review. *No other Catholic periodical was allowed to appear.*

The real reason behind these restrictions was not the lack of
paper but the determination to limit the extent of Church
influence. For their own publications the Communists had all
the paper they desired and of whatever quality they wanted.[10]
As a result 80% of the press fell into the hands of the Communists who were eager to get control of public opinion. The
few Catholic publications that appeared were forbidden to engage
in political controversy under pain of confiscation.

But control of the press did not satisfy the Soviet-controlled
Provisional Government. Since the stocks of books in libraries
and bookshops might prove an obstacle to the establishment of
Communism, an *Index* was drawn up with the names of books
that were to be withdrawn from circulation. In this way the
Communists succeeded in destroying a large number of Hungarian works of Catholic literature.[11]

From this gradual strangling of the Catholic press it was but
a step to the nationalisation of the twenty or so Catholic *printing
works* (April 1948) in spite of the many protests which the
Catholics addressed to the President of the Republic.[12]

The Church suffered a further blow when the existing
marriage laws were abrogated and new divorce facilities were
introduced by the Provisional Government.[13]

Beginning in July 1945 the Communist Party favoured the

---

[10] In 1948 the Communist editing house *Szikra* (Spark) could boast of having sold
in three years a total of 5,000,000 copies.

[11] *Vilagossag*, a Marxist daily, published on its front page in big print news such as this:
" In the library of the Benedictine Abbey of Pannonhalma two wagons of anti-democratic
books were seized." The truth is that not only books contained in the political " Index "
were removed, but many others, as for example the greater part of the publications
that appeared between 1919 and 1944. The same procedure was employed in the case
of the publishing house, *St. Stephen*, and the printing house, *Korda*. At the same time
Catholic reviews published between the two dates given above were seized, e.g.
Katolikus Szemle, *Elet*, etc.

[12] See the commentary on the Government decree in *Magyar Kurir*, 20 April 1948.

[13] Cf. Sipos, *Enchiridion*, 1954, p. 472.

organisation of debates against religion throughout the country. The former anti-clerical groups were restored to favour. Communist papers and periodicals began to represent the Church as " reactionary " and " the enemy of the people." [14]

Such was the atmosphere immediately preceding the general elections of autumn 1945. It was not without apprehension that the Church faced the possible results, and the Primate, Archbishop *Mindszenty*, felt obliged to address a special Pastoral Letter to the faithful. In it he recalled the " goodwill of the Church towards the rising democracy in Hungary," but went on to denounce the abuses and impositions of the new régime. In particular he said:

" We must regret that the matrimonial bond has been weakened by the Provisional Government which in our opinion had not the right to act thus and in doing so has contravened the will of the people . . . As regards the redistribution of land it has been presented as a means of destroying a certain class among the citizens, and the agrarian law has been put forward as a penal measure. Is such a motive in conformity with justice and the natural law? We do not find fault with the redistribution of land but with the spirit of vengeance shown in this instance. More dreadful still is the number of people who have been sent to prison through provincial tyrants' abuse of power or for paltry reasons. For intervening to prevent the dissolution of a Catholic association in his village a priest, who has been a victim of tuberculosis for many years, has been sentenced to hard labour. Another has been treated in the same way for preaching on the Feast of St. Stephen. The prefects of police have declared that priests who oppose the present rule will be deported to Siberia."

The Primate asked the faithful to vote for those candidates who " could be relied on to fight so that Hungary might be spared suffering, error, and immorality." [15]

---

[14] The (Communist) Hungarian Democratic Youth published 9 June 1945 a *Manifesto* containing violent attacks on St. Stephen, " a criminal blinded by incense . . ., who created the thousand year old system which has sullied our whole history in a loathsome way." Note that St. Stephen was the great organiser of the State and founder of the Catholic Church in Hungary. Attacks on him were but attacks directed against the Church.

[15] Cf. *Magyar Kurir*, 1 December 1945. The *Pastoral* was strongly attacked by the Government and by the Communists (Hungarian Radio), 2 November. Cf. also INS, 3 November.

This Pastoral Letter was read in all the churches of Hungary on 1 November 1945. The elections took place on 4 November and the results seemed to point to a future less full of uncertainties.

The Year 1946—The Suppression of Catholic Associations

Although the Communists were in a minority in the new Government, they relied on the support of the Soviet army of occupation and on their strong position in the Ministry for the Interior [16] to go ahead with measures calculated to reduce the influence wielded by the Church over the young through her schools and over the adult faithful through her various Catholic Action organisations.

From the beginning of 1946 the Catholic schools came under Communist fire. To suppress them from the outset would have been premature and would have proved a very arduous task. At first the Communists were content to diminish the standing of the Catholic schools in the eyes of the people and gradually to prepare the way for State intervention. To this end the Communist press launched a campaign of vilification, accusing the Catholic schools of " neglecting the children of the people and devoting themselves primarily to the children of the rich." [17]

---

[16] In the formation of the new Government the victorious Small-holders' Party reserved to itself the Ministry for the Interior. But Marshal Voroscilov, as President of the Commission of Control set up in Hungary by the victorious nations, by simply manifesting his displeasure succeeded in preventing this and in causing the position to be occupied by a Communist. Cf. Honti, *Le Drame hongrois*, p. 82.

[17] Cardinal Mindszenty answered this accusation in a discourse at Kalocsa, 30 May 1949: " There is a rumour that the Catholic schools, especially those directed by priests, neglect the children of the people and give their main attention to the children of the rich. I heard this accusation time and again at Budapest. Almost as soon as I arrived here I asked for the list of pupils in the Catholic institutions of the district and an indication of the parents' profession in each case. I have been able to gather the following data:

    (a) At the Jesuit College only 40% of the pupils belong to the well-to-do class —and I include minor employees in this; the other 60% are children of small-owners and workmen;

    (b) In the Catholic professional schools the percentages for the same categories are the following respectively: 35% and 65%; in the lyceum and normal schools, 17.5% and 82.5%; in the kindergarten, the respective figures are 233 and 366.

    (c) At the girls' Catholic normal schools the proportion is 104 to 488. All this proves the contrary of what we have been reproached with." Cf. Péterffy, *Le Cardinal Mindszenty*, Rome, 1949, pp. 123-126, and for the accusations against the Catholic schools: *Uj Ember*, 26 May 1946.

It was asserted over and over again that the Catholic schools could not stand comparison with the State schools either for their scholastic equipment or for the quality of their teaching personnel.   This allegation was clearly belied not only by a plebiscite among the parents who declared their preference for the Church schools but even by the reports of Government inspectors.

Finally the Communist press accused Catholic schools of lacking the democratic spirit and of evincing an anti-Russian bias, and therefore of being anti-Communist.   In the spring of 1946 reports were circulated of " plots " being hatched in the schools in Esztergom, Baja, Pécs, Keszthely, Nagykanizsa, Budapest, etc., plots which were supposed to be directed against the Red army. One report went so far as to say that in a certain school bombs had been discovered.[18]

The second Communist objective was to smash the Catholic Action associations.   Communist newspapers began to speak of dumps of arms discovered in the premises of some of the principal Catholic organisations and accused Catholic Action leaders of stocking propaganda leaflets and Fascist newspapers and insignia.

Meanwhile a Russian soldier was killed in Gyöngyös.   The murderer, a youth of 18, declared that he had committed the crime to avenge his mother who had been dishonoured and killed during the first days of the Soviet occupation.   During the trial it was discovered that the young man was a member of one of the Marian Societies and immediately there was talk of a plot. Father *Salesius Kiss*, president of the local Marian Society, was arrested along with about 20 young members whose ages were between 15 and 18.   The Communist press started its usual campaign and in Budapest Communist students were incited to march through the streets calling for the execution of Father *Kiss* and the dissolution of the Catholic associations.

Something similar happened in the summer of 1946 when a Russian officer was found murdered in front of a bar in Budapest.

---

[18] Cardinal Mindszenty reacted against such a monstrous piece of propaganda by a Memorandum to the Government at the beginning of the summer of 1946. He asked for proofs but there was no reply. Cf. Péterffy, *op. cit.* p. 125 for the text of the Memorandum, and pp. 129 *seqq.* for the Cardinal's discourse at Pécs.

The police searched the quarter and a young man who was a member of the KALOT (Catholic Young Peasants' Association) was held reponsible for the murder. Once more the Communist press hinted at a " conspiracy " and demanded the dissolution of KALOT and of all other Catholic associations.

General *Sviridov*, the Russian general commanding the occupation forces, then appealed to the Hungarian Ministry for Justice and complained of a conspiracy against the Russian military forces. He asserted that the Catholic associations were chiefly responsible and in the interests of general security and of democracy he asked the Government to suppress these organisations.

The General's letter to the Ministry for Justice was released in the press and was widely used by Communist propaganda organs. Demonstrations were organised, lists of petitions were circulated among the Communists and other cases were unearthed to lend weight to the accusation against the Catholic associations. In July 1946 the misdeeds of the associations were the dominant theme throughout the Communist press.

In the face of such charges the Catholics had no means of defence. Their two weeklies called in vain for an enquiry into the incidents alleged. Vain too were the appeals made to the Government by the presidents of the accused associations to protect them from attacks in the press and by the Party organisations.

The Government, although it was then under the presidency of a member of the Small-holders' Party, yielded to Communist pressure and issued the decree n. 7330/1946 M.E. which gave the Ministry for the Interior (Communist controlled) full liberty to dissolve or maintain organisations according as it judged opportune. By this decree the Communist Party became the *de facto* arbiter of the fate of the Catholic organisations and their property.[19]

---

[19] The Cardinal Primate in the name of the Hungarian episcopate protested vigorously to the President of the Council against this decree. Among other things his letter of 21 July 1946 stated: " We must solemnly protest against the grave measures, based on mere non-proven suspicions, which have been taken against our associations and against some of their members. We cannot keep silent on this matter any more than on the propagandist publicity." (Cf. Péterffy, *op. cit.* pp. 94-96).

The Ministry for the Interior made liberal use of the powers which it had received. About 4,000 Catholic associations were suppressed, many of their leaders arrested and their property confiscated. The few Catholic associations that were spared had to restrain their activity within ever-narrowing limits.[20]

Having disposed of the militant Catholics in one sweeping movement the Communists thought that the way was now open for a greater freedom of action among the masses.

* * *

To pour oil on troubled waters the Government addressed a proclamation to the clergy (not to the bishops) on 1 August 1946. In it the priests were asked

> " to join in supporting peaceful co-existence between the Hungarian people and the Russian army " and " to endeavour to convince the troublesome elements who opposed the results of the great changes that have come about, and who under pretext of some inevitable defects here and there are trying to arouse sentiments of antipathy against the Russian army and against the democracy . . . " The proclamation continued: " The Government of the Republic declares itself ready *to guarantee the rights of the Church* in future and to aid her in fulfilling her religious mission." [21]

On 10 August the Primate replied to this proclamation in a letter addressed to the President of the Council. After refuting the accusations implicitly contained in the document Cardinal *Mindszenty* gave a summary of all that had been done up to date against the Catholic Church. He recalled especially that

> " (a) Diplomatic relations with the *Holy See* have not yet been renewed, even though we are agreed on the person and on the mode of representation.

> " (b) Attacks on our *schools* and *institutions* are of daily occurrence. The press has refused our request to publish corrections on this subject. We have had to rest content with the confidence in our schools manifested by parents whose attitude in the matter has been a source of real encouragement to us.

---

[20] Cf. *Uj Ember*, 27 July 1947.   [21] Cf. Péterffy, *op. cit.* pp. 42-43.

" (c) Our associations have been attacked in connection with a
crime the details of which remain altogether obscure. Guilt
has been gratuitously imputed to us and in addition I have
never been permitted to see the details of the case. On
this matter we are still negotiating with the President of
the Council, but public opinion is disturbed because the
authorities do not tell the whole truth as I have requested.

" (d) Our processions and other activities of a purely religious
character have been banned, priests have been arrested and
examination of their cases has been excessively delayed.
Catholic daily papers no longer exist, there is no Catholic
Party, etc.

" (e) I have not yet examined the repeated attacks in certain
papers, including that issued by the Red army.

The Cardinal concluded: " So long as we continue to be the
target for accusations that lack all real proof it is impossible for
us to accede to the demand contained in the Government's appeal.
When however reparation has been made for the outrages inflicted
on the Church and when we have received an assurance that we
shall be allowed the free exercise of our religious activity, then
we shall be ready to give our unreserved collaboration."[22]

The Primate's letter had the further aim of rebutting the
Communists' manoeuvre by which they hoped to cause division
among the clergy. It is in this period that we must place the
first attempt to isolate the Primate by spreading the rumour
both orally and in the press that the bishops did not share the
Primate's attitude towards the Government and the Communist
Party.[23] The Communists did not relax their efforts in this
direction until the moment they put the Primate under arrest.

The Year 1947

In the beginning of 1947 Communist propaganda continued
to exploit the supposed pro-régime attitude of one section
of the clergy and the alleged differences among the Hungarian

---

[22] Cf. Péterffy, *op. cit.* pp. 44-47.
[23] The bishops in episcopal conference 6 September 1947 took a firm stand against
these attacks.

bishops.[24] At the same time *the Catholic schools* were the object of an increasing number of vicious attacks.

The Communist offensive of the previous year had consisted in a press campaign which accused the Catholic schools of pedagogical inefficiency, of lack of the democratic spirit and of counter-revolutionary sentiments. They now changed their tactics and, choosing as their instruments some members of the Small-holders' Party, they demanded the abolition of obligatory religious instruction in the State schools.[25]

Introducing a motion in favour of the abolition a speaker dared to say to Parliament on 12 March 1947: " The episcopate has accepted the proposal to make religious instruction *optional*." To contradict this offensive assertion the Cardinal Primate addressed a vigorous protest to the National Assembly.[26] The Government also received protests from Catholic parents.[27]

In the face of such strong opposition the Government plan failed.[28]

But by way of compensation for this failure and to limit still more the influence of the Church on Hungarian national life the Government decreed new restrictions on *the press*, supplementing those of 1945 which were still in existence though they had been introduced as " temporary." Notwithstanding the fact that the Constitution of 1946 guaranteed freedom of the

---

[24] Cf. *Magyar Náp* (Hungarian Sun), 22 January 1947 and *Friss Ujság* (Latest News), 27 April 1947. The bishops had to intervene officially against the press-campaign, 6 September 1947.

[25] Cf. Note in *Hungarian Telegraphic Agency* (MTI), 29 March 1947.

[26] Cf. Péterffy, *op. cit.* pp. 135-136.

[27] In the industrial town of Csepel alone 10,000 workers showed their displeasure at the projected law.

[28] Thus Mátyás Rákosi, Secretary of the Communist Party, in a discourse at Angyalföld —workers' quarter of Budapest—used this project as an arm against the Small-holders' Party: " Free teaching of religion . . . is an essential element of democracy, and as such is naturally approved and supported by the Communist Party . . . We know the religious feelings of the Hungarian people, and we are of opinion that it is necessary to avoid bringing up for discussion questions likely to give rise to new troubles and new disorders . . . Hence I feel bound to state here that the Communist Party disapproves of and condemns the carelessness and lack of responsibility of the Small-holders in making this question a matter for public discussion. According to us it is absolutely necessary to fix the relations between the Church and the Democracy, and may it be done as soon as possible and above all by first holding negotiations and then making an agreement with the directors of the Church . . ." *Szabad Nép*, 10 May 1947.

press the Government in 1947 approved a *Regulation* in virtue
of which:

1. No publication, including books and newspapers whether
   periodical or not, might be printed without the authorisation
   of the Ministry for Information.

2. This authorisation was likewise required for the continued
   appearance of papers that were at present being published.

3. The authorisation of the Ministry for the Interior was required
   for the circulation of every printed work.[29]

Theoretically, Pastoral Letters did not come under these
restrictions on the liberty of the press, but in practice they too
were subject to Government control. The bishops deemed it
their duty to make a protest on this subject, and on 16 June
1947 the Minister for Worship promised Parliament that he
would intervene in the question of Pastoral Letters. Actually
the protest of the episcopate went completely unheeded.[30]

*   *   *

Meanwhile there was no interruption in the Communist
campaign against the *Catholic Associations*.

Early in 1947 *Karitász* was singled out for attack. Through
its contacts with Western charitable associations *Karitász* had
been able to dispense a large volume of relief during the general
distress that followed the war.[31] Among other things it had
set up 126 relief kitchens; and to aid needy children it had
organised summer and winter holiday camps, even outside

---

[29] *Uj Ember* reporting these measures declared that they were contrary to the Constitution. This earned for it confiscation of that issue and suspension for two weeks.

[30] *Parliament Journal*, n. 75,556. Another protest is contained in a Pastoral Letter
11 November 1948. In this the bishops addressed themselves to the faithful as follows:
" Rather (than ask the *previous* consent of the Government) we give up all possibility
of keeping in touch with you through the press. Forced to withdraw to the Catacombs,
we shall speak to you now by the methods used 450 years ago, but never will we betray
the freedom and independence of the Church."

[31] With the approval of Cardinal Mindszenty help flowed to Hungary from the Catholics
of England, Ireland, Belgium and Holland, from the Holy See, Sweden and Denmark,
and above all from the Catholics of the USA thanks to the *National Catholic Welfare
Conference* (NCWC).

Hungary.[32]   In all this activity the Communists saw only the increased prestige that accrued to the Catholic Church. They made their decision—*Karitász* had to be liquidated.

* * *

On 6 May 1947 a Government spokesman attacked *Karitász* on the grounds that it was engaging in illegal political activity under the guise of charity, This theme was taken up in the Communist press which went on to affirm that *Karitász* was pursuing an " actionable " course by distributing foreign relief to persons on " List B " (i.e. those who were regarded as dangerous " anti-democratic " elements).   Accordingly the Government intervened and ordered *Karitász* to hand over 80% of foreign relief to the Ministry for Social Welfare, and to carry on individual distribution of the remaining 20% under the supervision of the local committees for social welfare which were Communist controlled.   As a result of these restrictions the flow of relief from foreign sources was suspended.   In Hungary itself the collection of gifts had become increasingly difficult since all producers had to merge their products in the national pool.   By such methods *Karitász* was forced to cease almost all its activity in the course of a single year (1947). This was precisely what the Communists wanted.

In May 1947 also there came a series of decrees *affecting external religious manifestations*, feast-days, pilgrimages and pro-cessions.[33]

* * *

The elections of 31 August 1947, as has already been stated, consolidated the position of the Communist Party in Hungary. With all political opposition removed the new Communist-

---

[32] To understand the extent of the work accomplished by *Karitász* it is enough to recall that in 1947 the NCWC alone had sent to Hungary help amounting to 2¼ million dollars. Collections were also made in Hungary itself.

[33] Here are some examples: In May 1947 in some places an attempt was made on various pretexts to prevent the Corpus Christi procession . . . The traditional pilgrimage at Budapest, Kakóczy Ut, was forbidden. The men who went in spite of the prohibition were arrested. On other occasions at Budapest, Csepel, Székesfehérvár, etc., the police tried to intimidate the faithful by taking the registration numbers of the cars of those who came to celebrate the religious feasts.

dominated Government was faced with only one obstacle to the introduction of Marxist principles. That obstacle was the Catholic Church which now became the sole repository of the hopes of all those who wished to prevent the sovietisation of their country.

For this reason the Cardinal Primate became the *champion of his nation's hopes and their chief protagonist in the struggle with the Hungarian Communists.*

Following the rise to power of the leftist parties pressure was brought to bear on Catholics to make them join the Communist Party. Speaking in the name of the Hungarian episcopate Cardinal *Mindszenty* voiced a strong protest against this violation of " democratic liberty " in a letter of 24 October 1947, addressed to the President of the Council, *Lajos Dinnyés*. The main points stressed by the Cardinal were: [34]

(a) *Enrolment in the Communist Party is being forced on people* who are not in sympathy with the Party programme, and even on those whose religious convictions are in direct opposition to it. Membership of the Party would exempt (and actually does exempt) from punishment and from the disabilities under " List B " (the " purge " list).

(b) *We also object to the spy system* carried on by the State security police, whose agents interrogate people, including priests, on the strength of fanciful and trumped-up charges. By means of threats these agents try to induce the accused persons to spy on the bishops and on Catholic associations and to report from time to time what they have seen and heard. It has even occurred that when the information furnished was unsatisfactory, the " spies " who already had suffered moral torture were subjected to physical violence as well.

The internal developments in Hungary, inevitably gave rise to grave apprehension as to the future of the Catholic Church.[35] Placing all their confidence in God the bishops held a conference

---

[34] See the complete text in Péterffy, *op. cit.* pp. 101-102. *Uj Ember* was suspended for having published the letter in its issue of 7 November 1947.

[35] Cf. *Magyar Kurir*, 29 November 1947. *Szabad Nép*, 13 December 1947 gives a violent discourse of the Party theorist, Révai, against Cardinal Mindszenty.

on 15 August 1947 at which they placed the whole Hungarian
nation under the protection of the Blessed Virgin and proclaimed
a Marian Year.[36]

The Year 1948

Now firmly established in power the Communists judged that
the right moment had come to withdraw the young from all
Church influence.

The first step was taken in March 1948 when the Minister
for the Interior instructed the director of *Karitász* to terminate
the activities of the organisation (most of which were concerned
with child welfare). The reason alleged by the Minister was that
" the conditions of the people are now so improved that activities
of this kind must be considered superfluous. The State will make
provision for exceptional cases that may arise."

Above all else the Communists were bent on destroying the
great influence which the Church exercised over the young in
her numerous schools. In this domain they planned a major
triumph. The Marxist leaders had already effected many changes
in the social structure of the country and they now considered
themselves in a position to launch a decisive attack on the
Catholic schools. As usual the preparatory stages were entrusted
to the propaganda machine.

In January 1948 the newspapers again began to criticise the
" inferior " conditions in Catholic schools, the pitiful state of
their teaching personnel, the lack of text-books, etc. For all
these deficiencies there could be only one solution—*the nationalisation of all Catholic schools*. During the month of May this was
the main topic in the Government press and in the Party publications.[37] To save appearances and to prove that nationalisation
was the will of the people the Communists decided to employ

---

[36] On the spiritual aims of the *Marian Year* see the Cardinal Primate's discourse at
Esztergom, 15 August 1947. Cf. Péterffy, *op. cit.* pp. 188, 189.

[37] Cf. *Kossuth Népe* (People of Kossuth), 19 May 1948 and *Népszava* (Voice of the
People), 1 May 1948. *Magyar Kurir*, 12 May 1948 reports a discourse of Rákosi against
the Catholic schools. Communist propaganda pretended that the nationalisation of
the schools was merely an administrative matter. Religious instruction would continue
to be obligatory. Once the law was voted this *obligation* was abrogated by Government
decree, 5 September 1949.

" democratic methods." Meetings were held, signatures collected and petitions in favour of nationalisation were presented to teachers, professors, employers, business employees and the labouring class. In case of refusal to sign, employees and labourers were dismissed, students expelled from their schools, professors suspended or transferred.

Cardinal *Mindszenty* took a firm stand against this procedure. Some time previously he had authorised a number of the bishops to approach the vice-Premier *Matayas Rakosi* [38] on the subject of the relations between Church and State. The negotiations achieved nothing when it came to the question of the denominational schools for which the Catholics demanded the maintenance of the *status quo*. Equally fruitless were the requests of the bishops for the re-establishment of the Catholic associations and the printing of one Catholic daily paper.

Since the virulent campaign against the schools continued Cardinal *Mindszenty* addressed a memorandum to *Gyula Ortutay*, Minister for Public Instruction. We shall quote this important document as it constitutes a serious indictment of Communist persecution technique:

" Mr. Minister,

Allow me to draw your attention to certain injustices that have been inflicted on us once again, contrary to both natural and divine law.

" The State continues to attack our schools and teachers and the campaign grows more intense every day. To-day, 29 May, one can say that the violence of the campaign against the Catholic schools and against the Catholic teaching body has reached its maximum.

" Both by artifice and by violence a ceaseless attempt is being made to induce our professors and teachers to support the nationalisation project, contrary to the terms of their oath. And even while extending an invitation to open negotiations, the Minister makes vague propaganda statements accusing our priests and

---

[38] Such was then the function officially carried out by Rákosi. Nobody however was ignorant of his real function as Soviet " proconsul " in Hungary.

teachers of religion of spreading political hatred rather than the Gospel teaching of love.

" I must accept the press accounts of such statements as being true since they have never been denied and the Minister has already spoken in such terms on other occasions.

" Pedagogical meetings are being held one after the other as is shown in the case of Esztergom; one cannot but note their very obvious moral failure. But have the authorities been informed of the precise reactions of public opinion as expressed at these meetings?

" So-called inspectors of studies visit educational institutions and by threats, lies and subterfuge induce and even force our teachers to disobey the legitimate ecclesiastical authorities . . .

" *Nicholas Tóth*, Doctor of Laws, member of the administrative commission of the Association of Catholic Parents, was arrested in his home by security police and was gaoled for having defended the rights of the Church in education.

" Agents, investigating the status of the personnel in business establishments in the capital, inquire about the schools attended by the children of employees and workmen. They also force the teachers to make a stand against the circulars issued by the episcopate . . .

" In a town in the Great Plain the police beat nine students and forced them to make a ' confession.' Using all possible means they extorted from priests a declaration in favour of the parish priest of Bakonykut against the Bishop of Székesfehérvár . . .

" Hatred of the Church is continually stirred up in Parliament, on the radio, in the press and in business offices and industrial concerns. Contrary to the terms of the peace treaty employees are dismissed and students expelled from the popular colleges solely because of their religious convictions.

" The tone of the press grows more vulgar and insulting and in face of this campaign of lies and calumnies the Church finds herself almost in the position of an outlaw. These are ' Kulturkampf ' tactics . . . all this means moral compulsion and permanent privation of religious liberty. To meet this onslaught the Minister and the Government fail to afford us their protection ' ex officio debita.'

" I cannot see how these facts, as well as many others which it would be almost impossible to enumerate, afford a favourable basis for serious peace discussions. [39]

" I remain, Mr. Minister,

Respectfully yours,

JOZSEF MINDSZENTY

Cardinal Primate and Archbishop."

Budapest, 29 May 1948.

A protest against the laicisation of the Catholic schools was also lodged by many citizens who were members of the Association of Catholic Parents.

On Government orders the police intervened to disperse public demonstrations of protest. [40]   Further severe measures were sanctioned and the police were ordered to occupy school buildings. [41]   Meanwhile the Government tried to soothe public

---

[39] Cf. Péterffy, *op. cit.* pp. 159-160—*Magyar Kurir,* 1 June 1948.

[40] At *Sopron* several persons, one a priest, Alajos Németh, were arrested for their opposition to State control of the schools. At Pócspetri during a riot a policeman was killed. This gave the press an excuse to start a new campaign against " ecclesiastical underhand methods." The Minister for Public Instruction, Ortutay, wrote to Cardinal Mindszenty on 4 June asking him to put a stop to the fight against the Hungarian " democracy." In his reply the Cardinal stated that the affirmations of the Minister were " altogether gratuitous." He furthermore denounced those who " act in a manner prejudicial to that peace and quiet which are so ardently desired by bringing up so disquieting a question and keeping it in the public eye by every means."—*Magyar Kurir,* 6 June 1948.

[41] The central director of the Association of Catholic Parents and secretary of the cultural section of Catholic Action, the Calasanctian Father, Edmond Lénard, had printed the list of protests, had added extracts from letters accompanying them and had sent everything to the dioceses for their information. The day after the approval of the nationalisation law the police broke into the premises of the cultural section of Catholic Action and arrested Father Lénard. The charge was based on these words of one of the letters: " We want to have nothing to do with Nazi individuals or with Nazi sympathisers. We do not want an atheistic youth, enemy of the Church, of the clergy and of the Pope; we therefore protest against State monopolisation of the schools "; and also a passage in which was deplored the capture of 26 persons who were afterwards inhumanly treated. Because Father Lénard had printed these two passages, and therefore approved of their contents, according to the officer in charge of the police his attitude was one of sedition and he had instigated revolt against two institutions of the Republic—the State school and the police. Furthermore Father Lénard according to Government authorities had favoured a clandestine press.

indignation by holding the episcopate responsible for the lack of progress in the discussions between Church and State.[42]

At this juncture the Minister for Education introduced the school nationalisation bill for immediate discussion in Parliament. The debate began on 16 June and in spite of the 3,000 telegrams of protest that reached the President's desk, the bill received the combined support of the Communists and Socialists and became law on 18 June by 230 votes to 63.[43] The new law decreed that the State should immediately take over all private schools and their possessions without granting any compensation other than the assurance that the teaching personnel would be maintained by the State. Church control and supervision were restricted to the teaching of religion (Law XXXIII, 1948). *By this law the Church lost 3,163 schools and 177 colleges and other educational establishments (with a total of about 600,000 students).*

The law became effective on 22 June and that same day a solemn protest, drawn up by the Primate in the name of the Hungarian episcopate, was read in all the churches.

* * *

At the very moment of striking this decisive blow at the Catholic Church the Communists were anxious to avoid stirring up too much public feeling. At the congress to unify the Communist and Social Democrat Parties, 12 June 1948, *Mátyás Rákosi* was careful to state:

" Religious instruction must continue to play its part in our schools even after nationalisation in conformity with the religious sentiment of the Hungarian people." [44]

Likewise the Minister for Education and for Worship, *Gyula Ortutay*, stated during the course of the parliamentary debate:

---

[42] See letter of the Minister for Public Instruction and for Worship to Cardinal Mindszenty, 14 June 1948 and the Cardinal's reply on the following day in Péterffy, *op. cit.* pp. 163-167, *Magyar Kurir*, 15 June 1948.
[43] See an account of the parliamentary debate in Péterffy, *op. cit.* pp. 167-171.
[44] Cf. *Szabad Nép*, 13 June 1948.

" I can say here that religious instruction remains obligatory
even in the State schools (and it will be imparted) by the same
teachers using the same texts and for the same number of hours
as before. We therefore guarantee the Church the right to
give religious instruction."

The same assurance was given by the General Secretary of the
Teachers' Union when he addressed Hungarian teachers on 17
June 1948. The events that followed show clearly to what extent
these declarations were sincere.

When the nationalisation law became effective there still
remained two grave problems:

(1) Should the Church accept the offer made by the State
to leave about ten schools, which were of historic importance,
in the hands of Catholics? By accepting the bishops would be
obliged to recognise formally the laicisation of all the other
schools, and that explicitly, for they would have to make a
declaration to the effect that they ratified all that had been done
in the name of the People's Democracy.

(2) The other question was whether religious should agree
to teach as State employees in their former schools, as the law
permitted. If they agreed they equivalently recognised the
validity of the law. There were several reasons why the Government had decided to " permit " the employment of teachers
formerly engaged in Church schools. For one thing there were
not enough lay teachers to replace them; secondly it was good
propaganda, since it helped to diminish the discontent of
Catholic parents; finally the Government hoped to win over
some of these teachers since they would be living in Communist
surroundings and would have to use Marxist text-books.

In a Pastoral Letter of 16 July 1948 the Hungarian episcopate
rejected the proposed compromise " acceptance of which would
have meant the abandonment of all our principles." [45]

* * *

The campaign against the Church was extended also to the
domain of religious broadcasts. From the beginning of 1948
radio sermons had to be submitted to the State censor and were

---

[45] Text in Péterffy, *op. cit.* pp. 176-180.

frequently rejected as being " unsuitable." The radio censorship was not satisfied that the Church should adopt a neutral attitude, but demanded that she lend moral support to the régime and its ideology. The Primate protested against this [46] and eventually the ecclesiastical authorities themselves decided to suspend religious broadcasts. As a propaganda measure the Communists tried to substitute other religious programmes which lacked the authorisation of the Catholic hierarchy.

With regard to the Marian Year which was proclaimed in August 1947 the Communists at first did nothing to prevent the religious ceremonies planned for the occasion and continued to make public declaration of their desire to guarantee religious liberty.[47] But they soon began to use various pretexts to prevent the faithful assembling at places of pilgrimage. Speaking in the name of the episcopate Cardinal *Mindszenty* addressed a letter of protest on this subject to the Minister for Worship (11 May 1948).

There was no change; and in its abuse of power the Government went so far as to forbid the holding of several religious manifestations, notably the traditional procession in honour of St. Stephen, to supplant which the Communists organised their " Bread Festival " (20 August 1948) along the route that had already been chosen for the procession.

Communist tactics to disturb public religious ceremonies embraced a whole series of measures from violent police methods to the lowest forms of subterfuge. In this connection there are two very significant documents: the first is a secret Communist circular and the other is a public declaration by the ecclesiastical authorities which treats of the Government's abuse of power and deals particularly with certain incidents that took place at the celebration of the second centenary of the Benedictine church at Celldömölk (11-12 September 1948).

The Communist circular, issued on 9 September, contains the following directives for elementary teachers and local Party secretaries:

---

[46] Cf. *Magyar Kurir*, 10 February 1948.

[47] More than 4 million of the faithful are estimated to have participated in the Marian Days organised in the Marian Year.

" 1. Discuss the nationalisation question with the peasants in their homes. Remind them that the Government has spent a million florins in the province of Vac to revive the schools. Not a word about the Church or the priests.

" 2. Party secretaries should mingle with groups going in procession or on pilgrimage and should carry on this kind of propaganda among them.

" 3. Keep repeating that the religious might have continued teaching in the schools if *Mindszenty* had not prevented them. Elementary teachers should follow the same line and try to make their propaganda convincing.

" 4. Propagandists and teachers should carry on this type of propaganda at Celldömölk among the men assembled in the hostels. They must try to draw the men away from *Mindszenty*, but while doing this they must give the impression that they too are faithful pilgrims. It must not become evident that they are engaged in propaganda.

" 5. Comrades who are engaged in this work should not wear any Party insignia.

" 6. Party secretaries and elementary teachers should in no case permit their friends to accompany them. During their work they must be penetrated with the spirit of their rôle as political propagandists. Let them watch carefully to find out what is being said, how the people react and whether there are any saboteurs at work. If they find anyone of that kind they must denounce him immediately to the local Party section."

In addition to these directives the Communists also employed the " external pressure " technique, which the Cardinal Primate denounced in a public statement.[48] The following are some revealing extracts:

On 15 August 1947, the Feast of the Patroness of Hungary, the bishops at their meeting in Esztergom proclaimed a Marian Year for Hungarian Catholics. Since then the faithful have flocked in tens and hundreds of thousands to places where Marian days have been arranged.

---

[48] Cf. *Magyar Kurir*, 14 September 1948.

Since spring 1948 the peaceful celebration of Marian devotions has been disturbed by interference which is obviously intentional. Everyone knows that not only have pilgrims been deprived of the most ordinary facilities, but that rights and privileges that are assured to all Hungarian citizens have been withheld from those who were on their way to exercises of prayer and expiation for the betterment of the state of their country.

1. The State railways withheld the usual facilities for people travelling in groups, and in some stations the ticket offices refused to give individual tickets even at full fare.

2. Buses were forbidden to carry pilgrims and this restriction was extended to apply to lorries that were suitable for carrying passengers. Cases were frequent in which trains left with less than the normal number of carriages.

3. Veterinary inspections of horses were arranged to prevent pilgrims who lived at great distances from arriving in time for the celebration of days of Marian devotion.

4. Quarantine regulations were drafted to keep the faithful at home.

5. In places where Marian devotions were being held, the use of loud-speakers was forbidden, or if at first permitted, the apparatus was removed just when it was about to be used.

These measures were but the prelude to a series of official hostile acts aimed at curbing the free exercise of religion. The climax was reached at Zalaegerszeg and especially at Celldömölk.[49]

* * *

During the course of the year 1948 Government policy with regard to the Catholic Church was wholly directed towards isolating Cardinal *Mindszenty* from the clergy and the faithful. Before adopting direct measures against the Primate the Communists tried every means to discredit him in the eyes of the masses. They began by limiting the opportunities for contact between the Cardinal and the faithful not only by making it

---

[49] See complete text in Péterffy, *op. cit.* pp. 193-195.

difficult for them to have access to him directly but also by restricting the relations he might have with his flock through the medium of the clergy.

At this time the bishops could still communicate with their people by means of Pastoral Letters, though their liberty in this respect was very much restricted. But in 1948 the *Press Regulations* were made more severe by the extending of the preventive censorship not only to all printed matter, but to *every kind of written work reproduced in several exemplars* whether by typewriter or poly-copying machine. In this way it was easy for the Government to prevent the publication of Catholic writings which did not meet with their approval. Pastoral Letters and episcopal circulars, though excepted from the provisions of the new regulation, were none the less subject to Government control indirectly, since printers were obliged to submit all texts without exception to the censorship authorities. In addition the Government was able to exercise control through the postal system and could prevent the despatch of anything it desired to suppress. As a result the sole means by which the bishops could express themselves freely was to have their Pastoral Letters polycopied by a reliable person and circulated privately.[50]

* * *

In her struggle with atheistic Communism the Church was fortified by the strong union existing between the clergy and the Cardinal Primate. To weaken and undermine this union the Hungarian Government adopted every possible means and many priests were arrested on various pretexts.[51]

Canon *József Jankovics* of Györ, who was parish priest of the cathedral, was arrested and later sent to a concentration camp for having refused ecclesiastical burial to a Communist who had died without giving any sign of repentance and whose marriage moreover was irregular. Sometimes the State salary was refused,

---

[50] In their collective Letter, 11 November 1948, the Hungarian bishops protested against the restrictions imposed on the liberty of the press.

[51] Cf. *Magyar Kurir*, 24 July 1948. The accusations against the clergy may be read in *Kossuth Népe*, 19 May 1948.

as happened to the Bishop of Györ and to the members of the diocesan chapters of Györ, Sopron, Kalocsa and Esztergom. Many priests were obstructed in the exercise of their ministry when Party officials ordered them not to read Pastoral Letters in public. Every day the newspapers named places where, it was stated, the Pastorals had not been read; this was used as an item of Communist propaganda to insinuate that the " lower clergy " did not share the bishops' point of view. Sometimes the Government sided with priests who had incurred ecclesiastical censure, thereby intending to show its " solidarity " with the persecuted " lower clergy " and thus to incite the faithful to adopt a hostile attitude towards the hierarchy.

The Communists also *tried to cause a rift between the Primate and the Hungarian episcopate.* During the autumn of 1948 the Government sent officials every day to complain to the bishops about the " aggressive policy " of the Cardinal, while at the same time Government information organs published episcopal statements which were certainly either fictitious or grossly misquoted.

The bishops replied with a declaration (3 November 1948) in which they expressed their entire confidence in the Cardinal Primate.

" The Hungarian episcopate is sincerely grateful to your Eminence for your invaluable apostolate. The bishops in union with the faithful express their amazement and sorrow at the unjust attacks to which your Eminence has been systematically subjected— especially quite recently—in the press, over the radio and at various meetings.

" Against these attacks the Hungarian episcopate voices a strong protest based on the right to religious freedom and other civic rights. We assure your Eminence of our confidence and sympathy and we express our solidarity and union with you in your work for the Church, the fatherland and the people of Hungary." [52]

But the attacks continued and on 18 November 1948 Cardinal *Mindszenty* judged it opportune to address a message to his people

[52] See complete text in *La Documentation Catholique*, 1949, col. 224.

in which he denounced the campaign which the Communist régime was waging against him. [53]

> " For several weeks and in different parts of our country a series of identical ' motions ' has been voted against me. I am judged guilty of having stirred up and fostered the counter-revolutionary and anti-democratic spirit during the Marian days organised in various centres in 1947-1948. The failure to reach an agreement between Church and State is deplored and it is requested that my harmful activities should be terminated.
>
> " I do not accuse my accusers. If at times I feel obliged to throw some light on the situation I do so merely as an act of justice towards my nation in view of her bitter sufferings, her tears, her appeals for justice . . . "

Arrest and Condemnation of the Cardinal Primate

At the beginning of 1948 *Mátyás Rákosi* had told Party functionaries during a discourse on the Party programme that the problem of relations between Church and State would be solved during that year in one way or another.

> " The Hungarian democracy," said the Communist leader, " has for three years tried every expedient to incorporate the Catholic Church in its reconstruction schemes but without success . . . Hungarian democracy must change the policy it has adopted so far. From now on we need to show no tolerance but rather unbending severity in our treatment of spies, traitors, traders in illegal exchange, and Fascists, who hide beneath the robes of priests or cardinals. It is incompatible with the stable organisation of our democracy that a Fascist and reactionary assault gang, such as that led by *Mindszenty*, should continue to disturb our reconstructive efforts ! "
>
> " Our evolution," concluded *Rákosi*, " demands that order should reign in this domain too, and if we cannot establish order by means of a reciprocal agreement, very well then ! we shall obey the will of the people and *establish it by the strong arm of the State.*"

The reciprocal " agreement " as understood by the Communists was meant to pave the way for the bolshevisation of the

---

[53] The police confiscated the letter. The complete text of this noble and courageous document may be read in *La Documentation Catholique*, 1949, col. 142-143.

country (the " reconstructive schemes " of *Rákosi*) by requiring the Church to make a declaration of loyalty and by obliging Catholics to profess obedience to the State and the so-called progressive democracy.[54] The heads of Protestantism had already agreed to adopt this attitude. The Catholic bishops however remained firm and constantly brought the discussion back to the necessity of first recognising that the Church possessed certain inalienable rights. A communiqué of the Hungarian episcopate dated 16 December 1948 stated more explicitly:

" It is our constant desire to reach a solution which will be in every way in conformity with the teaching of the Church and with her laws and rights. A proof of this desire can be seen in the negotiations already begun between representatives of the State and of the episcopate to solve a certain number of particular questions. We believe that the official authorities are of the opinion that a definitive settlement of these questions cannot be hoped for in the present circumstances without the intervention of the Holy See." [55]

In the eyes of the Communists the chief obstacle to the integration of the Catholic Church in the Marxist democracy was Cardinal *Mindszenty* and " Mindszentyism " (as *Rákosi* had clearly stated). Under the name " Mindszentyism " Communist propaganda included all the possible and imaginable evils that could affect the democracy; it was synonymous with stubbornness, ignorance, sabotage and backwardness.

It was decided to liquidate the Cardinal. At the beginning of the year *Rákosi* had referred to the " desire of the people." To implement this " desire " the Communists organised a series of public demonstrations in which students, workers and employees (intimidated by threats of dismissal) paraded before office buildings, Government departments and episcopal resid-

---

[54] The vice-President of the Council, Rákosi, deliberately ignoring the Primate, requested this declaration from Mgr. Julius Czapik, Archbishop of Eger, in a letter dated 7 May 1948. In the letter he reminded the archbishop that the Protestants had acceded to this request.
[55] Complete text in *La Documentation Catholique*, 1949, col. 150.

ences, and in the name of liberty demanded the removal of that
" reactionary," *Mindszenty*. The press took up the theme and
carried on a campaign of slander and contempt to discredit the
name of the Cardinal in the eyes of the people.[56]

On 19 November the police arrested the Cardinal's secretary,
Father *Andrew Zakar*, and on the 23rd they seized two other
priests attached to the Curia of Esztergom, Fathers *Imre Bóka*
and *János Fábián*. These arrests were devised to deprive the
Cardinal of some of his close collaborators.

On 20 December Cardinal *Mindszenty* addressed a letter to the
clergy in which he recommended constancy in the Faith. In a
message of the same date to his colleagues in the episcopate he
made the following statement:

> " Since I have not taken part in any plot I shall never resign.
> I shall not speak. If after this you hear that I have confessed this
> or that, or that I have resigned my office (even though this should
> be authenticated by my signature), you should realise that such
> a declaration is but the consequence of human frailty . . .
> Likewise I declare null and void any confession which may be
> attributed to me from this day forth . . . "

On 26 December 1948 Cardinal *Mindszenty* was arrested.
His trial began on 3 February 1949 and ended in the condemnation of the Cardinal to life imprisonment on charges of treason,
espionage, plotting against the safety of the State and illicit
trading in exchange.

For the Communists it was not only the Cardinal who was
no trial but the whole Christian civilisation and the values which
he had defended.

During the trial Cardinal *Mindszenty* became " his own
accuser." [57] The most horrible and sinister aspect of the trial
was that in 40 days the Communists succeeded in reducing the
" iron Cardinal " to a moral wreck.

---

[56] As an example see in *Szabad Nép*, 23 October 1948, the article, *The Preacher of Death*.

[57] Already during the trial the Cardinal had made his own " self-criticism." Cf.
The Yellow Book (Documents on the Mindszenty Affair), issued by the Hungarian Government,
Budapest, January 1949.

The Year 1949

During the period between the arrest and the condemnation of Cardinal *Mindszenty* the Government endeavoured to allay the disquiet caused by the imprisonment of the highest religious authority in the country. The press however did not cease to publish the vilest and at times contradictory accusations against the Cardinal.[58] Meanwhile Communist cells were busy in various meetings of workmen and peasants, in schools, factories, and villages, where they succeeded in getting motions passed calling for "an exemplary punishment," "the immediate departure of *Mindszenty*" and the "liquidation of the reactionary clergy." Representing these "decisions" as the will of "all Hungarians who desire peace" the Communists forwarded them to the Government; in reply *Dobi*, the President of the Council, stated that he "would respect the will of the people."

To prevent the clergy and the faithful from making a stand in favour of the Cardinal the Government continued to arrest those priests who because of their zeal were likely to offer resistance. *Many of these priests vanished without leaving a trace.*[59]

Immediately after the arrest of the Cardinal (end of December 1948) four bishops [60] were summoned to appear at the Ministry for the Interior in Budapest and were accused of being directly responsible for the way in which the situation had developed. The Government judged that this threat would be adequate to dissuade the bishops from engaging in active resistance.

In addition to this "truncheon" policy, the Government also made use of the "carrot" policy. Before the arrest of the Cardinal they had threatened to suppress the subsidies paid to the clergy;

---

[58] Cf. *La Documentation Catholique*, 1949, col. 137-138 and 214-215. Publications not adapting themselves to this line had to suffer the consequences. Thus *Világ* was suspended for a week because it gave news of the Cardinal's arrest "in a way open to false interpretation" and because it failed to insert a later Government statement on the matter.

[59] Cf. *La Documentation Catholique*, 1949, col. 160.

[60] Mgr. József Grösz, Archbishop of Kalocsa, Mgr. Dudás (Oriental Rite), Bishop of Hajdudorog, Mgr. Pétery, Bishop of Vác, and Mgr. Shvoy, Bishop of Székesfehérvár. Later a trustworthy person testified that they were told also that it would be better for them to resign as they had been compromised by a statement of the Cardinal and by the discovery in his palace of documents implicating them in illegal financial operations. The four bishops refused to resign. Cf. *La Documentation Catholique*, 1949, col. 135.

immediately after his arrest (28 December 1948) the Government sent for Mgr. *Julius Czapik*, Archbishop of Eger, to tell him that it was prepared to renew the subsidy agreement for another year after its expiration in 1948. By the terms of the agreement the clergy received a certain sum in compensation for the confiscation of Church property. Further Mgr. *Béla Witz*, Vicar General for Budapest,[61] was invited to take part in the Government reception on New Year's Day 1949. The Communist press described him as " the Cardinal's substitute and the representative of the Hungarian Catholics," and credited him with certain statements about the " cordial relations " that existed between Hungarian Catholics and the Communist Government.[62]

Negotiations between the episcopate and the Government recommenced on 4 January 1949 but no progress could be made and they ceased on 12 January. The Government seized the occasion to issue an official communiqué according to which President *Dobi* had received the bishops " with all the honours due to such an occasion." [63]

Likewise the Hungarian Government hoped to give clear proof of its " good dispositions " towards the Catholic Church by proposing to the Holy See that diplomatic relations between Hungary and the Vatican be renewed. By choosing this moment the Communists wished to create the impression that the Cardinal Primate alone was responsible for the fact that relations with the Holy See had not been re-established. Even though the Government had no illusions as to the outcome of such a proposal it could give it a propaganda value and use it as a weapon for " the moral disarmament " of the Catholics.[64]

---

[61] One of the vicars general of Esztergom resides traditionally at Budapest.

[62] Cf. *La Documentation Catholique*, 1949, col. 135 and 215-216.

[63] Cf. *La Documentation Catholique*, 1949, col. 216 and 1951, col. 91.

[64] Vatican Radio commented, 3 January 1949, on this Government step: " It is not clear how the desire of reaching agreement with the Holy See can be reconciled with the treatment inflicted on an archbishop—Primate and Cardinal—a treatment that is an offence against the Holy See. Furthermore it is known that the Holy See wishes to see the rights of the Church and of conscience safeguarded everywhere; it is for that reason that it demands not only freedom of religion but also freedom of preaching and propaganda and freedom for all Catholic institutions especially for the Christian education of youth . . . " Cf. *La Documentation Catholique*, 1949, col. 142.

The apparent truce, due in great part to the wave of indignation roused by the arrest of Cardinal *Mindszenty*, was nothing more than a change of tactics. Shortly afterwards the Communist Government set about organising a " fifth column " within the Catholic Church in Hungary. Scarcely a month after the condemnation of the Cardinal (March 1949) a *Peace Congress* was held in Budapest to which a number of priests was invited. The Communists had the effrontery to call these priest-delegates " representatives of the Church." [65]

The following month the Government selected Father *Ferenc Varga* whom it regarded as a Communist sympathiser for the task of organising the *Catholic Priests' Peace Movement* and of editing a paper called *A Kereszt* (The Cross) which was to be the official organ of the movement. [66]

Foreseeing the consequences of such a task and being unable to find any other way out of the moral dilemma in which he was placed Father *Varga* decided to flee the country. [67]

Nothing discouraged by this first failure the Communists turned to Canon *Miklós Beresztóczy* whom they had " taken in hand " and " convinced " during a period of imprisonment. Even though the inauguration of the " Peace Movement " did not take place till later the Communist leaders at this period began to do their utmost to attract as many priests as they could and if possible to win over some members of the episcopate. [68] They used the same methods as had proved effective in persuading the laity to join the Communist Party. Whoever refused to join was stigmatised as an enemy of the people and a war-monger. The Hungarian episcopate, constantly accused of lacking pliability, decided to give the lie to their persecutors. Since

---

[65] Of the clergy in favour of close co-operation with the Communists the ex-parish priest, István Bálogh, was specially active. He had already been suspended by his bishop, Mgr. Hamvas of Csanád. Cf. *La Documentation Catholique*, 1949, col. 146.

[66] The paper began publication 1 November 1950.

[67] The attempt failed and Varga, wounded at the frontier, was captured by the police and died shortly afterwards in Communist hands.

[68] As for the methods used by the Communists to obtain members for the movement, it will be enough to recall what the Minister for Popular Culture, Révai, wrote in *Szabad Nép*, 6 June 1953: " We cannot give material help to clerical reaction . . . only those who are loyal to the Workers' Fatherland can receive it. We are prepared to recompense those with a salary."

16

the Communists had asked the clergy to support the *Stockholm Peace Appeal* the bishops in a letter addressed 14 June 1949 to the Hungarian Committee at the World Peace Congress recalled, not only on their own behalf " but also on behalf of the secular clergy and the religious orders, that nothing is more natural for a Christian than to co-operate at all times for the establishment of a just peace among nations. Consequently the Hungarian bishops find no difficulty in subscribing to the desire for such a peace." After making this declaration the bishops were not prepared to endorse any other peace appeal.

The bishops had spoken of a noble concept of peace which was altogether different from what the Communists envisaged. *Their* peace was based on their own *political ideology*. No wonder then that they attacked the " ambiguity and mental reserves contained in the declaration of the hierarchy." They went further and accused the bishops of having " deepened the chasm between Church and State and especially between the clergy and the mass of believers." By such allegations the Communists were preparing the way for a new phase in the anti-Church campaign.

* * *

The Marxist régime was further consolidated by the results of the elections of 31 May 1949.[69]

Now that they had a firm grip on the reins of Government, and thinking that they had broken the back of the Catholic resistance, the Communists decided to introduce a new Constitution which would transform the country into a " proletarian state."

Although the Communists had collaborated in drafting the 1946 Constitution, it had been the creation of the Small-holders' Party and it enshrined both the democratic ideals of that period and some echo of the Atlantic Charter. Since that date with the growing influence of the Communist Party the official Government policy had travelled a great distance from its legal

---

[69] This time only the Communist Party went to the polls. The other parties had in the meantime been dissolved or forced to dissolve themselves or incorporated into the " National Front " (Communist).

basis. It was time to put an end to this disharmony. The new Constitution promulgated on 20 August 1949 modified the relations between Church and State.[70] Whereas the previous Constitution had ratified collaboration between Church and State their total separation was now proclaimed.

Articles 54 and 55 of the new Constitution read:

ART. 54 § 1.—" The Hungarian People's Republic guarantees its citizens liberty of conscience and the right to the free exercise of religion.

§ 2.—" In the interests of liberty of conscience the Hungarian People's Republic separates Church and State.

ART. 55.—" The Hungarian People's Republic *in conformity with the interests of the workers* guarantees freedom of speech, freedom of the press, and freedom of assembly."

The Hungarian Republic recognised freedom of religious practice but professed the principle of complete separation between Church and State. This did not mean that the Church became independent of the State but merely that the State no longer gave a solemn guarantee to protect the rights of the Church. By invoking the interests of the working classes or a similar motive, the State could act more freely with regard to the Church and could tamper with Church government without having to fear a storm of protest.

It was not long before the Church felt the consequences of the new Constitution. On 3 September 1949 the President of the Council of the Hungarian Republic issued a *decree having the force of law* to the following effect:

§ 1.—" In conformity with the principle of separation of Church and State and with the text of art. 54 of the Constitution of the Hungarian People's Republic, *religious instruction is not obligatory in schools.*

§ 2.—" The present decree, having the validity of law, becomes effective the day of its publication. The Minister for Public Instruction and for Worship is charged with its execution." [71]

---

[70] Cf. *Constitution of the Hungarian People's Republic*, Athenaeum Printing Press, Budapest, 1953.

[71] Cf. Ordinance 1101/1—1949/184 in the official newspaper *Magyar Közlöny*, 6 September 1949.

On the same day the responsible Minister, *Gyula Ortutay*, published order n. 5, in execution of the presidential decree:

§ 1.—" Beginning with the scholastic year 1949-1950 religious instruction is not compulsory.

§ 2.—" Parents who wish to have religious instruction given to their children must make known their intention to the school either orally or in writing before 15 September at the latest.

§ 3.—" The Minister for Public Instruction and for Worship will provide for the expenses of religious instruction.

§ 4.—" The present order becomes effective the day of its publication." [72]

---

[72] Cf. *Magyar Közlöny*, Hungarian Official Journal, 6 September 1949 and *Uj Ember*, 11 September 1949. In theory the decree allowed parents to enrol their children for the course of religious instruction; in practice it was a serious blow to all religious teaching. The local authorities and the school authorities by multiplying the formalities needed for enrolling made the task of the parents nearly impossible. Party members could not enrol their children at all. Religious instruction was to be given after all other classes and the teacher was not to be present until the exact hour fixed for the course. The religious instruction teacher was also limited to the simple exposition of the truths of religion without any mention of errors; he was not to hold meetings even in the Church with the pupils outside the hour of religious instruction. There was to be no punishment for non-attendance at the classes (cf. order 1101/11/IV. K/1950, 15 September 1950, signed by the sub-secretary, Magda Jóburu). Thus religious instruction was relegated to a very secondary and limited place in the curriculum and was in no way obligatory. In fact in this way it was hoped to destroy the influence of religion in public life.

In regard to this matter *La Civiltà Cattolica* (1954, IV, 270-284) gave the particulars which are here set out because they were common also to other countries under Marxist rule where the teaching of religion is " optional " in State schools. It is quite true that in the Hungarian schools, in virtue of the decree of 1950 (what is here in question is the above mentioned ordinance signed by Jóburu), religious teaching may still be given to those pupils whose parents ask for it. But several obstacles, created on purpose, aim at reducing either the number of students in such classes or the efficiency of the teaching. For instance according to article 4 of the decree the bishop presents the catechist to the Communal Committee to which belongs the right of nominating him. If a controversy crops up about his aptitude it is the Ministry, not the bishop, who decides the question. The Communists demand the presence of *both* parents for the child's enrolment even if the father must absent himself from work. On some occasions in the absence of the person competent to receive the request the parents are just laughed at. According to article 5 of the decree the priest giving religious instruction cannot remain in the school beyond the time assigned for the lesson, nor may he remain in any building belonging to the school. Another priest may not supply for him. Article 6 forbids every form of religious instruction to young people outside the schools, and this includes churches. The children may be assembled in the churches only for Confession, First Holy Communion and Confirmation. Finally the period permitted for such instruction is restricted to the limits defined by the State authorities; for First Communion, instruction is limited to two hours weekly for two months; for Confirmation to one hour. The Communal Committee must be informed in writing of the time and place of these instructions, of the name of the catechist, of the date of First Communion and of Confirmation. All this in order to guarantee " a well ordered development."

The Year 1950 ; the "Modus Vivendi"

The respite accorded the Church after the arrest of Cardinal *Mindszenty* was not of long duration. Once it was satisfied that the wave of indignation had subsided the Government launched a new assault during which the Hungarian Communists based their activity on what was being done in other Communist-dominated countries. It was no longer the Hungarian Government that dictated the tone of the anti-Church campaign; it preferred to leave the initiative to other Iron Curtain countries and to follow their lead, hoping by this means to attract less attention.

The campaign against the Catholic Church was waged on two fronts—the " peace " movement and the religious orders. For the Communists the " peace " question was closely linked with the signing of the *Stockholm Peace Appeal* and the *Peace Movement* recently organised among the clergy. On the other hand the Government had decided on a war of extermination against the religious who formed the backbone of the teaching personnel in the Catholic schools; in this they were merely advancing another step in their attack on the denominational schools and were endeavouring to rob the Church of the inestimable support of the religious orders. On these two fronts, either separately or simultaneously, the Communists kept up a relentless attack during the year 1950. Their tactics were carefully co-ordinated.[73]

The bishops were approached *individually*. At these meetings they were blamed for the failure to reach an agreement between Church and State—more especially after 14 April 1950 when the Catholic Church in Poland reached a *modus vivendi* with the Polish Government; the precarious situation of the clergy was referred to; the Protestants were held up as an example for the way in which they had submitted to the wishes of the Government.[74] Almost every day the clergy were pressed to

---

[73] Cf. Article in *Szabad Nép*, 14 May 1950: *Sworn enemies of our peace*, and that of 24 May: *Two Great Beasts of War; the Priest and the Kulak*. Already a Minister had denounced " the alliance between the Vatican and imperialism." (*Szabad Nép*, 2 April 1950).

[74] On the attitude of the Protestants in Hungary, see Ian Kanti, *La Hongrie douloureuse*, in *La Revue de l'Université Laval*, V, pp. 481-493.

make declarations of loyalty and to pledge themselves to support the Communist " peace " ideal. Priests found themselves faced with one case of conscience after another. In a word *everything possible was done to keep both bishops and clergy in a state of tension, living as they were in an atmosphere of ridicule, intimidation, terror and duplicity.*[75]

To help priests whom the Communists were forcing to support the Peace Movement the bishops published a new *Declaration* (28 April 1950) in which they explained the sense in which they understood the word " peace " and expressed their desire for a just peace. This declaration did not satisfy the Communists who wanted the bishops to declare themselves in favour of peace at it was understood by the Government. By failing to align themselves with the Government the bishops were still considered to be the " enemies of the people."

The situation of the religious orders was growing constantly worse.[76] After a conference on the problem the superiors of the various orders summarised their grievances in a *Memorandum* which they addressed to the Government on 15 April 1950.[77]

The bishops too foreseeing the coming storm had raised their voice on behalf of the religious in a Pastoral Letter of 25 May

---

[75] *La Documentation Catholique*, 1951, col. 99.

[76] The Calvary of the religious began with the struggle against denominational schools. The police began to discover plot after plot against the Democratic State in the colleges conducted by religious. Some religious (Edmond Lénard, Calasanctian; Salésius Kiss, Franciscan; Placid Olofson, Benedictine) were arrested and deported for this reason. After the nationalisation of the schools religious who had refused to teach in Communist schools gave their attention to the ministry and to charitable works. The political agents of the Government considered this as " subversive activity." The police got orders to prevent such priests from exercising their ministry in the country districts. At the beginning of 1950 the position had become very serious.

[77] Among other things the Memorandum says: " Very often we are forced to live as in a ghetto in our houses built at the cost of so much sacrifice and abnegation or we are forced to abandon them altogether. On the pretext of the law of nationalisation of schools, though very much contrary to the terms of that law, religious houses which never belonged to the schools or colleges are taken from us as are also the grounds, gardens, small orchards, movable goods and objects for domestic use. Practically everywhere we are deprived of our chapels, retreat houses, cultural institutes and printing presses. Our missions, retreats and pilgrimages are forbidden. At every instant we are prevented from going to the faithful for purely pastoral purposes, or from visiting the sick. Our seminaries and novitiates are confiscated. Our freedom of movement is restricted on unfounded suspicions (e.g. of making Church collections). We are forbidden to do as other citizens do. Sisters nursing in the hospitals are dismissed in great numbers contrary to the wishes of the doctors and the patients. The chance of employment and of a special reward is held out to anyone who would leave the order."

1950 in which they stated that the religious " are defenceless and find themselves at the mercy of their enemies without any possible means of assistance. The measures directed against them, far from ceasing, are becoming more numerous and more harrassing." [78]

The Hungarian Government had already decided on the *plan of action it was to adopt towards the religious.*[79]

During the night of 9-10 June the police notified 320 male religious and between 600 and 700 nuns in southern Hungary of the following expulsion order:

General Administrative Section IV
MINISTRY FOR THE INTERIOR
Secret Order

To.............................. religious, residing at .... By authority of decree 8130/1948 IV 6 B.M. r. § 2, I order your expulsion. You must immediately leave your place of residence and go to a place of detention. Reason: your continued residence in your present domicile is a danger to public order and security.

This order is without appeal. It must be immediately complied with by virtue of law 1929, § 56.

JOZSEF VERES,
Director General of the Department.

Budapest, 7 June 1950.

P.S. It is forbidden to leave the place of detention without special permission; any contravention of this order will entail administrative action. [80]

---

[78] Cf. *Magyar Kurir*, 25 May 1950.

[79] József Révai, Minister for Popular Culture, in a discussion in June 1950 gave expression to the Communist Leaders' view of the religious life: " A people's democracy has no need of religious for they not only do not fulfil their vocation but actually sabotage the aims of democracy. They must therefore be put as soon as possible in a position where they will be unable to harm the interests of the People's Democracy . . . " *Szabad Nép*, 6 June 1950.

[80] This order was carried out most rigorously. The police gave the religious half an hour to get ready and allowed them to take only baggage not exceeding 5 kilograms. All writings found in their houses were removed. To justify this action in the eyes of the people the police stated that they had found radio-transmission apparatus, writings exciting to revolution and sabotage, and certain spy material.

This wave of deportations caused grave anxiety to the ecclesiastical authorities. The superiors of the religious orders and congregations held a meeting on 17 June 1950 and Mgr. *József Grösz*, Archbishop of Kalocsa, convoked an episcopal conference for the 20th. Nevertheless the Government, convinced that it had now found the means of exercising the maximum pressure on the ecclesiastical authorities, proceeded to *deport an additional 1,500 to 2,000 religious* between 18-19 June, just one day before the opening of the episcopal conference. This time the reason given was not " continued residence . . . a danger to public order and security " but " transfer . . . in the public interest."

The position of the bishops in face of this new development was very difficult. By adopting an attitude of intransigence they might only aggravate the evil. The " Mindszenty complaint " which had been referred to the International Court of Justice at the Hague and to the United Nations Organisation was of no consequence to the Budapest Government. In this painful crisis the bishops needed the advice and the moral support of the Holy Father but the Hungarian Government had made it impossible for them to have recourse to the Holy See.[81]

In these circumstances the bishops asked for the re-opening of *discussions with the Government*, hoping that in the atmosphere of the conference chamber they might succeed in finding some solution. The discussions began on 28 June 1950.

It was the intention of the Government to draw the maximum profit from these meetings with the bishops. Instead of a free exchange of views the discussions were overshadowed by the threat of violence. To intimidate the episcopal delegation the Government ordered *the third series of deportations* between 10 and 12 July 1950.

While the discussions were still going on the Government adopted another expedient to " convince " the delegates. On 1 August 1950 the *Catholic Priests' Peace Movement* was officially inaugurated in Budapest. To ensure the greatest possible success for the new movement the Communists mobilised all the

---

[81] Cf. *La Liberté*, Fribourg (Switzerland), 11 October 1950.

resources of the Party. The inaugural session was attended by
150 priests who had been brought from all parts of the country
at Government expense.[82]

Once the movement was launched the Government was in
a position to inform the hierarchy that if the episcopal delegation
failed to come to terms with the Government, it was ready
to open negotiations with the priests who had joined the movement. Under this threat and with the hope that they might
yet save some of the religious the bishops finally decided to sign
an " agreement " which comprised two sections, one binding
the episcopate and the other the Government (30 August 1950).
The text of the " agreement " is as follows:

The Government of the Hungarian People's Republic and the
Hungarian Catholic episcopate, inspired by the desire to ensure
the peaceful co-existence of the State and the Catholic Church
and thus to favour the work of national reconstruction and
Hungarian unity and the peaceful development of the country,
have entered into negotiations and have concluded the following
agreement:

I

1. The episcopate recognises and in conformity with its civic
obligations supports the established order and constitution of the
Hungarian People's Republic. The bishops declare that according
to the laws of the Church they will deal severely with ecclesiastics
who act contrary to the legal orders and the reconstructive schemes
of the Hungarian People's Republic.

2. The episcopate strongly condemns all subversive activity of
whatever origin directed against public and social order within
the Hungarian People's Republic. The bishops declare that they
will not permit the religious sentiments of the faithful and the
Church to be used for political ends in opposition to the State.

---

[82] József Darvas, Minister for Worship, represented the Government. The movement
declared that priests were free and independent of their bishops and of the Holy See
as regards politics. In accordance with this point of view the movement in its first
Manifesto criticised bitterly the Hungarian bishops for their " political attitude," and
demanded that there be concluded at once agreements with the Hungarian State on all
outstanding religious questions. The Government on its side declared that the State
in the spirit of the Constitution would defend " the political liberty " of these priests
should the bishops decide to employ canonical sanctions against them. Cf. *Szabad Nép*,
27 September 1950.

3. The episcopate invites Catholics as patriotic citizens to co-operate fully in the great work undertaken by the Hungarian people under the direction of the Government of the People's Republic to realise the Five Year Plan, to raise the standard of living and to ensure social justice. The bishops ask parish priests especially not to oppose the co-operative agricultural movement which is a voluntary movement based on the moral principle of human solidarity.

4. The bishops support the Peace Movement. They approve the efforts of the Hungarian people and the Government of the Hungarian People's Republic to preserve peace, and they condemn all incitement to war. The bishops are opposed to the use of the atomic bomb and consider the first Government to use the atomic bomb as guilty of a crime against humanity.

II

1. The Government of the Hungarian People's Republic in conformity with the constitution guarantees Catholics freedom of worship and guarantees the Catholic Church freedom in the discharge of its duties.

2. The Government of the Hungarian People's Republic permits the restitution of eight schools (6 boys' schools and 2 girls' schools) to the Catholic Church and also agrees that a sufficient number of religious orders of men and women be maintained to ensure instruction in the denominational schools.[83]

3. The Government of the Hungarian People's Republic, in the spirit of the agreements signed with other denominations, will provide for the needs of the Catholic Church by means of subsidies over a period of eighteen years, that is until the Catholic Church is in a position to provide for its own needs. The amounts allocated to the Catholic Church will follow a descending scale and will be successively decreased at the end of every three or five year period. The Government of the Hungarian People's Republic intends by these subsidies to ensure that the clergy engaged in pastoral activity shall have the necessary minimum subsistence.

---

[83] By " denominational schools " is to be understood the eight schools mentioned above.

A commission, composed of an equal number of delegates from the Government of the Hungarian People's Republic and from the episcopate, will supervise the execution of the present agreement.

Budapest, 30 August 1950.

For the Hungarian Catholic episcopate:
Signed:

JOZSEF GRÖSZ,
Archbishop of Kalocsa.

For the Council of Ministers of the Hungarian People's Republic:
Signed:

JOZSEF DARVAS,
Minister for Worship and for Education. [84]

The obligations contracted by the two parties to this " agreement " (which might perhaps be better called a *modus vivendi*) were not of the same nature.

To silence accusations of sabotage and hostility to the order established by the Communists the bishops had engaged themselves to keep the clergy on the path of " loyalty " to the Hungarian People's Republic. Since the Government was not satisfied that the Church should follow a merely neutral course but required active participation in its schemes, the episcopate recommended the faithful to " co-operate fully " in the Five Year Plan and other Government schemes. Finally since Hungarian Catholics were required to take a stand with regard to international problems the bishops agreed to support the Peace Movement and to decry war and the use of atomic weapons. In return for such " concessions " the Government offered the Church freedom of worship and of " action ", in other words freedom to administer the sacraments and to preach, without making for example any reference to freedom of religious

---

[84] Cf. *La Documentation Catholique*, 1951, col. 92-93. The *Clergy Review*, October 1950, pp. 17-18: *Bulletin hongrois*, Budapest, 1 September 1950.

instruction in the schools. Eight colleges were restored to the
Catholics but the other confiscated schools remained in the
hands of the State.[85]

The Government promised to subsidise the Church for a
period of eighteen years—not quite one generation. It is to
be noted also that the present *modus vivendi* differs from the
Polish " agreement " in that there is no mention of Government
guarantees concerning the authority of the Holy See in the
religious domain.[86]   The aim of the Hungarian Communists
apparently was to separate the Catholics as much as possible from
the centre of their religion.[87]

Any hope that the Government would show itself more understanding as a result of the " agreement " was quickly dispelled.
The Government wished simply to make use of the "agreement "
to pursue its own " reforms " unimpeded.[88]   The religious orders
whose plight had constituted the focal point in the discussions
were shown no mercy. A decree of the Presidential Council of
the Hungarian People's Republic (n. 14, 1 September 1950)
ordered *the dissolution of 53 religious orders and congregations*.[89]

---

[85] From this point of view the Polish Agreement had obtained better conditions for it
guaranteed the free functioning of the Catholic university of Lublin.

[86] Cf. *La Documentation Catholique*, 1951, col. 95-96.

[87] Of its nature an Agreement between the Church and State can be made only by the
Holy See. The Hungarian bishops understood this clearly as is evidenced by the letter
of Mgr. Jozsef Grösz, president of the ecclesiastical delegation, to the Minister for
Worship: " The conference of bishops insists that this Agreement in no way prejudices
the rights of the Holy See in regulating relations between Church and State." They
only wanted to save, at a moment of calamity and isolation, what they deemed could
be saved. " The episcopal conference has taken this decision (i.e. to sign the Agreement)
in the hope that the difficulties existing between Church and State may be solved in
a spirit of reciprocal understanding, and that thus the religious may be treated in a
humane way especially in the matter of their appointment to the pastoral ministry."
Cf. *La Documentation Catholique*, 1951, col. 94. The bishops were not allowed to make
any public declaration of their reasons for signing.

[88] *Szabad Nép*, 4 September 1950, in an editorial headed, *After the Agreement*, wrote:
" The Government and our Party, guide of the Hungarian People's Democracy, will
do all in their power to have the letter and the spirit of the agreement put into practice."
The same paper on the following day in an article entitled, *Hollywood and Pius XII*, made
a scornful attack on the Holy Father.

[89] The decree appeared in *Magyar Közlöny* (Official Gazette), 7 September: " Some
days after the signing of the Agreement the Government issued the following legal decree
on the question of the religious orders:

1. " With the coming into force of this present decree the ' permit to function '

Only a few orders were spared so that they could provide the necessary personnel for the eight Catholic schools which were permitted to reopen.[90] *All the other religious were obliged to leave their houses within three months, lay aside the religious habit and enter into civilian employment.* An exception was made for 400 religious priests who were transferred to parochial duties but were not allowed to wear the habit of their orders. *All the monasteries and their property were confiscated.* The Communists could now boast of another victory over the Catholic Church.

The action of the Government caused stupefaction and profound sadness in the ranks of Catholics. On 10 September the Hungarian bishops issued a Pastoral Letter (censored in several places) protesting against the suppression of the religious orders but all to no avail.[91] Previous requests that the Government should permit the disbanded religious to leave the country were equally unsuccessful. *Rákosi* explained that the Government could not allow the religious to live in exile where they would suffer " profound nostalgic yearnings for the fatherland " !

On the other hand the Government made use of the " agreement " to ask the bishops to exhort the faithful to exercise the

---

of the teaching religious orders ceases to be valid in the territory of the Hungarian People's Republic. This enactment does not affect a certain number of orders of men and women needed to teach in the Catholic denominational schools.

2. " The religious orders whose ' permit ' expires according to section 1 must cease their activity in the territory of the Hungarian People's Republic as soon as this decree comes into force.

3. " In agreement with the Minister for Worship and Public Instruction the Minister for the Interior will draw up a list of religious orders which may continue their activity according to section 1.

4. " The present decree comes into force on the day of its promulgation. In agreement with the Minister for Worship and Public Instruction the Minister for the Interior will see to its execution, keeping in mind that the members of the religious orders whose ' permit ' ceases according to the terms of the present legal decree must leave their former conventual houses within three months."

[90] These were: *Benedictines* for the schools of Pannonhalma and Györ; *Calasanctians* for Budapest and Kecskemét; *Franciscans* for Esztergom and Szentendre; the *Sisters of Szeged* for the girls' schools at Budapest and Debrecen.

[91] The bishops stated that more than 10,000 religious (men and women) belonging to 53 orders were about to be forced to return to civilian life. They expressed their profound concern at the Government decrees that made this necessary and in face of which they could only protest. In spite of this the bishops asked God's blessing on the " agreement " while recalling that in their initial requests for discussions with the Government they were concerned only with alleviating the conditions of the religious orders.

franchise at the administrative elections fixed for the autumn
(1950). Accordingly to remain faithful to the " agreement "
the bishops in very measured terms dealt with the subject in a
letter of 10 October 1950.[92]

* * *

After the signing of the *modus vivendi* there was an apparent
lull in the attacks on the bishops. This truce did not last long
for the Communist Government planned to inveigle the bishops
into the political arena. In autumn 1950 the Government
insisted that the bishops sign the *Appeal of the World Peace
Committee* (the Stockholm Manifesto). In reply the bishops under
the leadership of Mgr. *Grösz*, Archbishop of Kalocsa, issued a
circular letter (11 December 1950) in which they spoke of peace
in the Gospel sense of the word. This letter displeased the
Communists and they renewed the attack. On the occasion of
the " Peace Congress " held in Berlin in February 1951 the
bishops were once more asked to sign the Peace Appeal drawn
up at the Congress. But this time to make it look like a " manifestation of the people's will " and to have an excuse for accusing
the bishops should they refuse to sign, the Communists sent
deputations of " Priests of Peace " and workers. Once again the
bishops stood firm and on 3 April issued another circular letter.[93]

The letter annoyed the Communists. To speak of peace
according to the Gospel and not according to Communist
teaching, to refer to UNO and to peace among peoples instead
of to the Kominform and to the peace of peoples under Marxism
—this was but to show that the bishops' way and the Communists'
way remained divergent. There were cries that the " agreement " had been violated. This date marks the beginning of a
new phase in the struggle against the Church in Hungary.[94]

To force the bishops to a compromise the Government made

---

[92] See for text *La Documentation Catholique*, 1951, col. 94. The letter was read in all
the churches, 15 October. Cf. *Magyar Kurir*, 15 October 1950.

[93] For text see *La Documentation Catholique*, 1951, col. 918.

[94] *Szabad Nép*, 13 April 1951, reported that Mgr. Grösz had refused to receive the
members of the " Peace Committee " of his city and that the same attitude was adopted
by Mgr. Hamvas of Csanád and Mgr. Pétery of Vác. " This means," *Szabad Nép* pointed
out, " that they do not support the Peace Movement and that therefore they brutally

use of priests belonging to the Peace Movement. Some parishes in Budapest were vacant. The Government, *usurping the authority of the bishops*, on 20 April 1951 announced a public meeting with a view to conferring the parishes on priests who were members of the movement. To meet this new threat and for the good of souls Mgr. *Endre Hamvas*, Bishop of Csanád and Administrator Apostolic of Esztergom [95]—in which capacity he had jurisdiction over Budapest—decided to sign the Appeal of the Berlin Congress. A little later the other bishops followed his example. The Government could consider that it had won the battle.

The Communists at once set about exploiting this victory to the full. Instead of the bishops the priests belonging to the Peace Movement were invited to discussions with the Government. On 26 April 1951 an official delegation of this movement met the Minister for Worship, *József Darvas*, to ask—certainly at the instigation of the Government—that the question of subsidies for the clergy be settled. The request was at once favourably received and the Government decided to double or treble the sum already being received by the clergy. This decision was however opposed to the principle of diminution of financial help announced in the " agreement " with the bishops. The new subsidy rates came into force four days after the beginning of the negotiations. The increase in emoluments was to be calculated from the date of the taking of the oath of fidelity to the Republic.[96] The Government had now given to the Peace Movement the prestige that follows success.

---

violate the agreement concluded with the Hungarian Government . . . Those who stand apart are the enemies of peace." Radio-Budapest also declared on 14 April: " The bishops have violated the agreement concluded with the State and signed by them." This meant that a new offensive in the old habitual form had begun.

[95] The Metropolitan Chapter of Esztergom proceeded, despite the Government's pressure in favour of Niklós Beresztóczy—a priest who had been bent to the will of the Communists by prison and it appears by torture—to the election of Mgr. Károly Gigler as Vicar Capitular. When he was placed under arrest two days later the canons elected Mgr. Zoltán Meszlényi, titular Bishop of Zarai, who was arrested twelve days later. Finally the Chapter elected the person acceptable to the Government, namely Beresztóczy. The Holy See then decided to intervene once again and nominated Mgr. Endre Hamvas, Bishop of Csanad, as Apostolic Administrator of Esztergom. Mgr. Meszlényi died in prison in January 1953, while Mgr. Gigler was set free after three years' imprisonment. In 1951, as will be seen later, the nomination of Beresztóczy as Vicar General was imposed by the Government.

[96] Cf. *A Kereszt* (The Cross), year III, number 11. *A Kereszt* is the organ of the movement of Priests for Peace.

In exchange for this concession the movement undertook to engage in propaganda that the lands remaining to the Church after the agrarian reform [97] should be " offered " to the State. In this way by an exchange of gifts it desired to cement the good relations established with the civil authority.

* * *

It could hardly escape the Government's notice however that there still existed among the Catholic clergy a strong opposition which was impeding every effort to lead the Church into the desired way. This obstacle had to be removed at all costs. So the Communists decided on new measures and chose new victims. On 15 May 1951 the police arrested the president of the episcopal conference, Mgr. *József Grösz*, Archbishop of Kalocsa, his secretary and some others on the pretext of illegal traffic in currency exchange, of hiding arms, of organising escapes, of assassination and incitement to assassination. The act of accusation stated that the plot had been prepared since November 1948 with the help of Cardinal *Mindszenty* who had entrusted Archbishop *Grösz* with its direction. After the success of the plot the latter was to become, *in case of impossibility on the part of Mindszenty and until the return of the king*, head of a Provisional Government and he was to appoint ministers of State in his capacity of " homo regius." The archbishop was also accused of having sent on 15 July 1951 a written declaration to the legation of an " imperialist " State at Budapest and to have been in close contact with other " imperialist " diplomatic representatives and with the Vatican.

A new trial was begun. It ended on 28 June 1951 with the following sentences: Mgr. *Grösz*, 15 years' imprisonment; the Cistercian Abbot, *Vendel Endrédy*, 14 years' imprisonment; the Cistercian Father *Hagyó-Kovács*, 13 years; three other persons 8 to 10 years' imprisonment. [98] The justification for these

---

[97] About 2,876 acres out of 1,254,530 acres in 1944.

[98] Even before the Archbishop of Kalocsa was condemned Radio-Budapest announced on 18 June 1951 the following charge against him: " Grösz aimed at overthrowing the Hungarian People's Government; his intention was to act himself as head of the State

sentences was given in these words: " The Court has held the accused guilty of the following crimes: organisation of means for the overthrow of the democratic régime, traffic in currency exchange, organisation of escapes from the country." In fact to the glory of the accused their only real " fault " was refusal to speak as the Communist régime would have them speak.[99] The Government believed that the arrest and condemnation of Mgr. *Grösz* had given them the opportunity to interfere more effectively in the life of the Church.[100]

On 15 May 1951 the *State Bureau for Ecclesiastical Affairs*— after the Soviet model—was set up. Its purpose was " to implement agreements between the State and the Churches and to superintend the aid given by the State to the different denominations." [101] *István Kossa*, one of the worst enemies of

---

until the restoration of the Hapsburgs. In collusion with his accomplices (the Americans and Marshal Tito, according to the Communist press) he had organised groups of armed terrorists. Finally he had been concerned in illegal transactions in foreign exchange and had committed acts of espionage." These accusations bore a striking resemblance to those announced by the same Radio in November 1948 against Cardinal Mindszenty: " The archbishop is the enemy of the people and of the People's Democracy; in his hatred of and hostility towards the republican régime he has now allied himself with foreign powers to destroy the Hungarian way of life and the People's Democracy." Cf. *La Documentation Catholique*, 1951, col. 197, and the article in *L'Osservatore Romano*, 22 June 1951.

[99] Cf. *Telegraphic Agency* (MTI) of 19 June 1951. Radio-Budapest gave great publicity to the act of accusation and to the Public Prosecutor Alapy's speech. The Catholic periodical *Sziv* was suppressed because it would not take sides in the trial. During the course of this trial the same metamorphosis and the same humiliating scenes for the venerable prelate were witnessed which had characterised the trial of Cardinal Mindszenty. See the typed account of the trial debate: *The trial of József Grösz and his accomplices*, State Publications, Budapest, 1951.

[100] On 2 June 1951 Radio-Budapest announced: " The National Committee of Catholic priests of Hungary (*sic*) has met to study the efforts already made to gather signatures for the international appeal for peace." Collaboration between the Government and the clergy in the movement for peace was therefore developing and what they were not able to obtain through the bishops they now wished to obtain by this means. Cf. *La Documentation Catholique*, 1951, col. 919.

[101] Law n. 1 of 1951, published in the *Magyar Közlöny* (Official Gazette) of 19 May 1951. The same number of this Gazette published the decree 110/1951 MT concerning the application of the above law. Article 1 of the decree determined the powers of the State Bureau for Ecclesiastical Affairs:

    (a) putting into force the covenants and agreements between the State and religious denominations;

    (b) personal and administrative affairs relating to State assistance to Churches and religious denominations;

    (c) settlement of personal and administrative subsidies for the upkeep of denominational colleges exempt from nationalisation;

    (d) payment of the expenses for religious teaching in the schools;

17

the Church, was put at the head of this *Bureau*. A month later, 15 June, all the Hungarian bishops had to pay *Kossa* a " courtesy visit " and begin new negotiations on questions still outstanding between Church and State. On this occasion the bishops made a vain attempt to intervene on behalf of the Archbishop of Kalocsa, Mgr. *Grösz*.[102]

In spite of all this the attitude of the Government grew stiffer every day. On 23 June 1951 Mgr. *Endre Hamvas* of Csanád, Mgr. *József Pétery* of Vác, Mgr. *Lajos Shvoy* of Székesfehérvár and Mgr. *Bertalan Badalik* of Veszprém (whom the Communists tried to involve in the trial of Mgr. *Grösz*), were put under police supervision and kept prisoners in their residences. Mgr. *Imre Kisberk*, Auxiliary Bishop of Székesfehérvár, met with the same fate on 25 June. On the following days the press published over the signature of two bishops, Mgr. *Hamvas* and Mgr. *Bárd*, declarations condemning the " conspiracy " of Mgr. *Grösz* and affirming their own loyalty.

With the bishops deprived of their freedom the Government decided to pave the way to have priests of the Peace Movement put in charge of the direction of the dioceses. So on 30 June 1951 Mgr. *Hamvas*, Bishop of Csanád and Apostolic Administrator of the Archdiocese of Esztergom, was (while still under house arrest) invited by the Government authorities " to present " a list of names from which a vicar general for Esztergom and one for Szeged might be chosen. Refusal would have meant more severe restrictions of his liberty and the impossibility of directing the two Sees dependent on him. Under these circumstances he preferred to make the Government-imposed nominations, and appointed *Miklós Beresztóczy*, head of the Peace Movement, as

---

(e) questions of the patrimonies of ecclesiastical foundations and other questions of ecclesiastical patrimonies;

(f) drawing up juridical rules of an ecclesiastical character and measures for their application;

(g) despatching business relating to liberty of conscience and the free exercise of religion; guarantee for the free exercise of religious ceremonies;

(h) all functions coming under and heretofore subject to the Ministry for Worship and for Public Instruction;

(i) carrying out decisions of the Council of Ministers on ecclesiastical matters and control of them.

102 Cf. *A Kereszt*, 21 June 1951.

Vicar General of Esztergom [103] and *Antal Széczy*, an important member of the same movement, as Vicar General of Csanád.

The Government tried to impose similar changes on the Bishop of Vác, Mgr. *József Pétery*. When he refused, his vicar general was forced to replace his own pro-vicar and chancellor by prominent members of the Peace Movement. Likewise Mgr. *Lajos Shvoy*, Bishop of Székesfehérvár, had to replace his chancellor. And a few days later Mgr. *Bertalan Badalik*, Bishop of Veszprém, was obliged to appoint a new vicar general.

After these changes the Government wanted to have proof of the loyalty of the bishops. An episcopal conference was called for 3 July at Budapest. The members of the episcopate still at liberty met under the presidency of Mgr. *Czapik*, Archbishop of Eger. At this meeting were also present the new vicars general, who outnumbered the diocesan bishops. A declaration previously approved by the Government was published. According to the text *as given by the Hungarian Telegraphic Agency*, the bishops protested their loyalty to the People's Republic, condemned every act of violence against the régime, undertook to observe " with ever growing care " the " agreement " signed with the State and above all *approved of the Peace Movement*. The Government demanded furthermore that in order to help production and increase working hours feasts of patrons, pilgrimages and days of Perpetual Adoration, which fell on week-days, be transferred to the following Sundays.[104]

But the Government was not yet satisfied. While the meeting of the Hungarian bishops was taking place, the *Presidential Council of the People's Republic* issued a new *decree on the formalities to be observed in filling vacant ecclesiastical sees*. It stipulated amongst other things that previous consent of the State was necessary in appointing titulars to vacant sees, and that the decree was retroactive to 1 January 1946.[105]

---

[103] The preceding year the Holy See had named the Bishop of Csanád Apostolic Administrator of Esztergom to prevent the Government candidate, Miklós Beresztóczy, from becoming vicar capitular. By its forcible intervention in June 1951 the Government attained its end and had him appointed vicar general.

[104] See the text of the declaration in *La Documentation Catholique*, 1951, col. 931-932. Cf. also *The Tablet*, 14 July 1951.

[105] Cf. *Hungarian Telegraphic Agency* (MTI), 3 July 1951.

This decree is a milestone in the history of the Catholic Church in Hungary. Two archbishops were in prison; four bishops were under house arrest; two diocesan ordinaries, five auxiliary bishops and the Abbot General of the Benedictines at Pannonhalma were not recognised by the State. There were only four bishops free and having State recognition. Furthermore on 9 July all junior seminaries were suppressed. By the autumn of 1952 the senior seminaries were closed at Szombathely, Veszprém, Székesfehérvár, Pécs, Kalocsa, Vác and Hejce. By then only five senior seminaries were functioning: the central seminary at Budapest, the seminaries at Esztergom, Eger, Györ and Szeged (all of which had now become inter-diocesan), and the seminary of the Oriental Rite at Nyiregyhaza (diocese of Hajdudorog).

By the decree the Government intended to place the bishops in a most serious dilemma: they must either accept the conditions laid down by the Government or be completely cut off from the religious life of the country. The conditions imposed by the State were: *an oath of loyalty to the Constitution and the appointment of outstanding members of the Peace Movement to positions of responsibility in the dioceses.* The episcopate decided that it would not allow itself to be completely isolated from the administration of the dioceses as this would bring in its wake incalculable consequences. So on 21 July 1951 the Hungarian hierarchy—with the sole exception of the Auxiliary Bishop of Székesfehérvár, Mgr. *Imre Kisberk*—considered it necessary to take the following oath before the Presidential Council of the People's Republic of Hungary:

> " I swear to be loyal to the Hungarian People's Republic, to its people and to its Constitution, to observe the Constitution and all lawful constitutional measures, to keep the State's secrets, to serve within the limits of my vocation the interests of the people, and by every means in my power to strive to contribute to the progressive strengthening of the Hungarian People's Republic." [106]

---

[106] Cf. *A Kereszt*, 1 August 1951. A previous declaration of loyalty by the Archbishop of Eger, Mgr. Czapik, was commented on by the official organ of the Party, *Szabad Nép*, 5 July 1951, in an editorial entitled *Better late than never.* The Archbishop of Eger, doyen of the bishops present, recalled in a brief speech at the taking of the oath the

The taking of the oath was followed by great changes in the personnel of the dioceses. The bishops had *to relieve the vicars general and chancellors of their office* and to appoint in their place members of the Peace Movement. Thus the movement only a year old was now practically governing the dioceses. The State had reached its goal. However so as to avoid all possibility of *deviationism* among the new diocesan directors, the Government placed in every episcopal see a Party man to supervise everything (correspondence, recruitment of clerics, theology courses, etc.), and to report to the State Bureau for Ecclesiastical Affairs.[107]

* * *

The first act of the new ecclesiastical " directors " was to offer to the State, in gratitude for the agreement concluded with the Government and as a " voluntary donation," all landed property still possessed by the Church.[108] Any priest having a benefice could now hold only 800 square metres of land. Ecclesiastical organisations had a right only to the same amount as an individual. Thus the clergy lost all economic independence. The lands acquired by the State were used to establish a *Fund* (rendelkezési alap), administered by the State Bureau for Ecclesiastical Affairs, which helped to pay a part of the clergy's salaries.

In the other fields of Church activity also the effects of this change were very much in evidence. Diocesan bulletins appeared in which it was attempted to prove from Sacred Scripture that the Communist social system was the ideal form of Christianity. In them the faithful were reminded of their obligation to bring their produce to the collecting centres, to complete as soon as possible their work in the fields,

---

obligation according to Catholic doctrine to respect the authority of the State and to observe the laws provided that they were not contrary to the divine law. In any case considering the nightmare atmosphere in which the episcopate had been plunged by the destruction of ecclesiastical organisation in Hungary, one can say the oath was extorted under pressure.

[107] This " Commissioner " of the State Bureau for Ecclesiastical Affairs effectively controlled the whole administration of the diocese: correspondence, appointments, advancement to orders, ordinations etc.

[108] Cf. *Magyar Kurir*, 14 August 1951.

to take part in production competitions, etc. Next parish priests were removed from their parishes without any canonical justification but merely to have members of the Peace Movement placed in the more important parishes. *Canonical penalties* were inflicted on priests who refused—remaining faithful to their vocation—to fall into line with State regulations.[109] Besides, whatever may have been its intention in professing submission to the Holy See in all questions of faith and morals, the movement in its external conduct so acted as to beget in the minds of the faithful, if not an aversion for, then at least mistrust of the Holy See.

Conclusion

From a general view of the religious situation in Hungary it is evident that the terms of the Constitution of 1949 guaranteeing liberty of religion while separating Church and State have not been put into effect. On the contrary the Church has been completely deprived of its freedom and subjected to the power of the State. The bishops cannot freely teach the Gospel or govern their dioceses. Indeed they do not enjoy even personal freedom. The influence of the Catholic Church in the public life of the country has been reduced to a minimum.

Three ecclesiastical circumscriptions have been suppressed: in 1951 the territory of the Abbacy *nullius* of Pannonhalma was divided between the dioceses of Györ and Veszprém; in 1952 the Vicariates of Nagyvarád and Kassa were officially attached to the dioceses of Csanád and Eger.

Of 3,344 Catholic schools only 16 remain in the hands of the Church. All junior seminaries were suppressed 9 July 1951, and 7 senior seminaries in the autumn of 1952. At the moment there are only 9 senior seminaries for both secular and religious clergy.[110] Before the Communists seized power there were 187 religious houses for men and 456 for women. Now there are only 6 for men and 2 for women. Only one Catholic hospital remains of the 9 existing in 1944. All Catholic associa-

---

[109] Cf. *A Kereszt*, 14 September 1951.
[110] 5 inter-diocesan seminaries of the Latin Rite; 1 seminary of the Oriental Rite; 3 seminaries for religious (Benedictine, Calasanctian, Franciscan).

tions have been " dissolved." Not a single Catholic printing-house remains. All Catholic newspapers and about 50 reviews have been suppressed; only 3 publications are still tolerated and these only under the most severe restrictions. Church activity outside the places of worship—and even within them the sermons are censored—is tolerated only if it is judged to be advantageous to the Government.

Furthermore the Church has lost many of its outstanding clergy. More than 130 priests have been imprisoned, 300 secular priests and 3,500 religious have spent more or less long terms in concentration camps and 8 priests are known to have been deported to the USSR.

The most notable victims of the persecution are the Cardinal Primate *Mindszenty* and Mgr. *Grösz*. Mention must also be made of Mgr. *Meszlényi*, Vicar Capitular of Esztergom, who died in prison and Mgr. *Pétery*, the heroic Bishop of Vác, whose place of internment is unknown.[111]

The Soviet Communists' plan to make the Catholic Church the slave of the State is clearly recognisable in the constant attempt to humiliate the hierarchy, to elicit more and more proofs of loyalty, to control to the greatest possible degree its activity and to surround it with priests belonging to the Peace Movement—in fact sometimes the hierarchy has been made subject to the Movement. But Hungarian Communism is preoccupied with a worry all its own: to wipe out the memory of Cardinal *Mindszenty* who to judge from the efforts of his enemies still holds a place of honour in the minds and hearts of his people.

* * *

After the new Constitution of *Imre Nagy* (July 1953) the persecution of the Church seemed to ease off a little. There was a noticeable revival in the practice of religion. But this must be regarded as merely part of the Communist " tactics." There were some difficulties within the State to be overcome

---

[111] It would seem that Mgr. Pétery was allowed to resume his duties at the beginning of 1956.

and the world outside had to be shown the possibility of peaceful " co-existence " between the Church and the Communist State.[112] This " favourable situation " however was of short duration. And in any case, as *L'Osservatore Romano* of 28 February 1954 pointed out, it must never be forgotten that " liberty of worship " is very far from complete religious liberty.

In June 1955 the Holy Office condemned two periodicals: *Bulletin catholique hongrois* [113] and *A Kereszt*. The Government replied by tightening its control on the clergy. Priests who as a result of the *Decree of the Holy Office* refused to take part in meetings of the " patriotic clergy " were threatened immediately with sanctions equivalent to suspension; in some cases they were driven from their dioceses and forbidden to exercise their ministry anywhere in the State.

Arbitrary control by civil functionaries of the *Bureau for Worship* is still in force in all episcopal Curiae. Every act of the bishops is supervised. A youth may not enter the seminary without the permission of these functionaries whose *nihil obstat* is again required before advancing to Holy Orders.[114]

On 16 June 1955 the Hungarian Government issued the following communiqué: " At the request of Cardinal *Mindszenty* himself and of the whole Hungarian episcopate, taking into account his great age [115] and the state of his health, the Minister for Justice has decided to suspend the application of the penalty to which the Prelate was condemned. As his place of residence the Cardinal has been assigned the ecclesiastical building proposed by the episcopate." [116]

---

[112] The Government continued to give its support to the Movement of Priests for Peace and to direct the activity of the Church by means of the Bureau for Ecclesiastical Affairs. Cf. pamphlet entitled: *The Hungarian Catholic Priests for Peace*, Budapest, 1953.

[113] The *Bulletin catholique hongrois* has been published for several years, and it is circulated also in foreign countries in several languages (Bolletino cattolico ungherese, Romisch-Katholische Rundschau aus Ungarn). This publication sets itself, under Government auspices, to " prove " that in the Hungarian Republic there reigns full religious liberty, and that consequently collaboration between the Catholic Church and the Communist Government is possible.

[114] Cf. *L'Osservatore Romano*, 26 November 1955.

[115] The Cardinal though ill was only 62 years of age.

[116] Cf. *L'Osservatore Romano*, 18 September 1955. A similar example of Communist " clemency " was the liberation of Mgr. J. Grösz, Archbishop of Kalocsa on 11 May 1956. Received on 13 May by the President of the Hungarian Council, Andras Hagedus,

Hungarian Communism continues to restrict religion to the churches and strives to prevent its spread and its influence on the life of the people. Every effort made by priests or people to give religion its true place is at once branded " political activity " and punished as such. One may have the Faith; but to live according to the Faith is at best tolerated and sometimes altogether forbidden. On the other hand no effort is spared to turn the clergy from the true work of their calling and to make them the instruments of Communist political propaganda.

Mgr. Grösz was authorised to take over again the administration of his diocese and his place at the head of the episcopal conference. Cf. *Szabad Nép*, 13 May 1956. *L'Osservatore Romano* of 20 May 1956 commenting on this measure of " clemency " and on the statement made on this occasion by Mgr. Grösz, concluded in these terms: " The statements that *Szabad Nép* attribute to Mgr. Grösz must be considered in the light of the real conditions of Catholicism in Hungary. When meticulous legislation attacks in practice the internal jurisdiction of the Church and legalises the intervention of the State in ecclesiastical and religious life, it is permitted to doubt the authenticity and spontaneity of the words spoken by Mgr. Grösz . . . The liberty accorded to the Archbishop of Kalocsa after five years of unjust imprisonment cannot be considered, when there is question of true liberty, as an adequate gesture of conciliation towards the Church. Oppression still exists; God grant that it may not become worse under the false appearances of ' a more moderate policy'."

Chapter 10

THE PERSECUTION OF THE CATHOLIC CHURCH

UNDER

Communist Rule in Poland

AFTER THE RUSSO-GERMAN invasion of 1939 the Polish Government went into exile. After many vicissitudes of fortune it found refuge first in Paris and later in London, and became known as the " London Government."

Later a " Provisional Government of National Unity " was formed in Lublin by Communist agents. At the end of the war this Government was recognised by the Western Powers as a consequence of the Yalta and Potsdam agreements.[1]

The first elections were held on 19 January 1947. But the Great Powers had certainly not foreseen the conditions under which these elections were held: suppression of all liberty of speech and of assembly, threats and arrests, withdrawal of the right to vote from about two million citizens . . . while the Red army still occupied Polish territory.

The Government bloc won 383 of the 444 seats. The Parties which adhered to the Government obtained 30. *Mikolajczyk's* Agrarian Party got only 27 seats. The remaining seats were gained by some Catholics who stood as independent candidates in only five districts.

On 6 February the Communist *Boleslas Bierut* was elected President of the Republic and on 8 February a new Government was formed of members of the Government bloc or supporters of it.

---

[1] This Government of " National Unity " set up on 28 June 1945 included some non-Communist members who had been attached to the former Government, then in exile in London.

The Catholic Church before the Establishment of the Communist Government

Before the war in 1939 the Catholic Church had 24 dioceses and 23,971,000 members.

In September 1939 under the terms of the *Ribbentrop-Molotov* agreement 180,000 square kilometres with approximately 12,000,000 inhabitants were handed over to the USSR.

After the defeat of National Socialism [2] the Conference of the " Big Three " at Potsdam decided that " while awaiting the final determination of the western frontiers of Poland the following territories should come under the control of the Polish State: former German territory bounded by a line starting from the Baltic Sea immediately west of Schwinemunde and continuing thence along the course of the Oder as far as its confluence with the Western Neisse, and following the course of the Western Neisse as far as the Czechoslovak frontier, including that part of East Prussia which is not placed under the Government of the USSR." There was question here of about 103,000 square kilometres of " recovered territory," to use the terminology employed thereafter by the Polish Government. The eastern boundaries on the other hand were fixed along the *Curzon-Ribbentrop-Molotov* line.

As a result of such territorial changes Poland lost the Orthodox minorities of the territories which had been transferred to the rule of the USSR (about 180,000 square kilometres), the Protestant minorities already living in pre-war Polish territory and more than 2,000,000 Lutherans out of the 4,422,000 Germans transferred by force from those districts which the Yalta and Potsdam agreements had placed " under the government of the Soviet and Polish States."

In the post-war period the Jews also found themselves much reduced in numbers though in 1938 they had constituted 15% of the population.

---

[2] The Catholic Church in Poland suffered heavy losses under the Nazi occupation. From 1939 to 1945 about 3,000,000 Poles were deported; of 21 ordinaries of the Latin Rite in 1939 only 6 remained in their Sees in 1945; priests were reduced in the same period from 12,200 to 8,605: 584 had been killed and 1,263 had died in concentration camps. Polish priests made up 80% of the Catholic clergy in the Dachau camp. Cf. Janicki, *Katolickie duchowienstwo polski w Dachau od 1940 do 1945* (MS.), (Polish Catholic clergy at Dachau from 1940 to 1945).

Thus in 1945 the Polish population had become almost entirely Catholic (22,546,000 i.e. 95%) with only small Protestant (280,000), Orthodox (500,000), and Jewish (80,000) minorities.

After seven years of reconstruction (1945-1952) the ecclesiastical divisions were re-arranged as follows: 4 archdioceses, Warsaw, Gniezno, Poznan and Cracow; 12 dioceses, Chelmno, Katowice, Czestochowa, Kielce, Lodz, Lomza, Lublin, Plock, Sandomierz, Siedlce, Tarnow and Wloclawek; 5 apostolic administrations for the dioceses east of the Oder and Neisse and in East Prussia, Breslau, Opole (Oppeln), Warmia, Danzig, Gorzow (Schneidemühl); 4 provisional residences (in dioceses only part of which had remained in Polish territory), Vilna (residence at Byalistok); Lwow of the Latins (residence at Lubaczow), Przemysl of the Ruthenians, Przemysl of the Latins.

In 1945 there were 8,615 priests and 6,192 parishes. At the beginning of 1952 there were 17 senior seminaries and 59 junior seminaries with almost 10,000 students. In addition there were the novitiates and seminaries of the regular clergy. At the end of 1951, 9 new ordinaries, 5 apostolic administrators and 15 auxiliary bishops had been appointed by the Holy Father to make up for the losses suffered during the years of war and occupation.

First Measures against the Church

The Communists having got into power took stock of the differences which existed between Poland and the other satellite countries. They took stock also of the difficulties which awaited them when enforcing their threefold revolution—political, social-economic and cultural. First of all Poland as a nation was a compact body of Catholics, while in other countries the existence of different religious groups offered an advantage to anyone who wanted to impose an ideological slavery on them. There it was easy to pit one group against the other and to set the different religions at variance with one another. In the second place a tradition of a thousand years testified that in the course of its history Poland had always fought at one and the same time for its Faith and for its independence.

During the first two years (1945 to the beginning of 1947) the Government [3] tried to show a formally correct attitude towards the Church. Besides the reasons already outlined this was due to the fact that the Government, occupied with consolidating its power in a country recently conquered by Soviet arms and with the reconstruction needed after the immense destruction caused by the war, did not think it expedient to attack the Catholic Church at once.[4] Yet even during those years there were acts of hostility and of terrorism, though somewhat isolated, as well as attempts to lessen the influence of the Church in public life.

Already on 18 July 1945 a campaign for a " new school " [5] was begun at the time of the " National Congress of Education " at Lodz. This Congress was presided over by *Skrzeszewski*, Minister for Education.

On 14 September 1945 the provisional Government unilaterally rescinded the Concordat with the Holy See which had been signed on 10 February 1925. It alleged that " . . . under the German occupation the Holy See had taken juridical steps opposed to the agreements set down in the Concordat." [6]

The *Polish Religious Bulletin* of 17 November 1945 announced that an apostate priest of the diocese of Warsaw, *Matuszewski*, had been named Minister for Propaganda in the provisional Government.

On 25 November 1945 this same Government promulgated a new marriage law which was plainly secular in character. It imposed the obligation of civil marriage, gave ample facilities for

---

[3] As is known the Holy See never recognised the Warsaw Government.

[4] In the years 1945-1947 funds were allotted for the reconstruction of some churches. The same thing was repeated in the following years, but the propaganda aim became ever more obvious.

[5] Cf. the article of T. Sulimiski which appeared in the review *Kultura*, 1952, III, 141.

[6] The news given by the BBC on 14 September 1945 was later confirmed by a communiqué of *Polpress*, 16 September. *L'Osservatore Romano* on 25 September 1945 published a statement in which it denied the accusation and explained that the nomination of certain prelates during the German occupation had been of a purely temporary nature, that this course had been taken to avoid leaving the faithful indefinitely without leaders, and that in any event these prelates were not appointed as residential bishops but simply as apostolic administrators.

divorce and transferred everything concerning marriage to the civil courts. [7]

From the beginning of 1946 the Government set out to weaken the power of the Catholic Church by encouraging proselytism on the part of the Protestant sects and the Orthodox communities [8] and by favouring the creation of a " Polish National Catholic Church."

On 30 September 1946 in spite of the opposition of the Catholic hierarchy [9] the Government officially recognised the new " Polish National Catholic Church," endowed it with *special funds* and procured for it all the facilities necessary for its organisation and development.

Four new Orthodox dioceses were established. With the approval of the Patriarch of Moscow Bishop *Macaryj* came from Lvov. An attempt was made to subject the remaining Greek-Catholics to his jurisdiction.

On 19 October 1946 the Government granted legal recognition to the two Churches, Baptist and Methodist. They had existed up to then but had not enjoyed any privileges.

On 15 February 1947 the " Ecumenical Council of the Churches " came into being. It was made up of 13 Christian non-Catholic religious organisations.

At the same time the Government pressed for the creation of the " Association of the Godless " and backed up *Glos Wolnych* (Free Speech), the Association's propaganda organ.

There was such undeniable evidence of a renewal of acts of terrorism that on 24 May 1946 the Polish hierarchy after a two

---

[7] On 7 December 1945 the Polish hierarchy published a letter protesting against abuses occasioned by the new marriage law: Cf. *Tygodnik Warszawski* 6 December 1945. Already in the course of a meeting held on 3 and 4 October at the monastery of Jasna-Gora the bishops had issued a joint statement which was published on 21 of that month. This statement warned the faithful to beware of resurgent Materialism and to oppose those who were trying to launch an attack on the Church in Poland. On 17 January 1946 the Holy Father in a letter to the Polish Catholics protested against all these persecuting measures and among others against " the new law which threatens the sanctity and stability of marriage." (*AAS*, vol. 38, 1946, p. 172).

[8] Cf. *Service oecuménique de presse et d'information* (SOEPI, April and June 1946).

[9] Already on 2 June 1946 the Catholic weekly *Tygodnik Warszawski* had unmasked the Government designs. On 20 July 1946 the Polish Primate, Cardinal Hlond, issued a " communiqué to Catholics " denouncing the Government move. Another communiqué was published by the hierarchy in the course of a plenary meeting held from 11 to 13 September 1946.

days' meeting at the Shrine of Czestochowa published a statement expressing its disapproval.[10]   The Government censorship however forbade the Polish press to publish this statement of the hierarchy.

In the years 1945-1947 through the instrumentality of the UB (State Security Bureau) about 100 priests disappeared. These were among the most outstanding and most active members of the clergy in the religious and social apostolate.

* * *

After the general elections of 19 January 1947 the struggle against the Church became more and more ruthless. It followed the usual pattern:

> gradual confiscation of all Church property in order to paralyse her activity;
>
> laicisation of the schools;
>
> transfer to the State of all works of charity (hospitals, kinder-gartens, homes, orphanages, etc.); [11]
>
> weakening of the link between the clergy and the hierarchy by stirring up internal disagreements.

Public institutions were laicised, special attention being paid to the schools.

On 10 March 1947 the Primate of Poland, Cardinal *Augustus Hlond*, protested against the Government's manoeuvres which tended to limit the activity of the Church to worship alone, [12]

---

[10] The declaration was given by the BBC in a broadcast in the Polish language; cf. *The Tablet*, 18 August 1946.

[11] After the charitable institutions had been taken from them the nuns were forced to live exclusively on alms. In the hospitals contact between priests and the patients was restricted by the fixing of the days and hours of visits (almost always twice a week). In Poland at the present time if the patients in hospitals do not go to confession on the days fixed for visits every request for spiritual assistance, even at the point of death, goes unheeded.

[12] Among other things he stated: " . . . These atheists wish above all to effect the disappearance of every religious principle in the education of youth. Their policy is calculated to eradicate the religion of the people and de-christianise them. The Church is attacked not only in the workshops and the factories but even in the humblest cottages

and on 8 September 1947 the Polish hierarchy published a joint
Letter which once again warned Catholics against atheistic
attacks: " We are faced with facts which are in flagrant contradiction with the dignity of Catholic moral teaching. They
are so numerous that we are forced to consider them as due to
a veiled struggle directed intentionally against God and against
the Church . . . " This Letter met with strong opposition from
Government organisations. On 29 October 1947 the Prime
Minister, *Joseph Cyrankiewicz*, described it before the Diet as " an
act of open opposition to the Government." It gave him the
excuse to organise a full-scale press campaign against the clergy
and the hierarchy.[13]

From the beginning of 1948 a series of arrests and of court cases
against the more prominent members of the clergy and the
hierarchy took place. The bishops and priests, already accused
of being opposed to the work of the Communist Government,
now found themselves being accused of " clandestine activity "
and " immorality." [14]

Meanwhile on 14 February 1948 a congress of the inspectors of
elementary schools was held at Sopot. During the congress the
Communist Minister for Education, *Skrzeszewski*, declared:
" . . . the whole teaching body should belong to the Communist
Party. The schools should be lay schools and there should be
nothing of religion in the classrooms. Within the walls of the
school every youth organisation of a denominational character
is forbidden." [15]

. . . Since the persecutions of Nero the Church has never experienced an attack that
can be compared with the present one . . . The independent mission of the Church
and its moral influence over men annoy the partisans of the totalitarian régimes. The
Church by refusing to keep rigidly inside the walls of its sacred buildings or to become
the tool of a political party exasperates them."

[13] Cf. *Glos Ludu*, 16 October 1947, and *Robotnik* (the organ of the Amalgamated Polish
Socialists), 17 October 1947.

[14] In February 1948 after a visit to Rome Cardinal Augustus Hlond was accused by the
press of having supported the " Vatican thesis " which, it was maintained, upheld the
German claim to the lands east of the Oder-Neisse line. The Cardinal was compelled to
reply to this accusation. He did so on 3 July in a message to the people of the " recovered
territories." On 22 October he died at the age of 67.

[15] The Polish hierarchy in a joint Letter to Polish youth, 15 April 1948, condemned
the Government's anti-religious stand on the question of the education of youth: " . . .
An effort is being made to base education on materialist teachings . . . The Church
will never accept this principle or condone the Godless education of youth. . . . "

In May 1948 the former Auxiliary Bishop of Pinsk, Mgr. *Karol Niemira*, was sentenced to six months in prison on a trifling pretext. Father *Buchala* of the diocese of Cracow was condemned to three years in prison for having " ridiculed the People's Democracy."

The following priests were also arrested and sentenced: *Pawlina*, former director of *Caritas*; *Grzechnik*; *Marchewska*; *Polowska*; *Jarkiewicz* (sentenced to penal servitude for " moral complicity in the assassination of three democrat agitators "); *Boleslas Stefanski* (sentenced to death on a charge of having enrolled his pupils " so as to form a secret gang "); *Krzeminski* (sentenced to six years in prison for alleged contacts with a secret movement); *Kacynski* (former Minister for Education in the Polish Government in exile in London, for having " taken part in activity detrimental to the State "); *Raczynski* and *Gurgesz* (for complicity in an organisation with subversive political aims).

Towards the end of September 1948 about 400 priests were either in prison or in concentration camps.

Enslavement of the Schools

In the meantime the sovietisation of the educational system went ahead. This was designed to bring about that cultural revolution which was an integral part of the general plan to sovietise the whole social life of the country. A detailed programme of education was introduced for the organisation of the " new school." [16] There were references to " paying attention to the democratic line in the education of children " [17] and of " education in the spirit of the new tasks." [18] In the elementary schools some " elements of economics," that is to say, some " elements of historic Materialism " [19] were introduced as " new matter."

---

[16] Cf. S. Bialas, *Organizacja Szkolnictwa*, p. 9.

[17] Cf. *idid.*, p. 59.

[18] Cf. *ibid.*, p. 61.

[19] During the period 1945-1948 pre-war textbooks continued in use. But in 1950-1951 the official newspapers could claim with pride that new Marxist-based textbooks had appeared. Cf. *Kalendarz Robotniczy* (Workers' Yearbook), 1951, p. 320.

For the school year 1951-1952, 133 other textbooks with an issue of 23 million copies were printed. Cf. *Informacja Prasowa* (Press Information) No. 274, 1951, p. 4. They conformed fully to Marxist teaching, certain passages being direct translations from the Russian model.

This change in the " scientific and pedagogic content " of the teaching in the elementary schools was accompanied by " the formation " of a new class of teachers while it was arranged that the Marxists rapidly took precedence over the others. All the teachers of the " elementary schools " were obliged to follow a special " political education course " in order to pass " an ideological examination " on the theory of Marxism-Leninism and on their efficiency " in putting the theory into practice." [20]

In order to hasten the preparation of the new teaching personnel courses of ten months were organised to run concurrently with the " re-education " of the old teachers.

The programme of instruction in the " secondary teachers' training schools " was based on the principle that every teacher ought to be a man " totally free from pseudo-moral and preconceived class ideas, from the world-outlook of the old régime and from the prejudices of bourgeois society." [21]

All teachers were obliged to belong " voluntarily " to the " Professional Association of Polish Teachers " (ZZNP). This association had the task of supervising closely the " educational work of the teachers " as well as their " fidelity to Marxist-Leninist principles."

In July 1948 all young people [22] were " enrolled " in a single mass organisation named ZMP (Zwiazek Mlodziezy Polskiej, Union of Polish Youth). [23]

Students for the universities were selected methodically on the basis of " programmes of orientation " drawn up by a " Commission of Admission " (a body similar to that which " directs " secondary school students). [24]

" Educational centres " were then set up for children of from

---

[20] The 15 June 1951 was prescribed as the very last date by which the course and examination must be completed.

[21] Cf. W. Ozga, *Rozbudowa Szkolnictwa* (The development of the school system), p. 59.

[22] In Poland the greater part of the youth pass on to the professional schools, which retain their old organisation and principles of formation, but only for the time being.

[23] The Union has a special university section, the ZAMP (*Zwiaczek Akademicki Mlodzieczy Polskiej*, Union of Polish University Youth).

[24] There was even a " university preparatory class " set up, reserved to artisans and manual workers under the age of thirty chosen by the Party. Manual workers after two years' instruction could pass directly to the chosen university faculty, certain of being admitted with priority over all other candidates.

4 to 7 years of age. These copied the pre-war kindergarten schools but gradually introduced the essence of the method devised in Russia by *Makarenko*, the "well-known Soviet expert in pedagogics." Women teachers for these schools were trained immediately in accordance with the principles of Marxist Materialism.[25]

"Nurseries," "children's palaces" (in the big cities), or "children's homes" (in the less important centres), and other establishments of a like nature, the educational systems of which were clearly stamped with atheistic principles, were opened for children of from one to four years.[26]

Every religious influence was eliminated from the schools. Gradually prayers were abolished; the time for religious instruction was reduced—in the higher schools it was completely suppressed; religious feast days were replaced by Party demonstrations. A campaign was organised to have the crucifix removed from the classrooms. Within the schools every activity was forbidden to the religious associations (The Crusade of the Blessed Sacrament, Sodalities of Our Blessed Lady, the Apostleship of Prayer, religious culture circles). Whenever possible more direct action was taken against religion by means of anti-religious school organisations such as the "Society of the Child's Friends," (TPD) whose rôle it is to take an interest in "workers' children so that they may be educated in the Marxist spirit." The task of replacing religion by Marxism was also taken up by the "Women's League" and the "Polish Youth League" (ZMP).

---

[25] In 1951 the National Congress of Polish professors and teachers was held. During this Congress Bierut declared that the most important task before the teaching profession was to "inculcate in youth a socialist morality," which he explained thus: "To eradicate from our educational system the legacies of the Old Order, to free it from the last traces of obscurantism which disguises itself behind a façade of false theories, and to lay bare and unmask the philosophy and social theory of the bourgeois era."

In January 1951 a "Science Congress" was held at Zakopane, in the course of which rules "based on the Marxist conception of the world" were laid down and "incorrigible" professors were deprived of their positions.

It was during the year 1951-1952 that the school system of the country was finally brought into line and the schools were transformed into easily manageable instruments of propaganda and of ideological pressure.

[26] The "Women's League" asked the Government to take over all the preparatory institutions for young children which were still under religious management (about 700), although in 1947-1948 already 287,940 children were enrolled in the 4,677 State kindergartens.

The struggle against religious instruction in the schools was based on the decree " on freedom of religious teaching." According to the decree religious instruction could be given only to children whose parents asked for it. But in Poland deceit and chicanery are widely used to prevent parents from expressing their wish in this matter. In the schools moreover sometimes there is no classroom available for religious instruction or again the pupils are invited to assist at cinema-shows or other amusements at the time for the lesson in religion.

It can scarcely be said that the Communist Government in Poland has proceeded with slow and measured steps in the conquest and enslavement of the scholastic and cultural machinery of the country.[27]

Campaign of Calumny and First Measures against the Clergy

On 14 March 1949 the Secretary of the Episcopal Commission, Mgr. *Sigismund Choromanski* received a note from the Government which affirmed that its attitude " in questions concerning the Faith and the Church " proved its " sincere intention of regulating its relations with the Church in a spirit of loyalty and sincere concern for its good." At the same time the Government drew the bishops' attention to " a growing anti-Government propaganda on the part of the clergy " which " was capable of creating anxiety and unrest in the minds of the people." [28]

---

[27] The new *Polish Academy of Science* was set up in November 1951. Jan Dembowski, noted for his leanings towards Communism, was elected president.

According to data furnished by the deputy Minister for the Sciences and for Secondary Schools, M. Golanski, " where there were only 28 university colleges in the period between the wars there are now 68 in Poland; the number of students has increased from 48,000 to 114,000. In place of the 4 higher technical schools then we now have 10, not mentioning the evening schools. The number of schools of economy has been raised to 10 and the number of faculties in them from 5 to 23, that is a five-fold increase. The number of medical training institutes has been doubled. Characteristic also is the rapid expansion in the field of art schools and teachers' training institutes . . . " Cf. *Problemy*, n. 5, 1951.

In 1950 in 118 teachers' training colleges there were 32,275 new teachers being instructed according to Communist (i.e. atheistic) methods.

[28] In a joint Letter signed by 24 bishops and archbishops on 24 April 1949 the hierarchy replied that they sought to " re-establish the truth" and among other things they affirmed

In the meantime the campaign of calumny against the clergy was intensified.

In July 1949 three bishops (Mgr. *Stanislas Adamski* of Katowice, Mgr. *Wenceslas Kaczmarek* of Kielce and Mgr. *John Lorek* of Sandomierz) were accused by the Government press, after a five year interval, of having collaborated with the Germans. The Auxiliary Bishop of Czestochowa, Mgr. *Czajka*, had similar allegations made against him by the Government radio.

On 5 July 1949 a decree obliged clerics to keep an " account book " which would permit the Government to control the offerings made by the faithful to the Church and the clergy.[29]

The moral authority of the clergy was undermined by a method having nothing of the merit of novelty. Their moral or political scandals, real or imaginary, were broadcast to the four winds. The consequent legal proceedings thus became a means of pressure and a show of force, while the number of accusations against the clergy for " crimes against morals " increased.[30]

On 18 July 1949 the hierarchy in a joint Letter had to protest against new abuses of power on the part of the Government. They gave as examples:

> the suspension of two Catholic weeklies, the *Tygodnik Powszechny* of Cracow and the *Tygodnik Warszawski*; these papers were alternately authorised and suppressed on several occasions.
>
> the nationalisation of all Catholic printing works (about fifteen);
>
> the removal of many nuns and almost all chaplains from hospitals;
>
> the suppression of several Catholic associations, etc.

" . . . Be convinced that it is certainly not by being traitors to God that you will build a better Poland."

The episcopate proposed the nomination of a mixed commission to examine the serious problems which had been awaiting solution for some time. The Government however nominated its delegates only on 26 July.

[29] Cf. *Dziennik Ustaw Rzeczypospolitej Polskiej* (Official Journal of the Polish Republic), 12 July 1949, n. 40.

[30] Already in 1948 the Minister for Education had given the following directive: " Public opinion must be brought to realise that Catholic morality is inferior to Socialist morality."

While a new propaganda campaign against the Pope [31] was being unleashed, there appeared on 5 August 1949 a decree " for the defence of consciences and of religious denominations." This decree threatened with very grave penalties (including that of death) any person who would utilise religion to disturb " public order."

Another decree of 5-6 August 1949 stated that the 1932 " Law on Associations " applied to pious associations and confraternities. This had not been the case formerly. For the purpose of drawing up a list of recognised associations a question-naire was sent to each organisation. It so resembled a police investigation that the bishops decided not to send in their applica-tions. When the time-limit for sending in applications had been exceeded the dissolution of the associations and confraternities followed automatically. The bishops then gave orders to con-centrate more on the individual apostolate but the police pursued with intense activity their inquiries to make sure that the associations were suppressed and were not carrying on any underground activity. [32]

According to *Wolski*, Minister for Public Administration, the religious orders were not bound to fill in this questionnaire. In spite of this and certainly by orders of the Government the official bureaux demanded that the religious orders do so. All the religious communities filled in the form and sent it through the post to the Minister on the last day allowed for receiving applications. Silence then enveloped the whole subject. The Government took no further steps. But many communities were deprived of the work which provided their income (hospitals, schools, welfare work, etc.). The result of this was that the religious, both men and women, were driven to devote them-selves to other activities in order to live. The hospitals of religious were first of all largely " socialised " and later " national-ised." [33]

---

[31] Cf. the newspaper *Trybuna Ludu*, 4 August 1949. The Holy Father's Letter to the Polish hierarchy, 1 September 1949, did not meet with the approval of the censor, who wanted to modify it considerably. It was made the object of press attacks and some priests were threatened with punishment if they read it from the pulpit.

[32] Cf. *Dziennik Ustaw Rzeczypospolitej, Polskiej*, 6 August 1949, n. 334.

[33] A law which nationalised hospitals still in the hands of the Church was approved on 21 September 1949, promulgated 1 October and already in operation on 3 October.

Another decree on 11 August 1949 obliged the clergy to hand over the baptismal registers to State officials.

A Government circular of 23 November 1949 placed further obstacles to the right to hold meetings and to exercise public worship. In this circular the Minister for Public Administration interpreted the decree of 11 March 1932 in such a way as to prohibit:

> the organisation of public pilgrimages as well as the solemnities held at their arrival and departure;
>
> processions on the public highway;
>
> the solemn blessing of the fields;
>
> the solemn blessing of crosses and statues on the public highways;
>
> the organisation of public demonstrations and religious processions;
>
> calling of meetings, plays, conferences, recitals at the Christmas crib;
>
> open-air parish meetings. [34]

All the foregoing measures were intended to intimidate [35] Catholics and emphasised the efforts already made to secularise public life.[36]

The censorship of the press became so rigorous that it was preferred to cease publication of the official diocesan papers.

By a decree of 23 December 1949 all the business and production of publishing houses and printing establishments were taken over and subjected to the control of a political body, the Central Office of Publications. This office replied as it thought fit to the various calls upon it and decided which works should or

---

[34] Cf. *Dziennik Ustaw Rzeczypospolitej*, *Polskiej*, 5 December 1949, n. 50.

[35] Towards the end of 1949 Fr. Brudnicki, a priest from near Warsaw, was sentenced to five and a half years in prison; the sentence was increased because of a speech he made in defence of the Holy Father: " . . . the democratic press," the Communist papers stated, " has shown the Pope to be the enemy of Poland; whoever opposes this contention thereby attacks the Government and the Democratic régime."

[36] In fact from the moment recreation centres had been set up in the villages and industrial centres (with dances in the open air) an effort was made to make the people forget the religious feasts; thus in 1949 the occasion of Stalin's birthday was utilised to the full to disturb the observance of the Feast of Christmas with which it coincided. We need not mention " Soviet Christmas trees " . . . !

should not be published. Many Catholic writers and scholars failed to have their works printed, even works they had already prepared.

The beginning of 1950 was noteworthy for a violent campaign against *Caritas*.[37] By a decree of 23 January 1950 nearly all the diocesan centres of the Association were searched and closed. Even before the investigation was completed a new Administrative Council was imposed on it in open violation of the laws then in force. This Council was made up of some priests and so-called " progressive Catholics." [38]

On 30 January more than 1,000 priests were brought together by fraud or by force in a pseudo-council in Warsaw Polytechnic School to " legalise " the steps taken by the Government against *Caritas*.[39] On its side the press concentrated on building up a whole fictitious and calumnious campaign against the Church and the bishops, accusing them of having knowingly tolerated the alleged abuses of *Caritas*.[40]

The Catholic bishops considered it their duty to make their

---

[37] At the beginning of 1950 *Caritas*, a huge relief organisation set up by the Church, had under its care:

   334 orphanages with 16,676 children;

   258 homes for the aged;

   38 convalescent homes for sick children;

   17 hostels for poor children;

   18 workers' hostels;

   346 public canteens (distributing approximately 100,000 meals per day). In Warsaw alone which three years previously was nothing but a shambles, *Caritas* owned in 1948, 19 kindergartens, 27 homes for infants, 18 homes for indigent students, 12 holiday camps for children, 12 rest houses, about 100 homes for the aged, 9 laboratories for students and 39 circulating libraries. *Caritas* received gifts from American relief organisations and from Poles residing in the USA.

[38] The press organs of the " progressive Catholics " were: the weekly *Dzis i Jutro* (To-day and To-morrow), established in 1945; the daily *Slowo Powszechne*, established in 1947; *Pax* publications, commenced in 1949, dealing with political matters and religious propaganda. One can see in these an obvious effort to encourage the building up of a socialist economy, while refusing to accept materialist philosophy.

[39] Even before this meeting other assemblies of Catholics, priests and religious, had been brought together under great moral pressure to accuse and condemn *Caritas*.
On 24 January 1950 Cardinal Sapieha, President of *Caritas*, protested to the President of the Republic in a telegram. (Text in *La Civiltà Cattolica*, 15 April 1950).

[40] According to the Government these abuses consisted in " administrative irregularities," and in the help given by *Caritas* not to the poor but to those in good circumstances and to the enemies of the People's Poland (e.g. to prisoners and to those who were in hiding in order to escape arrest by the police, etc.).

protest heard once more.[41]   But while continuing to clarify repeatedly their point of view they persevered in their determination to arrive at an agreement.

On 23 January following, the bishops again made new proposals; the negotiations, which had begun only on 6 March, were re-opened on 28 March.

Meanwhile on 20 March 1950 the *Dziennik Ustaw Rzeczypospolitej Polskiej* published the text of the law on the nationalisation of the remaining ecclesiastical property.

The ecclesiastical patrimony was almost entirely confiscated without any indemnification from the State.   To replace it an ecclesiastical " fund " administered by the Government was established, and parish priests got the assurance that parish lands would not be touched. The Government had also tampered with the *stole fees*.   Every priest had to pay a " tax " on offerings for Masses, funerals, religious functions, etc., and had to give the name of the donor.

---

[41] On 30 January 1950 the hierarchy sent a *memorandum* to President Bierut: " . . . *Caritas* is an integral part of the institutions of the Church. . . . The control imposed on this organisation by Government injunction is then contrary to the laws of the State in force in Poland . . . ".   At the same time a *circular* was sent to the clergy to make clear to them the reason why *Caritas* had been suppressed and urging them to refuse to take any part in the new organisation being sponsored by the Government.   A statement also was issued which was to be read from the pulpit on 12 February. (The authorities used threats and other forms of pressure to prevent its being read).

The Communist Government had several priests arrested not only for refusing to take part in the new administration of *Caritas* but also because they had read in public the bishops' statement.

These three documents were published in *L'Osservatore Romano* on 10 and 11 April 1950. See also the *Tablet*, 25 February 1950

The Primate, Archbishop Stephen Wyszynski, who had made his official entry into the Polish capital as new Archbishop Primate on 6 February 1949, addressed a Letter to the people recounting the history of *Caritas*. Cf. *L'Osservatore Romano*, 10 and 11 April 1950.

On 4 February 1950 Mgr. Choromanski addressed a letter to the Minister of State, Wolski, refuting the false statements made by him some days earlier at the meeting of *The National Council of the Caritas Organisation*.

On 16 February 1950 the bishops sent another *memorandum* to President Bierut in order to bring to the knowledge of the world the campaign being waged, in an ever more open and more bitter manner, by the Communist Government against the Catholic Church: " . . . We feel it necessary to emphasise that the struggle against religion long being carried on in Poland is being directed according to tactics which up to now it would have been impossible to imagine in the fight against God." (The document was signed by Cardinal Sapieha and Archbishop Wyszynski).

The Joint Declaration

On 14 April 1950 the hierarchy and the Government signed a " Joint Declaration," [42] as the bishops termed it, since there was no question of a true agreement much less of a Concordat.

We give here a translation of the document on account of its importance in the history of the relations between the Catholic Church and Communism in Poland, and also because the Polish Government authorities referred to it continually, often in a dishonest manner.

AGREEMENT CONCLUDED BETWEEN THE REPRESENTATIVES OF THE GOVERNMENT OF THE REPUBLIC AND OF THE POLISH HIERARCHY

With a view to ensuring for the nation, for the People's Poland and for its citizens, the best conditions for development, and also with a view to the possibility of working together peacefully, the Government of the Republic which recognises the principle of religious liberty, and the Polish hierarchy which has in view the well-being of the Church and the present political interests of the Polish State, define their relations in the following terms:

ART. 1.   The bishops will see to it that the clergy within the limits of its pastoral office teaches the faithful respect for the laws and for the State authorities.

ART. 2.   The bishops will see to it that the clergy within the limits of its pastoral activity encourages the faithful to work with greater enthusiasm for the reconstruction of the country and for the promotion of the nation's well-being.

ART. 3.   The Polish hierarchy recognises that economic, historical, cultural and religious rights demand that the recovered territories belong henceforward forever to Poland. Recognising the principle that these territories constitute an integral part of

---

[42] Official news of the matter was given by the *Polish Agency* PAP on 16 April 1950. On 22 April 1950 the hierarchy in the course of a communiqué to the faithful published in the Catholic weekly *Tygodnik Powszechny* defined the significance of the " Agreement." They also explained the circumstances in which the bishops had decided to sign it and about which the press and Communist propaganda in general had spread false and exaggerated rumours.

The hierarchy had accepted this compromise—this is what it really was—because they had seen in it a guarantee, however small, against future Communist violations of the liberty of the Church.

the Republic, the episcopate will request the Holy See that the ecclesiastical administrative centres which enjoy the privilege of resident bishoprics shall be permanently elevated to the rank of ordinary episcopal sees.

Art. 4. The bishops within the limits of their powers will oppose all hostile activity directed against Poland, and especially the anti-Polish and " revisionist " manoeuvres of a section of the German clergy.

Art. 5. The principle that the Pope is the supreme and decisive authority in the Church relates to questions of faith and morals, and also to matters of ecclesiastical jurisdiction. In all other affairs the hierarchy will act in conformity with the political interests of the Polish State.

Art. 6. Recognising that the mission of the Church can be fulfilled in harmony with different economic and social systems established by the civil authorities, the bishops will give instructions to the clergy not to oppose the development of agricultural co-operatives. The last mentioned have a moral foundation in human nature which tends towards voluntary social solidarity, having for its aim the common good.

Art. 7. The Catholic Church, which in conformity with its principles condemns all anti-national attitudes, will set its face particularly against the abuse of religious sentiments to the detriment of the State.

Art. 8. The Catholic Church, which in conformity with its principles condemns all crimes, will similarly oppose the criminal activities of underground groups, will stigmatise and apply canonical sanctions to those members of the clergy who are guilty of participating in clandestine movements or in any movement directed against the State.

Art. 9. The hierarchy in conformity with the teaching of the Church will endorse every effort having for its aim the maintenance of peace and will oppose as far as possible every tendency to provoke war.

Art. 10. Religious instruction in the schools:

(a) The Government does not intend to apply any restrictions to the manner of imparting religious instruction now obtaining in the schools. The programmes will be set by the school

authorities in agreement with the representatives of the
hierarchy. The schools will be provided with suitable
textbooks. Teachers of religion, whether lay or clerical,
will be placed on the same footing as teachers of other
subjects. Inspectors of religious instruction will be appointed by the school authorities in agreement with the
bishops.

(b) The school authorities will not place any obstacles in the
way of students who wish to participate in religious services
outside the school. (Supplement to Art. 10 (b): These
services include principally: Holy Mass on Sundays and feast-days and also at the opening and closing of the school year.
In addition the authorities will guarantee three days' holidays during Lent to students desiring to participate in
retreats and to receive Holy Communion. The school
authorites will fix the times for students wishing to receive
Confirmation during the bishop's visitation. The recitation
of prayers before and after class by the students who wish
to do so will not be opposed by the authorities).

(c) Catholic schools already in existence will be retained; nonetheless the Government will see to it that they loyally
conform themselves to the provisions of the State and carry
out the programmes of instruction laid down by the State
authorities.

(d) The free Catholic schools may enjoy the same rights as the
official schools in accordance with the general principles as
defined by the relevant laws and the arrangements made by
the school authorities.

(e) In case of the establishment or changing of a public school
into a school not providing religious instruction Catholic
parents who so desire will have both the right and the
opportunity to send their children to schools which do
provide it.

ART. 11. The Catholic university of Lublin will continue to
provide education in accordance with the arrangements at present
obtaining.

ART. 12. Catholic associations will continue to enjoy the
rights they have had up to the present when they have fulfilled
the requirements set out in the decree on associations. The same
conditions hold for sodalities of Our Lady.

ART. 13. The Church will have the right and the opportunity to direct within the framework of the laws already in force works of charity and assistance, and also to provide catechetical instruction.

ART. 14. The Catholic press and Catholic publications will enjoy in common with other sections of the press the rights defined by the relevant laws and the legal provisions of the authorities.

ART. 15. Public worship, pilgrimages and traditional processions shall not be hindered. These demonstrations however for the sake of maintaining order will be arranged or regulated by the ecclesiastical authorities in agreement with the administrative authorities.

ART. 16. Religious ministry for the army will be arranged by special statute drawn up by the military authorities in agreement with the representatives of the hierarchy.

ART. 17. In prisons religious ministry will be looked after by chaplains nominated by the competent authorities on the proposal of the ordinary. (Supplement to Art. 17: This ministry will comprise Mass on Sundays and feast-days, Holy Communion, Confessions and Sermons).

ART. 18. In State hospitals and also in independent ones, religious assistance for the sick who desire it will be provided by hospital chaplains who will receive remuneration in accordance with special agreements. (Supplement to Art. 18: The number of chaplains will be proportionate to the number of the patients; the chaplain will have a private apartment; he will have facilities for visiting the sick).

ART. 19. Religious orders and congregations within the limits imposed by their vocation and by the laws at present in force will enjoy complete freedom of action.

SUPPLEMENTARY PROTOCOL

ART. 1. In accordance with the agreement between the representatives of the Government of the Polish Republic and the hierarchy regarding *Caritas* and with a view to making normal the relations between Church and State, the Church organisation *Caritas* will become a Catholic association having for its object the dispensing of aid to the poor and needy. The association will conduct its activities within regions corresponding to the territorial and administrative divisions of the country. The hierarchy in conformity with the charitable ends of the association and also having regard to the principles and practice of the Catholic Church, will afford every facility to priests who ask permission to work in that association. (Supplement to Art. 1: With reference to the ownership of non-movable ecclesiastical goods at the disposal of *Caritas*, the Government will examine the possibility of paying compensation for losses sustained, either by sums taken from the Ecclesiastical Fund or by leaving the right of property to the Church, provided the Church guarantees the usufruct to the said association).

Art. 2. The Government of the Polish Republic, when putting into operation the law for the confiscation of goods in mortmain under Art. 2, Section 2 and 3 and Art. 7, Section 1, will examine the needs of the bishops and of religious institutions with a view to providing them with assistance. (Supplement to Art. 2: (a) Gardens, agricultural holdings of up to 125 acres, and livestock will be left in the hands of ordinaries; (b) ecclesiastical seminaries will also be allowed to retain gardens, agricultural holdings of up to 125 acres and livestock; (c) farms of less than 12½ acres adjacent to the grounds on which the houses of religious communities are built, and also the movable and non-movable goods for their use, will not be confiscated by the State).

Art. 3. The Ecclesiastical Fund will put suitable sums at the disposal of the diocesan ordinaries.

Art. 4. In applying the law on military service the military authorities will grant a delay to students in ecclesiastical seminaries, in order to allow them to complete their studies. Clerics once they are ordained priests, and religious once they have taken vows, will not be called to the colours, but will be enrolled in the reserve and assigned to auxiliary service.

Signed at Warsaw, 14 April 1950

WLADYSLAW WOLSKI, *Minister for Public Education*,
EDWARD OCHAB, *Vice-Minister for National Defence*,
ZYGMUNT CHOROMANSKI, *Secretary to the Episcopate*,
TADEUSZ ZAKSZEWSKI, *Bishop of Plock*,
MICHAL KLEPACZ, *Bishop of Lodz*.

As is obvious, the first nine articles of the agreement deal with the Government's demands. The articles, expressed in clear and forthright terms (e.g. the phrase: " political interests of the State "), try to compromise the Church by commitments on political (art. 1, 2, 6, 7, 8) or territorial (art. 3, 4) matters which are foreign to its mission. All these articles, as they are drawn up, are couched in terms which leave no doubt as to their intent. The other ten articles contain the requests of the hierarchy, all concerned solely with the salvation of souls.

The bishops speak in the tones of those who on being attacked defend their rights as best they can.

On 1 May 1950 General *Edward Ochab*, one of the signatories of the agreement and recently made Party Secretary, said in a speech: " Half measures and evasive insinuations will be useless and injurious . . . because we Marxists will continue to intensify our watchfulness in accordance with the realism propounded by *Marx*, *Engels*, *Lenin* and *Stalin*."

On 8 May 1950 the President of the Republic, *Bierut*, stated: " We will scrupulously fulfil the agreement which has been signed, but we will not permit re-actionary political intrigues to be planned as in the past, in violation of that agreement."

Meanwhile when the Ministry for Public Administration was suppressed and its duties transferred to national, regional and provincial administrative bodies, the whole Office for Religious Affairs was transferred to a special bureau, the direction of which after a long delay was given to *Anton Bida* who was a former director of the press censorship and who while occupying that post had been specially hostile to the Catholic press.[43]

In spite of the success of the negotiations the Minister, *Wolski*, who had headed the Government commission for the drafting of the agreement, was first expelled from the Party and later imprisoned.

But the agreement did not bring the hoped for truce in the struggle against the Church.

Some schools conducted by nuns (for example, the Sacred

---

[43] It was even said that the direction of Religious Affairs had been placed under the control of the Section for Denominational Affairs of the Soviet Embassy in Warsaw.

Heart Convent in Cracow) were laicised. In others permission
to teach catechism was refused.

The suppression of works and social institutions in the care
of the Church was intensified.

At the same time a campaign developed against the giving of
religious instruction in schools by " priests who are enemies of
peace." Committees of parents and even of pupils were set up
to demand the dismissal of these priests. About 500 ecclesiastics
were thus banished from their schools while others were arrested
for spreading " propaganda in favour of war."

A campaign was then started to obtain forcibly signatures to
the notorious Stockholm Appeal.

The newspaper *Trybuna Ludu* reproached two bishops, Mgr.
Ignatius Swirski of Siedlce and Mgr. *John Stepa* of Tarnow, for
having forbidden their priests to become members of the
Communist " peace committees." The same accusation was made
later against the whole hierarchy.

On 16 June 1950 Mgr. *Choromanski* published in the name of
the hierarchy a declaration in which he recalled that the Church's
mission was ever in favour of peace. He affirmed that the hierarchy and clergy do not fail to work for peace in the discharge
of their normal pastoral duties. The Government however
wanted a declaration which would constitute a commitment in
favour of the Stockholm Appeal. Some bishops signed as the
lesser of two evils. The Government hastened to make this
known by an official communiqué. Pressure was then brought
to bear on the other bishops who also decided to put their
signatures to the Appeal.

On 15 July 1950 *Trybuna Ludu*, the organ of the Communist
Party, drew the following conclusions from the signatures:
" Polish public opinion is entitled to demand that the attitude
taken by the Polish hierarchy in signing the Appeal should be
followed to its logical conclusion by their taking part henceforth
in the struggle against acts of aggression and incitements to war,
and also in the struggle to ensure peace."

Already however on 28 June 1950 Major *Dziemiduk*, in the
course of a press conference, had denounced the Catholic hierarchy's lack of respect for article 8 of the agreement. There

followed a new wave of arrests, together with the closing of schools and religious houses, which lasted throughout the summer of 1950.

The Hierarchy's Protest

A Plenary Session of the Assembly of the Hierarchy met at the Sanctuary of Czestochowa on 12 and 13 September 1950. On this occasion a Letter was sent to the President of the Republic, enumerating all the outrageous abuses of power of which the Church had been the victim in the period 1945-1950:

the unilateral breach of the Concordat;

the refusal on the part of the Government to recognise the ecclesiastical organisation in the reconquered territories;

the prohibition against the re-establishment of Catholic associations and organisations;

the continued and systematic closing of Catholic schools and institutions;

the severe restrictions imposed by the political censorship on Catholic newspapers and other publications with a view to their total extinction;

the handing over of Church property to relief societies which practically amounted to its nationalisation;

the seizure of all the diocesan printing houses and Catholic publishing establishments;

the effort on the part of the administrative authorities to interfere with the life of ecclesiastical confraternities and associations ending in the obligatory registration of monasteries and religious congregations;

the restrictions placed on freedom of public worship, going so far as to constitute an effort to prohibit the celebration of religious services and devotional exercises (such as the holding of missions, public processions, religious meetings and congresses);

the liquidation of *Caritas*;

the complete nationalisation of ecclesiastical property;

organised press campaigns of varying intensity against the Holy See and the hierarchy;

the curtailment of the rights of religion in the schools;

the expulsion and exclusion of many hundreds of priest-catechists from the schools;

the setting up of youth organisations of anti-Christian character and outlook;

support given to publications which were an insult to the teaching and life of the Church;

anti-religious propaganda through the press, books, lectures and formation courses;

restrictions on the liberty of conscience of members of Government associations and of professional organisations;

anti-religious propaganda in kindergartens, in schools, in holiday camps and in camps for children and for boys and girls;

the administrative annoyances inflicted by the civil authorities, by the police and by revenue officers on priests and bishops.

Having affirmed that " the past year especially since the signing of the Agreement was marked in a more serious manner by an accelerated suppression of social institutions and other Church organisations," the Memorandum went on to deal with

the materialist education of youth;

the precarious position of religious teaching in the schools and support given by the Government to the TPD schools (Society of the Child's Friends), in which religious instruction has been abolished and atheistic education is being imparted;

the reduction of the time allowed to religious instruction in classes I and II and the mass dismissal of priests who taught catechism (about 500);

the question of the recovered territories; [44]

---

[44] On this point the Letter stated: " The episcopate is ready to present this problem to the Holy See as soon as possible. In drawing up the Letter to the Holy Father however the episcopate was faced with serious difficulties which are of great import in the whole question. In recent weeks new events have taken place: at Wroclaw (Breslau) the seminary building has been expropriated; at Olsztyn the seminary authorities have been notified that its building must be evacuated; other ecclesiastical properties are already in the hands of the Government. The position at Opole is the same. In such circumstances the apostolic administrators cannot exert their influence in the most important matter of the formation of the clergy which is of decisive significance for the future of the life of the Church. All this has taken place through no fault of the Church. Many more examples could be given in other spheres of ecclesiastical life."

Government support for " patriot priests "; [45]

the Statute of the State Bureau for Worship, with the evident aim of hindering the activity of the Church;

press campaign against the Holy See;

the system of repression employed against the clergy, which is manifested in the great number of priests subjected to juridical inquiries, arrested without any legal reason or sentenced to long terms of imprisonment; [46]

the lot of religious communities and of religious forced to live " in exceptionally unjust circumstances " and subjected to " attempts to make them alter their attitude of non-interference in politics, which up to the present they have maintained ";

repeated violations of the Joint Declaration on the part of the Government.

In conclusion the Letter added: " . . . We limit ourselves to these problems while being aware however that we are far from having mentioned all that exist. It is our wish that this Letter should be a document for the record and that it will free us from the reproach of not having proclaimed the truth. Responsibility

---

[45] The Letter pointed out in this regard: " According to the view of the Government authorities under this title come priests ready to collaborate with the Government . . . The creation of a special group of ecclesiastics collaborating with the Government seems to be without meaning once an understanding (the agreement mentioned above) has been reached with the whole episcopate. A choice has been made—already sufficiently eloquent in itself—of men to whom under the title of ' patriot priests ' it is meant to give a special task to fulfil in Poland. Nearly all the heads of the Ecclesiastical Section of the Office for the Affairs of Worship have been for quite a long time now acting contrary to their moral and canonical duties. Some of them indeed have incurred ecclesiastical sanctions. To confide to such men the task of reforming ecclesiastical life in Poland is but to compromise your own authority in the eyes of the Catholic citizens who know their priests and know in whom they may place their trust. Furthermore the so-called ' patriot priests ' direct a publication (*Voice of the Priest*) which, although meant for the clergy, is printed without any ecclesiastical authorisation. This publication carries on a methodical attack on the Holy See, the Holy Father and the episcopate. It voices false moral and religious opinions. It does all in its power to undermine ecclesiastical discipline and tends to propagate heresy and schism among the clergy."

[46] The Letter affirmed: " Many priests have been taken directly from the churches, from the confessional and from the midst of children awaiting confession to the amazement and anxiety of the faithful. This is a singularly new occurrence in our life, for up to the present priests came very little into contact with the penal code. Even the bishops do not escape this supervision. During their pastoral rounds, meetings and visits they are surrounded by dozens of informers who make their presence known by their provocative behaviour. Many priests have been forced to collaborate with the Information Service. This has been brought about by methods of intimidation which have been used even on the assistants in the episcopal Curiae."

for the condition of the Church in Poland is not ours. We feel compelled to state this, because free Poland never persecuted the Church or religion. We see no way to that tranquillity of mind which is so indispensable and to national unity except by the ending of the struggle against religion." [47]

The Letter was signed by Cardinal *Sapieha* and by the Primate, Archbishop *Wyszynski*.

From October 1950 to February 1951 clergy and religious were constantly being arrested on various pretexts.[48]

In January 1951 Mgr. *Kaczmarek*, Bishop of Kielce, and his Vicar General were taken into custody.

On 26 January 1951 a Government decree ordered the removal from office and expulsion of the apostolic administrators appointed by the Holy See for the ecclesiastical circumscriptions in the German territories (Silesia and East Prussia) handed over to Poland until the Peace Treaty settled definite frontiers. They were: the Administrators of Danzig, Mgr. *A. Wronka*; of Wroclaw (Breslau), Mgr. *K. Milik*; of Opole, Mgr. *B. Kominek*; of Gorzow (Schneidemühl), Mgr. *Nowicki*; of Warmia, Mgr. *T. Bensz*. On 29 January the Government arbitrarily replaced them by " Vicars Capitular." [49]

Solely with the intention of clarifying the ecclesiastical situation in the " recovered territories " the Primate asked for and received permission to go to Rome.[50]

Two weeks after his return the Primate convoked a full meeting of the hierarchy. In a *Memorandum for the clergy* he gave the following instructions:

---

[47] The Letter was published by the *Kipa Agency*, 1 December 1950, and by *L'Osservatore Romano*, 14 February 1951.

[48] For example it was claimed that " sensational caches " of arms had been discovered on the premises of the Salvatorians of Mklolow, the Franciscans of Radecznica, and the Jesuits of Cracow.

[49] The Primate, Archbishop Wyszynski, intervened, and to avoid all danger of schism he sub-delegated ecclesiastical jurisdiction to five priests.

[50] In a Letter of 23 May 1951 to the clergy and faithful of his archdiocese he wrote: " . . . to enable you to share in the joy that was given me by seeing Peter in the person of the Holy Father . . . Our presence in Rome has borne witness to the world that Poland is Catholic and faithful to the Holy Father and that she can and must remain Catholic. We are conscious of having rendered the greatest possible service to our country and to the Church." Cf. *L'Osservatore Romano*, 30-31 July 1951.

" We desire that priests refrain from political activities and do not interfere in party questions. . . . We have only one duty— to announce the truth revealed by God and to help all to go towards God. It is therefore forbidden to priests to join secret or subversive movements or other social, economic or political movements. We have not been called to be the dispensers of the goods of this world." [51]

But the Communist newspaper *Trybuna Ludu* accused the Primate of having taken up the cudgels on behalf of the policy of the Holy See. It quoted against his attitude, " . . . the courageous decision of the Congress of Wroclaw, 12 December 1951, when 1,800 Polish Catholics, clergy and laymen, had on the contrary upheld the claims of the Government." This paper cited by way of example the statement of the clergy of Danzig who had declared " . . . we condemn the German clergy, who under the direction of Cardinals *Frings* and *Faulhaber* and influenced by the Vatican foster an atmosphere of hatred . . . " [52]

The Reign of Violence

The attack on the Catholic Church was intensified in 1952 just after the new general elections and the adoption of the new Constitution.

On 3 July throughout all Poland measures were quickly put through to close and take over all the junior seminaries belonging to various orders and religious congregations. Fifty-nine seminaries were taken over and nearly all the students were sent to labour-camps.

---

[51] In an interview given to the Cracow Catholic weekly *Tygodnik Powszechny* and published 16 December 1951 the Primate explained the mind and attitude of the Holy See on the problem of ecclesiastical organisation in the former German territories: " Even though the Holy See has not yet made a formal statement on the matter, its acts here surely speak for themselves. It is a fact indeed that the Holy See has taken cognisance of the ecclesiastical organisation established by the late Cardinal Hlond in the western territories. Furthermore the Holy See has authorised the re-establishment of diocesan Curiae, ecclesiastical courts, seminaries, etc., all well defined organisations which belong canonically to the independent life of a diocese. According as Church life develops its external organisation will not fail to take on better defined forms."

[52] Moreover from 17 July *Pravda* attacked the Primate's journey to Rome: " . . . Pius XII has approved and blessed the activity of the Polish higher clergy against the people; he has given the Primate Wyszynski yet more extensive powers."

The slanderous campaign was intensified against the priests and especially the bishops, who were accused of being instruments and victims of " Vatican policy " hostile to Poland, especially in connection with social problems and the questions of the western frontiers. The Holy Father himself was denounced as an accomplice of imperialist war-mongers and of the most hateful form of capitalism.[53]

On 8 November the Bishop of Katowice, Mgr. *Stanislas Adamski* was arrested with his coadjutor and his auxiliary, Mgr. *Herbert Bednorz* and Mgr. *Julius Bieniek*. All three were later expelled from the diocese of Katowice. Towards the end of 1952 it is estimated that about 1,000 priests were in prison, an average of 50 per diocese, in all 10% of the Polish clergy. From 21-27 January 1953 after a violent press campaign [54] four priests and three laymen were accused of:

illegal possession of 37,000 dollars and other foreign currencies;

receiving various valuable objects belonging to certain Polish aristocrats;

spying for the Americans.

At the same time a considerable number of other priests was arrested together with the Archbishop of Lwow and the Apos-

---

[53] In its issue of January 1954 the monthly review, *Nowe Drogi* (New Paths), official publication of a theoretical character of the United Workers' Party of Poland, gave the following list of polemic and critical works on the Vatican's political activity (these works appeared in Poland in 1952-1953):

Henry Korotynski: *Pytania ktore czekaja na odpozwied* (Questions which demand a reply), " Czytelnik," 1953.

Jurkiewicz: *Nuncjatura Achille Ratti w Polsce* (Nunciature of Achille Ratti in Poland), " Czytelnik," 1953.

A. Nowicki: *Papiez Pius XII w swietle przemowien i listow* (Pope Pius XII in the light of his Discourses and Letters), " Ksiazka i Wiedza," 1952.

A Nowicki: *Watykanski Bank Pacellich* (The Vatican Bank of the Pacellis), " Ksiazka Wiedza," 1952.

The titles of some of the articles appearing every day in the Communist press are worth noting. For the latter part of 1952 alone here are some examples: *The Vatican against Peace and Poland* (*Nowa Wies*, 21 December 1952); *Always on the side of War*, (*Dziennik Polski*, 22 November 1952); *A nest of robbers surround the Pope* (*Dziennik Polski*, 4 December 1952); *The Vatican Report* (*Trybuna Ludu*, 13 December 1952); *Genocidal Plans of Vatican Diplomats in Cardinal's Purple* (*Maly*); *His eye is in Heaven but his hand is in his Neighbour's Pocket* (*Poprostu*, 12 November 1952).

[54] As an example of the whole press see *Trybuna Ludu*, 18 January 1953, article entitled: *Centres of Conspiracy against the State which cannot be tolerated*. *Comments on the Espionage Affair of the Curia of Cracow*.

tolic Administrator of Cracow, Mgr. *Eugene Baziak*, the Auxiliary Bishop to the late Cardinal *Sapieha*, Mgr. *Stanislas Rospond*, and the Chancellor of the Curia, Mgr. *Stanislas Mazanek*.

After " full confession " very severe sentences were passed on the " guilty "; one of the four priests was sentenced to death.

There followed a new and shameful attack on the clergy in general, on the bishops and on the deceased Cardinal *Sapieha*.

The trial was used as a *moral alibi* by the Communists for a series of new legal enactments which violated the most elementary liberties of the Church.

On 9 February 1953 a decree was published on the nomination of ecclesiastics for various Church offices.[55]

ART. 1.   Church offices may be held only by Polish citizens.

ART. 2.   For the creation, transference or suppression of such offices, as well as for any alteration in their spheres of operation, the consent of the relevant civil authority is necessary.

ART. 3.   (a) Before charge of such offices is assumed the previous consent of the relevant civil authority must be obtained.

(b) The above provisions shall apply also to the case of dismissal or transference to other appointments.

ART. 4.   The proper authority for these cases is as follows: In what relates to the ordinaries of dioceses and to suffragans (?), the Bureau of the President of the Government; in all other cases, the Bureau of the President of the District National Council (in Warsaw and Lodz, the Bureau of the President of the National Council of these cities).

ART. 5.   Persons occupying such offices are to take an oath of allegiance to the Polish People's Republic at the Bureau for Religious Affairs, or at the office of the Praesidium of the competent National Council (for Warsaw and Lodz, the National Councils of these cities). [56]

---

[55] Published in *Dziennik Ustaw Rzeczypospolitej Polskiej* (official organ of the People's Republic of Poland), n. 10, 10 February 1953. Yet two successive Constitutions of 1948 and 1952 proclaimed the " separation " of the Church and State and promised " religious liberty " ! This decree on the contrary gave the State control over every act of ecclesiastical jurisdiction, and to some extent even over matters of personal conscience. In this decree use is made of the expression " ecclesiastico-spiritual dignity "—a phrase unknown to Catholic terminology—and a translation of the expression very often used in Russia: " Tserkovno-dukovnyja oblznoski " !

[56] See the text of the oath—*La Civiltà Cattolica*, 1953, III, p. 360.

ART. 6. Any priest occupying an ecclesiastical office who engages in activities contrary to law and public order or who supports or conceals such activities shall be removed from such office by order of higher ecclesiastical authority on its own initiative or at the request of the State authority.

ART. 7. The carrying out of this decree is the responsibility of the President of the Council of Ministers.

ART. 8. This decree is to take effect on the date of publication.

President of the Council of State:
A. ZAWADZKI.
Secretary of the Council of State:
M. RYBICKI.

On 5 May 1953 a directive was published for the implementation of the decree.

* * *

On 8 May 1953 the Cardinal Primate *Wyszynski* forwarded a lengthy memorandum to the President of the Council in which he exposed the pitiable condition to which the Church had been reduced by the Communist régime. He courageously denounced its misuse of power and its brutalities, pointing out clearly where the responsibility lay. He advised him paternally to follow the path of friendship, harmony, wisdom and respect for the rights of all. " Will the Government abandon its plan to enslave the Church and to make it a tool of the State? . . . Bear in mind that by the decree of 9 February 1953, which incidentally the Polish Constitution deprives of all juridical authority, the State has permanently arrogated to itself the right to interfere in the internal affairs of the Church and even with the liberty of conscience of priests. It has also arrogated to itself the right to subject ecclesiastical jurisdiction arbitrarily and systematically to its control. All this the Church expressly refuses to admit . . . "

The Government put its decree into effect by arbitrarily removing ecclesiastics from their charges and nominating men of their own choice. The bonds binding the clergy to the

Office for Religious Affairs were tightened; for their personal material needs all ecclesiastics must now apply to this Office, thereby giving it opportunities to *institute inquiries, to tighten control and otherwise oppress the Church.*

A small group of " progressive priests " served well to further the Communist design " to purify and reform the Church." On 18 June 1953 they held a congress at Warsaw; they adopted a report entitled " Prospects for the development of the Agreement between Church and State in the People's Republic of Poland." [57]

On 5 September 1953 eight bishops had either been removed from their sees or forbidden to fulfil their duties. They were as follows:

> Mgr. *Wenceslas Kaczmarek*, Bishop of Kielce;
>
> Mgr. *Stanislas Adamski*, Bishop of Katowice; [58]
>
> Mgr. *Herbert Bednorz*, Coadjutor of Katowice;
>
> Mgr. *Julius Bieniek*, Auxiliary and Vicar General of Katowice;
>
> Mgr. *Eugene Baziak*, Metropolitan Archbishop of Lwow and Apostolic Administrator of Cracow;
>
> Mgr. *Stanislas Rospond*, Bishop Vicar General of Cracow;
>
> Mgr. *Lucian Bernacki*, Bishop Vicar General of the Cardinal-Primate in the Archdiocese of Gniezno;
>
> Mgr. *Charles Splett*, Bishop of Danzig, who had been condemned to eight years' imprisonment in 1946 for " collaboration with the Germans."

---

[57] Statements of this kind are to be found in the Report: " Polish Catholic opinion protests against the attitude of the Vatican which shields with its authority the American politicians' war-plans . . . " As regards the bishops it is necessary " to find the moral courage and the intellectual arguments that will convince them and force on them an exact evaluation of the modern social and political reality." In the meantime it will be necessary " to purify the unhealthy atmosphere which even yet too often hangs with all its weight on the home form of Catholicism: a bourgeois and indeed a semi-feudal atmosphere explicable by the links that once bound the Church to the possessor-class in Poland."

[58] This had been re-named Stalingrad up to the time of Kruschev's attack on " the cult of personality."

For three years the Government opposed the installation of Mgr. *Adalbert Turowski*, and Mgr. *Anthony Pawlowski* in the dioceses of Czestochowa and Wloclawek respectively.

The more determined and influential of the clergy were removed from the scene either by imprisonment or by committing them to concentration camps; at the same time the better to upset Church organisation priests were transferred from one part of the country to another. Charge of the more important posts and centres was given to those who were either creatures of the new régime or who had yielded to most insidious and most brutal threats.

At the end of September 1953 the case against the Bishop of Kielce, Mgr. *Wenceslas Kaczmarek* (who had been arrested at the end of January 1951 and held in prison for 32 months without trial), was brought up for hearing. An endless and detailed " self-accusation " was staged in the course of which the bishop went back thirty years to the time when as a newly ordained priest he went to France to take his degrees at the Catholic university of Lille. The self-accusation involved other bishops, as well as the dead Cardinals *Hlond* and *Sapieha* and even the Holy Father himself.

Two days after a sentence of 12 years' imprisonment had been imposed on Mgr. *Kaczmarek*, Cardinal *Wyszynski* protested to the Government and in the name of the hierarchy denied that the Holy See had ever given political directives to the Catholic clergy and laity of Poland.

Mgr. *Kaczmarek* set free in February 1955 was again thrown into prison in March 1956.

On 26 September 1953, two days after Mgr. *Kaczmarek* was sentenced " for treason " and " complicity " with the Germans during the war,[59] a Government communiqué announced that Archbishop *Stephen Wyszynski* had been forbidden " to exercise the functions connected with the ecclesiastical charges devolving on him up to the present "; for all practical purposes this was

---

[59] The " treason " consisted according to his judges in having followed the "directives of the Vatican " and of his ecclesiastical superiors to the serious detriment of Polish National rights.

arrest.[60]   The reason alleged by the Government for " dismissing " and interning the Cardinal was " violation " of article 3 of the Agreement. In this article it was stated that the episcopate " starting from the view-point that the recovered territories were an integral part of the Republic shall have recourse to the Holy See to request that the ecclesiastical administrations already enjoying the rights of residential episcopal sees be transformed permanently into ordinary bishoprics." The episcopate however undertook to ask the Holy See to erect the ecclesiastical administrations in the " western territories " into dioceses. But the Holy See could not make a definite decision, i.e. to constitute dioceses, until the Peace Treaty had been signed by all the belligerents. In this it followed the usual practice. Had it acted otherwise it would have seemed to be taking sides, at least up to a certain point, in purely political matters which by their nature were outside its competence.[61]

The Memorandum makes it clear that after the Agreement the bishops had arranged to have the priests in charge of the circumscriptions in the " recovered territories " raised to the episcopal dignity. The Communist Government of Warsaw prevented the realisation of this step, pretending to see in it a purely political gesture.

During the infamous campaign against Cardinal *Wyszynski* after his arrest the Communist press painted him as a supporter of " German revisionism " and did not even hesitate to declare that his " internment " had been approved by all the other bishops. The Government spoke of " consignment to a comfortable

---

[60] Cf. *Trybuna Ludu*, 26 September 1953. " This decision," stated the Government, communiqué, " has been taken following Cardinal Stephen Wyszynski's persistent abuse despite several warnings, of his ecclesiastical office; he has violated the *Protocol of Understanding*, stirred up trouble and created an atmosphere favourable to subversive activities, as has been proved by the trial of Bishop Kaczmarek, activities particularly disastrous at a time when the integrity of the frontiers of the People's Republic of Poland is being threatened."

On 10 May on the occasion of a solemn procession at Cracow for the opening of the celebration of the seventh centenary of the canonisation of St. Stanislas, and again on 4 June at Warsaw on the occasion of the Corpus Christi procession, the Cardinal Primate was warmly cheered and acclaimed by the people.

On the eve of his arrest the Cardinal preached before a congregation of about 10,000 people in the Church of St. Anne.

[61] Cf. *L'Osservatore Romano*, 29 November 1953.

monastery," but an oppressive and unbroken silence prevented the Catholic world from knowing the place of his detention.[62]

Mgr. *Anthony Baraniak*, a close collaborator first of Cardinal *Hlond* and then of Cardinal *Wyszynski*, was also arrested. In 1955 he was released but was forbidden to carry out his pastoral duties.

According to Government information the ordinaries of the Polish dioceses met in the capital on 28 September 1953 and elected Mgr. *Michal Klepacz*, Bishop of Lodz, as president of episcopal conferences. According to the same sources they agreed on a declaration in conformity with the wishes of the Communist régime and re-affirmed the desire to work in harmony with the constituted authorities.[63] It was only on 3 October that the names of the bishops present became known. This taken in conjunction with the fact that the " statement " published on 29 September bore no signatures seemed to point to another instance of Communist trickery.

At the same time the bishops, vicars capitular and auxiliary bishops are supposed to have taken the oath of fidelity to the People's Republic at the presidential seat of the Council of Ministers. Mgr. *Klepacz* was said to have spoken in the name of the episcopate, and *Cyrankiewicz*, Minister of State, in the name of the Government.

It was stated that on 29 September a new episcopal " Praesidium " (made up of Mgrs. *Klepacz*, *Choromanski* and *Zakszewski*) was received in audience by President *Bierut*.

After the arrest of Cardinal *Wyszynski* and the " taking of the oath of fidelity " the Government began to push forward more vigorously the associations of " patriot priests " and " progressive Catholics." The " patriot priests " held their national congress at Warsaw on 15 October 1953. There it was decided to set up a " Central Committee of the National Front of Progressive

---

[62] The official account of the tenth session of the Commission for the Rights of Man (attached to UNO) enumerates 9,524 protests against the violation of religious freedom; 7,850 of these concerned the Communist régime in Poland and the " internment " of the Cardinal Primate. This however brought about not the slightest change either of heart or of practice on the part of the Communist authorities in Warsaw.

[63] See text of this unbelievable declaration in BEIPI, n. 104, 16-28 February 1954.

Priests and Laymen." This Committee was really a commission of 65 members clerical and lay having for aim, as was pointed out at the meetings of 17 and 18 November under the presidency of the Rev. Professor *John Czuj*, to " cement and strengthen the unity of the nation," to " oppose the calumnious propaganda of the enemies of our country " and " to expend every effort to fulfil the tasks which follow from the Declaration of the episcopate of 28 September 1953." [64]

In July 1954 a collection of sermons to mark the tenth anniversary of the Communist régime was distributed to both secular and regular clergy. This collection had been compiled by " progressive " elements. Great care had been taken to make it known that these sermons would continue in use until the spring of 1955.

In October 1954 the Government decided to suppress the faculties of Theology in the universities of Warsaw, Cracow and Poznan. University theological studies were allowed only in the university of Lublin [65] on which the Government imposed the appointment of five professors selected from among the " patriot priests." [66]

On 20 November 1954 the " Academy of Catholic Theology " of Bielany was solemnly inaugurated in the presence of representatives of the Government. The Reverend *John Czuj*, " a man in whom the Government had absolute confidence " was named rector.

In the course of an episcopal conference at Czestochowa from 15-17 August 1954 the bishops deplored the fact that about 1,200 nuns had been expelled from their convents situated

---

[64] At the end of 1954 Radio Warsaw announced that Anton Bida, who had directed the persecution during the previous two years up to the internment of Cardinal Wyszynski, had been replaced at the head of the National Office for Religious Affairs by Jan Izydorczyk —former Polish ambassador to the East German Democratic Republic.

This possibly marked the entry of a more subtle and diplomatic figure on the scene, one who had a wider knowledge of Polish mentality and for that reason was better able to apply Communist ideology in accordance with well-known tactical principles.

[65] Cf. *L'Osservatore Romano*, 17 October 1954. Meanwhile the news of the closing of the faculties of Theology in the universities of Warsaw and Cracow had been confirmed. Cf. *L'Osservatore Romano*, 20 January 1955; also the pro-Government interview concerning the academy given on 28 November 1954 by *Czuj* to the *Dzis i Jutro*.

[66] Cf. NCWC News Service, 26 October 1954.

mainly in Silesia [67] and that all religious instruction in public schools had been almost completely suppressed.

In the Catholic university of Lublin the faculties of Law and Economic Science were suppressed and more than 10 professors were arbitrarily dismissed. Furthermore there was reason to fear that the seminaries would be closed and replaced by an academy withdrawn from legitimate ecclesiastical jurisdiction and controlled by the public authorities through the medium of the Bureau for Worship. [68]

The teaching of Marxist doctrines was introduced in the senior seminaries of Wroclaw and Poznan. In all the other seminaries Communist infiltration in the formation of clerics is an established fact. [69]

Balance Sheet

Twelve years of Communist Government in Poland have brought with them heavy losses for the Church. [70]

Of the Catholic hierarchy 7 bishops are still in prison and 2 are not allowed to exercise their jurisdiction. The effort to split the clergy into two camps goes on relentlessly. The Government continues to help in every way the Commissions of Priests within the Communist Associations of Fighters for Freedom and Democracy. To help these " patriot priests " the

---

[67] The " liquidation " of communities of nuns was quietly carried on; one by one the convents were closed. A decree of 1954 confiscated without compensation the hospital of St. Joseph of Kamieniec Zabkowicki, maintained by the Sisters of St. Charles. The nuns " would be accommodated elsewhere." In Warsaw the Sisters of Mercy were expelled from the Hospital of Our Lord Jesus Christ founded by them two hundred years previously. In many other parts of the country also the confiscation of convents and the expulsion of religious took place.

[68] Cf. *L'Osservatore Romano*, 17 October 1954.

[69] See the revealing statements of the collaborator, Dr. Huet, Vicar General of Cracow in *Slowo Powszechne*, 26 February 1954 and the article: *The Atmosphere of Pastoral Work* in *Kuznica Kaplanska* (another organ of the " patriot priests "), 25 May 1954.

[70] Mgr. Adamski, 82 years old Bishop of Katowice, was liberated from forced residence in September 1956. Scarcely had he returned to his See when he made known to the " patriot priest " who had replaced him that he intended taking full charge of the diocese himself. As a result some 20 policemen, headed by the district attorney, broke into Bishop Adamski's home about 11 p.m. and in spite of his physical condition and his semi-paralysis carried him off to an unknown destination.

publication of the bi-weekly *Glos Kaplana* (Voice of the Priest) was encouraged. In December 1950 this title, already too compromised, was changed to *Ksiadz Obywatel* (Citizen Priest). There are also publications of less importance. Priests not joining these associations [71] are constantly branded in the Communist press as " enemies of the people ", " enemies of the people's Poland ", " Fascists ", accomplices of the Hitler criminals of the West ", etc. The Government demands the especial collaboration of the " patriot priests " for the realisation of its social plans and above all for its programme of collectivisation. [72]

The situation with regard to priests on 31 December 1953 was as follows: 37 killed, 260 disappeared, 350 deported, 700 imprisoned and 700 living in exile.

The fate of the regular clergy, and above all of the nuns, driven from their schools and prevented from carrying on their works of charity, has been no better. On 31 December 1953 the following were the statistics: 54 religious (men) killed, 200 deported, 170 in prison, 200 living in exile.

The nationalisation of ecclesiastical property was a very serious blow to the Church more especially in face of the flourishing " democratic " organisations for the de-christianisation of the people.

However it is in the domain *of the press* that the Church has been made to feel oppression most. The Catholic press has been all but wiped out. Publications are at present being passed off as Catholic and religious which come from the hands of so-called " progressive " individuals acting independently of all ecclesiastical control and with the full support of the Communist régime. In the years 1945-1950 there were only 32 really Catholic

---

[71] The number of " patriot priests," most of them suspended *a divinis* or under other ecclesiastical censures, was estimated at from 30-40 in 1950. In 1953 the number rose to about 100, i.e. about 1% of the whole Polish clergy. It is true that at the meetings of the " patriot priests " there were sometimes up to 1,000 priests from different dioceses present. But this is explained by the Communist methods of deceit, extortion and terrorism. There are actual cases of priests being brought to these meetings after having been taken by force from the altar or from their beds.

[72] See for example *Slowo Powszechne*, 24 April 1955.

religious publications.[73] In 1951 this number had been reduced to 12, the number of copies of each issue of these being reduced to a few thousand or even in some cases to a few hundred. In March 1953 the Communist authorities refused any further allocation of paper to Catholic periodicals. The last number of the great Catholic weekly *Tygodnik Powszechny* appeared on 9 March 1953. The monthly review *Znak* had appeared for the last time in February 1953. All the other Catholic papers and periodicals disappeared one after the other. *Tygodnik Powszechny* re-appeared in July 1953 no longer however edited by the archiepiscopal Curia of Cracow but by the editing house *Pax* which the Government had handed over to the " progressive Catholics." In May 1956 this weekly and *Dzis i Jutro* (condemned by the Holy Office in August 1955) announced that they had ceased publication in order to amalgamate and appear as a new periodical under the name of *Kierunki* (Orientations). *Slowo Powszechne*, organ of the Committee of " Catholic Intellectuals," presided over by the notorious *Boleslas Piasecki*, continues publication with full Government support.

This picture of the state of the Catholic press in Poland would be incomplete if, after pointing out the elimination of all Catholic periodicals and the encouragement given by the Government to " progressive " papers, no mention was made of the millions of publications for Communist propaganda purposes: 49,181,400 in 1948; 72,905,000 in 1949; and 122,253,000 in 1950.

The position in 1956 was even more gloomy and sad [74] than that described by the bishops in their Letter to the head of the State in September 1950. The words of the Holy Father addressed to the Polish hierarchy on 1 September 1951 were still entirely to the point:

" God bless your courage . . . Your battle is not against flesh and

---

[73] Before the war there were 329 Catholic publications. Of these 7 weeklies and 19 monthlies were of particular importance. *Rycerz Niepokalanej* (Knight of the Immaculate) alone had a circulation of almost one million.

[74] Take as an example the testimony of an English Labour Member of Parliament, a non-Catholic. After a visit to Poland with a British Parliamentary Delegation he stated that he had returned " depressed and dispirited " and that he was certain of the existence of a " cruel persecution." Cf. NCWC News Service, 29 November 1954.

blood, but against Principalities and Powers, against the rulers of darkness, against the evil spirits of this world." [75]

L'Osservatore Romano inquiring as to the whereabouts of Cardinal *Wyszynski* two years after his arbitrary removal from office and imprisonment wrote thus on " the drama of Catholicism " in Poland:

" We are dealing here with a great people almost completely Catholic with which Communism in its march westwards has come into contact. What will be the consequences of this meeting? What will be its effects? According to a very widespread opinion the possibility of ' co-existence ' between Catholicism and Communism will be tested in Poland.

" To attain this end recourse is had to self-styled ' progressive ' Catholics who are furnished with ample means for both domestic and foreign propaganda.

" Moscow needs an apparent ' reconciliation ' with Polish Catholicism, not for the purpose of consolidating its position in that nation which was made part of its sphere of influence at Yalta and Potsdam, but to exert a disintegrating influence on the forces of Catholicism, which in countries still free act as a barrier to Communism. In Poland the persecution has assumed a particularly insidious guise. An effort is being made to despoil Catholicism of its effective content in such a way that seen from the outside it will still appear unchanged. Even now an impossible Christian-Marxist syncretism destructive of all true spirituality is being subtly introduced within the framework of Catholicism." [76]

---

[75] Cf. Letter *Cum jam lustri*, 1 September 1951.
[76] Cf. *L'Osservatore Romano*, 3 July 1955. In November 1955 it was learned that the Primate was in a monastery formerly belonging to the Sisters of Nazareth at Komanza in the Beskid mountains.

Chapter 11

THE PERSECUTION OF THE CATHOLIC CHURCH

UNDER

Commnnist Rule in Romania

ON 23 AUGUST 1944 the Red army invaded Romania and imposed on it an unconditional armistice. One of the clauses of this armistice compelled Romania to enter the war against the Germans. Then followed a period of devastation during which the Soviet troops disposed of everything and everybody as they wished.

In March 1945 the Soviets replaced the Coalition Government which had signed the armistice by the " Popular Front " made up of elements of the Left. At the time the militant Communists in the whole of Romania numbered scarcely one thousand; but from the moment they acquired power, they set up a dictatorship which hastened to outlaw all existing parties. At the end of 1947 the King was obliged to abdicate and to leave the country. In the spring of 1948 the new régime brought in a Constitution based on the Soviet one and undertook social reforms and " the building of a socialist society."

One of the first pre-occupations of the new rulers was to destroy every obstacle opposed to the consolidation of their power. True to the lessons of Marx and Lenin, they saw in the Catholic Church one of the greatest of these obstacles.

In Romania Catholics numbered a little more than three millions of the twenty million inhabitants, scarcely 17% of the population. The Catholics belonged to two rites, the Oriental Rite and the Latin Rite.

The majority of the people belonged to the schismatic Orthodox Church, one of the most important self-governing

Churches of the Orient. It numbered about thirteen million adherents among whom the Communists found only too many elements ready to join them in the struggle against Catholicism.

The persecution of the Catholic Church in Romania will be dealt with under the following heads: (1) a brief reference to the history of the two Catholic Rites, (2) the preparation of the persecution through the press, (3) the anti-Catholic laws, (4) the direct persecution of the Church of the Oriental Rite, and (5) the attempt at creating schism in the Church of the Latin Rite.

The Greek-Catholic Church

The greater number of Romanian Catholics belongs to the Church of the Oriental Rite, called " The Uniate Church " or " The Greek-Catholic Church." In the Constitution of 1923 it was referred to as the Romanian Catholic Church, and as such enjoyed a certain position of dignity after the " dominant Church," namely the National Orthodox Church.

The Greek-Catholic Church had come into being at the end of the 17th century when a section of the Romanians of Transylvania decided at the synods of Alba Julia of 1698 and 1700 to unite itself to the Church of Rome. This union consisted essentially in the acceptance of certain Catholic dogmas: the primacy of the Sovereign Pontiff and three other dogmatic points which had separated the schismatic Church from the Catholic Church.

The Patriarch of Constantinople, the Archbishop of Valachie, and in a special way the Bishop of Karlowitz and his monks began a violent struggle against this union. But the Romanian bishops, first *Theophilus* and then *Athanasius*, remained firm in their decision to enter into the bosom of the Catholic Church, from which the Romanian people had been separated by Byzantine interests.

Once the initial difficulties had been overcome, the Uniate Romanian Church made rapid progress. A diocese was erected and under the direction of the bishop the first higher schools for the Romanians in Transylvania were opened. These schools were started in the little town of Blaj, which was also the seat of the episcopal See. Blaj thus became *the first centre of Romanian culture*. Around the Catholic schools sprang up a literary " Latinist " movement which marked a decisive turning point in the development of Romanian culture and in the re-awakening of national, political and social feeling.

Even non-Catholics recognised and appreciated the cultural importance of the Uniate Romanian Church. Already from the 17th century this Church had an organised administration and little by little increased its beneficent influence, united as it was to the centre of the Faith and of Catholic unity.

In 1948 when the Communists declared it " non-existent," the Romanian Uniate Church of the Oriental Rite was composed of a Metropolitan See with four suffragan dioceses: the arch-diocese of Alba Julia and Fagaras with its See at Blaj and the dioceses of Oradea Mare, Cluj, Lugoj and Maramures. After the last war the Vicariate of Bucharest had also been erected for the Catholics of the Oriental Rite who were outside Transylvania. The Romanian Uniate Church comprised according to the latest statistics about 1,570,000 faithful in 1,800 parishes with 1,810 priests.

The principal cultural institutions of the Romanian Church of the Oriental Rite were the theological seminaries of Blaj, Cluj and Oradea Mare and very many secondary and technical schools. From the middle of the 18th century training colleges for teachers, a college for the classics and the sciences, and com-mercial and professional schools were opened at Blaj. Each of these schools had a section for men and a section for women. Beius had a classical college and a scientific college, and two teachers' training schools existed at Oradea and Cluj.

Religious orders of the Oriental Rite were represented by the Basilians who had centres of intense religious life at Bixad, Moiseiu, Nicula, Prislope Obreja; by the Jesuits, with their novitiate at Totesti and a house in Bucharest; by the Assump-tionists, with their houses at Blaj, Beius and Bucharest. To render their apostolate among the Romanians more effective a number of the Conventual Franciscan Fathers and of the Brothers of the Christian Schools had embraced the Oriental Rite. The

Conventual Fathers served the parishes of Dragesti, Gruiulung and Decanesti, and had houses at Oradea Mare and at Bucharest.

There were in Romania only two religious orders for women of the Oriental Rite. The Sisters of the Mother of God had flourishing educational and charitable institutions at Blaj, Cluj, Juc, Sibiu, Sovata, Aiud and Gioagiu. At Moreni there was a monastery of contemplative religious, a recently founded institute.

The Uniate Church exercised moreover a notable influence on public opinion in Romania through its press. This comprised about twenty reviews, both weeklies and monthlies, and five printing houses which published many important books and religious brochures.

Within the Uniate Church was organised, especially after the First World War, every branch of Catholic Action. On the eve of its suppression Romanian Catholic Action of the Oriental Rite comprised 1,320 groups for men with more than 450,000 members, 730 Catholic Action groups for women with 340,000 members and many groups for young people.

The Church of the Latin Rite

The beginning of the Church of the Latin Rite in Romania goes back to the 13th century, when the diocese of Milcov (Moldavia) was created in 1228. The diocese of Sireth was established in 1370 and in 1413 that of Baia, then that of Bacau. Documents of the 14th century mention bishops of the Latin Rite at Turnu Severin and at Arges. From the 11th century there existed in Transylvania the dioceses of Oradea Mare and Alba Julia.

A great number of these dioceses disappeared in the course of the centuries. After the Concordat between Romania and the Holy See (1929) there was but one archiepiscopal See at Bucharest with four suffragan dioceses: Alba Julia, Satu Mare, Timisoara and Iasi.

The Church of the Latin Rite consisted mostly of Hungarians and Germans as well as a big number of Romanians of Moldavia and the members of the Italian and French colonies; in all ,174,000 faithful, with 694 parishes and 1,077 priests.

Under the control of the Catholic hierarchy of the Latin Rite there were 76 boys' schools with 15,396 pupils and 50 girls' schools with 13,300 pupils.

The press of the Church of the Latin Rite supplied the cultural needs of the different ethnical groups for which it was destined. There existed a daily paper in Hungarian and 23 periodicals in the German and Hungarian languages.

The Catholics of the Latin Rite had moreover all branches of Catholic Action. The most important were those of the Catholic men with 1,200 groups and 560,000 members and those of the Women's Catholic Action with 1,200 groups and 360,000 members.

* * *

In 1952 after seven years of Communist rule the whole structure of the Catholic Church in Romania was upset. The Catholic Church of the Oriental Rite was completely suppressed. Its dioceses and its parishes had been handed over to the Orthodox Church and its educational and charitable institutions had been nationalised. All the bishops were in prison, the priests were dispersed or imprisoned, and the faithful were compelled by force to join the Orthodox Church.

With regard to the Church of the Latin Rite the State recognised only two of the five dioceses which formerly existed; the bishops had been imprisoned, the schools were nationalised; Catholic Action, now turned into a schismatic movement, was to collaborate, according to the intention of the persecutors, in the complete annihilation of Catholicism in Romania.

Relations between the Catholic Church and the State

The relations between the Catholic Church and the State before the Soviet occupation were regulated by both the Romanian Constitution and the Concordat.

The Romanian Constitution of 1923 guaranteed freedom of worship and gave the Catholic Church of the Oriental Rite a certain priority over other Churches whose adherents were less numerous (art. 22). The Romanian laws even granted adequate subsidies for religious worship and for Catholic schools. Priests and professors of Catholic schools received from the State salaries proportional to their qualifications. In spite of the opposition of anti-Catholic circles and of the fact that the majority of Romanians were Orthodox, there were not, strictly speaking, any laws against the Catholic Church.

The relations between the Catholic Church and the Romanian State were regulated more precisely still by the Concordat drawn up on 10 May 1927 and ratified on 29 May 1929. The first article of the Concordat ensured the free exercise of Catholic worship throughout the whole country. The other articles regulated all questions relating to Catholics of the two Rites. Thus the number of the dioceses was fixed, as also the functioning of the Catholic schools and the activities of religious congregations and Catholic Associations.

If sometimes discussions arose between the Catholic press and that of the Romanian National Church they nearly always remained in the realm of theory, and in most cases spun themselves out in scientific explanations.

It can therefore be stated that before the setting-up of the Communist régime the Catholic Church in Romania enjoyed ample liberty which permitted it a continuous and promising development.

Struggle against the Church

From the beginning of the Communist occupation of Romania, the intention of the new rulers to undertake a war of extermination against Catholicism was manifest. However one of their first pre-occupations was to find an " ally " in the very camp of religion in order to be able to conduct more easily their campaign for the destruction of the Catholic Church. It was with this end in view that the Romanian Communist régime, making use of a cleverly thought-out tactic, began by taking control of the Romanian Orthodox Church.

In 1946 the Communists tried to enrol the Orthodox clergy in the Union of Democratic Priests, which was to constitute a subsidiary organisation of the Communist Party. The schismatic priest *Constantine Burducea* was appointed to find out and to bring together these democratic priests. The result was disappointing; the greater number of the priests refused to place themselves at the disposal of the Communist Party.

They then proceeded to replace the " elements " opposed to the régime. The Metropolitan *Irenaeus* of Suceava was obliged to resign on 22 July 1947. By decree n. 166 of 1947 Parliament decided that any priest of more than 70 years of age could no longer occupy a post either in the administration or in the government of the Church. This eliminated several bishops and old priests who were opposed to the régime. The Communists having discovered some priests who were disposed to collaborate with them placed them in positions of responsibility and authority.

On 28 February 1948 the Romanian Patriarch *Nicodemus* died; Parliament replaced him on 24 May 1948 by Bishop *Justinian Marina*; the new Patriarch was recognised as a man in whom the régime had confidence and who had more than once openly manifested his intention of serving the interests of the Communist Party.[1]

The legislation of the Orthodox Church was modified in such a way that all ecclesiastical questions were placed under the direct control of the Patriarch. As he took his orders from the Government, one can say that in order to attain their end the Communists had at their disposal the whole organisation of the Romanian Orthodox Church. This was made clearly evident in the course of the campaign for the destruction of the Romanian Catholic Church of the Oriental Rite.

Having got on its side the National Orthodox Church, which was the Church of the majority of the Romanian people, the régime began its attack on the Catholic Church without any further delay. There were *two phases* in this attack: in the first of these the whole Catholic Church without distinction of Rite was attacked; in the second the Churches of the Oriental

---

[1] On the new Patriarch and his complete dedication to Communist ideology and methods, see *La Civiltà Cattolica*, 1948, IV, 220, 223; 1949, II, 56-58. On the political significance of his election, see *Universul*, 28 August 1948.

and Latin Rites were attacked separately and the methods of attack were different.

Anti-Catholic Propaganda

It is a common tactic of all Marxist régimes to begin the struggle against religion by a campaign of calumny against the Church.

Every means of Communist propaganda was utilised from 1947 on to convince the Romanian people that Catholics were the enemies of the State and that the members of the clergy were spies in the service of imperialists. To forestall any chance of reply on the part of the Catholics, their press was totally suppressed, and in addition the Pastoral Letters of the bishops were by Government order subjected to a rigorous censorship.

The anti-Catholic campaign was conducted in the name of the Communist Party. On 22 February 1948 the Secretary of the Communist Party, *George Gheraghiu-Dej*, declared:

> " A number of the faithful of our country belong to the Catholic Church. We are obliged to state that the clergy are more or less opposed to the democratic régime in Romania and to the interests of the nation and of the people. The whole world over the Catholic clergy are subject to the Vatican whose reactionary and imperialistic activity is universally known. We cannot permit the clergy to abuse their powers in order to persuade the faithful to follow the directives of the Vatican or to make use of the Church as a means of propaganda against the democratic order." [2]

The press and the radio under the direction of the Propaganda Bureau of the Communist Party made attacks every day on the Church and the Holy Father.

> " The Pope," they declared, " is the head of Catholicism and at the same time the director of a political and financial organisation which makes use of religion to maintain the privileges of the dominant class. Everywhere the Catholic faithful are made use of by the Vatican to sustain its own prestige and to spread its

[2] Cf. *Biserica si Poporul* (The Church and the People), in *Lumina Crestina* (Christian Light) of 28 March 1948.

influence and its imperialism . . . The high dignitaries of the
Church possess immense wealth throughout the world . . . In
Italy 140 banks depend on the ' Banco di Roma ' (Bank of Rome),
of which Cardinal *Pacelli*, the present *Pius XII*, was a director,
and thus the Vatican controls to a great extent the finances of
Italy." [3]

According to the same vulgar accusations the Vatican was
called " a spying agency " and " an instrument of American
imperialism," " the protector of Fascist criminals," " the fifth
column of American expansion in Europe," etc. . . . [4] All
these unworthy imputations were directed against the Church
because, if one were to believe the Communists, she had forsaken
her Mission; and more than that, allied to Capitalism, she had
become a " spying organisation . . . which fights against
progress, against workers' movements, against Marxism and
against Communism." [5]   The wrong the Church had done
was to transform bourgeois egoism into a " divine mystery."
Anti-Catholic polemists did not hesitate to affirm: " The Vatican
practises an anti-Christian, anti-democratic and anti-national
policy." [6]

Moreover the supreme authority and the hierarchy of the
Church, as well as its whole organisation, were presented to
the people as being principally responsible for the war and for
all the misery after the war.

In order to give the greatest publicity to the calumnies against
the Catholic Church, Communist propaganda published a
pamphlet entitled: *Espionage and Treachery in the Shadow of the
Cross*, which was widely distributed among the working classes.
This slanderous pamphlet, which carried with it the blessing of
the Patriarch *Justinian Marina*, was presented by the Minister for
Worship, *Stanciu Stoian*, who wrote the preface for it, and was
printed under the aegis of the Government.   The highest

---

[3] Cf. A. Bratu and I. Manua, *Vaticanul Agentura a imperialismului american* in *Scanteia*
23 July 1948.

[4] See also as an example *Universul*, 19 August and 26 November 1949; *Romaniai
Magyar Szo* (Hungarian Voice of Romania), 7 and 27 January 1950.

[5] Cf. *Natiunea* (The Nation), 3 July 1948.

[6] Cf. *Romania Libera*, 23 July 1948.

authorities of the Orthodox Church and of the Communist régime were therefore associated in making known to the Romanian people the shameful mass of calumnies which were spread through chapters having as titles: " The anti-Christian and anti-national policies of the Vatican," " Nothing good for the people ever comes from the Pope," " The Sacred Patrimony of Treachery," " Poison beneath the Crucifix." [7]

The campaign of slander reached its height on the occasion of the denunciation of the Concordat and of the suppression of the Uniate Church.

The aim of this anti-Catholic propaganda was to prepare public opinion for the persecution the régime intended launching and to justify in anticipation the laws by which the Church was to be destroyed.

The Laws against the Catholic Church

The Patriarch *Justinian Marina* had been enthroned scarcely a month as head of the autocephalous Romanian Orthodox Church when the Government of Bucharest hastened to promulgate *a series of decrees and laws* which made manifest the reason for the campaign of slander against the Catholic Church. These were iniquitous measures against Catholicism in Romania.

On 17 July 1948 appeared decree n. 151: " The Concordat concluded between Romania and the Holy See on 10 May 1927 as well as the *agreements and conventions* approved for the carrying out of the aforesaid Concordat are to be considered revoked from the date of publication of the present Decree . . . The Law of 29 May 1929 ratifying the Concordat is abrogated as are all laws ratifying later conventions and agreements." [8]

This was the first direct measure taken by the Romanian Communists against the Catholic Church. In taking this step the Government violated every international custom, and paid no heed to article 23 of the Concordat, according to the terms of which the latter could not be rescinded unilaterally without six months' previous notice.

---

[7] Cf. Al. Radulescu-Cerna, *Spionaj si Tradare la Umbra Crucii*, Bucharest, 1948.
[8] Cf. *Monitorul Oficial*, n. 164, of 19 July 1948.

The reasons which incited the Government to take this grave step were exposed in an article by the Archimandrite *Valerian Zaharia*, spokesman of the Romanian Patriarchate.

" The denunciation of the Concordat," it is there stated, " is for the good of the country and of the people, for the Romanian State cannot renounce its sovereignty by tolerating ' a State within a State ' which Catholicism became after the Concordat. By the terms of the Concordat the Romanian State had all the obligations, while all the advantages were to the Vatican. The interests of the Catholic Church are contrary to the interests of the people. Since 23 August 1944 [9] the Vatican has conducted a reactionary policy against the efforts of the people. The denunciation of the Concordat brings back to the inheritance of the Romanian community the thousands given to the Vatican by former Parties. Now the division brought about in 1700 can be more easily healed, because with the Concordat disappears the instrument of reactionary Catholicism, destroyer of the national unity of the Romanian people; and so the return of the faithful of the Uniate Church will be at hand."

After giving all these " reasons," the spokesman of the Patriarchate ended by affirming that the Catholics would have greater liberty to express their sentiments and would be able

" to associate themselves with the people and to share in their aspirations, having been delivered from the slavery of the Grand Master of Rome, the Pope." [10]

These words of the Archimandrite *Valerian Zaharia* are reported because they express clearly in phraseology appropriate to persecutors the aim of this measure. Many other articles were published to prove that the Concordat was an error of the old régime which it was necessary to correct.

On 4 August 1948 appeared the *Decree on the general Regulations for Religions*, bringing under the control of the State the activity of all religious denominations in the country.

---

[9] On 23 August 1944 the Russian armies had begun the occupation of Romania, and an armistice had been signed between the USSR and the Government of Bucharest.
[10] Cf. Archimandrite Valerian Zaharia, *Denuntarea Concordatuli* in *Natiunea* of 18 July 1948.

This decree " formally guaranteed liberty of conscience and of religion " in the People's Republic of Romania (art. 1); it makes it the duty " of the faithful of all religions to obey the Laws of the State " (art. 10). Then we read: The organisation and functioning of any religious cult must have State recognition in the form of a decree of the National Assembly . . . recognition may be refused for sufficient reasons " (art. 13); the heads of religious organisations: " metropolitans, archbishops, bishops, superintendents, apostolic administrators, and administrative vicars," cannot take up office without the approbation of the National Assembly (art. 21).

After proclaiming the autonomy of the National Orthodox Church (art. 15), the decree declared that " religions organised in dioceses can have a number of dioceses proportional to the number of faithful . . ." A minimum of 750,000 faithful was required for the forming and the functioning of a diocese (art. 22).

In Chapter III the law treating of the activities of the different religions declares that " pastoral letters and circulars of general interest must be communicated at the proper time to the Minister for Worship " for preliminary censorship (art. 25); that the inscriptions and seals, as well as public meetings must be approved by the civil authority (arts. 19 and 24); that an inventory must be made of all goods, movable and non-movable; that an account of all these different operations should be addressed at the proper time to the Minister for Worship for verification and that all balance sheets ought to be approved by the same Minister (art. 29 and 30).

The section which struck directly at the Catholic Church was the following: " The relations of the various religions with foreign countries must be solely of a religious character. No religion, no representative of any religion whatsoever, can have any relations with other religions, institutions or official persons located outside the country except with the approbation of the Minister for Worship and through the intervention of the Minister for Foreign Affairs " (art. 40); moreover " no religious cult can, from a foreign country, exercise any jurisdiction over the faithful of the Romanian State " (art. 41).

As a measure specially directed against the Catholic Church of the Oriental Rite, the regulations concerning the change from one religion to another deserves special mention. " If at least 10% of one local community passes to another religion, that community loses its legal title to a part of its property proportional to the number of faithful who have abandoned it, and the part lost passes officially to the community of the adopted religion. If the majority of a local community changes to another religion, the church (place of worship, house of prayer) and all the annexes become the property of the religion adopted . . . If those who change to another religion represent 75% of the faithful of the abandoned religion all the property becomes by law the property of the adopted religion." (art. 37).

The law decrees that all relief works as well as all gifts received by religious organisations must be placed under the control of the State (art. 42). Under the same control are also placed institutions for the formation of the clergy which constitutes the personnel of the religion. The State must approve their administration and programme of studies (arts. 44 and 47). To the Orthodox Church was granted the right to have two institutions with power to grant university degrees, and only one with such power to the Catholic Church (art. 49). Finally the decree obliged all religions to submit to the Minister for Worship within three months from the promulagtion of the decree the statutes governing their manner of functioning (art. 56).[11]

As one can see, the decree on the General Regulations for Religions placed every religious denomination in Romania under the *absolute control of the State*. What was worse was that the Romanian State arbitrarily arrogated to itself the right to prevent the Sovereign Pontiff from exercising his spiritual jurisdiction over the faithful of Romania. The right and even the opportunity of having free relations with the head of the Church were withdrawn from the bishops. Besides, certain points of the decree clearly revealed the intention to strike at the Catholic Church and under the appearance of legality to prepare the way for the suppression of the Uniate Church.

The commentaries in the Communist press on the new law underlined this secret purpose of the Government. The Minister for Worship himself, *Stanciu Stoian*, declared on 24 August 1948:

---

[11] For " The Decree on the General Regulations for Religions " see *Monitorul Oficial* of 4 August 1948; J. B. Barron and H. M. Waddams, *Communism and the Church*, London, 1950 pages 76-82; *La Civiltà Cattolica*, n. 2,360, of 16 October 1948.

" Some of the Catholic clergy and faithful are turning towards the
People's Republic of Romania and are separating themselves from
their leaders . . . We expect that Catholics will re-examine their
attitude and this we hope for especially from Romanians of the
Uniate Church to whom we recall the example of their ancestors,
who in their time knew how to be one with the people and to
understand their sufferings." [12]

Another newspaper article recalled:

" Catholics took over the places of worship and other properties
of the pagan and Jewish religions." What wonder then if in
Romania, " the new law applies just measures to one of the most
controversial questions, and considerably facilitates the return of
our ' Uniate ' brothers to Orthodoxy; they know that from this
on they can all come back to the bosom of the Church they built
up, bringing with them the properties they had acquired." [13]

The allusion was clear; the Catholics of the Oriental Rite
should renounce their faith and join the National Church.

The law itself was moreover very explicit: if the Catholic
Church wished to exist and to develop its activity in Romania,
it must obtain permission from the Communist National
Assembly, submit completely to the control of the State and,
what was still more serious, it must renounce its submission
to the Sovereign Pontiff, to whom the law denied the right to
exercise his spiritual jurisdiction over the faithful living in
Romania.

The law on the General Regulations for Religions was destined
in truth only to prepare the ground for new Government
measures, which rapidly degenerated into *petty persecution and
abuse of power* and ended by practically forbidding all activity
on the part of the Church in Romania.

* * *

At the same time as the law on the regulation of Religions
there was promulgated the *Decree for the reform of public education.*

---

[12] Speech published in the paper *Natiunea* of 5 September 1948.
[13] Cf. Emilian Vasilescu, *Noua Lege pentru Regimul General al Cultelor*, in *Telegraful
Roman* of 22 August 1948.

The object of this was to give the young an education inspired by materialistic principles and by that means to draw them away from religion. By the terms of this law the State arrogated to itself the exclusive right to give public instruction and declared that all schools were " State schools."

The law began by declaring that:

" Public instruction in the People's Republic of Romania is a right equally enjoyed by all "; it can be organised only by the State and is lay in character (art. 1). The instruction has for end the education of youth "in the spirit of popular democracy" and tends to the formation of groups of specialists corresponding to democratic needs, and to the affirmation and realisation of socialism (art. 2). In order to render the teaching more democratic all denominational and private schools of whatsoever kind become State schools . . . All the goods, movable and non-movable, belonging to Churches, congregations, religious communities, and private societies, whether for the purpose of gain or otherwise . . . and which serve the functioning of schools for public instruction, become the property of the State (art. 35). The decree envisages the abolition of all associations and organisations having as their aim private education (art. 4).[14]

The law on public instruction is, according to Minister *Stanciu Stoian*, " a great reform which creates a new situation and a new mentality." [15]

The principles which inspired this new reform were introduced into the school programme. This obliged professors to bring up the pupils " in the political and social ideas of the historic time in which we live," and it gave precise directions for the struggle against " mysticism, prejudices and superstitions," it being understood that " all phenomena come from natural causes which science either knows or will know in the future . . . It is to be demonstrated that man by selection has the power to create new species of plants and animals." [16]

---

[14] Cf. *Monitorul Oficial*, Bucharest, of 3 August 1948.
[15] Cf. *Telegraful Roman* of 14 September 1948.
[16] Cf. *Programul Analitic pe anul scolar 1947-1948*, page 116.

The application of the law carried with it also *the reform of the text-books*. Already for the school-year 1948-1949 " unique " text-books were prescribed, mostly translated from Russian. Besides the defence of atheistic Materialism these books contained also a continual falsification of the history of the Church and the most perfidious interpretation of Christianity. In the first reader of the primary schools instead of the picture of Jesus among the little children the portrait of Stalin was substituted with the inscription: " Stalin is the children's greatest friend." [17]

To enforce the strict application of the new rules a Party agent was appointed for each school. He in turn was controlled by an " education counsellor " sent by the central Communist organisation. Further the " Pupils' Union," a kind of " school soviet " was set up. The pupils who formed part of this union were obliged to denounce their teachers if they did not appear to be sufficiently " democratic."

Party parades and sporting events were arranged in such a way as to render it impossible for the pupils to assist at Holy Mass. In the schools all religious teaching was forbidden. Thus the schools in Romania became an instrument for the propagation of anti-religious ideas and the young people began to be systematically educated in a purely materialistic and atheistic spirit.

* * *

About a year after the promulgation of the two laws mentioned above the Government of Bucharest issued another decree, dated 29 July 1949, forbidding religious orders to engage in teaching or relief works (art. 1), and ordering all members of religious orders of men to gather together in order *to continue to lead their religious life within the precincts of the Archbishops' palace of Bucharest and Alba Julia*. Nuns were obliged to go to three residences appointed by the régime at Radna, Ploesti and Timisoara (art. 2). [18]

In the space of twenty days the Government confiscated by virtue of this decree all the religious houses of Romania and

---

[17] Cf. *Abecedarul*, Editura de Stat, Bucharest, 1948, page 78.
[18] Cf. *Monitorul Oficial*, of 1 August 1949.

21

created in localities fixed by the decree itself residences, which were merely " concentration camps " for the members of religious orders. About 100 men and 1,800 nuns were affected by this decree.

After the publication and application of the laws concerning the Church of both Rites the persecution of the Catholics of the Oriental Rite began, followed immediately by that of the Catholics of the Latin Rite.

The Suppression of the Catholic Church of the Oriental Rite

Against the *Catholic Church of the Oriental Rite* the Communists adopted the same tactics as they had employed during the liquidation of the Catholic Church of the Oriental Rite in the Ukraine.[19]

In Romania the persecutors got valuable aid from the Orthodox hierarchy.

The Patriarch *Justinian Marina* soon after his election as head of the Romanian Orthodox Church declared in one of his first discourses on 6 June 1948:

> " I will strive in a special manner so that our Holy Romanian Orthodox Church, faithful to the new social evolution, may respond to the needs and the hopes of the people . . . Our thoughts go out to our brothers of the Romanian Greek-Catholic Church . . . It is precisely to the clergy of the Greek-Catholic Church, the only hope of Caesaro-papism in our country, that I address my paternal entreaties ; do not allow yourselves to be any longer deceived by your enemies. Show yourselves Romanians worthy of your ancestors who at the price of their lives preserved intact the patrimony of the Romanian people . . .
>
> What is it that still separates us ? Nothing other than the loyalty that you persist in according to Rome by your submission !

---

[19] The first attacks were launched by the Orthodox Ecclesiastical authorities. Already in the spring of 1948, when on a visit to Bucharest, the Patriarch Alexij of Moscow had declared that the Communist régime had placed Orthodoxy in the most favourable conditions in order to realise the union of the two Churches. Several people had the impression that the Muscovite Patriarch wished it to be understood by the heads of Romanian Orthodoxy that the Communists desired that the Uniate Romanian Church should be suppressed by the autumn of 1948, the date of the 250th anniversary of the establishment of the latter.

This supposition alone can explain the extraordinary zeal displayed by the Orthodox prelates in co-operating with the Romanian Government in the work of persecution as well as the urgency and violence employed in the destruction of one of the most glorious Romanian institutions.

Show now the same loyalty to the Church of our people and of our common ancestors . . . The greatest prospects are open to our future activity when we shall work no longer isolated, abandoned and persecuted as in the past but all re-united in a powerful National Church which will welcome into its bosom all the clergy and all the people of our dear Romanian country." [20]

Similar declarations were made by the patriarch on his return from the Congress of Orthodox Churches held in Moscow in July 1948.

An identical appeal was addressed to the Uniate Catholics by the Metropolitan of Sibiu, *Nicholas Balan*, one of the bitterest enemies of Catholicism. On the occasion of a national feast, celebrated on 15 May 1948 at Blaj, he declared in a solemn discourse:

" To-day when the People's Republic of Romania guarantees equal political, economic, cultural and religious rights to all the sons of our country without discrimination of race or religion, to persist in the spiritual separation brought about by the sad situation in which the Romanian people of Transylvania found themselves about 1700, means desertion from the one front of the new destinies held out to our hard-working people at the dawn of a near future.

" As successor of the former Metropolitans of Alba Julia who were protectors of the whole Romanian way of life in Transylvania, I address myself to you whom foreign interests have separated from your good Mother, the Orthodox Church, and invite you warmly and paternally to return to the common house. . . . The day of our national resurrection will be that day when we can embrace you and call you brothers. Come, we await you with open arms." [21]

These two appeals of the highest dignitaries of the Orthodox Church were the prelude to the suppression of the Catholic Church of the Oriental Rite. The commentaries in the newspapers made this clear. " The project of the Patriarch *Marina*,"

---

[20] Cf. Al. Radulescu and Al. Sadeanu, *Reintregirea Bisericii Romanesti din Ardeal* (Re-integration of the Romanian Church in Transylvania) Bucharest, 1949, page 5.

[21] Cf. Al. Radulescu and Al. Sadeanu, *Reintregirea Bisericii Romanesti din Ardeal*, 1949, pages 3-4, and *Legea Romaneasca* (Romanian Law), 16 May 1948.

wrote an authoritative collaborator of the Communists, " to bring back these brethren (the Uniate Catholics) to the liberty and beauty of Orthodoxy will be realised." [22] The Vicar of the Metropolitan See of Suceava, after having described in an article the " passage " of the Ukrainian Catholics to the Orthodox Church, concludes: " Will there be a similar joy for our people? We are convinced of it, even if we must wait till 21 October 1948 which will be the 250th anniversary of the act of union of Alba Julia." [23]

Direct action by the régime soon followed the appeals of the Orthodox hierarchy and the allusions of the press. During the month of August 1948, as we have seen, the general decrees against religion were published, and in September of the same year *some orders were approved* which in a special manner struck at the Uniate Church. Thus on 3 September a decree of the Government " deposed " Mgr. *John Suciu*, Apostolic Administrator of the Catholic Church of the Oriental Rite; on 16 September another decree contemplated the " deposing " of Mgr. *John Scheffler*, Bishop of the Latin Rite of Satu Mare, and on 18 September Mgr. *Alexander Rusu*, Uniate Bishop of Maramures, Mgr. *Valerius Trajan Frentiu*, Uniate Bishop of Oradea Mare, Mgr. *John Balan*, Uniate Bishop of Lugoj, Mgr. *Alexander Cisar*, Archbishop of Bucharest and Mgr. *Augustin Pacha*, Bishop of Timisoara, were " placed in retirement." The two last were of the Latin Rite.

Having thus deposed four of the six Uniate Bishops of the Oriental Rite and prevented two others—Mgr. *Julius Hossu*, Bishop of Cluj, and Mgr. *Basil Aftenie*, Vicar of Bucharest—from exercising freely their sacred ministry, the Communist authorities took the initiative in *convoking a synod*, which was to sanction the passage of the Uniate Catholics to the Schism.

The Congress of Cluj

Towards the end of September 1948 a letter was sent to all the Uniate priests, in which it was stated that the appeals of the Patriarch *Marina* and of the Metropolitan *Balan*, " who asked the

[22] Cf. Pr. I. Margineanu, *Un om si un program*, in *Universul*, 19 July 1948.
[23] Cf. Archimandrite Emilian, in *Semnanul* (Signal), 18 July 1948.

Romanians of the Greek-Catholic Rite to come back to the bosom
of the Romanian Orthodox Church," had made many Uniate
priests reflect on the problem of the union, and that they had
arrived " at the conclusion that the hour was come to unite the
two Churches."

> " Having been informed " continued the appeal, " of the meeting
> which is about to take place at Cluj on 1 October next, we the
> undersigned, Greek-Catholic priests of the respective parishes of
> the Department of .... delegate the Reverend .... of the parish
> of .... and the Reverend .... of the parish of .... to take
> part in this assembly and to represent us with full powers and with
> mandate to support with all their authority and to vote for the
> resolution on the return of the Greek-Catholic Church to the
> Orthodox Church. These proxies are authorised to sign in our
> name the aforesaid resolution, which we accept in advance." [24]

As can be seen from the text of the appeal, each priest was
invited to designate two parish priests from his department,
chosen before-hand by the Communist authorities, to represent
him at the Congress during the course of which it was intended
to " break the links " binding the Romanian Uniate Catholics
to Rome.

It is to be remarked that the appeal was not sent through
the post. A commission composed of representatives of the
Party and of the Government hastened to carry this document
directly to each priest, accompanying the delivery of it with
lying explanations, threats, promises, and summonses. It was
even explained to some of the priests that the coming Congress
had no intention of breaking " the links with Rome," (which aim
however was actually in the very text of the notice), but would
limit itself to discussing the problem of the reconciliation and
the collaboration of the two Romanian Churches. They even
spread the rumour that the Congress would be presided over
by Mgr. *Julius Hossu*, Uniate Bishop of Cluj.

Very many priests were thus led into error, all the more
easily as it was absolutely impossible for them to communicate

---

[24] Cf. the collection of documents on the persecution of the Church of the Oriental
Rite in Romania: *Biserica Romana Unita*, Madrid, 1952, page 308.

with the bishop or with their colleagues. However the greater number of them refused to sign the document.

The simple invitation to sign this document was followed by acts of violence. The greater number of the priests who refused to sign were placed *under arrest*. Some of those who signed did so only after having been tortured, sometimes even to the point where they lost control so that their signature was given while not fully conscious of what they were doing. The proof of this is given in the many cases cited in the account published by the Sacred Congregation of the Oriental Church.[25]

By such procedures as these 38 priests were " delegated." This was the same number as was present at the synod of 1698 which proclaimed the Union with Rome. These 38 priests were convoked for 1 October in the gymnasium of the Lycée Baritiu at Cluj. In the photographs taken during the Congress one can see, seated in the front rows, the representatives of the Government and the police.[26] Eyewitnesses at the Congress have confirmed the fact that the " delegates " were everywhere accompanied by police agents.

After the preliminary discussions which were all arranged before-hand, the following official report was drawn up:

I. The election of a president and a secretary was proposed.
Ad. I. The following were elected by acclamation: President, *Belascu Trajan*; Secretary, *Brumboiu Aurelian*; Auditors, *Geangalsu Nicholas* and *Madincea Paul*.

II. The delegating authorisations were read in alphabetical order.
Ad. II. The names were read of those given delegated authority from 22 provinces, showing 430 supporters.

III. The Archpriest *Belascu* then spoke, and having thanked the pious colleagues for the enthusiasm with which they responded to the invitation to unite the Churches (the initiative for this Union belonged to the priests), he pointed out the importance in the cultural and political order of the Act of 1700, which had as a consequence the fulfilment of the National ideal.

---

[25] Cf. SICO (Servizio Informazioni Chiesa Orientale) Rome, 1948, A. IV, n. 3, p. 1. On the subject of the reasons which induced several priests to sign the proxies, see: *La Documentation Catholique*, 3 July 1949, col. 845.
[26] Cf. Al. Radulescu and Al. Sadeanu, *Reintregirea Bisericii Romanesti din Ardeal*, p. 7.

The Archpriest *Sabin Truta* then showed how the Christian ideal had been hindered by misunderstandings among the priests. He underlined the desire of the people to see the union between the Churches realised.

The priest *Geangalsu* expressed the ardent desire of the priests to celebrate together.

The priest *Brumboiu* thanked the Government for the liberty granted to each of them to express his desires without the slightest hindrance.

The priest *Zagrai* read the resolution and the appeal, which were accepted and signed by all those present. *Belascu* closed the Congress by thanking all those present for the great enthusiasm manifested on the occasion of this historic act. [27]

The Congress having terminated, the " delegates " set off for Bucharest where they were received on 3 October by the Patriarch *Justinian Marina*, five Orthodox bishops and all the clergy of the capital. During the course of a solemn meeting held in the " Great Hall " of the Holy Synod, *Aurelian Brumboiu* read the resolution passed at the Congress at Cluj.[28] Then the Patriarch *Justinian Marina* and the Metropolitan of Transylvania *Nicholas Balan* both addressed the meeting. The resolution announced that the delegates gathered at Cluj had decided to come back " into the bosom of the Romanian Orthodox Church " and that they considered it their duty to convince the people to follow their example. After a eulogy of the Communist régime the resolution concluded by affirming that the new conditions of life in the People's Republic of Romania made it a sacred duty for all the people to break " the links with the Church of Rome, to which the interests of the people were foreign . . . In the light of these facts we proclaim our return into the bosom of the Romanian Orthodox Church, and in our own name and in the name of all those who delegated us to this meeting, *we decide to sever* relations with the Vatican. From this day we recognise as Superiors only those appointed by the authorities of the Holy Romanian Orthodox Church." [29]

---

[27] Cf. Al. Radulescu and Al. Sadeanu, *Reintregirea Bisericii Romanesti din Ardeal*, p. 14.

[28] The resolution was drawn up by the Minister for Religion and brought to Cluj by the priest, George Zagrai. Its approval by the Congress of Cluj was a mere formality.

[29] Cf. *Reintregirea Bisericii Romanesti din Ardeal*, pp. 18-19.

The Patriarch *Marina* expressed his satisfaction at seeing that his appeal had been listened to; he added: " In the name of the Holy Synod of the Romanian Orthodox Church and with great spiritual joy I record your resolution and your decision, and I receive you, with a father's arms wide open and a warm heart, into our holy sheepfold and our spiritual pasture." [30]

The Metropolitan *Balan* in his turn made a long dissertation proving that the union of the Romanians of Transylvania with the Roman Church was brought about only for political motives and temporal interests.

Immediately after the speeches in the Hall of the Holy Synod all those present went to the church of Saint Spiridion where the ceremony took place by which the " delegates " were received into the bosom of the Orthodox Church. The director of the Chancellery of the Holy Synod, *George Vintilescu*, read " the Act of the Synod " in which, after a resumé of the report of the Solemn Meeting and of the ceremony celebrated in Saint Spiridion's, it was announced that the separation between the Orthodox Church and the Uniate Catholic Church had ended.

" To bear witness to and confirm this we decide that this Act along with the resolution submitted to us, shall be inscribed in the Sacred Register of the Synod over our signature and the signatures of the 36 Greek-Catholic archpriests and priests, members of the delegation." [31] There followed the signatures of the patriarch, of the four Orthodox bishops present and of the members of the delegation. It is interesting to note that of these last there were 38 at Cluj while in the Act of the Synod there were but 36 signatures; two had succeeded in eluding the vigilance of the police and escaped from the forced journey to Bucharest.

The Communists after the ceremony at Bucharest considered *as liquidated the Roman Catholic Church of the Oriental Rite.*

While the Congress at Cluj and the solemnities at Bucharest were reserved for the clergy, the persecutors organised for the faithful a great popular Festival which was to take place at Alba

---

[30] Cf. *Reintregirea Bisericii Romanesti din Ardeal*, p. 23.
[31] Cf. *Reintregirea Bisericii Romanesti din Ardeal*, p. 31.

Julia on 21 October 1948, the 250th anniversary of the Union of the Romanians with the Church of Rome.

In the meantime the second step was taken. A form was to be signed by the faithful declaring that " freely and without being in any way forced " they re-united themselves with their brethren of the Orthodox Church, urged only by the desire of the spiritual unity of the Romanian people. In the majority of cases however the agents did not bother to get the individual signatures; the Communist official simply formed a commission which affirmed in the name of all their change over to " Orthodoxy." In many places the names of Jews and Orthodox Christians appeared on the list of signatures. In other places the " form " was said to be a " mere formality without any real importance," or a " declaration for world peace." Terrorism went hand in hand with fraud of this kind. Those refusing to sign were not allowed to perform any official act, even the registration of new-born infants. Local officials were threatened with instant dismissal if they attended Catholic functions. Threats of heavy taxes, deportation to Siberia, loss of pension and property, eviction—these were not the worst; in the end came the threat of being shot out of hand, and several of the faithful were maltreated.[32]

For the celebration on 21 October 1948 the Party had mobilised every one of its organisations in order to gather the greatest possible number at Alba Julia. They wished to give the impression that the Uniate Catholics had accepted with joy the suppression of their Church.[33]

The festival terminated with a " motion " voted by " acclama-

---

[32] There is a long and authoritative account of the methods used by the Communists in " L'Ora della prove per i cattolici di Romania," *La Civiltà Cattolica*, 1949, II, pp. 41-49. An account given by eyewitnesses may be read in *Christian Churches in Eastern Europe* (place of publication not given), 1956, pp. 69-71.

[33] The feast opened with the anthem of the People's Republic of Romania. They appointed as "president" of the feast, Trajan Belascu, the same who had been elected president of the Congress of Cluj, and as vice-presidents, all the arch-priests who had taken part in the same Congress, as well as 24 peasants and 12 intellectuals. All the priests present at Cluj constituted the " Committee of Initiative," which had as secretary Aurelian Brumboiu, the secretary of the Congress.

The city was decorated and the walls covered with slogans of this kind: " Long live the Romanian Republic "; " United in the faith of our ancestors, we fight for the rights of the people, for peace and for democracy."

tion " by all those present. The meeting declared among other things the following:

> " We break forever our relations, of what kind soever, with the Vatican and with Papal Rome. We incorporate ourselves with our whole being into the Romanian Orthodox Church.
>
> " We shall submit ourselves with filial love to all the decisions of the Holy Synod of our Romanian Orthodox Church."
>
> The motion ended thus : " Let us render the homage of our gratitude to the Grand Praesidium of the People's Republic of Romania and to the Government of the country for the freedoms guaranteed to all the children of the people and which have made possible the re-integration of the Romanian Church." [34]

After the popular manifestations a religious ceremony was held during which was read once again the motion, the resolution of Cluj, and the Act of the Synod. Finally both the Patriarch *Marina* and the Metropolitan *Balan* spoke.

At the dinner of " fraternisation " the patriarch and one of the Uniate priests spoke again.

The Communist press gave as usual long accounts of the festival at Alba Julia, and the police began to *occupy the churches of the Uniate Catholics* and *to hand them over to the ecclesiastical authorities of the Orthodox Church.*

*   *   *

The work of the persecutors was crowned by decree n. 358 of the Praesidium of the Great National Assembly of the People's Republic of Romania: " Definition of the rights of the former Greek-Catholic religion " which concluded thus:

> ART. 1. By reason of the return of the Greek-Catholic Church to the Romanian Orthodox religion and in conformity with article 13 of the decree no. 177 of the year 1948, the central

---

The first speaker, the president Trajan Belascu, drew attention to the importance of the event. Then the " peasant Andrew Avram " was called upon; he read at the microphone a discourse which repeated in general that of the president. Finally in the name of the Uniate intellectuals Professor Coriolan Tataru brought the speeches to a close.

[34] Cf. *Reintregirea Bisericii Romanesti din Ardeal*, pp. 58-59. The feasts of Alba Julia are described in detail in the book above quoted, pp. 44-47.

organisations of this Church (metropolitan sees, dioceses, chapters, orders, congregations, deaneries, monasteries, foundations, associations, as well as all other institutions and organisations) of whatsoever nature or name cease to exist.

ART. 2. The goods, movable and non-movable, belonging to the organisations and institutions mentioned in article 1 of this decree, with the exception of the goods of former parishes, return to the Romanian State which is to take immediate possession of them.[35]

The decree in question was dated 1 December 1948 and in virtue of it, in the eyes of the Romanian State, *the Romanian Church of the Oriental Rite* " *no longer existed*," and about a million and a half faithful who had not adhered even remotely to the " resolutions " or to the " motions " of the priests assembled at Cluj and at Alba Julia had no longer any right to profess their Faith. Thus was " legally " brought about the destruction of a nation's Faith.

* * *

The persecutors themselves, whose evident intention was the total annihilation of the Catholic Church of the Oriental Rite, reduced to a very minimum the possibility of defending the Roman Catholic Faith by making it practically impossible for the bishops and the priests to exercise their sacred ministry, by suppressing the Catholic press and by arresting a great number of the more prominent Catholic laymen.

When the Congress of Cluj was announced Mgr. *Julius Hossu*, bishop of that city, succeeded in sending out from his palace, where he was under house-arrest, a circular Letter which was surreptitiously delivered to many priests of the diocese. In this Letter, dated 30 September 1948, after having expressed his astonishment at learning that certain Uniate priests intended meeting at Cluj on 1 October 1948 to bring about the schism, he continued: " In virtue of the powers which I hold as Ordinary of Cluj, I apply the penalty of excommunication *ipso facto*

---

[35] Cf. *Monitorul Oficial*, of 2 December 1948.

incurrenda to all those who take part in the projected meeting. Those who unfortunately will be present at the Congress will be excommunicated by name by our decree which will be read in all the churches of the diocese." [36]

On 2 October 1948, the day following the Congress at Cluj, the Apostolic Nunciature of Bucharest sent to the Minister for Foreign Affairs of the People's Republic of Romania a *Verbal Note* to protest against the violence done to the Greek-Catholic Church of Romania by the Government.

The Note of the Nunciature recalled how the solemn engagements undertaken by the Romanian State at the time of the signing of the Paris Peace Treaty, 10 February 1947, " had been violated by a series of acts, carefully prepared and cleverly co-ordinated, perpetrated during these recent days against the Catholic Church of the Greek Rite in various provinces of Transylvania."

The Apostolic Nunciature insisted very specially on the action undertaken, not by irresponsible people, but by the civil authorities themselves, to compel the clergy of the Greek-Catholic Church to abandon their Faith . . . " This initiative of the civil power, which is itself in evident contradiction with the principles of liberty and equality of all religions in Romania, has clearly revealed its character of a religious persecution, especially by the methods taken to extort signatures. The priests, often conveyed by force to the Prefectures and to the police bureaux, were there terrorised, threatened with prison, with separation from their families, with deportation and with death. Those who resisted these first attacks were thrown into underground cells, ill-treated, subjected to unending interrogations and were set at liberty only when, completely exhausted by this inhuman treatment, they agreed to sign.

" This ill-treatment, of which the people of our country cannot but know and which must inevitably arouse public opinion throughout the world, has been confirmed by functionaries of the Patriarchate of Bucharest and by members of the so-called Congress for union with the Orthodox Church at Cluj,

---

[36] Cf. *Biserica Romana Unita*, pp. 311-312.

some of whom still bear the signs of the violence to which they had been subjected." [37]

The Minister for Foreign Affairs of Romania hastened to reply to this energetic Note by " rejecting categorically the protest of the Apostolic Nunciature against the return to the Orthodox Rite of the Greek-Catholic population of Transylvania, a protest which was an interference in the internal affairs of the People's Republic of Romania." Moreover " the Romanian Government rejected the gross calumnies contained in the above Note," denied the right of the Apostolic Nunciature to speak in the name of the " Catholic world " and " denounced the attempt at blackmail by the pretended threat that the violation of religious liberty on the part of the Romanian People's Republic would immediately stir up public opinion throughout the world." Finally the Romanian Government considered the protest of the Nunciature " an act of provocation " directed at the State and at the Romanian people." [38]

On 7 October the bishops of the Greek-Catholic Church in Romania addressed a collective Letter to the President, *Peter Groza*, informing him that administrative organisations and State police had begun their work of destroying the Uniate Romanian Church. The bishops, after protesting against the confiscation of another of their collective Letters by the police, wrote: "Mgr. *John Suciu* has been arrested on the public street by police agents while he was making one of his regular visits to the faithful under his charge. From 26 September to 4 October 1948 the Bishop of Cluj, Mgr. *Julius Hossu*, was confined to his palace in order that he might be unable to make contact with his clergy or hinder in any way the action being taken against the Church. In the capital of Transylvania the police arrested all the lay people and priests who, not knowing the steps that were being taken, tried to enter or leave the bishop's palace . . . For reasons of prudence we do not judge it opportune to enumerate here all the vexations and acts of violence to which the archpriests and priests whose signatures they wished to obtain were subjected." The Letter of the

[37] Cf. *La Documentation Catholique*, 1949, col. 869-870.
[38] Cf. *La Documentation Catholique*, 1949, col. 870-871.

bishops concluded by affirming that the Uniate Romanian Church had never been guilty of any acts of hostility against the nation or the Government, adding: " All of us, pastors and faithful, are resolved to remain in the bosom of the Catholic Church in whose service we wish to continue in life and in death." [39] The same day, 7 October, another collective Letter signed by the Catholic bishops of both the Oriental Rite and the Latin Rite was addressed to the head of the Government to protest against the vexations and abuse of power committed against the Church. The Letters were presented to the Minister for Worship, *Stanciu Stoian*, by Mgr. *Basil Aftenie*, Greek-Catholic Vicar of Bucharest. At the presentation of the documents the Minister urged the prelate himself to join the schism.

In order to prepare the faithful for the trials which awaited them, the bishops wrote a Letter recalling the grandeur of the Catholic Faith and unmasking the perfidy of the persecutors.[40]

* * *

Writing on the persecution of the Greek-Catholic Church in Romania, *L'Osservatore Romano* of 29 January 1949 stated: *" No similar story of moral violence, of persecution, of the ' Via Crucis ' of liberty, of personality and of human dignity can be read in all the pages of history."*

In truth we must go back to the pagan persecutions to find episodes of violence and cruelty comparable to the sufferings

---

[39] Cf. *Biserica Romana Unita*, pp. 321-324.

[40] Mgr. John Suciu, Apostolic Administrator of Blaj, was particularly active. During the period preceding the attack against the Uniate Church he visited all the parishes to exhort the people to remain steadfast in their faith.

The letters of this fearless pastor were awaited and read with devotion by all. His sermons were the surest spiritual guide in this time of uncertainty. Mgr. Suciu drew attention to the fact that the Romanian Uniate Church had never yet undergone the trial of martyrdom and that Providence offered it at this precise moment the grandest opportunity to undergo the " test of heroism " and to add to the glorious chapters of their history the still greater glory of martyrdom. The other bishops also devoted themselves to preparing the souls of the faithful for the persecution. Everywhere the churches were crowded and the evening devotions were never better attended. The priests followed the example of the bishops and the greater number of them preached fidelity to the Church, up to the moment when they were arrested by the police and relegated to concentration camps or put in prison. Cf. *Biserica Unita*, Madrid, 1952, p. 328.

inflicted by the Communists on the Uniate Catholics, clergy and laity, who refused to join the schism.

The persecutors " simplified " their attacks against the Catholics, putting " the priests in face of tragic dilemmas: their signature or prison; their signature or deportation; their signature or their lives." [41]

The signature, otherwise called " passing over to schism," was refused by the greater number of priests and faithful of the Uniate Church. Even if the numbers, certainly exaggerated, given by Communist propaganda be accepted, out of 1,810 priests scarcely 36 consented to play the game of the persecutors, and despite the methods employed by the Communist police only 430 signatures to the plan for the liquidation of the Uniate Church were received.

All the other priests without the formality of a trial were imprisoned and subjected to inhuman treatment. In hundreds they were packed together in the same room, when they were not shut up in underground cells or sent to forced labour.[42]

On 27 October 1948 Mgr. *John Suciu* was arrested, and on the night of 28-29 October all the other Uniate bishops were arrested: Mgr. *Valerius Trajan Frentiu*, Mgr. *Julius Hossu*, Mgr. *Alexander Rusu*, Mgr. *Basil Aftenie*, and Mgr. *John Balan*, as well as all the professors of the seminaries, all the members of the episcopal Curiae and, as has been already said, all the parish priests who approved of resistance to the provisions of the Government.

The bishops were first subjected to humiliations at the hands of the Communist police; they were then transferred to the summer villa of the Orthodox patriarch at Dragoslavele. The latter came from time to time to exhort them to join the schism. All his efforts were in vain and the bishops were transferred to the monastery of Caldarusani. About two years after they had been arrested it was learned that they were in the underground cells of the Ministry for the Interior and after that in the prisons of Vacaresti. *Nobody has ever learned precisely* how they were treated. The international press has published only news that could not

[41] Cf. *L'Osservatore Romano* of 29 January 1949, p. 3.
[42] Cf. SICO, 15 May and 2 December 1949.

be verified. It is certain however that on 10 May 1950 Mgr. *Basil Aftenie* died in a Communist prison from the ill-treatment he had received. Later the Communists brought to the prisons of Sighet the Greek-Catholic bishops together with the heads of the political parties who were most prominent in the past.

The priests were divided into two categories by the persecutors: the " higher clergy," and the " lower clergy." The professors of Theology, the Canonists and the personnel of the Curiae were considered as forming part of the " higher clergy."

The parish priests, according to the idea of the Communists, generally belonged to the " lower clergy." A good number of the priests who, according to the Marxist standard, formed part of the " higher clergy " were subjected to the same fate as the bishops, with this difference that they did not share their prisons and that a number among them was sent to forced labour.

The parish priests were kept in prison only for some weeks but when they were liberated they were subjected to constant supervision by the police.

The occupation of the cathedrals and churches of the Greek-Catholics by the religious authorities of the Orthodox Church gives us another aspect of the violence to which the Catholic Church was subjected.

The taking over of the cathedral of Blaj which was considered by everybody as the spiritual centre of the Romanian Uniate Catholics was surrounded with very special ceremony. On 28 October 1948 the police ordered the cathedral to be closed and the keys handed over to the priest *John Cisteian*. On the morning of 30 October the Metropolitan of Sibiu, *Nicholas Balan*, arrived to re-consecrate it. The Metropolitan was received at the gates of the city by the Prefect and a delegation from the Government while the priest *Cisteian* presented him with the keys. At the dinner which followed the occupation of the edifice *Balan* said among other things:

" The union of the Churches was always part of my programme. All my life I have held high this flag . . . I have always said that the Uniate Church was but a passing thing in the life of the Romanian people. To-day my prophecy has been fulfilled." [43]

On 31 October 1948 the last Mass was celebrated in the cathedral of Lugoj; after having driven away the many faithful who had assisted at it, the police put seals on the doors.

At Cluj the cathedral was occupied on 21 November. On this occasion the Orthodox bishop of the town, *Nicholas Colan*, declared in his discourse:

"We also honour the Pope, but at Rome, in his own home, for he has nothing to do with us here." [44]

From the end of October to the middle of November 1948 *all the parochial churches, all the chapels and all Catholic institutions were taken over by force.*[45]

This work had scarcely been accomplished before the heads of Romanian Orthodoxy tried to resolve the problem of the *assimilation of the Greek-Catholics*. To this end most of the 36 Uniate priests who had taken part in the Congress of Cluj were named vicars forane. Then a "conference" of all the vicars of the Metropolitan See of Transylvania was held. To this meeting which took place at Sibiu on 10 November 1948 all the Greek-Catholic priests who had gone over to schism were also admitted. In the opening discourse the Metropolitan *Balan* repeated the usual arguments against the primacy of the Sovereign Pontiff, accusing of pride the man who dared call himself " Vicar of Christ," and qualifying as absurd the claim of one bishop to exercise authority over the whole world. In conclusion he made an effort to demonstrate that the "transition" to schism had been a great benefit to the Romanian people and a precious help to the young " People's Republic." [46] During the conference anti-Catholic pamphlets were distributed, and the

---

[43] Cf. *Telegraful Roman* of 7 November 1948.

[44] Cf. *Renasterea (Rebirth)*, of 28 November 1948.

[45] Cf. *L'Osservatore Romano*, of 29 January 1949. Several times the police had to fight against those of the Catholic population still at liberty. The Communists paid no attention to the opposition of the Uniate Catholics or to the protestations of the ecclesiastical authorities; they simply pushed ahead with their own plans. The hierarchy of the Orthodox Church intoned a hymn of triumph, welcoming with joy the spoil offered them by Communist atheists.

[46] Cf. *Telegraful Roman* of 26 November 1948.

leader of the priests adhering to the schism, *Trajan Belascu*, declared that all would do their best to live in harmony with the Orthodox clergy. In order to consolidate the union a Greek Catholic priest, *Theophilus Herineanu*, was appointed Orthodox Bishop of Roman-Husi in Moldavia.[47]

All the efforts of the Orthodox hierarchy and clergy to " convert " the Uniate Catholics to the National Church were in vain. Many of the priests who had gone over to schism afterwards withdrew their signatures.[48]

The Uniate priests, now outlawed, were obliged to exercise their sacred ministry in secret. Many of them are still hidden in mountainous regions, supported by the faithful.

In order to suppress all activity of the proscribed Greek-Catholic Church, the Minister for the Interior issued a decree forbidding under threat of serious penalties all activity of the Uniate priests (referred to as " vagrants " in the text). Then large sums of money were promised to those who would denounce the Uniate priests who celebrated Holy Mass in secret. Finally any person giving hospitality or help to, and even anyone that did not denounce the Uniate priests of the Oriental Rite who had not embraced the schism, would incur the penalty of eight years in prison and the confiscation of his property.[49]

The Communist persecutors considered that by this last decree they had *definitely liquidated the Romanian Church of the Oriental Rite*. If it is living at the present moment, it is solely in the " catacombs " and by the spirit of faith animating the confessors of the Faith who still languish in Communist prisons.

The Persecution of the Catholic Church of the Latin Rite

The law on the General Regulations for Religions and on Public Education in Romania, published in August 1948, struck at both the Church of the Latin Rite and that of the Oriental Rite. However the Communist régime of Bucharest in the

---

[47] The Communist press made a great noise about this nomination and the writers set themselves out to prove that the Greek-Catholics who went over to schism were not merely " tolerated " but were welcomed by their brothers of the National Church. Cf. *Universul*, of 27 November 1948.

[48] Cf. *Biserica Romana Unita*, pp. 309 and 310.

[49] Cf. *Monitorul Oficial* of 20 August 1949.

first phase of the struggle against Catholicism limited itself to the legal destruction of the Church of the Oriental Rite. This was simply a question of tactics and of method.

The persecution of the Catholics of the Latin Rite was conducted in a different manner. The Government could not in this case have recourse to " invitations to return " nor make use of another religious organisation which would help it in its undertaking, as it had done in the case of the Romanian Orthodox Church for the liquidation of the Greek-Catholic Church.

Even the press seemed to have exhausted all its anti-Catholic arguments in its violent and clever campaign against the Greek-Catholic Church.

At first the Communists judged it sufficient for their purpose to combat Catholicism by favouring, as we have seen, the formation of a schismatic movement within the Church of the Oriental Rite, and by making laws which would take away all liberty from the Church of the Latin Rite.

The famous law on the General Regulations for Religions insisted that all religious denominations in the People's Republic of Romania must submit to the Minister for Worship their statutes; these had then to be approved by the competent civil authorities.

Compelled in order to survive to bow to the decisions of the Government, the Catholic episcopate of the Latin Rite in Romania had prepared the statutes demanded, at the very time that the régime was attacking with the greatest violence the Church of the Oriental Rite.

Some months before this, on 16 and 18 September 1948, Mgr. *Alexander Cisar*, Archbishop of Bucharest, Mgr. *Augustine Pacha*, Bishop of Timisoara, and Mgr. *John Scheffler*, bishop of Satu Mare, had been deposed. Only two bishops were recognised by the State, Mgr. *Aaron Marton*, Bishop of Alba Julia and Mgr. *Anthony Durcovici*, Bishop of Iasi.

The " Project of Statutes for the functioning of the Catholic Religion in Romania " was presented to the Government by these two bishops on 27 October 1948. The 46 articles treated of all the legal problems which should serve as the basis of the

relations between the State and the Church. Naturally this
project insisted on the spiritual structure of the Church and on
the rights of the Sovereign Pontiff who has spiritual jurisdiction
over all the members of the Catholic Church (art. 3). The
Minister for Worship said he was not satisfied with the statutes
presented, maintaining that the primacy of the Roman Pontiff
and his jurisdiction over Romanian Catholics constituted in the
view of the Government of the People's Republic an attack on
the sovereignty of the State. On the very day after this project
was presented the Communist police proceeded to arrest all
the Catholic bishops of the Oriental Rite.

The Government instructed the two " recognised " prelates
to have drawn up another project of statutes satisfying the
demands of the Communist régime and omitting all mention
of the right of jurisdiction of the Sovereign Pontiff. Attention
was drawn particularly to the necessity of bringing the Catholic
Church of the Latin Rite into line with the " spirit " of the
People's Republic of Romania; in a word the effective and
total submission of the Church to the civil authority was
insisted on.

In consequence of his refusal to yield to the proposals of the
Government Mgr. *Anthony Durcovici* was arrested on 24 June
1949, Mgr. *Aaron Marton* having been arrested three days before.
The Communists then turned to the vicars general to try to
get the desired statutes. The vicars general presented without
any modification the text drawn up a year before by the bishops,
adding that they had no authority to discuss these questions,
which were reserved to the supreme ecclesiastical authority.

Faced with the refusal of the hierarchy to yield to its desires,
the Communist Government devised a manoeuvre intended to
cause division among the Catholics, in order to bring about a schism
similar to the one the persecutors had tried to establish in
Czechoslovakia.

*   *   *

The attempt at schism and at causing discord among the
Catholics of the Latin Rite was conducted under cover of the
movement of " Struggle for Peace."

On 28 February 1950 the Holy Synod, supreme authority of the Romanian Orthodox Church, addressed a letter to all the clergy and Christian faithful of the People's Republic of Romania exhorting them to the fight for peace. This document extolled " the new style of peace " guaranteed by the Soviet Union and requested adherence to the appeal launched throughout the whole world by the Congress for Peace held in Stockholm. In the letter it was stated that, while the Christians of the East had taken their stand beside the defenders of peace, the Vatican and the Catholics had ranged themselves with the instigators of unbridled war and were preparing to let loose another world war.[50]

The letter of the Holy Synod was also sent to several Catholic priests and faithful of the Latin Rite, with the intention not only of defaming the Holy See, but also as a *first attempt to create division among Catholics.*

The Vicar General of Alba Julia, Mgr. *Louis Boga*, replied to the invitation by a letter addressed to the Minister for Worship, in which he explained the Catholic doctrine on peace.[51]   The letter reached the Minister on 24 April 1950, three days before the Congress announced by the Government, and to which were invited those Catholics prepared to co-operate with the régime.

This Congress took place on 27 April at Targu-Mures; it had been cleverly prepared over a long period of time by the agencies of Communist propaganda.[52]   Some priests and Catholic laymen, previously " worked on " by the police, were expected at this Congress to adopt an attitude hostile to the authority of the Church, under the pretext of the necessity of " the struggle for Peace." Those who assisted at the Congress scarcely numbered

---

[50] Cf. P. Gherman, *L'Ame roumaine écartelée*, Paris, 1955, pp. 165-168.

[51] Mgr. Boga expounded clearly the arguments developed by the Holy Father in his radio message at Christmas 1948, insisting specially on the idea that true peace must be based on charity and justice and deploring that the Catholic clergy though earnest in the service of peace were often accused of being its enemy and of being allied to the instigators of war. Cf. P. Gherman, *L'Ame roumaine écartelée*, pp. 165-168.

[52] The Congress of Targu-Mures like that of Cluj was organised by the Communists also with the intention—which they thought should succeed easily with the Latin Catholics of Transylvania—of restoring in schismatic form the "Status Catholicus Transilvaniensis." In this connection see *La Civiltà Cattolica*, 1950, III-IV.

one hundred; according to the arrangements made beforehand, they were to decide to sign the Stockholm Appeal launched by the Partisan Movement for Peace. Moreover they were to promise to work for the " bringing into line " of the Catholic Church of the Latin Rite with the spirit of the Communist laws of the People's Republic of Romania.

The Communist agents elected as president of the meeting the priest *Andrew Agotha*, who had already made it known that he was ready to collaborate with the régime.[53] In spite of ardent " indoctrination " several Catholics present at the Congress at Targu-Mures opposed the resolutions presented by the Communists. This did not prevent the Congress in its final meeting from appointing a " Catholic Committee of Action " which was to spread the idea of Communist peace, and especially to persuade the Catholics—and above all the priests—to sign the Appeal for Peace and to accept the fact of the break (on the part of the Government) with Rome. One of the first steps taken by this Committee was to bring pressure to bear on Mgr. *Louis Boga*, Vicar General of Alba Julia, to sign the decisions taken at Targu-Mures and to adhere to the " Movement for Peace." He refused however to collaborate in any way with the Committee. The evident object of this Committee was to create a schism in the Catholic community of the Latin Rite in Romania.

The Government attempt at creating a schism having failed, it was taken up again by this Committee which, in collusion with the Minister for Worship, tried to re-open the discussion about the Statutes of the Church of the Latin Rite in Romania. On 4 June 1950 the Episcopal Curiae of Alba Julia and Iasi received the text of the Statutes which had formerly been proposed by the bishops and then corrected by the Minister. This text was accompanied by a Note from the Minister, *Stanciu Stoian*, stating that these Statutes would be accepted only with the corrections made by the Minister.

The Statutes were made up of 39 Articles. At first sight they seemed acceptable enough, but in reality they were a cleverly

---

[53] It is precisely for this act of collaboration with the persecutors that Agotha was excommunicated on 5 May 1950.

thought-out instrument for the complete subjection of the Church to the atheistic State.

> ART. 1 affirmed that the Catholic Church could carry on its various activities according to its dogmas, canons and traditions, but always in conformity with the laws of the country.

We know what these laws were like.

> ART. 2 declared, " The Pope is the Supreme Authority in faith and morals, and in all matters concerning spiritual jurisdiction in the Roman Catholic Religion."

> ART. 13 speaks of the nomination of bishops as follows: " The right to name the Metropolitan and the Bishops belongs to the Holy See. These however must first be proposed by the Roman Catholic Church of the People's Republic of Romania, and be approved by the Government."

In the actual circumstances this meant that the Pope had to name the candidate proposed by the Government.

If some of the articles appear at first glance better than those quoted above, taken in conjunction with article 39 they leave little room for such an opinion. Article 39 revoked all previous concessions and added that all provisions of the present Statutes would be applied only with the approval of the Minister for Worship, " who will give approval after taking into account the dispositions of the Law on the General Regulations for Religions." [54]

The Communists knew well that it was impossible for the authorities of the Catholic Church to accept Statutes drawn up by the leading members of the schismatic movement; they hastened then to take radical measures against those who in their opinion would be in a position to make observations or remonstrances against the modified Statutes. So on the night of 10-11 May 1950 they arrested Mgr. *Louis Boga*, Vicar General of Alba Julia, and Mgr. *Mark Glasser*, Vicar General of Iasi who, while he was being interrogated, was subjected to such ill-

---

[54] *La Documentation Catholique*, April 8 1951, col. 429-432.

treatment that he died from the effects of it on 25 May 1950.
On 18 May Mgr. *Alexander Cisar*, Archbishop of Bucharest and
Mgr. *John Scheffler*, Bishop of Satu Mare, were both imprisoned.

Mgr. *Cisar* returned to his See after some years. On the other
hand, Mgr. *Scheffler* was killed in the Communist gaols.

Mgr. *Augustine Pacha*, who was " deposed " but still at liberty,
addressed a Pastoral Letter to the faithful in which he enumerated
all the abuses of power and acts of violence committed against the
Catholic Church by the Government. The prelate then deplored
that several priests had been deceived at the time of their signing
the Appeal for Peace. Only later on did they learn from the
newspapers " that from the fact of having signed they were
considered adherents of a Movement already condemned by the
Church as schismatic." " But what saddens us most," continued
Mgr. *Pacha*, " is that the Government, ignoring the lawful
Pastors, has not hesitated to make contact publicly and officially
with those who of their own accord have placed themselves
outside the Church." [55]

On 18 July Mgr. *Pacha* was arrested, and the schismatic
Movement pursued its activity with the full support of the
Government.

On 28 July 1950 the " Catholic Committee of Action," now
a subsidiary Communist organisation, launched a Manifesto filled
with accusations against the Catholic bishops who, it stated,
obstinately refused to accept the regulations proposed by the
State for all religions in the People's Republic of Romania,
preferring to take sides with the enemies of peace. The Manifesto
praised the spirit of the meeting at Targu-Mures, and exhorted
the Catholic clergy and faithful to accept the new Statutes of
the Catholic Church. The " Committee " claimed that it was
acting according to the laws of the Catholic Church; that was
precisely the reason, stated the Manifesto, why it sought to
translate into action the decisions taken at the congress of Targu-
Mures for the good of the people, of the Church, and of peace. [56]

---

[55] Cf. *La Civiltà Cattolica*, July 1950, p. 230.
[56] Cf. *La Documentation Catholique*, 8 April 1951, col. 432-434.

Expulsion of the representative of the Holy See

All the propaganda of the promoters of the " schismatic " movement was of no avail. The régime then returned to its old game of calumniating the Catholic Church and especially the Holy Father. To show that the representative of the Pope was nothing other than " a spy in bishop's clothing " a lawsuit was begun in which the Nunciature was accused of espionage. The trial was conducted in the classical Communist style : the decision was fixed in advance, the Communists made every effort to influence public opinion, and to prove that the Government was obliged to sever diplomatic relations with the Holy See, because the members of the Pontifical Nunciature were guilty of spying to the detriment of the Romanian State.

Among those accused there figured a certain *Nicholas Popescu*, ex-chauffeur of the Apostolic Nunciature. In the depositions of *Popescu* the Communist police inserted the " information " that the Apostolic Nuncio, Mgr. *Gerald O'Hara*, and the Counsellor of the Nunciature, Mgr. *Guy del Mestri*, had advised him to carry on propaganda among his friends in favour of America, " to boast of the power of atomic weapons, to gather information of military importance and to become a spy for the imperialists." The press drew special attention to these " crimes " of the Nunciature which it called " the centre of espionage." [57]

The newspapers went so far as to accuse the representative of the Holy See of being the head of a plot against the Romanian State. At the conclusion of the trial, besides condemning the seven " traitors " to sentences varying from seven years' forced labour to imprisonment for life, the Minister for Foreign Affairs demanded that the two members of the Pontifical Representation be compelled *to leave the country within three days.* Thus on 7 July 1950 the representative of the Pope was obliged to leave Romania. Before leaving he presented a Note of protest to the Minister for Foreign Affairs of the People's Republic. [58]

---

[57] The charge against the accused was published and commented on by the Romanian press. The French translation of the complete text of the trial was published in a supplement of the Communist paper *La Roumanie nouvelle*, n. 47, 15-31 July 1950.

[58] The Note deplored the hostile attitude of the Romanian Government to the Catholic Church and expressed " profound grief " at the attack on the Holy See, the Pope and his representatives. In face of this outrageous and unusual manner of acting

The Romanian people learned with astonishment and sorrow the decision of the Government to expel the representative of the Holy See. The people, with their common sense and honesty, knew the worth of the above-mentioned gross accusations.[59]

Congress at Gheorgheni and Meeting at Cluj

After the expulsion of the representative of the Pope the " Catholic Committee of Action " set about preparing another re-union of the Catholics. The brochures and circulars sent to the clergy and faithful referred to the Congress of Targu-Mures, renewed the accusations against the ecclesiastical authorities and invited Catholics to a new Congress which would debate more important problems than heretofore.

The Congress took place on 16 September 1950 at Gheorgheni and followed more or less the same routine as that of Targu-Mures. There were 120 priests and 150 laymen present. The greater number of those present was brought there by trickery and even by force, in ignorance of the matters to be discussed. The congress was presided over by the excommunicated priest *Andrew Agotha*, president of " The Catholic Committee of Action." The problem of peace, and the necessity of establishing normal relations between the Church and State were discussed. Then special attention was drawn to the duty of Catholics to collaborate in the progress of Socialism in the People's Republic of Romania. The congress ended by expressing the desire to see a *General Catholic Assembly* convoked.

The final motion read at the Congress was represented by Communist propaganda as having received the approval of *all the Catholics of the country*. In the meantime the police arrested several Catholic priests and attempted to induce others to

---

the Nunciature made a solemn protest and, with regard to the public affront offered to "the Church and to the representatives of the Holy See," it deferred with confidence and with calm to the judgment of the Romanian people. Cf. *La Documentation Catholique*, 10 September 1950, col. 1204-1206.

[59] *L'Osservatore Romano* of 10-11 July 1950 wrote: " The truth is that the Romanian Government had recourse to this mean and shameful expedient in order to realise a long premeditated plan: to get rid of the representative of the Sovereign Pontiff in order to carry out without any embarrassing witnesses the destruction of the whole organisation of the Catholic Church in Romania, to deprive the faithful of that nation of a capable guide in order that they might become more easily victims of the violence and deceit practised by the Government to separate them from their Supreme Pastor, the Pope."

collaborate with the partisans of the Movement. " Progressive " priests were placed in charge of several parishes. In order to strengthen the schismatic movement among Catholics, the " Catholic Committee of Action " kept its promise to organise a " General Assembly " and resolved to make it an occasion for a " popular " demonstration to confirm the realisation of the schism among Catholics.

Preceded by a re-union of 40 " progressive " priests at Bucharest on 14 March 1951, *a General Assembly of Catholics was held at Cluj on the following day.* " Representatives " of 601 parishes were present. The official speakers insisted once again on the theme of peace and on the necessity of imitating the example of the Catholics of Czechoslovakia and of Hungary who had put themselves on the side of their own People's Democratic Governments. It seems however that the principal object of the Assembly at Cluj had been to approve of the final wording of the Statutes of the Catholic Church proposed by the Government. The final motions of the Assembly mention almost exclusively these statutes presented as being inspired " by the teaching of Christ " and making their contribution to the activities of the partisans of peace. " In this spirit," concluded the motion, " the assembly confides to the directing Council of the statutes the sacred duty of making it possible for the higher administration of the two dioceses to proceed without delay to bring the Church within the framework of the legal order, thus responding to the desires of all the Catholics of the country who love peace." [60]

By this act the Communists thought that they had, at least in principle, brought about the schism within the Romanian Catholic Church of the Latin Rite.

To bring about this division in a practical manner they sought first of all to create the greatest confusion amongst the faithful. Priests in charge of parishes were changed frequently, so that the faithful could not themselves find out whether the new arrival was a " collaborator " with the Communists or a priest who had always remained true to Rome. Their minds were all

[60] *La Documentation Catholique,* 8 April 1951, col. 435-436.

the more upset on account of the insidious way in which the
" progressive " priests insisted, following the directions given
by the Communist persecutors, that they were in communion
with Rome and respectfully subject to the Sovereign Pontiff.

While these meetings were taking place and the press kept
on discussing ways and means to compel the bishops to agree
to the proposals of the Government, the Communist police did
not remain inactive.   Since the end of the year 1949 Father
Anthony Bisoc, Superior of the Conventual Fathers, and almost all
the Franciscans of Bacau had been imprisoned.   Similarly
the *priests who had not joined the schismatic movement were almost
all arrested* or sent to camps of forced labour.

In order to justify the measures taken against the Catholic
clergy the Communist leaders found no better means than to
stage *a new trial* to which were summoned the Bishop of
Timisoara, Mgr. *Augustine Pacha*, and a group of priests most of
whom were members of the Episcopal Curiae.   In the dock
were Fathers *Schubert*, *Boros*, *Waltner* and Father *Gatti* parish
priest of the Italian church in Bucharest.   During the trial the
press renewed all the old accusations against the Catholic Church
and insisted particularly that Mgr. *Pacha* and the accused priests
were guilty of treason because they belonged to a spy-ring
organised by the Regent of the Nunciature at Bucharest.   The
military prosecutor, Colonel *A. Ardeleanu*, stated among other
things in the course of the trial: " The bitterest enemy of our
people is the Vatican, a veritable international cancer."   The
prosecutor continued his harangue repeating the usual charges
of spying by the Catholic bishops and priests, the subversive
action of the clergy and their opposition to the Communist
movement for peace.[61]

After many accusations of this kind the accused were asked
to sign a declaration by which they threw themselves on the
clemency of the Communist tribunal and implored a reduction
of their penalties.[62]   The tribunal condemned the 81 years old
Mgr. *Pacha* to 18 years in prison and the other accused to
sentences varying from 10 to 15 years in prison.

---

[61] Cf. P. Gherman, *L'Ame roumaine écartelée*, p. 188.
[62] Cf. *Universul*, 12 September 1951.

To replace Mgr. *Joseph Schubert*, Vicar General of Bucharest, and Mgr. *Adalbert Boros*, Vicar General of Timisoara, condemned during the course of the trial, the Government nominated priests who had joined the schismatic movement. On 15 April 1951, a few days after the arrest of Mgr. *Schubert*, Canon *Trajan Jovanelli*, who had been set free a month earlier for this purpose, was appointed Vicar of Bucharest. To fill the post of chancellor of the Curia of Bucharest the Government named *Andrew Horn-Despina*, a priest of the diocese of Bucharest, who had been excommunicated *vitandus* by a decree of 4 April 1951. *Andrew Agotha*, head of the " Catholic Committee of Action," represented the Ministry on the Episcopal Curia.

The Communist régime by these nominations replaced forcibly the lawful pastors by apostates and excommunicated priests. Attention must be called to the fact that the Government discussed all questions relating to the Catholic Church solely with this group of priests.

In the meantime the bishops, who in the first period of the persecution had been kept in prison, found their sentences commuted to house-arrest.

For the time being, in spite of the resistance of the Catholics to the schismatic movement, the heads of this movement and especially the so-called " Catholic Committee of Action " continued to be active.

The faithful deserted the churches when they knew that a priest who collaborated with the Communists was celebrating Mass, refusing even to receive the sacraments from excommunicated priests.

To remove this distrust towards collaborating priests the organs of Communist propaganda had recourse to various expedients.

First of all there was a slackening off in direct anti-Catholic propaganda. The priests placed in responsible positions by the Communists were ordered to protest in the course of their sermons their attachment and their fidelity to the Holy Father. To the rare visitors from abroad it was constantly repeated that the priests, who had been authorised to live in the former episcopal palaces, were faithful Catholics subject to the Pope.

In reality it can be said that the attempt of the Communists to install in Romania a schismatic Catholic Church had failed. However it must be admitted that the absence for so long a time of all religious help sometimes resulted in a weakening of the faith, even among the most zealous of the faithful. Then again the atheistic and materialist education given to the young will in the near future produce in the country a generation not only lacking any religious formation but imbued with ideas hostile to Christianity and especially to the Catholic Church.

The schismatic movement on present day (1956) evidence of its development and activity is destined almost certainly to fail in its efforts. Even the Communists consider it simply as a *means of weakening the resistance of the Catholics* and of *creating a state of religious confusion* more favourable to anti-religious propaganda.

In any case one fact remains: only one of the Romanian bishops, Mgr. *Aaron Marton*, has been set free (in 1955). However his activity is subject to strict supervision by the Communist authorities who treat in the same way the excommunicated priests they substituted for the lawful pastors. The liberation of the Bishop of Alba Julia seems to form part of a plan to cause confusion in the ranks of the Catholics and to permit Communist propaganda to state that religious liberty is respected in Romania.

The authorisation given by the Government to hold in the cathedral of Bucharest the funeral ceremonies of Mgr. *Cisar*, who died in January 1954, was but another means of propaganda. This event allowed the régime to proclaim once again that in Romania religious liberty was so great that funeral services could be publicly celebrated for a bishop who had been kept under house-arrest since 1950 for his misdeeds.

Finally the schismatic movement favoured by the " Catholic Committee of Action " is only an instrument which the Communists use for the time being to satisfy " the old generation " and to give to the outside world proof of the much-vaunted religious liberty. In reality the Communists want only to make the way easy for the total liquidation of the Catholic Church in Romania.

Conclusion

From this statement of the facts which led to the suppression of the Catholic Church of the Oriental Rite and the formation of a schismatic movement among the Catholics of the Latin Rite in Romania it is very evident that the final objective of the Communist Government is the complete destruction of the Catholic Church in the country.

The losses inflicted on the Church by the Communist persecution are more clearly appreciated when we compare the state of the Catholic Church in Romania on the eve of the installing of the Communist régime with that of 1953, that is to say, after five years of unbridled persecution.

In 1945 before the Communists had seized power, there were in Romania: 1 Apostolic Nuncio, 12 archbishops and bishops, 2,995 priests, 3,795 churches and chapels, 2,494 parishes, 160 religious houses, 376 Catholic schools with about 53,000 pupils of both sexes, 30 newspapers and periodicals and 160 charitable institutions. In 1953 when the persecution against the Church had reached its peak, the Apostolic Nuncio had been expelled on the charge of spying and the 12 archbishops and bishops imprisoned; five of them had already died in prison. Of the 2,995 priests there were only 2,190 left; 55 were dead, 250 dead or dispersed, about 200 condemned to forced labour and 300 in prison. Of the 3,795 churches and chapels Catholics had the use of only about 700; 2,734 churches of the Catholics of the Oriental Rite had been handed over to the Orthodox; the others had been closed. All Catholic educational and charitable institutions, as well as religious houses, had been confiscated and declared the property of the State.[63]

Because the Catholics in Romania were in a minority, the

---

[63] *La Documentation Catholique* of 20 September 1953 published on its own account the following table:

	1945	1953
Apostolic Nuncio	1	Expelled.
Archbishops and Bishops ..	12	All imprisoned, condemned and deported—3 died in prison.
Priests and Religious ..	3,331	1,405: 55 killed—250 dead or missing—200 at forced labour—200 in prison.

persecutors could more easily accomplish the destruction of the Church. The Communists did not have to fear any resistance on the part of the whole population, which was non-Catholic and sometimes anti-Catholic. They found, as has been seen, an eager and docile helper in the National Orthodox Church.

For these reasons the persecution in Romania was more violent than any persecution to which predominantly Catholic countries were subjected and the destruction of the Church was pushed to its extreme limit. The Communist Government was able to proclaim that the Catholic Church of the Oriental Rite " no longer existed." As for the Church of the Latin Rite its activity was systematically hindered by the attempt to create a schism, organised with so much treachery by the Communist authorities.

In spite of the losses suffered by the Church and the cruelty of the persecution, the Romanian Catholics justly entertain great hopes of revival and of spiritual awakening. The sacrifice of those persecuted has been, even for non-Catholics, the most glorious proof of the supernatural spirit of Catholicism, while the alliance of the Romanian National Church with atheistic materialism has made many of our separated brethren examine their consciences, and has brought them closer to Catholicism.

The letters and the records of the persecuted tell us that they offered their sufferings for the triumph of the Church and the union of all Christians and that many among them are confident of the final victory of the reign of God.

The last testament of Mgr. *Alexander Cisar*, Archbishop of Bucharest, expressed this hope. " I am convinced," he writes, " that the Communist domination will pass and that Romania will win back her liberty . . . God has not forgotten us and our sufferings will bear fruit."

Churches and Chapels ..	3,795	700: 2,734 of the Oriental Rite handed over to the Orthodox Church.
Religious Houses	160	25: 85% suppressed.
Catholic Schools for boys ..	224 (28,000 pupils)	All suppressed.
Catholic Schools for girls ..	152 (23,000 pupils)	All suppressed.
Works of Charity	160	All suppressed.
Catholic Newspapers and Publications	30	All suppressed.

Chapter 12

THE PERSECUTION OF THE CATHOLIC CHURCH

UNDER

Communist Rule in Czechoslovakia

WHEN THE CZECHOSLOVAK State was set up in 1918 it gathered within its frontiers 8,700,000 Czechs and 3,400,000 Slovaks as well as large German and Hungarian minorities. In 1950 the population was roughly 12,500,000. Three quarters of these—more than 9,000,000—were Catholics.

The Czechs occupy the provinces of Bohemia and Moravia. These correspond to the two ecclesiastical provinces of Prague, with suffragan dioceses Budejovice, Hradec Králové and Litomerice, and of Olomouc with suffragan diocese, Brno.

Slovakia is divided ecclesiastically into the dioceses of Banska-Bystricá, Nitra, Spis, Kosice, Roznava and the Ruthenian diocese of Presov. This last serves the needs of the faithful of the Oriental Rite. As well as these there are also the vast Apostolic Administration of Trnava and that of Szatmar.[1]

From February 1948 the Communist persecution followed the same pattern in all parts of the country. After this date the different steps taken in Slovakia, Bohemia and Moravia correspond perfectly in degrees of violence and in timing. This renders it unnecessary to treat separately of each of these provinces in considering the various stages by which the almost complete suppression of the activity of the Catholic Church was achieved throughout the whole country.[2]

---

[1] Slovakia formed part of the kingdom of Hungary until 1918 and has not yet been organised as an ecclesiastical province with its own Metropolitan.

[2] Cf. *Der Neue Herder*, 1955. An important study, well documented, on the religious persecution in Czechoslovakia has been published by Ludvik Nemec: *Church and State in Czechoslovakia*, New York, 1954.

In the execution of their plans for the elimination of all Church influence the Marxist leaders proceeded step by step. This account of the measures taken against the Church, especially from 1948 on, will be divided into sections, each section dealing with one of these steps. Hence the following order of treatment which agrees very closely with the chronological order of events:

1. The religious and political situation in Czechoslovakia before 1948 with special reference to the persecution in Slovakia.

2. The laws against the Catholic press, Catholic schools and Catholic organisations.

3. The Government effort to create a schismatic movement.

4. The attempt to bring the episcopate and the clergy under Communist control.

5. Violent persecution of the Church.

1. THE RELIGIOUS AND POLITICAL SITUATION BEFORE 1948. THE PERSECUTION IN SLOVAKIA.

In Czechoslovakia the Communists proceeded with caution before openly attacking the Church and traditional institutions. The numerical strength of the Catholics, forming as they did 78% of the population,[3] was one reason for this cautious policy. Another was the natural antipathy to the Communist system felt by a people long outstanding for its attachment to the democratic freedoms.

On 16 May 1945 President *Benes* returned from exile at the

---

[3] Before the last war, according to statistics of 1930, Czechoslovakia had a population of 14,736,158. Of these 10,831,696 were Catholics of the Latin Rite and 585,041 were Catholics of the Oriental Rite; 1,129,758 were Protestants; 793,358 belonged to the Czechoslovak National Church; 145,598 were Orthodox; 357,000 were Jews; and 854,638 were without religion. After the war the frontiers of Czechoslovakia were re-adjusted so that on the arrival of the Communists to power, and after the expulsion of 1,912,000 inhabitants of German origin (Sudeten Germans), nearly all Catholics, the position was as follows: population, 12 million approximately; Catholics of the Latin Rite, 8,750,000, and of the Oriental Rite, 300,000; Protestants, 900,000; Czechoslovak National Church, 900,000; Orthodox, 60,000; Jews, 50,000; without religion, 970,000. The Church organisation in Czechoslovakia was as follows: 2 archbishoprics, 10 bishoprics, 2 apostolic administrations, with a total of 4,149 parishes, 5,779 secular priests, 1,363 religious houses and institutions, 1,163 religious priests, 1,102 lay religious and 10,868 nuns.

head of the Government he had formed during the German occupation. He had concluded on 12 December 1943 a treaty of mutual aid with Russia, in which he had agreed to help that State in its struggle against the Nazis. The war over, he considered that his country had a right to partake in the fruits of victory without thereby signifying acceptance of Communist domination. The elections of 26 May 1946 proved that the people were not at all willing to accept the system the Russians were trying to impose on them.

In the *Benes* Government the Communist minority, emboldened by the presence of the Red army, created all kinds of difficulties. By a *coup d'état*—a classic of its kind—the Communists succeeded on 25 February 1948 in changing the whole political structure of the country.[4] On the resignation from office of *Benes*, Parliament elected the Communist *Clement Gottwald* as President of the Republic.

As regards its attitude to the Catholic Church the *Benes* Government had from the start *sought to establish diplomatic relations* with the Holy See. On 13 May 1946 Mgr. *Xavier Ritter* was appointed representative of the Holy See with the rank of Internuncio Apostolic. Doctor *Arthur Maixner* became the Czechoslovak representative at the Vatican.

The difficulties arising in connection with the filling of the archiepiscopal See of Prague, vacant since 1941, were likewise solved under the *Benes* Government. At the death of Cardinal *Kaspar* in 1941 the political situation rendered impossible the nomination of a new archbishop. On 5 November 1946 Mgr. *Joseph Beran* was named Archbishop of Prague and Metropolitan of Bohemia.[5] The Government was represented at his consecration on 8 December 1946; among its representatives was the future President, *Gottwald*. On the same day Mgr. *Beran* received the medal of the Czech Resistance from the Minister for the Interior, *Vaclav Nosek*, who was himself a convinced Communist.

---

[4] Cf. Nemec, *op. cit.* pp. 221 *seqq.*

[5] The new archbishop had shown great courage during the Nazi occupation, when rector of the Prague seminary. This cost him three years' imprisonment in different concentration camps. On his appointment as archbishop on 14 November 1946 he received the Military Cross in recognition of his patriotism. Cf. Nemec, *op. cit.* pp. 202-203.

Up to the *coup d'état* of February 1948, despite numerous attacks,[6] the Catholic Church in Czechoslovakia enjoyed a certain liberty in the exercise of the sacred ministry, at least in Bohemia and Moravia. This was due in great measure to the courageous attitude adopted by the bishops towards a number of Government regulations.

A change came with the arrival of the Communists to power. Henceforth severe measures were taken against the Catholic Church. These measures were preceded by a campaign against the Church and the Holy See over the radio, in the press, in public speeches and in the cinema. The Communist press of Czechoslovakia can make the ignoble boast of having surpassed from 1948 its counterparts in all other Communist-dominated countries in *calumnies and insinuations of all kinds* against the clergy, the bishops and the Sovereign Pontiff himself.[7] The situation was rendered all the more difficult by the fact that the Communists at the same time deprived the Church of the means of replying to these attacks through the press.

The Persecution in Slovakia from 1944 to 1948

The anti-Catholic persecution in Slovakia from the end of the war up to the Communist *coup d'état* of 20 February 1948 deserves a special mention of its own. The Slovak nation, which fought in World War II against the USSR to save the independence it had won, learned from experience—even before its territory was overrun by Soviet troops—the treatment which the Catholic religion may expect from Communism.

During the summer of 1944 the Russians parachuted on to Slovak soil military and political instructors. They tried to win over to their cause the Government of the Slovak Republic by

---

[6] The Government had for example suppressed some traditional Catholic feasts on the plea that they " robbed the State of valuable working hours." Measures had also been taken against the teaching of religion in schools, reducing the hours devoted to it and making of it a second-class subject. A number of the clergy and of the Catholic laity accused of having plotted against President Benes was " purged." Most of these measures were due to the Ministry for the Interior, a key ministry which the Communists made sure to get hold of in the first Benes Cabinet. Cf. Nemec, *op. cit.* pp.204-220.

[7] In the course of this account frequent reference will be made to this press campaign against the Church. It is impossible however to give anything but a faint idea of the violence of anti-Catholic propaganda in Czechoslovakia during these last eight years.

proposing to it an alliance with Communism, and promising to respect the existence of a Slovak Soviet Republic.[8]

Making common cause with the local Communists and Protestants (these last-named were dissatisfied with the Government representing, as it did, the overwhelming Catholic majority), the Soviet " instructors " infused fresh life into the secret Communist and Democratic Parties, both of which served as the nucleus for the so-called *National Slovak Council*. This " Council " was clearly anti-Catholic, as was proved by the fact that one of its first decisions was the *nationalisation* (or more accurately the laicisation) *of the flourishing schools directed by priests and religious* and constituting three-fifths of all the schools in the country. In decree n. 5 of 7 September 1944 the Council laid down as follows:

(1) Schools of all categories and grades from the kindergarten to those of university standing are nationalised in Slovakia, dating from the coming into force of the present decree.

(2) The teaching staff and all the employees of the said schools become State functionaries.[9]

This decree was issued by the Council but remained a dead letter, for German troops were in occupation and the territory controlled by the partisans of the Council was limited.

A few months sufficed for the Communist partisans to show the extent of their anti-Catholic hatred. Presbyteries and episcopal residences were searched, property destroyed and threats made, backed by a display of armed force. Priests were thrown into prisons without any reasons being alleged. Religious were driven from their houses. Priests were killed independently of all military operations and the religious convictions of the victims were made a subject of mockery.[10]

When the Czechoslovak Republic was re-established, under the measure of self-government granted to Slovakia, the few local

---

[8] Cf. J. A. Mikus: *La Slovaquie dans le drame de l'Europe centrale*, Paris, 1955, p. 202.

[9] *Sbierka nariadení Slovenskej národnej rady* (Collection of the Decrees of the National Slovak Council), Banská Bystrica, 1944.

[10] For a documented account cf. *The Church of Silence in Slovakia* by T. J. Zubek, Whiting, Ind., 1956.

Communists found themselves in the position of masters of the country. The new National Slovak Council continued to be constituted by representatives of the two Parties, the Communist and the Democratic. The latter was still controlled by Protestants since Catholics were *de facto* excluded from public life. It was an easy thing in fact for the Communists to attribute the responsibility for this situation to the Church and to create an atmosphere of propaganda designed to prove that the Communists were opposed to the Catholics, solely because they were representatives of the former Slovak Republic. The Communist minority in this way aimed at making political precedents a " justification " for a series of decrees and regulations, inspired in reality by mere anti-religious hatred.

In the month of April 1945 two bishops were imprisoned. They were Mgr. *John Vojtassak*, Bishop of Spis, and Mgr. *Michael Buzalka*, auxiliary Bishop of Trnava, together with Mgr. *John Postényi*, director of the Society of Saint Adalbert (the great cultural organisation of Slovak Catholics), and other priests. The bishops were released after some months in prison in consequence of the repercussion, unfavourable to Communism, which their arrests had on the population.

By decree n. 34 of 16 May 1946 the National Council gave new force to the preceding decree on the nationalisation of all Catholic schools.[11]

> 1,800 primary schools with more than 25,000 pupils, 77 secondary schools with about 10,000 pupils, and 30 colleges with some 5,000 boarders besides many other educational establishments, were thus nationalised.
>
> It must be remembered that in Slovakia, where the school Law of the Emperor Francis Joseph—a law of liberalising tendency —had not been promulgated in view of the fact that the country formed part of Hungary, almost all the parishes had their own primary schools and in all centres there were secondary schools depending on ecclesiastical authority.

In virtue of decree n. 47 of 26 May 1945 *the confiscation of all*

---

[11] Cf. *Sbierka nariadeni Slovenskej národnej rady*, Bratislava, 1945.

school property was ordered.[12]   This measure struck a painful blow especially at those religious houses—and they were the greater number—which had been for a long time linked permanently with the schools. In many cases they had to surrender to the new lay tenants the cloistered parts of their religious houses.

In virtue of decree n. 80 (1945) all student hostels were confiscated from their ecclesiastical owners.[13]   Thus were lost the great Svoradov Institute for the university students of Bratislava and twenty-four other student hostels.

The Communists' aggressive measures in the matter of schools did not end here. Through the initiative of the Commissar for Education of the National Council (a noted Communist) members of the Party were named inspectors and directors of the schools. A " purge " of the teaching staffs was carried out by systematically retiring religious even from schools which up to this had belonged to them. The crucifix and every other religious emblem were banished from many classrooms. Religious instruction was relegated to the margin of the school programme and the period allotted to it was notably reduced.

Through the *referendum* promoted by the Central Catholic Bureau (or Central Catholic Secretariate—CCS) of Bratislava, signatures were collected by plebiscite in favour of the rights of the Church in the education of youth. But these had no value for the Communist *democracy*. The police confiscated the *dossiers* of signatures which were in the Bureau at Bratislava and in all the presbyteries of Slovakia, and arrested the director of the Bureau which had promoted the referendum.

By decree n. 51, 25 May 1945, *all Youth Associations of Catholic Action were dissolved* and their property—including libraries— was confiscated.

At the same time all religious works were excluded from public libraries, and Catholic periodical publications were restricted. As a result the reviews *Kultura* and *Obroda* ceased to appear, and the following Catholic publishing houses were

---

[12] Cf. *ibid*.   [13] Cf. *ibid*.

deprived of their printing presses: *Andrej* of Bratislava, *Spolok sv Vojtecha* of Trnava, and *Lev* of Ruzomberok.[14]

The formation of aspirants to the priesthood and the religious life suffered severely too. Many institutes had to hand over a large part of their buildings to serve as co-educational schools, and it was not unusual to hear rowdy laughter and the sound of noisy dancing at the very doors of the cloister. Seminarians and young religious were forced to attend public schools where Atheism and Materialism were taught.

The Slovak bishops protested in vain against all this in their collective Pastoral Letter of November 1945.

The elections on 26 May 1946 showed in no uncertain manner on what side the sympathies of the people lay: the Communists polled 30% of the votes, i.e. less than half of the Christian Democrat vote (61.5%).[15]

> Once again the will of the people was ignored. The result of the elections for the whole Czechoslovak Republic had in fact given a slight majority to the Communists supported by the Social Democrats (40% and 14% respectively). The bloc formed by Benes' National Socialists (24%) and the Popular Party (21%) (including 2 seats of the Slovak Independence Party) polled 45% of the votes. Supported by the Bohemian and Moravian Comrades, the Slovak Communists—not bothering now about the much vaunted Slovak independence—made use of this slight majority to hold on to their own position of authority. In this the weakness of the Democratic Party was also an advantage to the Communists.

After the elections there was some slight improvement in religious conditions, but they suffered none the less from the Communist manoeuvre. To cite only a few examples, law n. 248/1946 sanctioned work on Sundays and Church Holydays

---

[14] During the election period of 1946 there was a slight easing off in the ban on Catholics in public life. Taking advantage of this the reviews *Smer* and *Priatel dietok* (The Children's Friend) were able to appear again; *Novapráca* (New Work) and *Verbum*, two new reviews, took the place of those that had been suppressed.

[15] This was the result of the support given by the Catholics to the Democratic Party —a hard necessity aimed at preventing the Communists from gaining power. The Party under Protestant direction was not able to stop Communist expansion or prevent the more influential representatives of the Catholics from being arrested.

in spite of the fact that Catholic operatives declared themselves
ready to prolong the working hours on week-days; law n.
142/1947 *confiscated for the State all Church property*; many
Catholic Actionists were maltreated and imprisoned merely
because they wore on their breast a small metal cross as a
distinctive emblem.

The Communist *coup d'état* of February 1948 brought the
position of Slovakia in the persecution more closely into line
with that of Bohemia and Moravia.

2. THE LAWS AGAINST THE CATHOLIC PRESS, CATHOLIC SCHOOLS AND CATHOLIC ORGANISATIONS

One of the first steps taken by the new Government was the
suppression of *the bigger and more important of the Catholic newspapers* in Bohemia and Moravia.[16]   In this it was following the
pattern of Government procedure in all Communist-dominated
countries.   By a decree of the Ministry for Information, dated
26 February 1948, the publication of the following weeklies
was prohibited: *Rozsevac* (The Sower: 220,000 copies),
Nedele (The Sunday: 120,000 copies), *Katolík* (The Catholic:
30,000 copies).   The Slovak weekly, *Katolické Noviny* (Catholic
Journal) was not suppressed.   This special treatment was due
to the intention of the Government to transform this paper
later on into an organ of the schismatic movement.

The suppression of their newspapers deprived Catholics at
one and the same time of information concerning the life of
the Church and of the means of combating the attacks of their
adversaries.[17]

The Catholic reviews were attacked during the months that
followed.   Nearly all of them were suppressed by a decree of
the Minister for Information in November 1948.[18]

---

[16] Already under the preceding Government the Catholic press had suffered certain
restrictions.   In all Bohemia and Moravia it had been impossible to publish even one
Catholic daily, independent of the political parties.

[17] The protests of the hierarchy and of the faithful against this measure brought no
result.   The Government excused itself on the ground that scarcity of paper made such
proceedings necessary.

[18] The decree suppressing publications intended for youth laid down explicitly the
principle that such magazines should not be published by religious organisations.   Only
the one State Youth Organisation was entitled to publish them.

At the beginning of 1949 the Government set about implementing its desire " to bring to an end the capitalist exploitation and the anarchy prevalent in the book-publishing business." For this purpose two legal enactments were introduced: the first granted a monopoly to the non-periodical press, the second transferred to the State all ecclesiastical libraries. In the text of these laws among the bodies named as having a right to own a publishing business the Catholic Church was not mentioned. The State thus took over control of all the Catholic publishing houses. Bookshops, now under State control, excluded religious books,[19] prayer-books, the pronouncements of the Holy Father and all books on Theology. Only those books and periodicals could be got, in which Materialism was defended or the achievements of Socialism extolled. At the same time the Communist radio and press exhorted the people to distrust the " great enemy " i.e. all books attacking the Communist outlook.

The following list of Catholic publications, all suppressed by January 1949, gives an idea of the importance of the Catholic press and of the extent to which it suffered in the comparatively short period of 10 months of Communist rule:

1. Katolik (The Catholic)	weekly: 30,000 copies.
2. Nedele (The Sunday)	weekly: 120,000 copies.
3. Rozsevac (The Sower)	weekly: 220,000 copies.
4. Na Hlubinu (In Altum)	monthly: 4,000 copies.
5. Serafinsky Prapor (The Seraphic Banner) ..	monthly: 10,000 copies.
6. Mariansky Vestnik Svata Hora (The Marian Bulletin of the Sacred Mount) ..	monthly: 10,000 copies.
7. Ruze Dominikanska (The Dominican Rose)	monthly: 3,000 copies.
8. Apostolat Modlitdy (The Apostolate of Prayer)	monthly: 18,000 copies.
9. Vysehrad (Acropolis)	bi-monthly: 5,000 copies.
10. Cesta Pokoje (The Way of Peace) ..	quarterly: 1,200 copies.
11. Filosoficka revue (The Philosophical Review)	quarterly: 1,200 copies.
12. Andel Strazny (The Guardian Angel) ..	monthly: 60,000 copies.
13. Usvit (The Dawn)	monthly: 5,000 copies.
14. Radostne Mladi (Happy Youth)	monthly: 8,000 copies.
15. Akord (Accord)	monthly: 4,000 copies.

---

[19] The Ministry for Public Instruction appointed a Commission of so-called patriot priests in 1948 to issue a " corrected " version of the Catechism. This, needless to remark, was not approved by the hierarchy but was none the less made of obligation in the schools.

16. Hlasy Svatohostynske (Voice of the S. Mt. Hostyn)	monthly: 14,000 copies.
17. Vychovatelske Listy (Pedagogic Letters) ..	monthly: 6,000 copies.
18. Apostolat Sv. Cyrila a Metodeje (Apostolate of SS. Cyril and Methodius)	monthly.
19. Dobry Pastyr (The Good Shepherd) ..	weekly: 6,000 copies.
20. Vestnik Jednot Duchovenstva (Bulletin of the Association of the Clergy)	monthly: 4,000 copies.
21. Acta Academiae Velehradensis	quarterly: 3,000 copies.
22. Salesiansky Vestnik (Salesian Bulletin) ..	monthly: 10,000 copies.
23. Dorost (The New Age)	bi-monthly: 16,000 copies.
24. Vestnik Sv. Josefa (St. Joseph Bulletin) ..	monthly: 8,000 copies.
25. Farni Vestniky (Parochial Bulletins, in the Czech language)	
26. Verbum	monthly: 3,000 copies.
27. Smer (Direction)	monthly: 5,000 copies.
28. Plamen (The Flame)	bi-monthly: 18,000 copies.
29. Priatel Dietok (The Children's Friend) ..	bi-monthly: 50,000 copies.
30. Mladez a Misie (Missionary Youth) ..	monthly.
31. Jas (Splendour)	monthly: 8,000 copies.
32. Dobrocin (Good Action)	monthly.
33. Posol S. Srdca (The Messenger of the Sacred Heart)	monthly: 50,000 copies.
34. Hlasy z Domova a z Misii (The Voice of the Fatherland and of the Missions) ..	monthly: 50,000 copies.
35. Svata Rodina (The Holy Family)	monthly: 8,000 copies.
36. Slovensky Svet (The Slovak World) ..	weekly: 50,000 copies.
37. Serafinsky Svet (The Seraphic World) ..	monthly: 3,000 copies.
38. Frantiskansky Obzor (Franciscan Horizon)	quarterly.
39. Katolicka Jednota (Catholic Union) ..	monthly: 50,000 copies.
40. Marianska Kongregacia (Marian Congregation)	monthly: 3,000 copies.
41. Kralovna Maja (The Queen of May) ..	monthly.
42. Marianka	quarterly: 7,000 copies.
43. Svaty Ruzenec (The Holy Rosary) ..	monthly.
44. Zvesti Jezuitov na Slovensku (Jesuit News from Slovakia)	
45. Misionar (The Missionary)	monthly.
46. Cyril a Metod (SS. Cyril and Methodius) ..	monthly.
47. Trnavska Rodina (The Family of Trnava) ..	bi-monthly: 10,000 copies.
48. Vestnik Sdruzenia Sv. Josefa (Bulletin of the Congregation of St. Joseph)	
49. Salezianske Zvesti (Salesian News) ..	monthly.
50. Blagovestnik (The Good Bulletin) ..	bi-monthly.
51. Zivotm (Through Life)	bi-monthly: 50,000 copies.
52. Vestnik Ustr. Katol. Kancelarie (Bulletin of the Catholic Central Bureau)	
53. Farske Vestniky (Parochial Bulletins, in the Slovak language) [20]	

---

[20] This list, made out in 1949, is incomplete. In the Czech language alone 6 weeklies and 24 monthlies were suppressed while one weekly and one monthly were changed into pro-Communist organs.

In January 1949 also a " special Government Commissar " [21] was imposed on the following Catholic publishing houses:

1. The publishing firm of SS. Cyril and Methodius owned by *Gustav Francl*, Prague.
2. The publishing firm of *Bohuslav Rupp*, Prague.
3. The publishing firm of the Redemptorists, " Exercicní Dum," Frydek.
4. The publishing firm " Atlas," Prague.
5. The publishing firm of the " Vlast " Association, Prague.

The publishing house of the Missions of the Society of the Divine Word at Nitra was suppressed.

In April 1949 the official diocesan bulletins, " Acta Curiae," were suppressed. These bulletins had continued to appear even during the German occupation.

Finally a decree of the Minister for Information made it obligatory to have official authorisation for the reproduction of any text in any manner whatever (polycopies and the like included).[22] In principle the granting of this authorisation was reserved to the Ministry for Information; however in the case of notices and programmes of small dimensions the permission of the National Committee of the district sufficed. All violations of this rule were liable to punishment.

*   *   *

Among the very first pre-occupations of the new rulers must be mentioned *the suppression of Catholic schools* wherever such schools still existed.

Before the elections of 30 May 1948 the Government had presented to Parliament a Bill designed to secure for the State complete control of the schools. This Bill was passed on 21 April 1948, a bare two months after the Communist *coup d'état*.[23]

---

[21] His task was to examine publications, to withdraw from circulation or prevent the printing of anything not in harmony with the canons of the People's Democracy.

[22] N. 30965-48 T. O., according to the *Bulletin of the Catholic Clergy* (VKD), n. 3, of 10 June 1949. In regard to this *Bulletin* cf. note 43 *infra*.

[23] Cf. Law n. 95 in the *Collection of Laws and Regulations of the Czechoslovak Republic*.

Article 1 stated: " The school is exclusively a State institution." In consequence the goods belonging to the free schools became the property of the State.

Article 4 paragraph 2 stated however: " The Government has the power to make exceptions." Before the law came into force an agreement was reached between representatives of the Executive Committee and of the episcopate, whereby exemption would be granted to schools depending on ecclesiastical authority. The Ministry for Instruction immediately authorised the schools in question to enrol students for the academic year. But in spite of all assurances given [24] the Communist Minister for Instruction proceeded *per modum facti* to suppress nearly all the Catholic schools.

On 11 June the forthcoming nationalisation of primary and secondary schools was announced. This announcement was made at the exact time fixed for the meeting of a commission of bishops and representatives of the Government to discuss relations between Church and State.

On 30 September 1948 the law of 21 April came into force, *placing under State administration all primary and secondary schools.*

From November 1948 all kindergartens, though not expressly mentioned in the law, were likewise nationalised. In many cases the nuns in charge were expelled.

Even the junior seminaries did not escape the reform. Like all the other schools they too were obliged to submit their programmes of study for the prior approval of the Ministry for Public Instruction. Thus was it hoped to ensure that the studies of the pupils would be impregnated with Dialectic Materialism and Marxist Socialism.[25]

---

[24] This promise was made by the Minister for Justice, Cepicka, on behalf of the Government in order that the bishops might permit the singing of the *Te Deum* on the occasion of the election of President Gottwald.

[25] In the course of a conference to the Czech Youth League the Minister, Nejedly, outlined the principles which would henceforth inspire educators in the schools: " Education must be based on Marxism-Leninism so as to put an end to the exposition of other contradictory theories which serve only to create confusion in the minds of the young." At the meeting of the Central Committee of the Communist Party on 25 November 1948 Slansky proclaimed: "The world outlook of the working class, Marxism-Leninism, ought to occupy an important place in the programmes of instruction in all our schools. All the sciences should be explained in the light of our world outlook . . . " The school programmes are still more explicit as to the new line to be followed

At first for tactical reasons the Communist Government allowed religious instruction in the State schools. It was however made optional and from being first on the list of subjects it passed to the last place. Furthermore this concession was merely a manoeuvre to cloak the injustices committed against Catholic educational institutions. Soon afterwards a propaganda campaign was started to dissuade parents from allowing their children to attend the religious classes. This campaign was accompanied by all forms of obstruction.

The new law was enforced with extreme severity by the authorities. Teachers were watched by police agents, and pupils were often encouraged to inform on their masters.

On 3 June 1949 the text of a decree of the Ministry for Public Instruction in their regard was communicated to all the faculties and schools of Theology. In the decree it was noted that " the instruction given by them . . . was not in conformity with the People's Democratic Order." They were ordered to provide immediately a course in " social science, obligatory for all students." Success in the examination on the matter of this course would be " an indispensable condition for promotion to a higher class." The decree named the professor to be put in charge of the course and threatened with punishment all who did not follow out its instructions scrupulously and within the desired time.[26]

Thus within a year of the start of the open attack on the Church, Catholic schools had ceased to exist throughout the whole of Czechoslovakia; and the young everywhere were being instructed in Materialism, even those in the seminaries preparing for the priesthood.

* * *

in education: " The pupils should learn to seek the determining causes of all phenomena in economic sources and in the relations of class with class." In history manuals the Church, whenever treated of, is presented as a human institution which had its " feudal " form and was always the ally of the oppressors of the workers. Biological studies aim at showing that matter is the source of everything in nature, life included. Man is part of nature, is subject to its laws, but he knows these laws and in practice exploits them . . . From February 1948 the Communist Minister for Public Instruction ordered a portrait of Stalin to be placed in all the classrooms.

[26] See decree n. 77698/49/III—1 reproduced in the famous *Bulletin of the Catholic Clergy* (VKD), n. 3, of 10 June 1949. (Cf. *infra* note 43).

The suppression of Catholic organisations was another of the measures taken against the Church.

In Czechoslovakia there were two Catholic Action organisations—one for Slovakia, the other for Bohemia and Moravia. The Slovak organisation had at Bratislava a Central Bureau which served all its branches. A similar Bureau existed for the Czech Catholic Action organisation. Almost simultaneously the Prague Communist Government suppressed all the directing bodies of the various Catholic Associations. The Central Catholic Secretariate of Bratislava, through which the Slovak episcopate directed Catholic Action, was closed by a decree of the Ministry for the Interior dated 22 November 1948.[27] At the same time the director of the Secretariate was arrested and Slovak Catholic Action was considered dissolved.

About a month later the organisation " Czech Catholic Youth " was suppressed. Some days after this all other branches of Catholic Action in Bohemia and Moravia met the same fate.

The decrees of dissolution of these Catholic associations affirmed that these measures were being taken " in the public interest which demands the unification of all forces in conformity with the People's Democratic Order."

The ecclesiastical authorities and the directors of the Catholic organisations protested. The Communists responded by inviting them to join the Party organisations, and encouraged them to

---

[27] See decree of *The Commissariat for the Interior of Bratislava* n. 1008 I-V/3/1947. The reasons given for the closing are reproduced because they form a classic example of Communist " legality ":

" A study of the statutes of the Central Catholic Secretariate (CCS), submitted to the Commissariat for the Interior for approval, does not make clear the juridical position of this institution.

" According to the statutes this institution is based on the voluntary aggregation of its members and hence has not the character of an association. Articles 4 and 5 of these statutes lay down that the CCS is an executive organ of the Slovak bishops, its functions being: to serve as liaison between ecclesiastical institutions and offices; to co-ordinate and organise in agreement with the bishops the religious and moral instruction of the Slovak faithful through religious cultural conferences, courses, retreats, university summer-courses, libraries, cultural centres, the publication of books, reviews and other works, always with the exception of those dealing with politics; to keep in contact with Catholic organisations throughout the world, etc. From the foregoing it is difficult to see on what juridical basis this institution is founded. The end aimed at can be attained equally well by the already legally existing religious institutions, by the already

do so by threats and by arresting those who protested too strongly.

To overcome the unwillingness of the Catholics to comply with the foregoing the Government had recourse to the use of authority. In December 1948 a decree of the Commissariat for the Interior of Bratislava [28] ordered the fusion of the Slovak Catholic Women's Union, numbering about 100,000, and the Slovak Women's (Communist) League. This was done despite vigorous protests by the President of the Union; she denounced the order as contrary to Article 24 of the Constitution. The same month authority was likewise used to bring about the fusion of " The Catholic Youth of Bohemia " and the Czech Communist Youth League.

The motive for these measures against Catholic Action can be seen clearly in a speech delivered by the Minister for External Affairs, *Siroki*, in which he stated:

> " The unification of youth, the setting up of one single organisation, is the logical result of the political development which has taken place in Czechoslovakia. It is universally known that the People's Democracies guarantee freedom of worship to the various denominations; but we cannot allow the existence of youth organisations formed on a religious basis. These would destroy the unity of our youth and impede its efforts towards the building of a better future." [29]

The Communist authorities did not limit themselves to the suppression of Catholic Action associations; all other groups depending on the Church or drawing their inspiration from religion were also attacked. *Charitas*, an organisation which co-ordinated the charitable work of Catholics, was not spared. A large number of kindergartens and works of charity depended

---

existing juridically founded associations, and eventually by other legal cultural or social institutions.

" For these reasons the setting up of the CCS is contrary to the present juridical situation; hence in the public interest its statutes cannot be approved nor can its activity be permitted."

[28] See decree n. 35002/I-III/2 of 22 December 1948 in the *Collection of Laws and Regulations of the Czechoslovak Republic*.

[29] Cf. Nemec, *op. cit.* p. 307.

on this organisation. All these were confiscated by the Government, one after the other. At the same time an attempt was made to turn *Charitas* itself into an instrument of Communist propaganda. To this end a priest entirely devoted to the Government was placed at its head and thus this well-deserving organisation was transformed into a Government and Communist tool. By a law of 19 July 1948 the hospitals too were nationalised.[30]

Finally among the measures introduced during 1948 against the Church *the nationalisation of all ecclesiastical real estate* must be mentioned. This left the Church impoverished, and placed the clergy at the mercy of the State in economic matters.[31] During the year 1948 also the press continued to attack with extreme violence the Church and the Holy See.[32]

* * *

The above series of outrages was denounced by the Czechoslovak episcopate in a *Memorandum* addressed to the Government and dated 16 August 1948. The denunciation was repeated on 13 October in a Pastoral Letter,[33] publication of which was forbidden by the Government. Among other things the *Memorandum* stated:

" Despite promises of religious liberty and repeated affirmations of good will a campaign was conducted which was anti-religious and basely anti-clerical. This campaign proceeded in accordance with a well-established programme exactly similar to that followed in other countries where the Catholic religion and the Catholic Church have been attacked."

On 5 December 1948 the Minister *Nejedly* made the following statement in a speech delivered over the radio:

---

[30] Cf. *Lidová Demokracie* (People's Democracy) of 20 July 1948.

[31] See Law n. 10835/48-A-II-1162 in the *Collection of Laws and Regulations of the Czechoslovak Republic*, as well as Nemec, *op. cit.* pp. 256-257 for interesting statistics.

[32] See for example the attacks which appeared in *Obrana Ludu* (Defence of the People) of 27, 28, 30 November and 2 December 1948 (*The Vatican, Apostle of Imperialism*); in *Rudé Pravo* (Red Right) of 3 December; in *Lidová Demokracie* of 9 December; in *Narodni Obsvobozeni* (National Liberation) of 3 December.

[33] See *Agency APA*, 16 October 1948.

" Our Catholic people will not have to undergo any test of fidelity to the Church in matters of religion. Nobody, the State, its institutions, or the Government, envisages anything whatsoever of this kind. Neither do the people, who have other cares and who consider questions of belief as of little importance . . . The people have at last realised where the so-called ' service ' of God and of the different saints has led them. This service was being used to turn them into slaves under the domination of the rich and of their henchmen . . . The policy of the Government, in full keeping with the sentiment of our people, is this: Believe what you wish, that is your own business, a matter of opinion and of taste. Even attend whatever Church you like. But let these things remain outside the public life of the citizens and of the State." [34]

The end which the Communist Government hoped to attain by these measures [35] was clear: to eliminate everything which could in any way hinder the " realisation of Socialism " and the triumph of Communism. In November 1948 this aim was again stressed at the ninth Congress of the Czechoslovak Communist Party. At this Congress the Communist leaders set about the task of building in Czechoslovakia a " new world " based on the ideology of Dialectic Materialism and on the social principles enunciated by Marx, Lenin and Stalin.

From this time onwards the " tactical attacks " against the Catholic Church ceased, and a campaign for its " total enslavement " to the State started.

3. THE GOVERNMENT EFFORT TO CREATE A SCHISMATIC MOVEMENT

The Catholic Church in Czechoslovakia met its " Munich " in 1949. The name Munich has a sinister sound in Czech ears. It was in that city in 1938 that the three Great Powers decided the fate of the Fatherland without even consulting those most

---

[34] Cf. *Lidová Demokracie*, 7 December 1948.

[35] To these may be added the law on marriage. From 1 January 1950 civil marriage was made of obligation and might not be preceded by any religious ceremony whatsoever —not even by the publication of the banns. Divorce was legislated for *ex novo*. Cf. *The Tablet* of 26 November 1949.

concerned. This is exactly what happened to the Catholic Church in 1949 when it suffered its most serious reverses at the hands of the Communist Government.

In January and February negotiations for an agreement between Church and State came to an end. The episcopate stood firm in its demand for the recognition of the neutrality, the liberty and the autonomy of the Catholic Church, while at all times it admitted and preached the duty of loyalty to the State. The Government on the other hand aimed at turning the Church into a docile instrument to be used for the furtherance of Government policy.[36]

Realising that the negotiations had failed the Communist rulers decided to try with all the means at their disposal to make the most of the " clerical reaction."

At the beginning of 1949 the Ministry for the Interior sent certain written instructions to the provincial directors of National Security, and through them to the district directors, on the procedure to be adopted in dealing with the Roman Catholic Church. In particular it was directed that

1. Orders be given to the local agrarian committees to proceed immediately to the execution of their decisions to confiscate the lands of parochial benefices.[37]

2. All pilgrimages and all religious functions held outside the Church be prohibited; inside the Church only those ceremonies be permitted which could be controlled publicly.

3. The printing of ecclesiastical publications be in principle forbidden.

4. All remaining religious associations be dissolved.

---

[36] No statement was issued concerning the negotiations. On 17 March 1949 in an interview granted to the *International News Service* Archbishop Beran, having recalled that at that date approximately 120 priests were in prison, stated that the negotiations had failed for three reasons: (1) the Government had demanded that the Church make a declaration of loyalty to the régime; (2) he had been asked to revoke the suspensions of the Rev. Plojhar and two other Slovak priests—all three in Government posts contrary to the direct orders of the episcopate; (3) the Government envisaged a further confiscation of ecclesiastical property. Besides the Government refused to allow the Holy See take part in the negotiations. Cf. *La Documentation Catholique*, 1949, col. 999, also *The Tablet* 2 April 1949.

[37] According to the terms of law n. 10833/48-A-II-1162 which deprived the Church of all remaining real estate.

5. A watch be kept to discover whether the faithful supplied the priests with food and clothing coupons, or provided the parochial houses with food. The houses of suspected persons be thoroughly searched.

6. Priests willing to collaborate with the Communists be helped, but be not trusted blindly.

Subsequently the district directors of National Security were ordered to communicate these instructions orally only, to the local bodies and to the local " men of confidence." [38]

These directives of the Ministry for the Interior marked a new departure in the attack on the Church, calling, as they did, on police aid.

Through the implementation of these directives the Government hoped:

1. To separate the bishops and the priests by the suppression of the *Acta Curiae*; to weaken the religious spirit of the priests by the prohibition of all meetings—retreats, clerical congresses, etc. included.

2. To separate the priests from the laity who might help them.

3. To limit religious activity to the inside of church buildings and to control it even there.

4. To liquidate whatever remained of Church property and thus to deprive the clergy of all economic independence.

As has been already seen in part the first months of 1949 also witnessed:

1. Repeated attacks on the Holy Father and on the Catholic Church.

2. Prohibition of the printing of religious books, even of the prayers for the Holy Year.

3. The giving of help to a section of the press which was Catholic only in name so as to make of it an instrument of Government propaganda.

4. The placing of Commissars in Catholic publishing houses, the censoring of books, the destroying of books already printed.

---

[38] There were three " men of confidence " in each village; none of them knew who the others were.

5. The Marxist indoctrination of youth in direct opposition to the assurances given on 11 June 1948. [39]

6. The control of parochial libraries in accordance with the law concerning libraries. [40]

7. The registration of religious associations and confraternities (in certain places the names of the members were demanded).

8. Administrative measures against religious, including the searching of their houses.

9. Control of all sermons and all religious functions.

On 29 April 1949 the episcopate protested against these different measures in a *Memorandum* addressed to President *Gottwald*. The *Memorandum* stated:

" To-day we have a further and undeniable proof that the Government has launched an all-out campaign against the Church, using all the means at its disposal, in the fact that orders and precise instructions to that end have been transmitted to the police authorities in the provinces and districts.

"We know that these orders are only the first phase of the final and decisive blow." [41]

In May 1949 seeing the failure of all efforts to conciliate the bishops the Communists decided to separate the episcopate from the clergy and faithful. They invited these to detach themselves from the hierarchy, who alone were responsible for the failure of the attempts to reach an agreement between Church and State. This, stated the Communist propaganda, was the only way to settle the differences which imperilled the religious life of the country.

To put this plan into execution, which was in fact *to form a separate Schismatic Church*, the Communist Government proceeded as follows:

---

[39] The Czechoslovak Youth League (CSM) spared no effort to win the youth to its side. The Government for its part suppressed even the eucharistic meetings of Catholic youth and forbade all meetings outside church buildings.

[40] Cf. *Decree of the Ministry for Public Instruction*, n. P. 20076/49-9/6 of 19 January 1949.

[41] Cf. *La Documentation Catholique* of 31 July 1949, col. 1006-1009; cf. *The Tablet* of 25 June 1949.

(1) It organised a violent campaign of vilification against the episcopate and against the Holy See.[42]

(2) " The Bulletin of the Catholic Clergy " (VKD) was published from 11 May 1949 under the direction of the Ministry for Public Instruction.[43]

(3) Further restrictions were imposed on the liberty and the authority of the bishops by three new decrees:

(a) On 20 June 1949 a decree of the Ministry for Public Instruction made it obligatory " on all ordinaries *to submit henceforth directly to the Ministry for examination all documents (pastoral letters, circulars, instructions,* etc. . . .) destined for the

---

[42] Cf. the articles published in *Lidová Noviny* (The People's Journal), 13 March 1949: *The Vatican, Ally of Reaction* by Jar Putik; 18 March: *Religion has nothing to do with it* by St. Budin; 25 March: *The Philosophy of the Vatican* by J. Putik; 31 March: *The Vatican and the Germans*; 10 April: *In what Waters fish the Fishers of the Vatican*; in *Nove Slovo* of 26 March: *Vatican Policy as seen from the texts*; in *Lidova Demokracie* of 30 June; in *Rudé Pravo* of 29 June: *The evil Shepherds*; in *Prace* of 28 June; in *Svobodne Slovo* (The Free World) of 25 June. Cf. also Radio-Prague broadcasts of 15, 20, 23, 30 March. The defamation reached its height with the book *Conspiracy against the Republic* published 6 December 1949. This book was published and 100,000 copies of it printed under the direction of the Ministry for Information, inspired by the Minister, Cepicka. It presented the Catholic clergy as the greatest enemy of the State and the Vatican was held up to the contempt of the citizens for having tried to establish a " reactionary dictatorship " with the aid of " western imperialists." In Slovakia the Commissariat for Information undertook the diffusion of a work by one N. M. Segel, entitled *The Vatican in the service of American Reaction* (Bratislava, Tatran, 1949).

[43] In its letter of 17 May to the Minister, Nejedly, the Czechoslovak episcopate protested strongly against the publication of the *Bulletin* edited, as is known, under the directions of the Ministry for Public Instruction and written by apostate or suspended priests, or by members of other religious denominations. The bishops objected especially to the abuse of the title. Archbishop Beran warned the faithful on 28 May against the false news spread by the Government in the *Bulletin* concerning the relations between the Church and the State. The *Bulletin* had as aim to give to the clergy " objective information " regarding the situation, and to publish Government decrees concerning ecclesiastical matters. With the idea of replacing the Catholic press the following publications were launched: *Kristanska Zena* (Christian Woman), *Lidova Demokracie* and *Lidova Obroda* (Renaissance of the People). All these publications paraded as Catholic, the better to cloak the struggle of the State against the Church. They were sold near the churches and were presented to the people as " the Catholic press." The *Bulletin*, condemned at different times by the bishops, later became the organ of the schismatic *Catholic Action* movement in Bohemia and Moravia. In Slovakia a new weekly appeared on 17 June 1949 with the title of the old Slovak Catholic publication, *Katolicke Noviny*. 800,000 copies of the first number were printed. (This publication was eventually condemned by the Vatican in 1955). In fact the two papers were distributed *free* to all priests by the Government. The *Pastyr Duchovni* (The Spiritual Pastor) made its appearance later on in the pseudo-Catholic cause with the support of the Government. Cf. *Archives of the SS. Cyril and Methodius League* (CML), Fitzjohn Avenue, London and *The Tablet* of 21 May 1949; cf. also *L'Osservatore Romano* of 24 July 1955.

priests or for the public. No document of this kind may be either published or distributed without the previous approval of the Ministry." [44]

(b) A second decree, emanating from the same Ministry, informed the bureaux of parishes and deaneries that *notification of all clerical meetings, whether held in private or in public,* should be given at least three days in advance to the National Committee of the district. This latter was empowered to have a delegate present at each meeting. [45]

(c) The third decree declared to be null and void all ecclesiastical penalties inflicted on priests " for political reasons." [46]

(4) A *Catholic Action Committee* was founded, which in the designs of the Communists would aid in promoting and provoking divisions and schisms within the Church itself.

Czechoslovakia was in advance of all the other " Progressive Democracies " in the use of this last method.

In February 1949 the mode of procedure to be adopted by Communist Governments towards the Catholic Church was discussed by the Kominform at its Congress in Karlovy Vary (Carlsbad). It was then decided to form a dissident Movement to meet the particular case of Czechoslovakia. [47] The Movement was to be called *Catholic Action,* and its organisation was to be placed in the hands of a group of apostate or deluded priests who had shown themselves willing to collaborate with the Communist Government.

Already even before the founding of the *pseudo-Catholic Action* Communist propaganda had spoken of setting up a special Committee which would take the initiative in the bringing about of normal relations between Church and State in Czechoslovakia.

The bishops were thus fore-warned and could condemn as it were in anticipation the schismatic movement of the *pseudo-Catholic Action.* [48]

---

[44] Cf. *Bulletin of the Catholic Clergy* (VKD) n. 4 of 25 June 1949.
[45] Cf. *ibid.* [46] Cf. *ibid.*
[47] Cf. *L'Osservatore Romano* of 2 July 1949, and *The Clergy Review* of 5 June 1951.
[48] See Archbishop Beran's Letter to the clergy of 31 May 1949 in *La Documentation Catholique* of 31 July 1949, col. 1013.

Despite the warnings of the Archbishop of Prague, on 10 June 1949 a number of priests and lay people came together on the initiative of the Government in the Smetana Hall, Prague, for the purpose of forming the " Catholic Action Committee." The greater part of those present was unaware of the real purpose of the meeting; many had consented to attend only because they believed that means apt to bring about peace between Church and State were to be discussed.

A *Proclamation* was drawn up in which the amelioration of relations between Church and State was set forth as the end aimed at by the Movement. The signatories of the document added:

> " We hope that our bishops will regard our action with under-standing. However we exhort those who might dare to penalise in any way our priests or the Catholic people because of their attitude to the State to note well that we have with us the over-whelming majority of the faithful . . . We cannot accept any order of a political nature from outside the country." [49]

In the course of the meeting a *Programme* was outlined for the Movement, which made it for all practical purposes the representative of the Catholic Church in all dealings with the Government. Before all else the controlling Committee aimed at reaching an agreement at any cost which would bring back to " normal " the relations between Church and State. When the approval of those present was sought for this *pseudo-Catholic Action* programme about sixty priests gave their sig-natures; many of them did this thinking they were merely attesting their presence at the meeting. [50]

---

[49] The text of the *Proclamation* can be found in all the newspapers of 11 June 1949. The *Lidova Demokracie* of the same date commented as follows: " The Catholics pronounce themselves in favour of an agreement between the Church and the State."

[50] It is to be noted that one of the Communists' most intimate collaborators, the sus-pended priest, Joseph Plojhar, did not sign the *Proclamation*. Evidently the Communists considered that his support might compromise the document in the eyes of the faithful. The names of priests to whom the question was never put or who refused energetically their support later appeared on the list of signatories. The names of priests long dead, or who never existed, also appeared. Many signatures were extorted by trickery, by threats, or by insistence carried to extremes.

Henceforth the *Catholic Action Movement* was presented to the public by the Government as the only true representative of the Catholic Church.[51]

The new Committee of Catholic Action was officially formed on 17 June 1949. *M. Pujma*, producer at the National Theatre, was elected President, and *Vojtech Torok*, an active member of the Communist Party, Secretary. The new Committee immediately announced that 1,500 priests had already joined the Movement, and added: " The bishops have not responded to the appeal addressed to them. In consequence a special delegation will be sent to inform them of the programme of the new Movement, and of the repercussions throughout the country to this action. [52]

Aware of the danger the bishops had however already acted. Two days earlier, 15 June 1949, the episcopate warned the clergy and the people of the danger of schism in a Letter to be read in all the churches on Sunday 19 June. This Letter contained the following:

> " A pseudo-Catholic Action is in process of formation against the will of the bishops. It aims at confusing the faithful, and rendering it impossible for the bishops to defend the liberty and the rights of the Church.
>
> " From these facts it clearly follows that there is not question here of an agreement between Church and State, but rather of the subordination of the Roman Catholic Church to an anti-Christian ideology which aims at replacing religion by Marxism and claims for the State the right to intervene in matters of conscience, faith and morals—a claim no Christian may admit." [53]

On the same Wednesday, 15 June, on which this letter was drawn up, a group of police agents visited the episcopal palace

---

[51] The rôle of the *Bulletin of the Catholic Clergy* (VKD) was to spread the schismatic movement and to repeat the theses put forward in the *Proclamation* issued on the occasion of the founding of the *pseudo-Catholic Action*, namely: " Under Communist rule the rights of the Church and religious liberty will be respected "; " The movement is in submission to the Pope in matters of Faith and Morals "; and " The bishops alone are responsible for the failure to reach an agreement between Church and State."

[52] Cf. *La Documentation Catholique*, 31 July 1949, col. 1001.

[53] Cf. *La Documentation Catholique*, 31 July 1949, col. 1014.

during the absence of Archbishop *Beran*. Invoking gratuitously an Austrian law of 1874, they demanded access to all Curia documents, claiming that these should have been countersigned by a representative of the Government. On his return the Archbishop found a Government Commissar already installed in the archiepiscopal secretariate, charged with *controlling and countersigning all documents of the Curia, and with keeping a strict watch over the whole administration of the archdiocese.*

Meanwhile the police had searched the Curia and arrested two priest members of the Curia staff. They took away official notepaper and the archiepiscopal seal. These they later used to forge an order purporting to come from the Curia and forbidding the reading on 19 June of the bishops' Letter. This forged order was shown by the police to the parish priests. The Government Commissar did his utmost to isolate the Archbishop, preventing his mail from reaching him and forbidding visitors.

On Friday, 17 June, Archbishop *Beran* protested to the Minister for Public Instruction against the arbitrary acts of which he was the victim.

On Saturday, 18 June, he addressed a protest directly to the Minister for the Interior, claiming the right in his capacity as archbishop to demand of his subordinates a clear declaration of loyalty made under oath.[54]

On the same day the Archbishop decided to put the faithful on their guard against the schismatic manoeuvres of the Government. In the church of the Premonstratensian Monastery at Strahov he preached a courageous sermon to many thousands of people.[55] The Abbot of the Monastery, Dom *Jarolimek*, was immediately arrested by the police.

The Communist organisations notified their members to attend on the following day, 19 June, at Prague Cathedral for the purpose of preventing the faithful from attending, and also to interrupt the sermon to be preached during Mass by the Archbishop. At the appointed time the Communist supporters filled the cathedral and constantly interrupted the Archbishop's

---

[54] Text in *La Civiltà Cattolica* 1949, III, pp. 473, 474.
[55] Cf. *La Documentation Catholique*, 31 July 1949, col. 1002.

sermon by shouts and whistles.[56]   That evening Archbishop *Beran* was confined to his palace and forced to remain there.[57]

On Sunday and on the days preceding the parish priests were visited by police agents.   Some were threatened with arrest if they read the bishops' Letter, others were shown the forged order from the Chancellery at Prague.

For its part the Communist Government declared in the press and over the radio through some of its better informed members that " it could not tolerate that the hierarchy should terrorise patriotic Catholic priests and deprive them of freedom of opinion in political matters."   It blamed Archbishop *Beran* primarily for this state of affairs.[58]

Eventually on the same 19 June the bishops drew up another Letter which succeeded in reaching the priests despite a most careful watch on the part of the police.   This Letter was to be read in all churches on Sunday, 26 June.   In it the Communist methods were denounced in an overwhelming manner.[59]   The following were the chief things denounced:

1. The systematic campaign conducted over the radio and in public speeches against the Catholic Church;

2. The ignoring of the right of parents to choose the kind of education to be given to their children;

3. The suppression of the religious press with a few unimportant exceptions;

4. The forbidding of all meetings whatsoever outside church buildings;

5. The confiscation of what remained of Church property.

---

[56] The Minister for Public Instruction blamed seminarists, theological students, and the religious orders for these disturbances; he offered to submit them to an inquiry and, if needs be, to form a Commission. (Circular n. 95124/49—III/1, of 9 July 1949, kept in the *CML Archives*).

[57] The Minister for the Interior later notified Archbishop Beran that he had provided him with a police-escort " to protect him."   The Bishop of Hradec Kralové, also placed under surveillance, protested in vain.   Cf. *L'Osservatore Romano* of 10 July 1949, *A protest by Mgr. Picha*.

[58] The Prime Minister, Zapotocky, delivered a violent speech over the radio.   Cf. *La Documentation Catholique*, 1949, col. 1008.   On 25 June 1949 the Minister, Cepicka, in his turn attacked vehemently.

[59] Full text in *La Civiltà Cattolica*, 1949, III, pp. 206-211;   an English translation appeared in *The Tablet* of 2 July 1949.

The Letter also recalled that

1. Religious schools were almost non-existent, and the treatment meted out to those still functioning gave very little hope for the future.

2. Teachers of religion were examined as to their philosophical views, and received instructions on the manner of teaching religion in accord with the spirit of Materialism.

3. In seminaries and faculties of Theology teachers have been installed to teach the so-called " Social Sciences," their aim really being to impregnate gradually the minds of future priests with materialist philosophy.

4. An effort is constantly being made to deprive the Church of buildings used for religious purposes. The taking over of religious houses and of houses destined for the education of students for the priesthood is spoken of. In Slovakia in particular some religious houses have been forcibly evacuated and the priests taken away.

5. A conference of the bishops at Dolni Smocovec had to be adjourned because of the discovery in the conference room of a concealed recording apparatus. [60]

6. The last meeting of the bishops at Prague was disturbed by the police.

In conclusion the Letter affirmed that there was question here of " a systematic persecution of the Catholic Church in Czechoslovakia, well prepared and methodically executed."

On 20 June the Holy See condemned the *pseudo-Catholic Action*. [61]

At the same time police guarded the doors of each bishop's house so as to control all the bishop's movements. *A Government Commissar was placed in every Chancellery : he claimed the right to interfere in an unheard of manner in ecclesiastical matters.* [62]

---

[60] This episode is described in *La Documentation Catholique*, 31 July 1949, col. 1006.

[61] Cf. *L'Osservatore Romano* of 20 June 1949, and *Acta Apostolicae Sedis (AAS)*, 2 July 1949, p. 33. The decree of the Holy Office was read in nearly all the parish churches in Czechoslovakia. Of the 5,779 secular priests it is thought that about 170 continued even after the condemnation to take part in the new organisation. On 17 July 1949 the Catholic priests of Czechoslovakia rejected in a public declaration " the pseudo-Catholic Action as anti-Catholic and schismatic."

[62] Examples of the " ecclesiastical circulars " issued by these Government Commissars may be read in Nemec, *op. cit.* pp. 316-324.

On 5 August Archbishop *Beran*, still under house-arrest, protested to the Attorney General against the injustices of which he was the victim, and requested that the legality of the measures taken be examined.[63]

In particular the Archbishop wrote:

" I wish to ask the Attorney General if the Government Commissar has the right

1. to act on behalf of the archbishop without having received from him any mandate to do so;

2. to use the seals and the official note-paper of the archbishopric without any delegation from the archbishop;

3. to take control of the funds of the archiepiscopal administration, and to let it be known, without informing the person in charge, that he has full powers to deal with current accounts;

4. to take control likewise of the central funds of the diocese of Prague, which in law do not belong to the archiepiscopal administration, and thereby to render impossible the payment from these funds of the wages due to employees in the archiepiscopal palace;

5. to prevent the normal functioning of the archiepiscopal administration, the archbishop not being allowed even to receive official correspondence.

. . .

These are some questions which I respectfully ask the Attorney General to answer."

During this time the Government continued to encourage in every way the *pseudo-Catholic Action*,[64] openly persecuting the priests who refused to support it. During July and August 1949 *priests were arrested in dozens*; those were selected who by virtue

---

[63] *L'Osservatore Romano* of 19 August 1949 gave the Archbishop's letter as received through a press agency. The text may also be found in *La Documentation Catholique*, 6 November 1949, col. 1465, 1466.

[64] The " League of Atheists and Heterodox " encouraged the Czechoslovak women to leave the Catholic Church. The Secretary General of the Party, Slansky, in a circular of 12 July, asked the secretaries of Party cells to visit priests who had signed the Catholic Action Proclamation, so as to prevent all retractions. Cf. *CML Archives* and *La Documentation Catholique*, 6 November 1949, col. 1468; also *The Tablet*, 6 August 1949, where a resolution of the Executive Council of the Party of the Czechoslovak People may be read.

of their authority or by their personal qualities were in a position
to exercise influence over the other priests and over the people.

But the very great majority of the clergy and of the faithful
showed themselves hostile to the Government's efforts to set
up a Church separated from Rome. To cloak the failure and
the unpopularity of the schismatic movement the Communists
began to organise pilgrimages to the better-known of the
country's holy places. The Catholics refused to take part in
these manifestations, in the course of which " meetings " were
held and the Pope and the bishops insulted. In spite of this
the pilgrimages took place, the " pilgrims " being drawn from
members of the Party, specially got together for the occasion.

Despite the means used to impose the schismatic movement
on the people, the hoped-for success was not achieved.

With the exception of a small group of deluded priests and
some Catholic Communists, nobody wished to hear mention of
the new *Catholic Action*. Eventually the leaders of the Government concluded that violence was the only method which would
achieve the destruction of the Catholic Church. This explains
why in the last phase of the struggle the Prague Government
made no pretence of good will towards the representatives of
the Church, and showed very little further interest in the
schismatic movement.

Trial, prison, concentration camp—these would henceforth
be the lot of those who dared proclaim their Catholic Faith or
resist Communist rule.

4. THE ATTEMPT TO BRING THE EPISCOPATE AND THE CLERGY UNDER COMMUNIST CONTROL

On 9 May 1948, a few months after the *coup d'état*, the
Communist Government introduced a new Constitution based
on Marxist principles.[65]

Czechoslovakia was declared " a People's Republic founded
on work." The new Constitution guaranteed liberty of conscience
(Art. 15) and laid down that " all religious denominations as

---

[65] Cf. *La Constitution de la République tchécoslovaque* (Loi constitutionelle du 9 mai
1948) in *Bulletin de Droit tchécoslovaque*, 1948, pp. 109 and following. Cf. also *La Documentation Catholique*, 1949, col. 1451-1454.

well as non-adherence to any particular denomination are equal before the law " (Art. 16, 2).

Further the Constitution adopted for the People's Republic of Czechoslovakia an economic system based on the nationalisation of the means of production and on the dictatorship of the proletariat with one Chamber of 300 deputies.

The Constitution merely referred to the general principles governing the relations between the different denominations and the State. Law 23 of 6 September 1948, " for the defence of the People's Democratic Republic," gave further information on this subject. Article 28 specified: " Whosoever abuses his office, religious or other, by influencing politics in a way detrimental to the People's Democratic Order, will incur a penalty of from one to twelve months' imprisonment." This article made it possible for the Government to lend a semblance of legality to injustices of all kinds. [66]

But it is especially by the laws of October 1949 that the Communist Government regulated the relations between the State and religious denominations. Among the latter the Catholic Church as " the religion of the majority of the people " held the leading place.

On 14 October 1949 Parliament passed two laws which became operative on 1 November of the same year. [67]

The first (decree n. 217/49) set up a *State Bureau for Ecclesiastical Affairs*; the second regulated the question of salaries in regard to the religious denominations in general (decree n. 218/49) and the Catholic Church in particular (decree n. 219/49). [68]

The State Bureau for Ecclesiastical Affairs

In taking this step the Czechoslovak Communist Government was to a certain extent, adopting the legislative system of the Soviet Union. In Russia a kind of Commissariat had been dealing

---

[66] In fact many priests were arrested on the strength of this article, on the most varied pretexts, often simply for having shown fugitives the way to the frontier.

[67] Cf. *Lidova Demokracie* and *Rudé Pravo* of 15 October 1949, which gave prominence to the two laws. Cf. also *La Documentation Catholique*, 1949, col. 1451-1454.

[68] These laws as well as the others cited in this section are included in the *Digest-Index of Eastern European Laws*.

with religious questions for a number of years. Article 1 of the new law stated: the head or director of the new Bureau will be appointed by the President of the Republic. The Bureau had as duty: " to see that ecclesiastical and religious life develop in harmony with the Constitution and the People's democratic régime and thereby to ensure that each citizen enjoy the liberty of conscience guaranteed by the Constitution on the basis of religious toleration and the juridical equality of all denominations " (Art. 2). The Bureau also reserved to itself the right of dealing with all religious questions whatever their nature (Art. 3).

Thus as is clear from the tenor of the law the State sought to deprive the Church of the right " to watch over the religious life " of the faithful. To infuse into the " organism of the Church " the spirit of " the People's Democracy " was the aim set itself by the Government. All Church activity was brought through the new Bureau under the control of the State.[69]

This measure was also applied to Slovakia, with however this difference: the head of the Bureau there was appointed by the Government and his powers were limited to ecclesiastical problems of that region.

The Law concerning the Budgets and the Salaries of Ministers of Religion

So as to get more deeply into ecclesiastical affairs the Czecho-slovak Communist Government published on 14 October 1949 decree n. 218/49. This dealt with " the defraying of expenses arising in connection with the personnel and the material up-keep of the Church and of religious associations recognised by the State." [70]

The law laid down as a general principle: " Activities of a sacred character proper to the Churches and to religious societies may be performed only by persons who have been so authorised by the State and who have taken an oath, the text of which will be determined by special Government decree.

---

[69] The Bureau was suppressed in 1956 and its functions devolved on the Ministry for Culture. This was merely a transfer of powers because legal enactments which were inacceptable to the Catholic Church remained unchanged.

[70] Cf. *La Documentation Catholique*, 18 December 1949, col. 1650-1651.

The filling of all positions, whether by election or by nomination, is subject to the prior approval of the State " (Art. 7).

To regulate the application of this law to the Catholic Church decree 219/49 was published on 18 October 1949. In this it was set down that " priests must be loyal in the way demanded by the State, giving no cause for criticism, and must fulfil the conditions generally required for entry into the service of the State " (Art. 18, 1). If a priest is judged by the State to be unfit to enter *its* service " the position he holds should be considered vacant " (Art. 18, 2). In spite of these provisions the decree did not hesitate to affirm that " priests are employees of the Church " (Art. 1).

These few citations are sufficient to show that the Church was regarded by the Communist State as an institution depending on the civil power.[71]

The State, having arrogated to itself the right to name the " ecclesiastical employees," proceeded to appoint to various positions of responsibility a number of perjured priests who were prepared to collaborate with the persecutors of the Church.[72]

To compel in a certain sense the clergy to accept the new measures the Government proceeded, as has been already stated, *to confiscate whatever was left of ecclesiastical property.* The law further laid down that all " charities, private or public," were transferred to the State (Art. 11 of decree 218/49) and demanded that all budgets be submitted for approval within a certain time (Art. 9).

---

[71] *Rudé Pravo*, the official organ of the Party, commented as follows on these laws: " The new laws signify a complete change in the economic means of the Church and in the position of the lower clergy. It is not surprising that such a reform should be condemned by those who relied on the oppression which they exercised on their priests . . . These latter admit having been obliged to sign a resolution against these laws, while on the contrary they are impatient for their coming into force. This is a great defeat for the liars who have sold themselves to the Western Powers and who talk of religious persecution . . . "

[72] A typical example of the inadmissible interference of the State in the internal affairs of the Catholic Church deserves mention here, if only because it is the first of its kind: The Ordinary of the diocese of Banska Bystrica having died on 8 January 1950, the Government appointed the Rev. John Dechet, " faithful servant of the Republic," as " ecclesiastical administrator " of the diocese. The bishops protested on 17 January against this illegal interference of the Government, and the Holy See excommunicated Dechet on 19 January. Cf. *L'Osservatore Romano*, 19 February 1950 . . . This was the first of a long series of illegal appointments by the Government.

As compensation for the confiscated goods the State took upon itself to pay a salary proportioned to their work to priests employed in parishes, chancelleries, hospitals and cathedral chapters. The same was decided with regard to superiors of religious houses, bishops, apostolic administrators and vicars general (Arts. 2, 3, 4, of decree n. 219/49).

Communist propaganda insisted particularly on the fact that by the new law the State intended to provide for the needs of the clergy and to reward them in proportion to the value of their contribution to the common good. During the discussions on the bill the newspapers published photographs of priests invited (or forced) to assist at the Parliamentary debates.

Nevertheless the clergy of the different dioceses protested to the Government in two *pro memoria* dated, respectively, 11 and 14 October. They denounced therein the *State Bureau* as " an unheard of violation of the internationally recognised rights of the Church, and an attempt to annihilate it." They renounced " spontaneously the pecuniary benefits provided for in the law." Finally they demanded that religious liberty be guaranteed to the people, and that the clergy be allowed to attend without hindrance to their spiritual duties.[73]

On 18 October 1949 as the new law was being passed in Parliament, the clergy made a public declaration of fidelity and attachment to the episcopate.[74] The bishops for their part drew the Government's attention on 21 October 1949 to the fact that the new laws

" take from the Church its autonomy which consists in freedom to deal with its own organisational and constitutional questions. Henceforth the State claims the right to interfere by ecclesiastical appointments in its internal structure, and to refuse consent for ideological or political reasons to the appointment of ecclesiastical persons to ecclesiastical offices. These provisions place the *Church outside the law* and are contrary to the fundamental laws of the Republic concerning freedom of worship, since this

---

[73] Cf. *La Documentation Catholique*, 6 November 1949, col. 1467, 1468.
[74] Cf. *La Documentation Catholique*, 6 November 1949, col. 1463.

freedom includes in its concept the liberty of the internal order of the Church." [75]

The Government chose to regard these protests of the bishops and the clergy as " the refusal of some members of the clergy " to fulfil their duties as citizens. [76]

The State Bureau for Ecclesiastical Affairs commenced to function. Ecclesiastical property was confiscated, and the clergy were henceforth regarded by the State as a category of employees in its service. [77]

The breaking off of Diplomatic Relations with the Holy See

The breaking off of diplomatic relations with the Holy See formed another part of the Government effort to enslave the Catholic Church to Communist rule.

In April 1949 the Czechoslovak Government asked the Secretariat of State to recall Mgr. *Gennaro Verolino*, the acting Chargé d'Affaires of the Holy See in Prague. Since the Government gave no reason for such a demand the Holy See considered

---

[75] In article 20 of the law concerning payment of the clergy it is required that they take an oath of loyalty to the Czechoslovak Republic in the following terms "I N.N. . . . promise before God to be loyal to the Czechoslovak Republic and to its People's democratic régime and to do nothing against its interests, its security and its integrity. As a citizen of the Czechoslovak People's Republic I will fulfil conscientiously the duties of my office and will do my utmost to help the constructive efforts being made to procure the well-being of the Czech and Slovak people."
Concerning this oath the bishops gave the following directives to the clergy in their Letter of 21 October: " You are required to make the promise before God; it follows necessarily that you may not promise, nor may the State demand that you promise anything except that which is in keeping with the inalienable rights of which God is the direct and indirect author for it is on his Commandments as expressed in the Decalogue that all valid laws are founded. The rectitude of your conscience therefore commands you to add, either by word of mouth or in writing, ' in all that is not contrary to divine and ecclesiastical laws and the natural rights of man '."

[76] *Rudé Pravo*, 30 October 1949. The newspaper falsified completely the directives of the bishops, reporting them as having " recommended the ecclesiastics to accept their salaries and to take the oath prescribed in the law."

[77] In November 1949 the President of the Republic, Clement Gottwald, in an interview with the French Communist paper *L'Humanité* made the position clear: " The conflict is not between the Catholic Church and the Czechoslovak Republic, but between the Republic and certain high dignitaries of that Church. The majority of the clergy and of the faithful is in agreement with the State. The State is striving to strengthen this agreement as is proved by our religious laws which guarantee the material existence of all the Churches, so that being free from economic worries they may devote themselves to their religious mission. The conflict between the State and certain high dignitaries of the Church has nothing to do with religion. It arises from the political activity against the State of a group of the higher clergy." Cf. *L'Humanité*, 5 November 1949.

it necessary to protest. However to avoid aggravating the situation Mgr. *Verolino* was recalled, but it was demanded that he be allowed to remain in Prague until the arrival of the new Chargé d'Affaires, Monsignor *Bertoli*, Counsellor of the Apostolic Nunciature in Switzerland. At the same time application was made for an entry visa for Mgr. *Bertoli*.

The Minister for External Affairs hastened to give assurance by verbal note that the Czechoslovak Legation in Berne had already been instructed to issue the required visa without delay to the new Chargé d'Affaires.

During this time serious police measures were taken against Mgr. *Verolino*. Members of the Party and of the Government launched violent attacks on him in the press and over the radio. [78]

Finally on 13 July 1949 the Representative of the Holy See was ordered to leave Czechoslovakia. The Czechoslovak Legation in Berne had still not granted to Mgr. *Bertoli* the visa promised by the Minister for External Affairs.

Once the Chargé d'Affaires had left it was impossible to get the required visa either for Mgr. *Bertoli* or for two other diplomats appointed successively to the Inter-nunciature in Prague. [79] In the meantime in accordance with diplomatic practice the Secretary of the Inter-nunciature took control as Chargé d'Affaires. The Government, supported by a second virulent press campaign, refused to acknowledge the right of the Secretary to direct the Inter-nunciature until the arrival of the new Chargé d'Affaires, and interfered in various ways with the Pontifical representation. Finally on 16 March 1950 the Secretary was asked, in a statement made over the radio, to leave within three days the territory of the Czechoslovak Republic.

The break in diplomatic relations between the Holy See and the Government in Prague was thus complete, in accordance with the desires of the Communist leaders. [80]

---

[78] Cf. *L'Osservatore Romano*, 11 and 12 July 1949. Cf. also *The Tablet* of 9 July in which are reproduced the attacks of the Minister, Cepicka, over the radio on 25 June 1949.

[79] Cf. *L'Osservatore Romano*, 27 July 1949.

[80] *L'Osservatore Romano*, 29 March 1950. The last member of the Czechoslovak Legation to the Holy See left Rome without even informing the Secretariat of State of his departure. Cf. *The Tablet*, 6 May 1950.

The Liquidation of the Greco-Catholic Diocese of Presov

Another episode in the enslavement of the Catholic Church by the Government was the liquidation of the Greco-Catholic diocese of Presov.

This diocese of the Oriental Rite had 321,000 Catholics with 341 priests. It was transformed by a *Government measure* into an Orthodox diocese and joined to the " Autocephalous Orthodox Church of Czechoslovakia " which had been formed at the instigation of the Communists. The following are the circumstances of the transformation:

First the Bishop, Mgr. *Pavol Gojdic*, was arrested and his Auxiliary deported; the stage was thus set for the application of the Government plans elaborated at Moscow.

On 28 April 1950 the Orthodox Metropolitan, *Eleutherius*, convoked at Presov an assembly of self-styled delegates of the clergy and faithful of the Greco-Catholic diocese of Presov. The assembly in a proclamation denounced the union with the Church of Rome which had taken place in 1649, and asked to be united to the Russian Orthodox Church.

On 27 May 1950 a decree of the Communist Government granted legal recognition to this transfer in spite of the almost unanimous opposition of the population.[81] On 1 July the Metropolitan *Eleutherius* announced that the union was a *fait accompli* and hastened to transmit the news to the Patriarch *Alexij* of Moscow.

On 29 July 1950 a new Orthodox bishop was chosen by a People's Ecclesiastical Assembly composed of 238 lay people and 21 priests. Thus by a simple Government decree a Catholic diocese " disappeared " in Czechoslovakia, and its faithful were all forced to become members of another denomination.

5. VIOLENT PERSECUTION OF THE CHURCH

During the different stages of the struggle against the Church the Czechoslovak Communist Government tried to avoid as far as possible a violent conflict with the hierarchy and the Holy

---

[81] See text of the communication of the Minister Fierlinger to Eleutherius in *La Civiltà Cattolica*, 19 August 1950.

See. This conflict was however inevitable, given the bad faith of the Government, which aimed at the complete enslavement of the Church and at no time paid any heed to the repeated protests of the bishops.

The bitterness of the struggle was specially due to the Government's failure to make a success of the schismatic movement through the intermediary of the *pseudo-Catholic Action*, and to the decree of the Holy Office of 13 July 1949 condemning membership of the Communist Party. This decree was published on the very day that Mgr. *Verolino* was called upon to leave Prague.[82]

The Communist press continued its campaign of vilification against the Church. At the same time the President of the Republic, *Clement Gottwald*, intervened personally in the struggle, declaring: " The higher clergy of the Catholic Church in Czechoslovakia are enemies of the régime; they are opposed to all agreement with the Government and are the centre of internal reaction. All Czechoslovak reactionaries at home and abroad are in touch with the higher Catholic clergy and are preparing to attack our democratic Republic." [83]

Suppression of Religious Houses

By the breaking off of diplomatic relations between the Holy See and the Czechoslovak State the Communists considered they had rid themselves of an indiscreet observer. They could now proceed with less misgiving to intensify the persecution, having recourse even to force should the need arise.

---

[82] Two days later, 15 July, the Minister Cepicka, commenting on the decree of the Holy Office and the departure of Mgr. Verolino, stated: " On the evening of the day of Verolino's departure forever from our country, which he wished to lead to civil war, a decree issued over the radio of the Holy See announced the excommunication of all Catholic Communists and of those who collaborate with them . . . This is only an expression of rage at the success of the workers in their struggle against those who exploit them. Those who try to carry out the orders of the Vatican are without doubt traitors to the State and to the people." *Rudé Pravo*, 17 July 1949.

For the Communists the decree of the Holy Office against atheistic Materialism constituted an offence against the People's Democratic States. The organ of the Czechoslovak Communist Party wrote: " The aim of the Pontifical decree is clear; it obliges all the faithful to undertake subversive activity against the régime and the law. It thus constitutes an unheard of interference in the internal affairs of the State." *Rudé Pravo*, 23 July 1949.

[83] *Rudé Pravo*, 29 February 1950.

On 14 and 15 March 1950 two agents arrived in every religious house, one charged with the " re-education " of the occupants, the other to take over administrative control. In reality the mission of these two agents was to study and prepare a plan for the taking over of religious houses by the State.[84]

The reason to be given for this latter measure was that " the religious houses are centres of espionage and activity in favour of the Vatican." [85]

As a psychological preparation of public opinion for such a step a *great court-case* was staged at Prague lasting from 30 March to 5 April 1950. In the dock were *11 superiors or outstanding members of different religious congregations.* A number of these had been arrested only a few days previously. The penalties imposed ranged from life imprisonment to 10 years, accompanied by heavy fines and the loss of civic rights. Only one of the accused was acquitted; he nevertheless was sentenced to 2 years' imprisonment " for not having denounced the group to the authorities, knowing of their high treason and espionage." [86]

During the nights of 13 to 14 and 21 to 22 April 1950 militant Communists occupied all the religious houses of men in Czechoslovakia.[87] The religious were taken to the so-called " concentration monasteries " or to the labour camps. In Slovakia in numerous places (Zlaté Moravce, Pezinok, etc.) the police had to turn out in force to prevent popular uprisings. In September of the same year the religious houses of women suffered the same treatment.

The Communist press explained to the people, while availing itself of the occasion to insult the religious, that there was no question of these latter being arrested. They were merely being " brought together in more suitable houses " where they could freely apply themselves to their own formation and live under good conditions.[88]

---

[84] The juridical basis for these measures was made clear in the Prague trial of 30 March 1950: " The existence of a religious order, which demands full and exact obedience, is manifestly in contradiction with the legislation at present in force in the Czechoslovak Republic." Cf. *Svobodné Slovo,* 4 April 1950.

[85] *Mlada Fronta,* 1 April 1950; *Rudé Pravo,* 16 April 1950.

[86] Cf. *La Documentation Catholique,* 1951, col. 1088.

[87] *Novy Zivot,* May 1950.

[88] *Rudé Pravo,* 20 and 25 April 1950. *Tvorba,* 12 April 1950.

A Government communiqué of 18 April 1950 tried to justify these things especially in the eyes of international public opinion. It stated:

> " It has been proved recently that the Catholic religious orders had become instruments in the hands of the external enemies of the Republic. In the course of court proceedings dealing with subversive activities it has been established that a number of religious houses had concealed enemy agents, spies and even assassins . . . Efforts have been made to bring these religious orders back to their true pristine religious mission. It has also been observed that big religious houses were occupied only by a few persons, who did no work, and who spent the greater part of their time instigating the people to crime. It is for these reasons that religious have been gathered together in a number of monasteries where they will be able to devote themselves to a purely religious mission in conformity with the rules of their orders." [89]

For its part the Bureau for Ecclesiastical Affairs stated that not only had the religious houses become " almost empty " buildings but they had become as well " nests of subversive activity against the State."

> " It is for this reason that religious have been gathered together in bigger and more suitable monasteries. This regrouping has been done in such a manner as to disturb as little as possible the interior life demanded by the rules. A great chance is being given to all religious thus united to fulfil their religious duties and to increase their productive capacity under conditions much better than those existing in their monasteries which were often badly administered . . . The days of the monasteries are over; little by little their social usefulness has disappeared. We are acting in accordance with the spirit of the present time and in the interests of our worker people." [90]

Approximately *2,000 religious* were placed in the " concentration monasteries " according to figures established by the police. At first all religious superiors were put in the

[89] *Czechoslovak News Agency* (CTK), 18 April 1950. Cf. also *The Tablet*, 13 May 1950 which reproduces the text.
[90] *Bulletin of the Catholic Clergy* (VKD), 20 May 1950.

monastery of Zeliv (Bohemia); the Jesuits and the Franciscans were put together in the monastery of Bohosodov; the
Dominicans, the Capuchins, the Premonstratensians and others
in that of Kraliky, while the Salesians, the Calasanctians and
the Augustinians were interned at Osek and Hejnice. Eventually
only two or three of these monasteries remained; in these were
kept the religious who were unsuitable for work or who were
considered " politically " dangerous. All the others were employed in the industrial works of the country.

In the concentration monasteries the religious were forced
to follow a course of Marxist " re-education." Their teachers
were " cultural agents " of the Party. The religious wore similar
uniforms, each having a number.

During the autumn of 1950 the younger religious and the
novices were called to the army. At the same time a great
number of the older religious were enrolled in the " voluntary
work brigades " or sent to the mines or the forced labour camps.[91]

As regards women religious, already in September 1950 it
was said that 1,500 nuns were " guests " of the central " convents."
These " convents " were in reality forced labour camps where
the nuns were obliged to work in the factories and in the fields
. . . Besides the Government tried to win over the nuns to
its cause; for this reason many meetings of General and Provincial Superioresses were called at Prague. The effort failed.
As a result *the greater number of the 10,000 Czechoslovak nuns*
were expelled from their houses and employed in industrial
works. Some were allowed to remain in the hospitals because
of a shortage of lay nursing staff and because of the opposition
of the doctors in charge to their departure; they had, however
to submit to the supervision of a member of the lay staff.
Others were permitted to remain in houses for the old, the
incurable, the ill, etc., in other words they were allowed to

---

[91] On 12 July 1950 a new Penal Code, promulgated under n. 86 in the Collection
of Laws, came into force in Czechoslovakia. In article 36 it lays down that anybody
who has given proof of hostility towards the People's Democracy and who has not changed
his attitude during the serving of his sentence is liable on its completion to be sent
to a forced labour camp for a period of from three months to two years. In 1949 and 1950
about 70 forced labour camps came into being in Czechoslovakia; this number increased
later. Cf. *L'Osservatore Romano*, 29 October 1950: " Approximately 2,000 priests are
in prison or interned in labour camps."

stay with the " non-productive " people. But they were systematically and regularly removed from schools, orphanages,
kindergartens, nurseries, etc., that is, from all places where
people might be susceptible of education.

By the end of 1951 *not a single religious house existed in all
Czechoslovakia* with the exception of some " concentration
monasteries " which were in reality concentration camps.[92]
The houses of the religious were taken over by the Government
and used for purposes anything but spiritual. The Benedictine
Abbey of Prague-Brevnov, for example, was transformed into
a school for the State police. Other religious houses became
military barracks. The libraries of the different houses were
" liquidated "; some of the books were sold, the rest destroyed.
Thus did Communist rule put an end to the cultural and religious
forces represented by the regular clergy in Czechoslovakia.

Suppression of the Seminaries

Seminaries and faculties of Theology are a source of strength
to the Church as well as a guarantee for the future. These also

----

[92] Cf. *L'Osservatore Romano*, 3 May 1950, *Concentration Monasteries in Czechoslovakia.*
La Civiltà Cattolica (1954, III, pp. 8-9) gives these detailed items of information.
In the prisons of Ilava in Slovakia there are from 225 to 270 priests whom some gaolers
do not allow to recite the breviary; the more particularly dangerous internees remain
continually locked in their cells; the others are subjected to the very hardest labour.
Not a few are in the uranium mines of Jachymov. Those who have been condemned to
the more severe sentences are subjected in the prisons of Leopoldov to the worst
possible conditions; among these latter are Bishops Vojtassak, Buzalka, Gojdic. After
four years the lot of the religious has not changed much. For the most part—except
for the few engaged in agriculture as at Kraliky in Bohemia—they were condemned to
labour in factories and in the public shipyards or with the road-repair gangs. For the
youngest of these prisoners this already severe treatment was exchanged for military service
in which they were assigned the heaviest fatigue-duties. Their period of service was also
extended beyond the normal period of two years. The same lot generally awaited
seminarists who were considered untrustworthy by the Government. In the spring
of 1953, 240 religious were interned in the monastery of Zeliv. At Osek at the same time
there were also about 200 religious who worked in a nearby factory, or else were brought
every day to the port of Usti on the Elbe to load coal and metal.
Certain " concentration monasteries " were suppressed in the spring of 1953, but
those confined there had little cause for rejoicing. In the Hajek " monastery " for example
before its evacuation the Communists condemned a number of priests to from two to
twenty months' forced labour. The others were for the most part sent to the army,
a fate which, as has been said, meant a change of place but not of conditions. Even the
oldest and those who were ill did not get full liberty. They were not allowed to return
to their monasteries which were occupied by the Communists. Hence in order to
make a living they were obliged to look for civilian employment.

were an object of attack by the Communists who wished to have them under their absolute control.

Decree n. 112 of 14 July 1950 *fixed the programme of religious instruction* [93] *and regulated the functioning of schools of Theology.* It stated that the appointment of teachers of religion was exclusively within the competence of the Bureau for Ecclesiastical Affairs (sec. 3, 1). Only " a master who had given proof of great political wisdom " could be considered for such a post.

This same decree *suppressed all Catholic faculties* and schools of Theology. At the same time for the formation of the clergy of all Czechoslovakia it set up two seminaries having " State " faculties of Theology, one at Prague (later transferred to Litomerice), the other at Bratislava.

The deans of these two faculties were to be appointed by the Minister charged with the direction of the State Bureau for Ecclesiastical Affairs, and were to be responsible to the Minister himself for the conduct of the faculties.

Section 4, § 2 of the decree declared that the Government together with the Church would ensure that " the education of the theological students would proceed according to the spirit of the People's Democracy and the precepts of the Church." [94]

The entire decree tended to limit the influence of the Church and of religion in theological education; it sought thereby to secure absolute control for the Government.

Theological students who refused to attend these Government-controlled faculties, where the study of Marxism-Leninism was of obligation, were obliged to report for work to the labour exchanges, or were called up for compulsory military service. In spite of many appeals in the Government press and over the radio very few students attended the two faculties of theology. [95] The Government's aim was clear: to form with jealous care future " priest-collaborators."

---

[93] Religious instruction had been authorised, although with many Government restrictions and controls, by Law n. 95 of 21 April 1948. There is question here of new regulations.

[94] Cf. *The Clergy Review*, February 1951.

[95] Cf. *Novy Zivot*, May 1951.

Court Proceedings against Priests and Bishops

The agents of the Communist police received at the beginning of 1950 very detailed instructions as to the watch they should keep on the personal activity of each priest. By secret circular they were asked to supply information concerning the personality of the priests, their work, their tastes and the relations they had with their bishops, the people, and the Government. The political outlook of the priests and especially their attitude to the Communist Catholic Action Movement were to be noted. The agents were asked to find out likewise what part, if any, the priests had played in the campaign against the measures decreed by the Government; had they read or not read the Pastoral Letter for the Feast of Corpus Christi 1949; what did they think of the religious publications of the Communists; how had they reacted to the decree condemning Communism; when condemned by the Communist authorities had they asked to be pardoned; what were their reactions to the measures of the State in regard to the payment of the clergy.[96]

The agents began to watch the priests day and night so as to obtain the required information. They subjected them in general to continual questionings, sometimes even resorting to force.

The police investigations into the activity of the priests were only a preparation for *court proceedings* which would bring the supposed faults of the clergy before the public. In fact during the first four months of 1950 *dozens of priests were condemned by the Czechoslovak People's tribunals.*[97] Most of them were accused of having read the Pastoral Letters of the bishops. The names are known of over 20 priests and religious condemned during January and February 1950.[98]

---

[96] Cf. *La Documentation Catholique*, 1951, col. 1088, which gives the text of the Circular published by the Agency *KIPA*, 17 February 1950.

[97] To give more " legality " to the trials of the clergy and the hierarchy the Communist Government approved a new administrative Penal Code on 12 July 1950 which came into force on 1 August. Articles 123, 173 and 174 dealt with " crimes " connected with sacerdotal activity. The exercise of the sacerdotal ministry in conformity with the instructions of the lawful ecclesiastical superiors constituted a " crime." In these conditions the prisons began to be filled with priests. The text of the new Code may be read in the *Digest-Index of Eastern European Laws*, 24-25.

[98] Cf. *La Liberté* of Fribourg, 25 and 26 July 1950, which gives the names of the condemned priests as well as the " crimes " of which they were accused.

All during the year 1950 the Czechoslovak Communist Government tried to intimidate the clergy by means of much-publicised court proceedings.

The appointment of vicars general and of Government officials, to which the Bureau for Ecclesiastical Affairs proceeded systematically, greatly increased the pressure on the bishops. It was the intention of the Communists to exclude eventually these latter entirely from the government of the dioceses.

The arrest of the better known among the clergy had the result of isolating the bishops and depriving them of valuable counsels. Further steps were then taken to restrict their liberty. Their residences were watched by the police; their presence in the cathedrals was forbidden; finally they were placed under house-arrest or, as was often the case, thrown into prison.

Between July and September 1950 the following were placed under arrest:

Mgr. *Pavol Gojdic*, Greco-Catholic Bishop of Presov.
Mgr. *Michal Buzalka*, Auxiliary Bishop of Trnava.
Mgr. *Ian Vojtassak*, Bishop of Spis.
Mgr. *Stanislas Zela*, Auxiliary Bishop of Olomouc.
Mgr. *Stefan Barnas*, Auxiliary Bishop of Spis.
Mgr. *Basil Hopko*, Greco-Catholic Auxiliary of Presov.
The Bishops of Litomerice and Budejovice, Mgr. *Stefan Trochta* and Mgr. *Josef Hlouch* were placed under police surveillance in their houses. The Bishop of Hradec Kralové, Mgr. *Picha*, was arrested and confined in a cell in the monastery of Broumov.

At the same time the Government removed all vicars general loyal to the Church. In their places they put vicars chosen from among the " patriot priests."

From 27 November to 2 December 1950 the trial took place in the notorious prison of Pankrac of *the Auxiliary Bishop of Olomouc, Mgr. Stanislas Zela, and 8 other accused.*[99] They

---

[99] Four of the accused were close co-operators of Archbishop Beran of Prague: Mgr. John Boukal, his first secretary; Mgr. Joseph Cihac, Archdeacon of the Metropolitan Chapter; Mgr. Jaroslav Kulac, of the Archiepiscopal Chancellery; and the Rev. Anthony Mandl, secretary for Catholic Action in the archdiocese. Two others had served in the Apostolic Inter-nunciature: Mgr. Otokar Svec as counsellor, and the Salesian Father, Vaclav Martvy, as translator. Finally on the list came two well-known religious: the Rev. Stanislas Jarolimek, Abbot of the Premonstratensian Monastery of Strahov; and the Rev. John Opasek, Abbot of the Benedictine Monastery of Brevnov.

were charged with having attempted the overthrow of the People's Democratic régime and the economic and social order of the Republic. They were also accused of spying for foreign powers. In the plans of the persecutors this trial was meant to impress the crowds and to show conclusively to the people that the higher clergy were opposed to the Communist authorities. The accused " confessed " their faults.[100]

Mgr. *Stanislas Zela* was condemned to 25 years' imprisonment and was fined 150,000 crowns. The other accused were condemned to penal servitude for life or to terms of imprisonment.[101]

About a month later, 10 January 1951, another trial commenced at Bratislava. This time the accused were three Slovak bishops: Mgr. *Ian Vojtassak*, Bishop of Spis, aged 73 years; Mgr. *Pavol Gojdic*, Bishop of the Oriental Rite of Presov; and Mgr. *Michal Buzalka*, Auxiliary Bishop of Trnava. Again on this occasion the charges were chosen to suit propaganda purposes. As was becoming the custom in such trials the accused " admitted " their faults and almost asked pardon for having taken part in espionage against the People's Democracy. The defending

---

[100] The following are some examples from the publication mentioned below (101). It should be remarked that there is question here of courageous and zealous priests, most of whom had faced fearlessly the threats of the Nazis. " Yes, I wish to confess, as a penitent, my activity . . . " (p. 131). " Do you admit your guilt? " " Yes " answered Canon Cihac, " I am fully conscious of my activity against the State " (p. 66). " Are you by profession a spy? " was asked of the Rev. Martvy, and he answered: " I admit that such is the case " (p. 116). " Do you know why you have been arrested? " to which the Abbot Jarolimek promptly replied: " For crimes against the law " (p. 119). " Do you feel guilty? " " Yes, the cause of my arrest was my activity against the State," answered hastily the Rev. Mandl. And to the question: " Can you describe the connection between the Vatican Catholic Action and your subversive and spying activity? " " Yes," replied Mandl, " and I wish to state it openly " (p. 104). (As seen earlier, there was a Communist " Catholic Action " in Czechoslovakia as well as the real Catholic Action).

[101] So as to make these accusations public the celebrated legal expert Hobza published under the direction of the Ministry for Information and People's Culture a work entitled: *The Trial of the Vatican Agents in Czechoslovakia : Bishop Zela and companions* (Prague, Orbis, 1951). According to this the accused were guilty of spying and of high treason. They confessed their faults and showed themselves thankful to their judges for the mercy shown them and for permission to express publicly their repentance for the evil they had done against the workers. Hobza explained that " Canon Law and ecclesiastical rules are not valid in Czechoslovakia. Every Church dignitary or ecclesiastical functionary who gives primacy to canonical obedience over loyalty to the State should be considered a traitor and a culprit against the laws of the State." In consequence direct contact with the Pontifical Representative or with the Pope was forbidden to Czechoslovak citizens. Cf. *Novy Zivot*, December 1950, pp. 16, *seqq*.

lawyers stated that the culpability of their clients was so evident that any defence was rendered difficult.[102] The trial lasted only five days and the sentences were extremely severe: Mgr. *Pavol Gojdic* and Mgr. *Michal Buzalka* were condemned to life imprisonment; Mgr. *Ian Vojtassak* was sentenced to 24 years' imprisonment.[103]

At the beginning of February 1951 *the trial of four ecclesiastics began; the series continued thus for several months*. The accusations in all cases were almost identical and the sentences were given the appearance of acts of mercy by the people's tribunals. As a result of these trials parishes and rectories were frequently left without priests. In the meantime the " patriot priests," not

---

[102] Cf. *The Trial of three traitor bishops of Slovakia; Vojtassak, Buzalka, Gojdic*, issued under the direction of the Ministry for Information and People's Culture. (Prague, Orbis, 1951).

[103] Cf. *L'Osservatore Romano*, 1 and 2 December 1950. Below is an extract from the interrogation of Mgr. Vojtassak, as cited by Michel in his book: *Problémes religieux dans un pays sous régime communiste* (Paris, Ed. Fleurus, p. 73).

President: Which suited you better? (the capitalist system or the socialist system).

Bishop: The capitalist system.

President: In what way?

Bishop; From the material and economic point of view the bishopric was somehow better provided for . . .

President; Can you affirm that violence was used against the Church and against religion when the workers came into power? Did they close the churches?

Bishop: I cannot affirm it.

President: What did you fear on the overthrow of the capitalist system? You have said that capitalism assured the economic position and the power of the Church . . .

Bishop: Yes.

President: You have said that of the two systems, capitalist and socialist, you preferred capitalism; that means that you have chosen it with all its consequences: its riches on the one hand and its misery and unemployment on the other . . .

Judge (*Bedrna*): Why did you ally yourself with the reactionary forces against the People's Democratic Order?

Bishop: Ultimately because of the question of ecclesiastical property.

Judge's comment: Here Vojtassak tells the whole truth. It was a question of Church property. That also worried the high ecclesiastical hierarchy in Austria-Hungary, in the first Czechoslovak Republic, in the Slovak State and again now after the Liberation.

Judge (addressing the bishop): For you it was a question of Church property. Why did you not question the faithful? Were the workers of your opinion?

Bishop: No.

Michel comments: " Mgr. Vojtassak, an exemplary bishop and well-known for his great charity, his apostolic zeal and his detachment, was not responsible for the answers he gave. He fought against atheistic Communism for many other reasons besides that of Church property. His answers before the tribunal were those learned from the Communist ' producers.' I cite this example only to show in what manner Communism attacks the Church and the clergy and tries to discredit them." See a full analysis of the trial and interrogations of the three accused based on the original documents in *La Civiltà Cattolica* (1952, II, 604-614).

occupying themselves overmuch with the care of souls, were holding congresses and meetings to approve the Stockholm Appeal for Peace.

On 15 January 1951 the vicars general and the vicars capitular appointed by the Government met at Prague. This meeting of " diocesan ordinaries " was meant to give the impression that a regular conference of the bishops had been held, and that as a result the government of the dioceses was proceeding normally.

On 13 February four new titular canons were installed in the cathedral of Olomouc. Representatives of the Bureau for Ecclesiastical Affairs were present, and the ceremony was accompanied by an oath of loyalty to the State.[104]

On 28 February a vicar general and a number of canons were installed at Brno; the cathedral of Kosice then had its turn, getting seven new canons. In the diocese of Spis a vicar capitular was appointed while the bishop and the two Vicars General, Mgr. *Stefan Barnas*, Auxiliary Bishop, and Mgr. *Josef Tomanocy* were in prison.

On 10 March the Communists moved Archbishop *Beran* to the Castle of Rozmital, then to Nova Rise, after having fined him 50,000 crowns for his " negative attitude in regard to the new ecclesiastical legislation in Czechoslovakia." [105]   Such a

---

[104] The Law of 14 October 1949, n. 218, and the executive decrees, n. 219-223, of 18 October formed the basis for these appointments. True, this law declared that ecclesiastics are employees of the Church, not of the State; still it demanded that " they satisfy all the general conditions imposed on Government employees " (Law 218—decree 219, art. 7). Further no ecclesiastic may exercise his powers without the consent of the Government (Law 218, art. 7, I—decree 219, art. 16) and the previous consent of the Government is necessary for all appointments (Law 218, art. 6, 2). Government salaries are paid only to ecclesiastics who have obtained the consent of the Government. The Bureau for Ecclesiastical Affairs is authorised to draw up a list of posts to be filled with the consent of the Government. A post occupied without Government consent is to be considered vacant (decree 219, art. 88).

If within 30 days a vacancy is not filled in the desired manner, the Government takes upon itself by way of administration the function of the ecclesiastical authority. Decree 219, article 30 gives the Government the right of patronage in the presentation of candidates to the competent ordinary. The names for a vacant post must be sent by the bishop to the episcopal consistory. They must then be submitted to the Government with the names of those judged unsuitable for the post indicated. The Government chooses a candidate from those not eliminated by the consistory. The bishop is *bound* to appoint the person whose name is thus presented to him. In other words *appointments to all ecclesiastical posts are under Government control*. " Priests like all others are employees of the State . . .", a statement *inadvertently* made over Radio Prague !

[105] Cf. *L'Osservatore Romano*, 15 March 1951.

fine rendered vacant the Archiepiscopal See of Prague according to the Communist Penal Code.[106] On 3 March four new canons had already been appointed; some days later one of these was elected Vicar Capitular of Prague, the Vicar General, Mgr. *Theophilus Opatzny*, appointed by the Archbishop, having been forced to resign.

On 15 March three new canons were appointed to the cathedral of Budejovice against the will of Mgr. *Josef Hlouch*. A vicar general was likewise imposed on the diocese of Lito-merice, while the Bishop, Mgr. *Stefan Trochta*, was excluded from the exercise of his pastoral ministry.[107]

In June 1951 the Minister, *Zdenek Fierlinger*, who had succeeded *Cepicka* as Director of the Bureau for Ecclesiastical Affairs, proceeded to the nomination of nine vicars general in as many Czechoslovak dioceses, thus setting up *a new hierarchy of patriot priests*.[108]

In the course of the year 1951 the position of the Church became more and more precarious. More than 3,000 priests, regular and secular, were deprived of their liberty; of these, 2,000 were in " concentration monasteries." Many others were relieved of their posts with the result that many parishes were for a certain time at least deprived of priests.[109]

Pressure was continually brought to bear on the bishops,

---

[106] Declaration of the Bureau for Ecclesiastical Affairs in *Rudé Pravo*, 11 March 1951.

[107] The *Sacred Congregation of the Consistory* on 17 March declared all these appointments null and void and recalled all the acts of violence endured by the Church in Czechoslovakia where " the rights of the Church have been violated in a continued and unheard of manner and ecclesiastics are the victims of iniquitous attacks . . . The authors of these misdeeds are reminded of the various canons which inflict on them the penalty of excommunication reserved to the Holy See *simpliciter* or *speciali modo* according to the gravity of the case." This pronouncement led to an intensification of the persecution by the Government.

[108] The Communists tried to give as much appearance of canonical legality as possible to these appointments (election for the vicars capitular, approval by the bishop for vicars general).

[109] In the middle of this general disarray the Communist propaganda continued to repeat that there had never been greater religious freedom than in Czechoslovakia. The organs of propaganda devoted themselves to the distribution especially abroad of publications in which figured declarations of liberty made by " patriot priests," and photographs of churches and religious ceremonies attended by great crowds of people. The Czechoslovak Legation in Rome undertook the distribution of one of these publications: " *Czechoslovak Documents*." The relevant commentary in *L'Osservatore Romano* drew attention to the suppression of religious liberty in Czechoslovakia from the moment the Communists judged themselves sufficiently strong to impose on the country the dictator-

isolated in their houses or in prison, to induce them to take the oath of loyalty to the State.

On 12 March the Government spread the news that Mgr. *Picha* of Hradec Kralové, Mgr. *Carsky* of Kosice, Mgr. *Trochta* of Litomerice, Mgr. *Lazik* of Trnava, Mgr. *Onderek*, Apostolic Administrator of Cesky Tesin, and the " new Vicar Capitular " of Prague, the Rev. *Stehlik*, had taken the *oath of loyalty* to the People's Republic. On this occasion Mgr. *Carsky* was obliged to read aloud a declaration, evidently extorted. The declaration refused " recognition of ecclesiastical penalties " (inflicted according to the Communists for " political " reasons), and attested that " the activities of our People's Democratic Order are in full harmony with the moral principles of our holy Church." The declaration contradicted all the principles for which these bishops, especially Mgr. *Carsky*, had up to then courageously fought.

The Communists to lessen the great popularity of the bishops had confined them to their residences, forbidding all contact with priests or people. After this period of isolation *all* the bishops with the exception of Archbishop *Beran* of Prague, Archbishop *Matocha* of Olomouc, Mgr. *Skoupy* of Brno, Mgr. *Hlouch* of Budejovice, and Mgr. *Trochta* of Litomerice had been imprisoned and then " indoctrinated " (after the manner special to the Communists) in order to get from them the declaration under oath of 12 March 1951. Later Mgr. *Necsey* of Nitra joined the signatories named above. The Communists did not fail to make the most of the alleged political activity of this bishop during the war.

Pressure was brought to bear on other bishops also, for example on Mgr. *Skoupy* of Brno. The Bishop of Budejovice, who like Archbishop *Beran* had been exiled from his diocese, and the Archbishop of Olomouc remained unshaken in their refusal to sign the declaration.

---

ship of the proletariat—thus exposing the duplicity and the perfidy of such propaganda. Cf. *L'Osservatore Romano*, 29 October 1950.

The same type of Communist propaganda led to the publication of *For the Glory of God* by the so-called " Catholic Charity of Bohemia," in 1955. This book which has many photographs aims at proving that Catholic life is in no way hampered by the rule of the Communists.

If it is recalled that Mgr. *Zela*, Auxiliary of Olomouc, Mgr. *Vojtassak* of Spis, and Mgr. *Buzalka*, Auxiliary of Trnava, had already been condemned at the beginning of 1951, one can realise that the position of the remaining Czechoslovak bishops became truly tragic after the declaration of 12 March.

The Communists tried to profit by this situation of the epis-copate. Those who had sought by taking the oath to be in a position to remedy in some way the bad administration of their dioceses, were now asked to give new declarations favourable to the Government. Thus did the Communists try to give an appearance of *ecclesiastical legality* to their measures, although from 1952 it was clear that the Government had no further need of the bishops. The dioceses were for the greater part governed by creatures of their own, chosen from the ranks of the " patriot priests."

All the bishops' statements, of which even the signatures were often forged, must be taken with caution from this time onwards, especially when one remembers the methods used by the Communists to extort signatures in favour of the so-called Catholic Action and of the Ecclesiastical Laws of October 1949.

On 28 September 1951 the Bureau for Ecclesiastical Affairs organised a Congress at Prague to which all the clergy were invited. The Minister, *Fierlinger*, declared that those present represented all the clergy of Czechoslovakia.[110] In fact, the Government considered as " no longer existing " the bishops it had imprisoned and the religious it had confined in the " concentration monasteries." In its eyes the Church was represented by the small group of perjured priests who had collaborated with the State in the formation of the schismatic movement.

In the following years the Communist rulers continued to declare the existence of religious liberty for international propaganda purposes. At times they showed " good will " towards the Church,[111] but their close watch on her activities

---

[110] All means were used to get the clergy to attend this Congress. But after Minister Fierlinger's attacks on the person of the Holy Father, the Congress became the occasion for a great manifestation of loyalty to the Holy See and to the Pope.

[111] This "good will" reduced itself in substance to the revival of salaries for the clergy and the giving of subsidies for the repair of certain churches of historical or artistic interest.

and their efforts to destroy all religious life never abated. The secret tribunals continued to condemn the clergy and the faithful,[112] and there was no relaxation in the watch kept over the State seminaries for the education of the clergy. No effort was spared to separate the people from the Church, and priests were forced to attend courses of Marxist indoctrination.

In 1953 two other bishops were arrested: Mgr. *Robert Pobozny*, Vicar Capitular of Roznava, and Mgr. *Charles Skoupy*, Bishop of Brno—the latter, according to information from Czechoslovakia, for having organised the Marian Year. The dioceses continued to be directed by the men appointed by the Communists. Thus came into being what has been called the *Theocracy of the atheistic State in Czechoslovakia*.[113]

In 1954 Mgr. *Trochta* was tried and sentenced to 25 years' penal servitude for " having spied in the interests of the Vatican." The same penalty was imposed on his Vicar General, Mgr. *James Kuska* and on another priest Fr. *Francis Vlak*. It was learned in 1954 (it has not however been possible to check this) that the Archbishop of Olomouc, Mgr. *Matocha*, was imprisoned following a general round-up in which a hundred priests and thousands of lay people were arrested. Later on Archbishop *Matocha* re-appeared in public, weary and ill, but without any clarification of the mystery of his long silence.

Conclusion

This account of the different stages in the persecution of the Catholic Church in Czechoslovakia does not claim to have recounted fully all the facts or cited all the pronouncements made by the Czech and Slovak bishops in their efforts to resist the persecution. It limits itself to insisting on the methods adopted by the Communists to nullify the activity of the Catholic Church, beginning with the laws conceived and passed by them, and finally arriving at the acts of violence against the bishops, the secular clergy, and the religious.

---

[112] To quote only one example, shortly before Christmas 1952 thirty members of Catholic Action were called for trial and condemned to from 3 to 22 years' imprisonment. *Not a syllable appeared in the press concerning this trial.*

[113] Cf. *L'Osservatore Romano*, 19 February 1950.

It is to be noted that the persecution in Czechoslovakia reached its height in a relatively short time. In fact it took the Communist rulers in Prague only three years, from 1948 to 1950 inclusive, to promulgate the laws which effectively brought the activity of the Church under State control. During that time the Catholic schools were confiscated, an effort was made to create a schismatic movement and to form a national " hierarchy," while the lawful pastors were held in concentration camps, in prisons, or forced to remain in their houses.

The Oriental diocese of Presov was the only diocese formally abolished in Czechoslovakia. The 2 archdioceses, the 9 other dioceses, and the 2 apostolic administrations have passed however under State control. The bishops where still free are free only *pro forma*; all the administration is done by the agents of a Government opposed in principle to religion. The State appoints the priests to the parishes, and for the important posts it chooses them as far as possible from among those who have shown themselves loyal collaborators of the Communists. To this sad list may be added the confiscation of all Church property, and the loss of 1,363 religious houses and educational and charitable institutions which belonged to the Church.

L'Osservatore Romano of 24 July 1955 gives the following:

1. 13 bishops, residential or auxiliary, have been removed from office; 5 of them are listed in *L'Annuario Pontificio* of 1955 as " in prison for the Faith," while the 8 others are " detained in an unknown place." It is rumoured that some of these latter have been granted supervised freedom. (The most complete mystery continues to surround the fate of the Archbishop of Prague, Mgr. *Josef Beran*, as late as March 1957).

2. The better known of the secular clergy got the same treatment as the bishops; the others are still closely watched in all their pastoral activities.

3. Up to this the Communist Government has paid no heed to the points raised by the Czechoslovak bishops—in their collective Pastoral Letter of 1949—as essential for co-existence. These are (i) respect for the consciences of the young and recognition of the educational mission of the family and of the

Church, (ii) recognition of the jurisdiction of the Pope and the bishops, (iii) the repeal of oppressive measures.

4. The attitude of the Czechoslovak Communist Government towards the Catholic Church is still marked by an interference in Church government which is becoming ever stronger and more far-reaching.

The eight and a half million Czech and Slovak Catholics are at present bereft of their spiritual guides, while " new " priests are being prepared for them.[114] The Government continues its effort to cause confusion in the Catholic ranks, and hopes eventually to be able to destroy the very structure of the Church. Its hopes are founded on the youth now being formed in Atheism and in contempt for everything spiritual. The faithful in Czechoslovakia see the danger and pray God to spare their Fatherland this misfortune.

---

[114] This is being brought about above all by means of courses of " re-education." To refer only to Prague there are two different courses of instruction to which Catholic priests are obliged. The first lasts about two weeks, and from 30 to 35 ecclesiastics take part in it, all unwillingly except for one or two. They remain together for a fortnight. At the beginning of this period each participant presents his personal papers as well as his *curriculum vitae*. A series of conferences follows, confided to functionaries of the State Bureau for Ecclesiastical Affairs and to other Government agents charged with developing the propagandist report dear to the régime. To the same end are directed the monthly conventions which take place at Prague in the House of St. Ignatius, from which in April 1950 the Jesuits were expelled, and which the Administration has now taken over as a house for the clergy. Discussions on sacred subjects are held at these meetings. However the speeches of the functionaries of the State Bureau or of some of the " patriot priests " predominate.

With this action of a collective nature there is also action on the individual level. This is exercised on each priest by the so-called secretaries of Ecclesiastical Affairs, some of whom are women. They watch over the activity of the individual priest particularly his sermons; they insist that he should persuade the people of the excellence of the present administration and induce them to co-operate willingly with it. The priests are expected to do this in their sermons, in their private conversations and even in the confessional.

Chapter 13

THE PERSECUTION OF THE CATHOLIC CHURCH

UNDER

Communist Rule In Viet-Nam

As is generally known it was the Geneva Armistice Agreements in July 1954 which led to the setting up in Viet-Nam of a real Communist State with sovereign power over a whole well-defined, unified, and compact territory.

According to the terms of these agreements the country was divided into two zones along the line of the 17th Parallel. These were described officially as " military re-groupings," but became in reality two distinct States, as had already happened in the case of Germany and Korea.

The northern zone which was immediately proclaimed the *Democratic Republic of Viet-Nam* (*DRVN*) corresponds in fact to the part of the country in which Catholics were most numerous. Church institutions, colleges and schools, and works of charity were numerous and flourishing there. The territory comprised the following nine vicariates apostolic: *Bacninh, Buichu, Haiphong, Hanoi, Hung-Hoa, Langson* and *Caobang, Phat-Diem, Thai-Binh, Vinh* and a part of the Vicariate of *Hue* (cut in two by the 17th Parallel). A Papal representative, Mgr. *John Dooley*, resided at Hanoi with the title of Apostolic Delegate.

The Tragedy of the Refugees

The entry of the Communists into Hanoi coincided with the beginning of the *tragedy of the refugees*.[1] Clause 14 of the Armistice

---

[1] On the question of refugees, cf. the following: *Terror in Viet-Nam*, published under the auspices of the NCWC, Washington, 1955; *Les Viet-Minh et les Accords de Genève*, Saigon, 1955; articles in *L'Osservatore Romano* from which relevant passages will be quoted; the Information Bulletins of the *Fides Agency*; also " *Extrait du rapport sur la siuatio n des refugiés du Nord-Viet-Nam, envoyé à la Sacrée Congrégation de Propaganda Fide;* " Saigon, October 1955.

Agreements granted the people of Viet-Nam a delay of 300 days
to decide in which zone they would choose to have their homes.
The exodus of the northern population, already begun before
the armistice at the time of the evacuation of the Tonking delta
by the French forces, assumed in some months the proportions
of a full-scale and irresistible emigration. To stop it the Communist authorities used every means of persuasion, obstruction
and coercion: blockading of roads and rivers, commandeering
of boats even of those employed in fishing, moral and physical
violence, threats and arrests.[2]

Next they set up a complicated bureaucratic procedure for
" travel permits." Each person who wished to travel had to apply
individually, giving the reasons for his journey. This led to
meticulous enquiries by the administration and a long wait for
the reply which was almost invariably negative. Nevertheless
considerable numbers of the population of Tonking (the vast
majority of them Catholics) forced their way through the
blockades on their journey to the coast. In small groups they
spread across the country, across the rice fields and the canals,
dragging along a few miserable belongings—a small bag of rice,
some clothes, always some holy images and sometimes even the
bells which they had devoutly taken from their little churches.
There were bloody encounters with the Viet-Minh. Frail
overloaded sampans struggling against the rough sea were
wrecked trying to join the French and American boats anchored
off the shore.[3]

The entry of the Communists into Hanoi on 9 October 1954
had made the places of embarkation more difficult of access.
The Viet-Minh control over the whole province became stricter
and more oppressive. Yet there was a constant flow of refugees
towards the coast from Upper-Tonking where the permission

---

[2] They went so far as to hold back one or two members of each family so as to dissuade
the others from leaving. Small children were separated from their parents, sons from
their fathers, etc. Cf. *Terror in Viet-Nam*, p. 7.

[3] At Tra-ly in November 1954 about 6,000 natives of Tonking were marooned for
some days in desperate straits on a sand bank in danger of being washed away by the tide.
Informed of this, the French rushed boats to bring them to safety. The Viet-Minh
then protested to the CIC (International Commission of Control) about the violation
of territorial waters and the Commission admitted that the authorities of the Democratic
Republic of Viet-Nam alone had authority over this territory!

to transfer to the southern zone became known only in November.[4] This time the Communists had recourse to a vast deployment of forces. They surrounded villages, deported the population and placed sentries in front of each house. As a result of complaints and desperate appeals which reached it from all parts, the Commission Internationale de Controle (CIC) sent mobile sections into different localities to conduct an enquiry. The members of the Commission however, armed only with International Law, were practically powerless in the face of the concerted obstruction of the Communist authorities. If, as happened most often, the CIC did not succeed in stopping the violation of the agreements, its reports served at least as a record.[5]

The dreadful significance of this enormous exodus of peasants, artisans and workers continued to worry the Communists. They pretended that there was no question of a spontaneous exodus, but that it was the result of pressure by the Catholic clergy on the consciences of the faithful, of fear of war and of the atom bomb or again of the promise of happiness held out by the " Diem clique " and the " American imperialists " in order to entice the people to the South.

---

[4] From September the CIC had recommended the two parties to give ample publicity to the right of free transfer which was almost unknown.

[5] The CIC did not show evidence of much energy. Each section, composed of a Polish, an Indian and a Canadian delegate, was expected to come to definite decisions but had neither coercive powers nor means of transport at its disposal.

It drew up four reports which were not published officially. The world press however published large extracts from them. In the fourth report, drawn up by the Canadian Commissioners, the " Minority Report " is significant. Cf. *Bulletin of the Canadian Catholic Conference* of December 1955.

Denouncing the " atmosphere of fear and suspicion " which prevented any efficacious enquiry, the Canadian Commissioners affirmed that " at Phat-Diem, Tra-ly, Ba-lang, Luu-my, Thuan-nghia and Tho-ninh there were good reasons for thinking that the local authorities had taken special measures before the investigation to prevent the discovery of certain facts and to prevent effective contact between those who wished to emigrate and the representatives of the International Commission . . . Soldiers and militia mounted guard in front of Catholic houses so as to prevent the occupants from leaving . . . meetings were organised at the time of arrival of the Commissioners . . . in other cases the refugees had been assembled at the Church which the Commissioners were advised not to enter, on the grounds that they would upset the ceremonies. Very often the clergy had been threatened and sometimes even imprisoned or put under house arrest . . . It happened frequently that the members of the Commission found themselves faced by organised groups of persons who presented protests concerning the ' compulsory emigration.' These noisy and disorderly demonstrations caused the Commissioners to lose much of the time at their disposal . . . "

Aside from the question of whether it was possible for " American " propaganda to have more success than that of the Marxists in a territory controlled exclusively by Communists, it is enough to recall, in the face of such gratuitous assertions, some known and established facts.

In ten months 860,000 persons passed from the North to the South, while in the same period there were not 5,000 persons prepared to make the journey in the opposite direction.

At the request of the Communists the CIC conducted an enquiry in the refugee camps of the South to find out whether anyone was being held there by force. In the camps inspected by the Commissioners 25,000 of the 121,000 emigrants were questioned individually. Not one of them asked to be allowed to return to the North. [6]

What explanation is there for this emigration, immense in its proportions?

That this movement was due to religious motives is shown by simple statistical data: of 860,000 refugees, 676,000 were Catholics. [7] They have not concealed from anyone that they fled in order to preserve their own faith and that of their children. The international press re-echoed this fact. Led by their parish priests whole parishes have faced a journey of some 1,250 miles in order to rebuild their parishes in the South around small new churches which they placed under the protection of the same holy Patron they had at home. [8] There is no question of course of excluding other social-economic motives, such as exorbitant taxes, the impossibility of carrying on a small business or a trade, confiscation of lands. Yet when all these factors are taken into account and when it is realised that the Capitalist population of Tonking did not number hundreds of thousands,

---

[6] Cf. *Bulletin of the Canadian Catholic Conference*, December 1955.

[7] Cf. *Les Refugiés du Nord-Viet-Nam*, Saigon, October 1955.

[8] " These are very fervent Catholics," wrote an eye witness. " They ask for very little, are never sorry for themselves and are satisfied with the most niggardly concessions. In the evenings they gather together in the precincts of the church and pray on their knees for an hour or two. They are the poorest of the poor and take with them their handful of possessions . . . " *L'Osservatore Romano*, 7-8 January 1955. Cf. also *Le Courier de Genève*, 25 January 1955; *Figaro* of 21 January 1955; *La Croix* of 1 February 1955; *L'Osservatore Romano* of 22 January and 13 February 1955.

it must be admitted that this " choice of liberty " on the scale of a plebiscite was made chiefly for religious motives.[9]

Religious Policy of the Government

This exodus of refugees, which had profound repercussions on the national and international plane, undoubtedly influenced also the *religious policy* of *Ho Chi- Minh's* Government.[10]

Before the armistice liberty of worship was recognised in the territories controlled by the Viet-Minh. On the official, legislative, or statutory level it was hard to find enactments discriminating exclusively against Catholics. There was nevertheless a *de facto* persecution. Several vicars apostolic, with more than a hundred priests and perhaps as many religious, had been imprisoned or put into concentration camps. The other members of the clergy had been virtually confined to their residences. A large part of Church property had been confiscated or " taken charge of " by parish committees, while the remainder was subjected to taxes which were so heavy that they amounted to confiscation. The clergy were treated as " exploiters " or as " rich proprietors " and were accused publicly in the people's assemblies convoked to " unmask re-actionaries." Catholic schools and seminaries, although officially open, found it practically impossible to continue by reason of the high taxes levied on them and the obligation imposed on them of adopting programmes inspired by Marxism.[11]

In 1945, out of a population of 22 millions, Viet-Nam counted little more than 2 million Catholics, that is about 10%. Of the 14 vicars apostolic, 3 (twelve years later, 9) were native born; while native priests were far more numerous than foreign missionaries (1,500 as compared with 400 French, Spanish and Canadian). Despite their small numbers in comparison with the total population, the Catholics formed a compact

[9] Ho Chi-Minh himself in his Christmas message of 1954 assured the people of Tonking who had emigrated to the South that the Communist authorities had taken great care of their homes and rice-fields, and awaited their return to the North. It was not then a question in this instance of rich landowners. Cf. *L'Osservatore Romano*, 13 February 1955.

[10] Ho Chi-Minh's attempt at appeasement with regard to Catholics is in itself proof that the exodus of people was due primarily to religious motives.

[11] Cf. *L'Osservatore Romano*, 19 May 1955.

group, united in the Faith and representing a great spiritual force. For this reason President *Ho Chi-Minh* was very careful in the early stages not to take measures against the Church. The country, galvanised by the desire for independence, closed its ranks around him, while yet showing no tendency to favour a Marxist form of government. There were even certain signs of interest in Catholicism. At every big religious solemnity President *Ho Chi-Minh* never failed to broadcast messages assuring Catholics of his solicitude for them. Nobody however had any illusions; a government directed by men trained in Moscow and in Communist China could not but translate sooner or later its atheistic doctrines into action. A first " tightening up " against the Church began to manifest itself in October 1946; a perfidious propaganda, backed by intimidating measures, was unleashed against the *Lien-Doan-Cong-Giao-Viet-Nam* (Viet-Nam Catholic Federation), accusing it of being an anti-national, foreign-inspired movement. When civil war broke out the Communists were able to give full scope to their anti-Catholic hatred. An open persecution was begun. All the security measures employed against suspected persons were applied to foreign missionaries, to native priests and to militant Catholics. Summary executions took place, and the entire religious life of the people was mercilessly controlled. Everything was done to discredit the priests and to prevent contact between them and the faithful. From this period date the well-known Viet-Minh concentration camps with their " re-education courses." [12]

After the armistice almost all the prisoners were released (in conformity with a clause in the armistice) and direct propaganda against the Church abated. There were even attempts, sometimes ridiculous, to win over the Catholics.[13] Great proclamations concerning " liberty of belief and worship " were made, crowned by the Resolution of the National Assembly, 26 March 1955, which contains these six points:

  1. Freedom of " belief and worship " as well as of religious teaching " in religious organisations "; freedom of the religious press

---

[12] See for particulars *Tabor*, pp. 306-313, an article by Fr. Joseph Vang.
[13] Cf. *L'Osservatore Romano*, 19 May 1955.

"within the framework of the laws of the Government of the Democratic Republic."

2. Recognition of civic rights and duties for all those who profess a religion; exemption from certain civic duties for ministers of worship so that they may attend to their pastoral duties.

3. "Respect for and protection" of places of worship.

4. "Protection" of the law for "organisations engaged in religious teaching."

5. In the application of agrarian reform, the granting to churches, pagodas and other places of worship, of rice-fields sufficient —in the judgment of the local population and of the authorities —" to provide for the maintenance of worship and the needs of the ministers of religion."

6. "Those will be punished who under the pretext of religion or priding themselves on their religious motives endanger peace, unity, independence and democracy; subvert the unity of the citizens; turn their adherents from the fulfilment of their civic duties; interfere with the liberty of thought of others, or commit other illegal acts." [14]

It is evident that these principles limit religious freedom to "freedom of belief and of worship." They permit people's organisations to fix the details for the maintenance of worship and of the clergy; they give the political and administrative authorities by paragraph 6 the right to revoke the above-mentioned freedoms under the pretext of "repressing abuses."

This Resolution of the Assembly was interpreted by the decree of President *Ho Chi-Minh* dated 14 June 1955.[15] Here are its more significant passages:

On the subject of freedom "to preach religion in the temples" it is stated clearly that "in the course of these sermons ministers of religion have the duty to teach the faithful love of their fatherland, the meaning of their civic obligations, respect for the people's authority, and for the law which obtains in the people's Republic of Viet-Nam" (article 1).

---

[14] Cf. *L'Osservatore Romano*, 19 May 1955.
[15] Cf. *Freedom of Belief in the Democratic Republic of Viet-Nam*, Hanoi (Edit. in foreign languages) 1955, pp. 18-23.

Religious schools " must follow the Government programme of instruction " (article 9).

The area of rice-fields or of land leased to the Churches " will be determined by the peasants in a democratic gathering sanctioned by the provincial authority " (article 10).

Ministers of religion " who own real estate, though not classified as rich owners, must nevertheless conform strictly to the agrarian policy of the Government " (article 11).

" Relations in religious matters between the Church in Viet-Nam and the Vatican are an internal matter for Catholicism," in which " the administrative authorities do not want to be involved " (article 13).

" Freedom of belief and freedom of worship " are rights of the people, and the authorities of the Democratic Republic respect them and help the people to exercise them (article 15).

Those who know the standard practice of People's Democracies will not be led by such pronouncements to harbour any illusions about the intentions of the régime: Catholic preaching and teaching are legal, but only in so far as they are in agreement with the propaganda of the Government which continues to declare itself atheistic; [16] exemptions regarding the confiscation of land are in theory granted to priests, but can be democratically revoked at any moment; relations with Rome are unhindered " in religious matters," but can be forbidden whenever a doubt arises concerning the " religious " character of the question discussed; finally article 15 gives the People's authorities the power of interfering in the internal life of the Church under the pretext of " helping " the faithful to exercise freedom of belief.

This last article is designed to favour the activities of " Catholic patriots " against the hierarchy of the Church. In fact a " Committee of Catholics loving their country and peace " was set up in Viet-Nam. This committee, which numbers scarcely ten priests and a few laymen, organises demonstrations " of loyalty to the Government," sends delegations to peace congresses,

---

[16] " The Party," writes the Communist journal of Hanoi, *Nhan Dan,* " believes absolutely in the scientific correctness of Marxism-Leninism." Cf. *L'Osservatore Romano* of 5 August 1955.

invites and receives " patriotic " delegations from other Communist countries, and sows suspicion of and inspires hatred towards those bishops and priests who have no part in it. The authorities grant facilities and protection to the Committee. While the vicars apostolic and parish priests are refused permission to move about their districts the " patriot priests " can come and go as they wish in Government vehicles under police protection.

Balance Sheet

Towards the end of 1955 the situation of the Church was approximately as follows. Still in their vicariates were Mgr. *Khue*, in Hanoi; Mgr. *Mazé* in Hung-Hoa; Mgr. *Duc* in Vinh; Mgr. *Hedde* and his Coadjutor Mgr. *Jacq* in Langson and Caobang; Mgr. *Tao*, Apostolic Administrator of the Vicariates of Haiphong and Bacninh. But over the whole of the country about twenty priests were imprisoned under various pretexts; others were under house arrest; all including the bishops laboured under the quasi-impossibility of leaving their residences, even in order to visit their flock in remote places. All missionary preaching was suppressed. Catechism lessons and divine services were thwarted by incessant village or workshop meetings held at the same time. The young people were held to far-away and ill-defined statute-labour. Practically all the Catholic schools were closed—the last secondary school of Hanoi having been taken over by infiltration of Communist professors and pupils. Catholic periodicals no longer existed.[17]

However the worst has undoubtedly yet to come. *Ho Chi-Minh* is hoping for the general elections which were promised to him by the Geneva Conference in order to " unite " the country. So long as he entertains this hope he does not exert extreme pressure.

---

[17] Cf. *L'Osservatore Romano* of 5 August and 13 August 1955.

Chapter 14

THE PERSECUTION OF THE CATHOLIC CHURCH

UNDER

Communist Rule in Yugoslavia

IN YUGOSLAVIA in contrast to what happened in the other satellite countries of the USSR the Communists during the Second World War, acting under the name of the Popular Liberation Front (*Osvobodilna Fronta*: OF), seized power from within the country. They were aided in a very decisive manner by the Allies to the detriment, it must be said, of the other groups also fighting against the forces of occupation. So from the end of 1945 no other satellite country, with perhaps the exception of Albania, was so thoroughly under Communist domination.

The National Army of Liberation (*Naroda Osvobodilna Vojska*: NOV) entered Zagreb on 8 May 1945. A coalition Government was formed immediately, having at its head Marshal *Tito*. Besides the Communists it was composed of members of the Yugoslav Government in exile in London, and national elements, members of the National anti-Fascist Council of Liberation of Yugoslavia (AVNOY). But a few months sufficed to show the true intentions of the Communist Party: to keep complete control, stifling—in blood if necessary—every attempt to establish a really democratic Government. When elections were held, staged according to the well-known Communist plan, the voting was *unanimous* in favour of Marshal *Tito* and the Republic (99.89%).[1]

---

[1] The *People's Federated Republic of Yugoslavia* was then proclaimed. It comprises six Federated Republics: Slovenia, Croatia (with Slavonia and Dalmatia), Bosnia-Herzegovina, Serbia (with Vojvodina), Montenegro and Macedonia.

In June 1948 Yugoslav Communism was denounced by the
Kominform. Having become the declared " enemy " of all the
countries owing obedience to the Soviets and especially of its
neighbours, *Tito's* régime sought from this time to obtain
favours from the Western Powers especially in economic and
military matters.

Whatever about the sincerity of this " reversing of alliances," [2]
it is a fact that there resulted from it no change in the hostile
attitude of the Government with regard to the Catholic Church.
Tito went so far as to make it known clearly after June 1948
that the régime *remained purely and integrally Communist*, faithful
in every way to Marxist theories. And experience has unfortunately proved that the People's Federated Republic of
Yugoslavia (PFRY) differed in no way in its anti-religious
character from the other " People's Democracies," no matter
what was said by official propaganda, or by Yugoslav Communist
diplomats to foreign countries or even by tourists returning
from visits to the country where they had been guests of the
régime. *Religious persecution there is inspired by the same principles
and follows the same methods as in all Communist countries.*

It is not easy to expose briefly and clearly the legislation with
regard to the Church in Yugoslavia; for in addition to the
Federal Laws we must take into account here the special laws
of the different Republics and remember that their application
varies from one Republic to another.

But better than all the legislative texts a summary table of
the situation of the clergy, of the press, of Catholic establishments, etc., will show in a clear light the situation of the Catholic
Church in Yugoslavia.

Liberty of Worship

The Constitution of the Yugoslav State, and those of the
Constituent Republics, formally recognise " liberty of conscience
and liberty of worship "; they demand " the separation of Church
and State "; they forbid " the abuse of the Church and of religion

---

[2] On 15 March 1952 Tito, receiving a group from the universities, stated : " We
have always stood firm in our position and we have granted no concessions either in our
internal or our external policy." Cf. *Borba* (Struggle) 16 March 1952.

for political ends "; they declare illegal " political organisations
with religious backgrounds "; they authorise religious communities " whose teachings are not opposed to the Constitution "
to exercise their religious functions and to celebrate their
religious rites. What follows shows the value in practice of these
constitutional guarantees.[3]

The expression " separation of Church and State " has quite
a different meaning under the People's Democracies from what
it has under the secular Governments of the West. By this phrase
must be understood the separation of the people themselves from
the Church and an inexorable war against the latter.[4]

In the same way " liberty of worship," does not at all mean in
Yugoslavia *liberty of religion*. This " liberty of worship " does not
guarantee to the Church the complete accomplishment of its
mission, such as the Christian education of youth, the preaching
of the Gospel, the social apostolate, works of charity, the
organisation of the hierarchy of the country, free intercourse
with the Holy See, etc.; it obtains only in the interior of the
church buildings which have not been destroyed or taken over
for secular use.[5]

---

[3] In all the proletarian dictatorships, in accordance with their constitutions, religion
is a private affair. But the *Party* cannot consider it as such, since it has the duty to fight
against " anti-scientific prejudices " by every means: propaganda, persuasion and if
necessary " elimination."

[4] See how clearly the President of the People's Assembly of Croatia Vicko Krstulovic
expressed himself in a meeting of the Communist Party held at Osijek: " The revolution
has enabled us to break the old middle class framework, to destroy the main foundations
of this middle class and to take over control of everything. But we cannot destroy the
Church as an institution. Not that our country or our government is lacking in power
to do so, but because in the conscience of many citizens, especially the peasants, there
still exist tenacious remnants of faith. We know that the Church as an institution
is nearing its end; our struggle against it must be in the political and cultural arenas,
enlightening the conscience of the people at the same time as we raise their standard
of living, so that they may come to understand better that the world did not develop
under the guidance of the Holy Spirit (*sic*), but according to the laws of Nature. We
must mobilise public opinion in the villages and in the towns against the destructive
work (of priests) . . . "
Cf. *Naprijed* (Forward), 1 June 1952, cited by *L'Osservatore Romano*, 6 December 1953.

[5] " . . . The Church should confine itself to what ought to be its only end, the
celebration of religious ceremonies, and on this point it enjoys full liberty in the eyes
of the State and in relation to other organisations, whether of a religious or an anti-
religious character. But liberty of religion does not merely signify liberty to practise
such and such a religion; it also allows the liberty of the ideological struggle against
religious mysticism and religious prejudices."
Cf. *Nedeljne informativne novine* (Weekly News), 4 May 1952.

Certainly the people come in crowds to the churches in which a priest is permitted to officiate. This fact often makes an impression on foreign tourists when they see it and leads them to draw false conclusions about " religious liberty " existing in the country. To get the right view one must read the *Memorandum*, drawn up for Marshal *Tito* by the Catholic bishops at a meeting held at Zagreb from 23 to 26 September 1952, presided over in the forced absence of Mgr. *Louis Stepinac* by the Archbishop of Belgrade, Mgr. *Joseph Ujcic*.[6]
This *Memorandum* states:

> " The Catholic bishops call attention to the fact that there exists in Yugoslavia no effective religious liberty; the liberty of conscience and the free exercise of religion of which the Constitution speaks in article 25 have been in practice reduced to a mere partial liberty of worship, or as the laws put it, to liberty of religious ceremonies."

The bishops speak of "mere partial liberty" because in certain spheres liberty of worship has been so circumscribed that it has in practice ceased to exist. This liberty of worship does not exclude for example the fact that

—the Section for National Defence (OZNA), in other words the Secret Police, lists the names of the faithful who frequent the churches;

—the accomplishment of their religious duties often becomes for the faithful whose names are on the list a source of serious difficulties, sometimes even of deliberate discrimination; before 1951 they could not obtain ration cards, and at the present moment they are deprived of employment, etc.;

—frequenting the church is rigorously forbidden to all military personnel or anyone wearing any kind of uniform whatsoever;

---

[6] This *Memorandum* was addressed to Marshal Tito, but was returned without comment to the Archbishop's Palace in Belgrade. When in December 1952 seven bishops were called to an interview by Marshal Tito, they presented to him personally this document which is of capital interest on the history of the relations between Church and State in the People's Federated Republic. The text can be found in *Une Eglise du silence*, *Catholiques de Yougoslavie*, Paris, 1954.

—liberty of *obstruction* and that of disparaging religion and its ministers are authorised even in the very churches; [7]

—all religious ceremonies are forbidden outside the churches; [8]

—the administration of the Sacraments to the sick in hospitals, to prisoners, and especially to those condemned to death is forbidden;

—sermons in the churches are strictly supervised by the police. This obliges the priest to take exasperating precautions. It is for him a torture to recognise in the congregation a police agent, sometimes ignorant and fanatical, sometimes living in the fear that he in his turn is being watched by a secret agent, and consequently obliged, whether he likes it or not, to denounce supposed " abuses in the pulpit." A sermon which prudently holds to the simple Catholic doctrine could be interpreted wrongly and considered as an invitation to sabotage, to struggle against the régime, to revolt; [9]

---

[7] On 27 September 1953 Tito condemned these excesses which were very many especially that year: " There was question," he said in substance, " of errors of tactics, for religion and the Church should be fought by other methods particularly by the ' education ' of the young people." The Marshal said among other things: " As you know, deplorable excesses under the form of acts of violence have been committed among us. These happened in certain places on account of the bitter and hostile policy of certain ecclesiastical leaders with regard to the present situation. The people were exasperated by it . . . We cannot take their part and we condemn such proceedings, for we possess much more efficacious arms in our struggle. . . . We do not desire acts of violence; we are opposed to them . . . We must make use of political means; it must be explained that our conquest has cost one million seven hundred thousand lives, and we cannot permit a few priests to dream of destroying it. Tell them that we cannot allow them to become the agents of foreign powers. The priest too must serve the people . . . enlighten the masses on political matters, fight for our young people, not with guns and fists, but on the contrary by organising them, by working with them." Cf. *Vjestnik* (News), 28 September 1953.

[8] Processions through public thoroughfares were authorised again in 1951 in certain Republics but only in principle, for in practice the excessive Government taxes to which they were subject, placed them out of reach. Moreover processions must not impede traffic. Wherever it had been possible to organise them they had been disturbed in all sorts of ways, even by loud whistles and jeering. On this question the *Memorandum* of the bishops stated: " Processions are forbidden in many regions. The important religious feasts, bringing together the faithful of different parishes, have been subjected to all sorts of annoyances. This is specially notable on the occasion of the ceremonies for a First Mass. The gifts which according to ancient custom are offered to the young priests have been confiscated by the ODB " (Administration of National Security), that is to say the NKVD of Yugoslavia).

[9] The *Oslobodjenje*, 8 March 1952, accused priests of abusing the democratic liberty which reigned in Yugoslavia because they dared to say that " Christ was a workman and also the Apostles," and for having upheld the existence of God. By doing this they were said to have incited their parishioners to religious intolerance. The parish priest *of*

—the press seizes every opportunity to attack religion, the Catholic Church and especially the Holy See.

On this last point innumerable examples could be cited. For consistency and vulgarity it would be difficult to find anything in any of the other Communist-controlled countries to equal the insults of the Yugoslav Government and Communist press. The Holy Year was described as " a huge financial ramp "; the Vatican was called " the representative of Italian Imperialism," the " age-old enemy of our people," " the home of re-action," a " shameless calumniator," etc. A book was published by the Serbian, *Mihajlo Petrovic*, entitled *The Vatican and the Imperialist Policy of the Reactionary Western Powers* (Belgrade, 1947).[10] The State radio for its part broadcast a stupid " travesty " of the *Pater Noster*. It gave great publicity to blasphemous " litanies " of the Blessed Virgin. The cinemas showed as documentary films the most detestable falsehoods called " crimes of the clergy."

The Note of the Vatican Secretariate of State to the Minister for Foreign Affairs of the PFRY, dated 15 December 1952,[11] cited some examples taken from the *more recent* events, and

---

Crikvenica on 14 October 1951 took as the text of his sermon the Gospel of the Sunday: " Render to Caesar the things that are Caesar's and to God the things that are God's." He was attacked at great length in the *Vjestnik*, 18 October: " The priest, respecting the sense of the passage of the Gospel, had indeed exalted the love of country, but," said the paper, " the exhortation was tendentious, for in the second part of his sermon he had specified the limits of obedience to the laws of the State, putting in the first place God and the Divine Laws." For the city of Djakovo, residence of the Bishop of Srijem, a list of subjects was drawn up, about which priests were forbidden to preach under penalty of being arrested : atheism, the sacrament of marriage and its indissolubility, the fifth commandment, the patience of Job, the *non est pax impiis*, etc. To speak of the Papacy from the pulpit was in certain districts to undermine the unity of the people and the State; to speak of " wolves in sheep's clothing " was attacking the régime. Several priests were condemned to three or six months in prison for having treated of these forbidden subjects.

We read in the *Memorandum*: " Freedom of preaching is also threatened. Priests are accused for having quoted Holy Scripture. Positive explanations of the truths of Faith are considered as attacks on the security of the State and on the new social order. It was even forbidden to priests to speak to the children in Catechism class against atheistic propaganda. ' Priests,' says a direction issued by the local People's authority of Bosnia Herzegovina, ' must not exercise any influence over parents to prevent their children from becoming atheists.' It was even demanded of one priest that he should advise the people not to come to church any longer."

[10] Cf. also the pamphlet : *Tajni Dokumenti o odnosima Vatikana i Ustaka NDH*, Zagreb, Ognjen Prica, p. 144, also the documented refutation of this text in *La Civiltà Cattolica*, 1952, IV, pp. 428-435.

[11] Published in *L'Osservatore Romano*, 14 January 1953.

concerning only Croatia and Slovenia, where the great majority of the population was Catholic:

(a) On 9 February 1952 the *Slovenski Porocevalec* (Slovenian Messenger) of Ljubljana published a circular addressed to the different sections of the Communist Party of Slovenia : " During the school year it is necessary to help young people to understand by the aid of arguments based on science the negative and re-actionary influence of religion and of obscurantism . . . " This circular carried among others the signature of *Edward Kardelj*, Vice-President of the Council of Ministers and Yugoslav Minister for Foreign Affairs, and also that of *Boris Kidric*, President of the Economic Council of the Central Government.

(b) The *Vjestnik* of 20 April 1952 reported the following statement of Doctor *Milos Zanko*, Minister-President of the Council for Civilisation and Culture of the People's Republic of Croatia: " Whoever thinks that in virtue of the liberty of conscience guaranteed by the Constitution he can introduce aims in education opposed (to Marxism) does not fulfil his duty as an educator; it is just as if he were to teach that $2 + 2 = 7$."

(c) At Belgrade *Borba* (Struggle) of 7 November 1952 reported that *Alexander Rankovic*, Minister for the Interior, speaking at the Sixth Congress of the Yugoslav Communist Party, had underlined the necessity of a " fight, resolute, obstinate and incessant against the manifestations and ideas of the middle class, of the clergy and of the Kominformists."

(d) The *Vjestnik* of Zagreb of 9 November 1952 explained the way in which this struggle was to be understood in an article by the academician, *Marko Kostrencic*, well-known propagandist of Communist ideas : " The morality of Christ must be rejected because it is unworthy of man, and it condemns him to a life of negation. Christian morality urges you to cruelty on a grand scale. Socialist morality draws its inspiration from the Marxist conception of the world; it denies the existence of another and better world, of a transcendent celestial kingdom, with all its supernatural terrors and its consolations, mounting from Satan, the spirits, and the saints up to god (*sic*) and to gods of all descriptions. This conception of the world has killed god (*sic*) as well as all the gods. For only the visible, material world exists . . . "

(e) Other *official* declarations of the Communist Party are in accordance with these statements. *Nova Makedonija* of Skoplje of 2 March 1952 affirmed: " Our Party has never been indifferent with regard to religious ideology and the Church, but to-day we must organise an ideological, systematic and daily struggle, by means of the press, of mass organisations and of cultural institutes, in order to destroy all religious concepts of the universe, all prejudices, all religious traditions . . . "

(f) In the same strain *Borba* of Belgrade of 1 March 1952, reporting the conclusions of the Fifth Plenary Session of the Central Committee of Macedonia, wrote: " The ideological work of the Party with regard to our workmen consists in the effort to withdraw them from the influence of religion and of mysticism . . . "

(g) At Sarajevo the newspaper *Oslobodjenje* of 13 September 1952 reported that during the course of a meeting of the Communist Party held at Foca and at Kiseljak it was deplored that some members of the Party " thought they were permitted to perform their religious duties, on the grounds that this was guaranteed by the Constitution of our country and by law to all citizens, forgetting that members of the Party ought to be in the vanguard of progress, and the first to fight against superstition,' primitivism,' and all the remnants of re-action."

(h) At Ljubljana *Slovenski Porocevalec* of 13 September, giving an account of the meeting of the Communist Party held at Notranje Gorice, wrote: " Speeches were made about the necessity for the struggle against religious obscurantist prejudices and above all against the clergy who keep them alive . . . "

(i) *Ljudska Pravica*, the organ of the Slovene Communist Party, stated clearly on 16 February 1952 that " a Communist is not free to go to Church, to assist at religious ceremonies, to contract marriage before a priest, to have his own children baptised. For the Communist religion is the opium of the people . . . "

These few citations, *which are only a specimen* of the numerous anti-religious statements which flooded the daily press, are in complete accord with the statutes of " The Union of Communists of Yugoslavia." These declare: "The mere fact of belonging to the Union of Communists of Yugoslavia is incompatible with the profession of religion and the practice of religious rites . . . "

Besides, Marshal *Tito* himself in an address to the representatives of the Congress of the Associations of Professors, Teachers and Masters of Yugoslavia, declared, as was reported in *Borba* of 30 April: "I know that in foreign countries they reproach us with withdrawing young people from god (*sic*) and from the Church. But we cannot tolerate that these men practise superstition, and all that is but superstition. We must fight against superstition."

About a year after the rupture between *Tito* and the Kominform some signs of easing off in the struggle against religion could be noticed as well as care on the part of the Government to avoid any serious new conflicts with the Church. In truth the persecutions did not cease, no amends were made for the injuries done to the Church, and the liberties which had been suppressed were not restored. Nevertheless the régime began to be careful—without much success however—not to give the Church new reasons for complaint. But as there was no ideological change in the relations between the State and the Church, there was no guarantee that these tactical concessions would be respected or that they would be applied without discrimination. In fact Communism in Yugoslavia continued to pursue its main objective: the application of the law of dialectic Materialism to every way of life, including religion.[12]

Among these "easing-off" gestures made for "propaganda" purposes the following may be noted:

In 1949 the printing of a prayer book and catechism was authorised for the first time since 1945, but the number of copies was strictly limited. In 1950-51 the nomination of six new bishops was permitted; priests who till then had been excluded from their parishes were now allowed to take charge of them; repairs to certain churches and parochial residences

---

[12] On this see the report presented by the theorist of Yugoslav Communism, Milovan Djilas, at the Eleventh Plenary Session of the Central Committee of the Yugoslav Communist Party in *Kommunist*, a. 4, n. 1 (1950).

were authorised; in a limited measure the seminaries which had not been suppressed were allowed to seek funds from abroad for their upkeep; the faculty of Theology of Zagreb was again allowed to confer academic degrees.[13] On 1 January 1951 an amnesty was granted to 11,000 prisoners including some priests; in certain localities the nuns could live again in community (the civil authorities closed their eyes to this move) and could unobtrusively appear in the streets in their religious habits; in Bosnia-Herzegovina, and especially at Sarajevo, a few convents were restored to the nuns. In other places the giving of religious instruction was not opposed as openly as in the past, and a few catechists were authorised to teach in the schools.

Marshal *Tito* also tried to solve the case of Mgr. *Stepinac* by offering the Holy See to set him free if he would go into voluntary exile.[14] This step having failed, on 5 December 1951 the sentence of imprisonment on Mgr. *Stepinac* was commuted to " conditional liberty." [15]

All this merely proved *that the persecution, from being " virulent " which it had been till then, was entering into a " quieter " phase, and that the authorities were counting on the time factor to do its work.* To induce the people to abandon the Faith continued to be the immediate objective of Communism in Yugoslavia; but for the future it sought above all to strike at the pastor in order to disperse the flock and it accentuated the work of the " indoctrination " of youth.[16]

In the course of the first four years of their Government the

---

[13] A decree dated 29 January 1952, over the signature of the President of the Government of the PFR of Croatia, suppressed the faculty of Theology of the University of Zagreb. A few days after, the Government of the PFR of Slovenia passed a similar measure against the faculty of Theology of the University of Ljubljana. The suppression of the title of *State faculty* brought with it automatically the suppression of a subsidy. But in fact the State continued its subsidy to this second faculty of Theology, because its doyen, Dr. Stanko Cajnkar, and some of the other professors were the leading figures of the " People's Priests " of the Ciril-Metodijsko-Drustvo (CMD). The Communists boasted freely of this help given by them to a faculty of Theology. In reality their tactics were evident: the existence of these faculties, without any private means of support, must depend on Government subsidies, and these would not be forthcoming except under definite conditions, which meant an absolute control of the teaching in the direction of Communist social progress.

[14] Cf. *L'Osservatore Romano*, 9-10 July 1951.

[15] Cf. *L'Osservatore Romano*, 7 December 1951.

[16] See *La Civiltà Cattolica*, 1950, I, pp. 581-592.

Communists had, so to speak, tied the hands of the Catholic Church by innumerable decrees: the press suppressed, social institutions liquidated, the material situation of the clergy more and more compromised, priestly ministry interfered with in a thousand ways, every obstacle raised to prevent the practice of religion by the citizens, and finally, a number of priests and faithful imprisoned and put to death. From 1949, not being able to add anything further to these measures, they confined themselves in this new phase to keeping in force the legislation against religion and the Church while at the same time striving by a methodical campaign to de-christianise the soul of the people and especially to detach the young people from God and from religion.[17]   *To the " destructive " phase of the first years there now succeeded the " anti-religious constructive phase."* [18]

---

[17] Of all the synchronised campaigns against religion which abound in the history of the persecution in Yugoslavia the one which started in the beginning of 1952 may be cited as typical. The radio and the press—especially that devoted to the young people—gave the signal for a systematic course of propaganda against all forms of religion, which was presented as an invention of capitalism for the exploitation of man, as an irrational mysticism, as a ridiculous superstition, as a monument of obscurantism; this propaganda spoke in shameful terms of prayer, of the sacraments, of miracles, of Christian " mythology," of the faults of the Church. *Oslobodjenje*, organ of the Popular Front of Bosnia-Herzegovina, began the attack in its editions of 29 and 30 January. This was followed in the first days of February by *Pobjeda* (Victory) of Cetinje, organ of the Popular Front of Montenegro, by *Naprijed* (Forward), a weekly paper of the Communist Party in Croatia (of 8 and 15 February), by *Ljudska Pravica* (The People's Right), organ of the Communist Party of Slovenia (of 16 February), and in the first days of March by the *Nova Makedonija* (New Macedonia), organ of the Popular Front in Macedonia. The following also joined the chorus: the *Knjizevni novine* (Literary Journal) and the *Trideset Dana* (The Thirty Days) of Belgrade, the *Voce del Popolo* (Voice of the People) of Fiume, and the *Svobodna Dalmacija* (Free Dalmatia) of Split. It was not by pure chance, notes Cavalli in *La Civiltà Cattolica* (1952, II, 135-149), that the duty of leading this campaign was confided to newspapers almost completely unknown outside Yugoslavia; the idea was to reach the people without attracting the attention of the western world which was meant to believe that the religious strife was nothing but a legend fabricated by the Vatican. In substance all these papers only paraphrased what had been expressed very clearly by M. Kangrga in the *Naprijed*, mentioned above: " Religion is the greatest depravation of man." It must be fought by every means. *And several times during the year in different parts of the country* campaigns of this kind were inaugurated.

They increased considerably in the course of the months of April and May 1952. See for example: *Politika* of Belgrade, on 5 and 21 May; *Nedeljne Informativne Novine* also of Belgrade, 4 May; *Republika* also of Belgrade, 6 May; *Vjestnik* of Zagreb, 9 and 18 May; *Partiski radnik* (The Party Worker), organ of the Communist Party in Serbia, 15 May; *Borba* (The Struggle) of Belgrade, 27 May; *Slovenski porocevalec* (The Messenger of Slovenia), of Ljubljana, 11 May.

[18] Marshal Tito had no hesitation in affirming at Mostar on 14 September 1951: " Yugoslavia is not a country which tries to annihilate religion by the aid of decrees; religion as a private affair cannot be destroyed by administrative means." To priests

In 1952 after another turn of the screw aimed at paralysing economically the Catholic Church the régime attempted to force the clergy to accept its persecuting decrees, and even more to join in applauding the Government. Religious liberty had already become a mere possibility of holding well supervised ceremonies; now a " spontaneous " movement of acceptance of the régime was inaugurated among the clergy.

The Catholic Press

The hunt for Catholic books began in Yugoslavia, as *Tito's* troops " liberated " towns and villages.   Bookshops, Catholic printing presses, prayer books, books of devotion, artistic as well as popular editions,[19] were systematically destroyed;   even antique shops were not spared.   Pictures, crucifixes and all religious objects were confiscated.

The confiscation of printing houses was legalised by condemning as " collaborators " *all the Catholic directors and editors.*[20]

With regard to the Catholic press Yugoslavia showed itself more intransigent than any of the other countries professing Marxist doctrines. With one blow *the Catholic press was completely wiped out* by an ordinance which required Government authorisation for all publications.   Under various pretexts authorisation was refused for several publications, while other requests did not even receive a reply.   In Croatia for example in 1939 the Catholic press printed 700,000 copies every month.   Now only two or three Catholic pamphlets continued to appear under miserable conditions, with a much reduced production and constantly censored; but the OZNA never ceased creating difficulties.   The State was the only supplier of printing paper and refused it to the Catholic press.

From 20 September 1945 the bishops could state undeniably:

he had said: " You are permitted to occupy yourselves with religious affairs, but on the other hand you should not meddle with political affairs and must not propagate religious fanaticism."   These two phrases simply mean that it was forbidden to priests to offer the least resistance to the powerful means used to spread atheism.   Cf. *Borba*, 15 September 1951.

[19] The Communists went so far as to declare war even on Latin grammars through hatred of Rome, " the age-long enemy."

[20] Cf. *La Civiltà Cattolica*, 1947, II, pp. 561-572.

" To-day there remains not one newspaper of the hundreds (in Croatia and Slovenia) which existed before the war."

Ten years after these first measures the situation could be summed up thus :

Before the installation of the Communist régime there were in Yugoslavia 152 Catholic periodicals (dailies, weeklies, reviews and bulletins etc.). These numerous publications required a proportional number of publishing houses and printing presses; 24 of these were particularly important. At the moment *all Catholic printing and publishing houses* are in the hands of the State. Almost all Catholic publications—from daily papers to parish bulletins—have been suppressed in one way or another. For some time with a very limited issue certain papers survived, as the *Verski List* (Religious Journal) of Maribor, *Oznanilo* (Gospel) of Ljubljana, *Gore srca* (Sursum Corda) of Zagreb. These three papers, one after the other, had to cease publication.[21] It was the same with the monthly review of Belgrade, *Blagovest*. In 1955, the Catholic press was represented only by a monthly bulletin for clergy entitled *Vjestnik*,[22] published under great difficulties at Djakovo, and by the review *Druzina* (The Family) of Nova Gorica, which appeared twice a month on eight pages demy-format.[23] These Catholic periodicals would evidently be confiscated immediately if they attempted to reply to the calumnies and blasphemies systematically published by the Communist press.

It was practically impossible to print any book of a religious character in Yugoslavia.[24] In Slovenia the only religious book

---

[21] For example *Oznanilo* could in the beginning appear *only once a week*, made up of four pages on *very bad paper*. Then it was authorised to appear only every two weeks, made up of two pages demy-format. Only 30,000 copies were allowed, when it could sell 500,000. Since 1952 it has had to cease publication.

[22] This Catholic Bulletin for the clergy must not be confounded with other publications having the same title (meaning: News) and in particular with the periodical published by the Association of Saints Cyril and Methodius.

[23] The Apostolic Administration of Nova Gorica is the proprietor of this review, but it is interesting to note that the editing is done at Ljubljana at the office of the Co-operative of " the People's Priests," members of the CMD.

[24] This is the truth. But that did not prevent Marshal Tito from declaring on 31 August 1951 to some foreign journalists: " The Churches in this country have their newspapers, print brochures and books. Perhaps *they do not publish as many as formerly*, because we have to buy paper at a very high price. However they have their own papers, books and pamphlets, as well as their own schools where they educate their priests."

that could be reprinted was the New Testament (only 10,000 copies), edited by the Society of St. Ermagora of Celje.

Finally it must be mentioned that priests belonging to the Association of Saints Cyril and Methodius (CMD), protected by the Communist Government, have one periodical *Nova Pot* (New Life); this is just a propaganda sheet at the service of Government policy, and besides it contains nothing of a religious character. On a par with it is the *Organizacijski Vjestnik*, a political paper of the régime for the Catholic clergy.

Educational Establishments

From the moment it took over power the Communist Government determined before all else to establish a " new " school system, that is to say, a system that was to make everything that recalled the past disappear from the school. Educational establishments were ordered to spread Marxist theories, and for that purpose the Party sought as professors men who were ardent revolutionaries rather than competent teachers.

Article 38 of the Constitution of 31 January 1946 [25] lays down:

" The schools belong to the State. The Law alone can authorise the opening of private schools, but they remain under the control of the State. Primary education is free of charge and compulsory. The school is separated from the Church."

As the school belongs to the State, it is the latter which makes the " regulations " for the education of the pupils. Before everything else the school must tend to bring up the pupil as a socialist citizen steeped in materialist principles " the study of which permits teachers to form in their pupils a sound outlook on the world, which withdraws them from the influence of the clergy and the diverse ideological theories of the middle classes." [26]

---

[25] This article has remained unchanged in the new Constitution passed on 13 January 1953.

[26] Thus Milovan Djilas, one of the principal theorists of the Communists of Yugoslavia in " L'Ecole nouvelle, discussions sur les problèmes de l'école." Vol. II, p. 7, 1950.— At the Fourth Congress of the Party Tito, after complaining of the results of the socialist education among university students, thus traced the programme for future work:

In these conditions it is not surprising that all religious teaching, especially the teaching of the Catholic religion, is banished from such schools.

In Bosnia-Herzegovina, where the Catholics were one third of the population, the authorities attacked the teaching of religion even in the churches, arguing that these churches were thereby transformed " unconstitutionally " into private schools. The same thing happened in Montenegro.

A decree of the Slovene Republic of 31 July 1951 displayed the same severity.

In Croatia, where the majority of the population was Catholic, the local authorities in the small towns allowed the priests to give instruction in the schools, but outside the ordinary school hours and only if the parents asked for it in writing. But by decree of 31 January 1952 the Council for Education and Culture of the People's Republic of Croatia suppressed all religious teaching in the schools. It was also forbidden by the decree to gather children of school age in offices or parish halls, or even in private apartments, in order to teach them catechism or to undertake any work of instruction or education.

In some districts where the teaching of Christian Doctrine in the public schools is theoretically recognised by law, the situation is far from satisfactory. First of all religion can be taught only in the primary schools and in the lower classes of the secondary schools. In the first four years of primary education it is for the parents to decide whether their child ought or ought not to receive religious instruction; on the other hand, in the higher classes of the primary schools, it is for the pupils themselves to decide. Such " liberty " is in reality but a bitter farce, invented by the Communist Party to make people believe there is liberty of religion in Yugoslavia. In practice every possible and imaginable obstacle is raised by official organisations to prevent parents from asking for religious instruction for their children and also to induce the children not to ask for it either.

" To take the necessary measures for the formation of the young in the secondary schools, in order that these young people may become, in the more or less distant future, the true socialist ' intelligentsia.' The quicker we set to work the sooner shall we withdraw our ' intelligentsia ' from the influence of various foreign ideas, and the sooner shall we have a sure support to bring to success the building of the new society."

Usually the time for receiving these requests is limited to a single day at the expiry of which none is considered. The requests themselves are subjected to an extremely rigorous examination and the slightest error in form is sufficient to render them null.[27] The school authorities do everything possible to render this concession useless. Often they even advise the children to leave school before the hour for catechism, or they organise, during the hour reserved for the teaching of religion, walks and games. Generally the catechism lesson is fixed for the last hour, so that in the schools that have afternoon classes it cannot be held at all, the hour being too late to allow the children to reach their homes before nightfall. On the other hand in the schools which have class only in the morning the lessons on religion are fixed for the afternoon, to compel the children to make additional long journeys to assist at them.

As for the priests who desire to be authorised to teach Christian Doctrine, they must furnish three copies of their requests, one for the local Communist Committee, the second for the Committee of the district, the third for the provincial Committee. After interminable bureaucratic delays, even when the authorisation is granted, the priest can give instruction for only one hour a week for a maximum of three months of the school year. In a word it is possible to teach religion only for a maximum of eight or ten hours each year.

In Croatia for example, during the school year 1949-50, out of about 350,000 pupils scarcely 30,000 received any religious instruction, and that only in a superficial way. This instruction was rendered still more difficult by the complete lack of suitable books.

In order to remedy these deficiencies the priests sought to give lessons in the churches, but the Communist Government intervened immediately.

---

[27] In general things happened like this: at the beginning of the school year the master announced to the pupils that on the following day the parents who desired their children to receive instruction in Christian Doctrine must present their requests in writing. He usually added: " We will see to-morrow who are the re-actionary parents who wish their children to listen to the nonsense of the priests, and also who are those among you who are so stupid as to waste their time at catechism lessons. Those who do not assist at the lessons on religion may play football or go for a walk."

As for the houses of Catholic education, these had been in a flourishing condition, but they were decimated. The nuns alone had 65 secondary schools with 5,044 students, and 86 primary schools with 16,405 pupils, 142 kindergartens with 8,296 children, 41 boarding schools with 2,378 students. But of all these not one remains; in the same way 11 colleges conducted by religious orders of men were closed. The buildings were taken over and used by the Communists for their own needs.

The Note of the Vatican Secretariate of State of 15 December 1952 thus sums up the situation:

" All the Catholic educational institutions, which numbered hundreds with tens of thousands of pupils, have been closed. In all the State schools from the lowest to the highest religious instruction has been eliminated and the teaching of atheistic Materialism is obligatory. Many teachers who would not teach or would not practise Atheism were dismissed, and many pupils accused of going to church were not allowed to attend school." 28

For its part the *Memorandum* of the bishops of Yugoslavia to Marshal *Tito* in 1952 with regard to *religious instruction* declared:

" Priests have been forbidden to give religious instruction not only in the schools, but also in private houses, and even in the

---

28 Some extracts from Communist publications will suffice to confirm what has just been said.

Very many pupils were expelled from secondary schools for *religious faults*, that is to say, for having been absent from class on the Feast Days of Christmas time. Cf. *Vjestnik*, 22 February 1952.

In June 1951 the National Congress of Teachers in the primary and secondary schools decided to intensify the struggle against " religious prejudices and mysticism." Cf. *Politika*, 12 July 1951.

The school books, even those in the hands of the pupils of the primary schools, speak with contempt of this " means of mystification which is religion." Cf. *Testo di storia per le scuole elementari per l'anno scolastico 1950* (Italian edition), pp. 17-18, Tipografia cittadina, Pola.

Countless are the articles which demand that " clerical education " be eliminated and that " care must be taken of the purity " of instruction in the schools. Cf. *Vjestnik*, 25 April 1952. This can be seen, for example, in *Nasi Razgledi* (Our Horizons), 31 October 1952 (article on *Moral Education*, by Marika Dekleva); *Rijeski List*, 20 February 1952; *Zasavski Vjestnik*, 3 April 1952; *Slovenski porocevalec*, 22 February and 2 April 1952. Also see the documentary articles of Cavalli which appeared in *La Civiltà Cattolica* in 1952 (II, pp. 135-149) and 1953 (IV, pp. 135-150; 531-546; 627-639).

Borba of 10 March 1952 attacked a schoolmaster because he attended church, and asked how could it be possible for one who practised religion to teach properly Marxism, the origin of man, etc.

churches. There are numbers of cases where the priests were forbidden to instruct children in the churches. Even their preparation for First Communion was forbidden. For having disobeyed these prohibitions priests have been harassed, fined and condemned to prison."

On the subject of the *Catholic Educational Institutions* it stated:

" We are compelled to mention the liquidation of all the Catholic schools throughout the whole territory of our Republic. A whole series of our secondary schools, both classical and commercial, of our training colleges for teachers, of our schools of arts and crafts, of our primary schools, and even of our infant and kindergarten schools, has been suppressed with one stroke of the pen. The buildings have been confiscated."

Seminaries and Religious Institutions

The functioning and existence of the seminaries, indispensable for the proper formation of the clergy, meet with many difficulties. Many seminaries have been closed; the buildings of some others which are still open, such as those at Zagreb, and Ljubljana, have in part been occupied. The seminaries that still exist are subjected to constant annoyances and they have to struggle against serious economic difficulties on account of the confiscation of Church funds and of the almost complete impossibility of receiving any gifts from the faithful of the country (either in money or in kind) or help from Catholics abroad.

Because the buildings had been occupied or confiscated the junior seminaries of Maribor, Ljubljana, Senj, Skoplje (Prizren), Subotica, Sarajevo (at Travnik) had to close their doors. In all Slovenia there is but one junior seminary; the boarding school opened at Vipava in the Apostolic Administration of Nova Gorica [29] cannot be classed as a junior seminary. Neither are there any junior seminaries in Montenegro, Bosnia-Herzegovina, Vojvodina and Macedonia. As for Croatia the Minister President of the Council for Civilisation and Culture, *Milos Zanko*, ordered by a circular of 31 January 1952 that all young boys under 15

---

[29] This boarding school was occupied in October 1953 at the time of the tension between Italy and Yugoslavia.

years of age attend the State schools where, everyone knows, Marxist doctrines are taught. In this way the junior seminaries can have no pupils in the first four classes of the secondary school.[30]

To sum up: of the 18 junior and senior seminaries in which the secular clergy were educated, there remained only 9. To these no boys under 15 could be admitted; that meant that they had to spend eight years in the official schools, veritable " seminaries " of Atheism.[31]

The number of seminaries was subsequently reduced by the suppression in 1955 of the junior seminary of Rijeka (Fiume) and in 1956 of the theological seminary of Split, closed for eight years by sentence of the Tribunal.[32] At the end of August 1956 the senior seminaries of Yugoslavia were reduced to 4 in number: Zagreb, Ljubljana, Djakovo, Krizevci.

The religious orders had 20 novitiates, 22 apostolic schools, 11 colleges and 9 theological colleges. Of these only 9 houses (novitiates and apostolic schools) remain.

A sentence pronounced by the Tribunal of Split ordered in August 1956 the closing for 5 years of the Episcopal High School and of the Franciscan High School of that city.[33]

Catholic Associations and Charitable Works

From the first days of the new régime a Government decree forbade any meeting which had not been authorised. This decree applied even to choir practices in church. The bishops themselves decided on the suppression of Catholic associations when they learned that OZNA were ordered to make out lists of the members.

---

[30] See the Note from the Vatican Secretariate of State of 15 December 1952, already quoted.

[31] With regard to Atheism in Yugoslavia the *Memorandum* to Marshal Tito stated: " There is also the sad question of the official teaching of Atheism in the schools and in public life in Yugoslavia. Atheism is the religion of the régime. It is propagated in all the schools of the State, by conferences, and by the press, and it is imposed on all functionaries and in the army. It is formally forbidden to teachers and professors of the High Schools to attend church; those who disobey this ruling are dismissed. *To belong to the Catholic religion is considered the gravest fault for a functionary.* The officers of the Yugoslav Army are denied the liberty of having their children baptised.

[32] Cf. *Politika*, 2 August 1956.

[33] Cf. *Politika*, 2 August 1956.

Many of the directors of Catholic Action were dismissed from their positions in the Administration or retired without pension. Some were arrested at the same time as their chaplains, others had to pay fines, others still were condemned to forced labour or to prison, and a number had all their property confiscated.

The charitable institutions also felt the heavy hand of Communist totalitarianism which tolerated neither opposition nor rivalry in any field whatsoever. To-day there does not exist one single orphanage or home for old people conducted by Catholics; about one hundred institutions of this kind have been suppressed, and the people they took care of, more than 5,000, have been either expelled or taken care of by Communist Commissars. To justify in the eyes of public opinion this inhuman treatment of so many unfortunate people the Communists launched a campaign of calumny against the Catholic charitable institutions.[34]

The purely religious associations like the Third Orders, the Sodalities of Our Lady and the Confraternities of the Blessed Sacrament, met with innumerable difficulties if, as in some places, they were not forthwith dissolved.

Places of Worship

In the *Memorandum* of the bishops presented to Marshal *Tito* in December 1952 it is stated:

> " The churches, it is true, are still open. But many of them, as for example the church of the Trappists at Delibasinoselo near Banja Luka, have been used for some time as granaries and as sheds for agricultural machinery in spite of their artistic value. The magnificent church of St. Joseph at Ljubljana, a jewel of religious art, was simply taken from the Catholics and handed over to the sect of Old Catholics who in fact are very few in number in this city.[35]
>
> " Along the roads many crucifixes and images of the saints have

---

[34] In this strain were the infamous caricatures of the nuns of Ljubljana which depicted them as gaolers of the babies entrusted to their care; some nuns were accused of ill-treating them and of allowing the children of partisans to die of hunger; other charges were that orphans were compelled to become priests, etc.

[35] Since then it has been transformed into a cinema studio.

been taken away and it has not been possible to discover the authors of these profanations. In Slovenia and in other parts of the country similar profanations took place in many chapels. In November 1949 the grand and beautiful church of the Holy Saviour in Rijeka (Fiume) was destroyed by a mine during the night, though it was situated right in the centre of the city. In the same manner were also wrecked the church of the Carmelites at Selo, near Ljubljana, and the very beautiful chapel built on a hill called " Mount Calvary " near Rijeka. According to information received *several Catholic churches of Banat* have suffered the same fate. In different parts of the country many public churches served by members of religious congregations were closed by force. The church of the Blessed Virgin of Ptujska Gora, which was the church of the greatest pilgrimages in the diocese of Maribor, was seized and converted into a museum in spite of the protests of the ecclesiastical authorities.

" The civil authorities *grant no authorisation for the building of new churches.* [36] Besides it is very difficult to obtain permission for any work of *restoration of the old churches.*"

The Government moreover continued the confiscation of monasteries, religious schools, Catholic institutions, etc., handing them over for secular use. In such cases it was the custom to allow the clergy or religious only one or two rooms—and that only temporarily—while the remainder of the building was occupied by police bureaux and the offices of Communist organisations. In Bosnia and in Herzegovina the confiscation of ecclesiastical buildings was more thorough.

From what is known of these confiscations there is no doubt that the loss suffered by the Church amounts to a very considerable sum. This mode of attack on the Church had as its aim to paralyse practically all its activities.

With regard to the parish archives the *Memorandum* already quoted states:

" The registers of births, deaths and marriages were taken from the churches in 1946. Since then the Government Bureaux have reserved to themselves the right to control the new registers

---

[36] At Osiek, Biroljic near Simj, at Novo Selo near Rakovica, and in many other places, this authorisation was refused.

established since 9 May 1946. The old registers have never been given back to the churches, in spite of the promise to hand them back at latest in 1951."

The Persecution of the Priests and the Hierarchy

In the beginning the Government tried to obtain the " collaboration " of the clergy; officially, it was said, this was to remove any obstacles which might render it more difficult for the two parties to accomplish their double duty, religious and national; but in reality the idea was to make use of the clergy to strengthen the régime.

It is well known that divisions among the clergy favour the designs of the Communist authorities. That is why in Yugoslavia the Communists have always tried, and are still trying, to bring about a separation between the " higher " and the " lower " clergy, or to speak in terms of the struggle of the classes, between the " exploiters " and the " exploited."

But having come up against the unanimous resistance of the clergy, the Party quickly adopted other measures.

The first was that of propaganda. The Communists tried to persuade the people that the resistance of the clergy to the régime was inspired by no reasons other than those of a material order; in particular the Church, being a capitalist organisation, would oppose agrarian reform with all its strength.[37]

Then recourse was had to various measures against the clergy. In many parts of the country priests were deprived of ration cards for food and clothing (these were in use in Yugoslavia up to the autumn of 1951). Collections in kind, made for churches or any other ecclesiastical institutions, were conditional on special permission being granted by the authorities, while money collections were absolutely forbidden. The priests were constantly at the mercy of the police, and received no protection from organised attacks.

In 1945 there appeared an ordinance obliging each priest to ask for a special authorisation, like the one issued to artisans, entitled *permit to exercise the calling of the care of souls.* This

---

[37] In reality it was quite otherwise. The greater number of the clergy, just as poor as the faithful, had nothing to lose from the agrarian reform.

authorisation in Slovenia alone was refused to about a hundred priests, while others had to wait a very long time before receiving it.

In the course of the months of June and July 1945 dozens of priests and Catholic laymen were arrested; charged with having collaborated with the former Governments, they were brought before military tribunals and the greater number of them was condemned to death.

The most unlikely accusations were then made against the clergy, among which like a recurring theme continually appeared those of " enemies of the people," " fascists," " re-actionaries," " traitors "; this indeed is in no way astonishing, since if one did not show sympathy towards Communism, that was quite sufficient in the eyes of the accusers to be regarded no longer as a citizen but as a traitor to the people.

The Catholic bishops denounced this bloody persecution in a Pastoral Letter dated 20 September 1945. Referring to the massacre of the priests and the conditions under which justice was administered the bishops stated:

" The sad and terrible lot of many of our priests brings sorrow and uneasiness to our hearts. Already during the war many of them had fallen not only on the field of battle but under the guns of the civil and military authorities. When hostilities ended the condemnations to death of Catholic priests continued.

" According to our information *the number of victims was 243 dead, 169 detained in prisons or in concentration camps, 89 missing —a total of 501.*

" To this number must be added 19 seminarists, 3 brothers and 4 nuns killed.

" This is something *that was unheard of in the Balkan countries for centuries.* But the crowning of our sorrow is the fact that these victims, as well as hundreds and thousands of others, were refused the solace of their religion *in their last moments,* which in any civilised country is accorded even to the worst criminals.

" These judgments were passed in a summary manner by the tribunals. The accused for the most part did not know what charges were preferred against them till they appeared in court; very often they were not permitted to defend themselves in accordance with proper legal procedure either by calling witnesses or by having the help of a lawyer."

At the moment when the bishops of Yugoslavia made this solemn protest against the wrongs inflicted on the clergy, several of their own number were already victims of the persecution.

Mgr. *Joseph Srebnic*, Bishop of Krk, was arrested in his residence on 16 April 1945, and interned for some time in a village in the mountains about 6 kilometres from Crikvenica.

At the time that the Communists entered Zagreb, Mgr. *Joseph Carevic*, Bishop of Dubrovnik, Ragusa, disappeared in a most mysterious manner. Some time afterwards some peasants discovered at the bottom of a well a heap of decaying bodies, and believed they recognised the body of the bishop from scraps of clothing.

On 15 May 1945 Mgr. *John Simrak*, Bishop of Krizevci for the Catholics of the Byzantine Rite, was arrested on the charge of hostility to the liberation movement and Communist forces. On 28 June he was condemned to death. He was kept in prison for two months and was subjected to such brutal treatment that his health was gravely undermined. Transferred to the Mercy Hospital at Zagreb he died there a few months later.

On 21 August 1945 an action by non-appearance was begun in Ljubljana against the Bishop of that city, Mgr. *Gregory Rozman*, accused of " collaboration." It ended on 28 August by condemning the prelate to 18 years of confinement, 10 years' loss of civic rights and the confiscation of all his property.

In Bosnia Mgr. *John E. Saric*, Bishop of Sarajevo, escaped into Austria on the advance of the Communists, taking with him the Bishop of Banja Luka, Mgr. *Joseph Garic*, who was suffering from cancer and who died on 30 June 1946 at Gratz.

Not being able to wreak their vengeance on the two bishops the Communists singled out the two dioceses, deprived of their pastors, for their particular hatred. In 1946 the diocese of Sarajevo counted 50,000 Catholics less than in 1939; it is presumed that a good number of them escaped into Croatia, but there is good reason to believe that *about 10,000 were assassinated* by the Communists whose intention it was to exterminate the

Catholic Church in Bosnia. Of 92 diocesan priests in 1939 36 had disappeared by 1946: 9 were killed, generally without trial, 9 imprisoned and the others had fled. Thus half the parishes of this diocese were deprived of the aid of religion. The seminaries had been closed and occupied; the Catholic schools as well as the charitable institutes for children had been suppressed; the press had been muzzled. The Vicar General, Mgr. *Anthony Buljan*, had been arrested immediately, and after two months of extremely harsh imprisonment was taken to Zagreb where he was subjected to rigorous supervision by the police.

In Bosnia also the treatment inflicted on the diocese of Banja Luka was not any less severe. A short time after the arrival of the Communists half the parishes had been deprived of their priests. The diocesan clergy had lost half their number, the schools and charitable works had been suppressed with the exception of one hospital. After a mighty movement of the people to the north of the country, which indeed lasted but a short time, the Catholic population fell from 130,000 to 40,000. Of the priests, 7 were executed without trial, 6 imprisoned and 9 fled the country.

These are but a *few episodes* of Communist violence in the course of the first years of the Government.[38] The persecution reached its height at the time of the " very sad trial "[39] of Mgr. *Louis Stepinac*, the Archbishop of Zagreb, who was arrested in September 1946.[40]

This trial began on 30 September. It was conducted according to a plan fixed beforehand based on accusations of a political character which had no foundation. Several witnesses for the

---

[38] A more complete and documented account will be found in *La Civiltà Cattolica*; 1946, III, pp. 318-324; 1954, I, pp. 716-730; 1954, II, pp. 105-120.

[39] Pius XII spoke of it as the " tristissimo processo."

[40] At first the régime tried to break the resistance of Mgr. Stepinac by employing " gentle means," inviting him to attend " popular celebrations." Then they resorted to stronger measures, attacking him in the press as a " war criminal," keeping him in prison for 15 days, scarcely a month after the arrival of Tito's troops. Gunmen were hired to assassinate him while he was going to the inauguration of a new parish in November 1945. While the implacable persecution was raging against priests and faithful, Mgr. Stepinac, as President of the episcopate, had written courageous letters protesting against the violence of the Communists (24 March and 20 September 1945, and 27 August 1946) These letters decided the fate of the archbishop.

prosecution were called and practically none for the defence; all those who might have given evidence in favour of the archbishop had been arrested from 24 to 30 September. Mgr. *Stepinac* refuted every charge made against him, in spite of the sinister atmosphere of hostility and prejudice of the court. Even though the tribunal did not succeed in proving any of the charges against him, the archbishop was condemned on 13 October 1946 to 16 years of forced labour, and to the loss of his political and civic rights for five more years.[41]

Soon after the trial Marshal *Tito* admitted at a meeting at Zagreb: " We are accused of having arrested *Stepinac* in order to get rid of him. When Mgr. *Hurley*, representative of the Pope, called on me, I said to him: ' Take him away to avoid his being sent to prison; if not we will arrest him.' And we waited for several months before doing so." By striking thus at the Archbishop of Zagreb the leaders of the Communists wished to convey to the other bishops that they would have to yield to the demands of the Government. The Yugoslav régime gave the lead to all the other " People's Democracies " in this respect, and began a series of other and still more sad trials. Mgr. *Stepinac* had stated but the truth when he declared before the tribunal: " My only crime is that I have not acceded to the demands of the Communists, the sole rulers of this country."

The persecution in Yugoslavia did not stop with the Stepinac trial. A second trial took place in 1948. Arrested on 22 April of that year Mgr. *Peter Cule*, Bishop of Mostar, was brought in July before the People's Court on the charge of " collaboration with the Ustachia régime." The charge was so vague that false witnesses had to be called. Mgr. *Cule* himself proved that their evidence was false. He declared before his judges that the only reason he was appearing in the dock was because as bishop he had defended the rights of the Church and of religion. And he added, that was a right recognised by the Constitution. Nevertheless he was condemned to 11 years in prison. His secretary, Father *Mate Nuic*, was condemned to 8 years in prison

---

[41] The account of the trial can be found in *Il processo dell' Arcivescovo di Zagabria*, by Fiorello Cavalli, Rome 1947.

because he had not given evidence against his bishop (18 July 1948).

Mgr. *Cule*, after having undergone an extremely hard term of imprisonment, was sent to forced labour, and while being transferred there was injured in a railway accident.

In the history of the persecution in Yugoslavia we must not omit to mention innumerable acts of intolerance, of Communist fanaticism and of coarseness towards the clergy in the discharge of their religious duties.[42]   One could draw up a disgraceful list. Rotten eggs were thrown at priests during the celebration of Mass, sermons were violently interrupted by fanatics, bishops were attacked on their way to administer the Sacraments. These attacks, accompanied with the grossest insults and directed against priests and bishops, were frequent from the very beginning of the régime. They were the " popular and spontaneous " accompaniment to all the pressure brought to bear on the clergy and on the Church by official Government organisations.   The Communist propagandists loved to daub the walls with the slogan: popovi = lopovi, opatice = svercerice   (priests = robbers, religion = smuggling).

The arrests of priests continued during the course of the years 1947-50.   In the first few months of 1949 and *in one province alone* 15 priests were condemned for their " anti-national attitude."

On 26 April 1950 the Archbishop of Belgrade, Mgr. *Joseph Ujcic*, in the name of all the bishops of Yugoslavia drew attention to the extent of the persecution by the Government in a *Memorandum* addressed to the Direction of Worship. It replied on 19 May 1950 by stating that the *Memorandum*

" was the fruit of an impossible mentality and consequently could
    not serve as a basis for discussion or negotiation between the
    Government of the PFR of Yugoslavia and the Catholic epis-
    copate . . . "

The year 1951 saw the renewal of the attacks against the bishops, especially on the occasions of their pastoral visits. The following are a few examples:

---

[42] The following newspapers were particularly active in this work of stirring up the people: *Politika* of Belgrade, *Slovenski porocevalec* of Ljubljana, and *Viestrik* of Zagreb.

In May 1951 Mgr. *Maximilian Drzecnik*, Apostolic Administrator of Maribor, was the object of serious molestations on the
part of the police, because his visit to the district of Ptuj had
stirred up great enthusiasm among the faithful. Mgr. *Cyril Banic*,
Apostolic Administrator of Sibenik, was the object of several
attacks in the course of one pastoral visit. Another very serious
attack was made on 20 January 1952 on Mgr. *Anthony Vovk*,
Apostolic Administrator of Ljubljana. At the station of Novo
mesto, under the eyes of the police, a group of fanatics accused
the prelate of imaginary war crimes and attempted to burn him
alive. Mgr. *Vovk* was seriously burned. But the individual who
was principally responsible, when brought to court, was condemned only to 10 days in prison, which he did not serve. To
this act of violence, witnessed by the whole population, many
others could be added.

One should recall here also the " interrogations " which the
bishops had to undergo on their return from the pastoral visits
they had been able to make in spite of every obstacle. After a
conference of the bishops held at Zagreb from 23 to 25 September
1951, which had been declared illegal by the Communists,
the twenty bishops present had to appear before Government
functionaries who threatened them with the severest penalties
if they did not withdraw the *non licet* they had issued against the
Associations of the People's Priests. Very often these interrogations lasted several days.

The Communists were never at a loss for pretexts to attack
the bishops. Here are some further examples taken from the
years 1952-53:

Three months after the attack of which Mgr. *Vovk* had
been the victim, the press launched a violent campaign against
him because he had dared in his Letter to the clergy to recall
that Christians had the duty to profess their faith to the point
of heroism. Such language was considered a provocation and
heavy fines were imposed on the bishop. The same prelate was
later brought into court and condemned for having recalled to
the faithful the words of *Pius XII* on the crime of abortion; the
law of Yugoslavia legalised the use of means to procure abortion
and the circular of Mgr. *Vovk* was looked upon by the Com-

munists as an attack on its legality. Mgr. *Salis-Seewis*, Auxiliary
Bishop of Zagreb, was attacked by *Vjestnik* for having dared
to publish a Pastoral Letter in which he explained how Christians
should regard the Person of Jesus Christ, and exhorted them to
remain faithful to God. For *Vjestnik* this text amounted to
an attack on Socialism. In a general way during the whole of
1953 the press tried in a venomous manner to excite the people
against the bishops, seeking all kinds of pretexts. It denounced
for example the behaviour of the Ordinaries of Split, of Zadar,
and of Sibenik, and in general of all the clergy of Croatia, with
regard to the census of 31 March 1953. The law enacted on
this occasion that every citizen should declare whether he was
an atheist or belonging to some religious denomination. The
prelates had then recommended their faithful to state clearly
that they professed the Catholic religion. The Communists said
there was in this a violation of conscience, and that the bishops
by doing this were following the orders of the Vatican which
wished " to exploit the census to create confusion and a psychosis
of religious persecution." [43]

In the course of these three years also numerous episodes
of brutal and calculated violence took place in very many places
in Yugoslavia. The perpetrators of these acts, who according to
the Communists were always " irresponsibles," were never
identified and these acts of violence remained unpunished.

In connection with *the acts of violence against the members of the
episcopate* it may be noted the Central Committee of the Communist Party of Yugoslavia meeting at Brioni on 16 June 1953
sent to all the surrounding organisations the order to accentuate
the struggle against the Catholic bishops, to prevent them from
any public activity and from coming in contact with the faithful.
After that one should not be astonished at the assaults on, among
others, Mgr. *Charles Celik*, Apostolic Administrator of Banja Luka,
on 22 August 1953; on Mgr. *Cyril Banic*, Apostolic Administrator of Sibenik, on 4 August 1953; on Mgr. *Anthony Radic*,
Vicar General of Sibenik, in August 1953; on Mgr. *Francis Franic*,
Auxiliary Bishop of Split, and Mgr. *Bonefacic*, Bishop of Split,

---

[43] Cf. *Borba*, 5 March 1953.

in July and August 1953; on Mgr. *Louis Budanovic*, Apostolic Administrator of Backa, on 6 September 1953; on Mgr. *Joseph Pavlisic*, Auxiliary Bishop of Senj, on 3, 5 and 16 July 1953; and on Mgr. *Francis Salis-Seewis*, Auxiliary Bishop of Zagreb, on 8 August 1953.[44]

The Economic Blockade of the Church [45]

From 1945 the Government of Belgrade decreed a sweeping agrarian reform. This was immediately applied to ecclesiastical properties at the moment when the same authorities suppressed all contributions of the State to Church expenditure and to the support of the pastors. Thus the resources of the Church were reduced to extreme limits at one blow. For example the few establishments tolerated for the formation of the clergy had no longer any right to more than the ten hectares (25 acres) authorised by the law. In addition the officers appointed for the application of the agrarian reform to Church property did not even keep to the rulings of the law and went beyond its prescriptions in the matter of expropriations.

However the bishops of Yugoslavia, while deploring these spoliations in their collective Letter to the faithful on 20 September 1945, accepted that the Church be reduced to a state of great poverty, and even of destitution. They counted on the aid of the Catholic population for the support of the clergy, for the maintenance of the few seminaries, of the diocesan organisations and of the few religious communities left.

Such was the position up to 1952. But 1952 marked a new stage in the struggle of Communism in Yugoslavia for the destruction of the Church, viz. the economic blockade.[46]

In nearly all the parishes of Croatia and of Bosnia-Herzegovina, to mention only these two Republics, the custom existed of

[44] The details of these attacks are given in articles in *La Civiltà Cattolica*, 1954, I, pp. 716-730, and II, pp. 105-120.

[45] To give an example of the methods employed by the Government authorities and the police in Yugoslavia to enslave the clergy the next paragraph is based on the book already quoted: *Une Eglise du silence*, pp. 90 *seqq*. The Communists made use of similar means to paralyse also the other activities of the clergy.

[46] The taxes which already weighed heavily on those subject to taxation (particularly the peasants) were augmented in the case of those who showed themselves generous to the Church. " If they can give to the priests," say the police, " they can also give to the State."

making collections in kind from the people for the Church. A group of parishioners, men and women, undertook this collection. The Communist authorities forbade all collections outside the Church. The collectors were abused and even punished by fines and imprisonment.

In Slovenia this kind of collection was forbidden from the time of the " liberation " and, in addition, the collections made inside the churches are often reserved to-day for the " People's Priests " under the arbitrary control of the police.

In Yugoslavia, as in many other Christian countries, it is the custom to have houses blessed every year by the priests. On these occasions an offering is made by the faithful. The police immediately saw in this a form of begging, which was forbidden by law.

The police carried their zeal to the point of confiscating money collected for bells, for repairs to the churches, and the stipends for Mass.[47]

During the first months of 1952 there was a very active campaign for the recovery of taxes on the clergy. Up to then they had to pay 4% of their income. Although no legal dispositions on this matter existed it is certain that a verbal order to increase taxes was given throughout the whole territory of the Federated Republic. The functionaries in charge of checking income tax returns presented themselves at the bishops' residences, at the presbyteries and at the convents, claiming to check all the books, looking up every entry, not forgetting the ordinary collections, where they were still authorised, the stipends for Masses, the offerings made at baptisms, marriages and deaths, etc. And when the total of these different items of revenue did not amount to the figure they judged to be " a just figure," they took this latter as the basis on which to levy the tax.[48]

---

[47] Here are some more examples : nuns reduced to begging have been punished because they accepted a gallon of milk offered them to thank them for care given to the sick.

In a parish in Slovenia in June 1952 a priest was to celebrate his first Mass. His family was very poor, so the neighbours got together something for the occasion. On the evening before, the police came and confiscated everything.

[48] " You are an intelligent man," they said to the parish priest. " To live you need a certain sum, X, every month, which comes to so much, Y, a year." This sum, Y, was the amount they took to assess the tax due, a purely imaginary figure, which was often enormous.

In this year 1952 they went back over the years 1951, 1950, 1949, 1948 and even 1947, to calculate the income tax on these years, which had already been paid. The total " on which tax was payable " mounted up in this way to hundreds of thousands and even millions of dinars.[49]

It was no use for the priest to claim that he had to defray the expenses of the church, to pay for repairs, to send to the bishop's palace or to his colleagues the stipends for Masses which he himself could not acquit. If he could not pay the amount of the tax demanded by them, the collectors seized everything they could take away easily: radios, typewriters, sewing machines, furniture and even clothing.

Moreover no matter how carefully the income tax returns were made out, the police could always claim that they were not complete, that there was an attempt to conceal part of the revenues, and then there followed a court action in which the priest was condemned to a heavy fine or even to prison.[50]

---

[49] Here is how the tax collector proceeded. For example a community was composed of 50 nuns. Ten of them were able to work, the others were too old, or ill or simply had no work. The community was considered a " physical person." The total of the salaries of the ten nuns who were working represented a revenue which would be considerable for one person alone. It was this total, multiplied three or four times, according to the number of years for which the collectors demanded arrears of tax, which served as a base on which to reckon the tax. If the 10 nuns in question earned 50,000 dinars a month, that is 600,000 a year, it would be entered as a revenue of 2,400,000 dinars for the four years. And the collector could then demand another million dinars !

[50] The Communist newspapers themselves demonstrate with what animosity the Income Tax Commissioners in Yugoslavia utilised the system for the spoliation of the clergy. In its number of 31 December 1952 Slovenski Porocevalec denounced as examples of people who did not pay the taxes due, at Maribor: Bishop Drzecnik, Apostolic Administrator, the parish priest of the cathedral and the Diocesan Chancellor. The Tax Commissioners claimed 558,749 dinars and stopped the current account of the bishopric in order to recover this sum. Mgr. Drzecnik maintained that it was impossible for him to pay this exorbitant tax and appealed to the Supreme Court. It was of no avail. After this decision the Minister for Finance confiscated the total amount in the current account of the bishopric, which the Communist paper asserted came to over a million dinars. This account was made up of legacies, stipends for Masses and other resources of the same kind . . . At Ljubljana the issue of 6 December 1952 of Ljudska Pravica reproached the Municipal People's Committees for not making the clergy pay the taxes due by them according to the law. And to prove that the parish priests of several parishes in the district had not paid the proper taxes the Communist paper gave opposite the items declared by the parish priests on which the tax was calculated, statements made by private individuals who pretended to have paid for a marriage, for a funeral or for some other ceremony, sums of money greater than those shown by the priest. At Belgrade also, Borba, 9 December 1952, joined the chorus and accused the parish priests of making false declarations.

It must not be forgotten that, if the priest did not have a special authorisation from one of the official organisations, he could not receive any gift whatsoever from the faithful under penalty of a heavy fine or a corresponding term in prison, with confiscation of the offering. Needless to say this particular clause concerned only the clergy. Any citizen of Yugoslavia was entitled to receive any gift whatsoever from his relations, friends or acquaintances.[51] Any of the faithful who were generous enough to offer their help freely to the priest to look after the church, to replace the sacristan or the man who rang the bell—and no priest was in a position to pay these men any longer—these people suffered the same fate as their pastors. The heavy hand of the tax collector fell on them and often they were summoned to the police barracks to answer unending questions and listen to exhortations, the trend of which it is easy to surmise. They were especially advised never to give anything to the priests.

In the same way as the parishes the religious communities of men and women were harassed by these assessments.

With regard to the dioceses the custom in Yugoslavia is that each parish takes up a collection on one or more Sundays for the bishop, and the amount collected is sent to the diocesan Curia. But the income tax collectors insisted that the amounts of these collections should appear on the parochial tax returns, and that they should be again entered on the income tax returns of the bishop. In this way the tax was paid twice.

It was possible, it is true, to appeal against the decisions of the local authority. In some cases the higher authorities admitted to some extent the inaccuracy of the total of the taxable revenue, and reduced this total sometimes by an appreciable amount. Still in spite of this partial " correction," the injustice remained.

The police gladly made use of the collection of the taxes as a means of forcing the hand of the clergy. The Associations of the People's Priests received very favourable treatment on this question of taxation. Should any priest refuse to join these associations he was immediately so overtaxed that he could not possibly pay. He was told that if he consented to join his taxes

---

[51] No exception was made; everything the priest received must be considered as an offering, for which a previous authorisation had to be obtained.

would be reduced and even remitted. *It would be interesting to learn how many priests had joined because of these tactics.*

It is perfectly clear that such a policy on the part of the Government authorities had for its end *to convince the priests that their subsistence depended solely and entirely on the civil authority which would come to their aid only in the measure in which they gave their support to Communism.*

The Religious Orders of Women

In Yugoslavia there were still a few religious houses of men though many had been destroyed during the war or had been suppressed by special edicts of the Government. Of course all their activity outside their houses had been completely curtailed. It was not a rare thing to find in their buildings the offices of the UBDA, of organisations of the Communist Party and of the army.

But the congregations and orders of women have been much more harshly treated. From 1945 the schools, colleges, homes and other institutions of that kind conducted by nuns had been confiscated. A little later on the nuns were driven from the hospitals and finally they were forbidden to wear their religious habit.

In Bosnia-Herzegovina, the most " progressive " of the Yugoslav People's Republics, there is not in existence a single religious institute of women. The 64 houses, having more than 1,000 nuns of different congregations, which existed in 1949, have disappeared.

The most important congregation of nuns in Yugoslavia was that of the Sisters of Charity of St. Vincent de Paul. The mother house was in Zagreb. In 1941 the congregation comprised 4 provinces, 145 houses, 2,174 professed nuns and 145 novices. These nuns had charge of 51 hospitals or clinics, 7 hospices for the poor, 6 orphanages, 32 kindergartens, 26 primary schools with 4,305 pupils, 5 preparatory schools, 11 industrial schools, 2 higher schools for young girls with 1,172 pupils, 18 colleges with 658 students, and various other houses of education. It is difficult to say at the moment what remains of all these various activities.

The nuns have been literally driven from their convents and all their institutions have been confiscated. The Government authorities have forbidden the nuns, who had to wear secular dress, to have any contact with their superiors. Some were even obliged to attend Communist meetings. In the beginning they were put to work cleaning the streets, or doing like tasks, particularly on Sundays.

In Croatia in 1939 there were 27 religious congregations of women, with 397 convents, 3,980 nuns and 247 novices, not to mention the Croat nuns who were working in 26 convents in foreign countries.[52] At the moment about 250 convents have been closed and only a small number of nuns is able to live in community under the greatest difficulties.

In 1950 there were about 40 Sisters of Charity in Communist prisons. One can say the same for the other orders and congregations. The nuns are always numbered among those who have to complete their sentences to the last hour.

It is certain that about 13 nuns belonging to three different religious congregations were assassinated after the coming of the Communist régime, while a still greater number disappeared; they are in all probability dead.

Ecclesiastical Associations

Towards the end of 1949 Marshal *Tito*, receiving a group of self-styled " People's Priests " asked them: " Now that we are separated from Moscow, why cannot you separate yourselves from Rome? "[53]

The Communist régime attempted at different times to create a division amongst the priests. It began in Slovenia by establishing a special bureau for religious questions, entitled *The Religious Commission accredited to the Presidency of the Council of Ministers of the People's Republic of Slovenia.* Extensive powers were given to this bureau, and it was considered by the Government as the

---

[52] Cf. K. S. Draganovic, *Le Système général de l'Eglise en Yougoslavie*, Sarajevo, 1939, pp. 472, 525, 560-561.

[53] Cf. *Nova Pot*, Year I, n. 2.

organ of liaison between the Government and the hierarchy.[54]
The Communist authorities named as president of this commission the excommunicated priest, *Joseph Lampret*, who had
been suspended *a divinis* by his superiors.[55]

The second attempt to divide the clergy was the foundation
of *The Association of Saints Cyril and Methodius* (CMD). This is
how it began: the president of the commission in Slovenia,
Joseph Lampret, had founded in the spirit of Communism the
*Secretariate for the Pioneering Projects of Priest-members of the
Liberation Front* (*Osvobodilna Fronta*, a Communist political
organisation). In the beginning this Association had but few
members, the priests knowing that they could not form part
of a Communist organisation and still less of an organisation of
the political character of the OF (*Osvobodilna Fronta*).

In order to sow dissension among the clergy the Secretariate
published the *Bilten*, a small paper of from 4 to 6 pages, filled
with hatred against the faithful priests, against the bishops, against
the Vatican and against the Pope. The Sacred Congregation of
the Council by its decree of 12 April 1949 condemned and
forbade the *Bilten*, as spreading false doctrines with the intention
of undermining and destroying ecclesiastical discipline and as
deliberately defaming the hierarchy. The Sacred Congregation
pointed out that this pamphlet was already forbidden by the terms
of Canon 1,399, § 6, of the Code of Canon Law.

Since this paper had but very little success among the clergy,
the Government which wanted at all costs to have priests on its
side, began organising conferences and meetings for that purpose,
but without result. On account of the outrageous propaganda
of the Secretariate against the Holy See and its representatives,
and against the bishops, the priests would not co-operate. Then
there was a change of tactics.

During the summer of 1949 there was held at Ljubljana a

---

[54] Often the Government authorities opened the bishops' letters, and then sent them
back to the writers telling them to submit the matter " through the channel of the
Religious Commission."

[55] Some years before the war the priest, Joseph Lampret, had already been arrested
on the charge of being a Communist; afterwards he left his own diocese of Maribor.
He fled into Dalmatia. There he was found by the Communists themselves during the
war.

General Assembly of all the members of the *Secretariate for the Pioneering Projects of Priest-members of the OF*, in the course of which was founded the *Association of Saints Cyril and Methodius of the Catholic priests of Slovenia*. The *Bilten* ceased to appear and was replaced by the *Nova Pot* (New Way); soon after was established the *Organizacijski Vjestnik* (Organisation Bulletin), which adopted a more moderate tone than that of the *Bilten*. The direction of the new association was however in the hands of the same persons.[56]

The ends of this association were not long in manifesting themselves, and the bishops of Yugoslavia in their conference of 26 April 1950 had to pronounce a *non expedit* which aroused protestations from the Communist press. Still a certain number of priests thought they could interpret this *non expedit* in a wide sense, and despite the attitude of their superiors joined the movement.

To help in the development of this association the Government favoured its members in the exercise of their ministry.[57] Besides it brought pressure to bear on those priests who were imprisoned. It is very significant that the priests who were set free showed themselves zealous propagandists of the association. Many priests condemned to several years in prison and even forced labour were set at liberty when they promised to become members of the movement. The secretary of the association in 1953, who had been condemned to 16 years of forced labour, had been liberated after serving only four years, and now become a passionate propagandist spent himself in the work of the organisation.

---

[56] *L'Osservatore Romano*, 10 November 1950, published the following declaration: "Since the Yugoslav priests, Anthony Bajt, Joseph Lampret and Victor Merz, in spite of repeated warnings from the Sacred Congregation of the Council, have persisted in their disobedience, this Sacred Congregation by its sentence of 30 August 1950 declared that the afore-mentioned priests have incurred excommunication reserved *speciali modo* to the Holy See."

[57] A letter coming from Ljubljana in 1951 stated: "The priests who are members of the Association enjoy certain rights and privileges. Unlike the other priests they may teach religion, move around freely, receive wine for Mass and flour to make hosts, and they enjoy many other privileges. It is certain that the Communists have not obtained from the organisation all that they expected from it. The clergy have not been divided, and it is not with this nucleus grouped in the organisation that the Communists will be able to found a new Sect of 'the National Slovene Church,' as they had strongly hoped."

The spirit that animates this movement of the " People's Priests of Slovenia " may be stated thus: it wishes to be a faithful tool in the hands of the Communists, and to work in close co-operation with the *Socialist Union of Workers of Slovenia* (*Socialisticna Zveza Delovnega Ljudstva Slovenije*, SZDLS), which is a mass political organisation. Among its members the Association of Saints Cyril and Methodius propagates the economic ideas which inspire Communism, but it wishes also to prepare the way for seeking a *modus vivendi* between the Church and State. Already it has obtained for its priests a kind of insurance, gladly conceded by the Government which thus gets a greater grip on the clergy.

On the central committee depend 8 provincial committees and on them 19 district committees. The programme is the same for them all, more civil and political than sacerdotal. Here for example are some of the subjects discussed at their meetings: The priests and their civic duties of the moment; The ideal of the people's priests in civil society; What is clericalism? How to work for peace? It is only very exceptionally that they treat of priestly duties and problems.[58]

The attitude of the bishops of Slovenia with regard to the CMD has always remained negative; the bishops however have shown understanding for those priests who, on account of the economic difficulties of the clergy, agreed to become members of the association.[59]

The bishops made every effort to the extreme limit to save at least something, and they declared that they were ready to accept the statutes of the association, if they were modified on a few points and submitted for the approbation of the Holy See. At the congress in the autumn of 1952 the statutes were amended according to the desires of the bishops, with the proviso

---

[58] Cf. *Organizacijski Vjestnik*, where the more recent programmes are published.

[59] Many ecclesiastics joined either because they were promised greater freedom in their ministry, or because the economic advantages which social insurance would bring them, were painted for them in glowing colours. The members of the CMD and other similar associations enjoy in fact an insurance contract, in virtue of which priests would have the same privileges as those accorded to workmen and to functionaries: medical assistance, insurance against illness and old age, and the right to pension.

When these promises were without effect, they were often compelled to join by threats and by violence.

however that they were not to be sent to Rome for approbation.[60]

In the course of local meetings of the CMD petitions were
drawn up addressed to the bishops asking that the penalty of
excommunication should be withdrawn from those priests who
had been excommunicated. But it must be remarked that these
protestations coming from meetings held in various localities
were practically stereotyped; account was no doubt taken of
each particular situation, but over and above all of the directives
of the Government. Besides, the representatives of public
authority very often assisted at these meetings, and in the
presence of the priests criticised the bishops, denouncing their
misdeeds and attacking the Church. As has already been said the
CMD worked in strict collaboration with the Communists
through the OF.

At the time of the breaking-off of diplomatic relations between
the Holy See and the Government at Belgrade the Communist
press published some articles by priest members of the CMD,
which were simply a reproduction of the Government commentary, viz. there is no longer any need of a third intermediary
in the consultations about the *modus vivendi*. When in the first
days of January 1953 *Tito* received some of the bishops and
discussed with them the question of an " agreement," the
Communist press published interviews with certain priests, who
again expressed the Government's sentiments.

After the CMD of Slovenia there followed in Bosnia-Herzegovina an association of " People's Priests." The Government
and the police did everything to favour the establishment of
similar associations in the territories of the People's Republics
of Croatia and Montenegro. In fact some groups of priests
first founded " *project committees* " and later established real
associations in these Republics (in Croatia on 12 November,
1953).

In their *Memorandum* to Marshal *Tito* the bishops of Yugo-

---

[60] According to the *Nova Pot* the reasoning of the directors of the CMD was as follows:
we have given satisfaction to the bishops by modifying the statutes; therefore we are
in agreement with them, and by that fact the CMD is approved without any further
sanction.

slavia declared that these associations had not the required qualifications to accomplish the great tasks which they had set themselves; first of all because they had always been under the influence of the State authorities and in the second place because the bishops considered the instructions given to the CMD a provocation to ecclesiastical indiscipline and a progressive diminution of religious life, rather than a working towards their definite end which was to prepare a *modus vivendi* between the Church and the State. The bishops laid down as conditions for the recognition of these associations of priests that the statutes must be brought into line with the Code of Canon Law and that their work should be brought under the direct control of the ecclesiastical authorities.

In conclusion the CMD and similar associations have shown themselves to be dangerous organisations tending to divide the clergy; these so-called Catholic organisations in the hands of the Communists could not but deceive the clergy and the faithful. The great majority of the faithful however understood well their true aim, and did not accept the priests who were members of these associations. Were it not for the pressure brought to bear on them, and the threats and the lies of the police, very few priests would be disposed to join a movement of this kind. On this matter in the *Note* of the Secretariate of State dated 15 December 1952 it is stated:

" The problem of the associations called ' People's Priests ' must be examined in view of the general situation in which the Church finds itself. We know that these associations were originated by the civil authorities. A great number of priests have been and still are being influenced to join them by threats, or by the promise of being able to exercise more freely their parochial ministry, or by desire of the economic advantages granted to priests who have joined.

" Besides by the very fact that they do not belong to these associations some priests meet with great difficulties in the accomplishment of their sacred ministry; others have not yet been able to take possession of the parishes to which they were appointed by the bishop, or have not been able to take up residence there.

" In the above-mentioned associations those who exercise the greatest influence, under external instructions, are frequently priests who are at variance with divine faith, or with ecclesiastical discipline and who thus have incurred canonical sanctions.

" The police assist at these meetings, and political personalities often intervene. In the speeches made the action of the bishops and even of the Church is openly and publicly criticised. These associations have always been united in close collaboration with the ' Popular Front ' and through it with the Communist Party as at the present moment it unites them to the Communist Union of Yugoslavia."

The Rupture of Diplomatic Relations

On 22 October 1945 the Holy See, uneasy at the sad turn of events in Yugoslavia and with the hope of bringing peace, had appointed Mgr. *Joseph Patrick Hurley* as Apostolic Nuncio to Belgrade. The Government of Yugoslavia did not reply to this gesture and its Legation to the Holy See continued to be under the control of a simple secretary to the embassy. In consequence of the hostility shown by the Government the Nunciature was unable to accomplish its mission with any degree of success.

The pretext for breaking off diplomatic relations was given towards the end of 1952 to the Government by the controversy on the *ecclesiastical associations*. The reservations made concerning these by the bishops of Yugoslavia [61] were attributed to the intervention of the Holy See; according to a *Note* of 1 November 1952 addressed to the Nunciature at Belgrade, to be transmitted to the Secretariate of State, the Holy See had unduly intervened in the internal affairs of the People's Federated Republic. [62]

The Secretariate of State replied by a *Note* on 15 December, enumerating the more recent abuses of power of which the Catholic Church had been the victim. [63] This document was handed to the Yugoslav Minister for Foreign Affairs, who later stated, when *L'Osservatore Romano* published the text on 14 January 1953, that he had never received it. What really

---

[61] Cf. circular of the Yugoslav episcopate to the clergy, dated 25 September 1952, the text of which can be found in the book; *Une Eglise du silence*, pp. 160-161.

[62] Cf. *Une Eglise du silence*, pp. 141-144.

[63] Cf. *ibid.*, pp. 144 *seqq.*

happened was that the portfolio, handed to the Minister by the
Chargé d'Affaires of the Holy See at Belgrade, had been sent
back a few hours later still closed and sealed, apparently intact. [64]

But the unilateral decision to break off diplomatic relations
with the Holy See had already been announced; it was justified,
claimed the Communists, not only on account of the " inter-
ventions " of which there was question, but also by the news
that Mgr. *Louis Stepinac* had been made Cardinal. This, according
to Marshal *Tito, constituted a provocation.* [65]

On 17 December 1952 the Chargé d'Affaires of the Holy See,
Mgr. *Silvio Oddi*, was compelled to close the Apostolic Nun-
ciature at Belgrade and on the 27th of the month to set out for
Rome. Thus came to an end the diplomatic relations between
Yugoslavia and the Holy See. [66]

Marshal *Tito* in his speeches and interviews never ceased
repeating that Yugoslavia would not consent to re-open the
question of diplomatic relations with the Holy See as long as the
latter continued to interfere in the internal affairs of his
country. [67]

The Law against Religious Communities

After the rupture of diplomatic relations the newspapers of
Yugoslavia began to publish, with perfect synchronisation,
articles stating that, now that all possibility of foreign inter-

---

[64] Cf. *L'Osservatore Romano*, 18 January 1953.

[65] On 29 November 1952 news was received that the Archbishop of Zagreb was
among the number of Cardinals that Pius XII had decided to create on 12 January 1953.
The Government of Belgrade and the press denounced this nomination as an intolerable
provocation and let loose a violent campaign against the Sovereign Pontiff and the
Catholic Church.

[66] Commenting on the departure of the Chargé d'Affaires, *L'Osservatore Romano*
wrote: " If the Apostolic See were a State like the others it would long ago have had
plenty of reasons for recalling its own representative at Belgrade. But having in view
always the good and the care of souls it has manifested unbounded forbearance, because
the existence of a diplomatic link would have rendered the study of a *modus vivendi*
possible, in the case where an act of goodwill or of repentance would have given the
indispensable premises. This link by the initiative of the Government of Belgrade is
now broken; nothing remains for us but to take cognisance of this act with great sadness
after having shown the ill-disposed and gratuitous character of this decision."

[67] Cf. for example the interview given to the correspondent of the *Associated Press*
at Belgrade, 10 August 1953.

vention had been removed, the relations between Church and State would without doubt improve very soon.

Towards the end of February 1953 some bishops, with Mgr. *Joseph Ujcic* at their head, were called into consultation by Marshal *Tito* in order to establish an *agreement* or *modus vivendi* between the People's Republic and the Catholic Church. It was on that occasion that the Vatican Acting-Secretary of State for Extraordinary Affairs addressed a letter to Mgr. *Ujcic* reminding him that any agreement between the Church and Governments was not within the legitimate jurisdiction of the ordinaries, and that according to ecclesiastical law this was reserved solely to the Holy See. This letter was sent through the ordinary mail and naturally the authorities of Yugoslavia knew about it.

On 22 May 1953 the Parliament of Yugoslavia passed a *Law concerning Religious Denominations*, which placed in the hands of the Government a new means of paralysing religious activity in the future. During the course of the discussions on this law the Minister for the Interior, *Alexander Rankovic*, attacked with extreme violence the new " uncalled for " intervention of the Holy See in the internal affairs of the Republic, quoting in support of his argument, the Letter addressed on 16 February by Mgr. *Dominico Tardini*, the Acting-Secretary of State, to Mgr. *Ujcic*.[68] The law was passed. *L'Osservatore Romano* of 6 December 1953 commented on it in these terms:

> " The law pretends to interpret the constitutional guarantees. At first sight it would seem, if not actually liberal, at least not very different from the ' laicist ' legal rulings of bourgeois Governments. But for example what value can be attached to the legal power to punish ' abuses ' of religion (art. 5) when it is a Communist authority which defines these abuses? And how can one not wonder, still considering this article 5, whether the prohibition

---

[68] This Letter recalled in a few phrases the good dispositions of the Holy See, which said that it was ready to open negotiations with the Yugoslav Republic, on condition that the latter was disposed to respect the essential rights of the Church. *Borba* reproduced on 23 January a " facsimile " of the letter, in which this passage was omitted. *L'Osservatore Romano* on 31 May reproduced side by side the original text and that given by *Borba*, concluding that evidently the Communists did not want public opinion to know the real sentiments of the Holy See.

' of the provocation and the instigation to religious intolerance, to hatred and to discord ' or the command not ' to disturb religious meetings, religious instruction, religious ceremonies ' are not cynical irony, when the whole press of Yugoslavia is nothing but a chorus of hatred against Catholicism, the Church and the Holy See, while the bishops on their pastoral journeys are attacked even in the churches and during the ceremonies ?

" And while article 7 affirms that ' the rights of citizens cannot be interfered with on account of their religious convictions,' it is impossible to forget that many employees and members of the liberal professions have been relieved of their functions because for example they had sons in the seminary; that pupils have been expelled from schools because they did not attend on Christmas Day. In art. 4 it is laid down that communities ' are free to establish special religious schools for the formation of priests.' But we know the conditions under which seminaries are allowed to function.

" Article 3 prescribes that ' religious communities can publish and distribute religious literature '; this again is but bitter irony, when we compare the written law with the facts. To-day in all Yugoslavia there are but two Catholic monthly pamphlets: the *Vjestnik* of Djakovo [69] and *Druzina* of Nova Gorica. The *Blagovest* of Belgrade has been suppressed.

" Everything leads us to believe that the law concerning religious communities was designed with an eye to propaganda in foreign countries rather than to regulate ecclesiastical life. The Government which has no scruples about violating almost every one of its clauses or of interpreting them to suit itself, wants to see one clause only applied, that contained in article 9, which says: ' The priests of different denominations have the right to found their own associations of priests.'

" This ' right ' which at least in the case of Catholics and Orthodox has for its end to bring the clergy into opposition with the bishops, is the origin of all the unlawful acts of violence of which Yugoslavia is the scene and which contravene not only justice but all the practices of civilisation . . .

" This criterion is common to all the ' People's Democracies.' The Governments dominated by the Communists wish to compel the Church to renounce its own internal laws and adapt itself

---

[69] Cf. above note 22.

to the ecclesiastical law of the State, which is inspired by
materialist and anti-religious ideologies. In brief, an *atheistic
absolutism.*"

Balance Sheet

(1) *The Faithful.*—The education of youth is still a monopoly
of the Communist Party. The religious feasts can scarcely be
observed because work is obligatory in the offices, the schools and
the factories, under serious penalties. Any religious ceremony
outside the churches is still forbidden. Religion is banished from
public life and Atheism is imposed on all functionaries, soldiers,
and all those who by their employment have any connection with
the State, etc. While all religious propaganda is forbidden, anti-
religious propaganda is not only permitted, but looked upon with
favour in public life, including even outrageous and blasphemous
inscriptions on the walls of the churches and the presbyteries.

All religious help for prisoners is forbidden under any form
whatsoever. In the hospitals it is permitted only on the written
demand of the sick person, but it is severely forbidden to a priest
under grave penalties to suggest to the sick person even in the
vaguest way that he should receive the sacraments and Holy
Viaticum.

The Yugoslav Communist régime, which remains anchored to
its position of ideological Materialism, remains faithful to its
programme of de-christianising the people, in spite of some
tactical concessions occasionally made to the Church.

The Communists in spite of their system of repression and
their lying propaganda have gained among the faithful results
which fall far short of those they expected. The profound attachment of the Yugoslav Catholics to their bishops and priests is
remarkable; they are regular in attending the churches and in
the reception of the sacraments. However it cannot be denied
that the Communists have succeeded in detaching the young
people from their parents and from the Church, without indeed
obtaining even there the results their thorough programme had
led them to expect.[70]

---

[70] See the article *Religion under Tito, impression of a visit in July 1950*, published by
the *Tablet*, 19 August 1950.

(2) *The Priests.*—There were in Yugoslavia in 1940 about 6,000 priests, secular and regular. To-day there are less than 4,000: 400 were killed during the war; about thirty were massacred immediately after it; 500 were obliged to seek refuge in foreign countries; others have died in prison, have been executed or have disappeared. Among those who remain at least a thousand have been in Communist prisons, and in 1953 some 200 were still detained in them.[71]

In the *Memorandum* of 25 September 1952 to Marshal *Tito* the bishops of Yugoslavia observed:

> During the eight years that this régime has lasted a very great number of the Catholic clergy has had to undergo the humiliations and sufferings of the penitentiaries. Among those still in prison, is the Bishop of Mostar, Mgr. *Peter Cule*. The Archbishop of Zagreb, Mgr. *Louis Stepinac*, although he has been released from prison, is under house arrest and is not allowed to perform his duties.
>
> Is it not truly astonishing that the clergy, who in civilised countries never or scarcely ever come into conflict with the penal code, should in our country have become so incorrigibly criminal?

Annoyances, humiliations and outrages, not to mention the heavy financial burdens, are the daily bread of the clergy. From time to time some action is brought into court against one or other of them. The last in order of time was the trial, concluded on 2 August 1956, of Mgr. *Anthony Pilepic*, formerly Rector of the Theological Seminary of Split, Father *Ostrojic*, professor in the same seminary and two clerics. Mgr. *Pilepic* was condemned to five and a half years', Father *Ostrojic* to four and a half years' severe imprisonment, while one student received a sentence of two years and the other of one and a half years " for propaganda against the State and the existing social order of the country, for spreading Fascist ideas and for the misuse of religion for political ends." [72] The seminary and the Franciscan high school

---

[71] In the month of March 1953 M. Rankovic, Minister for the Interior, declared in Parliament that there were still 141. *L'Osservatore Romano*, reproducing this figure, 24 May, cast doubts on its accuracy.

[72] Cf. *Politika*, 2 August 1956.

were closed for five years. Included in this progressive suppression of the Catholic Church as represented by its ministers and its seminaries, must also be counted the trials and condemnations carried out in Slovenia against priests in charge of schools for alleged violation of the laws in force. [73]

The religious orders and institutes of women are still deprived of juridical personality.

(3) *The Episcopate.*—The Catholic hierarchy, though perhaps less disturbed in its organisation than in other countries under Communist domination, has nevertheless been subjected to acts of violence perpetrated against the persons of many of its leaders.

Cardinal *Louis Stepinac*, Archbishop of Zagreb, condemned to sixteen years of forced labour was liberated after serving six years, but is compelled to remain in retirement in his native village of Krasic under the strict supervision of the police.

Mgr. *Peter Cule*, Bishop of Mostar, condemned to eleven and a half years of forced labour was until recently still in prison, where he was not allowed either to celebrate Mass or to say his Breviary. It is not known where he is imprisoned at present.

Mgr. *John Simrak*, Bishop of Krizveci, died from the savage treatment he endured in prison.

Mgr. *Joseph Carevic*, former Bishop of Dubrovnik, died under mysterious circumstances, but everything leads to the suspicion that he was assassinated.

Mgr. *Joseph Garic*, Bishop of Banja Luka, died in exile.

The Archbishop of Sarajevo, Mgr. *John Saric*, and the Bishop of Ljubljana, Mgr. *Gregory Rozman*, are still in exile.

The Apostolic Administrators of Ljubljana and of Maribor cannot enter the parts of their dioceses which border on the frontier. It is the same for the Coadjutor and the Auxiliaries of the Archbishops of Zagreb and of Antivari (Bar).

Certain prelates continue to be confined to their residences for more or less long periods, according to the arbitrary decisions of the Communist authorities. This is particularly the case of Mgr. *Salis-Seewis*, Auxiliary Bishop of Zagreb and of Mgr. *Nezic* and Mgr. *Garkovic*, Apostolic Administrators of Pazin and Zara.

---

[73] *L'Osservatore Romano*, 5 August: *The Church in Yugoslavia.*

The bishops are often insulted and sometimes brutally attacked during their pastoral visits or when they go to the villages to administer the sacrament of Confirmation.

In their *Memorandum* of 25 September 1952 to Marshal *Tito*, the bishops concluded:

> All these facts prove that there does not exist in Yugoslavia either liberty of conscience or liberty of religion and that the Catholic Church is seriously threatened in its essential liberties and in its vital rights.[74]

---

[74] In August 1956 the Federal Procurator of the PFRY vetoed the printing and diffusion of the Apostolic Letter *Dum maerenti animo* (29 June 1956), directed to the bishops and the faithful of the Church of Silence, asserting that the Pontifical document contained " numerous calumnious assertions " on conditions in Yugoslavia, and was a " gross attempt to abuse religion for political ends," constituting even an " intolerable interference in the internal affairs of our country." The press and in particular *Borba* echoed the assertions of the Procurator, calling the Holy See " the implacable enemy of Yugoslavia." *Borba* wrote: " The last letter of the Pontiff is only one of the expressions of this hatred. Besides, the Vatican has not limited itself to giving expression to its hatred (*sic*) against Yugoslavia, but incites our people directly to revolt against the legitimate government . . . " After stating that in the PFRY full liberty of religion exists, *Borba* added that " The Vatican is not concerned with religious liberty but with the fact that . . . the Yugoslav people through Socialism have freed themselves from mediaeval mysticism and conservatism, as well as from subjection to ecclesiastical hegemony . . . " It is to be noted that the Letter *Dum maerenti animo* does not contain particular references to the Yugoslav situation, but is restricted to expressing the Holy Father's participation in the trials of millions and millions of his children everywhere in the Church of Silence, and to recomending steadfastness in the Faith through the help of prayer. Cf. *L'Osservatore Romano*, 17-18 August 1956.

Chapter 15

Recent Events

IN THE AUTUMN of 1956 tragic events revealed once more
to the world the true and terrifying character of Communism
—the merciless and logical outcome of the teaching of Marx and
Lenin. The denial of the spiritual, moral and civic rights of the
human person, and of the legitimate aspirations of the peoples
in countries crushed under Marxist rule has been further confirmed by the bloody repression of the Hungarian revolt against
the yoke of Communism.

On this occasion the truth of the words of *Pius XI* in the
Encyclical *Divini Redemptoris*, 1937, shone out like a beacon:

> " Nor can it be said that these atrocities are a passing phenomenon
> which habitually accompanies great revolutions . . .; no, they
> are the natural fruits of the system."

It is outside the scope of this work to deal with the tremendous
lesson which from the political and social aspect must be drawn
from what happened in the period from the Warsaw upheaval to
the Soviet intervention in Hungary. These events have shown the
world—if it needed to be shown—what ten years of Communist
domination have given to the peoples behind the Iron Curtain:
misery, injustice, oppression, humiliation, and despair. They
have proved too the impossibility of normal democratic development under Marxist rule. Where there is no freedom there can
be no bounds to oppression, no limits to the shedding of blood.

As a complement to the theme of this book a very brief
outline of the events from August 1956 up to the present
moment (July 1957) is given.

The Ukraine

After the congress of the Soviet Communist Party in February 1956, remarkable for Kruschev's anti-Stalinist speech, it seemed as if the Muscovite atheist régime had assumed a more liberal attitude towards the Catholic Church in the Ukraine.

Many Ukrainian priests, condemned to forced labour in Siberia, were allowed to return home. They were however strictly forbidden to exercise their pastoral ministry in public. Among those permitted to return were two bishops, Mgr. *John Latyszewskyj*, former Auxiliary Bishop of Stanislav and Mgr. *Nicholas Czarneckyj*, Apostolic Visitator for Volynia. According to recent reports the Metropolitan, Mgr. *Joseph Slipyj*, is still in Siberia. Only in December 1956 did the news come through of the death in Karaganda, Siberia, on 6 October 1949, of Mgr. *Niceta Budka*, Auxiliary Bishop of Lvov.

It was difficult for those returning from Siberia to get permission to reside in any district and to find work by which they might earn a livelihood. This was due in great part to the hostility of the Orthodox hierarchy which began protesting to the Central Government against the return of Catholic priests. More recently the Orthodox hierarchy, taking advantage of events in Hungary and of the sympathy shown by the people of the Ukraine towards the Hungarian insurgents, took a more open stand and publicly opposed the return of Catholic priests. As a reason for their attitude they asserted that this return constituted a public danger not only for the Orthodox Church but also for the safety of the Soviet Union, since these priests, always at the service of the Vatican and of the American Imperialists, were preparing the ground for a rebellion of the bourgeois nationalist elements in the Ukraine.

As a result of this agitation the Government took from all the priests returned from Siberia their personal papers and certificates of release from the concentration camps. On account of this these priests were forced to leave the Ukraine, and this invariably meant that they were again deported to Siberia. It is known with certainty that many priests were in this way sent back to Siberia and with them were deported thousands of the faithful. In fact it is believed on good authority that at the moment a third of the Catholic population of the Ukraine is in Siberia. The period of " less strained relations " as part of the anti-Stalinist *thaw* has passed and the persecution has begun again with greater violence against the Catholics of the Constantinopolitan-Slav Rite still left in the Ukraine. Although the Communist Government has forced youth of both sexes to enrol themselves in the *Komsomol* (Communist Union of Youth) and although by every means at its disposal it has carried on for twelve years an intense atheistic propaganda, recent trustworthy accounts from the Ukraine affirm that the young people are not entirely lost to the Catholic Church and to the cause of civilisation.

Orthodox propaganda, in which it is easy to recognise a first step towards State Atheism, has been no more successful among Catholic youth.

The fact that the Communists have set aside the policy of " relaxation " and have begun a new era of religious persecution must be attributed to the heroism of many Ukrainian Catholics and to certain courageous manifestations of their faith particularly on the part of the young people of the Ukraine.

* * *

Czechoslovakia

In mid-October 1956 Czechoslovak Government sources announced that two " high dignitaries " of the Catholic Church had been pardoned and set at liberty: Mgr. *John Vojtassak*, (former Bishop of Spis according to the official communiqué) and Mgr. *Michael Buzalka*, Auxiliary Bishop of the Apostolic Administration of Trnava. The two prelates were transferred to an unnamed place in Slovakia, where they were " guests " in one of the *Caritas* houses; they were allowed " to travel freely in the country," but not to return to their respective dioceses.

This act of " clemency " had an exclusively propagandist value serving to prove to the superficial and to those ignorant of the real facts the " desire for less strained relations " on the part of the Communists of Prague. In fact it followed on the deportation

in August and September 1956 of the nuns still employed as
nurses in the nationalised hospitals; it did not allow Mgr.
Vojtassak to resume the government of his diocese in place of
the vicar capitular whom the *Bureau for Ecclesiastical Affairs* had
imposed; this " liberty " was not extended to Mgr. *Gojdic*,
Bishop of Presov (for the Oriental Rite), one of the three bishops
condemned in the trial of January 1951.

On 12 November 1956 the 87 year old Bishop of Hradec-
Kralové, Mgr. *Maurice Picha*, died. He was free at the time but
his " freedom " was more apparent than real as the " competent
authorities " had imposed on him a vicar general of their own
choosing. Mgr. *Picha's* successor as administrator of the vacant
see, appointed by the supreme ecclesiastical authority, would
have been Mgr. *Charles Otcenasek*, titular Bishop of Chersonesus
in Crete. But the Government authorities had foreseen this for
a long time and had removed the young bishop, only 37 years
of age, to an unknown destination. There he is still detained
(March 1957).

In Czechoslovakia more completely than in other Communist-
controlled countries the external organisation of the Church
continues to be oppressed. Ecclesiastical jurisdiction is being
limited continually by the Communist State bureaucracy which
incessantly proclaims the separation of Church and State and
insists that religion is a private affair of the citizen.

The full liberty of worship which according to Communist
propaganda exists in Czechoslovakia is in fact no more than
freedom of worship in the churches, for the priest in the exercise
of his ministry must restrict himself to the administration of the
sacraments and to giving very limited religious instruction. If
he is zealous, if he has influence with the faithful, he becomes
suspect and is in serious danger.

Police and Party supervision goes on. Interference by the
civil and political authorities is such that the ordinaries and the
parish priests are not free to arrange even the hours for Mass.
These must be fixed according to the real or supposed demands
of so-called voluntary but actually obligatory labour.

In the summer of 1956, in the atmosphere of " relaxation of
tension," liberty was offered to many religious still held in the

" concentration monasteries," provided they undertook not to
wear the religious habit or get in touch with their superiors.
Almost all refused and remained in the places of concentration.
At about the same time (July 1956) some religious—Salesians
and Jesuits—were tried secretly and sentenced to severe
penalties. Their crime was that they had escaped some time
previously from a concentration monastery and had secretly
exercised their priestly ministry. They were tortured but did
not lose their calm dignity before their judges. One of the
accused, the provincial superior of a religious order in Slovakia,
declared that he alone as superior was responsible for the acts
of his subjects. This statement resulted in a more severe penalty
for him but did not save the others.

Marxist Materialism continues to be the basis of education in
all the schools. In primary education up to the fourth standard
religious instruction is still given. But according to a new regulation this must be asked for by *both the parents*. Formerly the
signature of one of the parents was sufficient. The spirit of the
new regulation will be clear to anyone who considers the
position among his fellow-workers of the father of a family who
asks for such instruction for his children.[1]

* * *

Poland

On 28 October 1956 it was announced that Cardinal *Wyszynski*,
Primate of Poland, had been set free. The Warsaw authorities,
shaken by the risings that had disturbed the country, intended
this gesture to prove that they had no part in the grave respon-

---

[1] Towards the end of June 1957 *Rudé Pravo* announced the arrest and—some days
later—the condemnation to various terms of imprisonment of a group of Salesian priests,
guilty of " illegal activity " and of spying for a " foreign power." *L'Osservatore Romano*
of 13 July 1957, in an article entitled " Una Republica esemplare," put itself the question:
how could the Prague authorities have ever revived the method of terror-trials, which,
as was universally known, the anti-Stalinists had declared to be " monstrosities " ? The
paper answered its own question by pointing out how the Central Committee of the
Czech Communist Party, in its meetings of 14 and 15 June, was pre-occupied with
the Church's persistent influence on youth, and decided to intensify anti-religious
propaganda, without however (according to the well-worn reservation) touching in
any way " freedom of religion." For *L'Osservatore Romano* the arrests and condemnations
pointed in an obvious direction, since the return to methods and systems which for
some time had been put aside as " monstrosities " of the Stalinist tyranny could not
be without significance.

sibility that devolved on their predecessors for the act of violence of 26 September 1953. The Cardinal Primate himself sent a telegram to the Holy Father informing him of his release. The Pope replied at once that he hoped the event would mean for Poland that peace " which is founded on justice and charity and on the freedom that belongs to the Church."

Michalski, mouthpiece of the Communist régime, commented on the news over Radio-Warsaw:

> " The return of the Primate does not belie what we have been saying for a year, namely, that even in that period (of Stalinist oppression) the Church enjoyed freedom of worship; it was not unlimited freedom, but it was freedom nevertheless. Catholics were not alone in their opposition to the removal of the Primate from public life. The decision to put the Cardinal away belongs to the Stalinist period in the politics of our country. The return of the Primate proves that that period is at an end and that we have reverted, at least in the Church-State sector, to bi-lateral discussion of controversial matters. This does not mean that such matters do not now exist, nor does it mean that the Church may again take part in political life. Separation of Church and State is a definite formula for the co-existence of civil society with ecclesiastical society. Separation is a constitutional advance which we are not alone in having achieved. . . .
>
> " The return of Cardinal *Wyszynski* to his see is a return to the good method of interchange of views and the casting aside of the method of unilateral decisions."

In a word this situation is at most a *return to the position existing after the joint Declaration of the Government and the episcopate on 14 April 1950.* It would seem that this is the sense too in which *Gomulka's* words are to be taken when he promised that confiscated Church property would be restored and that the other bishops would be reinstated in their sees.

On 6 November it was announced that five bishops had returned to the duties they had been obliged to abandon when they were arrested during the reign of the Stalinist " clique." These were: Mgr. *Adamski*, Bishop of Katowice; his Coadjutor, Mgr. *Bernorz*; his Auxiliary, Mgr. *Bieniek*; the Auxiliary Bishop of Gniezno, Mgr. *Baraniak*, and the Vicar General of the same diocese, Mgr. *Bernacki*.

Realising that satisfactory relations with the Church were a necessity in a country predominantly Catholic, the Gomulka Government in the month of November favoured the setting-up of a mixed State-Church Commission to settle outstanding problems between the Government and the episcopate. This Commission was made up as follows: for the Government, M. *Sztachelski* and M. *Morawski* a member of the Politburo; for the episcopate, Mgr. *Klepacz* and Mgr. *Choromanski*, both of whom had signed the 1950 agreement.

In a communiqué dated 8 December the Commission announced an Agreement in principle on a certain number of questions. The most important dealt with the re-introduction of religious instruction in the schools. It was laid down that this should be an optional, extra-curricular subject, given by teachers appointed jointly by the school and Church authorities and paid for by the State. The Commission also recommended the abrogation of the decree of February 1953 which gave the State power to arrange all ecclesiastical appointments, and the drafting of a new law to provide for consultations between the episcopate and the Government before new appointments were made. The Commission further called for provision to be made for religious care of the sick and those in prison and for the return of nuns and priests expelled from the " western territories " in 1953. Finally the Commission referred to the Agreement entered into between the Government and the episcopate on 4 December which accepted the temporary compromise solution proposed by the Holy See and the bishops in 1951 for the administration of the dioceses situated in the " western territories." In virtue of this Agreement the titular bishops nominated by the Holy See were acknowledged. These titular bishops would be created ordinaries when a peace treaty finally settled the status of the " western territories."

On 10 December with the permission granted to the editors of the weekly *Tygodnik Powszechny* and of the monthly *Znak* to resume the posts from which they had been dismissed in 1953, it could be said that the monopoly of the Catholic press, held up to this by the " progressive " Catholics of the *Pax* association, was broken.[2]

Towards the end of January 1957 the Polish elections marked clearly the success of *Wladislaw Gomulka* and the so-called " National Front." The Polish people had freedom to choose only between a " new Communist road " based especially on the personality and former attitude of *Gomulka*, and a Communism imposed from outside as in Hungary with all its ruinous consequences. In such circumstances only one choice could be expected: the National Front.

Shortly before the elections the ecclesiastical authority limited itself to reminding Catholics of their duty to vote. Their one desire was to spare the Polish nation strife, bloodshed and ruin. Abstentionism or voting against the National Front would in fact have brought with it tragedy within the country and armed intervention from without.

At the moment it is impossible to say how lasting will be the re-establishment of certain fundamental religious freedoms in Poland. Communism if it remains loyal to its principles cannot renounce the anti-religious struggle. But a State directed by Communists can in a moment of supreme difficulty and under the immediate threat of a tragedy such as happened in Hungary renounce the application of certain of its ideological prejudices and undertake an apparent change of policy. The situation in Poland continues to be difficult; the elections of January 1957 evidently have not solved the Polish political problem nor have they shown, as some try to pretend, that in this country at least co-operation between Catholicism and Communism has been achieved.

Many grave problems regarding the liberty of the Church still

[2] The " progressive " movement is at present on the wane in Poland. Its leader, M. Piasecki, was a protégé of one of the most Stalinist members of the Politburo and therefore had no choice but to support the Stalinists during recent events in Poland. Until October 1956 the Communists continued to try to use the movement to undermine the influence of the Church, but it has always been rejected by the great majority of Polish Catholics. Since his release Cardinal Wyszynski has again condemned the movement. Some of its members are now trying to form new, less compromised groups and have dissociated themselves from M. Piasecki. But an " All Polish Club of Progressive Catholic Intellectuals," formed on 5 November under the leadership of those who had been victimised previously, appears to be the most popular and promising Catholic grouping

await solution in Poland.   It is not the time to indulge in optimism.   Future relations between the Communist State and the Catholic Church will depend on how the Government puts into practice the new agreements.   The Polish Government so completely disregarded the spirit of the 1950 Agreement that the bishops complained of the régime's " implacable hatred " of the Church.   It is better to wait and see what will be *in fact* the attitude of the Communist *Gomulka*.

More recent information (March 1957) about the practice of religion in Poland is as in the past consoling.   The Catholic Church guided by the noble figure of the Cardinal Primate *Wyszynski* manifests a spiritual and intellectual fervour which oppression has only ripened and invigorated.

In the uncertainty that must remain as regards the future this constitutes one element of certainty.[3]

* * *

Hungary

In Hungary, 30 October 1956, regular army formations and a group of insurgents liberated Cardinal *Mindszenty* from Felsöpeteny prison to which he had been transferred some days previously from his " forced residence." A communiqué of the Council of Ministers of the *Nagy* Government dated 1 November stated that the Primate could again exercise his ecclesiastical functions and his civil rights, because his condemnation had been *devoid of all justification*.

---

[3] The latest more outstanding events during the summer of 1957 have to do with Cardinal Wyszynski's visit to Rome.   On returning to Poland, the Primate published a Pastoral Letter, dated 19 June 1957. This appeared however only on 7 July in the weekly *Tygodnik Powszechny*.   The Cardinal emphasised the *purely religious nature* of his visit and indicated as a programme for the celebration of the thousandth anniversary of the propagation of the Christian Faith in Poland " the struggle to remain faithful to God, to the Cross, to the Gospel, to the Church and her pastors, and to our Fatherland, advance-guard of Christianity."   After the Cardinal's return, the Polish censorship prevented the publication of one of his communications in which he forbade ecclesiastics to publish books through the agency of the " progressive " editing organisation " Pax " or to collaborate in any way whatsoever in its periodical publications.   As is well known, even under the Gomulka Government and in spite of repeated protests by the Polish Hierarchy and explicit condemnations by the Holy See, Piasecki's " progressive " political group, " Pax," continues to call itself *Catholic* and to pursue its aim of " conciliation " of Polish national-Catholicism with the policy of the Communist régime.

It is scarcely necessary to recall the sad turn of events in Hungary shortly after the insurrection had restored the democratic liberties of the people.

When with the help of Soviet tanks the fierce and repressive rule of *Janos Kadar* had been consolidated the persecution in Hungary increased in violence. In January 1957 several priests were arrested and brought before the courts, accused of " counter-revolutionary activity." Religious instruction in the schools, re-established during the short-lived period of the *Nagy* Government, has come under bitter attack from the President of the Council, *Kadar*. He has not been ashamed to state publicly: " We will not allow the re-actionary elements to continue to exercise their influence over women and to torture (*sic*) our children by teaching them the knowledge of God."

Indications of the present situation in Hungary are to be seen in the attacks made by members of the Government and by the Party press on some members of the episcopate. These attacks have been directed especially against Cardinal *Mindszenty*. After his liberation by the insurgents he had been living in the vicinity of the USA Legation in Budapest. Since 5 November when Russian tanks advanced into the city he has found refuge in the Legation.

The official paper of the Communist Party, *Nepszabadzag*, in the first days of February accused Cardinal *Mindszenty* of being behind the action taken by the Bishops of Vac and Székesfehérvár against " democratic and progressive priests " in preventing them from " taking part in religious functions . . . " The paper contested the bishops' " right to discredit and set aside faithful sons of the country and of the Church, among them deputies and most important directors of the National Committee of Catholic Priests for Peace . . . "[4]

The truth is that the Hungarian bishops had merely put into

---

[4] The attack of the Communist paper gave the American Legation in Budapest the opportunity to clarify its position. It declared that " while the personal safety and well-being of the Cardinal were being looked after in the best possible way within the Legation, at the same time nothing was left undone and nothing is being left undone on the part of the diplomatic representation of the United States to ensure that the Cardinal does not in any way make use of the Legation to carry on political activities or activities connected with politics."

effect the letter and the spirit of a decree of the Sacred Congregation of the Council, 21 January (*AAS*, XXXXIX, 38-39),
which threatened with grave penalties about a dozen Hungarian
priests who already for some time had been suspended *a divinis*
because they had accepted without any authority ecclesiastical
offices from the Communists. Should they not submit to certain
prescriptions of that Congregation (renunciation of the offices
arbitrarily assigned them and now held without authority) they
would incur excommunication reserved *speciali modo*. The
Cistercian priest, *Horvath*, in virtue of this decree incurred
excommunication immediately for his evident reluctance to
comply with the prescriptions of the competent ecclesiastical
authority.

The Sacred Congregation of the Council by this decree simply
applied permanent norms of Canon Law.

* * *

The hope that events in Poland and Hungary in October-
November 1956 marked the beginning of the end of an era of
persecution, of abuse of power, of tears and blood, has up
to now proved illusory. The attitude of the Communist
Governments towards religion has not changed. In spite of
the " new road " announced at first, in spite of the promised
" democratisation " and the vaunted elimination of the " criminal
cliques " of the past, everything points to the fact that with
the reinforcing of the Iron Curtain the forces of " counter-
revolution," represented primarily for the Communists by the
Catholic Church, will feel the strain more keenly as the *screw
gets one more turn*. Marxist Communism, whether it assumes the
guise of savage Stalinist tyranny or of the smiling " relaxation " of
Bulganin, or of the " peaceful co-existence " of *Kruschev*, can never
mean anything but slavery and oppression. Neither can the
Church expect anything from the re-habilitation of the " devia-
tionists " and the " Titoists." *National Communism is no less the
enemy of the Church than is Soviet orthodoxy.*

At a time so full of sorrow for Hungary and so fraught with
danger for the countries of Eastern Europe the voice of Pope

Pius XII has been raised in three Encyclicals[5] and in an Appeal (10 November 1956) to the world—something entirely new in the history of the Church and in Pontifical procedure.

On 28 October 1956, asking for public prayers to obtain peace based on justice for the Hungarian people torn by bloody war, the Pope wrote in *Luctuosissimi eventus*:

> " Let it be clear to everybody that when order has been destroyed among nations it cannot be restored by force of arms, the bearer of death, or by oppressing the citizens by violence which cannot stifle their innermost feelings, or by deceptive theories which corrupt the heart and violate the rights of the Church and of all civic and Christian conscience. The longing for true liberty can never be smothered by force."

And on 5 November 1956 in *Datis nuperrime*:

> " Conscious of our duty we cannot but deplore and condemn these tragic events which have aroused the indignation and deep sorrow not only of Catholics everywhere but of all free peoples. . . . For the word of the Lord to Cain: ' The voice of thy brother's blood cries to me from the earth,' is still true to-day; the blood of the people of Hungary cries out to the Lord. And if the Just Judge often does not punish man for his sin till after death, His vengeance sometimes falls even in this life—as history teaches—on rulers and on nations for the injustices they have inflicted on others."

And in his world-wide Appeal on 10 November *Pius XII*, having recalled " the outrage culminating in the ruin of the beloved people of Hungary, whose crime was to have sought respect for the fundamental rights of human beings," he proclaimed:

> " But the import of the sorrowful events in Hungary weighs on the hearts of men more than all other anxieties. The universal and spontaneous emotion of the world, which the attention given to

---

[5] *Luctuosissimi eventus*, 28 October 1956, *Laetamur admodum*, 1 November 1956, *Datis nuperrime*, 5 November 1956.

other grave events has not been able to diminish, shows how necessary and urgent it is to give back liberty to those who have been deprived of it.

" Can the world allow itself to be indifferent to the lot of our brothers and *abandon them to the fate of a degrading slavery?* Surely Christian conscience cannot escape the moral obligation of trying by every permissible means to restore their dignity and give them back liberty."

The terrible crime against Christianity, civilisation and human dignity perpetrated in Hungary has recalled to the free world the imminent peril represented by Communism which brings in its train the spiritual, moral and economic oppression of whole nations.[6] The drama of the Church of Silence continues. The struggle in Hungary is not, as Communist propaganda would have men believe, a struggle between the proletarian revolution and bourgeois re-action. It is a fight between tyranny and the spirit of liberty, a fight for the defence of all that is noblest and best in the heart of man.

---

[6] See the impressive documentation on this matter in the two volumes of the United Nations' *Report of the Special Committee on the problem of Hungary*, dated 12 June 1957. The Special Committee, made up of representatives from Australia, Ceylon, Denmark, Tunisia, and Uruguay, was established following on a Resolution of the United Nations' General Assembly on 10 January 1957. The Report is particularly striking for the fact that an organ of the United Nations—contrary to what happened on other occasions —was able to pronounce so clear and unanimous a condemnation of Soviet aggression. In spite of this condemnation however the system of savage repression and of prison and death sentences continued under the Kadar régime.

It is enough to recall here the wave of arrests of Catholic clergy which took place at the end of July and the beginning of August 1957. A communiqué of the Ministry for External Affairs gave as reasons for these arrests charges such as: " compilation and printing of large numbers of pamphlets and other propagandist material, which was distributed chiefly in the counter-revolutionary armed centers." The Encyclicals of the Holy Father were called " the injurious circulars of Pope Pius XII on events in Hungary." All this however did not prevent the Kadar Government from bringing pressure to bear on the bishops and faithful in an effort to make them side with the régime, in the hope perhaps of obtaining a kind of moral re-adjustment. It is in the light of this " policy " too that one should consider the favour shown in these last months to a new organisation for ecclesiastics called " Opus Pacis " and belonging to the equivocal *National Committee for Peace*.

Documents of His Holiness Pope Pius XII on the Persecution of the Catholic Church

Besides frequent references to the persecution of the Church which may be found in the many messages and discourses of the Holy Father, the following documents on particular aspects of the Church's sufferings have been published. Also, to Pius XII is due the amazing expression " Church of Silence " to signify that part of the Christian community whose " hands are bound and whose lips are closed " (Radio Message, Christmas 1951).

1945—23 December: Encyclical *Orientales omnes Ecclesias*, published on the occasion of the 350th anniversary of the re-union of the Ruthenian Church with the Holy See. *AAS* XXXVIII (1946), pp. 36-63.

1949—11 January: Apostolic Letter *Acerrimo mœrore*, in which the Holy Father deplores the arrest of Cardinal Mindszenty. *AAS* XXXXI (1949), pp. 29-30.

1949—14 February: Secret Consistory. Allocution against the condemnation of Cardinal Mindszenty. *AAS* XXXXI (1949), pp. 41-45.

1949—16 February: Discourse of the Sovereign Pontiff to the plenary audience of the Diplomatic Corps after the Budapest sentence. *AAS* XXXXI (1949), pp. 73-74.

1949—20 February: Discourse to the Romans on the sacred rights of the Church. *AAS* XXXXI (1949), pp. 74-76.

1949—1 September: Letter *Decennium dum expletur* to the Polish
                       Episcopate. *AAS* XXXXI (1949), pp. 450-453.

1951—1 September: Letter *Cum jam lustri* to the Polish Episcopate.
                       AAS XLIII (1951), pp. 775-778.

1951—28 October: Apostolic Letter *Impensiore caritate* to the
                       Episcopate, clergy and faithful of Czecho-
                       slovakia, on the suffering of the Czechoslovak
                       Church. *AAS* XLIII (1951), pp. 768-772.

1952—18 January: Apostolic Letter *Cupimus imprimis* to the
                       Episcopate, clergy and faithful of China.
                       AAS XLIV (1952), pp. 153-158.

1952—27 March: Apostolic Letter *Veritatem facientes* on the
                       persecution of the Church in Romania.
                       AAS XLIV (1952), pp. 249-253.

1952—7 July: Apostolic Letter *Sacro vergente anno* to all the
                       peoples of Russia. *AAS* XLIV (1952), pp.
                       505-511.

1952—14 November: Discourse of the Holy Father on the occasion
                       of the 20th anniversary of the foundation of
                       the College Saint Josaphat at Rome (summary
                       of the persecution of the Catholic Church in
                       the Ukraine). *AAS* XLIV (1952), pp.
                       876-878.

1952—15 December: Encyclical Letter *Orientales ecclesias* on the
                       persecution of the Catholic Church of the
                       Oriental Rite in Bulgaria and Czechoslovakia.
                       AAS XLV (1953), pp. 5-14.

1953—16 July: Apostolic Letter *In Poloniae annalibus* to the
                       Episcopate, clergy and faithful of Poland, on
                       the occasion of the 7th centenary of the
                       canonisation of St. Stanislas. *AAS* XLV (1953),
                       pp. 498-502.

| 1953—19 November: | Discourse of the Holy Father to the Heads of Mission of the Diplomatic Corps accredited to the Holy See, on the occasion of the molestations inflicted on Cardinal Wyszynski. *AAS* XLV (1953), pp. 755-756. |

| 1954—7 October: | Encyclical Letter *Ad Sinarum gentem*. *AAS* XLVII (1955), pp. 5-14. |

| 1955—8 December: | Apostolic Letter *Gloriosam Reginam* to the Polish Episcopate, on the occasion of the 3rd centenary of the miraculous protection of the Sanctuary of Our Lady at Jasna Gora (Czestochowa). *AAS* XLVIII (1956), pp. 73-77. |

| 1956—29 June: | Apostolic Letter *Dum maerenti animo* to Cardinals Mindszenty, Stepinac and Wyszynski, and to the archbishops, bishops, clergy and faithful of Albania, Bulgaria, Czechoslovakia, Yugoslavia, Poland, Romania, Hungary and East Germany, on the occasion of the 5th centenary of the Bull of Calistus III, announcing prayers and other devotions against the Turkish threat. *ASS* XLVIII (1956), pp. 549-554. |

| 1957—19 July: | Prayer composed by the Holy Father for "The Church of Silence." Cf. *L'Osservatore Romano*, 19 July 1957. Here is a translation of the prayer: |

O Lord Jesus, King of martyrs, comfort of the afflicted, support and consolation of all those who suffer for love of You and because of their loyalty to Your Spouse, Holy Mother the Church, in Your kindness hear our fervent prayers for our brothers of the "Church of Silence." Grant that they may never weaken in the struggle nor waver in the Faith. Rather may they experience the sweetness of the consolation You reserve for those souls whom You deign to call to be Your companions on the height of the cross.

To those who must bear torments and violence, hunger and toil, may You be the unshakeable strength which supports them in their trials and fills them with the certainty of the rewards promised to those who persevere to the end.

To those who are subjected to moral constraints, often all the more dangerous because they are more deceitful, may You be the light which illuminates their understanding so that they may clearly perceive the straight road of truth. May You be the strength which supports their will, enabling them to overcome every crisis, every vacillation and weariness.

For those who cannot openly profess their Faith, practise the Christian life regularly, receive the holy sacraments frequently, consult in a filial way with their spiritual guides, may You Yourself be the hidden altar, the invisible temple, superabundant grace and paternal voice, which helps them, encourages them, heals their afflicted spirits and gives them joy and peace.

May our fervent prayer be of help to them. May our fraternal solidarity make them feel that they are not alone. May their example be edifying for the whole Church, especially for us who think of them with so much affection.

Grant, O Lord, that the days of trial be shortened and that very soon—together with their converted oppressors—they may freely serve and adore You, who with the Father and the Holy Spirit livest and reignest for ever and ever. Amen.

Partial Indulgence of 3 years for those who devoutly recite this prayer.

Certain other references will be found in footnotes throughout the book.

Bibliography

||||||||

LIST OF SOME USEFUL WORKS ON CERTAIN ASPECTS OF THE COMMUNIST PERSECUTION

I.—Communism and Religion

Different authors: *Le Communisme et les Chrétiens*. Paris, 1946.

BERDIAEFF N.   *Le Marxisme et la Religion*. Paris, 1947.

COMBES J.   *L'Assaut contre le Christ au XXe siècle*. Paris, 1948.

HERNANDEZ J. M.   *La Iglesia del Silencio*. Madrid, 1953.

MAC EOIN G.   *The Communist War on Religion*. New York, 1951.

SHUSTER A.   *Religion behind the Iron Curtain*. New York, 1954.

REGONDI L.   *Rose e Sangue oltre la cortina di ferro*. Roma, 1953.

PLAMER G.   *I Partigiani di Dio*. Milan, 1953.

BREVI G.   *Russia, 1942-1953*. Milan, 1954.

ESCOLA D.   *Nosotros y los catolicos del Este*. Barcelona, 1955.

XXX   *La Chiesa del Silenzio*. Rome, 1952.

XXX   *Der Kampf des Kommunismus gegen die Religion*. Aschaffenburg, 1952.

XXX   *Kirche in Not—Priesternot—Kirche in Not—Bolschewismus-Ersatzreligion*. Königstein, 1952, 1953, 1956.

XXX   *Communisme et Religion* (La doctrine, les méthodes, les faits). *La Documentation Catholique*, col. 1129-1130, 7-21 September 1952.

GUSSONI l .   *The Silent Church*. New York, 1954.

XXX   *Christian Churches in Eastern Europe*. A survey of Communist tactics. July, 1956 (without indication of place).

Tabor (year VII, vol. XIII), *La Chiesa del Silenzio*.

III.—USSR

A.—RUSSIA

SCHWEIGL G.   *Il Cristianesimo nell'Unione Sovietica*. Rome, 1948.

AMMAN A. M.   *Storia della Chiesa Russa*. Turin, 1948.

MAC CULLAGH F.   *The Bolshevik Persecution of Christianity*. London, 1924.

EMHARDT E.   *Religion in Soviet Russia Anarchy*. London, 1929.

HARDER B. — *Die Religion in Rot-Russland.* Harz, 1928.
D'HERBIGNY M. — *La Guerre antireligieuse en Russie soviétique.* Paris, 1930.
MARTEL R. — *Le Mouvement antireligieux en U.R.S.S.* Paris, 1922.
TIMASHEFF N. S. — *Religion in Soviet Russia (1917-1942).* London, 1943.
VON ECKAROTT H. — *Russisches Christentum.* Munich, 1947.
BRIEM E. — *Kommunismus und Religion in der Sowjetunion.* Basel, 1948.
ANDERSON P. — *People, Church and State in Modern Russia.* New York, 1944.
ZERNOV N. — *The Russians and their Church.* London 1945.
DE VRIES W. — *Christentum in der Sowjetunion.* Heidelberg, 1950.
CAPUCCIO — *Russia, regno dell'anticristo.* Milan, 1953.

B.—LATVIA

XXX — *The Soviets against Church. Persecution in Soviet Latvia.* Latvian Central Committee, Germany, 1950.
XXX — *The Catholic Church of Latvia under the bolshevik torture.* Stockholm, 1950.

C.—LITHUANIA

XXX — *Appeal to the United Nations on Genocide.* Published by Lithuanian Foreign Service. Washington, 1951.
LATU R. — *L'Eglise derrière le rideau de fer.* Paris, 1948.
MAUCLERE J. — *La situation de l'Eglise catholique en Lithuanie.* Le Raincy, 1950.

D.—UKRAINE

XXX — *Primi Incatenati—Libro bianco sulla persecuzione religiosa in Ucraina.* Rome, 1953. There are also editions of the book in English: *First victims of Communism,* Rome, 1953, and in German: *Die ersten Oper des Kommunismus,* Munich, 1953.
CHOMIK M. — *La Lutte de l'Eglise catholique de l'Ukraine contre le Communisme.* Logos, I, 1950.
DE VRIES G. — *Cattolici Ruteni.* La Civiltà Cattolica, 1950, vol. I.
DE VRIES G. — *Soppressione della Chiesa greco-cattolica nella Subcarpazia.* La Civiltà Cattolica, 1950, vol. II.
BUCKO G. — *Il Metropolita Andrea Szeptyckyj, grande figura della Chiesa cattolica Ucraina.* Albano Laziale (s.a.).
ACTS OF THE SYNOD OF LWOW — (In Ukrainian), Lwow, 1946.

IV.—Albania

CAVALLI F. — *Persecuzione religiosa nell'Albania Communista.* La Civiltà Cattolica, 1947, 7 June and 19 July.
FIDES (International Agency) — Documentation. Fascicle of March 1953.

VI.—Bulgaria

CAVALLI F.   *Persecuzione religiosa nella Repubblica Popolare Bulgara.* La Civiltà Cattolica, 17 January 1953.
XXX   *Les Lois sur les Cultes en Bulgarie.* La Documentation Catholique, 1949, col. 1205-1209.

VII.—China

DUFAY F.   *L'Etoile contre la Croix.* Hong Kong and Paris, 1954.
MONSTERLEET J.   *Les Martyrs de Chine parlent.* Paris, 1953.
REMY   *Pourpre des Martyres.* Paris, 1953.
CAVALLI F.   *Indipendenza e libertà della Chiesa nella Cina Communista.* Rome, 1951.
DRANSARD L.   *Vu en Chine.* Paris, 1952.
DE LEFFE J.   *Chrétiens dans la Chine de Mao.* Paris, 1955.
DE ECHALAR P.   *Il Communismo contra il Cristianesimo in Cina.* Rome, 1951.
BONNICHON A.   *La Persécution en Chine et l'Encyclique* Ad Sinarum gentem. Rome, 1955.
LEFEUVRE J.   *Shanghaï; Les enfants dans la ville.* Cronique de la vie chrétienne a Shanghaï, 1949-1955. Paris-Tournai, 1956.
CICR   *Livre Blanc sur le Travail forcé et les Institutions concentrationnaires dans la Republic Populaire de Chine.* Paris, 1957.

VIII.—Korea

" GENTES "   (Special issue, March 1949).
CHANG L.   *Le Clocher de la Croix sur la Terre Rouge.* Fusan, 1951.
O'CONNOR P.   *Faith behind barbed Wires.* NCWC News Service, 1953.
XXX   *Schicksal in Korea, Deutsche Missionaere berichten.* Abbey of St. Ottilia, Germany (no date).
XXX   *Trois ans de captivité d'une religieuse dans la Corée du Nord.* Annales des Soeurs de Saint-Paul-de-Chartres, July 1953.
LANE R. A.   *Ambassador in Chains.* The Life of Bishop Patrick James Byrne. New York, 1955.

IX.—Hungary

XXX   *Livre Blanc.* Quatre années de lutte pour la défense de l'Eglise Hongroise. Paris, 1949.
HONTI F.   *Le drame hongrois.* Une grande bataille de la civilization chrétienne. Paris, 1949.
NAGY F.   *La Lotta dietro la cortina di ferro.* Milan, 1950.
PETERFFY S.   *Il Cardinale Mindszenty.* Rome, 1949.
BOER N.   *Il Cardinale Mindszenty.* Milan, 1950.
FABIAN B.   *Cardinal Mindszenty, the story of a modern martyr.* New York, 1949.
MIHALOVICS S.   *Mindszenty—Ungarn Europa—Ein Zeugenbericht.* Karlsruhe, 1949.
JUST B.   *Un procès préfabriqué, l'affaire Mindszenty.* Paris 1949.
DOMENACH   *Le procès des évêques hongrois.* Esprit, September 1951.
XXX   *The Case of Archbishop Grösz.* Clergy Review, August 1951.

XXX — *La persecution religieuse en Hongrie.* La Documentation Catholique, 1949: col. 131-161; 209-230; 257-280; 321-352.

CAVALLI F. — *La Chiesa Cattolica nella Repubblica Popolare Ungherese.* La Civiltà Cattolica, 15 September 1951.

XXX — *Recent Events in Hungary.* Clergy Review, October 1950.

VON VARNA KELEMEN A. — *Die Stimme des Rufenden—Das Leben des Kardinal Fürstprimas von Ungarn.* Saarlouis, 1950.

UNITED NATIONS. — *Report of Special Committee on the problem of Hungary.* Volumes I and II, dated 12 June 1957.

X.—Poland

XXX — *White Paper on the persecution of the Church in Poland.* London, 1954.

XXX — *New moves in the Communist struggle against the Church in Poland.* London, 1955.

LEVEQUE M. — *Persécution en Pologne.* Paris, 1954.

XXX — *L'Eglise et l'Etat en Pologne.* La Documentation Catholique, 1946, col. 1028-1041.

XXX — *La situation de l'Eglise catholique en Pologne.* La Documentation Catholique, 1950, col. 727-735 and 807-829.

TUROWICZ — *L'expérience polonaise.* Terre Humaine, April 1952.

LENTEN A. P. — *Situation du Catholicisme en Pologne.* Dossier de la Semaine, 7 July 1952.

NAUROIS, C. — *Dieu contre Dieu?* Drame des Catholiques progressistes dans une Eglise du Silence. Fribourg-Paris, 1956.

XI.—Romania

XXX — *Biserica Romana Unita* (different authors). Madrid, 1952.

MARKHAM H. R. — *La Roumanie sous le joug soviétique.* Paris, 1949.

GHERMAN P. — *L'Ame roumaine écartelée.* Paris, 1955.

STEFANESCU G. — *Le Calvaire des Catholiques en Roumanie.* Paris, 1953.

XXX — *Reintregirea Bisericii Romanesti Unite din Ardeal.* Bucharest, 1949.

HERBERT L. — *Le Drame de l'Eglise Unie en Roumanie.* La Documentation Catholique, 1949, col. 833-891 and 923-936.

JANIN R. — *L'Eglise catholique en Roumanie.* La Documentation Catholique, 1951, col. 423-436.

XXX — *Persecution of Religion in Rumania.* Washington, 1949.

MIRCEA A. — *Persecución comunista de la Religión en Rumania.* Madrid, 1954.

POP N. — *Kirche unter Hammer und Sichel.* Die Kirchenverfolgung in Rumänien 1945-1951. Berlin, 1953.

XII.—Czechoslovakia

CAVALLI F. — *Governo comunisto e Chiesa cattolica in Cecoslovacchia.* Rome, 1950.

MANNOY R. — *Comment on bolchevise un pays.* Louvain, 1951.

MICHEL A. — *Problèmes religieux dans un pays sous régime communiste.* Paris, 1955.

NEMEC L. — *Church and State in Czecoslovakia, theologically, juridically and historically documented.* New York, 1954.

ROSSETI M. V. — *Un viaggio oltre cortina.* Turin, 1955.

ZUBEK T. — *The Church of Silence in Slovakia.* Passaic, 1956.

XIII.—Viet Nam

XXX   *Terror in Viet-Nam: a record of another broken pledge.* Washington, 1955.

XIV.—Yugoslavia

XXX   *Une Eglise du Silence—Catholiques de Yougoslavie.* Bruges, 1954.

PATEE R.   *The Case of Cardinal Aloysius Stepinac.* Milwaukee, 1949.

CAVALLI F.   *Il processo dell'Arcivescovo di Zagabria.* Rome, 1947.

MIGLIORATI V.   *La Chiesa nella Repubblica Federativa Popolare Jugoslava.* *La Civiltà Cattolica,* 1946: 6 July, 7 September and 19 October; 1947: 21 June.

Analytical Index

" Agit-Prop "
27.

Agrarian Reform
See under various countries.

Agreements, Accords, etc.
10; and see under various countries.

ALBANIA
110-127 ; Agreements, Accords, etc., 119-125; Arrests, 113, 115, 116, 117, 118, 119, 120; Bishops, 112, 118, 119, 121, 122, 123, 125; Catholic Action, 113; Catholic Press, 112, 113, 126; Catholic Works, 112, 126; Celibacy, 124; Church Organisation before the Persecution, 111; Church Property, 124; Communist Accession to Power, 110; Communist Congress of Parmeti, 110; Communist Propaganda, 113, 116; Constitution, 111; Democratic Front, 110; Deportations, 113; Dissident National Church, 119, 120; Elections, 110; Expulsions, 114, 115, 117; Freedom of Religion, 110; Mohammedans, 111, 119; National Anti-Fascist Committee, 110; Nuns, 126; Oath of Fidelity, 124; Official Church Language, 121; Orthodox Church, 111, 119; Parishes, 111, 123, 124; People's Republic of Albania, 110; Persecution, 112 *et seq.*; Priests, 111, 112, 117, 120, 124, 125, 127; Religious, 124, 125; Religious Houses, 111, 112, 117, 126; Schools, 114, 115, 116, 126; Seminaries, 113, 116, 121, 126; Separation, 111; Statutes, 119, 120; Trials and Sentences, 114, 116, 118; Vicars Capitular, 122, 123; Worship, 124; Youth Organisations, 113, 116.

Anti-religious Laws, Decrees, etc.
See under various countries.

Anti-religious Propaganda
27 *et seq.*; and see under various countries.

Apathy (Christian)
1.

Arrests
9; and see under various countries.

Atheism
1; and passim Chapters 3-15.

Bishops
See under various countries.

BULGARIA
152-161 ; Anti-religious Propaganda, 155, 158; Arrests, 154, 159, 160, 161; Bishops, 154, 158, 160; Catholic Press, 154, 157; Church Organisation before the Persecution,

153; Communist Press, 160, 161; Confiscations, 155, 157, 158, 159; Constitution, 152, 156; Education, 153, 157; Elections, 152, 153; Expulsions, 154, 159; Freedom of Conscience and of Religion, 153, 156, 159; Marriage, 153; Nuns, 160, 161; Orthodox Church, 156; Priests 154, 156, 157, 160, 161; Religious, 153; Religious Denominations, 156, 157, 158; Religious Houses, 153, 155, 161; Schools, 153, 155; Seminaries, 159; Soviet Occupation, 152; Trials, 159, 160; Worship, 156; Youth Organisations, 157.

Bureaux for Ecclesiastical Affairs

10-13, 16; and see under various countries (*State Bureau for Ecclesiastical Affairs*).

CARPATHO-UKRAINE

102-109 ; Agrarian Reform, 103; Annexation, 101, 103, 109; Arrests, 101, 109; Basilian Fathers, 104, 106, 107; Bishops, 103, 104, 106; Church Organisation before the Persecution, 99; Communist Press, 103, 104; Confiscations, 103, 104, 105; Constitution, 104; Department of Worship, 103; Deportations, 105, 106, 109; Dissident National Church, 101, 105; Greek Catholic Church, 102, 105, 106, 108, 109; Manifesto, 102; Orthodox Church, 99, 101, 102, 103, 104, 105, 106, 107, 109; Outrages, 101, 107; Parishes, 99, 103, 104; Places of Worship, 99; Preaching, 104; Priests, 99, 103, 104, 106, 109; Re-education, 109; Religious Houses, 99; Religious Teaching, 99, 104; Schismatic Synod, 105; Schools, 99; Soviet Occupation, 100; Treaties, 98; Uniate Church, 102, 104, 105, 108; War, 98, 99; Worship, 103.

Catechism
See under *Religious Teaching*.

Catholic Action
See under various countries.

Catholic Associations
7, and see under various countries.

Catholic Press
See under various countries.

CHINA

162-184 ; American Imperialism, 175 (*et passim*); Anti-religious Propaganda, 165, 166, 167, 173, 176; Arrests, 168, 177, 178, 179, 180, 181, 183; Atheism, 166, 167; Bishops, 163, 169, 171, 175, 176, 178; Catholic Press, 172, 177; Church Organisation before the Persecution, 163; Churches, 168, 170, 177; Civil War, 162, 163, 164; Communist Ideology, 162; Confiscations, 167, 169, 172; Constitution, 165, 171, 175; Dissident National Church, 173 *et seq.*, 175; Expulsions, 177, 178, 182; Freedom of Religion, 165, 166, 171, 172; Imprisonment, 178, 180, 181, 183; Kuomintang, 169; Legion of Mary, 172, 177, 179, 180; "Long March" 162; Marriage, 167; Marxism, 165, 170, 171, 172, 175; Missionaries, 163, 164, 167, 168, 169, 170, 171, 174, 178, 181, 183; Outrages, 170; People's Courts, 168, 170, 180; People's Republic, 163; Persecution, 164, 165, 171, 181; Poverty, 177; Preaching, 166, 174; Priests, 163, 164, 170, 171, 174, 175, 177, 178, 179, 180, 183; Re-education, 165, 167, 174, 175, 180; Religious Teaching, 167; Schools, 164, 166, 167, 168, 172, 177; Seminaries, 177; Statutes, 175, 176; Systematic Persecution, 164, 165; Taxes, 167; Trials, 168, 169, 170; Triple Autonomy, 173, 175, 178, 179; Universities, 164, 167, 172; War, 162; Worship, 165, 172, 177; Youth Organisations, 178.

Church of Silence
15 *et seq.* ; 451.

Church Organisation before the Persecution
See under various countries.

Church Property
See under various countries; and cf. *Confiscation, Spoliation*.

" Co-existence "
16, 17, 21 *et seq.*, 24, 29, 30.

Collaboration
12-13.

Communism, Meaning of
1.

Communist Associations
See under *Korea, Poland, USSR.*

Communist Persecution
Methods of, 2 *et seq.*; mode of, 3 *et seq.*; permanent features of, 6 *et seq.*; compared
with former persecutions, 14, 15; results of, 15-20.

Communist Press
See under various countries.

Communist Propaganda
22 *et seq.*; and see under various countries.

Concordat
See under various countries.

Confiscation
See under various countries.

Constitutions
See under various countries.

CZECHOSLOVAKIA

341-394 ; Anti-Catholic Laws, 342, 345, 346, 347, 348, 349 *et seq.*, 352 *et seq.*,
354, 355, 356, 357, 358, 359, 362 *et seq.*, 371 *et seq.*, 374, 388, 391, 393; Arrests,
345, 346, 349, 356, 366, 369, 371, 379, 385, 389, 392; Atheism, 348, 392 (Atheistic
State), 394; Bishops, 342, 344, 346, 348, 353, 355, 359, 360, 361, 362, 363, 364,
365, 367, 368, 370, 374, 375, 378, 382, 384, 385, 388, 389, 390, 391, 393; Catholic
Action, 347, 349, 355, 356, 362, 363, 364, 392; Catholic Associations, 342, 347,
349, 355, 356, 359; Catholic Press, 347, 349, 350, 351, 352, 359, 360, 362, 367;
Charitable Works, 356, 357, 373, 393; Church Organisation before the Persecution,
341 *et seq.*; Communist Press, 344, 350, 357, 367, 374, 376, 379, 383; Communist
Propaganda, 344, 346, 354, 357, 358, 361, 362, 363, 367, 376, 389, 390; Confiscation,
346, 347, 349, 350, 357, 359, 360, 367, 373, 374, 375, 393; Congress at Prague
(1951), 391; Constitutions, 356, 370, 371, 372; Coup d'État (1948), 343, 344,
349, 352, 370; Deportations, 455; Dissident Catholic Action, 363, 364, 365, 368,
369, 370, 378, 384, 386, 391; Dissident National Church, 363; Education, 347, 353,
354, 367, 456; Elections, 343, 348, 352; Expulsions, 353, 381; Freedom of Worship,
356, 357, 358, 359, 360, 365, 370, 372, 374, 389, 391, 455; Greek Church, 377;
Illegal Appointments, 373, 388, 389; Jews, 342; Kominform, 363; Latin Rite, 342;

Decrees against the Church

Deportations

Dissident Associations

Dissident Catholic Action

Dissident Congresses

EAST GERMANY

Education
See under various countries; and cf. *Schools, Seminaries, Universities.*

Elections
See under various countries.

ESTONIA
53-55; Arrests, 54; Catholic Press, 54; Charitable Organisations, 54; Church Organisation before the Persecution, 53; Church Property, 54; Churches, 54; Confiscation (see under *Church Property*); Expulsions, 54; Lutheranism, 53, 54; Orthodox Church, 53, 54; Peace Appeal, 54; Places of Worship, 53; Priests, 53, 54; Religious Teaching, 54; Soviet Occupation, 53, 54; Taxes, 54.

Expulsions
9; see under various countries; and cf. *Deportations, Rupture with the Holy See.*

Famine
See under *USSR*; and cf. *Pontifical Relief Mission.*

Freedom of Religion
26; see under various countries; and cf. *Worship, Freedom of Worship.*

" Freedom of Worship "
13, 26; see under various countries; and cf. *Worship, Freedom of Religion.*

HUNGARY
194-253; Agrarian Reform, 196, 200, 201, 203, 344; "Agreement" (1950), 237-239, 240, 241, 242, 243, 247; Anti-religious Propaganda, 203, 215; Arrests, 203, 205, 208, 211, 215, 216, 222, 224, 226, 227, 234, 244, 460; Bishops, 208, 209, 210, 212, 214, 217, 218, 220, 222, 223, 224, 227, 228, 229, 230, 233, 234 (Declaration on "Peace"), 236, 237, 238, 239, 240, 241, 242, 243, 246, 247, 248, 250, 251, 252, 461; Bureau for Worship, 252; Catholic Action, 197, 198, 202, 205; Catholic Associations, 197, 198, 199, 204, 205, 206, 207, 210, 250; Catholic Press, 197, 201, 202, 208, 209, 210, 222, 251; Censorship, 222, 241, 251; Charitable Works, 211, 250; Church Organisation before the Persecution, 195; "Co-existence," 262, 462; Communist Index of Books, 202; Communist Press, 202, 204, 205, 206, 208, 209, 213, 215, 223, 226, 227; Communist Pressure to join Party, 212; Communist Propaganda, 199, 203, 204, 206, 220, 223, 225, 227, 228, 252; Communist Spy System, 212; Confiscations, 201, 217, 228, 241; Constitutions, 194, 196, 230, 231, 248, 250, 251; Convictions, 244; Decree on Vacant Ecclesiastical Sees, 247, 462; Deportations, 234, 236; Education, 196, 228; Elections, 194, 195, 203, 204, 211, 230, 242; Expulsions, 200, 235; Five-Year Plan, 239; Freedom of Religion, 199, 215, 219, 221, 223, 228, 231, 238, 239, 246, 252; Insurrection, 452, 461; Karitász, 210, 211, 213; Marian Year, 213, 219, 220, 221, 224; Marriage Laws, 202, 203; Modus Vivendi, 233, 239, 240, 242; Negotiations, 214, 217, 224, 228, 236, 237, 246; Oath of Fidelity, 243, 248; Parishes, 199, 200; Pastoral Letters, 200, 203, 204, 210, 218, 222, 223, 234, 241; Patriot Priests ("Priests of Peace"), 242, 243, 245, 246, 247, 248, 249, 251, 252, 461; Peace Appeal, 230, 233, 242; Peace Congresses, 229, 230, 242, 243; Peace Movement, 229, 233, 234, 236, 238, 239, 243, 247, 248, 249, 250, 251; People's Republic, 194; Places of Worship, 200, 251, 253; Preaching, 203, 218, 228; Priests, 197, 199, 203, 207, 214, 215, 220, 222, 223, 227, 237, 238, 241, 249, 250, 251, 252, 253, 461; Protestants, 196, 233; "Relaxation," 462; Religious, 251; Religious Broadcasts, 218, 219; Religious Feasts, etc., 211, 219, 247; Religious Houses, 197, 241, 250; Religious Orders, 233, 234, 236, 238, 240, 241; Religious

Religious Orders
See under various countries; and cf. *Religious.*

Religious Teaching
See under various countries.

Resolution of November 1954
27, 28.

ROMANIA

294-340 ; Abdication of King, 294; Agreements, Accords, etc., 327-332; Anti-Catholic Laws, 299, 303 *et seq.*, 326 *et seq.*, 331; Anti-Catholic Propaganda, 301 *et seq.*, 309, 325, 333, 337, 338; Arrests, 298, 314, 319, 321, 322, 323, 328, 331, 332, 334, 336, 339; Bishops, 295, 297, 298, 300, 301, 306, 312, 315, 319, 321, 322, 323, 324, 328, 330, 332, 336, 337, 339; Catholic Action, 297, 298; Catholic Associations, 299, 308, 339, 340; Catholic Press, 297, 298, 299, 301, 319, 339, 340; Church Organisation before the Persecution, 295 *et seq.*, 298; Colleges, see *Schools*; Communist Press, 301, 306, 318, 326, 333, 336; Concordats, 297, 298, 299, 303, 304; Confiscation, 309, 339; Congresses at Cluj, etc., 312 *et seq.*, 319, 320, 325, 334, 335; Constitutions, 294, 295, 298; Decrees, 303, 304, 305, 306, 307, 308, 309, 312, 318; Democratic Priests, 299, 300; Depositions, 312; Disappearance of the Catholic Church of the Oriental Rite, 312 *et seq.*, 319; Divisions among Catholics, 328, 329; Education, 307, 308, 309, 326, 338; Expulsions, 333, 339; Festival at Alba Julia, 316 *et seq.*; Freedom of Worship, 298, 305; Greek-Catholic Church, 295, 310, 313, 318, 320, 321, 326, 327; Latin Rite, 294, 297, 298, 301, 310, 312, 322, 326, 327, 328, 329, 330, 335, 339, 340; Latinist Movement, 296; Manifesto of 1950, 332; National Church, 299, 300, 305, 307, 311, 326, 340; Nationalisation, 298, 308; Oriental Rite, 294, 296, 297, 298, 300, 305, 307, 310, 311, 312, 313, 316, 319, 322, 326, 327, 328, 339, 340; Orthodox Church, 294, 298, 299, 300, 303, 306, 310, 311, 312, 313, 315, 316, 317, 320, 321, 324, 325, 327, 329, 340; Paris Peace Treaty (1947), 320; Pastoral Letters, 332; Peace Movement, Congresses, etc., 328 *et seq.*, 332, 335, 336; Persecution 295, 299, 307, 310, 322, 326, 339, 340; Places of Worship, 306, 307, 324, 325, 339; Popular Front, 294; Preaching, 322, 337; Priests, 298, 299, 300, 313, 314, 315, 319, 320, 321, 322, 323, 324, 326, 330, 332, 335, 336, 339; Progressive Priests, 335, 337; Religious Orders, 296, 297, 299, 306, 309, 339, 340; Religious Teaching, 309; "Re-union," 315 *et seq.*, 325, 334; Schism, 322 *et seq.*, 327, 328, 330, 331, 332, 335, 336, 338, 339, 340; Schools and Colleges, 295, 296, 298, 299, 308, 309, 339, 340; Seminaries, 296, 323; Soviet Occupation, 294, 299, 304; Statutes, 306, 327, 328, 330, 332, 335; Synods, 295 (Alba Julia), 312, 316, 329; Text-books, 309; Trials, 333, 336; Uniate Church, 295, 296, 297, 303, 304, 306, 307, 312, 316, 321, 322, 323, 325; War, 302, 329; Worship, 299.

Rupture with the Holy See
See under various countries; and cf. *Deportations, Expulsions.*

Schism
See under various countries; and cf. *Dissident Associations, National Church, Rupture with Holy See.*

Schools
See under various countries; and cf. *Education, Seminaries.*

Secular Clergy
See under *Priests.*

Seminaries
See under various countries.

Separation of Church and State
See under various countries.

Separation of Hierarchy from Priests and Faithful
8.

Soviet Occupation
See under *Carpatho-Ukraine, Estonia, Hungary, Latvia, Lithuania, Korea, Poland, Romania, Ukraine.*

Sovietisation
4; and passim Chapters 3-15.

Spoliations
See under *Confiscations.*

" Statutes," Official
10; and see under various countries.

Taxes
See under various countries.

Treaties
See under various countries.

Trials
8, and see under various countries.

Triple Autonomy
9, 16; and see under *China.*

Twentieth Soviet Congress
21.

UKRAINE

82-98 ; Agreements, Pacts etc., 82; Anti-religious Laws, 84; Arrests, 84, 87, 92, 95; Atheism, 454; Bishops, 84, 90, 92, 93, 98; Catholic Action, 83; Catholic Press, 83, 84, 89, 98; Catholic Synod, 86; Church Organisation before the Persecution, 82, 83; Collectivisation, 84; Confiscation, 84, 92; Congress, Communist Party, 453; Constitutions, 84, 86, 89, 94; Deportations, 87, 88, 92, 95, 453; Dissident Associations, 93, 94; Dissident Priests, 93; Education, 85, 86; Expulsions, 84; Freedom of Worship, 84, 89; Komsomol, 454; Modus Vivendi, 90; Nationalisation, 84; Orthodox Church, 83, 88, 90, 91, 94, 95, 97, 98, 453, 454; Pacts etc. (see *Agreements*); Parishes, 93; Pastoral Letters, 86; Persecution (renewed), 454; " Pioneer Group," 94, 95, 96, 98; Priests, 83, 85, 86, 88, 89, 93, 95, 97, 98, 453; Re-education, 90; "Relaxation," 454; Religious Feasts, 89; Religious Houses, 83, 84, 89; Religious Teaching, 83, 85, 89; " Re-union," 94; Schismatic Synod, 96; Schools, 83, 98; Seminaries, 83, 89, 92; Separation (of Church and State), 94; Soviet Occupation, 82, 83, 84; Taxes, 89; Treaties, 82; Trials, 92; Uniate Church, 83, 84, 88, 90, 91, 95, 97; War, 83, 87, 88; Worship, 84, 89; Youth Organisations, 454.

Uniate Church
See under *Carpatho-Ukraine, Ukraine, Romania.*

Universities
See under *China, Czechoslovakia, Poland.*

USSR (RUSSIA)
31-53 ; Anglican Church, 50; Annexations, 52, 53; Anti-religious Laws, 31 *et seq.* 38, 39, 41, 42, 48; Anti-religious Propaganda, 32 *et seq.*, 39, 46, 47, 48, 51, 52; Apostolic Administrations, 47; Arrests, 41, 42, 47, 49; Atheism, 32, 40, 52; Bishops, 37, 38, 45, 46, 50; Charitable Associations, 37; Church Organisation before the Soviet Régime, 36 *et seq.*, 40; Church Property, 38, 39, 41, 42; Civil War, 31; Code for Ecclesiastical Affairs, 36, 37; Collectivist Systems, 49; Communist Press, 32, 33, 41, 50; Communist Propaganda, 31, 44; Confiscation (see under *Church Property*); Constitutions, 32, 36, 48, 51; Ecclesiastical Organisation, 40; Education, 32; Expansion of Soviet Power, 52, 53; Famine, 34 *et seq.*, 41, 45; Komintern, 31; Komsomol, 33; Latin Rite, 40; Militant Atheists, 47, 48, 51; Mussolini, 41; New Economic Policy, 48; New Offensive (1929-1932), 47-51; New Plan of Campaign (1924-1928), 46, 47; Orthodox Church, 32, 33, 36, 38, 39, 42, 46; Parishes, 48; Penal Code, 42, 43, 44; Pontifical Relief Mission, 34 *et seq.*, 45; Priests, 48, 50, 51; Religion, 31, 32, 33, 48; Religious Associations, 48; Religious Liberty, 36, 37, 48, 50, 51; Religious Teaching, 32, 37, 38, 39, 46; Seminaries, 32, 37; Separation (of Church and State), 32, 38, 42, 49; Taxes, 46, 49; Treaty of Riga, 39, 40; Trials, 42, 43, 44, 49, 52; War, 31, 39, 52; Worship, 41, 48, 51; Youth Organisations, 33.

VIET-NAM
395-403 ; Agrarian Reform, 401, 402; Arrests, 396, 399, 403; Atheism, 402; Bishops, 403; Catholic Federation, 400; Catholic Press, 400, 403; Charitable Associations, 395; Church Organisation before the Establishment of the Régime, 395; Communist Propaganda, 400, 402; Confiscation, 398, 399, 402; Deportation, 397; Dissident Associations, 402; Elections, 403; Executions, 400; Exodus of Population, 397, 398, 399; Freedom of Worship, 399, 400, 401, 402; Geneva Armistice (1954), 395, 400; Marxism, 399, 400; Missionaries, 399; Parishes, 398; Patriot Priests, 403; Persecution, 399, 400; Places of Worship, 398, 401; Preaching, 401, 403; Priests, 398, 399, 400, 402, 403; Re-education, 400; Refugee Camps, 398; Refugees, 395 *et seq.*; Religious, 399; Religious Teaching, 400, 401, 402; Resolution of National Assembly, 400 *et seq.*; Schools and Colleges, 395, 399, 402, 403; Seminaries, 399; Taxes, 398, 399; Travel Permits, 396; Vicariates Apostolic, 395; War, 400.

World Opinion
5.

Worship
See under various countries; and cf. *Freedom of Worship, Bureau for Worship* (Hungary).

Youth Organisations
See under various countries.

YUGOSLAVIA
404-451 ; Agrarian Reform, 425, 433; Agreements, Accords, etc., 446-448; Anti-religious Propaganda, 409; Apostolic Letter to the Church of Silence (1956), 451;

32

Index of Names

A

Adamski (Mgr.), 265, 282, 285, 290, 457.
Adenauer, C., 129, 140.
Aftenie (Mgr.), 312, 322, 323, 324.
Agotha, A., 330, 334, 337.
Alapy, 245.
Albats, H., 57.
Alexyj, 91, 93, 96, 109, 310.
Anthony, 107.
Apor (Mgr.), 200.
Arata (Mgr.), 54, 57.
Ardeleanu, 336.
Aspiniks, P., 60.
Athanasius, 295.
Avram, A., 318.

B

Badalik (Mgr.), 246, 247.
Bagaratian (Mgr.), 49.
Baigner, M. (Fr.), 190.
Bajt, A., 440.
Bakalscki (Fr.), 160.
Balan, J. (Mgr.), 312, 323.
Balan, N., 311, 312, 315, 316, 318, 324, 325.
Bálogh, 229.
Banic (Mgr.), 431, 432.
Baraniak (Mgr.), 288, 458.
Bárd (Mgr.), 246.
Barnas (Mgr.), 385, 388.
Baumtorg (Mgr.), 47, 49.
Baziak (Mgr.), 283, 285.
Bednorz (Mgr.), 282, 285.
Bekers, E., 60.
Belascu, T., 314, 315, 317, 318, 326.
Belovejdoff, 154.
Benedict XV, 34.
Benes, 342, 343, 344, 348.
Bensz (Mgr.), 280.
Beran (Mgr.), 343, 359, 362, 363, 366, 367, 369, 385, 388, 390, 393.
Beresztóczy, M., 229, 243, 246.
Bernacki (Mgr.), 285, 458.
Bernorz (Mgr.), 457.
Bertoli (Mgr.), 376.
Bida, 275, 289.
Bieniek (Mgr.), 282, 285, 457.
Bierut, B., 254, 263, 269, 275.
Bisoc (Fr.), 336.
Boga (Mgr.), 329, 330, 331.
Boka, I., 226.
Bonati (Mgr.), 118.

Bonefacic (Mgr.), 432.
Booth (Fr.), 191.
Borisevicius (Mgr.), 79.
Boros (Mgr.), 336, 337.
Bossilkov (Mgr.), 160, 161.
Boukal (Mgr.), 385.
Brennan (Mgr.), 191.
Brizgys, 74, 80.
Brudnicki (Fr.), 267.
Brumboiu, A., 314, 315, 317.
Buchala (Fr.), 261.
Bucynski, 90.
Budanovic (Mgr.), 433.
Budka (Mgr.), 92, 98, 453.
Bukharin, 32.
Buljan (Mgr.), 428.
Burducea, C., 300.
Butkiewicz (Mgr.), 41, 44, 45.
Buzalka (Mgr.), 346, 382, 385, 386, 387, 391, 454.
Byrne (Mgr.), 191, 192.

C

Cajnkar, S. (Dr.), 413.
Carevic (Mgr.), 427, 450.
Carneckyj (Mgr.), 92, 98.
Carsky (Mgr.), 390.
Cavalli, F., 414, 429.
Celik (Mgr.), 432.
Centoz (Mgr.), 67.
Cepicka, 353, 362, 367, 378, 389.
Chang, B. (Fr.), 176.
Chen, I., 179.
Chen, M. (Fr.), 176.
Chiang Kai-Chek, 6, 162, 163.
Chira (Mgr.), 104.
Chomysyn (Mgr.), 92, 98.
Choromanski (Mgr.), 264, 269, 274, 276, 288, 457.
Chou En-Lai, 173.
Ciarnas, 44.
Cicerin, 42.
Cieplak (Mgr.), 41, 43, 44, 45.
Cihac (Mgr.), 385, 386.
Cisar (Mgr.), 312, 327, 332, 338, 340.
Cisteian, J., 324.
Coba (Mgr.), 127.
Colan, N., 325.
Crustov (Fr.), 160.
Cule (Mgr.), 429, 430, 449, 450.
Curti (Fr.), 118.
Cyrankiewicz, 260, 288.
Czajka (Mgr.), 265.

M. H. GILL AND SON LTD., PRINTERS, DUBLIN.

Da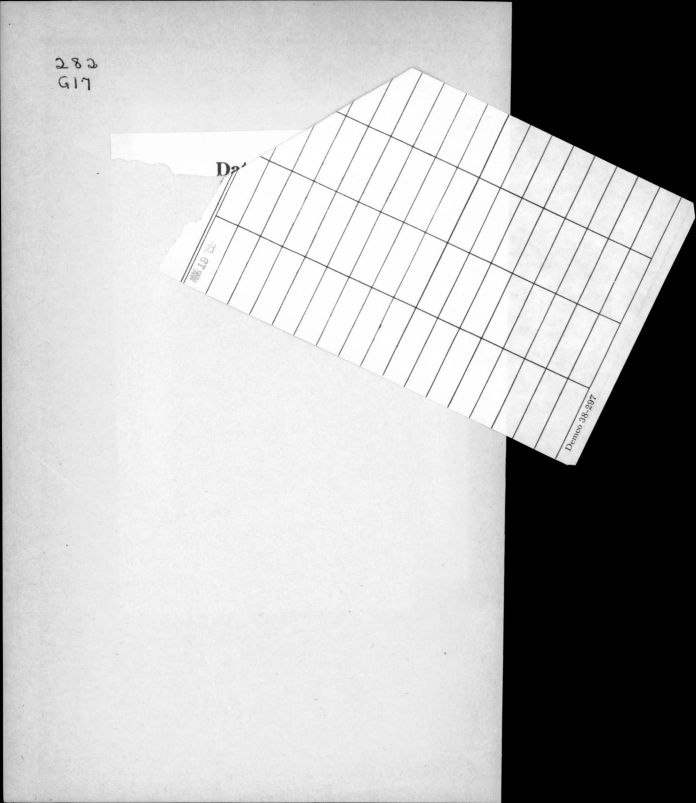